350

# THE BEST PLAYS OF 1938-39

## "ABE LINCOLN IN ILLINOIS"

Abe: Yes—we've fought the good fight—in the dirtiest campaign in the history of corrupt politics. And if I have won, then I must cheerfully pay my political debts. . . . I have been gambled all around, bought and sold a hundred times.

*(Raymond Massey)*

# THE BEST PLAYS
# OF 1938-39

### AND THE
### YEAR BOOK OF THE DRAMA
### IN AMERICA

EDITED BY
## BURNS MANTLE

*With Illustrations*

## DODD, MEAD AND COMPANY
NEW YORK  -  -  -  1939

20767

# INTRODUCTION

IT takes the theatre a year, and sometimes two or three years, to turn around and set about the business of developing a trend. The trend this last season, insofar as one appeared, was largely patriotic. At least in the sense that several outstanding plays took on a political coloring.

Not only was Robert Sherwood's "Abe Lincoln in Illinois" the most outstanding of the dramatic successes, but it had as Broadway companions at one time or another Maxwell Anderson's "Knickerbocker Holiday," Elmer Rice's "American Landscape" and the George Kaufman-Moss Hart "The American Way."

All these plays, or the inspiration from which they stem, can be traced, I think, to the political discussions and the national problems that have arisen within the last few years to plague and confound the voting citizens. These discussions have made several of our dramatists nation conscious, if not race conscious. Mr. Sherwood would bring his country back to a sane and open-minded review of those constructive philosophies Abraham Lincoln preached as a people's champion, and without prejudice as a capitalist's critic. Mr. Anderson found many of his personal conclusions regarding a true democracy amusingly pointed up in the experiences of the New Amsterdam that was Peter Stuyvesant's early stamping ground. Mr. Rice hoped to call the attention of the more violent contenders of the present to the crises of the past through which our embattled forefathers fought that their liberties might be preserved. And the Messrs. Kaufman and Hart thought also to review forty years of recent American history to prove that where there has been tolerance and a free, open, healthy national life in this great melting pot of a nation there also has been peace and happiness in the family groups that are the foundation of the nation.

There was a definite note of criticism sounded in these plays on nationalistic themes, but happily they were also good dramas. Two have been included in this year's selection of ten, the Sherwood "Abe Lincoln" and the Kaufman-Hart "The American Way."

There was also some suggestion of criticism of native character and national tendencies in two or three other popular plays.

v

Lillian Hellman, by exposing the sordid selfishness ruling a family of Southern manufacturers in "The Little Foxes," plainly asked her audience-public to pause and consider the net results of encouraging these and similar tendencies of the predatory natives.

Mr. S. N. Behrman, deciding finally that his play of the year might reasonably reflect a state of mind such as any thinking dramatist could encounter, wrote "No Time for Comedy." In his discussion of the titular subject he was able to unburden himself of a good many conclusions sprung from the European chaos.

Clare Boothe, accused of having written "Kiss the Boys Good-Bye" "as a parody of Hollywood's search for a Scarlett O'Hara," replied with considerable spirit that "this play was meant to be a political allegory about Fascism in America. . . . I deliberately chose that most exportable, highly praised and consistently sentimentalized of Dixie products—the Southern Belle—to examine her, not only for her own Fascist leanings but for her potentialities as a proselyter to the cause. In satiric terms, she is an American version of a Brown Shirt street brawler from Munich in a swank Berlin coffee house, circa 1930."

Mr. Odets' "Rocket to the Moon" is, on face value, a modern domestic triangle comedy, the story of a discouraged small income husband, harassed by a well meaning but utterly depressing wife and inspired with hope and confidence by the familiar sympathetic office companion. But it is also strongly significant in a social sense in stating the case for those groping humans born of the present family set-up—common victims of the times and of circumstance.

Mr. Barry's "Here Come the Clowns" was both mystifying and provocative. Even the drama critics, confessing the mystery, were willing to sit through two performances of the play in a search for its meaning. Those who decided that they had found it were convinced that the troubles of the world, and of humans trying to decide as to whether good or evil ruled the world, were chiefly in Mr. Barry's mind as he wrote. The author later confirmed and simplified these conclusions. Whatever may be wrong with the world it is within the power of man to correct it in the Barry conviction. Which makes his play well worth pondering.

"The Philadelphia Story" has, happily, no particular social significance. Here Mr. Barry is again writing in the mood of his earlier and more successful comedies of the "Holiday" and "Paris Bound" period. But he is still writing brilliantly and incisively of recognizable humans and giving Katharine Hepburn a prayed-for opportunity to prove that a good part of her success as an actress has been entirely justified.

Mr. Carroll's "The White Steed" is a drama for a reasonably restricted public. Probably not all the readers of a year book of the drama in America are devoted to the Irish or to the problems of that volatile race. But there is beauty in the Carroll script and appeal in the Carroll story that entitle "The White Steed" to the New York Drama critics' citation as the worthiest of the plays brought from abroad last season.

"Family Portrait" is another of the season's most interesting dramas that is also of restricted appeal. Not for any lack of merit as a drama, but because of its subject. Lenore Coffee and William Joyce Cowen have dared to write an imaginative and entirely reverent story of the life of Jesus Christ, colloquially phrased as to dialogue, simply pictured as to incident. They have found their excuse in a verse of the Bible (St. Mark 6: 1-5), in which the brothers and sisters of the Savior are named. Their sincerity and the reverent playing of a cast headed by Judith Anderson helped "Family Portrait" to a consistent if not popular success.

"The Best Plays of 1938-39" brings us to the twentieth anniversary of the series' inception, which occurred the season of 1919-20. Its features have been checked and modestly expanded from issue to issue, and there is satisfaction in the endorsement of the book's readers. I trust the current volume will not unduly crowd your shelf.

B. M.

Forest Hills, L. I., 1939.

# CONTENTS

# CONTENTS

# ILLUSTRATIONS

# THE BEST PLAYS OF 1938-39

# THE BEST PLAYS OF 1938-39

## THE SEASON IN NEW YORK

THIS particular theatre season, being that of 1938-39, will be classified by historians, in all probability, as the first of the N. Y. World's Fair seasons. But, as a matter of record, the advent of the Fair had little effect upon it until near its close. It was then, belatedly, and a little sadly, discovered that history's greatest show, in its early stages at least, offered competition that could not possibly be met. The showmen were a little stubborn at first, and kept their attractions playing at a loss in the belief that the crowds would turn to Broadway as soon as the novelty of the Fair had passed. But the crowds refused to turn. Then it was decided that there would be little hope for the theatres through the Summer. Such interest as they might arouse would come in the Fall, at the normal opening of a new season. Then there would be the lure of first-night excitement as well as that of the new plays to attract theatre-minded visitors. It will be another year before I can tell you how this prognostication worked out.

Otherwise the season in New York was steadily interesting but never very exciting. It missed the note of experimentation that added so much to the previous season, and while the quality of the attractions offered was good and of an even standard, it lacked both novelty and those high-lighted incidents that usually give a season distinction and character.

Divisionally the season's greatest single triumph, I think, was that marked by the advent of the Playwrights' Producing Company, an organization composed of Robert Sherwood, Maxwell Anderson, Sidney Howard, S. N. Behrman, and Elmer Rice, banded together for the purpose of producing plays written by its members. An auspicious start was made with the production of Mr. Sherwood's "Abe Lincoln in Illinois." This fine historical and biographical drama scored the success of the year. It was fortunately followed by the success of Mr. Anderson's and Kurt Weill's "Knickerbocker Holiday," Mr. Weill furnishing the musical score for Mr. Anderson's first musical comedy libretto. Mr.

3

Rice's "American Landscape" failed to win popular acclaim, but Mr. Behrman's "No Time for Comedy," plus Katharine Cornell, gave the playwrights' company a third success. Mr. Howard did not get his contribution finished in time, but is scheduled to lead off with it next season.

The Theatre Guild, on the other hand, suffered a series of defeats through the season and was thus temporarily displaced as the leading play producing unit of the American theatre. The Guild sponsored five productions and scored a single success—that of Philip Barry's "The Philadelphia Story," with Katharine Hepburn featured. It still owes its subscribers a sixth play.

The Group Theatre, the Guild's lustiest offspring, made definite progress, producing two new plays successfully, Clifford Odets' "Rocket to the Moon" and Irwin Shaw's "The Gentle People," and reviving Odets' "Awake and Sing" for forty-four well-attended performances.

The Federal WPA theatre consolidated its position, in a way, and then began slipping toward the liquidation that followed in the Spring. This people's theatre completed a run of 237 performances for ". . . one-third of a nation . . . ," one of 168 performances for "Haiti," another of 167 performances for "Prologue to Glory," and one of fifty-four performances for "On the Rocks." "The Big Blow," by Theodore Pratt, its most important dramatic production of the season, continued for 157 performances and was well liked. A children's story that also amused adults, "Pinocchio," ran on and on from December to June. The Federals created considerable first-class excitement by staging the first of the jazzed "Mikados" in Chicago and importing it later to New York, as is more fully recorded hereafter, and boldly challenged Broadway competition with a left-wing revue, "Sing for Your Supper." At the season's close WPA theatre activities seemed threatened with extinction, due to the gradual liquidation of the arts projects born of a three-year-old relief program. A valiant effort is still being made to salvage the best features of the project's achievements.

It proved to be a fairly active Summer season in New York. There were still thirteen attractions playing in the Broadway theatres when we quit the record in June, 1938. These included the English school comedy "Bachelor Born," which was not withdrawn finally until the succeeding January; the popular musical comedy, "I Married an Angel," which hung on until February, and three that are still with us—the six-year-old "Tobacco Road," the two-year-old "Pins and Needles" and the year-and-a-half-old

American high school comedy "What a Life."

Of the others "Our Town" and "On Borrowed Time" ran into November, "Shadow and Substance" was through in October and the rest quit variously in June and July.

The new season started belatedly and uncertainly with an English attempt at the American type of gangster play, one called "Come Across," by Guy Beauchamp and Michael Pertwee. It lasted a scant two weeks. This was mid-September, and the next two weeks were not only fairly lively with new plays, but two of them registered resounding hits. One was the somewhat amazing "Hellzapoppin," which the experts found a little on the loud and common side, but which the laugh-starved crowd literally gobbled. Olsen and Johnson, veteran comics of the two-a-day, were the producers, and, as it turned out, they knew their public better than the experts did. "Hellzapoppin" proved so popular it was afterward transferred to the Winter Garden, and for months was a riotous sell-out.

The other September hit was Clare Boothe's satirical comedy, "Kiss the Boys Good-bye," a satirical comedy presumably inspired, as previously noted, by the picture producers' search for someone to play Scarlett O'Hara in the screen version of *Gone with the Wind*. It was Miss Boothe's later contention that the American South's contribution to the theories and aims of Fascism was what moved her to write the play. As we have included excerpts from "Kiss the Boys Good-bye" in this volume readers are privileged to draw their own conclusions.

There were also three rather ambitious failures scored during the season's first fortnight. One was the Theatre Guild's first entry, "Dame Nature," a story of adolescent romance and tragedy adapted by Patricia Collinge from André Mirabeau's original, which closed after five weeks. Another was Max Gordon's attempt to capitalize on the "Pins and Needles" excitement with an uptown copy of a down-town success called "Sing Out the News," and a third was Guthrie McClintic's hopefully produced "Missouri Legend," being Elizabeth B. Ginty's biographical drama with Jesse James as its hero. Jesse as a misguided but otherwise more or less noble romantic struggled through forty-eight performances and was gone.

Fred Stone had some personal success with a revival of the Winchell Smith and Frank Bacon record-breaker of other years, the comedy called "Lightnin'," which John Golden did for him. It held out for seven weeks. Mr. Stone had previously played the Bacon part with several stock companies.

October brought in four of the season's early hits. Topping these were the Playwrights' Producing Company's "Abe Lincoln in Illinois" and "Knickerbocker Holiday," the Maurice Evans "entirety" Hamlet, an imported "Oscar Wilde," and a return engagement of Helen Hayes and "Victoria Regina." The personal success note was strong with all four, as so frequently is the case with popular hits. The Robert Sherwood "Lincoln" would have lost much without the fine performance of Raymond Massey in the name part. "Knickerbocker Holiday" revived memories of Walter Huston's happy years in vaudeville. The uncut "Hamlet," naturally, was greatly dependent upon the fine interpretation of young Mr. Evans. The "Oscar Wilde" owed much to the English actor, Robert Morley, and, of course, to think of "Victoria Regina" without Helen Hayes is, for Americans, quite impossible.

The major disappointment of the season's second month was the lingering illness that took off Moss Hart's and George Kaufman's "The Fabulous Invalid," after sixty-five performances. It was a heavy and handsome production and the overhead proved too much for the box-office to meet. Being an echo, or a series of echoes, of theatrical history during the last thirty years, the play seemed to fall between two publics—a young public that was not particularly interested in the glamorous stage celebrities of the past, and an older public that was a little saddened by the recollections the imitations inspired.

Mr. Morley carried "Oscar Wilde," an honest tribute to the unhappy genius, through the season. Mr. Evans played "Hamlet" ninety-three times. Mr. Massey is threatened with a lifetime of "Abe Lincoln," and Mr. Huston was taken on tour with "Knickerbocker Holiday," after 168 performances in New York.

A second costly incident of this period was a biographical musical comedy devoted to the lives and works of William S. Gilbert and Arthur Sullivan called "Knights of Song." This production was also hopefully and handsomely staged by Laurence Schwab. Public response was delayed and it was closed after two weeks.

J. B. Priestley's "I Have Been Here Before" also proved a minor disappointment. England's popular novelist has been having a determined try at popularizing the metaphysical drama ("Time and the Conways" being last season's contribution), but he has not so far succeeded in finding a sufficiently interested public to support him.

The first of the musical successes was "Leave It to Me," this being Bella and Samuel Spewack's adaptation of their own comedy, "Clear All Wires," which failed some seasons back. Cole Porter supplied lyrics and score, and two favorite comedians, Victor Moore and William Gaxton, organized the fun. They were teamed with Sophie Tucker from vaudeville and Tamara from Russia.

A couple of uninteresting weeks after this George Abbott brought in his own and a couple of other fellows' version of Shakespeare's "The Comedy of Errors." By the time it reached Broadway there was but a single line of the Shakespearean text left in the script, but the story of the two dromios, he of Ephesus and his twin of Syracuse, as well as the super-heated romances of their respective masters, were fairly recognizable. Richard Rodgers and Lorenz Hart provided lyrics and score and sat in on the comedy interludes.

There was also one dramatic success to save November from being a month of rather sorry failures. This was Clifford Odets' "Rocket to the Moon," which has been included with the play selections for this volume.

The more ambitious of the productions that failed included the Mercury Theatre's "Danton's Death," a compressed staging of the expansive Georg Buchner drama that Max Reinhardt first brought to America. Orson Welles, who had temporarily turned from the Mercury Theatre enterprise when he began causing sensations and making money with radio drama, produced and played in "Danton's Death," but did not try to force a run after three weeks.

A comedy, "Ringside Seat," by Leonard Ide, dramatizing the somewhat extravagant adventure of a murder trial fan, brought Grant Mitchell back from the cinema to play the lead, but failed to bring enough patrons to the box office to support him.

Holiday time brought little to cheer about, though some cheering was done. Inspired by Bramwell Fletcher and a few other enthusiasts, William A. Brady took a hand in the organization of a Playhouse Company which revived "Outward Bound" with the idea of going on from there with other revivals of remembered plays. "Outward Bound," however, proved so definite a success that they continued with it through the season. This was a significant happening of the theatre year, made even more significant because it brought back to the theatre the Laurette Taylor who is one of its outstanding comediennes and a luminous figure in its recent history—the first of the popular stars to achieve a two-season run in the same part, as she did with "Peg-o'-My-Heart." in both New York and London.

It was early December when the Playwrights' Producing Company suffered its first failure with a patriotic and lightly historical drama by Elmer Rice called "American Landscape." In this play Mr. Rice, through the employment of the ghosts of dead Americans who had had a hand in bringing the nation through several important crises, had the same theme in mind that the Messrs. Kaufman and Hart afterward employed in "The American Way." "American Landscape" was the more seriously written of the two plays, but less direct in its appeal. The Playwrights withdrew it after five weeks.

An item of the December list was the production by Eddie Dowling of Philip Barry's "Here Come the Clowns," which has also been included with the best plays of the year in this volume. It proved a mystifying play, in the playing, but commanded the respect of its audiences and moved many patrons to a strong defense of its purpose as a searching inquiry into the problems of living.

For the rest, as intimated, holiday time in the theatre was a time of disappointment. The Theatre Guild suffered a second failure with Thornton Wilder's "The Merchant of Yonkers," which proved a fanciful comedy that even the art of Jane Cowl could not hold up past a subscription period of five weeks. Marc Connelly tried valiantly to do something with and for Arnold Sundgaard's "Everywhere I Roam" (it being Mr. Sundgaard's contention that he did altogether too much), but nothing very promising came from the collaboration. And as for the rest of the December contributions, it were kindness to forget them.

And then came the new year and another round of hits. Ethel Waters started it with the DuBose Heywards' "Mamba's Daughters," a typical melodrama of the South made plausible and interesting by the performance of the colored singer. The next night brought George Abbott's production of a rowdy dramatization of Victoria Lincoln's "February Hill," though the adapters, R. L. Buckner and Walter Hart, were careful to change the locale from Massachusetts to northern New York, and to change the names of all the characters, thus avoiding some sort of copyright interference that threatened at the time. The common tale of three generations of prostitutes, the play's fun and frankness saved it for the playgoing public that takes its drama neat.

Following close upon these two was "The Gentle People," a New York gangster folk drama in the Odets manner written by Irwin Shaw and played with considerable success by Franchot Tone, Sylvia Sidney and Sam Jaffe, all popular throwbacks from the movies. Soon after this came Paul Vincent Carroll's "The White Steed," which greatly pleased the same public that had liked Mr. Carroll's "Shadow and Substance" so well the season before.

With these hits out of the way the D'Oyly Carte troupe started a nine-week repertory season of Gilbert and Sullivan favorites, with nary a break in the popularity that has greeted previous engagements. A week later Beatrice Lillie came in with a Noel Coward compilation of Coward tunes and sketches called "Set to Music." As usual Miss Lillie brought her own crowd up standing—literally standing at the rear of the theatre the first few weeks. And then came "The American Way." This timely opus so vividly recalled the American scene of the last forty years that its audiences received it with cheering and a crowded theatre for many months. Excerpts from its diffused but exciting text are included herein.

Maurice Evans, having worn himself a little thin playing the complete "Hamlet" for ninety-three performances, turned to the first part of "Henry IV" and put on a lot of flesh very rapidly. Playing Sir John Falstaff in a crinoline-and-springs costume that completely encircled him he scored a second success and won additional praise for his artistic insight and a demonstrated versatility that no other young actor of his day has earned.

Early in February the Theatre Guild, rapidly achieving an inferiority complex that was devastating, made its third production, that of Stefan Zweig's "Jeremiah." This biblical story of a worried prophet was dealt with severely by a majority of the reviewers and scorned by all save the most loyal of subscribers. Five struggling weeks and it was gone.

Now came "One for the Money," a right-wing revue, staged, it was rumored, with Jock Whitney backing, and opulently produced in direct contrast to the left-wing success, "Pins and Needles." It was aimed directly at, and staged for, New York's café society set. Its start was slow, but gradually the cleverness of Nancy Hamilton's lyrics, she being the program's chief inspiration, became noised about and a total of 132 performances were chalked up before it was decided to stop for the Summer. Immediately there followed a bid from Chicago, and "One for the Money" was shipped West for a Summer run.

John Kirkland, who has acquired something more than a competence from the six-year success of "Tobacco Road," and lost only a part of it with "Tortilla Flat," returned to producing with a rowdy piece built by himself and Leyla Georgie around the legendary life and romances of the original "Florodora" sextette. This was called "I Must Love Someone," and included, as its most diverting episode, a revived staging of the long popular "Tell Me, Pretty Maiden" sextette. There did not at first appear to be great interest in these lights of love, but Mr. Kirkland persisted, tinkering with the script and finally inducing the first Mrs. Kirkland, Nancy Carroll, to abandon her motion picture commitments and come East to play the lead for him. In the early Summer business took an upturn and the run continued.

Another of the larger musicals, "Stars in Your Eyes," brought Jimmy Durante back from Hollywood and Ethel Merman back from whatever she was doing at the time. Together with Tamara Toumanova, a Russian ballerina, they scored a first night success that was as promising as that of "I Married an Angel," also the enterprise of Dwight Deere Wiman. Interest was feverish for many weeks. When it began to subside in late May Mr. Durante decided he had better get back to pictures.

Now Tallulah Bankhead, who had been waiting ever so long for a real drama, found one in Lillian Hellman's "The Little Foxes." No single audience of the year had been moved to a sincerer demonstration of approval than was that which greeted Alabama's favorite daughter. She played through the season to an increasingly enthusiastic response and was thrilled in the Spring when she divided honors with Raymond Massey and "Abe Lincoln in Illinois" in the vote of the New York Drama Critics' Circle aimed at selecting the best play of American authorship produced during the season. Miss Hellman's play is one of the more important exhibits of this year book.

Joe Cook, one of the more dependable of the native zanies, hopefully tried a vaudeville farce called "Off to Buffalo." The bankroll was not strong enough to permit a month's tinkering with the material, which might have saved it, and the piece was withdrawn after a week's playing.

Judith Anderson, the brilliant Australian who has scored many a success as a heroine of somewhat exotic impulse, surprised and incidentally thrilled her admirers by appearing as, of all persons, Mary, Mother of Jesus, in a drama called "Family Portrait." Herein the family life of the Savior is imagined in terms of contemporary drama, as may be seen by a reference to the excerpts herein printed.

"Rocket to the Moon," giving signs of having gone as far as it could, the Group Theatre revived Author Odets' first success, "Awake and Sing." Curiously, many playgoers who had not pre-

viously discovered it as an outstanding drama of Jewish family
life in the New York Bronx now raised their voices in excited
trebles of praise and the revival almost equaled in popularity the
original run of the play.

About this time attention became focused on what was jour-
nalistically accepted as a "war of the Mikados." Early in March
the Federal WPA Theatre had moved from Chicago its most successful mid-Western production, which was a swing version of the
Gilbert and Sullivan classic. "The Swing Mikado" immediately
duplicated its Chicago success and continued for many weeks to
capacity crowds at Federal theatre prices, $1.10 being the highest.

An envious showman named Michael Todd, also from Chicago,
thereupon tried to buy "The Swing Mikado" from the Federal
producers. Failing in this he appropriated the idea and staged a
rival syncopated version which he called "The Hot Mikado."
This, having all the aids to success the Chicago relief enterprise
lacked, including selected performers, handsome scenery, tasteful
costumes and professional orchestrations and arrangements, not to
overlook Bill Robinson, popular colored champion of the tap
dancers, naturally outdistanced the WPA version, despite the difference in cost.

Again an envious pair of commercial producers thought to take
a hand in the contest. Bernhard Ulrich and Melvin B. Ericson
succeeded in separating "The Swing Mikado" from the government and presented it in direct competition with the "Hot" number. The result was disastrous. "The Swing Mikado" lasted but
a few weeks in the Broadway competition, none of which turned
a profit. "The Hot Mikado" ran on for a time and was then
selected by Grover Whalen and his advisers for a trial flight at
popular prices at the Fair's magnificent Hall of Music.

It was late March before Katharine Hepburn was ready for
another try at reclaiming the approval of Broadway. She had
made her first bid some years back, at the height of her motion
picture popularity, with a play called "The Lake," and the experience had been unhappy. Now she came with a new play by
Philip Barry called "The Philadelphia Story," and under the auspices of the Theatre Guild, which had hoped to bring her back
last year in "Jane Eyre." The result on this occasion was entirely satisfying to everybody interested, including the drama
critics, as more fully appears in later pages.

The season, drawing toward an early close, had few exciting
moments its last few weeks. A drama from London, Charles Morgan's "The Flashing Stream," with the importation of which a

good deal of hope had been involved, proved a bit heady for Broadway audiences. Its cast was headed by Geoffrey Tearle and Margaret Rawlings, popular players abroad, but they could not save it.

A weird experimental drama by William Saroyan, "My Heart's in the Highlands," received what is known professionally as a "mixed reception." Those who found it poetically and symbolically inspiring liked it very much. Those who did not thought it formless, purposeless and lacking in all the basic qualities necessary to legitimate drama.

Happily this was quickly followed by a new S. N. Behrman play, "No Time for Comedy," with the long-absent Katharine Cornell as its star. This was the fourth production and the third hit scored by the Playwrights' Producing Company and carried the First Actress triumphantly into the Summer.

An interesting but unprofitable experiment of the late season was a good-will gesture financed by the Republic of Mexico. A "Mexicana" revue was sent North from the City of Mexico in the hope that New York would approve and Mexican stage art and prestige would be profitably expanded. It was not a bad revue, and was pointed with several exceptionally clever sketches, but as soon as it had exhausted the interest of the Latin-American public resident in New York the local public was found to be no more than mildly interested. Hot weather and the opening of the World's Fair also had something to do with "Mexicana's" closing after five weeks.

There was an attempt to stir interest afresh in the European mess with the production of a reasonably conservative anti-Hitler drama, "The Brown Danube," by Burnett Hershey. This one detailed the attempted escape of a noble Austrian family from Vienna at the time of the German invasion, and, though biased, was also blessed with a happy ending. The head of the Von Tornheim family, whose daughter was being ruthlessly pursued by a Nazi leader, was able to turn the tables on the fellow by proving that his mother had forsworn her Jewish ancestry to marry his father.

A new subscription organization, the American Lyric Theatre, in association with the League of Composers, produced two native folk operas, Stephen Vincent Benét's "The Devil and Daniel Webster," with a musical setting by Douglas Moore, and "Susanna, Don't You Cry," built around twenty-nine of the Stephen Foster songs by Sarah Newmeyer and Clarence Loomis. The native works were richly staged and professionally cast. The recep-

tion, by society subscribers principally, was friendly and the outside public reaction was at least encouraging.  A Ballet Caravan
program of native ballets was also a feature of the engagement.

The season ended in a flurry of excitement and hope connected
with the opening of the World's Fair, conceded to be the greatest
of all similar exhibits staged within the memory of man.  The
showmen were hopeful the Fair would bring crowds to town and
that they, naturally associating New York with the theatre, would
spend a part of their time and a little of their money at the theatre wickets.  Disappointment followed closely upon the heels of
hope, for the crowds did no such thing.  They had come to see
the Fair, and there they went and stayed.  As the season advanced and the crowds were more generally representative of the
West and Middle West business improved, but by that time most
of the theatres that had been hanging on with the weaker attractions of last season's list had put up the shutters.

There were approximately eighty new entertainments produced,
dramatic and musical, and the traditional percentage of hits and
misses—one money success for every four failures—remained unchanged.

# THE SEASON IN CHICAGO

## By CECIL SMITH
### Dramatic Critic of the *Chicago Tribune*

AFTER several depression years in which the graph of Chicago's theatrical activity persistently showed a downward course, the season of 1938-39 eased off into a plateau. While it would be fatuous to pretend that the Chicago stage abruptly took a new lease on life, at least it did not come within closer hailing distance of the abyss. The total of playing weeks in the commercial theatres between June 1, 1938, and May 31, 1939, virtually duplicates the 1937-38 figure. More productions (26 as against 19) were revealed to the local public, but runs were shorter, and the year's aggregate box office intake probably matched closely that of the preceding year.

The external scene of what we whimsically call the "Randolph Street Rialto" (none of the playhouses being on Randolph Street) remains unchanged. Four theatres—the Harris, the Selwyn, the Erlanger and the Grand Opera House—carried the major burden of the season. The vast Auditorium Theatre, busy most of the time with opera, ballet, and concert bookings, attempted to enter the legitimate arena with engagements of "I'd Rather Be Right" and "The Women." In four weeks "I'd Rather Be Right" grossed over $150,000 in the huge house. But even a hastily installed public address system failed to make George M. Cohan audible to the balcony, and the historic old house made more enemies than friends by its venture. Late in May the Civic Theatre, a small unit in the $30,000,000 Civic Opera building (known as "Insull's Folly") attempted to lift itself out of the white elephant classification by initiating a popular price repertory. As these paragraphs go to press the ultimate fate of the project remains to be seen.

There are other theatres in Chicago waiting to be used, whenever the traffic demands their reinstatement. The Studebaker, the Princess, the Majestic, the Blackstone and the Great Northern remain as mementoes of an earlier day, still unsullied by such Hollywood interior decoration as has ravaged the Garrick, the Apollo (the old Olympic), the United Artists (the old Apollo) and the Clark (the old Adelphi). The Federal Theatre Project

14

has been using the Blackstone and the Great Northern, but their tenancy can hardly be called permanent.

Within the city's shrunken theatrical zone the season brought to light nineteen plays known to Broadway, in most cases with all or part of the original company, five new undertakings with Broadway aspirations (in every case but one quickly frustrated), and the opening stock company effort at the Civic. The Federal Theatre Project was represented by fourteen efforts, ranging from dissertations on syphilis and electric power to the all-Negro "swing" version of Gilbert and Sullivan's "The Mikado," whose twenty-two weeks at the Great Northern Theatre made it the most smashing hit of the year. A single Yiddish drama, not classified above, spent a week at the Studebaker—Jacob Ben-Ami in Maurice Schwartz's production of "Who Is Who."

On the artistic side of the ledger the season maintained a high level. Most of the arrivals from New York were tried and true successes, whose Chicago careers depended more upon the fickle taste of a midwestern audience than upon the resolution of any doubts about the intrinsic merits of the plays themselves. Along in the Fall and early Winter, for instance, the public decided that it did not care much for plays about death, religious asceticism and kindred sobering subjects. Consequently "On Borrowed Time" and "Shadow and Substance" took it in the neck, while "Susan and God," "I'd Rather Be Right" and "Kiss the Boys Good-bye" proceeded to clean up.

There is a good deal to be said in extenuation of this attitude. Plays were booked into the city in helter-skelter fashion, whenever their touring schedules made a Chicago engagement desirable from a purely managerial point of vantage. No attempt was made to balance the schedule with a carefully selected assortment of plays and musicals of varying character. Thus from September to January the local playbills were crowded with such serious items as "Golden Boy," "Of Mice and Men," "On Borrowed Time," "Whiteoaks," "Shadow and Substance," "The Sea Gull" and "Our Town." Except for a horrid revival of "The Women," the city waited until January 15 for its really raucous comedy, "Kiss the Boys Good-bye." Meanwhile Gertrude Lawrence in "Susan and God" and Mr. Cohan in his presidential spoofery attracted most of the cash customers in town, for they alone presented the lighter side of life in terms attractive to the laity. And during this period the Federal Theatre Project with its light-hearted "Mikado" for once was able to outsmart the commercial theatre.

Consequently the public began to grasp the undeniable fact that a Chicago season is chiefly composed of cast-offs from New York—often very worthy cast-offs, to be sure, but presented in no particular order and with no sensitivity to the specific theatrical tastes of this city. Against this lethargy there proved to be only one effective counteragent—stars. Except for "On Borrowed Time," which enjoyed the matchless services of Dudley Digges, every production boasting the name of a first-line star for its marquee enjoyed good business.

Indeed, Chicago has not seen such a display of major luminaries in many a long season. Gertrude Lawrence started off the procession in early October. Although she had not played in the city for years and years, her path was prepared by magnificent promotion, and she became a reigning favorite overnight. Her welcome not worn out by twelve weeks in "Susan and God," Miss Lawrence returned in April in Samson Raphaelson's "Skylark." This time she was hampered by a mediocre vehicle and bad notices, and she fared less well, though reasonably prosperously, for a four-week period.

In the week of November 27 the concentration of star performers reached its peak, with Miss Lawrence, Mr. Digges, Mr. Cohan and Ethel Barrymore all in town, and the Lunts only a week away. Such rich fare jaded the public palate for a time, with the result that Sir Cedric Hardwicke, Frank Craven and Cornelia Otis Skinner—big names, but smaller than those to whom the town had become accustomed—drew less well than they might have with less eminent predecessors. It remained for Vera Zorina, as the year's best exploited new personality, to restore the full drawing power of the star system. With Dennis King and Vivienne Segal as co-workers, Miss Zorina turned "I Married an Angel" into a smash that could have continued long after the closing date imposed upon it by impending Hollywood duties.

Deferring comment upon the five professional tryouts which brought an air of novelty to the season, I have put in chronological order the season's record, omitting Federal Theatre and other peripheral items:

"Pins and Needles," Labor Stage revue; "Golden Boy" (Group Theatre production), with Luther Adler, Frances Farmer and Morris Carnovsky; "I Am Different," with Tallulah Bankhead; "Susan and God," with Gertrude Lawrence; "Blossom Time," revival with Everett Marshall; "Of Mice and Men," with Guy Robertson and Claire Luce; "The Women," revival with Lois Wilson;

"Dame Nature" (Theatre Guild production); "On Borrowed Time," with Dudley Digges and Frank Conroy; "I'd Rather Be Right," musical comedy with George M. Cohan and Taylor Holmes; "Whiteoaks," with Ethel Barrymore; "Amphitryon 38," with Alfred Lunt and Lynn Fontanne (Theatre Guild production); "Golden Boy," return engagement with Phillips Holmes and Jean Muir; "Shadow and Substance," with Sir Cedric Hardwicke; "The Sea Gull," with A. Lunt and L. Fontanne (Theatre Guild production); "Kiss the Boys Good-bye," second company with Lucia Lull; "Our Town," with Frank Craven; "Candida," with Cornelia Otis Skinner (her first performance in the role); "Bachelor Born," with original New York company; "What a Life," second company with Eddie Bracken; "I Married an Angel," musical comedy with Vera Zorina, Vivienne Segal, Dennis King, Walter Slezak, and original New York cast; "Angela Is Twenty-Two," by Sinclair Lewis, with Philip Merivale; "Knickerbocker Holiday," musical comedy with Walter Huston, Ray Middleton and New York cast; "Skylark," with Gertrude Lawrence; "My Dear Children," with John Barrymore and Doris Dudley; "Petticoat Fever," revival with Guy Robertson.

First of the season's extra-Broadway experiments was "I Am Different," a comedy adapted from the Hungarian of Lily Hatvany by Zoe Akins. Miss Tallulah Bankhead, with bass voice and tousled hair, undertook to make convincing the authors' thesis that a woman who thought she was very, very different was hardly different at all. The dialogue and situations alike were feeble, and the company set a new record for listlessness before they finished a stand of three and a half weeks. The troupe toured the South after leaving Chicago, and folded up sadly in Washington at Thanksgiving time.

On January 24 Cornelia Otis Skinner offered her brand-new version of Bernard Shaw's "Candida." The dialogue moved slowly, as Miss Skinner dwelt sententiously upon her lines, as though waiting to hear an imaginary answer from one of the vaporous entities of her solo-dramas. She had neither the pace nor the feel of co-operative playing, and even the hysterical, rather neurotic Marchbanks of John Cromwell did not work up sufficient excitement. After two weeks played in Chicago to slim attendance, "Candida" went off on the road and died a premature death not unlike that of "I Am Different."

Sinclair Lewis's "Angela Is Twenty-Two" was a puzzling play because despite a good many straightforward, penetrating bits of Lewis writing, its plot (a close cousin to "Accent on Youth") would not jell. Mr. Lewis himself had originally played the part of a middle-aged doctor seeking to keep up with his youthful wife. I saw him in Milwaukee, and quite concurred in the managerial move which brought Philip Merivale in to replace him before the Chicago engagement. Mr. Merivale, however, knew he had a turkey on his hands, and was evidently psychologically unable to contribute much support toward a bad cause. Soon after it left Chicago, the piece bit the dust.

Riding high on the crest of the popularity occasioned by "Susan and God," Gertrude Lawrence came back to town in April in "Skylark," a new comedy of marital misunderstanding by Samson Raphaelson. Having foregone an earlier opportunity to act in "No Time for Comedy," Miss Lawrence, along with John Golden, the producer, pinned high hopes on "Skylark." As things eventuated at the premiere, Mr. Raphaelson seemed not to have written a play, but merely a first or second draft. Everybody forgot lines, some of which had been provided only an hour or two before the curtain. The whole business was a flop, though some reviewers tried to be kind and helpful, and though a good number of Miss Lawrence's admirers came to see her.

The one success among untried plays came at the tag end of a season that had looked pretty well washed up. John Barrymore, returning to the stage after an absence of sixteen years, took the city by storm in a farce called "My Dear Children." Adroitly written by Jerry Horwin and Catherine Turney to exploit the Barrymore style and mannerisms, and to capitalize upon the actor's domestic history, the farce was made to order for a rehabilitated star who did not wish to take himself too seriously. Early in the engagement Mr. Barrymore went to bed for six days with a heart attack. Under the care of a physician he soon recovered and gave more consistent performances than before his illness. Although one never quite knew what to expect on any given night, Mr. Barrymore's playing was always diverting, even when he ad libbed generous portions of the script. The whole performance was strengthened by a cast of unusual quality, numbering among its members Doris Dudley (hurriedly brought in when Elaine Barrie left both the company and Mr. Barrymore's hearth in St. Louis), Tala Birell, Lois Hall, Dorothy McGuire and Philip Reed. The play is still running as I submit this record, sharing the limelight with "One for the Money" and the Civic Theatre repertory.

The Civic Theatre venture still hangs in the balance. The opening bill, "Petticoat Fever," was fair to middling, with Guy Robertson less roistering at the opening than he became later. If

future casting can bring interesting new faces to the theatre and
eliminate several incompetent hangers-on from radio studios, the
project may serve to keep open the most comfortable theatre in
Chicago.  The entrepreneur is J. Charles Gilbert, former "Blossom Time" leading man, and present manager of the Civic Opera
House and the Civic Theatre.

Throughout the year the Federal Theatre Project consistently
improved its gait.  The swing "Mikado," employing an all-Negro
cast and an imaginative set of costumes by John Pratt, set the
city by the ears.  It played at the Great Northern for 22 weeks,
and was withdrawn then only because the New York project
wanted to borrow it to bolster up its feeble prestige.  If the show
had been allowed to remain in Chicago, it might have drawn
audiences for a year or more.

In the second half of the year the Federal Theatre gave up
its preoccupation with living newspapers and social issues, and
turned to Shakespeare.  Ian Keith, having already played in a
WPA revival of "The Copperhead," directed and acted in
"Othello" and "Hamlet."  After his resignation from the local
project to go to Australia, the remaining company gave "As You
Like It"—but that belongs in the 1939-40 story, since it did not
open until June.

None of the other Federal Theatre productions won much acclaim, though Ruth Page's modernized version of "Carmen," set
in the midst of a Spanish civil war and called "Guns and Casta-
nets," was provocative if unfinished.

In the past few years Chicago has seen a mushroom growth of
little theatre units.  Except for the Chicago Repertory Group,
the Institute Players of the Jewish People's Institute, and the
Chicago Mummers Theatre, the standards are none too professional.  The Repertory Group gave capable performances of "The
Cradle Will Rock" and ". . . One third of a nation. . . ."  The
Mummers sponsored the successful return of Francis X. Bushman
to the stage in "The Bishop Misbehaves."  The Uptown Players
are semi-professional in quality, and would be better if they did
not try plays like "Elizabeth the Queen," which they have not
the means to produce.

Summer theatres likewise seem to be sprouting now.  For the
most part they run on an amateur basis.  An important exception
is the Coach House Theatre in Oconomowoc, Wisconsin, where the
repertoire is limited to new plays, performed by casts sprinkled
with capable professionals.

The season was encouraging to the extent that the theatre did not lose ground in Chicago. Probably it is idle to look for any positive improvement until the city develops some self-assurance as a production center, and until a better rapport is established between New York producers and the public they are seeking to attract in Chicago. The lion's share of the deficiencies in any Chicago season may be attributed to the evils of absentee land-lordism. The stage in Chicago is ripe for a genuine revival, but careful, intelligent planning will be necessary to bring it about.

# THE SEASON IN SAN FRANCISCO

By Fred Johnson

Drama Editor of *The Call-Bulletin*

EVEN in a business as accustomed to the unexpected as the showman's, San Francisco's theatrical year came to a close in the midst of changes as surprising as they were swift.

With two smash hits on its hands and a third to its credit since early January, the Federal Theatre was compelled to close the last pair in the face of turn-away business. This ironical procedure followed within a day the Senate's failure to include expected support of the WPA project in Uncle Sam's relief measure.

In the same week one of the town's leading legitimate houses, which has complemented the Federal organization's work of keeping the theatre alive, went the way of motion pictures, with a lowly "grind" policy. This was no less a playhouse than the Geary, opened as the Columbia and the first of its class to be erected downtown some thirty years ago, following the city's disaster of 1906.

But despite the theatre's seeming low estate in this section of the coast, new hope loomed with announcement that if the town was to get along for the present with but one home of the legitimate, that house would be kept continuously alight. This would be the Curran, newer than the adjoining Geary, and which has housed most of the leading road attractions since its construction.

Here Capitalist Louis Lurie, who had gradually moved into the rialto scene, entered partnership with Homer Curran, whose production activities with Edward Belasco once meant much to San Francisco theatregoers. Abandoning his leasing interest in the rival Geary, Mr. Lurie proclaimed that what this town needed most was an undarkened theatre. And the Curran-Lurie firm would bring it about with its own productions to supplement those too infrequent ones from what is now laughingly called the road.

With assurances that worthy plays acted by "name" players and even stars would be forthcoming, he said there was nothing definite to report under that heading as this record was completed.

But there was still the cheering certainty that Helen Hayes and Herbert Marshall would be on the scene July 10 with a premiere of "Ladies and Gentlemen," a comedy laid in California and the work of Ben Hecht and Charles MacArthur. Moreover it was to mark Gilbert Miller's first Summer absence from England in 25 years, so that he might join authors and stars here for the opening rites.

His visit was to have further significance as a long-delayed follow-up of his father Henry's practice of giving San Francisco a Summer theatrical feast each year, with a premiere of at least one new play destined for Broadway. (Note—When drama critics hereabouts get into the mood of harking back, it is usually a hark to the Henry Miller seasons. And the harkers are always at their best in lean days of the legitimate.)

Returning from cheerful matters to the Federal Theatre obsequies, let it go into the record that it was "The Swing Mikado" which so gloomily closed at the government's playhouse at the Golden Gate International Exposition on Treasure Island as "Two a Day," a vaudeville cavalcade, from Los Angeles, was shut down at the Alcazar, the Federal mainland base, after a run of five weeks and prospects for as many more. The organization's third hit, Hall Johnson's "Run, Little Chillun," had previously hung up a city record of more than four solid months. This had definitely ended the project's period of poverty and its toying through the theatrical year with plays old and new and such alternates as "Murder in the Cathedral" and "Having Wonderful Time," "Night Must Fall" and "Room Service."

San Francisco's exposition had been looked to for a rejuvenation of the town's legitimate theatres, besides adding to the year's entertainment on its own account. By early summer it had not increased the number of touring attractions expected to be drawn to the city to entertain a larger body of visiting theatregoers than usual.

But the Fair by that time had not only done well for itself on the amusement score, but in the case of Clifford C. Fischer's "Folies Bergère" had given San Francisco a brand of spectacular vaudeville and beauty show it otherwise would never have seen. Mr. Fischer was so impressed by the acclaim given his offering on an early visit that he returned it from Hollywood for a second run and made plans to import an even more Parisian show for late Summer, bringing over his costumes and scenery in bond with a company of seventy-five people.

There was more than the difference of a titular "l" in the "Follies" which J. J. Shubert whipped up in Hollywood under the name of Ziegfeld for the exposition's California Auditorium

between the Fischer dates. Its unanimous panning by the critics
was as severe as their praise for the French attraction was ful-
some.

Mr. Shubert provided better known names—Al Trahan, Everett
Marshall and Ruby Mercer—more and newer costumes and lush
settings, more songs and dances. But his glorified girls lacked
the glamour and training of their rivals in the "Folies Bergère."

Most massive of spectacles, on what was probably the world's
largest stage, was the "Cavalcade of the West," a pageant set
for the Fair's duration and a consistent draw. There was disappointment that Thomas Wood Stevens of nearby Stanford University had not provided a counterpart of the Globe Theatre
company to present Shakespearean tabloid plays as an exposition attraction. Similar productions were left to the Federal
Theatre in its three playhouses at the government building, too
soon terminated by Washington's official closing order.

In the city's two leading theatres the year was barer of legitimate entertainment than at any time since the gold rush of 1849.

Gertrude Lawrence relighted and vastly brightened the Curran
in late Summer with five big weeks in "Susan and God." Tallulah
Bankhead followed with an average fortnight in "I Am Different," to be overshadowed by Ann Harding's excellent run for the
same period in a revival of "Candida."

A decided casualty was Victor Victor's new play, "Soliloquy,"
with which John Beal ventured into New York later for a similar
fate, but with more merciful brevity. Swinging to another revival, Homer Curran and Luther Greene took a chance with
George Kelly's "The Torch-Bearers," starring Constance Collier,
with Clay Clement and Maude Eburne in support. The response
was but fair.

Cornelia Otis Skinner scored impressively in her first one-
woman play, "Edna His Wife," but the ill-advised Cissie Loftus
returned to the stage in disappointing fashion with characteriza-
tions old and new. In her older guises she was the more successful. Trudi Schoop, continuing the mimic cycle, found more favor.

Irene Rich had cause for repentance in daring a stage come-
back in the new play, Jacques Deval's "A Broom for the Bride."
Ending her run midway of the second week, she returned to radio
and screen assignments.

An annual light opera season, probably to be extended to four
weeks next year, seemed assured with the success of Helen
Gahagan in a revival of "The Cat and the Fiddle" and the return of John Charles Thomas in "The Gypsy Baron," an operetta

based on Johann Strauss' "Zigeunerbaron." The Strauss music and a modernized book by George Marion enlivened the production, but not so much as did Thomas, reveling in the part of a strolling lion tamer. In his support appeared Soprano Vivian Della Chiesa, Hope Manning and Billy Gilbert.

Miss Gahagan, who scored in "The Cat and the Fiddle" here a half dozen years ago, was supported in the new cast by George Houston and Odette Myrtil. Thomas had played a record-breaking engagement at the same theatre last season in "Blossom Time."

Jed Harris's production of "Our Town," starring Frank Craven, was announced to run for two weeks only when the town failed to respond at once to Thornton Wilder's prize play as expected. Patronage increased after the first five days, but plans to disband the company had been made and the engagement was terminated as planned.

"On Borrowed Time," another Broadway success in which Death was an unaccustomed theme as entertainment, received more attention and a longer run at the Geary Theatre, with Victor Moore in the starring role of "Gramps" and Guy Bates Post as Mr. Brink. Opening on the same night as "Our Town" in the adjoining theatre, "Of Mice and Men" was well supported for one week longer than the Wilder play. Wallace Ford brought out the production in association with Sam H. Harris, resuming his role of George and with Lon Chaney, Jr., of Hollywood as Lennie.

The New York company in "Pins and Needles," the garment workers' musical revue, did a fair business, as did Ethel Barrymore in "Whiteoaks." Brock Pemberton personally accompanied his third company for a moderately successful run of "Kiss the Boys Good-bye."

Heading the special events of the year was Max Reinhardt's production of "Faust" in the Civic Auditorium. It was massively staged, with Conrad Nagel in the title role, George Houston as Mephistopheles and Lenore Ulric and Margo in other roles. The California Festival Association's sponsorship and the Reinhardt name were well publicized, but the general public responded indifferently.

Santa Clara University's seventh production of its famed Passion Play by the late Clay M. Greene led the near-by collegiate offerings in importance. Stanford University, which had done most of Alumnus Maxwell Anderson's plays under special concessions as to rights, turned its attention to Shakespeare, concentrating on "The Tempest," and followed with Gorky's "The Lower Depths," "Tobias and the Angel" and "Knickerbocker Holiday."

The University of California Little Theatre, on its postage stamp platform in Wheeler Auditorium, continued to work prodigiously, featuring "Murder in the Cathedral," "The Cradle Will Rock" and "Anna Christie."

The revived Players Club of San Francisco put on a 1939 Summer festival in which Novelist Charles Caldwell Dobie's dramatization of Frank Norris's "McTeague" was a highlight. The Wayfarers, one of the city's sturdiest little theatres, continued its varied programs, with periodical delvings into Shakespeare. And the Berkeley Playmakers announced its sixteenth annual prize in a national one-act playwriting contest.

## THE SEASON IN SOUTHERN CALIFORNIA

### By Edwin Schallert
### Drama Editor of the *Los Angeles Times*

CLASSIFYING trends in the theatre during the season of 1938-39 in Southern California is, perhaps, one of the most difficult tasks to face the appraiser in recent years. Not to sing the blues, but to face facts, it is probably the lack of progress in any direction in the professional sphere of the play that makes this particularly true of the twelve-month ending this mid-annum. Tendencies that promised much in the 1937-38 period, notably the revival of road attractions, have been severely hit by what commentators are pleased to call the recession. From the standpoint of the showgoer, who had previously entertained high anticipations for real development, a far more appropriate word would be depression. It was symbolized by the almost total absence of visiting companies during the earlier part of the season, and the inactivity likewise for long spaces in Coast production, plus the futility from a commercial angle of most efforts to put life and liveliness into the languishing drama.

Yet in this very season of seeming setbacks was witnessed simultaneously the extended runs of two Federal Theatre offerings, "Run, Little Chillun" by Hall Johnson, and the "Two-a-Day" vaudeville revue by Gene Stone and Jack Robinson, as well as the strengthening, if anything, of the community playhouse fortress, with its attendant scholastic adjuncts.

Max Reinhardt and Henry Duffy are now forces in this domain, which is ruled, of course, by the Pasadena Community Playhouse. Both Reinhardt and Duffy broke away from student presentations, as such, at least once during the year to offer productions of larger significance, and furthermore Reinhardt was represented by the financially unfortunate "Faust" offered in the summer of 1938 as a festival event at the Pilgrimage Play outdoor theatre.

Reinhardt's other bid for larger public favor, his revival of the old Goldoni comedy, "At Your Service," was inherently more interesting and attractive, even though not essentially professional. Duffy's testing of the appeal of a new play, "Mrs. Lincoln," by Ramon Romero, in which his wife, Dale Winter, was starred in the title part, did not meet happiest fate, despite it had certain distinct merits. It had not been properly condensed prior to the premiere.

The big question of the moment is: What do the protracted engagements of the Federal's "Run, Little Chillun" and "Two-a-Day" prove regarding the Southern California theatre? What especially can they prove with the present tumult and turmoil in the project itself, due to its possible abandonment? One production, "Run, Little Chillun," with an all-Negro cast, a genre affair of the colored race, quite extraordinary of its type, ran nearly a year, most of the time at one theatre, and has lately been experimented with as a commercial venture. The other, a piquant vaudeville revue, as rare as old wine, namely "Two-a-Day," had more than a six months' stay in a Hollywood playhouse.

The same vital elements may possibly be detected in these two offerings, that characterize "The Drunkard," now in its seventh year at the Theatre Mart, namely their novelty. It is this same element, incidentally, that caused a sort of tabloid revue, the "Folies Bergère," which came to Los Angeles from the San Francisco exposition, to play a good healthy engagement at that citadel of the motion pictures, Grauman's Chinese Theatre, on a three-a-day basis.

The freakish nature of all these victories for showmanship do not, regrettably, spell any well-defined policy for theatrical advancement. They are heartening hits only because they show that there is a potential public willing to attend on the footlights, but this public probably would just as readily pursue a big gridiron contest or an exciting midget auto race. There is, in other words, no integrated audience that may be depended on for its devotion to the play in Southern California. Only exception that might be cited to this are the Pasadena Community adherents. The fickle nature of the theatregoer in Los Angeles itself is evidenced now even in reception according the motion picture, which has endured its uncertainties during the year in Southern California.

Remedy for all this now being suggested is a subscription plan to insure better play-giving and possibly the visits of primary New York productions, with their original companies, a plan which is beginning to find a place in eastern cities. On the Coast it is still but talk, without much official sanction. One hears occasionally that the Music Foundation of the Junior Chamber of Commerce in Los Angeles will embark on play-sponsoring. The Junior Chamber itself, though a separate organization, has lately been promoting the destiny of "Where Liberty Dwells" by Austin Strong as a festival offering for the Fall of 1939, and that may crystallize into further enterprises. "Where Liberty Dwells," concerning Lafayette and Washington, expounds the theme of democracy and Americanism.

The Music Foundation on the other hand has had some negotiations with Arthur Beckhard, noted for his efforts a year or so ago in the production field in Santa Barbara. Intentions of this body seem to be germinating with promise, but it may be a year before there is actual fulfillment.

Meantime Helen Hayes' starring in "Ladies and Gentlemen" with Herbert Marshall in Santa Barbara, San Francisco and Los Angeles is at least somewhat of a restorative to wavering theatrical hopes. This is a July-August (1939) happening and therefore beyond the scope of this review. It may be noted that the play is by Charles MacArthur and Ben Hecht (names in that order) based on an original by Ladilaus Bus-Fekete, the Hungarian. The Hayes glamour was undeniable during the 1937-38 season, and the new premiere looms more importantly than anything that took place in 1938-39. So maybe the curtain of the auspicious is raised once again—for the 1939-40 season.

Of the Burns Mantle ten-best plays only two have been seen on the Coast—"Susan and God," by Rachel Crothers, starring Gertrude Lawrence, and "Kiss the Boys Good-bye," by Clare Boothe, offered by a fair-to-middling road company. Other road and Coast offerings in the professional class included "On Borrowed Time," starring Victor Moore; "Candida," with Ann Harding; "I Am Different," starring Tallulah Bankhead; "Soliloquy," with John Beal; "Torch-bearers," with Constance Collier; "Whiteoaks," starring Ethel Barrymore; "Of Mice and Men," with Wallace Ford, Lon Chaney, Jr., and Isabel Jewell, and most of the original New York supporting cast; "Our Town," with Frank Craven; "Tobacco Road," third or fourth return, with John Barton.

Too much cannot be said of the effectiveness of the majority of these attractions. Best in general qualities were "Of Mice and Men," "Our Town," and needless to say "Susan and God." Lon Chaney, Jr., turned out to be quite an astonishing Lennie in "Of Mice and Men," deserving of stage recognition in the future, without doubt. "Our Town" did not seem to possess full-fledged popular appeal, even though admired for the fine writing of Thornton Wilder. "I Am Different" by Zoe Akins missed rather completely on its premiere in Los Angeles. "Soliloquy" did slightly better but failed of audience approval. "Whiteoaks," despite the Barrymore presence, was adjudged dull. Scarcely anything was distinguished, and that fact is no aid or benefit to the theatre in the western area.

Light opera was triumphant again, due to the presence of John Charles Thomas in a so-called streamlined version of Johann Strauss' "The Gypsy Baron," contrived by Ann Ronell and George Marion, Jr., from the films. Music was interestingly arranged, but neither book nor lyrics were illuminative. A point was made of the fact that only 40 per cent of the original "Gypsy Baron" melodies were used. The rest was made up largely of Strauss Viennese waltzes. With Thomas as star the production enjoyed packed houses.

Allan Jones also proved a magnet in "The Desert Song," while "The Cat and the Fiddle," with Helen Gahagan and George Houston, was commendable. "The Waltz Dream" rather missed fire, and the standard of the season, particularly openings, was below the par established the previous year. Light opera will proceed as an institution regardless.

Again one finds himself face to face with a theatrical perplexity in the case of Earl Carroll, who has had eminent good fortune in the dual roles of revue producer and night club proprietor. Ordinarily one would scarcely take cognizance of an activity such as this in a strictly theatrical review of the year. But in Southern California the Earl Carroll establishment seems to be regarded as theatre rather than restaurant. His net profits within about six months are supposed to have attained almost $100,000. His entertainment center is known from Coast to Coast, and lures the tourists. He has staged two of the most elaborate revues ever seen in Los Angeles, and has the most modern stage equipment to accomplish this. For a brief while he had Willie and Eugene Howard as the stars of his second show, but their material was, as a whole, not adaptable. Eye appeal of beautiful girls is the pre-eminent facet in the Carroll contribution. He chose a name for his second show related to the current exposition mood of New York and San Francisco in "The World's Fairest," and Carroll seems to have had no trouble in finding the charmers to live up to that description in the pulchritudinous mazes of the film colony.

Everything in Pasadena Community's chronicles for the year seemed to build up nicely to a dramatic climax when that creative center premiered "The Great American Family," adapted by Robert Chapin and Charles King from a book of the same name by Lee Shippey, Los Angeles columnist. Simple, unaffected, and even untheatrical this impression of a pulp-magazine writer and his family held undeniable interest, which received initial stimulus from the fact that the author is so well known in the locality. The Pasadena surpassed its own record for runs with the play, previously held by "Lazarus Laughs" of Eugene O'Neill, and commercial production was subsequently contemplated.

The summer festival of Maxwell Anderson plays at the theatre opened even more auspiciously than the past four adventures of the same type. "Elizabeth the Queen" was staged with art, and the casting was exceptionally good. This initial festival piece was given toward the end of June, and "Valley Forge," "The Wingless Victory," "The Masque of Kings," "Both Your Houses," "Gods of Lightning," "Winterset" and "The Star-Wagon" were programed through the remainder of the summer as a fine demonstration of accomplishment of a native dramatist and poet. In 1938 the Irish-British Bernard Shaw reigned with his "Arms and the Man," "Major Barbara," "Heartbreak House," "On the Rocks" and "Back to Methuselah."

Between the festival pyramids, so to speak, the repertoire of the playhouse included "Autumn Crocus," C. L. Anthony; "O Evening Star," Zoe Akins (first time on Coast); "Tovarich," Jacques Deval; "And Stars Remain," Philip G. and Julius J. Epstein (first Coast); "Paradise Plantation," Shirland Quin (new); "Yes, My Darling Daughter," Mark Reed; "The Boy David," James M. Barrie (first American); "You Can't Take it With You," Kaufman and Hart; "Ah Wilderness," Eugene O'Neill; "Stage Door," Ferber and Kaufman; "Where the Blue

Begins," Christopher Morley (first American); "Brother Rat," Finkelhoff and Monks; "Olympia," Molnar; "The Unguarded Hour," Bernard Merivale (first Coast); "To Quito and Back," Ben Hecht, and the three J. B. Priestley plays, a minor festival, including "Time and the Conways," "People at Sea" and "I Have Been Here Before." There stands, of course, the progressiveness of the Southern California theatre.

Besides "Run, Little Chillun" and "Two-a-Day," the Federal Theatres offered some very creditable presentations of "Alien Corn," "High Tor," "Having Wonderful Time," "Volpone," and gave also "Excursion," "Judgment Day," "Bird of Paradise," "Prologue to Glory," "The Amazing Dr. Clitterhouse," "To the Ladies," "The Milky Way," "The Alarm Clock" and various others. Total plays produced during 1938-39 season was 22, and the total attendance is recorded as 496,874. Quality improved over previous years.

Sporadic activities, commercial and otherwise, comprised a revival of "White Cargo" for quite some duration, production of Schiller's "William Tell" by an assemblage of refugee European actors; "Horrorscope" revue, Cornelia Otis Skinner in her one-woman repertoire; "The Shattered Lamp," "Hobohemians," vaudeville; "Gettysburg," Will Morrissey revue, etc.

Needless to say, there is no abatement of the community and little theatre doings, and there won't be, so long as there is a chance for talent to be trained and be discovered for pictures in Hollywood, as well as the inherent urge toward play-giving which still, in one form or another, seems to be a national manifestation.

# ABE LINCOLN IN ILLINOIS
## A Drama in Three Acts

### By Robert E. Sherwood

A CERTAIN lightly suppressed excitement followed the approach of Robert Emmet Sherwood's drama, "Abe Lincoln in Illinois," which reached Broadway in mid-October, 1938. For one thing it had been preceded the season before by another Lincoln play, which was E. P. Conkle's "Prologue to Glory," produced with considerable success by the Federal WPA Theatre. Speculation was stirred, though it did not become exactly rife, as to how the two dramas would compare. Secondly, "Abe Lincoln in Illinois" was the first production sponsored by a newly organized Playwrights' Producing Company, operating through which five leading American dramatists, including in addition to Mr. Sherwood, Maxwell Anderson, Sidney Howard, Elmer Rice and S. N. Behrman, had banded together to produce their own plays. Formerly similar co-operative ventures among the playwrights had not proved either artistically inspiring or commercially successful. Thirdly, there had been some suggestion that the employment of a Canadian-British actor, Raymond Massey, to play the role of America's most idolized hero might easily present a handicap of sentiment and personality which the play would have to overcome.

As it turned out no one of these three items, unless it be that of the play's sponsorship, exerted the least bias in the drama's reception. Comparison with the Conkle drama was quickly eliminated, save in the broadest sense, by the fact that the two plays were studies of differing Lincolns, the one an awkward youth of slumbering ambition, the other a rapidly maturing and solemnly apprehensive young man. An interested enthusiasm for the success of the author-producers helped the venture and Mr. Massey's quick and complete personal success in characterization included his performance as an asset rather than a liability.

The critical reception of "Abe Lincoln in Illinois" was largely on the rapturous side. A majority of the reviewers were unashamedly ecstatic in their praise of the drama, and of Mr. Sherwood's writing and Mr. Massey's performance. "Mr. Sher-

wood has written his finest play," declared Brooks Atkinson.
" 'Abe Lincoln in Illinois' is part of the living truth of America."
" 'Abe Lincoln in Illinois' is the great American drama," declared
Heywood Broun, who had been handicapped in discovering the
great American drama for some years by reason of other em-
ployment.

There were more modest estimates, and one or two mild dis-
senters. It was John Mason Brown's contention, for example,
that Mr. Sherwood had been helped materially by collaborators,
including the audience's fore-knowledge of the hero's greatness, as
well as Mr. Lincoln's own contributions to the script. "Had
there been calls of 'Author! Author!' " wrote Mr. Brown, "Mr.
Sherwood would have had to appear behind the footlights hand
in hand with Honest Abe. Failing him he would have been compelled to walk on with a copy of the Lincoln-Douglas debates
in his hand and point to it, even as conductors point with proper
gratitude to the members of their orchestras without whom there
would have been no music."

There was general admission, however, that this was the greatest of the Lincoln plays to date, and to this admission the general play-going public quickly and whole-heartedly subscribed.
"Abe Lincoln" ran through the season, playing to consistently
large and enthusiastic audiences.

We first meet Abe Lincoln in Mr. Sherwood's play in the cabin
of Mentor Graham, schoolmaster, in New Salem, Ill. It is late
at night. Abe, long, loose, gaunt, tired, though intent, is sitting
at a rude table across from Graham, who has been giving him a
lesson in grammar. Abe is dressed in the ragged clothes of a
backwoodsman. One arm is swung awkwardly across the back
of his chair and his long legs stretch out before him.

Mentor is describing the moods. "Every one of us has many
moods," he is explaining. "You yourself have more than your
share of them, Abe. They express the various aspects of your
character. So it is with the English language—"

One by one the moods are taken up and analyzed. The in-
dicative, imperative, potential, subjunctive and infinitive. Now
Mentor has found a newspaper and from it he asks Abe to read
a part of a Congressional speech by Daniel Webster: "A fine
document and a perfect usage of the imperative mood in its horta-
tory sense," explains Mentor.

Abe begins the speech with some crude idea of declamation,
but Mentor is not satisfied. "Imagine that you're making the
speech before the Senate, with the fate of your country at stake,"

he corrects. And Abe, raising his voice commandingly, proceeds:

" 'When my eyes shall be turned to behold for the last time the sun in heaven, may I not see him shining on the broken and dishonored fragments of a once glorious Union; on States dissevered, discordant, belligerent; on a lane rent with civil feuds, or drenched, it may be, in fraternal blood! Let their last feeble glance rather behold the glorious ensign of the Republic, now known and honored throughout the earth, not a single star of it obscured, bearing for its motto no such miserable—' "

" 'Interrogatory—' "

" 'Interrogatory as "What is all this worth?" Nor, those other words of delusion and folly, "Liberty first and Union afterwards"; but everywhere, spread all over in characters of living light, that other sentiment, dear to every true American heart—Liberty and Union . . .' "

"Emphasize the 'and.' "

" 'Liberty *and* Union, now and forever, one and inseparable!' "

Abe thinks that Webster must have had his hearers up on their feet and cheering with that speech. Mentor explains that while some cheered others spat—"depending on which section they came from."

"What was he talking about?" Abe wants to know.

"It was in the debate over the right of any State to secede from the Union," explains Mentor. "Calhoun had pleaded South Carolina's cause—pleaded it ably. He said that just as we have liberty as individuals—so have we liberty as States—to go as we please. Which means, if we don't like the Union, as expressed by the will of its majority, then we can leave it, and set up a new nation, or many nations—so that this continent might be as divided as Europe. But Webster answered him, all right. He proved that without the Union, we'd have precious little liberty left."

They have arrived at the potential mood. "That signifies possibility, usually of an unpleasant nature," announces Abe. "Like, 'If ever I get out of debt I'll probably get right back in again.' "

"Why did you select that example, Abe?" Mentor asks.

"Well—it just happens to be the thought that's always heaviest on my mind."

"Is the store in trouble again?"

"Yes. Berry's drunk all the whiskey we ought to have sold, and we're going to have to shut up any day now. I guess I'm my father's own son, all right. Give me a steady job and I'll fail at it."

Mentor cannot agree with that conclusion. Abe, he insists, is as well-liked as any man in the community and everybody is anxious to help him. Abe admits that. Even now Josh Speed and Judge Green are trying to get him appointed postmaster. "I've got my friends, all right," Abe agrees, "the best friends. But they can't change my luck, or maybe it's just my nature."

"What you want to do is get out of New Salem. This poor little forgotten town will never give anyone an opportunity."

Abe has thought of moving. His family have always been movers. "My old father ambled from Virginia to one place after another in Kentucky, where I was born," he says. "And then into Indiana and then here in Illinois. About all I can remember of when I was a boy was hitching up and then unhitching, and then hitching up again. . . . But wherever I go—it'll be the same story—more friends, more debts."

"Well, Abe, just bear in mind that there are always two professions open to people who fail at everything else; there's school-teaching and there's politics."

"Then I'll choose school-teaching. You go into politics, and you may get elected."

"Yes—there's always that possibility."

"And if you get elected, you've got to go to the city. I don't want none of that."

"What did I say about two negatives?"

"I meant, any of that."

It appears that Abe's objection to cities comes from his experience the two times he has been to New Orleans. It was the people that scared him. He was scared they might kill him. Yet he doesn't know why he thought so.

"You think a lot about death, don't you?" Mentor suggests.

"I've had to," answers Abe, quite solemnly, "because it has always seemed to be so close in the forest where I grew up. When I was no higher than this table, we buried my mother. The milk sick got her, poor creature. I helped Paw make the coffin—whittled the pegs for it with my own jack-knife. We buried her in a timber clearing beside my grandmother, old Betsy Sparrow. I used to go there often and look at the place—used to watch the deer running over her grave with their little feet. I never could kill a deer after that. One time I catched hell from Paw because when he was taking aim I knocked his gun up. And I always compare the looks of those deer with the looks of men—like the men in New Orleans—that you could see had murder in their hearts."

"You're a hopeless mess of inconsistency, Abe Lincoln."

"How do you mean, Mentor?"

"I've never seen anyone who is so friendly and at the same time so misanthropic."

"What's that?"

"A misanthrope is one who distrusts men and avoids their society."

"Well—maybe that's how I am.  Oh—I like people, well enough—when you consider 'em one by one.  But they seem to look different when they're put into crowds, or mobs, or armies."

Abe is about to leave when Mentor finds something else he wants him to read.  It's a poem.  He hands it to Abe, and Abe reads—

" 'On Death—written at the age of 19 by the late John Keats.

" 'Can death be sleep, when life is but a dream,
And scenes of bliss pass as a phantom by?
The transient (*He hesitates on that word.*) pleasures as a
    vision seem,
And yet we think the greatest pain's to die. (*He moves closer
    to the light.*)
How strange it is that man on earth should roam,
And lead a life of woe, but not forsake
His rugged path—nor dare he view alone
His future doom—which is but to awake.' " (*He looks at*
    MENTOR.)

"That sure is good, Mentor.  It's fine!"

He is reading it again, to himself as the lights fade.

It is noon of July 4.  In a rude tap-room of New Salem's Rutledge Tavern there are a table and two chairs with a stool and an old keg to serve as a stool when needed.  There is a bench in front of a fireplace, and another along the back wall. On the wall bench Ben Mattling, a veteran of the Revolutionary War and one of New Salem's minor social problems, is waiting for service when Ninian Edwards, Judge Bowling Green and Josh Speed come in.  Mr. Edwards is a visitor, "young, handsome and prosperous."  Judge Green is "elderly, fat and gentle," and Mr. Speed is a "quiet, mild, solid, thoughtful and well-dressed" citizen.

His escorts have brought Mr. Edwards to the Tavern looking

for Abe Lincoln. While Josh Speed goes in search of Abe the others order whiskey from Ann Rutledge, the young and attractive mistress of the Inn, and settle down to wait. Soon it appears from their talk that Mr. Edwards is down from Springfield in search of a candidate for the Assembly who will, if elected, help even in a small way "to frustrate that tyrant, Andy Jackson."

"I assure you that I yield to no one in my admiration for the character of our venerable President," declares Mr. Edwards; "but when he goes to the extent of ruining our banking structure, destroying faith in our currency and even driving sovereign states to the point of secession, then, gentlemen, it is time to call a halt."

"We got two more years of him—if the old man lives that long," says Judge Green. "You can't make headway against his popularity."

"But we can start now to drive out his minions here in the government of the State of Illinois. We have a great battle cry, 'End the reign of Andrew Jackson.'"

Jack Armstrong, leader of the Clary's Grove Boys, has burst into the room, followed by three of his crowd. They have come to demand a keg of liquor and are rough about it. They only laugh at Miss Rutledge's order that they leave.

"If my father were here he'd take a gun to you," says Ann; "just as he would to a pack of prairie wolves."

"If your Paw was here he'd be scareder than you," boasts Jack. "'Cause he knows we're the wildcats of Clary's Grove, worse'n any old wolves, and we're a-howlin' and a-spittin' for drink. So get the whiskey, Miss Annie, and save your poor old Paw a lot of expenses for damages to his property."

They are getting ugly now, and are ready to fight. Picking out one possible opponent after another they come finally to the stranger, Ninian Edwards, and recognize him as the Governor's son. Jack doesn't like Ninian, who is trying to be amiable.

"No wonder you've got a New Orleans suit of clothes and a gold fob and a silver-headed cane," sneers Jack, picking up the cane. "I reckon you can buy the best of everything with that steamin' old pirate land-grabber for a Paw. I guess them fancy pockets of yourn are pretty well stuffed with the money your Paw stole from us taxpayers—eh—Mr. Edwards?"

"Let's take it offen him, Jack," suggests one of the other Grove boys.

"Let's give him a lickin', Jack," puts in a third.

They are ready to close in on Ninian when Ann brings them a mug of liquor apiece. They are about to start in to help themselves to the keg when Ann makes a last protest—

"Aren't there any of you men can do anything to protect decent people from these ruffians?" she pleads.

Ninian Edwards is quick to answer. He will be glad to do whatever he can, despite the hasty advice of Judge Green that probably it would be better if he were careful. This suggestion serves to whet Jack Armstrong's confidence. He is prowling around his intended victim, promising to give him a taste of the Clary's Grove boys' talent as bone crushers, when the door opens and Abe Lincoln quietly walks in.

Abe is now wearing a "battered claw-hammer coat and pants that have been 'foxed' with buckskin." He is carrying the mail, and has brought a letter for Ann. He is a little surprised that the Grove boys aren't drunk yet, but not at all surprised that they are spoiling for a fight. But why should they want to fight Edwards?

"Put a stop to it, Abe," pleads the Judge. "It'd be next door to murder."

"You stop your trap, Pot Green," advises the surly Jack. "Murder's too good for any goose-livered enemy of Andy Jackson. Come on, boys!"

ABE—Wait a minute, boys. Jack, have you forgot what day it is?

JACK—No, I ain't! But I reckon the Fourth of July is as good a day as any to whip a politician!

ABE (*amiably*)—Well, if you've just got to fight, Jack, you shouldn't give preference to strangers. Being postmaster of this thriving town, I can rate as a politician, myself, so you'd better try a fall with me— (*He turns to* NINIAN.) And as for you, sir, I haven't the pleasure of your acquaintance; but my name's Lincoln, and I'd like to shake hands with a brave man.

NINIAN (*shaking hands with* ABE)—I'm greatly pleased to know you, Mr. Lincoln.

ABE—You should be. Because I came just in time to save you quite some embarrassment, not to mention injury. Got a couple of letters for you, Bowling. Here's your Cincinnati *Journal*, Trum.

JACK—Look here, Abe—you're steppin' into something that ain't none of your business. This is a private matter of patriotic honor . . .

ABE—Everything in this town is my business, Jack. It's the only kind of business I've got. And besides—I saw Hannah down by the grove and she says to tell you to come on to the

picnic and that means *now* or she'll give the cake away to the
Straders children and you and the boys'll go hungry.  So get
moving.

FEARGUS (*to* JACK)—Are you goin' to let Abe talk you out
of it?

ABE—Sure he is.  (*He turns to* TRUM COGDAL.)  Say, Trum—
if you ain't using that *Journal* for a while, would you let me
have a read?

TRUM—By all means, Abe.  Here you are.  (*He tosses the
paper to* ABE.)

ABE—Thanks.  (*He turns again to* JACK.)  Better hurry, Jack
—or you'll get a beatin' from Hannah.  (*He starts to take the
wrapper off, as he goes over to a chair.*)

JACK (*looks at* ABE *for a moment, then laughs.  To* NINIAN)—
All right!  Abe Lincoln saved your hide.  I'll consent to callin'
off the fight just because he's a friend of mine.

ABE—And also because I'm the only one around here you can't
lick.

JACK—But I just want to tell you, Mr. Ninian Edwards,
Junior, that the next time you come around here a-spreadin' pisen
and—

ABE—Go on, Jack, Hannah's waiting.

JACK (*over to* ABE)—I'm going, Abe.  But I warn you—you'd
better stop this foolishness of reading, reading, reading morning
noon and night or you'll be getting soft, and you won't be the
same fighting man you are now.  And it would break my heart
to see you licked by anybody—including me.

The Clary's Grove boys are ready to leave.  Abe notices the
one called Feargus with the keg of liquor he has taken from Ann's
kitchen, and orders him to put it back.  After the Grove boys
have stormed out the talk turns again to the object of Mr. Edwards' visit.

"Abe—how would you like to run for the State Assembly?"
asks Josh Speed.

"When?"

"Now—for the election in the Fall."

"Why?"

NINIAN—Mr. Lincoln, I've known you for only a few minutes,
but that's long enough to make me agree with Josh Speed that
you're precisely the type of man we want.  The whole Whig
organization will support your candidacy.

ABE—Is this your idea, Josh?

JOSH (*smiling*)—Oh, no, Abe—you're the people's choice.

TRUM—What do *you* think of it, Bowling?

BOWLING (*heartily*)—I think it's as fine a notion as I ever heard. Why, Abe—I can hear you making speeches, right and left, taking your stand on all the issues—secession, Texas, the National Bank crisis, abolitionism—it'll be more fun than we ever had in our lives!

ABE—Isn't anybody going to ask what *I* think?

JOSH (*laughs*)—All right, Abe—*I'll* ask you.

ABE (*after a moment's pause*)—It's a comical notion, all right —and I don't know if I can give you an answer to it, off-hand. But my first, hasty impression is that I don't think much of it.

BOWLING—Don't overlook the fact that, if elected, your salary would be three whole dollars a day.

ABE—That's fine money. No doubt of that. And I see what you have in mind, Bowling. I owe you a considerable sum of money; and if I stayed in the legislature for, say, twenty years, I'd be able to pay off . . . $2.50 a day— (*He is figuring it up on his fingers.*)

BOWLING—I'm not thinking about the debts, Abe.

ABE—I know you ain't, Bowling. But I've got to. And so should you, Mr. Edwards. The Whig party is the party of sound money and God save the National Bank, ain't it?

NINIAN—Why, yes—among other things . . .

ABE—Well, then—how would it look if you put forward a candidate who has demonstrated no earning power but who has run up the impressive total of fifteen hundred dollars of debts?

BOWLING (*to* NINIAN)—I can tell you something about those debts. Abe started a grocery store in partnership with an unfortunate young man named Berry. Their stock included whiskey, and Berry started tapping the keg until he had consumed all the liquid assets. (*Chuckles.*) So the store went bankrupt, and was non compos mentis, through drink—and Abe voluntarily assumed all the obligations. Fifteen hundred dollars' worth! That may help to explain to you, Mr. Edwards, why we think pretty highly of him around here.

NINIAN—It's a sentiment with which I concur most heartily.

ABE—I thank you one and all for your kind tributes, but don't overdo them, or I'll begin to think that three dollars a day ain't enough.

It is Josh Speed's idea that election would give Abe the thing he most wants, a chance to learn, a chance to associate with the finest lawyers in the State. Abe isn't sure the finest lawyers

would welcome association with him.  Ninian Edwards is convinced Abe is the kind that knows how to handle men.

"I can handle the Clary's Grove boys because I can out-wrassle
them—but I can't go around Sangamon County throwing all the
voters," laughs Abe.  Besides, how do they know that his political
views would agree with theirs?

"We need good, conservative men to counteract all the radical
fire-brands that have swept over this country in the wake of
Andrew Jackson.  We've got to get this country back to first
principles."

"Well—I'm conservative, all right," admits Abe.  "If I got
into the legislature you'd never catch me starting any movements
for reform or progress.  I'm pretty certain I wouldn't even have
the nerve to open my mouth."

"I told you, Ninian—he's just the type of candidate you're
looking for," laughs Josh.

It is Mr. Edwards' opinion that Abe, as postmaster, is in an
excellent position from which to conduct a campaign and dis-
tribute literature.  "We want to spike the rumor that ours is the
party of the more privileged classes," he adds.  "That is why we
seek men of the plain people for candidates."

"Would you supply me with a suit of store clothes?" Abe
wants to know.  "A candidate mustn't look *too* plain."

Mr. Edwards thinks that can be arranged.  "So—think it over,
Mr. Lincoln, and realize that this is opportunity unlimited in
scope.  Just consider what it means to be starting up the ladder
in a nation which is now expanding southward, across the vast
area of Texas; and westward, to the Empire of the Californias on
the Pacific Ocean.  We're becoming a continent, Mr. Lincoln—
and all that we need is men!"

Ninian Edwards and the others have gone when Ann Rutledge
comes back to clear the table.  Abe would have a talk with Ann,
if she will listen to him.  She will, but she doesn't consider that
just because he's postmaster, and happens to know that she has
had a letter from a certain Mr. McNeil, that it's any concern
of his—

"I know that, Ann," Abe quickly admits.  "But it appears to
me that you've been crying—and it makes me sad to think that
something could have hurt you.  The thing is—I think quite a
lot of you—always have—ever since I first came here, and met
you.  I wouldn't mention it, only when you're distressed about
something it's a comfort sometimes even to find a pair of ears to
pour your troubles into—and the Lord knows my ears are big

enough to hold a lot."

Abe's reward is a tender smile and the assurance that, in Ann's eyes, he is a Christian gentleman. She is willing to admit, too, that perhaps she was silly to have promised herself to Mr. McNeil. She guesses she couldn't really love anybody as faithless as that. Which is all right with Abe, and he thinks she would be very foolish fretting any more about it. Perhaps, he admits, he doesn't know much about females, as Ann suspects, but he certainly spends a lot of time thinking about them. And he thinks Ann would be very foolish if she were to let what the New Salem gossips may say about her having been rejected, and all that, make her unhappy—

"I told you it's just weakness—it's just vanity," Ann is saying. "It's something you couldn't understand, Abe."

She has crossed the room and is staring out the window. Abe has twisted around in his chair to look at her.

"Maybe I can understand it, Ann," he says, slowly. "I've got a kind of vanity myself. Josh Speed said so, and he's right . . . It's—it's nothing but vanity that's kept me from declaring my inclinations toward you. (*She turns, amazed, and looks at him.*) You see, I don't like to be sniggered at, either. I know what I am—and I know what I look like—and I know that I've got nothing to offer any girl that I'd be in love with."

ANN—Are you saying that you're in love with me, Abe?

ABE (*with deep earnestness*)—Yes—I am saying that. (*He stands facing her. She looks intently into his eyes.*) I've been loving you—a long time—with all my heart. You see, Ann—you're a particularly fine girl. You've got sense, and you've got bravery—those are two things that I admire particularly. And you're powerful good to look at, too. So—it's only natural I should have a great regard for you. But—I don't mean to worry you about it, Ann. I only mentioned it because—if you would do me the honor of keeping company with me for a while, it might shut the old gossips' mouths. They'd figure you'd chucked McNeil for—for someone else. Even me.

ANN (*goes to him, puts her hand on his hand which is clutching a lapel*)—I thought I knew you pretty well, Abe. But I didn't.

ABE—Why do you say that? Do you consider I was too forward, in speaking out as I did?

ANN (*gravely*)—No, Abe . . . I've always thought a lot of you—the way I thought you were. But—the idea of love be-

tween you and me—I can't say how I feel about that, because
now you're like some other person, that I'm meeting for the first
time.

ABE (*quietly*)—I'm not expecting you to feel anything for
me. I'd never dream of expecting such a thing.

ANN—I know that, Abe. You'd be willing to give everything
you have and never expect anything in return. Maybe you're
different in that way from any man I ever heard of. And I can
tell you this much—now, and truthfully, Abe— If I ever do
love you, I'll be happy about it—and lucky, to be loving a good
decent man . . . If you just give me time, Abe—to think about
it . . .

ABE (*unable to believe his eyes and ears*)—You mean—if you
took time—you might get in your heart something like the feeling I have for you?

ANN (*with great tenderness*)—I don't know, Abe. But I do
know that you're a man who could fill anyone's heart—yes, fill it
and warm it and make it glad to be living. (*He stares at her so
hard that she again looks away from him. He takes her hand
between both of his and works it around in his terrific grasp. It
is some time before he finds words.*)

ABE—Ann—I've always tried hard to believe what the orators
tell us—that this is a land of equal opportunity for all. But I've
never been able to believe it, any more than I could believe God
made all men in his own image. But—if I could win you, Ann—
I'd be willing to disbelieve everything I've ever seen with my
own eyes, and have faith in everything that I've ever dreamed of.
(*Both are silent for a moment.*) But—I'm not asking you to say
anything now. And I won't ask you until the day comes when
I know I've got a right to. (*He lets go of her hand, picks up
the newspaper, rises, and walks quickly toward the door.*)

ANN—Abe! Where are you going?

ABE—I'm going to find Bowling Green and tell him a good
joke. (*He grins. He is standing in the doorway.*)

ANN (*worried*)—A *joke?* What about?

ABE—I'm going to tell him that I'm a candidate for the Assembly of the State of Illinois.

He goes out as the light fades.

The sitting room in Bowling Green's house near New Salem
is small and home-like. The walls are lined with books and
family pictures, there are comfortable chairs and a sofa. A ladder
at back leads to an attic room in which Abe Lincoln has been

sleeping. He has been away over a year now and has run down to New Salem because Ann Rutledge has been very ill. Abe is with Ann now.

Bowling and Nancy, his wife, have been sitting up waiting for Abe. They have been reading Dickens' *Pickwick Papers* when Josh Speed knocks on the door. Josh is also anxious about Abe. He has found him pretty moody of late, and in the Assembly Abe has just sat there drawing his three dollars a day without apparent interest in anything. Perhaps his being in love with Ann Rutledge explains it. It would be better for both of them if Abe were to marry Ann, Nancy thinks. But Bowling isn't so sure. Might ruin Abe—

"He could go to Springfield and set up a law practice and make a good thing of it. Ninian Edwards would help him to get started. And he'd soon forget little Ann. He has just happened to fasten on her his own romantic ideal of what's beautiful and unattainable. Let him ever attain her, and she'd break his heart."

Josh isn't sure he agrees with Bowling on that. He has been watching Abe ever since he met him the time Abe was piloting a steamboat. He thought for a long time he could help him to fame and fortune. But he soon learned differently—

"I found out that he has plenty of strength and courage in his body," says Josh, "but in his mind he's a hopeless hypochondriac. He can split rails, push a plow, crack jokes, all day—and then sit up all night reading "Hamlet" and brooding over his own resemblance to that melancholy prince. Maybe he's a great philosopher—maybe he's a great fool. I don't know what he is."

Nancy persists that neither Josh nor Bowling is of much help to Abe. They think of him as they might of a problem they had found in a book. Abe is a man, and he is miserable, insists Nancy, and all they do for his misery is to laugh at his comical jokes, vote for him on election day and give him board and lodging when he needs it. "All that doesn't give a scrap of satisfaction to Abe's soul and never will," insists Nancy, with some fervor, "because the one thing he needs is a woman with the will to face life for him."

"You think he's afraid to face it himself?"

"He is! He listens too much to the whispers that he heard in the forest where he grew up, and where he always goes now when he wants to be alone. They're the whispers of the women behind him—his dead mother—and *her* mother, who was no better than she should be. He's got that awful fear on him, of not knowing what the whispers mean, or where they're directing him.

And none of your back-slapping will knock that fear out of him. Only a woman can free him—a woman who loves him truly, and believes in him. . . ."

There is a knock on the door. It is Abe. He is bareheaded and wet from the storm when he comes in, his face drawn. "He now wears a fairly respectable dark suit of clothes. He looks considerably older and grimmer."

Abe's greetings are perfunctory. Suddenly he turns to Nancy. "Ann's dead," he tells her, simply. "Tonight, the fever suddenly got worse. They couldn't seem to do anything for it."

Nancy goes to him and takes his hand sympathetically. "Oh, Abe—I'm sorry," she says. "She was such a dear little girl. Everyone who knew her will join in mourning for her."

"I know they will. But it won't do any good. She's dead."

They would have him sit down, but he will not. "I'm not fit company for anybody," he says. "I'd better be going." But they won't let him go. Josh Speed is the first to stop him—

"You're the best friends I've got in the world," says Abe, "and it seems a pretty poor way to reward you for all that you've given me, to come here now, and inflict you with a corpse."

BOWLING—This is your home, Abe. This is where you're loved.

ABE—I know that. And I love you, Bowling and Nancy. But I loved her more than everything else that I've ever known.

NANCY—I know you did, Abe. I know it.

ABE—I used to think it was better to be alone. I was always most contented when I was alone. I had queer notions that if you got too close to people you could see the truth about them, that behind the surface, they're all insane, and they could see the same in you. And then—when I saw her, I knew there could be beauty and purity in people—like the purity you sometimes see in the sky at night. When I took hold of her hand, and held it, all fear, all doubt, went out of me. I believed in God. I'd have been glad to work for her until I die, to get for her everything out of life that she wanted. If she thought I could do it, then I could. That was my belief. . . . And then I had to stand there, as helpless as a twig in a whirlpool; I had to stand there and watch her die. And her father and mother were there, too, praying to God for her soul. The Lord givith and the Lord taketh away, blessed be the name of the Lord! That's what they kept on saying. But I couldn't pray with them. I couldn't give any devotion to one who has the power of death, and uses it. (*He has stood up.*) I'm making a poor exhibition of myself—and I'm sorry—but—I can't stand it. I can't live with myself any longer. I've got to die and be with her again, or I'll go crazy! (*He goes to the door and opens it and stands looking out.*) I can't bear to think of her out there alone!

BOWLING (*going to* ABE, *with great tenderness*)—Abe . . . I want you to go upstairs and see if you can't get some sleep. . . . Please, Abe—as a special favor to Nancy and me.

ABE (*after a moment*)—All right, Bowling. (*He turns and goes to the ladder.*)

NANCY (*taking candle from bookcase*)—Here's a light for you, dear Abe. (*She hands him the candle.*)

ABE—Thank you, Nancy. . . . Good night. (*He goes up the ladder into the attic. They all look up after him.*)

NANCY (*tearful*)—Poor, lonely soul. (BOWLING *cautions her to be quiet.*)

JOSH (*putting on his coat*)—Keep him here with you, Mrs. Green. Don't let him out of your sight.

BOWLING—We won't, Josh.

JOSH—Good night. (*Closes the door.*)

BOWLING—Good night, Josh.


"He bolts the door, then comes down to the table and picks up the lamp. Nancy looks up once more and then goes out. Bowling blows out the lamp and follows her out. He closes the door behind him, so that the only light on the stage is the beam from the attic." The curtain falls.


## ACT II

The law office of Stuart and Lincoln in Springfield is on the second floor of the Court House. It is a small room and variously furnished. There is an old desk, a table and chair and a ramshackle sort of bed with a buffalo robe thrown over it. A row of law books adorns a sagging shelf and an old wood stove is ready for use when needed.

"On the wall above the desk is hung an American flag, with 26 stars. Between the windows is an election poster for Harrison and Tyler, with a list of Electors, the last of whom is Ab'm Lincoln of Sangamon."

Billy Herndon, a youthful and eager law student, is at work at the table. Shortly Abe Lincoln comes up the stairs and into the room. "Abe wears a battered plug hat, a light alpaca coat, and carries an ancient threadbare carpet bag. He is evidently not in a talkative mood. His boots are caked with mud."

Abe has been away on a trip around the circuit. He hasn't been very well, he tells Billy, but the Doctor dosed him up to keep him going. Nothing particular had happened, though they had got him up on the stump once or twice. Once he ran into Stephen Douglas and they had had some argument in public. Nothing serious.

As for the office, Billy reports that not much has happened. Judge Stuart is in Washington and reports the campaign is getting as hot as the weather. The Elijah P. Lovejoy League of Freemen would like to have Mr. Lincoln speak at their abolitionist rally—

"It's funny, Billy," says Abe. "I was thinking about Lovejoy the other day—trying to figure what it is in a man that makes him glad to be a martyr. I was on the boat coming from Quincy to Alton, and there was a gentleman on board with twelve Negroes. He was shipping them down to Vicksburg for sale—had 'em chained six and six together. Each of them had a small iron clevis around his wrist, and this was chained to the main chain, so that those Negroes were strung together precisely like fish on a trot line. I gathered they were being separated forever from their homes—mothers, fathers, wives, children—whatever families the poor creatures had got—going to be whipped into perpetual slavery, and no questions asked. It was quite a shocking sight."

Josh Speed and Bowling Green have arrived. Passing through Springfield they decided to check up on Abe. A lot of folks in New Salem would like to know how he is getting on. Abe cannot report much in the way of law business, but he is already a great social success, being invited to the home of Ninian Edwards for all the more elegant functions. And the Edwards folks, he would have them know, are very high-grade people. They have a house "so big you could race horses in the parlor," and Mrs. Edwards is one of the Todd family from Kentucky. "They spell their name with two Ds—which is pretty impressive when you consider that one was enough for God," says Abe.

Also in Rochester not long since Abe had met and shaken the hand of the President of the United States, Martin Van Buren.

"Was the President properly respectful to you?" Bowling would know.

"Indeed he was," reports Abe. "He said to me, 'We've been hearing great things of you in Washington.' I found out later he'd said the same thing to every other cross-roads politician he'd met."

Billy Herndon, who is a red-hot abolitionist, isn't at all satisfied with Abe's course. "He wants me to get down into the blood-soaked arena and grapple with all the lions of injustice and oppression," explains Abe, and Bowling Green is entirely sympathetic with that sentiment.

Otherwise Abe is able to report some progress. "I've been able to pay off my debts to the extent of some seven cents on the dollar, and I'm sound of skin and skeleton."

"But why don't we hear more from you and of you?" demands Bowling.

ABE—Josh can tell you—I've been busy.

BOWLING—What at?

ABE—I'm a candidate.

JOSH (*points to poster over the bed*)—Haven't you noticed his name? It's here—at the bottom of the list of electors on the Whig ticket.

ABE—Yes, sir—if old Tippecanoe wins next Fall, I'll be a member of the Electoral College.

BOWLING—The Electoral College. Is that the best you can do?

ABE—Yes—in the limited time at my disposal. I had a letter from Seth Gale—you remember him—used to live in New Salem and was always aimin' to move West. He's settled down in Maryland now—and has a wife and son. He says that back East they're powerful worried about the annexation of Texas.

BOWLING—They have reason to be. It would probably mean extending slavery through all the territories, from Kansas and Nebraska right out to Oregon and California. That would give the South absolute rule of the country—and God help the rest of us in the free states.

JOSH—It's an ugly situation, all right. It's got the seeds in it of nothing more nor less than civil war.

ABE (*crossing to bed and stretching out on it*)—Well, if so, it'll be the abolitionists' own fault. They know where this trouble might lead, and yet they go right on agitating. They ought to be locked up for disturbing the peace, all of them.

BOWLING—I thought you were opposed to slavery, Abe. Have you changed your mind about it?

ABE—No. I am opposed to slavery. But I'm even more opposed to going to war. And, on top of that, I know what you're getting at—both of you. (*He speaks to them with the utmost of good nature.*)  You're following Billy Herndon's lead—troubling your kind hearts with concerns about me and when am I going to amount to something?  Is that it?

BOWLING—Oh, no, Abe.  Far be it from me to interfere in your life.

JOSH—Or me, either.  If we happen to feel that, so far, you've been a big disappointment to us, we'll surely keep it to ourselves.

ABE (*laughs.  He has ambled over to the window*)—I'm afraid you'll have to do what I've had to do—which is, learn to accept me for what I am.  I'm no fighting man.  I found that out when I went through the Black Hawk War, and was terrified that I might have to fire a shot at an Indian.  Fortunately, the Indians felt the same way, so I never saw one of them.  Now, I know plenty of men who like to fight; they're willing to kill, and not scared of being killed.  All right.  Let them attend to the battles that have to be fought.

BOWLING—Peaceable men have sometimes been of service to their country.

ABE—They may have been peaceable when they started, but they didn't remain so long after they'd become mixed in the great brawl of politics.  Suppose I ran for Congress, and got elected. (*Sits up.*)  I'd be right in the thick of that ugly situation you were speaking of.  One day I might have to cast my vote on the terrible issue of war or peace.  It might be war with Mexico over Texas; or war with England over Oregon; or even war with our own people across the Ohio River.  What attitude would I take in deciding which way to vote?  "The Liberal attitude," of course.  And what is "the Liberal attitude"?  To go to war, for a tract of land, or a moral principle?  Or to avoid war at all costs?  No, sir.  The place for me is in the Electoral College, where all I have to do is vote for the President whom everybody else elected four months previous.

BOWLING—Well, Abe—you were always an artful dodger—and maybe you'll be able to go on to the end of your days avoiding the clutch of your own conscience.

Ninian Edwards has come to invite Abe to another dinner. This time he includes Bowling and Josh and promises all three of them that they are going to meet a very charming young woman named Mary Todd.  Mary is Ninian's brilliant sister-in-law. "She speaks French like a native, recites poetry at the drop of a hat, and knows the names and habits of all the flowers," promises Ninian.  "And I'd better warn you," he adds, "she's going to

survey the whole field of matrimonial prospects and select the one
who promises the most.  So, you'd better be on your guard, Abe,
unless you're prepared to lose your standing as a free man."

"I thank you for the warning, Ninian," laughs Abe.

"I'm sorry, Abe, that I shan't be able to hear you carrying on
a flirtation in French," says Bowling, after Ninian has gone.

"I'm not pretending with you, Bowling—or you, Josh," confesses Abe, seriously.  "I know what you're thinking about me,
and I think so too.  Only I'm not so merciful in considering my
own shortcomings, or so ready to forgive them as you are.
(*Rises.*)  But—you talk about civil war—there seems to be one
going on inside me all the time.  Both sides are right and both
sides are wrong and equal in strength.  I'd like to be able to rise
superior to the struggle—but—it says in the Bible that a house
divided against itself cannot stand, so I reckon there's not much
hope.  One of these days I'll just split asunder, and part company with myself—and it'll be a good riddance from both points
of view.  However—come on.  (*He takes his hat from desk.*)
You've got to get back to Nancy, and Josh and I have got to
make a good impression upon Miss Mary Todd of Kentucky."

He is waving them to the door as the lights fade out.

The parlor of Ninian Edwards' house is comfortably furnished
in "moderately elegant" style.  This November evening, six
months after the meeting in Abe Lincoln's office, there is a fire
burning in the grate and Ninian is standing before it.  He has
been talking with Elizabeth, his wife, "a high-bred, excessively
ladylike" young woman who, at the moment, is displaying signs
of considerable agitation.

The talk is about the possibility of Elizabeth Edwards' sister,
Mary Todd, having serious matrimonial designs upon Abe Lincoln.  The idea is quite preposterous to Elizabeth, but not at all
so to Ninian, though Ninian would like to warn Elizabeth that if
she thinks Abe would be overjoyed "to capture an elegant, cultivated girl, daughter of the President of the Bank of Kentucky,
descendant of a long line of English gentlemen," she may find
herself greatly mistaken.

Mary Todd comes suddenly into the room, and they try to
change the subject quickly, but Mary is too smart for them.  She
senses that they have been talking about her and so accuses them.
Elizabeth is quick to admit the charge.  Also free to confess that,
to her, the idea of Mary's being even lightly interested in Abe
Lincoln as a possible husband is quite beyond the bounds of

credibility.

Mary is prepared with her answer and has no hesitancy in stating it. "I shall answer you, Elizabeth," she says. "I have given more than one moment's thought to the possibility you mentioned —and I have decided that I shall be Mrs. Lincoln. I have examined carefully the qualifications of all the young gentlemen and some of the old ones in this neighborhood. Those of Mr. Lincoln seem to me superior to all others, and he is my choice."

"Do you expect me to congratulate you upon this amazing selection?" snaps Elizabeth.

"No! I ask for no congratulations, nor condolences, either."

"Then I shall offer none."

"Forgive me for prying, Mary," adds Ninian; "but have you as yet communicated your decision to the gentleman himself?"

"Not yet. But he is coming to call this evening, and he will ask humbly for my hand in marriage; and, after I have displayed the proper amount of surprise and confusion, I shall murmur, timidly, 'Yes.' "

Elizabeth gives up a little pitifully. Ninian is only interested in one phase of Mary's decision—

"Understand, my dear," he is saying, "I'm not quarreling with you. My affection for Abe is eternal—but—I'm curious to know —what is it about him that makes you choose him for a husband?"

"I should like to give you a plain, simple answer, Ninian, but I cannot," confesses Mary, for the first time a trifle uncertain.

"Of course you cannot," insists Elizabeth. "You're rushing blindly into this. You have no conception of what it will mean to your future."

"You're wrong about that, Elizabeth. This is not the result of wild, tempestuous infatuation. I have not been swept off my feet. Mr. Lincoln is a Westerner, but that is his only point of resemblance to Young Lochinvar. I simply feel that of all the men I've ever known, he is the one whose life and destiny I want most to share."

She could not, says Mary, be content with a "happy marriage" in the conventional sense. She has no craving for comfort and security. Never having tried poverty she does not know how she might cope with that. But she does feel that with Abe there would be before her the chance for high adventure—"so long as I can know that I am always going forward, with my husband, along a road that leads across the horizon."

"And how far do you think you will go with anyone like Abe

Lincoln, who is lazy and shiftless and prefers to stop constantly along the way to tell jokes?"

"He will not stop, if I am strong enough to make him go on," answers Mary, furiously, turning on her sister. "And I am strong. I know what you expect of me. You want me to do precisely as you have done—and marry a man like Ninian—and I know many—that are just like him. But with all due respect to my dear brother-in-law—I don't want that—and I won't have it. Never! You live in a house with a fence around it—presumably to prevent the common herd from gaining access to your sacred precincts—but really to prevent you yourselves from escaping from your own narrow lives. In Abraham Lincoln I see a man who has split rails for other men's fences, but who has never built one around himself."

"What are you saying, Mary? You are talking with a degree of irresponsibility that is not far from sheer madness."

"I imagine it does seem like insanity to you. You married a man who was settled and established in the world, with a comfortable inheritance, and no problems to face. And you've never made a move to change your condition, or improve it. You consider it couldn't be improved. To you, all this represents perfection. But it doesn't to me. I want a chance to shape a new life, for myself, and for my husband. Is that irresponsibility?"

Before Elizabeth can answer, Mr. Lincoln is announced by the maid. A moment later, Abe, wearing a new suit and with his hair "nearly neat," is shown into the room. He senses the electricity in the atmosphere and makes a particular effort to be affably casual. He has been delayed, he explains, by Hannah, who is Jack Armstrong's wife. Ninian will remember Armstrong, the bully of New Salem. His wife is in Springfield to ask Abe to defend their son, Duff, who is in jail for murder.

"I went over to the jail to interview the boy and he looks pretty tolerably guilty to me," admits Abe. "But I used to give him lessons in the game of marbles while his mother foxed my pants for me. That means, she sewed buckskin around the legs of my pants so I wouldn't tear 'em to shreds going through underbrush when I was surveying. Well—in view of old times, I felt I had to take the case and do what I can to obstruct the orderly processes of justice."

"And the boy will be acquitted. I tell you, Abe—this country would be law-abiding and peaceful if it weren't for you lawyers."

With the excuse that they must hear the children's prayers Elizabeth and Ninian retire, though Elizabeth is plainly reluctant to leave.

Now, at Mary's gracious invitation, Abe has crossed to the
chair before the fire. He is sitting opposite Mary, and she is
looking at him with melting eyes as the light fades.

On the afternoon of New Year's Day, a few weeks later, Abe
Lincoln is sitting slumped in his chair before his desk in his law
office. He has his hat on and a muffler is hanging untied about
his neck. Half-sitting on the nearby table Josh Speed is reading
a long letter, and apparently giving its contents serious attention.
When he has finished the letter Abe would like to have his opinion
of it.

Josh frankly does not like it. He has no quarrel, he says, with
Abe's choice of words, but the letter is brutal and heartless and
how Abe could have thought to deliver it is beyond his understanding. "This letter isn't written to Mary Todd," exclaims
Josh; "it's written to yourself. Every line of it is intended to
provide salve for your own conscience."

Josh not only refuses to deliver the letter, as Abe has requested,
but strongly counsels that it be not sent until Abe is a little
calmer in his mind. Abe is determined to find another messenger.
He might ask the minister to hand it to the bride, suggests Josh,
sarcastically. But Abe continues to insist that he cannot hope to
be calm in his mind until the matter is settled once and for all.

"I just feel that I've got to the end of my rope," says Abe,
miserably; "and I must let go, and drop—and where I'll land I
don't know, and whether I'll survive the fall, I don't know that,
either. . . . But this I do know: I've got to get out of this thing
—I can't go through with it—I've got to have my release!"

Ninian Edwards can be heard coming up the stairs, hailing them
heartily in the name of the New Year. He is wearing a handsome, fur-trimmed great-coat and carrying two silver canes.
Ninian is at some loss to understand Abe's dejected spirits and
would make light of them, until he hears that at least one con-
tributing cause is the fact that Abe is just back from the funeral
of his oldest friend, Bowling Green. Ninian is moved by the
news. He is glad that Abe was at the funeral. Yet, Ninian is
of the opinion that Bowling would be the first to expect Abe to
put aside his sadness on this, his wedding day.

"I'm only sorry that our old friend didn't live to see you two
fine people married," says Ninian, making a gallant effort to
assume a more nuptial tone. "I've made all the arrangements
with the Rev. Dresser, and Elizabeth is preparing a bang-up
dinner—so you can be sure the whole affair will be carried off

handsomely *and* painlessly."

Ninian would also deliver himself of a few words of advice to Abe—advice of a fairly personal nature. He is eager that Abe's and Mary Todd's marriage shall be a success. It will be, he feels sure, if Abe will make it a point to keep a tight rein on Mary's ambition. From childhood Mary has been known to have delusions of grandeur; has even boasted that the man she would marry would one day be President of the United States. She never has entirely lost those youthful delusions. "So I urge you to beware," Ninian concludes. "Don't let her talk you into any gallant crusades or wild goose chases. Let her learn to be satisfied with the estate to which God hath brought her. . . ."

Billy Herndon has come in. He has a bottle in his pocket and is more than a little drunk. After Ninian has gone, Billy decides to offer his congratulations to Abe in a toast which Abe accepts without any response. Billy is frank to confess that he never has really approved of Abe's marrying, but now he is eager to apologize.

"I doubt that Miss Todd and I will ever get along well together," he tells Abe, "but I'm now convinced that our aims are the same—particularly since I've heard the warnings delivered by her brother-in-law. (*A note of scorn colors his allusion to* NINIAN.) If she really is ambitious for you—if she will never stop driving you, goading you—then I say, God bless her, and give her strength."

Billy would like to offer a second toast: "To the President of the United States and Mrs. Lincoln," but Abe will have no more.

"There is not going to be a wedding," he says simply, turning to Billy. "I have a letter I want you to deliver to Miss Todd. Give it to him, Josh."

In place of handing over the letter Josh Speed puts it in the stove. When Abe protests Josh admits he had no right to do such a thing, but there it is. "In that letter," he explains to Billy, "Mr. Lincoln asked Miss Todd for his release. He told her that he had made a mistake in his previous protestations of affection for her, and so he couldn't go through with a marriage which could only lead to endless pain and misery for them both."

"If that isn't the truth, what is?" asks Abe, deeply distressed.

"I'm not disputing the truth of it. I'm only asking you to tell her so, to her face, in the manner of a man."

"It would be a more cruel way. It would hurt her more deeply. For I couldn't help blurting it *all* out—all the terrible things I didn't say in that letter. (*He is speaking with passion.*) I'd

have to tell her that I have hatred for her infernal ambition—that
I don't want to be ridden and driven, upward and onward through
life, with her whip lashing me, and her spurs digging into me!
If her poor soul craves importance in life, then let her marry
Stephen Douglas. He's ambitious, too. I want only to be left
alone!"

"May I say something?" asks Billy.

"I doubt that you're in much of a condition to contribute," Abe
starts to protest, but Josh urges the young man on. "What is
it, Billy?"

BILLY—It's just this. Mr. Lincoln, you're not abandoning
Miss Mary Todd. No! You're only using her as a living sacrifice, offering her up, in the hope that you will thus gain forgiveness of the gods for your failure to do your own great duty!

ABE—Yes! My own great duty. Everyone feels called upon
to remind me of it, but no one can tell me what it is.

BILLY—I can tell you! I can tell you what is the duty of
every man who calls himself an American! It is to perpetuate
those truths which were once held to be self-evident: that all
men are created equal—that they are endowed with certain inalienable rights—that among these are the right to life, liberty
and the pursuit of happiness.

ABE—And are those rights denied to *me?*

BILLY—Could you ever enjoy them while your mind is full of
the awful knowledge that two millions of your fellow beings in
this country are slaves. Can you take any satisfaction from
looking at that flag above your desk, when you know that ten
of its stars represent states which are willing to destroy the
Union—rather than yield their property rights in the flesh and
blood of those slaves? And what of all the states of the future?
All the territories of the West—clear out to the Pacific Ocean?
Will they be the homes of free men? Are you answering that
question to your own satisfaction? That's your flag, Mr. Lincoln, and you're proud of it. But what are you doing to save it
from being ripped into shreds?

ABE (*jumping to his feet*)—I'm minding my own business—
that's what I'm doing! And there'd be no threat to the Union
if others would do the same. And as to slavery—I'm sick and
tired of this righteous talk about it. When you know more about
law, you'll know that those property rights you mentioned are
guaranteed by the Constitution. And if the Union can't stand on
the Constitution, then let it fall!

BILLY—The hell with the Constitution! This is a matter of the rights of living men to freedom—and those came before the Constitution! When the law denies those rights, then the law is wrong, and it must be changed, if not by moral protest, then by force! There's no course of action that isn't justified in the defense of freedom! And don't dare to tell me that anyone in the world knows that better than you do, Mr. Lincoln. You, who honor the memory of Elijah Lovejoy and every other man who ever died for that very ideal!

ABE—Yes—I honor them—and envy them—because they could believe that their ideals are *worth* dying for.

Abe gives in. He will go and talk with Mary, and then he will go away. He doesn't know where. And thus he leaves them, Billy shouting down the stairs after him that he is quitting; that he is running away from his obligations to God and to his own immortal soul. There is no answer.

Josh understands. "He'll be in such a state of emotional upheaval," says Josh, "he'll want to go away by himself for a long time. Just as he did after the death of poor little Ann Rutledge. He'll go out and wander on the prairies, aimlessly, trying to grope his way back into the wilderness from which he came. There's nothing we can do for him, Billy. He'll have to do it for himself."

"May God be with him!" prays Billy fervently as the curtain falls.

Two years have passed. On the open prairie near New Salem Seth Gale and his wife have made camp. There is a smoldering fire in the foreground and around it packing cases, blanket rolls, etc. The rear end of a covered wagon juts out into the open. Near the fire Gale is standing, holding his eight-year-old son, Jimmy, in his arms.

Jimmy has been ill with swamp fever for days. He is burning up now, and would have the blanket taken off. His father, fearful of the chill night air, tries to quiet him.

Through Jack Armstrong Seth has got in touch with Abe Lincoln, after some difficulty, and Jack reports that Abe has gone to fetch Dr. Chandler. This news serves to give Mrs. Gale some little hope. Jimmy's fight with the fever has been pretty hard on his mother. They make a bed for the boy in the wagon.

It has been seven or eight years since Seth has seen Abe. He should expect changes, Jack warns him. "He's changed plenty since he went to Springfield. He climbed up pretty high in the world, but he appears to have slipped down lately. He ain't much like his old comical self."

A few moments later Abe can be seen coming across the prairie toward the camp. "My God, look at him!" explodes Seth, in greeting. "Store clothes and a plug hat!"

Abe has not been able to get Dr. Chandler, but he knows where he can find him later. Meantime if there is anything he can do he would like to help. There is nothing—unless, as Mrs. Gale suggests, he knows where there is a preacher. She would like to have a preacher say a prayer for Jimmy. So far as anybody knows there isn't a preacher within twenty miles.

"Why don't you speak a prayer, Abe?" Jack suggests. "You could always think of something to say."

"I'm afraid I'm not much of a hand at praying," protests Abe. "I couldn't think of a blessed thing that would be of any real help."

"Never mind. It's just a religious idea of Aggie's," Seth explains. The talk turns to other things.

The Gales, having been crowded out of Maryland when "the city grew right over our farm," are on their way West and have stopped in New Salem hoping that Abe will join them. They are heading for a place called Westport, Kansas, and after they have outfitted there they will join with a lot of others and press on to Oregon. The country's settling fast in the West. Jack Armstrong has counted as many as two hundred wagons in a single week, carrying people from Pennsylvania, Connecticut, Vermont and all over to the new land of promise.

"I'm going, too," says Jack, "soon as I can get me a wagon. They'll need men like me to fight the Indians for 'em and they'll need men with brains, like you, Abe, to tell 'em how to keep the peace."

"It's a temptation to go, I can't deny that," admits Abe.

"Then what's stopping you from doing it? You said yourself you've just been drifting."

"Maybe that's it—maybe I've been drifting too long. Is it just the three of you, Seth?"

"That's all. The three of us and Gobey, the nigger."

"Is he your slave?"

"Gobey? Hell, no. He's a free man! My father freed his father twenty years ago. We've had to be mighty careful about Gobey. You see, where we come from, folks are pretty uncertain how they feel about the slave question, and lots of good free niggers get snaked over the line into Virginia and then sold down the river before you know it. And when you try to go to court and assert their legal rights, you're beaten at every turn by the damned, dirty shyster lawyers. That's why we've been keeping well up in free territory on this trip."

Seth is convinced that Oregon is going to be free. If it isn't, if the United States isn't strong enough to protect its citizens from slavery, "then we'll cut loose from it and join with Canada," says he with some warmth. ". . . I love this country and I'd fight for it. And I guess George Washington and the rest of them loved England and fought for it when they were young—but they didn't hesitate to cut loose when the Government failed to play fair and square with 'em."

"By God, if Andy Jackson was back in the White House, he'd run out them traitors with a horse-whip!" interjects Jack.

"It'd be a bad day for us Americans, Seth, if we lost you, and your wife and your son," says Abe Lincoln, grimly.

SETH—My son!—Oh—I've been talking big—but it's empty talk. If he dies—there won't be enough spirit left in us to push on any further. What's the use of working for a future when you know there won't be anybody growing up to enjoy it. Excuse me, Abe—but I'm feeling pretty scared.

ABE—You mustn't be scared, Seth. I know I'm a poor one to be telling you that—because I've been scared all my life. And seeing you now—and thinking of the big thing you've set out to do—well, it's made me feel pretty small. It's made me feel that I've got to do something, too, to keep you and your kind in the United States of America. You mustn't give up, Seth. Don't let anything beat you—don't you ever give up.

AGGIE (*coming out of wagon and running to* SETH)—Seth!

SETH—What is it, Aggie?

AGGIE—He's worse, Seth. He's moaning in his sleep, and he's gasping for breath. (*Breaks down.*)

SETH (*taking her in his arms*)—Never mind, honey—never mind. When the doctor gets here, he'll fix him up in no time. It's all right, honey. He'll get well.

ABE—If you wish me to, Mrs. Gale, I'll try to speak a prayer.

JACK—That's the way to talk, Abe.

SETH—We'd be grateful for anything you might say, Abe.

ABE (*taking off his hat*)—Oh, God, the Father of all living, I ask You to look with gentle mercy upon this little boy who is here, lying sick in this covered wagon. His people are traveling far, to seek a new home in the wilderness, to do your work, God, to make this earth a good place for your children to live in. They can see clearly where they're going, and they're not afraid to face all the perils that lie along the way. I humbly beg you not to take their child from them. Grant him the freedom of life. Do not condemn him to the imprisonment of death. Do not deny him his birthright. Let him know the sight of great plains and high mountains, of green valleys and wide rivers. For this little boy is an American, and these things belong to him, and he to them. Spare him, that he too may strive for the ideal for which his fathers have labored, so faithfully and for so long. Spare him and give him his father's strength—give us all strength, O God, to do the work that is before us. I ask you this favor, in the name of your son, Jesus Christ, who died upon the Cross to set men free. Amen.

GOBEY (*with fervor*)—Amen!

SETH AND AGGIE (*murmuring*)—Amen!

ABE (*putting his hat on*)—It must be getting near midnight. I'll go after the doctor.

SETH—Thank you, Abe.

AGGIE—Thank you—thank you, Mr. Lincoln.

GOBEY—God bless you, Mr. Lincoln!

The lights fade quickly as the curtain falls.


A few days later Mary Todd is sitting in the parlor of the Ninian Edwards' home reading. It is evening. Shortly the maid announces Mr. Lincoln. Miss Todd, at some pains to control her emotions, hesitates for a moment and then asks that Mr. Lincoln be shown in.

Mary has turned to face Abe as he enters. There is a trace of nervousness in his manner as he tries to explain his present visit and offer free apology for the things he had said at their last meeting.

Mary is understanding. She knows that he has been through a long and severe illness. She is glad that he is again restored to health, and hopes that he will soon be able to resume his onward march. For whatever happened at their last meeting she feels that she was largely at fault.

"I was blinded by my own self-confidence," Mary confesses, as her voice momentarily wavers. "I—I loved you. . . . And I believed I could make you love me. I believed we might achieve a real communion of spirit, and the fire of my determination would burn in you. You would become a man and a leader of men! But you didn't wish that. (*She turns away.*) I knew you had strength—but I did not know you would use it, all of it, to resist your own magnificent destiny."

"It is true, Mary—you once had faith in me which I was far from deserving," insists Abe, humbly. "But the time has come, at last, when I wish to strive to deserve it. (MARY *looks at him sharply*.) When I behaved in that shameful manner toward you, I did so because I thought that our ways were separate and could never be otherwise. I've come to the conclusion that I was wrong. I believe that our destinies are together, for better or for worse, and I again presume to ask you to be my wife. I fully realize, Mary, that taking me back now would involve humiliation for you."

"I am not afraid of humiliation, if I know it will be wiped out by ultimate triumph," says Mary.

She would want to feel that he himself is sure and would like to know what has impelled his proposal. He tells her of his meeting an old friend on the prairie and of the urge he felt to join the pilgrimage to the West. Suddenly he had realized that that was not his direction. "The way I must go is the way you have always wanted me to go," he says. "I promise, Mary—if you will have me—I shall devote myself for the rest of my days to trying—to do what is right—as God gives me the power to see what is right."

"Then I shall be your wife. I shall fight by your side until death do us part." There is a note of triumphant exaltation in her voice. "Abe, I love you—oh, I love you. Whatever becomes of the two of us, I'll die loving you!"

She is sobbing on his shoulder. "Awkwardly he lifts his hands and takes hold of her in a loose embrace. He is staring down at the carpet over her shoulder" as the curtain falls.

## ACT III

It is a Summer evening in 1858. A speaker's platform has been erected in a small Illinois town. A strong light shines down upon the speaker now standing at the front of the platform. He is Ninian Edwards and he has been serving as moderator in a debate between Judge Stephen A. Douglas, seated to his right at the rear of the platform, and Mr. Abraham Lincoln, seated to his left. They are candidates for the high office of United States Senator from Illinois.

"This series of debates between these two eminent citizens of Illinois," Mr. Edwards is saying, "has focused upon our state the attention of the entire nation, for here are being discussed the vital issues which now affect the lives of all Americans and the whole future history of our beloved country. According to the usual custom of debate, each of the candidates will now speak in rebuttal . . . Judge Douglas."

Judge Douglas steps forward with some deliberation. "He is a brief but magnetic man, confident of his powers. He carries a few notes which he places on the lectern and studies for a moment before he speaks."

"My Fellow Citizens: My good friend, Mr. Lincoln, has addressed you with his usual artless sincerity, his pure, homely charm, his perennial native humor. He has even devoted a generously large portion of his address to most amiable remarks upon my fine qualities as a man, if not as a statesman. For which I express deepest gratitude. But—at the same time—I most earnestly beg you not to be deceived by his seeming innocence, his carefully cultivated spirit of good will. For in each of his little homilies lurk concealed weapons. Like Brutus, in Shakespeare's immortal tragedy, Mr. Lincoln is an honorable man. But, also like Brutus, he is an adept at the art of inserting daggers between an opponent's ribs, just when said opponent least expects it. Behold me, gentlemen—I am covered with scars. And yet—somehow or other—I am still upright. Perhaps because I am supported by that sturdy prop called 'Truth.' Truth —which, crushed to earth by the assassin's blades, doth rise again."

Mr. Lincoln, continues Judge Douglas, is so adept at skirting the fringes of truth that he has kept entirely concealed from his audiences the plight of the textile workers of Massachusetts, even now on strike against the fourteen-hour day and all the frightful injustices that accompany it. What kind of liberty is *this?* Mr. Lincoln has also seemingly overlooked the condition of the workers engaged by the Illinois Central Railroad who also are on strike because they, too, demand a living wage. "All through the North," trumpets Mr. Douglas, "hungry men, marching through the streets in ragged order, promoting riots, because they are not paid enough to keep the flesh upon the bones of their babies! What kind of Liberty is *this?* And what kind of *equality?*"

Mr. Lincoln, says Judge Douglas, is a great one to harp upon the question of equality, and the argument of the Abolitionists that the Declaration of Independence has declared all men free and equal, by divine law, thus establishing the equality of the

Negro as an inalienable right in the very face of the verdict of
the Supreme Court in the case of Dred Scott, which declares the
Negroes to be an inferior race of beings, "subjugated by the
dominant race, enslaved, and therefore *property* like all other
property."

"Mr. Lincoln is a lawyer," protests the Judge, vehemently,
"and I presume, therefore, that he knows that when he seeks to
destroy public confidence in the integrity, the inviolability of the
Supreme Court, he is preaching *revolution!* He is attempting to
stir up odium and rebellion in this country against the constituted
authorities; he is stimulating the passions of men to resort to violence and to mobs, instead of to the law. He is setting brother
against brother! There can be but one consequence of such in-
flammatory persuasion—and that is *Civil War!* He asks me to
state my opinion of the Dred Scott Decision, and I answer him
unequivocally by saying, "I take the decisions of the Supreme
Court as the law of the land, and I intend to obey them as such!"
Nor will I be swayed from that position by all the rantings of
all the fanatics who preach "racial equality," who ask us to vote,
and eat, and sleep, and marry with Negroes! And I say further—Let each State mind its own business and leave its neighbors alone. If we will stand by that principle, then Mr. Lincoln
will find that this great republic can exist forever divided into
free and slave states. We can go on as we have done, increasing
in wealth, in population, in power, until we shall be the admiration and the terror of the world!"

Mr. Douglas glares at the audience. He is mopping his brow
as he turns to resume his seat.

Mr. Edwards introduces Mr. Lincoln simply by name. "Abe
glances at his notes, takes his hat off, puts the notes in it, then
rises slowly and comes forward. His words come from an emotion so profound that it needs no advertisement."

"Judge Douglas has paid tribute to my skill with the dagger,"
begins Abe. "I thank him for that, but I must also admit that
he can do more with that weapon than I can. He can keep ten
daggers flashing in the air at the same time. Fortunately he is
so good at it that none of the knives ever falls and hurts
anybody. He can condone slavery in the South and protest hotly
against its extension to the North. He can crowd loyalty to the
Union and defense of state's sovereignty of the South into the
same breath. You have heard the Judge make allusion to those
who advocate voting and eating and marrying and sleeping with
Negroes. Whether he meant me specifically, I do not know. If

he did, I can say that just because I do not want a colored woman for a slave I don't necessarily want her for a wife. I need not have her for either. I can just leave her alone. In some respects she is certainly not my equal, any more than I am the Judge's equal in some respects. But in her natural right to eat the bread she earns with her own hands without asking leave of anyone else, she is my equal, and the equal of all others. And as to sleeping with Negroes—the Judge may be interested to know that the slave states have produced more than four hundred thousand mulattoes—and I don't think many of them are the children of abolitionists."

The word "abolitionist" reminds the speaker of New England. He, too, has been there. He has seen "those cheerless, brick prisons" called factories; he is familiar with the lives of those white slaves of the North who weave into cloth the cotton picked by the black slaves of the South, and as an American he is not proud that such conditions exist. Nor does he think any of the striking workers of the North would like to change places with the slaves in the South—

"Will they not rather say: 'The remedy is in our hands'? And still as an American I can say—thank God we live under a system by which men have the *right* to strike! I am not preaching rebellion. This country, with its institutions, belongs to the people who inhabit it. Whenever they shall grow weary of the existing government, they can exercise their constitutional right of amending it, or their revolutionary right to dismember or overthrow it. If the founding fathers gave us anything, they gave us that. And I am not teaching disrespect for the Supreme Court. I am only saying that the decisions of mortal men are often influenced by unjudicial bias—and the Supreme Court is composed of mortal men, most of whom, it so happens, come from the privileged class in the South. There is an old saying that judges are just as honest as other men, and not more so; and in case some of you are wondering who said that, it was Thomas Jefferson."

The purpose of the Dred Scott Decision, the speaker points out, is to make property and nothing but property of the Negro in all the states of the Union. "It is the old issue of property rights versus human rights. . . . It is the same spirit that says, 'You toil and work and earn bread and I'll eat it.' Whether those words come from the mouth of a king who bestrides his people and lives by the fruit of their labor, or from one race of men who seek to enslave another race, it is the same tyrannical principle."

There was no exception to the rule that all men were created equal in the Declaration of Independence, Mr. Lincoln reminds his hearers, and yet there are those who would now amend the statement by adding to it "except the Negroes." How long will it be before they will also want to add "except Negroes, foreigners, Catholics, Jews or—just poor people"?

Many people, both North and South, Mr. Lincoln admits, were opposed to stirring up trouble; they would let each state mind its own business. That might be the safer course for the time being. But let them beware lest the demon they could create through slavery does not turn and rend them. "When you begin qualifying freedom, watch out for the consequences to *you*," he thundered. "And, he added firmly, "I am not preaching civil war! All I am trying to do—now, and as long as I live—is to state and restate the fundamental virtues of our democracy, which have made us great and can make us greater."

"I believe most seriously that the perpetuation of those virtues is now endangered," continued Mr. Lincoln, "not only by the honest proponents of slavery, but even more by those who echo Judge Douglas in shouting, 'Leave it alone.' This is the complacent policy of indifference to evil, and that policy I cannot but hate. I hate it because it deprives our Republic of its just influence in the world; enables the enemies of free institutions everywhere to taunt us as hypocrites; cause the real friends of freedom to doubt our sincerity; and especially because it forces so many good men among ourselves into an open war with very fundamentals of civil liberty, denying the good faith of the Declaration of Independence and insisting that there is no right principle of action but self-interest. In his final words tonight, the Judge said that we can be 'the terror of the world.' I don't think we want to be that. I think we would prefer to be the encouragement of the world, the proof that man is at last worthy to be free. But—we shall provide no such encouragement, unless we can establish our ability as a nation to live and grow. And we shall surely do neither if these states fail to remain *united*. There can be no distinction in the definitions of liberty as between one section and another, one class and another, one race and another. 'A house divided against itself cannot stand.' This government cannot endure permanently, half slave and half free."

As the speaker returns slowly to his seat the lights fade.

On an afternoon in the Spring of 1860 Abe Lincoln is sitting in the parlor of his home in Springfield telling his three sons, Tad, who is 7, Willie, who is 9, and Robert, a young Harvard student of 17, just now sitting by the window smoking a pipe with an air of great importance, the story of his going for the doctor to help Seth Gale's son the time he had met the Gales on the prairie near New Salem. Josh Speed is also a quiet listener.

He had found the doctor, Abe relates, after a considerable search, and induced him to come back and see the boy. The doctor had given the boy a lot of medicine (which probably tasted bad, as Tad suspects) and it had cured him.

"I never saw those nice people again," says Abe, "but I've heard from them every so often. That little boy was your age, Willie, but now he's a grown man with a son as big as Tad. He lives on a great big farm, in a valley with a river that runs right down from the tops of the snow mountains. . . ."

Mary Lincoln interrupts the story. She is terribly put out to find Robert smoking when he knows it is against her orders, and she soon hustles the children out to make ready for their supper.

It is nearing the time of Abe's appointment with three men who have come from the East to see him on a political matter, Josh suggests. Mary had not heard of this visit, and is a little excited by the news. Certainly these are the most important guests who have ever crossed the threshold of her house, especially if they are coming, as Abe suspects, to look him over as a possible candidate for the Presidency. But, insists Abe, they are coming not as guests but merely on business—

"Yes! Rather important business, it seems to me," snaps Mary. "They want to see us as we are—crude, sloppy, vulgar Western barbarians, living in a house that reeks of foul tobacco smoke."

"We can explain about having a son at Harvard," suggests Abe.

But Mary is not to be easily pacified. Why has she not been told? Why has Abe not dressed himself properly in his best suit? Why are his boots not clean?

"You probably think, just as all the others do, that I'm a bitter, nagging woman, and I've tried to kill his spirit, and drag him down to my level," Mary protests to Josh, when Abe has gone to clean his boots. "There never could have been another man such as he is! I've read about many that have gone up in the world, and all of them seemed to have to fight to assert themselves every inch of the way, against the opposition of their enemies and the lack of understanding in their own friends. But he's never had any of that. He's never had an enemy, and every one of his friends has always been completely confident in him.

Even before I met him, I was told that he had a glorious future, and after I'd known him a day, I was sure of it myself. But he didn't believe it—or, if he did, secretly, he was so afraid of the prospect that he did all in his power to avoid it. He had some poem in his mind, about a life of woe, along a rugged path, that leads to some future doom, and it has been an obsession with him. All these years, I've tried and tried to stir him out of it, but all my efforts have been like so many puny waves, dashing against the Rock of Ages. And now, opportunity, the greatest opportunity, is coming here, to him, right into his own house. And what can I do about it? He *must* take it! He *must* see that this is what he was meant for! But I can't persuade him of it! I'm tired—I'm tired to death! (*The tears come now.*) I thought I could help to shape him, as I knew he should be, and I've succeeded in nothing—but in breaking myself. . . ."

"I know, Mary," says Josh, tenderly. "But—there's no reason in heaven and earth for you to reproach yourself. Whatever becomes of Abe Lincoln is in the hands of a God who controls the destinies of all of us, including lunatics, and saints."

Abe has come back into the room with his boots at least partly cleaned. Mary has gone to prepare refreshments for the expected guests. Abe and Josh have a moment to consider the importance of the visitation from the East. It is Josh's idea that these men are pretty influential in the pivotal states. Also that if they should offer Abe the nomination, and he should get it, there would be a fine chance for his election.

"There'll be four candidates in the field, bumping each other, and opening up the track for a dark horse," says Josh.

"But the dark horse might run in the wrong direction," smiles Abe. And adds: "It seems funny to be comparing it to a horse-race, with an old spavined hack like me. But I've had some mighty energetic jockeys—Mentor Graham, Bowling Green, Bill Herndon, you, and Mary—most of all, Mary."

"They don't count now, Abe. You threw 'em all, long ago. When you finally found yourself running against poor little Douglas, you got the bit between your teeth and went like greased lightning. You'd do the same thing to him again, if you could only decide to get started, which you probably won't. . . ."

When the committee arrives it consists of a politician named Crimmin, a manufacturer named Sturveson and the Rev. Dr. Barrick of Boston. As the maid lets them in Sturveson is seen to be "elderly, wealthy and blank, Barrick a soft Episcopalian dignitary and Crimmin a shrewd, humorous fixer."

There are pleasant words by way of greeting and then the visitors are ready to come directly to the point.

STURVESON—It is no secret that we are desperately in need of a candidate—one who is sound, conservative, safe—and clever enough to skate over the thin ice of the forthcoming campaign. Your friends—and there's an increasingly large number of them throughout the country—believe that you are the man.

ABE—Well, Mr. Sturveson—I can tell you that when first I was considered for political office—that was in New Salem, twenty-five years ago, I assured my sponsors of my conservatism. I have subsequently proved it, by never progressing anywhere.

BARRICK—Then you agree that you are the man we want?

ABE—I'm afraid I cannot go quite that far in self-esteem, Dr. Barrick, especially when you have available a statesman and gentleman as eminent as Mr. Seward, who, I believe, is both ready and willing.

STURVESON—That's as may be. But please understand that this is not an inquisition. (*Both laugh.*) We merely wish to know you better, to gain a clearer idea of your theories on economics—religion—and National affairs in general. (CRIMMIN *nods wisely.*) To begin with—in one of your memorable debates with Senator Douglas, your opponent indulged in some of his usual demagogery about industrial conditions in the North, and you replied shrewdly that whereas the slaves in the South . . .

ABE—Yes, I remember the occasion. I replied that I was thankful that laborers in free states have the right to strike. But that wasn't shrewdness, Mr. Sturveson. It was just the truth.

STURVESON—It has gained you substantial support from the laboring classes, which is all to the good. It has also caused a certain amount of alarm among business men, like myself.

ABE—I cannot enlarge on the subject. It seems obvious to me that this nation was founded on the supposition that men have the right to protest, violently if need be, against authority that is unjust or oppressive. The Boston Tea Party was a kind of strike. So was the Revolution itself. So was Nicholas Biddle's attempt to organize the banks against the Jackson administration.

STURVESON—Which is all perfectly true—but—the days of anarchy are over. We face an unprecedented era of industrial expansion—mass production of every conceivable kind of goods—railroads and telegraph lines across the continent—all promoted and developed by private enterprise. In this great work, we must have a free hand, and a firm one, Mr. Lincoln. To put it bluntly, would you, if elected, place the interests of labor above those of capital?

ABE—I cannot answer that, bluntly, or any other way; because I cannot tell what I should do, if elected.

STURVESON—But you must have inclinations toward one side or the other. . . .

ABE—All I can say is, if it came to a conflict between those two forces, I should attempt to consider them as equals.

BARRICK—I applaud your purpose, Mr. Lincoln, in steadfastly proclaiming the rights of men to resist unjust authority. But I am most anxious to know whether you admit One Authority to whom devotion is unquestioned?

ABE—I presume you refer to the Almighty?

BARRICK—I do.

ABE—I think there has never been any doubt of my submission to His will.

BARRICK—I'm afraid there is a great deal of doubt as to your devotion to His church.

ABE—I realize that, Doctor. They say I'm an atheist, because I've always refused to become a church member.

BARRICK—What have been the grounds of your refusal?

ABE—I have found no churches suitable for my own form of worship. I could not give assent without mental reservations to the long, complicated statements of Christian doctrine which characterize their Articles of Belief and Confessions of Faith. But I can promise you, Dr. Barrick—I shall gladly join any church at any time if its sole qualification for membership is obedience to the Saviour's own statement of Law and Gospel: "Thou shalt love the Lord thy God with all thy heart and with all thy soul and with all thy mind, and thou shalt love thy neighbor as thyself." . . . But—I beg you gentlemen to excuse me for a moment. I believe Mrs. Lincoln is preparing a slight collation, and I must see if I can help with it. . . .

In the discussion that follows Barrick is convinced that Abe unquestionably is an infidel. Sturveson is as certain that he is a radical. Crimmin, the politician, is amused at their anxiety. Of course Abe is all the things they say, and that is what makes him the marvelous vote-getter that he is. All the party should demand of its candidate is to get himself elected and Lincoln can do that.

"In that uncouth rail splitter you may observe one of the smoothest, slickest politicians that ever hoodwinked a yokel mob," asserts Crimmin, pitching his voice low. "You complain that he evaded your questions. Of course he did, and did it perfectly! Ask him about the labor problem, and he replies, "I believe in democracy." Ask his views on religion, and he says, "Love thy neighbor as thyself." Now, you know you couldn't argue with that, either of you. I tell you, gentlemen, he's a vote-getter if I ever saw one. His very name is right—Abraham Lincoln! Honest Old Abe! He'll play the game with us now, and he'll go right on playing it when we get him into the White House. He'll do just what we tell him. . . ."

Abe has come back to invite them into the dining room where Mrs. Lincoln is prepared to serve tea. "Bring your seegar with you, Mr. Crimmin," he advises. The lights fade as they pass through the door.

It is the night of Election Day, November 6, 1860. The Lincoln campaign headquarters in the Illinois State House are littered and noisy. Two high windows at the back let onto a balcony. Between them is a huge chart of the thirty-three states and their electoral votes. A map of the United States on the left wall is dotted with miniature red, white and blue flags. The noise of an election crowd, occasionally punctuated with band music, seeps through from the Square outside and the clatter of telegraph instruments comes from the next room.

Abe Lincoln, wearing his hat and spectacles, is reading newspaper clippings at one side of the room. Mrs. Lincoln is sitting near, her eyes fixed alternately on the chart and map. Robert Lincoln, Josh Speed and Ninian Edwards are smoking and gossiping in the center of the room.

The election has been close up to now, telegraph reports from the doubtful states indicating that Douglas leads Lincoln in New York City and they are running neck and neck in Illinois. Maryland is all for Breckinridge and Bell. Pennsylvania looks safe for Lincoln. Speaking generally, Douglas is still ahead, but Lincoln is gaining.

Billy Herndon, a little drunk and greatly excited, is in, protesting the ignorant enthusiasm of the mob that is willing to cheer anything and anybody. He also has been asked by a group of reporters to find out what will be Mr. Lincoln's first official action after he is elected. Mr. Lincoln thinks he will try growing a beard. A little girl has written him to suggest that whiskers would give him more dignity.

The bulletins continue to arrive. Connecticut is safe for Lin-

coln; Douglas is ahead in Missouri; Breckinridge and Bell are
trailing. Lincoln has picked up a clipping from the Chicago
*Times.* He reads:

"Lincoln breaks down! Lincoln's heart fails him! His legs fail
him. His tongue fails him. He fails all over! The people refuse to support him! They laugh at him! Douglas is champion
of the people! Douglas skins the living dog."

"I can't stand it any longer," says Mary, her voice trembling.

"Yes, my dear, I think you'd better go home," says Abe, coming
to her. "I'll join you presently."

"No! I won't go home!" Mary is hysterical now. "You
only want to get rid of me. That's what you've wanted ever
since the day we were married—and before that. Anything to
get me out of your sight, because you hate me! And it's the
same with all of you—all of his friends—you hate me—you wish
I'd never come into his life."

Abe has stood up quickly. "He himself is in a fearful state of
nervous tension—in no mood to treat Mary with patient in-
dulgence." He asks Josh Speed, Ninian and the others please
to step out. When they have gone he turns on Mary—

"Damn you! Damn you for taking every opportunity you
can to make a public fool of me—and yourself. It's bad enough,
God knows, when you act like that in the privacy of our own
home. But here—in front of people! You're not to do that again.
Do you hear me? You're never to do that again!"

Mary has stood aghast before this outburst. Her hysterical
temper has given way to blank terror. "Abe! You cursed at
me," she is saying, in a faint, strained voice. "Do you realize
what you did? You cursed at me!"

"I lost my temper, Mary," says Abe, controlling himself with
an effort. "I'm sorry for it. But I still think you should go
home rather than stay here and endure the strain of this—this
Death Watch."

Mary is staring at him uncomprehendingly. "This is the night
I dreamed about when I was a child," she is saying; "when I was
an excited young girl, and all the gay young gentlemen of Springfield were courting me and I fell in love with the least likely of
them all. This is the night when I'm waiting to hear that my
husband has become President of the United States. And even
if he does—it's ruined for me. It's too late."

She has opened the door and gone out. Abe, anguished, follows her with his eyes. He calls Robert and sends him home
with his mother.

The cheering outside the window increases. Now the crowd has begun to sing "Old Abe Lincoln Came Out of the Wilderness." It looks like seventy-four electoral votes sure for you," Ninian reports to Abe. "Twenty-seven more probable. New York's will give you the election." Abe is seemingly little impressed. "I'm just thinking what a blow it would be to Mrs. Lincoln if I should lose," he says.

"I'm afraid that the loss to the Nation would be somewhat more serious than that," says Billy Herndon.

Mr. Crimmin has come in, beamingly contented. Nor is he the least depressed to hear that Mr. August Belmont is claiming New York state for Mr. Douglas. The next bulletins bear him out. Lincoln is gaining.

"The next bulletin from New York will show you winning," Mr. Crimmin assures Abe, expansively. "Mark my words, Mr. Lincoln, this election is all wrapped up tightly in a neat bundle, ready for delivery on your doorstep tonight. We've fought the good fight, and we've won!"

"Yes—we've fought the good fight—in the dirtiest campaign in the history of corrupt politics," answers Lincoln, seriously. "And if I have won, then I must cheerfully pay my political debts. All those who helped to nominate and elect me must be paid off. I have been gambled all around, bought and sold a hundred times. And now I must fill all the dishonest pledges made in my name."

The doleful winner has left the room. Mr. Crimmin is puzzled. Can it be that Lincoln does not want to win?

"The answer is—yes," Josh Speed assures him. This is a refreshingly new experience for Mr. Crimmin.

"Would you like to become President of the United States at this time?" demands Billy Herndon. "Haven't you been reading the newspapers lately?"

"Why, yes—I try to follow the events of the day."

"Don't you realize that they've raised ten thousand volunteers in South Carolina? They're arming them. The Governor has issued a proclamation saying that if Mr. Lincoln is elected the state will secede tomorrow, and every other state south of the Dixon line will go with it. Can you see what that means? It means WAR! Civil War! And he'll have the whole terrible responsibility for it—a man who has never wanted anything in his life but to be let alone, in peace."

"Calm down, Billy. Go and get yourself another drink," advises Ninian. The next minute confirmation has come. Ninian reads the dispatch—

"'At 10.30 tonight the New York *Herald* conceded that Mr. Lincoln has carried the state by a majority of at least twenty-five thousand and has won the election.' He's won! He's won! Hurrah!"

Jed, the messenger, has thrown open the window and shouted: "Lincoln is elected! Honest Old Abe is our next President!"

There is a terrific cheer outside. The band is blaring out "Illinois." The men in the room are embracing each other and engaging in a lively game of backslapping as they move toward Lincoln to offer their congratulations.

"God be praised!" shouts Billy. "You're President, Mr. Lincoln. You're President of the United States!" "And my congratulations, Mr. President," adds Crimmin. "This is a mighty achievement for all of us."

They are all trying to shake Abe's hand. He solemnly thanks them all. But he will not go near the window. Nor step out on the balcony. "I guess I'll be going on home to tell Mary," he says, moving toward the door.

At the door Captain Kavanagh stops him. He has been detailed to accompany the new President.

"I'm grateful, Captain. But I don't need you," says the President.

"I'm afraid you must have us, Mr. Lincoln," the Captain replies. "I don't like to be alarming, but I guess you know as well as I do what threats have been made."

"Well, good night, Josh, Ninian, Mr. Crimmin—Billy. Thanks for your good wishes."

"With your permission, sir, I'll go first," says Captain Kavanagh.

The Captain goes on. Mr. Lincoln follows. Two officers close in behind them. The cheering grows fainter. The lights fade to darkness.

There is a shrill train whistle. The date is February 11, 1861. A train of cars has been backed into the station at Springfield, Ill. The station is draped with flags and bunting and there is a crowd held back by two files of state militia drawn up along the platform. The soldiers carry rifles with bayonets fixed and packs on their backs.

Captain Kavanagh is pacing up and down, nervously chewing a dead cigar. To the Captain of Militia he admits his nervousness, and explains it. "For three months I've been guarding the life of a man who doesn't give a damn what happens to him," he says. "I heard today that they're betting two to one in Richmond that he won't be alive to take the oath of office on March the 4th."

The Captain of Militia would be willing to take some of that money, and Kavanagh respects his confidence in his men. But just the same, he suggests that a close watch be kept of every window in every car.

In the distance a brass band is heard playing "Old Abe Lincoln Came Out of the Wilderness." The crowd begins to sing the words. There is some little commotion as Ninian and Elizabeth Edwards, Josh Speed, Billy Herndon and Crimmin make their way through the crowd.

"How is the President feeling today?" Crimmin would know.

"Just as gloomy as ever," Ninian assures him.

"He came down to the office, and when I asked him what I should do about the sign, 'Lincoln and Herndon,' he said: 'Let it hang there,' reports Billy. 'Let our clients understand that this election makes no difference to the firm. If I live, I'll be back some time and then we'll go right on practicing just as if nothing had happened.'"

"He's always saying that—'If I live—'" says Elizabeth Edwards.

A tremendous cheer starts in the distance and swells toward the crowd. "The President has arrived!" runs the report. The militia is brought to attention. The crowd is pushed back from the platform. The cheering grows louder. The militia is brought to "Present—Arms!" The Lincoln party arrives—

"Abe . . . will be fifty-two tomorrow. He wears a beard. Over his shoulders is his plaid shawl. In his right hand he carries his carpet bag; his left hand is leading Tad. Behind him are Mary, Robert and Willie, and the maid. All, except Mary, are also carrying bags. She carries a bunch of flowers."

Mary and the children are helped into the car. The soldiers have some difficulty keeping back the crowd. Mr. Lincoln is the last to mount the platform. There are cries for a speech. Mr. Lincoln has taken off his hat and turned to wave a half-hearted gesture. When there is silence he speaks—

"My dear friends—I have to say good-by to you. I am going now to Washington—with my new whiskers—of which I hope you approve—"

There is a shout of laughter and now the crowd presses forward with such force the militia is worried. It is the President who suggests that the people be permitted to come on. They are all old friends of his, he says. The soldiers fall back and the crowd surges happily forward. Soon there is silence again. Mr. Lincoln continues—

ABE—No one, not in my situation, can appreciate my feelings of sadness at this parting. To this place, and the kindness of you people, I owe everything. I have lived here for a quarter of a century, and passed from a young to an old man. Here my children have been born and one is buried. I now leave, not knowing when nor whether ever I may return. I am called upon to assume the Presidency at a time when eleven of our sovereign states have announced their intention to secede from the Union, when threats of Civil War increase in fierceness from day to day. It is a grave duty which I now face. In preparing for it I have tried to inquire what great principle or idea it is that has kept this Union so long together. And I now believe that it was not the mere matter of separation of the Colonies from the mother-land, but that sentiment in the Declaration of Independence which gave liberty to the people of this country and hope to all the world. This sentiment was the fulfillment of an ancient dream, which men have held through all time, that they might one day shake off their chains and find freedom in the brother-hood of life. We gained democracy, and now there is a question whether it is fit to survive. Perhaps we have come to the dreadful day of awakening, and the dream is ended. If so, I am afraid it must be ended forever. I cannot believe that ever again will men have the opportunity we have had. Perhaps we should admit that and concede that our ideals of liberty and equality are decadent and doomed. I have heard of an eastern monarch who once charged his wise men to invent him a sentence which would be true and appropriate in all times and situations. They presented him with the words, "And this too shall pass away." That is a comforting thought in times of affliction—"And this too shall pass away." And yet— (*Suddenly speaks with quiet but urgent authority.*) let us believe that it is not true! Let us live to prove that we can cultivate the natural world that is about us, and the intellectual and moral world that is within us, so that we may secure an individual, social and political prosperity, whose course shall be forward, and which, while the earth endures, shall not pass away. I commend you to the care of the Almighty, as I hope that in your prayers you will remember me.   Good-by, my friends and neighbors.

The President is leaning over the rail, shaking hands with the friends closest to him.   The crowd has begun to sing "John Brown's Body."   There is mingled cheering and shouts of affectionate farewell—"Good-by, Abe!"   "Good luck!"   "We trust you, Mr. Lincoln!"

"Time to pull out, Mr. Lincoln; better get inside," suggests Captain Kavanagh, touching the President's arm.

Abe Lincoln gives one last wistful wave to the crowd.   The people are singing "Glory, Glory, Hallelujah!"   The soldiers are clambering aboard.   The lights fade out.

THE CURTAIN FALLS

# THE LITTLE FOXES
## A Drama in Three Acts

### By Lillian Hellman

IN 1934 Lillian Hellman, who had been quietly attending to her knitting as play reader for Herman Shumlin, as a reviewer of books for the New York *Times* and, occasionally, as a press agent for the theatre, burst suddenly upon Broadway as the author of a dramatic sensation among the plays of that year. This was "The Children's Hour," which she afterward did over as a motion picture scenario entitled "These Three."

Nothing more was heard of Miss Hellman as a playwright (she having gone to Hollywood to capitalize her success) until 1936, when she stepped forth again as the author of a labor problem play called "Days to Come." There was merit in this drama, too, but it was a definite letdown from the promise aroused by "The Children's Hour" and was received with disappointing indifference by both critics and playgoers.

For another three years Miss Hellman went back to the cinema and then turned in a third script to Mr. Shumlin. This bore the title of "The Little Foxes," and again the Hellman-Broadway impact was terrific. "The Little Foxes" was received by both reviewers and playgoers with much, though not quite, the same enthusiasm as "The Children's Hour." Because of the superb craftsmanship of its writing, coupled with the soundness and originality of its theme and character creation, topped by the unusual fitness of Tallulah Bankhead and her supporting players for their jobs, "The Little Foxes" became the talked-of drama of the year. When award time arrived in the Spring the New York Drama Critics' Circle gave Miss Hellman's play one more vote than it gave Robert Sherwood's "Abe Lincoln in Illinois," the Pulitzer prize winner, as the best play of the year by an American author. It continued a favorite drama with thousands of playgoers for the next several months.

"In outline 'The Little Foxes' might be called a psychological horror story, so virulent is its contemplation of a hateful and rapacious Southern family at the turn of the century," wrote Richard Watts, Jr., in his *Herald Tribune* review of the play. "By its implications, though, it is far more than that. Through

75

its thoughtful indignation it becomes a scornful and heartfelt parable of the rise of the industrial South in all its ruthlessness, its savage sense of realism and its fine scorn for the older trappings of Confederate romanticism."

We are in the living room of the Giddens home, in a small town in the deep South, when the curtain rises on "The Little Foxes." It is the Spring of 1900, and early evening. The living room, from which a stairway at back leads to a landing and on to the upper floors, is a pleasant room, and good looking. "The furniture is expensive, but it reflects no particular taste," writes the author. "Everything is of the best, but that is all."

There are folding doors at back, under the stairway, leading to the dining room. They are closed at the moment, and the sound of voices can be heard through them. In the living room, Addie, "a tall nice-looking Negro woman of about 55," has been briefly startled by the appearance of Cal, a middle-aged Negro, who has come from the cellar carrying a bottle of the family's choicest old port. Cal is headed for the dining room. The port has been specially ordered by Miss Regina for the "mighty honored guest," and when Miss Regina orders like that she knows what she is doing. . . .

The dining room doors are opened suddenly. Birdie Hubbard lets herself quietly into the room and quickly closes them. "Birdie is a woman of about 40, with a pretty, well-bred, faded face. Her movements are usually nervous and timid, but now, as she comes running into the room, she is gay and excited."

Birdie has come to send Cal over to her house to fetch a music album from her desk. But before Cal can go the dining room doors are again opened and quickly closed to let Oscar Hubbard in. Oscar, a rather unpleasant person in his late 40's, is Birdie's husband, and he quickly countermands Birdie's instructions to Cal about the music album. Furthermore, Oscar would like to know what Birdie means by leaving the table and running about like a child? Also what has she meant by chattering like a magpie all evening to Mr. Marshall?

Birdie would protest that she had no intention of boring Mr. Marshall. He seemed interested in music and they talked about music. She had found Mr. Marshall a very educated, cultured gentleman. And he wasn't bored.

"You have had too much wine," growls Oscar. "Get yourself in hand now."

"What am I doing?" protests Birdie. "I'm not doing anything.

What am I doing?"

"I said get yourself in hand. Stop acting like a fool."

"I don't believe he was bored. I just don't believe it. Some people like music and like to talk about it. That's all I was doing."

Again the dining room doors are opened quickly and Leo Hubbard comes hurrying through. "He is a young man of 20, with a weak kind of good looks."

Leo has come to report, as a warning to his mother and father, that the dinner guests are coming in. A moment later Cal opens the doors wide and the hostess, Regina Giddens, and her guests enter the room. Regina is with William Marshall. "She is a handsome woman of 40. Marshall is 45, pleasant-looking, self-possessed."

They are followed by Alexandra Giddens, Regina's daughter, "a very pretty, rather delicate-looking girl of 17," and by Benjamin Hubbard, "55, with a large jovial face and the light graceful movements that one often finds in large men."

"Mr. Marshall, I think you're trying to console me," Regina is saying. "Chicago may be the noisiest, dirtiest city in the world, but I should still prefer it to the sound of our horses and the smell of our azaleas. I should like crowds of people, and theatres, and lovely women—*very* lovely women, Mr. Marshall?"

"In Chicago?" Mr. Marshall answers, smiling pleasantly. "Oh, I suppose so. But I can tell you this: I've never dined there with three *such* lovely ladies."

Addie has started passing the port and has included Alexandra, who hesitates about taking a glass until her mother sweetly suggests that she may drink in Mr. Marshall's honor—

"Mr. Marshall, this will be the first taste of port I've ever had," Alexandra confesses.

"No one ever had their first taste of a better port," replies the perfect guest, raising his glass in a toast. Now he has turned to Regina. "Well, I suppose it is all true, Mrs. Giddens."

"What is true?"

MARSHALL—That you Southerners occupy a unique position in America. You live better than the rest of us, you eat better, you drink better. I wonder you find time, or want to find time, to do business.

BEN—A great many Southerners don't.

MARSHALL—Do all of you live here together?

REGINA—Here with me? (*Laughs.*) Oh, no. My brother

Ben lives next door. My brother Oscar and his family live in the next square.

BEN—But we are a very close family. We've always *wanted* it that way.

MARSHALL—That is very pleasant. Keeping your family together to share each other's lives. My family moves around too much. My children seem never to come home. Away at school in the Winter; in the Summer, Europe with their mother—

REGINA (*eagerly*)—Oh, yes. Even down here we read about Mrs. Marshall in the society pages.

MARSHALL—I dare say. She moves about a great deal. And all of you are part of the same business? Hubbard Sons?

BEN (*motions to* OSCAR)—Oscar and me. (*Motions to* REGINA.) My sister's good husband is a banker.

MARSHALL (*looking at* REGINA, *surprised*)—Oh.

REGINA—I am so sorry that my husband isn't here to meet you. He's been very ill. He is at Johns Hopkins. But he will be home soon. We think he is getting better now.

LEO—I work for Uncle Horace. (REGINA *looks at him*.) I mean I work for Uncle Horace at his bank. I keep an eye on things while he's away.

REGINA (*smiling*)—Really, Leo?

BEN (*looking at* LEO, *then to* MARSHALL)—Modesty in the young is as excellent as it is rare. (*Looks at* LEO *again*.)

OSCAR (*to* LEO)—Your uncle means that a young man should speak more modestly.

LEO (*hastily, taking a step to* BEN)—Oh, I didn't mean, sir—

But Mr. Marshall has turned to Birdie. Where is the Wagner autograph she had promised to show him? Birdie is all nervous apologies. She has, she says, developed a headache—and—

"My wife is a miserable victim of headaches," puts in Oscar Hubbard quickly, and as quickly turns to suggest to Birdie that, seeing Mr. Marshall wishes it, she should play for him. Mr. Marshall would be pleased and Birdie and Alexandra prepare to offer a duet—

The talk has turned to the Southern aristocracy. Mr. Marshall is surprised to find how remarkably the aristocrats have kept together, and kept what belonged to them. But Ben Hubbard is quick to correct him. Southern aristocrats have not kept together, nor do the Hubbards belong to that class. Oscar's wife, Birdie, is the only true aristocrat among them, Ben admits.

As for the Hubbards, they came along about the time Birdie's great-grandfather owned the fine plantation called "Lionnet," and he and his kind were enjoying the best of everything in the way of living. They were there when the aristocrats were riding off to war, leaving their cotton, and their women, to rot. When the war was over and these fine Southern gentlemen returned to their deserted plantations they were unable to adapt themselves to anything and too high-toned to try.

"Sometimes it is difficult to learn new ways," suggests Mr. Marshall understandingly.

"You're right, Mr. Marshall," admits Ben, determined to bring his guest's attention back to the discussion and away from the interest he is taking in the duet that Alexandra and Birdie have started. "It is difficult to learn new ways. But maybe that's why it's profitable. *Our* grandfather and *our* father learned the new ways and learned how to make them pay. They work. (*Smiles nastily.*) They are in trade. Hubbard Sons, Merchandise. Others, Birdie's family, for example, look down on them. (*Settles back in chair.*) To make a long story short, Lionnet now belongs to *us.* (BIRDIE *stops playing.*) Twenty years ago we took over their land, their cotton, and their daughter. (BIRDIE *rises and stands stiffly by the piano.* MARSHALL, *who has been watching her, rises.*)"

"May I bring you a glass of port, Mrs. Hubbard?"

"No, thank you, sir. You are most polite."

Regina is quick to sense the situation and would turn Ben from pursuing the subject further. Her brothers, she suggests, are obviously trying to convince Mr. Marshall that this is the time for the ladies to withdraw so the men can talk business, but Ben denies the charge. He is intent only on reassuring Mr. Marshall as to the creed of the Hubbards.

"I am a plain man and I am trying to say a plain thing," explains Ben, speaking to Regina. "A man ain't only in business for what he can get out of it. It's got to give him something here. (*He puts his hand to his breast.*) That's every bit as true for the nigger picking cotton for a silver quarter, as it is for you and me. (REGINA *gives* MARSHALL *a glass of port.*) If it don't give him something here, then he don't pick the cotton right. Money isn't all. Not by three shots."

MARSHALL—Really? Well, I always thought it was a great deal.

REGINA—And so did I, Mr. Marshall.

MARSHALL (*leaning forward. Pleasantly, but with meaning*)—

Now you don't have to convince me that you are the right people for the deal. I wouldn't be here if you hadn't convinced me six months ago. You want the mill here, and I want it here. It isn't my business to find out *why* you want it.

BEN—To bring the machine to the cotton, and not the cotton to the machine.

MARSHALL (*amused*)—You have a turn for neat phrases, Hubbard. Well, however grand your reasons are, mine are simple: I want to make money and I believe I'll make it on you. (*As* BEN *starts to speak, he smiles.*)   Mind you, I have no objections to more high-minded reasons. They are mighty valuable in business. It's fine to have partners who so closely follow the teachings of Christ. (*Gets up.*)   And now I must leave for my train.

REGINA—I'm sorry you won't stay over with us, Mr. Marshall, but you'll come again. Any time you like.

BEN (*motions to* LEO, *indicating the bottle.*)—Fill them up, boy, fill them up. (LEO *moves around filling the glasses as* BEN *speaks.*)   Down here, sir, we have a strange custom. We drink the *last* drink for a toast. That's to prove that the Southerner is always still on his feet for the last drink. (*Picks up his glass.*)   It was Henry Frick, your Mr. Henry Frick, who said, "Railroads are the Rembrandts of investments." Well, *I* say, "Southern cotton mills *will be* the Rembrandts of investment." So I give you the firm of Hubbard Sons and Marshall, Cotton Mills, and to it a long and prosperous life.

Leo and Alexandra are to drive Mr. Marshall to the train. Ben and Oscar have gone to see them to the carriage. Regina and Birdie are for the moment alone. Regina is exultant. Marshall is the man who is to open the door of the future for them. She thanks Birdie for being charming to him at dinner, and Birdie, always surprised when anyone notices her, is pleased to report that Mr. Marshall was quite impressed with Regina, too.

"He said to me, 'I hope your sister-in-law will come to Chicago. Chicago will be at her feet.' He said the ladies would bow to your manners and the gentlemen to your looks."

Regina is happy to hear that. It helps to clear the Chicago picture in her mind. Mr. Marshall is undoubtedly a very lonely man. He has said that his wife is away a good deal, very social and high-tone. Regina will go to Chicago one day, and Mrs. Marshall will introduce her. "It won't take long with an introduction from her," muses Regina.

But Birdie is worried. How can Regina leave Horace? How can she go to Chicago? Regina's flight of fancy is way beyond such problems.

"There'll be millions, Birdie, millions. You know what I've always said when people told me we were rich? I said I think you should either be a nigger or a millionaire. In between, like us, what for? (*Laughs. Looks at* BIRDIE.) But I'm not going away tomorrow, Birdie. There's plenty of time to worry about Horace when he comes home. If he ever decides to come home."

And now Ben and Oscar are back. They are similarly exultant. The deal is practically set. There should be a drink to celebrate. They are all thrilled by the outlook. Even Oscar is smiling. He, too, is thinking ahead as he reminds Regina of what a fine-looking couple Leo and Alexandra make and how Mr. Marshall had remarked what fine young people they were.

Regina has told her brothers that she and Birdie had been doing a bit of daydreaming about the future. Now she would like to know what they think of doing with their shares.

The brothers had not thought much about it. Ben is reluctant to count the chickens just yet. Still, he has thought he might have a stable. He knows where there is one. "A rich man's pleasure, the sport of kings," muses Ben. "Why not the sport of Hubbards? Why not?"

Oscar thinks perhaps the pleasure of seeing the bricks grow will be enough for him. Yet, he and Birdie might take a few trips. He might even consider buying the Cornelly place on Jekyll Island. A change of climate would be good for Birdie—and there's fine shooting on Jekyll Island.

As for Birdie, she would like two things: First she would like to have Lionnet back—not as it is, but as it used to be the way her father and mother kept it, with a fresh coat of paint every year, and the smooth lawn all the way down to the river. They could have the organ fixed, and restore the cutting garden, just as her mother had it—

"Oh, I do think we could be happier there," cries Birdie, excitedly, not realizing that they all have long ceased listening to her. "Papa used to say that *nobody* had ever lost their temper at Lionnet, and *nobody* ever would. Papa would never let anybody be nasty-spoken or mean. No, sir. He just didn't like it."

As her second gift, after they have restored Lionnet, Birdie would like to have Oscar's promise not to shoot so much, not to kill so many birds and animals just for the joy of killing. There are so many poor people who need the food—it is wicked to

shoot food just because you like to shoot. But no one is paying
any attention to Birdie or her wishes. No one is paying a great
deal of attention to anyone, so Ben decides to take charge of the
conversation. When he has their attention he continues—

"I said that I had, and I do, estimate the profits very high—
for myself, and Oscar, of course."

"And what does that mean?" demands Regina, slowly. Ben
shrugs his shoulders and turns to Oscar. Oscar clears his throat
and endeavors to explain—

OSCAR—Well, Regina, it's like this. For forty-nine per cent
Marshall will put up four hundred thousand dollars. For fifty-
one per cent— (*Smiles archly.*) a controlling interest, mind
you, we will put up two hundred and twenty-five thousand dollars besides offering him certain benefits that our (*Looks at* BEN.)
local position allows us to manage. Ben means that two hundred
and twenty-five thousand dollars is a lot of money.

REGINA—I know the terms and I know it's a lot of money.

BEN (*nodding*)—It is.

OSCAR—Ben means that we are ready with our two-thirds of
the money. Your third, Horace's I mean, doesn't seem to be
ready. (*Raises his hand as* REGINA *starts to speak.*) Ben has
written to Horace, I have written, and you have written. He
answers. But he never mentions this business. Yet we have
explained it to him in great detail, and told him the urgency.
Still he never mentions it. Ben has been very patient, Regina.
Naturally, you are our sister and we want you to benefit from
anything we do.

REGINA—And in addition to your concern for me, you do not
want control to go out of the family. (*To* BEN.) That right,
Ben?

BEN—That's cynical. (*Smiles.*) Cynicism is an unpleasant
way of saying the truth.

OSCAR—No need to be cynical. We'd have no trouble raising
the third share, the share that you want to take.

REGINA—I am sure you could get the third share, the share
you were saving for me. But that would give you a strange
partner. And strange partners sometimes want a great deal.
(*Smiles unpleasantly.*) But perhaps it would be wise for you
to find him.

OSCAR—Now, now. Nobody says we *want* to do that. We
would like to have you in and you would like to come in.

REGINA—Yes. I certainly would.

"THE LITTLE FOXES"

Regina: I'm sorry you won't stay over with us, Mr. Marshall, but you'll come again. Any time you like.

Ben: Down here we have a strange custom. We drink the *last* drink for a toast.

*(Lee Baker, Tallulah Bankhead, Carl Benton Reid, Dan Duryea, Charles Dingle)*

BEN (*laughs, puts up his hand*)—But we haven't heard from Horace.

REGINA—I've given my word that Horace will put up the money. That should be enough.

BEN—Oh, it was enough. I took your word. But I've got to have more than your word now. The contracts will be signed this week, and Marshall will want to see our money soon after. Regina, Horace has been in Baltimore for five months. I know that you have written him to come home, and that he hasn't come.

OSCAR—It's beginning to look as if he doesn't want to come home.

REGINA—Of course he wants to come home. You can't move around with heart trouble at any moment you choose. You know what doctors are like once they get their hands on a case like this—

OSCAR—They can't very well keep him from answering letters, can they? (REGINA *turns to* BEN.) They couldn't keep him from arranging for the money if he wanted to—

REGINA—Has it occurred to you that Horace is also a good business man?

BEN—Certainly. He is a shrewd trader. Always has been. The bank is proof of that.

REGINA—Then, possibly, he may be keeping silent because he doesn't think he is getting enough for his money. (*Looks at* OSCAR.) Seventy-five thousand he has to put up. That's a lot of money, too.

OSCAR—Nonsense. He knows a good thing when he hears it. He knows that we can make *twice* the profit on cotton goods manufactured *here* than can be made in the North.

BEN—That isn't what Regina means. (*Smiles.*) May I interpret you, Regina? (*To* OSCAR.) Regina is saying that Horace wants *more* than a third of our share.

OSCAR—But he's only putting up a third of the money. You put up a third and you get a third. What else *could* he expect?

REGINA—Well, *I* don't know. I don't know about these things. It would seem that if you put up a third you should only get a third. But then again, there's no law about it, is there? I should think that if you knew your money was very badly needed, well, you just might say, I want more, I want a bigger share. You boys have done that. I've heard you say so.

BEN (*after a pause, laughs*)—So you believe he has deliberately held out? For a larger share? (*Leaning forward.*) Well, I *don't* believe it.  But I *do* believe that's what *you* want.  Am I right, Regina?

REGINA—Oh, I shouldn't like to be too definite.  But I *could* say that I wouldn't like to persuade Horace unless he did get a larger share.  I must look after his interests.  It seems only natural—

OSCAR—And where would the larger share come from?

REGINA—I don't know.  That's not my business.  (*Giggles.*) But perhaps it could come off your share, Oscar.

Oscar is furious, but the others are inclined to laugh at him. When he accuses Regina of talking big, but without any assurance that she can even get Horace to come home, to say nothing about his putting up his third of the money, she calmly reminds him that she is not one to be asking for things she does not think she can get and as for Horace, she can promise them that he will come home when she sends for him—

"I will send Alexandra to Baltimore," she explains, when they demand to know how she will get Horace home.  "She will ask him to come home.  She will say that she *wants* him to come home, and that *I* want him to come home."

"Well, of course she wants him here," Birdie suddenly interposes; "but he's sick and maybe he's happy where he is."

Regina ignores Birdie's suggestion.  They will, she thinks, admit that she can get Horace home.  But before she does she must know what he is going to get.  What does she want?  Just twice as much as they have offered.

Again the brothers are explosive in their protestations.  Again they assure Regina that she must be crazy to expect any such share.  But Ben has a counter proposition:

"You're holding us up, and that's not pretty, Regina, not pretty," says Ben, shaking a roguish finger at her.  "But we need you, and I don't want to fight.  Here's what I'll do: I'll give Horace forty per cent, instead of the thirty-three and a third he really should get.  I'll do that, provided he is home and his money is up within two weeks.  How's that?"

"All right."

"I've asked before: where is this extra share coming from?" Oscar wants to know.

"From you.  From your share," Ben answers pleasantly.

"From me, is it?"  Oscar is almost inarticulate with rage. "That's fine and dandy.  That's my reward.  For thirty-five years I've worked my hands to the bone for you.  For thirty-five years

I've done all the things you didn't want to do. And this is
what I—"

"My, my. I am being attacked tonight on all sides," says Ben,
turning slowly to look fixedly at Oscar, who has suddenly stopped
talking. "First by my sister, then by my brother. And I ain't
a man who likes being attacked. I can't believe that God wants
the strong to parade their strength, but I don't mind doing it if
it's got to be done. (*Leans back in his chair.*) You ought to
take these things better, Oscar. I've made you money in the
past. I'm going to make you more money now. You'll be a
very rich man. What's the difference to any of us if a little more
goes here, a little less goes there—it's all in the family. And it
will stay in the family. I'll never marry. (ADDIE *enters, begins
to gather glasses from the table.* OSCAR *turns to* BEN.) So my
money will go to Alexandra and Leo. They may even marry
some day and— (ADDIE *looks at* BEN.)"

"Marry—Zan and Leo—" The thought is not pleasant to
Birdie.

"That would make a great difference in my feelings, if they
married," agrees Oscar.

Regina is not ready to discuss this prospect. There is plenty
of time. Besides the fact that Alexandra and Leo are first
cousins should be remembered.

"That isn't unusual," Oscar is quick to point out. "Our grandfather and grandmother were first cousins."

"And look at us," giggles Regina.

It is agreed finally that Regina will seriously consider what
they have been discussing; that she will send for Horace and
that she is pretty sure Horace will do what she tells him to
do. . . .

The children are back from having seen Mr. Marshall off on
his train. And now her mother has told Alexandra of the trip
that has been planned for her to Baltimore. The fact that she
is going alone adds to her excitement, but it is not at all to the
liking of Addie. Addie feels sure Mr. Horace ain't going to like
his daughter's traipsing up there by herself. Mr. Horace will be
expecting Addie to be along. Alexandra, too, thinks it would be
more fun if Addie could go—

Regina is firm and of no mind to compromise. Alexandra
should like going alone. Addie has babied her too much. Let
her set about her packing. And let her not worry about her
father's being too ill to travel—

"You are doing this for Papa's own good," Regina explains,

taking Alexandra's hand. "You must let me be the judge of his condition. It's the best possible cure for him to come home and be taken care of here. He mustn't stay there any longer and listen to those alarmist doctors. You are doing this entirely for his sake. Tell your papa that I want him to come home, that I miss him very much."

"Yes, Mama."

Regina has gone upstairs to superintend Addie's packing. The Hubbard brothers and Leo have left. Now only Birdie is left, and she is worried.

"I don't understand about my going, Aunt Birdie," Alexandra is saying. "But anyway, Papa will be home again. (*Pats* BIRDIE's *arm.*) Don't worry about me. I can take care of myself. Really I can."

"That's not what I'm worried about, Zan," says Birdie, shaking her head ominously.

ALEXANDRA (*coming close to her*)—What's the matter?

BIRDIE—It's about Leo—

ALEXANDRA (*whispering*)—He beat the horses. That's why we were late getting back. We had to wait until they cooled off. He always beats the horses as if—

BIRDIE (*whispering frantically, holding* ALEXANDRA's *hands*)— He's my son. My own son. But you are more to me—more to me than my own child. I love you more than anybody else—

ALEXANDRA—Don't worry about the horses. I'm sorry I told you.

BIRDIE (*her voice rising*)—*I am not worrying about the horses.* I am worrying about *you.* You are *not* going to marry Leo. I am not going to let them do that to you—

ALEXANDRA—Marry? To Leo? (*Laughs.*) I wouldn't marry, Aunt Birdie. I've never even thought about it—

BIRDIE—But they have thought about it. (*Wildly.*) Zan, I couldn't stand to think about such a thing. You and— (OSCAR *has come into the doorway on* ALEXANDRA's *speech. He is standing quietly, listening.*)

ALEXANDRA (*laughing*)—But I'm not going to marry. And I'm certainly not going to marry Leo.

BIRDIE—Don't you understand? They'll make you. They'll make you—

ALEXANDRA (*taking* BIRDIE's *hands, quietly, firmly*)—That's foolish, Aunt Birdie. I'm grown now. Nobody can make me do anything.

BIRDIE—I just couldn't stand—

OSCAR (*sharply*)—Birdie. (BIRDIE *looks up, draws quickly away from* ALEXANDRA. *She stands rigid, frightened. Quietly.*) Birdie, get your hat and coat.

ADDIE (*calling from upstairs*)—Come on, baby. Your mama's waiting for you, and she ain't nobody to keep waiting.

ALEXANDRA—All right. (*Then softly, embracing* BIRDIE.) Good night, Aunt Birdie. (*As she passes* OSCAR.) Good night, Uncle Oscar. (BIRDIE *begins to move slowly towards the door as* ALEXANDRA *climbs the stairs.* ALEXANDRA *is almost out of view when* BIRDIE *reaches* OSCAR *in the doorway. As* BIRDIE *quickly attempts to pass him, he slaps her hard, across the face.* BIRDIE *cries out, puts her hand to her face. On the cry,* ALEXANDRA *turns, begins to run down the stairs.*) Aunt Birdie! What happened? What happened? I—

BIRDIE (*softly, without turning*)—Nothing, darling. Nothing happened. (*Quickly, as if anxious to keep* ALEXANDRA *from coming close.*) Now go to bed. (OSCAR *exits.*) Nothing happened. (*Turns to* ALEXANDRA *who is holding her hand.*) I only —I only twisted my ankle. (*She goes out.* ALEXANDRA *stands on the stairs looking after her as if she were puzzled and frightened.*)

THE CURTAIN FALLS

## ACT II

A week later, in the early morning, before Addie has finished cleaning up the Giddens living room, Oscar Hubbard is over to inquire if anything has been heard from Alexandra and her father. They had said that they would be home Thursday night and here it is Friday morning and no sign of them. It is puzzling, and a little worrying to Oscar. And to Addie, too. She has been up all night waiting for them.

Regina comes to the stair landing in a dressing gown when she hears Oscar. She isn't worried. Any number of things could have happened to delay Alexandra and her father. They may have missed connections in Atlanta. Or their train may have been delayed. A hundred things could have kept them.

Cal has brought in a tray with hot coffee. He is a little surprised to find that Mr. Oscar ain't out shooting this morning. First morning in a long time, Cal is willing to bet. And it is, Oscar admits—first morning since he had his head cold, and that must have been eight years ago. But he had had a good morning the day before—

"Bet you got enough bobwhite and squirrel to give every nigger in town a Jesus-party," chuckles Cal. "Most of 'em ain't had no meat since the cotton picking was over. Bet they'd give anything for a little piece of that meat—"

"Cal, if I catch a nigger in this town going shooting, you know what's going to happen."

"Yes, sir, Mr. Oscar."

Leo has arrived from the bank to report that there has been no word received from his Uncle Horace. He thought he'd better come to let them know. He thought, rather, suggests his father, that he had an excuse to take an extra hour off. Leo should have stayed at the bank and done his work. It is time he was thinking of settling down and getting married.

"You also got to stop with that woman in Mobile," continues Oscar, seriously. "You're young and I haven't got no objections to outside women. That is, I haven't got no objections so long as they don't interfere with serious things. Outside women are all right in their place, but *now* isn't their place. You got to realize that."

"Yes, sir. I'll tell her. She'll act all right about it."

"Also, you got to start working harder at the bank. You got to convince your Uncle Horace you're going to make a fit husband for Alexandra."

Leo is wondering what might happen if his Uncle Horace doesn't come home, or doesn't put up the money. They would only have to get the money from the outside, his father explains. That would be easy enough. Leo thinks also that it was a damned shame, what the others had done to his father.

"Don't talk so loud," cautions Oscar, with a hasty glance upstairs. "Don't you worry. When I die, you'll have as much as the rest. You might have yours *and* Alexandra's. I'm not so easily licked."

"You think Uncle Horace don't want to go in on this?"

Oscar (*giggling*)—That's my hunch. He hasn't showed any signs of loving it yet.

Leo (*laughing*)—But he hasn't listened to Aunt Regina yet, either. Oh, he'll go along. It's too good a thing. Why wouldn't he want to? He's got plenty and plenty to invest with. He don't even have to sell anything. Eighty-eight thousand worth of Union Pacific bonds sitting right in his safe deposit box. All he's got to do is open the box.

OSCAR (*after a pause. Looks at his watch*)—Mighty late breakfast in this fancy house. Yes, he's had those bonds for fifteen years. Bought them when they were low and just locked them up.

LEO—Yeah. Just has to open the box and take them out. That's all. Easy as easy can be. (*Laughs.*) The things in that box! There's all those bonds, looking mighty fine. (OSCAR *slowly puts down his newspaper and turns to* LEO.) Then right next to them is a baby shoe of Zan's and a cheap old cameo on a string, *and*—nobody'd believe this—a piece of an old violin. Not even a whole violin. Just a piece of an old thing, a piece of a violin.

OSCAR (*very softly, as if he were trying to control his voice*)— A piece of a violin! What do you think of that!

LEO—Yes, sirree. A lot of other crazy things, too. A poem, I guess it is, signed with his mother's name, and two old school-books with notes and— (LEO *catches* OSCAR's *look. His voice trails off. He turns his head away.*)

OSCAR (*very softly*)—How do you know what's in the box, son?

LEO (*stops, draws back, frightened, realizing what he has said*) —Oh, well. Well, er. Well, one of the boys, sir. It was one of the boys at the bank. He took old Manders' keys. It was Joe Horns. He just up and took Manders' keys and, and—well, took the box out. (*Quickly.*) Then they all asked me if I wanted to see, too. So I looked a little, I guess, but then I made them close up the box quick and I told them never—

OSCAR (*looking at him*)—Joe Horns, you say? He opened it?

LEO—Yes, sir, yes, he did. My word of honor. (*Very nervously looking away.*) I suppose that don't excuse *me* for looking— (*Looking at* OSCAR.) but I did make him close it up and put the keys back in Manders' drawer—

OSCAR (*leaning forward, very softly*)—Tell me the truth, Leo. I am not going to be angry with you. Did you open the box yourself?

LEO—*No, sir, I didn't.* I told you I didn't. No, I—

OSCAR (*irritated, patient*)—I am *not* going to be angry with you. (*Watching* LEO *carefully.*) Sometimes a young fellow deserves credit for looking round him to see what's going on. Sometimes that's a good sign in a fellow your age. (OSCAR *rises.*) Many great men have made their fortune with their eyes. Did you open the box?

LEO (*very puzzled*)—No. I—

OSCAR (*moving to* LEO)—Did you open the box? It may
have been—well, it may have been a good thing if you had.
LEO (*after a long pause*)—I opened it.

Nobody had seen him, Leo adds. He was in the bank alone.
And his Uncle Horace never knew. Uncle Horace only looked
in the box once every six months, when he cut the coupons.
Sometimes he even let Manders do that. "Imagine not looking
at all that," suggests Leo. "You can bet if I had the bonds I'd
watch 'em like—"

"If you had them," repeats Oscar; "*if* you had them. Then
you could have a share in the mill, you and me. A fine, big
share, too. (*Pauses, shrugs.*) Well, a man can't be shot for
wanting to see his son get on in the world, can he, boy?"

Leo is beginning to see what is in his father's mind. But of
course he hasn't the bonds and Uncle Horace has. True, admits
Oscar, but perhaps Uncle Horace would be willing to lend Leo
the bonds if he decides not to use them himself. A loan of them
for three or possibly four months! That should be simple!
Here it is April. Horace won't likely look at them again until
Fall. He wouldn't even miss them! Not if he never looks at
them! And it wouldn't hurt Horace. People ought to help
each other—

Ben has arrived. Regina, looking down from the staircase
landing, is amused to find her relatives gathered so early, and so
eagerly. She still is convinced there is no cause for alarm. She
comes downstairs and soon has them all in the dining room for
breakfast.

Addie is gathering up the coffee cups when she hears voices
outside. A moment later she has run into the hall and when she
reappears she is supporting Horace Giddens with her arm around
his shoulders. "Horace is a tall man of about 45. He has been
good-looking, but now his face is tired and ill. He walks stiffly,
as if it were an enormous effort, and carefully, as if he were
unsure of his balance."

Soon Alexandra has followed them in, explaining as she comes
that they had to stop in Mobile because of Papa's condition, and
that there was no way to send a message. Alexandra is fluttery,
having taken on the responsibilities of a nurse. It is very important that nothing should happen to papa's medicine. And he
must have his wheel chair—

"He doesn't feel all right," Alexandra corrects her father.
"He just says that. The trip was very hard on him, and now

he must go right to bed."

Alexandra would call her mother, but her father stops her. He would like to have a cup of Addie's coffee. They just can't make good coffee up North.

It would be just as well, thinks Addie, if Alexandra would clean herself up a bit before she does anything else, and Alexandra is willing, but she must first be sure Addie knows about the medicine—

"The pills Papa must take every four hours," she explains. "And the bottle only when—only if he feels very bad." Turning to her father she adds, anxiously: "Now, don't move until I come back and don't talk much and remember about his medicine, Addie—"

Horace has his coffee and would have some of the family news. He would like to know why Zan was sent to fetch him home.

"I don't know," protests Addie. "All I know is big things are going on. Everybody going to be high-tone rich. Big rich. You too. All because smoke's going to start out of a building that ain't even up yet."

"I've heard about it."

"And, er—" Addie has some little reluctance about going on. "And—well, Zan, she going to marry Mr. Leo in a little while."

"What are you talking about?" Horace is looking fixedly at her.

"That's right. That's the talk, God help us."

"*What's* the talk?"

"I'm telling you. There's going to be a wedding— (*Angrily turns away.*) Over my dead body there is."

Now Horace is ready to have the family called. Addie still hesitates, but finally opens the doors and the Giddenses troop in. There is considerable excitement mixed with the greetings, and a good deal of explaining. In the midst of it all Birdie runs in, wearing a flannel kimono, her face flushed and excited. Birdie's greeting is the sincerest of them all, but her husband is terribly distressed at the way she looks. The idea of her crossing the square dressed that way! He sends her home, even before she can see Alexandra.

The others have gone back to finish their breakfasts, at Regina's urging, and Regina and Horace are alone. Immediately they become awkward and self-conscious. Regina would laugh the awkwardness away—

"Well. Here we are. It's been a long time," she says, and Horace smiles. "Five months. You know, Horace, I wanted to come and be with you in the hospital, but I didn't know where my duty was. Here, or with you. But you know how much I *wanted* to come."

HORACE—That's kind of you, Regina. There was no need to come.

REGINA—Oh, but there was. Five months lying there all by yourself, no kinfolks, no friends. Don't try to tell me you didn't have a bad time of it.

HORACE—I didn't have a bad time. (*As she shakes her head he becomes insistent.*) No, I didn't, Regina. Oh, at first when I—when I heard the news about myself—but after I got used to that, I liked it there.

REGINA—You *liked* it? (*Coldly.*) Isn't that strange. You liked it so well you didn't want to come home?

HORACE—That's not the way to put it. (*Then, kindly, as he sees her turn her head away.*) But there I was and I got kind of used to it, kind of to like lying there and thinking. (*Smiles.*) I never had much time to think before. And time's become valuable to me.

REGINA—It sounds almost like a holiday.

HORACE (*laughing*)—It was, sort of. The first holiday I've had since I was a little kid.

REGINA—And here I was thinking you were in pain and—

HORACE (*quietly*)—I was in pain.

REGINA—And instead you were having a holiday! A holiday of thinking. Couldn't you have done that here?

HORACE—I wanted to do it before I came here. I was thinking about us.

REGINA—About us? About you and me? Thinking about you and me after all these years. (*Unpleasantly.*) You shall tell me everything you thought—some day.

HORACE (*after a minute's silence*)—Regina. (*She turns toward him.*) Why did you send Zan to Baltimore?

REGINA—Why? Because I wanted you home. You can't make anything suspicious out of that, can you?

HORACE—I didn't mean to make anything suspicious about it. (*Hesitantly, taking her hand.*) Zan said you wanted me to come home. I was so pleased at that and touched, it made me feel good.

REGINA (*taking away her hand, turns*)—Touched that I should want you home?

HORACE (*sighing*)—I'm saying all the wrong things as usual. Let's try to get along better. There isn't so much more time.

Horace would know first about the crazy talk he's heard regarding Zan and Leo marrying. When Regina assures him it is no more than foolish gossip, fed by an absurd notion she has permitted Oscar to toy with, he would have her go further and stamp it out of Oscar's mind entirely. He never wants to hear of it again, not as long as he lives.

Horace has been wondering a little why after he has been in the hospital for five months, his wife is not sufficiently interested to inquire about his health. Probably they have written her that he cannot live long.

That is a subject, Regina coldly suggests, that people do not talk about. But what did the doctors think caused his bad heart? It could not be, by any chance, his fancy women—

"I don't think that's the best scientific theory," Horace answers with an unpleasant smile. "You don't catch heart trouble in bed."

"I didn't think you did," snaps Regina angrily. "I only thought you might catch a bad conscience—in bed, as you say."

"I didn't tell them about my bad conscience. Or about my fancy women. Nor did I tell them that my wife has not wanted me in bed with her for— (*Sharply.*) How long is it, Regina? (REGINA *turns to him.*) Ten years? Did you bring me home for this, to make me feel guilty again? That means you want something. But you'll not make me feel guilty any more. My 'thinking' has made a difference."

Regina is prepared to apologize and promise to be nice, but when Horace rises to go upstairs she is again excited. He must wait and talk to Ben. Ben has something very important to tell him about, something very important to them all, including his beloved daughter. Hurriedly she summons Ben from the breakfast room, and finally, by continued pleading, gets Horace to sit down.

Ben is willing to wait, if Horace is not feeling well, but given the chance he proceeds to have his say. "You know what I've been telling you for years," Ben is saying. "How I've always said that every one of us little Southern business men had great things (*Extends his arm.*) right beyond our finger tips. It's been my dream: my dream to make those fingers grow longer. I'm a lucky man, Horace, a lucky man. To dream and to live to get what you've dreamed of. That's my idea of a lucky man. (*Looks at his fingers as his arm drops slowly.*) For thirty years

I've cried bring the cotton mills to the cotton. Well, finally I got up nerve to go to Marshall Company in Chicago."

Horace has opened his medicine bottle and taken a dose. He knows all that Ben has told him, and is again inclined to leave them. Again Regina holds him back. He may know what Ben has told him, but he doesn't know that her brothers have promised to give him a larger share—a much larger share—thanks to her bargaining. He's getting more and Oscar is getting less. Which Horace can understand when he hears the proposition— an investment of seventy-five thousand dollars that is sure to make them a million. And what has Ben promised the Marshall Company besides the money?

"Water power. Free and plenty of it," Ben reports.

"You got them that, of course."

"Cheap. You'd think the Governor of a great state would make his price a little higher. From pride, you know. (HORACE *smiles.* BEN *smiles.*) Cheap wages. 'What do you mean by cheap wages?' I say to Marshall. 'Less than Massachusetts,' he says to me, 'and that averages eight a week.' 'Eight a week! By God,' I tell him, *'I'd* work for eight a week myself.' Why, there ain't a mountain white or a town nigger but wouldn't give his right arm for three silver dollars every week, eh, Horace?"

"Sure. And they'll take less than that when you get around to playing them off against each other. You can save a little money that way, Ben. (*Angrily.*) And make them hate each other just a little more than they do now."

"What's all this about?" demands Regina, sharply.

"There'll be no trouble from anybody, white or black," laughs Ben. "Marshall said that to me. 'What about strikes? That's all we've had in Massachusetts for the last three years.' I say to him, 'What's a strike? I never heard of one. Come South, Marshall. We got good folks and we don't stand for any fancy fooling.' "

"You're right. (*Slowly.*) Well, it looks like you made a good deal for yourselves, and for Marshall, too. (*To* BEN.) Your father used to say he made the thousands and you boys would make the millions. I think he was right."

"Millions for us, too," Regina reminds him, with a nervous laugh.

"Us? You and me? I don't think so. We've got enough money, Regina. We'll just sit by and watch the boys grow rich."

They turn and watch Horace's movements tensely. Slowly he goes to the staircase and starts up. Regina is protesting furiously.

He stops on the stairs to listen to her tell how they have waited
all this time for his coming. Now they cannot wait any longer.
Oscar has to be in Chicago by the end of the week, and with the
money.

Still Horace is unimpressed. He is very tired, he repeats. He
is going to his room. But Regina is not to be put off. She
wants a reason. She is going to have a reason. She is going to
talk to Horace now. And she follows her husband upstairs.

"Sometimes it is better to wait for the sun to rise again," Ben
calls after her, softly. "And sometimes, as our mother used to
tell you, it is unwise for a good-looking woman to frown. Soft-
ness and a smile do more to the heart of men."

Regina has disappeared down the upstairs hall. Soon there is
the sound of voices, voices raised in anger, from upstairs. Oscar
is worried. What if Horace does hold out? What if they do
have to go outside for the money? The very suggestion is unpleasant to Ben.

Leo might be able to help in case he was needed, suggests
Oscar. Leo has a friend who owns eighty-eight thousand dollars
in Union Pacific bonds, and Leo's friend doesn't look at the
bonds for five and six months at a time—

Ben's attention is caught by the suggestion. He doesn't want
to know who Leo's friend is—not even his name—nor where he
keeps his bonds, but if the friend would like to loan them, until
Fall, say—

"Why not? Why not?" chuckles Ben. "Good! We are
lucky. We'll take the loan from Leo's friend—I think he will
make a safer partner than our sister." He nods toward the
stairs, and turns to Leo. "How soon can you get them?"

"Today. Right now. They're in the safe-deposit box and—"

"I don't want to know where they are."

"We will keep it a secret from you," agrees Oscar, as he laughingly pats Ben's arm.

"Good. Draw a check for our part. You can take the night
train for Chicago," says Ben.

Leo slyly suggests that he thinks he should get something out
of the deal—perhaps Uncle Horace's share—but he is quickly
put in his place by Uncle Ben, and also by his father.

A moment later there is a sound of running feet in the upstairs
hall, followed by Alexandra's voice calling out hysterically, as she
comes hurrying down the stairs—

"Mama—Mama—don't . . . Uncle Ben! Uncle Ben! Please
go up. Please make Mama stop. Uncle Ben, he's sick, he's so

sick. How can Mama talk to him like that—please, make her stop. She'll—"

"Alexandra, you have a tender heart," smiles Ben.

ALEXANDRA (*crying*)—Go on up, Uncle Ben, please— (*Suddenly the voices stop. A second later there is the sound of a door being slammed.*)

BEN—Now you see. Everything is over. Don't worry. (*He starts for the door.*) Alexandra, I want you to tell your mother how sorry I am that I had to leave. And don't worry so, my dear. Married folk frequently raise their voices, unfortunately. (*He starts to put on his hat and coat as* REGINA *appears on the stairs.*)

ALEXANDRA (*furiously*)—How can you treat Papa like this? He's sick. He's very sick. Don't you know that? I won't let you.

REGINA—Mind your business, Alexandra. (*To* BEN. *Her voice is cold and calm.*) How much longer can you wait for the money?

BEN (*putting on his coat*)—He has refused? My, that's too bad.

REGINA—He will change his mind. I'll find a way to make him. What's the longest you can wait now?

BEN—I could wait until next week. But I can't wait until next week. (*He giggles, pleased at the joke.*) I could but I can't. Could and can't. Well, I must go now. I'm very late—

REGINA (*coming downstairs towards him*)—You're not going. I want to talk to you.

BEN—I was about to give Alexandra a message for you. I wanted to tell you that Oscar is going to Chicago tonight, so we can't be here for our usual Friday supper.

REGINA (*tensely*)—Oscar is going to Chi— (*Softly.*) What do you mean?

BEN—Just that. Everything is settled. He's going on to deliver to Marshall—

REGINA (*taking a step to him*)—I demand to know what— You are lying. You are trying to scare me. *You haven't got the money.* How could you have it? You can't have— (BEN *laughs.*) You will wait until I— (HORACE *comes into view on the landing.*)

BEN—You are getting out of hand. Since when do I take orders from you?

REGINA—Wait, you— (BEN *stops.*) How *can* he go to

Chicago? Did a ghost arrive with the money? (BEN *starts for the hall.*) I don't believe you. Come back here. (REGINA *starts after him.*) Come back here, you— (*The door slams. She stops in the doorway, staring, her fists clenched. After a pause she turns slowly.*)

HORACE (*very quietly*)—It's a great day when you and Ben cross swords. I've been waiting for it for years.

ALEXANDRA—Papa, Papa, please go back! You will—

HORACE—And so they don't need you, and so you will not have your millions, after all.

REGINA (*turning slowly*)—You hate to see anybody live now, don't you? You hate to think that I'm going to be alive and have what I want.

HORACE—I should have known you'd think that was the reason.

REGINA—Because you're going to die and you know you're going to die.

ALEXANDRA (*shrilly*)—Mama! Don't— Don't listen, Papa. Just don't listen. Go away—

HORACE—Not to keep you from getting what you want. Not even partly that. (*Holding to the rail.*) I'm sick of you, sick of this house, sick of my life here. I'm sick of your brothers and their dirty tricks to make a dime. There must be better ways of getting rich than cheating niggers on a pound of bacon. Why should I give you the money? (*Very angrily.*) To pound the bones of this town to make dividends for you to spend? You wreck the town, you and your brothers, *you* wreck the town and live on it. Not me. Maybe it's easy for the dying to be honest. But it's not my fault I'm dying. (ADDIE *enters, stands at the door quietly.*) I'll do no more harm now. I've done enough. I'll die my own way. And I'll do it without making the world any worse. I leave that to you.

REGINA (*looking at him slowly, calmly*)—I hope you die. I hope you die soon. (*Smiles.*) I'll be waiting for you to die.

ALEXANDRA (*shrieking*)—Papa! Don't— Don't listen— Don't—

ADDIE—Come here, Zan. Come out of this room.

"Alexandra runs quickly to Addie, who holds her. Horace turns slowly and starts upstairs" as the curtain falls.

## ACT III

Two weeks later, on a rainy afternoon, Horace Giddens is sitting in the living room of the Giddens house looking out the window. "On the table next to him is a safety-deposit box and a small bottle of medicine."

At the piano Alexandra Giddens and her Aunt Birdie are sitting. Alexandra is having a lesson and Birdie is counting for her. Birdie is talkative this day, and reminiscent. She remembers so many interesting things—the days when she and Alexandra's father used to play together, he the fiddle and she the piano; the day that Oscar first brought her to the Hubbards' to supper, and she saw all the family together for the first time—

"Birdie, when did Oscar get back from Chicago?" Horace interrupts.

"Yesterday. Hasn't he been here yet?"

"No. Neither has Uncle Ben since—since that day."

"Oh, I didn't know it was *that* bad. Oscar never tells me anything—"

"The Hubbards have had their great quarrel," muses Horace, smiling. "I knew it would come some day. It came."

"It came. It certainly came all right," agrees Alexandra.

"But Oscar was in such good humor when he got home, I didn't—" Birdie's amazement is profound.

"Yes, I can understand that," says Horace.

Addie has brought cookies and a carafe of elderberry wine. It is almost like a party, thinks Alexandra. A nice party, too. They have all been so happy together, with the house to themselves. Just quiet and restful, as Addie agrees. But it won't be that way long—

"Little while now, even sitting here, you'll hear the red bricks going into place," Addie prophesies. "The next day the smoke'll be pushing out the chimneys and by church time that Sunday every human born of woman will be living on chicken. That's how Mr. Ben's been telling the story."

And she believes it. Everybody believes what Mr. Ben orders. "There ain't been so much talk around here since Sherman's army didn't come near," insists Addie.

Birdie has taken an extra glass or two of the elderberry wine, and is remembering again. Remembering that she and Horace never played together after that first night. Oscar didn't like it. Music, said Oscar, made him nervous. But Horace has always been mighty kind to Birdie. Several times he has stepped in and saved Birdie's embarrassing experiences, and once he stopped Oscar from— Birdie catches herself and there are no further revelations for the moment.

Horace has sent for Cal to go on an errand. Cal is to go to the bank, and around to the back door. He will find Mr. Manders and Mr. Leo going over the day's business. He is to say to Mr. Manders that Mr. Horace says he is much obliged to him for bringing the safety deposit box. And he is to ask Mr. Manders to come over that night and bring Mr. Sol Fowler with him.

It is a pretty foolish errand to Cal. Mr. Manders already knows he brought the box around. But, Horace repeats, that is to be the message just the same. . . .

"Miss Birdie, that elderberry going to give you a headache spell," protests Addie, as Miss Birdie returns to the wine.

"Oh, I don't think so," gaily answers Birdie. "I don't think so. Mama used to give me elderberry wine when I was a little girl. For hiccoughs. (*Laughs*.) You know, I don't think people get hiccoughs any more. Isn't that funny? (BIRDIE *laughs*. HORACE *and* ALEXANDRA *laugh*.) I used to get hiccoughs just when I shouldn't have."

ADDIE (*nodding*)—And nobody gets growing pains no more. That is funny. Just as if there was some style in what you get. One year an ailment's stylish and the next year it ain't.

BIRDIE (*turning*)—I remember. It was my first big party, at Lionnet I mean, and I was so excited, and there I was with hiccoughs and Mama laughing. (*Softly. Looking at carafe.*) Mama always laughed. (*Picks up carafe.*) A big party, a lovely dress from Mr. Worth in Paris, France, and hiccoughs. (*Pours drink.*) My brother pounding me on the back and Mama with the elderberry bottle, laughing at me. Everybody was on their way to come, and I was such a ninny, hiccoughing away. (*Drinks.*) You know, that was the first day I ever saw Oscar Hubbard. The Ballongs were selling their horses and he was going there to buy. He passed and lifted his hat—we could see him from the window—and my brother, to tease Mama, said maybe we should have invited the Hubbards to the party. He said Mama didn't like them because they kept a store, and he said that was old-fashioned of her. (*Her face lights up.*) And then, and *then* I saw Mama angry for the first time in my life. She said that wasn't the reason. She said she was old-fashioned enough not to like people who killed animals they couldn't use, and who made their money charging awful interest to poor, ignorant niggers and cheating them on what they bought. She was very angry, Mama was. I had never seen her face like that. And then suddenly she laughed and said, "Look, I've frightened Birdie out of the hiccoughs." (*Her head drops. Then softly.*) And so she had. They were all gone. (*Moves to sofa, sits.*)

ADDIE—Yeah, they got mighty well off cheating niggers. Well, there are people who eat the earth and eat all the people on it like in the Bible with the locusts. Then there are people who stand around and watch them eat it. (*Softly.*) Sometimes I think it ain't right to stand and watch them do it.

BIRDIE (*thoughtfully*)—Like I say, if we could only go back to Lionnet. Everybody'd be better there. They'd be good and kind. I like people to be kind. (*Pours drink.*) Don't you, Horace; don't you like people to be kind?

HORACE—Yes, Birdie.

BIRDIE (*very drunk now*)—Yes, that was the first day I ever saw Oscar. Who would have thought— (*Quickly.*) You all want to know something? Well, I don't like Leo. My very own son, and I don't like him. (*Laughs gaily.*) My, I guess I even like Oscar more.

ALEXANDER—Why did you marry Uncle Oscar?

ADDIE (*sharply*)—That's no question for you to be asking.

HORACE (*sharply*)—Why not? She's heard enough around here to ask anything.

ALEXANDRA—Aunt Birdie, why did you marry Uncle Oscar?

BIRDIE—I don't know. I thought I liked him. He was kind to me and I thought it was because he liked me too. But that wasn't the reason— (*Wheels on* ALEXANDRA.) Ask why *he* married *me*. I can tell you that. He's told it to me often enough.

ADDIE (*leaning forward*)—Miss Birdie, don't—

BIRDIE (*speaking very rapidly, tensely*)—My family was good and the cotton on Lionnet's fields was better. Ben Hubbard wanted the cotton and (*Rises.*) Oscar Hubbard married it for him. He was kind to me, then. He used to smile at me. He hasn't smiled at me since. Everybody knew that's what he married me for. (ADDIE *rises.*) Everybody but me. Stupid, stupid me.

Alexandra has gone to her father and taken his hand. Perhaps, she suggests, they can go away somewhere when he is better. Just by themselves. And her father thinks perhaps they can.

Again Addie has tried to keep Miss Birdie still, but Birdie is having her day of confession now and will not be stopped. Headache? She's never had a headache in her life. That's only the family's excuse. Birdie drinks. She always has drunk. Alone, by herself, in her room. And when the family wanted to hide it they have always said she had a headache—

"Even you won't like me now," says Birdie, turning away from the sympathetic Alexandra. "You won't like me any more."

"I love you. I'll always love you," protests Alexandra.

"Well, don't. Don't love me," snaps Birdie furiously. "Because in twenty years you'll just be like me. They'll all do the same things to you. (*Begins to laugh hysterically.*) You know what? In twenty-two years I haven't had a whole day of happiness. Oh, a little, like today with you all. But never a single, whole day. I say to myself, if only I had one more *whole* day, then— (*The laugh stops.*) And that's the way you'll be. And you'll trail after them, just like me, hoping they won't be so mean that day or say something to make you feel so bad—only you'll be worse off because you haven't got my mama to remember—"

"I guess we were all trying to make a happy day," sympathizes Alexandra. "You know, we sit around and try to pretend nothing's happened. We try to pretend we are not here. We make believe we are just by ourselves, some place else, and it doesn't seem to work. (*Kisses* BIRDIE'S *hand.*) Come now, Aunt Birdie. I'll walk you home. You and me."

Addie thinks it may have been good for Miss Birdie to talk that way, but she's sorry Miss Zan had to hear it. But Zan's father is glad Zan did hear. It would be nice for her to stay innocent, but it is better that she should know—

"How else is she going to know that she's got to get away? I'm trying to show her that. I'm trying, but I've only got a little time left. She can even hate me when I'm dead, if she'll only learn to hate and fear this."

Horace would have Addie promise to take Zan away if anything should happen to him. He'll fix it so the family can't stop her. Horace is going to make a new will as soon as Sol Fowler arrives. And upstairs, in a certain drawer, he has left seventeen hundred-dollar bills in an envelope with Addie's name on it. . . .

Regina is back. In the hall she shakes out her umbrella and tosses a damp coat over the banister. Finding Horace there she is displeased. Their agreement had been that he was to stay in his part of the house and she in hers. But Horace has something to tell Regina. It is about the bonds. About their having disappeared from the safety deposit box and, so far as Horace knows, been already invested in the Hubbard Sons and Marshall enterprise.

"I wasn't there, but I can guess what happened," Horace explains. "This fine gentleman (Leo) to whom you were willing to marry your daughter, took the keys and opened the box. You remember that the day of the fight Oscar went to Chicago? Well, he went with my bonds that his son Leo had stolen for him. (*Pleasantly.*) And for Ben, of course, too."

REGINA (*slowly*)—When did you find out the bonds were gone?
HORACE—Wednesday night.
REGINA—I thought that's what you said. Why have you waited three days to do anything? (*Suddenly laughs.*) This *will* make a fine story.
HORACE—Couldn't it?
REGINA (*still laughing*)—A fine story to hold over their heads. How could they be such fools?
HORACE—But I'm not going to hold it over their heads.
REGINA (*the laugh stops*)—What?
HORACE (*turns his chair to face her*)—I'm going to let them keep the bonds—as a loan from you. An eighty-eight-thousand-dollar loan; they should be grateful to you. They will be, I think.
REGINA (*slowly smiles*)—I see. You are punishing me. But I won't let you punish me. If you won't do anything, I will. Now. (*She starts for the door.*)
HORACE—You won't do anything. Because you can't. (RE-GINA *stops.*) It won't do you any good to make trouble because I shall simply say that I lent them the bonds.
REGINA (*slowly.*) You would do that?
HORACE—Yes. For once in your life I am tying your hands. There is nothing for you to do. (*There is silence. Then she sits down.*)
REGINA—I see. You are going to lend them the bonds and let them keep all the profit they make on them, and there is nothing I can do about it. Is that right?
HORACE—Yes.
REGINA (*softly*)—Why did you say that I was making this gift?
HORACE—I was coming to that. I am going to make a new will, Regina, leaving you eighty-eight thousand dollars in Union Pacific bonds. The rest will go to Zan. It's true that your brothers have borrowed your share for a little while. After my

death I advise you to talk to Ben and Oscar. They won't admit anything and Ben, I think, will be smart enough to see that he's safe. Because I knew about the theft and said nothing. Nor will I say anything as long as I live. Is that clear to you?

REGINA (*nods, softly, without looking at him*)—You will not say anything as long as you live.

HORACE—That's right. And by that time they will probably have replaced your bonds, and then they'll belong to you and nobody but us will ever know what happened. (*Stops, smiles.*) They'll be around any minute to see what I am going to do. I took good care to see that word reached Leo. They'll be mighty relieved to know I'm going to do nothing and Ben will think it all a capital joke on you. And that will be the end of that. There's nothing you can do to them, nothing you can do to me.

REGINA—You hate me very much.

HORACE—No.

REGINA—Oh, I think you do. (*Puts her head back, sighs.*) Well, we haven't been very good together. Anyway, I don't hate you either. I have only contempt for you. I've always had.

HORACE—From the very first?

REGINA—I think so.

HORACE—I was in love with *you*. But why did *you* marry *me?*

REGINA—I was lonely when I was young.

HORACE—*You* were lonely?

REGINA—Not the way people usually mean. Lonely for all the things I wasn't going to get. Everybody in this house was so busy and there was so little place for what I wanted. I wanted the world. Then, and then—Papa died and left the money to Ben and Oscar.

HORACE—And you married me?

REGINA—Yes, I thought— But I was wrong. You were a small-town clerk then. You haven't changed.

HORACE (*nods, smiling*)—And that wasn't what you wanted.

REGINA—No. No, it wasn't what I wanted. (*Pauses, leans back, pleasantly.*) It took me a little while to find out I had made a mistake. As for you—I don't know. It was almost as if I couldn't stand the kind of man you were— (*Smiles, softly.*) I used to lie there at night, praying you wouldn't come near—

HORACE—Really? It was as bad as that?

REGINA (*nodding*)—Remember when I went to Doctor Sloan and I told you he said there was something the matter with me and that you shouldn't touch me any more?

HORACE—I remember.

REGINA—But you believed it. I couldn't understand that. I couldn't understand that anybody could be such a soft fool. That was when I began to despise you.

HORACE (*puts his hand to his throat, looks at the bottle of medicine on table*)—Why didn't you leave me?

REGINA—I told you I married you for something. It turned out it was only for this. (*Carefully.*) This wasn't what I wanted, but it was something. I never thought about it much but if I had (HORACE *puts his hand to his throat.*) I'd have known that you would die before I would. But I couldn't have known that you would get heart trouble so early and so bad. I'm lucky, Horace. I've always been lucky. (HORACE *turns slowly to the medicine.*) I'll be lucky again.

Horace, his hand to his throat again, has taken the cork from the bottle of medicine and is reaching for a spoon when the bottle slips from his hand and breaks on the table. With a gasp he calls to Regina to tell Addie to bring the second bottle from upstairs. Regina does not move. He stares at her and understands. Hoarsely he tries to call Addie. Realizing she cannot hear "he makes a sudden, furious spring from the chair to the stairs, taking the first few steps as if he were a desperate runner. On the fourth step he slips, gasps, grasps the rail, makes a great effort to reach the landing. When he reaches the landing, he is on his knees. His knees give way, he falls on the landing, out of view."

Regina has not turned. She waits a moment, then goes to the foot of the stairs and calls her husband's name. Getting no reply she climbs the stairs hurriedly and a second later is calling excitedly for Addie and Cal.

A moment later Leo Hubbard arrives at the door. Getting no response he lets himself in and calls loudly for his Aunt Regina. Cal appears on the stairway to quiet him. Now Ben and Oscar have followed Leo into the house. They hear the news of Horace's bad attack. They don't know whether to go upstairs or not.

Before they can decide Leo manages to get a message across to them. He has been looking for his father all day. He has wanted to tell him that Uncle Horace knows about the bonds. Leo was in the bank when Cal came with the message to Manders. Uncle Horace has known since last Wednesday— And he has sent for his lawyer, Sol Fowler. Leo would quietly take the box back, but Ben is against that. There is a chance that Horace has not told Regina. Horace and Regina, he knows, have not been on such good speaking terms recently. And if she doesn't know, it may work out all right.

"If she does know, you're to say he lent you the bonds," Ben advises Leo. Then Regina comes slowly down the stairs.

They are all three staring at her as she calmly seats herself and reports that Horace has had a bad attack; that at the moment he is unconscious; that Horace had that afternoon told her about the bonds; that Horace had said Leo had stolen the bonds and given them to his father, and that it was Horace's plan to pretend that he had loaned the bonds to Ben and Oscar as a present from Regina.

"He said there was nothing I could do about it," concludes Regina. "He said the rest of his money would go to Alexandra. That is all."

Ben and Oscar are visibly perturbed. Leo is inclined to be rather jittery. Regina remains calm. Horace had repeated, she says, that there was nothing she could do as long as he was alive to say that he had lent her brothers the bonds.

Ben would put a cheerful face on the matter. The bonds are safe and will be returned safely to Regina. That was the understanding. On a more appropriate day they will talk it all out. Now he thinks perhaps he had better go and help find a doctor.

"I don't think you had better go yet," says Regina commandingly. "I think you had better stay and sit down."

"Since when do I take orders from you?" snaps Ben.

"You don't—yet," answers Regina. "Come back, Oscar. You, too, Leo."

"My dear Regina—" begins Oscar.

BEN (*softly patting* REGINA's *hand*)—Horace has already clipped your wings and very wittily. Do I have to clip them, too? (*Smiles at her.*) You'd get farther with a smile, Regina. I'm a soft man for a woman's smile.

REGINA—I'm smiling, Ben. I'm smiling because you are quite safe while Horace lives. But I don't think Horace will live. And if he doesn't live I shall want seventy-five per cent in exchange for the bonds.

BEN (*steps back, whistles, laughs*)—Greedy! What a greedy girl you are! You want so much of everything.

REGINA—Yes. And if I don't get what I want I am going to put all three of you in jail.

OSCAR (*furiously*)—You're mighty crazy. Having just admitted—

BEN—And on what evidence would you put Oscar and Leo in jail?

REGINA (*laughing gaily*)—Oscar, listen to him. He's getting ready to swear that it was you and Leo! What do you say to that? (OSCAR *turns furiously towards* BEN.) Oh, don't be angry, Oscar. I'm going to see that he goes in with you.

BEN—Try anything you like, Regina. (*Sharply.*) And now we can stop all this and say good-by to you. (ALEXANDRA *comes slowly down the steps.*) It's his money and he's obviously willing to let us borrow it. (*More pleasantly.*) Learn to make threats when you can carry them through. For how many years have I told you a good-looking woman gets more by being soft and appealing? Mama used to tell you that. (*Looks at his watch.*) Where the hell is Sloan? (*To* OSCAR.) Take the buggy and— (*As* BEN *turns to* OSCAR, *he sees* ALEXANDRA. *She walks stiffly. She goes slowly to the lower window, her head bent. They all turn to look at her.*)

OSCAR (*after a second, moving toward her*)—What? Alexandra— (*She does not answer. After a second,* ADDIE *comes slowly down the stairs, moving as if she were very tired. At the foot of steps, she looks at* ALEXANDRA, *then turns and slowly crosses to door and exits.* REGINA *rises.* BEN *looks nervously at* ALEXANDRA, *at* REGINA. *As* ADDIE *passes him, irritably to* ALEXANDRA.) Well, what is— (*Turns into room—sees* ADDIE *at foot of steps.*)—what's? (BEN *puts up a hand, shakes his head.*) My God, I didn't know—who could have known—I didn't know he was that sick. Well, well—I— (REGINA *stands quietly, her back to them.*)

BEN (*softly, sincerely*)—Seems like yesterday when he first came here.

OSCAR (*sincerely, nervously*)—Yes, that's true. (*Turns to* BEN.) The whole town loved him and respected him.

ALEXANDRA (*turning*)—Did you love him, Uncle Oscar?

OSCAR—Certainly. I— What a strange thing to ask! I—

ALEXANDRA—Did you love him, Uncle Ben?

BEN (*simply*)—He had—

ALEXANDRA (*suddenly starts to laugh very loudly*)—And you, Mama, did you love him, too?

REGINA—I know what you feel, Alexandra, but please try to control yourself.

ALEXANDRA (*still laughing*)—I'm trying, Mama. I'm trying very hard.

BEN—Grief makes some people laugh and some people cry. It's better to cry, Alexandra.

ALEXANDRA (*the laugh stops. Tensely moves toward* REGINA.) —What was Papa doing on the staircase? (BEN *turns to look at* ALEXANDRA.)

REGINA—Please go and lie down, my dear. We all need time to get over shocks like this. (ALEXANDRA *does not move.* REGINA'S *voice becomes softer, more insistent.*) Please go, Alexandra.

ALEXANDRA—No, Mama. I'll wait. I've got to talk to you.

REGINA—Later. Go and rest now.

ALEXANDRA (*quietly*)—I'll wait, Mama. I've plenty of time.

Regina's plans are quite definite. She will be going to see Judge Simmes the next day. She will tell the Judge about Leo. She will have enough proof to be convincing. And what if they should deny it!

"You couldn't find a jury that wouldn't weep for a woman whose brothers steal from her," ventures Regina, calmly. "And you couldn't find twelve men in this state you haven't cheated and hate you for it."

There is nothing else for Regina to do. She is one of those people who must finish what they have started. Whether her brothers are convicted or not doesn't greatly matter. Regina will by that time be in Chicago and they will be ruined. Mr. Marshall will not want to be involved in a scandal—

"Now, I don't want to hear any more from any of you," concludes Regina. "*You'll do no more bargaining in this house.* I'll take my seventy-five per cent and we'll forget the story forever. That's one way of doing it, and the way I prefer. You know me well enough to know that I don't mind taking the other way."

"None of us have ever known you well enough, Regina."

Oscar is moved to protest, but has no other solution. Regina decides that the matter is settled. She has forgotten everything, and they can draw up the papers tomorrow.

Now they have gone, Oscar and Leo bewildered and angry; Ben with a laugh and a compensating bit of philosophy—

"Well, I say to myself, what's the good?" says Ben. "You and I aren't like Oscar. We're not sour people. I think that comes from a good digestion. Then, too, one loses today and wins tomorrow. I say to myself, years of planning and I get what I want. Then I don't get it. But I'm not discouraged. The century's turning, the world is open. Open for people like you and me. Ready for us, waiting for us. After all, this is just the beginning. There are hundreds of Hubbards sitting in rooms like this throughout the country. All their names aren't Hubbard, but they are all Hubbards and they will own this country some day. We'll get along."

"I think so."

Ben has gone. Regina has turned to Alexandra. What is it Alexandra wanted to talk to her about? Alexandra has changed her mind. There's nothing to talk about now.

Regina would be sympathetic. She realizes that Alexandra has had a bad shock, that she loved her father very much—

REGINA—It will be good for you to get away from here. Good for me, too. Time heals most wounds, Alexandra. You're young, you shall have all the things I wanted. I'll make the world for you the way I wanted it to be for me. (*Uncomfortably.*) Don't sit there staring. You've been around Birdie so much you're getting just like her.

ALEXANDRA (*nodding*)—Funny. That's what Aunt Birdie said today.

REGINA (*nodding*)—Be good for you to get away from all this.

ADDIE (*entering*)—Cal is back, Miss Regina. He says Dr. Sloan will be coming in a few minutes.

REGINA—We'll go in a few weeks. A few weeks! That means two or three Saturdays, two or three Sundays. (*Sighs.*) Well, I'm very tired. I shall go to bed. I don't want any supper. Put the lights out and lock up. (ADDIE *moves to the piano lamp, turns it out.*) You go to your room, Alexandra. Addie will bring you something hot. You look very tired. (*Rises. To* ADDIE.) Call me when Dr. Sloan gets here. I don't want to see anybody else. I don't want any condolence calls tonight. The whole town will be over.

. ALEXANDRA—Mama, I'm not coming with you. I'm not going to Chicago.

REGINA (*turning to her*)—You're very upset, Alexandra.

ALEXANDRA (*quietly*)—I mean what I say. With all my heart.

REGINA—We'll talk about it tomorrow. The morning will make a difference.

ALEXANDRA—It won't make any difference. And there isn't anything to talk about. I am going away from you. Because I want to. Because I know Papa would want me to.

REGINA (*puzzled, careful, polite*)—You *know* your papa

wanted you to go away from me?

ALEXANDRA—Yes.

REGINA—And if I say no?

ALEXANDRA (*looking at her*)—Say it, Mama, say it. And see what happens.

REGINA (*softly, after a pause*)—And if I make you stay?

ALEXANDRA—That would be foolish. It wouldn't work in the end.

REGINA—You're very serious about it, aren't you? (*Crosses to stairs.*) Well, you'll change your mind in a few days.

ALEXANDRA—You only change your mind when you want to. And I won't want to.

REGINA (*going up the steps*)—Alexandra, I've come to the end of my rope. Somewhere there has to be what I want, too. Life goes too fast. Do what you want; think what you want; go where you want. I'd like to keep you with me, but I won't make you stay. Too many people used to make me do too many things. No, I won't make you stay.

ALEXANDRA—You couldn't, Mama, because I want to leave here. As I've never wanted anything in my life before. Because now I understand what Papa was trying to tell me. (*Pause.*) All in one day: Addie said there were people who ate the earth and other people who stood around and watched them do it. And just now Uncle Ben said the same thing. Really, he said the same thing. (*Tensely.*) Well, tell him for me, Mama, I'm not going to stand around and watch you do it. Tell him I'll be fighting as hard as he'll be fighting (*Rises.*) some place where people don't just stand around and watch.

REGINA—Well, you have spirit, after all. I used to think you were all sugar water. We don't have to be bad friends. I don't want us to be bad friends, Alexandra. (*Starts, stops.*) Would you like to come and talk to me, Alexandra? Would you—would you like to sleep in my room tonight?

ALEXANDRA (*taking step towards her*)—Are you afraid, Mama?

"Regina does not answer. She moves slowly out of sight. Addie comes to Alexandra and presses her arm."

**THE CURTAIN FALLS**

# ROCKET TO THE MOON
## A Drama in Three Acts

### By Clifford Odets

IN its eighth season the Group Theatre, which started as a protest of the younger workers in the Theatre Guild vineyard against a sort of forced mental and physical unemployment, successfully topped the record of its august progenitor in the popularity of its productions.

The record was not particularly impressive, save in a competitive sense, but it did seem to indicate that while the older organization was suffering a kind of circulatory arthritis the younger was taking on fresh injections of vim and vigor with cumulative experience.

The Group was again helped immensely by its favorite and most dependable dramatist, the Clifford Odets whose "Awake and Sing" and "Waiting for Lefty" were among the hits that stimulated its early growth. Mr. Odets, again forsaking the easier money of Hollywood for the sake of his art, delivered a play of middle-aged romance called "Rocket to the Moon" which his severest critics were ready to admit contained some of the most forceful writing of his career.

There was some disposition on the part of the reviewers to regret that the new drama did not end as strongly as it began, and Mr. Odets, who is not one of the playwrights boasting contempt for what critics write, proceeded to do a bit of rewriting that strengthened his play.

As a social criticism "Rocket to the Moon" is less florid and less exciting than earlier Odets dramas, but it is promising in that it indicates the same facility in expression, in dialogue writing and in the creation of individually stirring and holding dramatic episodes, that characterized those plays written in the heat of a crusader's campaign.

Ben Stark, dentist, had established the office into which we are shown at the opening of "Rocket to the Moon" in the New York neighborhood in which he had grown up. He shares the waiting room with another dentist, Philip Cooper, whose operating room is off to the right. Looking straight ahead you can see

Dr. Stark's dentist's chair and a part of the furniture in his operating room. It is a hot June afternoon. Dr. Stark, a smallish, worried man in his late thirties, and his wife, Belle, an angular and persuasively managerial type, are in the midst of an argument that has distressed Dr. Stark, though he has tried to take it casually. The talk has arrived at the stage where Mrs. Stark is saying:

"No, I want you to make up your own mind, or see that I'm right."

To which Dr. Stark replies significantly: "Aren't you always right, Belle?" This, to Mrs. Stark, is an entirely uncalled-for remark.

It now appears that the argument has been over the question of the Doctor's taking new offices in a better location. He has always wanted to specialize and when his father-in-law offered to bear all the expense of a change he felt that it was an opportunity that should not be missed.

It is Mrs. Stark's contention that even though her father was to pay the original cost, the upkeep of the rent would be more than Ben could afford; that his patients would not follow him because they would be frightened by the grandeur of the new location. It would take years to build up a new practice, she is convinced.

"I was a pioneer with Gladstone in orthodontia once," Stark recalls moodily, as he goes to the water cooler. "Now I'm a dentist, good for sixty dollars a week, while men with half my brains and talents are making their twenty and thirty thousand a year!"

As he waters the flowers Belle suggests that he may have missed his calling. He should have been a botanist, or at least a florist. But would Belle have married a florist? Ben would know. Belle thinks it probable, considering the state of her nerves, and the unhappiness of her home life, with her poppa and mama quarreling incessantly, that she would have married a shoemaker, almost. Ben can think of a lot of answers to that one, but restrains himself. It is agreed that when Belle's father comes Ben will tell him, gently but firmly, of his decision not to move. Furthermore it is to be made plain to Poppa that he cannot come to live with the Starks. Belle won't have that, either—

"If you'd seen the life of hell he gave my mother, you'd understand," she snaps.

"All right, but your mother's been dead a year. He's an old

man, lonely—"

"He'll manage—he's been to school."

"I only mean that he's alone in the world—"

"A man and his wife should live alone always," says Belle seriously. "Poppa would be an intruder in our house. We wouldn't have a minute to ourselves. And out of sheer respect for my mother's memory—"

"Your father isn't a villain—"

"Why do you take his part?"

"I'm not, but after all, a man wants to spend thousands of dollars putting me in a better practice and you expect me to think he's a villain?"

"Now, Ben, you know he'd be in the way, don't you?"

"I guess so. . . ."

"Don't you know it?"

"Yes, mam. . . ."

Next they get around to the question of Ben's new secretary. "A fancy lady" she must be, Belle thinks, if she takes two hours for lunch. And she the one whose salary Ben raised the third week. What if she *was* only getting $12 a week? Belle could live on that, if she had to. Thank God, they don't have to. But—

"It's not God who keeps us off the dole," declares Belle.

"It's you, Belle. I don't know what I'd do without you," admits Ben, putting his arms around her.

"Take the pipe out of my face," says Belle, and then she kisses him. The quarrel is practically over.

There are still a few little items, like the ad in the paper offering the Stark apartment for rent during the Summer. And the three months' rent Dr. Cooper owes for his part of the office. Ben will have to stiffen his backbone about Cooper. Belle would also like to see some promise of a regular vacation that will take them far away from home, and their home routines.

Belle's father has stuck his head in the door, caught a glimpse of Belle's back, and hastened away. Belle doesn't like her father. Once she heard him say: "The mother ate sour grapes and the daughter's teeth are set on edge." She has never forgotten that.

And now it comes out that Belle has been feeling blue all morning. This happens to be an anniversary with her, and Ben has forgotten all about it— The anniversary of her baby's birth and death. And the doctors have said she could never have another—

Cleo Singer, the secretary, is back from lunch. She is a bright,

pretty girl, smartly gowned a little beyond the secretary average.
Sensing the tautness of the atmosphere Cleo is for escaping into
the office as soon as possible.  But she is not going to escape
Belle.  Dr. Stark is sent peremptorily on his way to wait for his
wife in the drugstore downstairs.  Belle remains behind to have
a talk with Cleo.

First, Mrs. Stark would point out, when Cleo has been summoned, there is the rather extravagant angel-skin satin dress the
secretary is wearing.  It is the coolest she has, insists Cleo.  Then
there is the habit Cleo has of going without stockings.  That
doesn't make a good impression on the patients.  And she might
also put her hair down, seeing she is no longer modeling dresses.

Dr. Cooper is in from the adjoining office.  He has come to
inquire about a phone call, and to get a drink of water.  The
doctor is thirsty and the day is hot.  There is no water cooler
in his room.  Cooper is not only hot but discouraged.  "In my
younger days I was inclined to poetry," says he.  "In my older
days I'm inclined to poverty."

Everything has gone wrong for Dr. Cooper.  As a last blow his
young son has fallen on the ice and broken his arm—

"And that's the only break I've had in years," he cracks.
"Yes, I went through the whole war and nothing happened to
me.  They could have left me there—"

"You . . . owe us a few months' rent here," ventures Belle a
little hesitantly.

"You have my sympathies."

"I know it's a bad time to remind you—"

"To tell the truth, I'm waiting for a call from the loan company.  I'll see what they have to say."

Cooper drinks too much.  That is Belle's opinion.  He must
know that patients don't like the smell of liquor on a doctor's
breath.  Cooper resents the bawling out, but he knows Belle is
right—  For looking out for her husband's interests he doesn't
blame her.  And if he gets the loan—

The phone is ringing.  But—  There is to be no loan.

"Stay another month," suggests Belle, genuinely touched by
his abject attitude.

Belle is going now, leaving a message for Dr. Stark that "his
terrible wife" will expect him home at 7.  At the door she meets
her father, Mr. Prince, coming in.  "Prince is near sixty, wears
an old panama hat, a fine Palm Beach suit of twenty years ago
and a Malacca cane.  There is about him the dignity and elegant
portliness of a Jewish actor, a sort of aristocratic air.  He is an

extremely self-confident man with a strong sense of humor which, however, is often veiled. He is very alive in the eyes and mouth, the rest of him relaxed and heavy."

Father and daughter exchange glances and Belle goes on. Mr. Prince comes into the room, seats himself in a chair, leans on his cane, stares at Cleo and begins a sort of cross examination.

In her replies Cleo gives him as good as he sends, but very little information. Finally Prince manages to learn that Cleo has few opinions regarding life in general. She has been a dancer with several shows. She is apparently willing to take life as it comes.

"In my opinion," volunteers Prince, "the universe is governed by a committee; one Man couldn't make so many mistakes."

Cleo is willing to admit that that is funny. She can even believe that Mrs. Stark is right when she says that Mr. Prince is a clown. But when he suggests that if he were a young girl he would get somebody to support him she begins to bristle. Nobody supports Cleo. She comes from a very good home—

"I heard enough from you," she tells Prince, with some spirit. "In fact I heard enough all day! I don't need this job. They burn your ears off around here for sixteen dollars a week. That's chicken feed!"

"Less! Pigeon feed!"

"I don't have to stand in Macy's window and let people throw rocks at me!"

Nor is she the kind of girl who has to stand around and let anybody make suggestive remarks to her. Mrs. Stark can't order her around as though she were a dummy, and as for Prince, he's just an old fool.

"I thought Dr. Stark was a nice man when I came here. But his wife just twists him around her little finger like a spit curl."

"Correct! And any woman could do the same."

"He stands there like a big shepherd dog and she tells him what to do!"

"Correct!"

"He's afraid of his own shadow!"

"Correct!"

"You can't get in my good graces by agreeing with me in everything I say. I see right through you, Mr. Prince, like cellophane."

Cleo has worked herself into quite a temper and Mr. Prince is constrained to quiet her—

"Calm down," he orders sharply. "You have expressed your-

## "ROCKET TO THE MOON"

Stark: Listen, Cleo. . . . Think! What can I give you? All I can offer you is a second-hand life, dicated to trifles and troubles . . . and they go on forever. This isn't self-justification . . . but ts are stubborn things, Cleo. . . . This is how it must end. . . .

Prince: And I offer you a vitalizing relationship: a father, counselor, lover, a friend!

*(Eleanor Lynn, Luther Adler, Morris Carnovsky)*

self enough! You work here in an office—a regular insect society—so don't act like a tiger. Unless you don't want the job."
And now Cleo is quite apologetic. She is sorry for some of the
things she has said. She is even a little dewy-eyed about them.
Perhaps, she thinks, there is something in her eye. Mr. Prince
is making a casual examination with the corner of his silk handkerchief when the door opens and Dr. Stark stands for a second
observing the scene with evident disapproval. Prince and Cleo
do not see him.

"Is it out?"

"I think so."

"Don't rub it."

"No."

"You use nice toilet water. It smells like thousands of
flowers—"

"Gardenia."

"Pleasant."

"Forty dollars an ounce."

"Unpleasant."

They have seen Stark, "the shepherd dog." The Doctor moves
on into the office, suggesting curtly that Cleo had better take the
ad offering the apartment down to the *Times*. Cleo delivers Mrs.
Stark's message that the Doctor should be home by 7, and goes
on. Then Ben would like to know from Prince just what has
been going on in his absence. Poppa, he knows, is a great hand
with the girls, but Poppa is quick to deny the soft impeachment.
Poppa has sauntered casually over to a side window, and is at
the moment greatly interested in a building over the way. It is,
Dr. Stark explains, the back of the Hotel Algiers, a name to stir
the imagination of Mr. Prince. He knows a bookie who lives at
the Hotel Algiers and he suspects they rent out rooms to couples.
Perhaps some night he'll come back and look—just as if it interested him.

"Tell me, what interests you, Poppa?"

PRINCE—I love to gamble; cards, the races, the market . . .

STARK—Wine, women and song.

PRINCE—In all my life I never took a drink, and I don't sing.
Yes, Benny, *I* started from an idealist, too, believe it or not.
Now I'm a villain. . . . What does your friend Shakespeare say
on this point?

STARK—What point?

PRINCE—The point of all points—happiness! Where is she

hiding, happiness? (*After giving* STARK *a quizzical glance.*) So when do you expect to move?

STARK (*nervously*)—Move?

PRINCE (*picking up the dental magazine*)—I see you turned down the pages—the machinery—

STARK—That Ritter outfit is a beauty. . . .

PRINCE (*seeing the other's hesitation*)—But?

STARK—I've decided to stay here for the present, Poppa. Not that your kindness—

PRINCE—Why?

STARK—Belle thought . . . she thinks it won't be wise.

PRINCE (*pursing his lips*)—I see. And you, what do you think?

STARK—After all, it's an economic risk. . . . (*He flushes off into silence.*)

PRINCE (*almost vehemently*)—Crazy boy, I offer it to you on a silver platter—

STARK (*painfully*)—That's how it is, Poppa.

PRINCE—Your nose is just the right shape to fit your wife's hand!

STARK—Is that a right thing to say?

PRINCE—Well, it's your life—yours and Mrs. Belle Stark!

STARK—Why do you insist, Poppa?

PRINCE—Because I like to do some good to a man who needs it! A lovable being!

STARK—Why don't you make it up with Belle?

PRINCE (*with a smile*)—How's business?

STARK (*smiling*)—Slow. . . .

PRINCE—The Summer slump?

STARK—Yes. Why don't you get along with Belle, Poppa?

PRINCE (*wryly*)—It's a pleasant June afternoon, Benny.

STARK—It grieves her very much.

PRINCE (*reluctantly*)—Benny, my daughter don't like me; she claims I ruined her mother's life. I claim her mother ruined *my* life!

STARK—How?

PRINCE—There are two kinds of marriages, Benny—where the husband quotes the wife, or where the wife quotes the husband. Fact? Fact!

STARK—But you didn't speak to her for ten years.

PRINCE—Because she insulted my soul, me, a first-class man, a lover of his brother man—

STARK—And his sister!

PRINCE—Never! *But never!* Not once did I make a sexual deviation! And what did I ask from my wife? To be a companion, to help me succeed—

STARK—You did—you're worth a fortune.

PRINCE—In spite of her! I shouldn't be ambitious. Go work for somebody else for twenty dollars a week—a man with my brains! Play safe! A housewife's conception of life! In the bargain, she had more respectability under the blankets than you have on Fifth Avenue! A man of my strength, my fire! (*Now masking his feelings again.*) Drip, drip, the matrimonial waters go, and a man wears away. My wife is dead, I'm an old man who missed his boat. Ida Prince had her revenge . . . her husband has disappeared in the corner, with the dust, under the rug.

Without marriage, Poppa is convinced, he would have been one of the world's greatest actors. All his life—but the subject is unpleasant. So is the succeeding topic, for that matter. Dr. Stark again protests Mr. Prince's attitude toward his daughter. Belle is lonely. The Doctor is sure she is eager to bury the hatchet.

She is, agrees Prince—"Right in my head." They don't like each other, he and his daughter. Mr. Prince cannot be moved from that conviction. If he wants to live with the Starks it is only because he likes Ben. And now he would change the subject—

The only sensible woman he ever knew, observes Mr. Prince, killed herself and left a note reading, "I am a pest!" . . . He had made six thousand dollars that morning. . . . The more money he makes the more heartaches he has. . . . To whom will he leave it? . . . Maybe Jascha Heifetz. . . . Why should he go to Saratoga? . . . Drinking the waters would only prolong his life. . . . Whenever a man tells him his wife is wonderful he looks in his face for the truth. . . . He has looked into Ben's face and knows him for a better liar than he had suspected—

"I don't know what you mean," says Ben.

"A life where every day is Monday," explains Prince. "There used to be a week-end, but now it's always Monday. Awnings up, awnings down, coat on, coat off. Sweat in Summer, freeze in Winter—a movie, a bridge game, an auto ride to Peekskill. Gas is twenty cents a gallon, worry about the bills, write a budget— the maid is too expensive—you bought a pair of shoes *last* month. You're old, you're getting old—she's old. Yesterday you didn't look in my face. Tomorrow you forgot I'm here. Two

aspirin pills are good for headaches. The world is getting . . .
so dull, let me sleep, let me sleep! You sneeze, you have a cold.
No, that was last month. No, it's now. Which is now and
which is then? Benny . . . you used to be a clever boy!"

"Yes, a certain man once said that in our youth we collect
materials to build a bridge to the moon; but in our old age, he
says, we use the materials to build a shack."

"Yes, *this is it!* But you, you graduated first in the class!
You played tennis, you were full of life and plans. Look, you
don't even resent me now."

"I'm what I am. . . . It's not Belle's fault," protests Stark.
Prince would deny that assertion. He knows. Belle knows.

"She's got you where she wants you. . . . Like an iceberg,
three-quarters under water. . . . I mightn't live forever. I want
you to know what I think." And then, as he prepares to go on
to his broker's to watch the board, he adds:

"Iceberg, listen . . . why don't you come up and see the world,
the sea gulls and the ships to Europe? When did you look at
another woman last? The year they put the buffalo nickel on the
market? Why don't you suddenly ride away, an airplane, a
boat! Take a rocket to the moon! Explode! What holds you
back? You don't want to hurt Belle's feelings? You'll die soon
enough—"

"I'll just have to laugh at that!"

"Laugh. . . . But make a motto for yourself: 'Out of the coffin
by Labor Day!' Have an affair with—with—with this girl . . .
this Miss Cleo. She'll make you a living man again."

"You're a great joker, Poppa." Both men laugh.

". . . Never look away from a problem, Benny."

"I never know when you're serious."

"When you look away from the problem, it don't disappear.
But maybe *you* might disappear. Remember I told you!"

Prince has vanished through the door. "Sonofagun!" murmurs
Stark, laughing. But suddenly he stops laughing, and looks a
little frightened as Dr. Jensen, a chiropodist with offices down
the hall, enters the room. Dr. Jensen is commonly called
Frenchy, probably because he is an American with Swedish parents. He is "aged thirty, realistic and alert, fast and practical."

Dr. Jensen has come for a drink of water. He finds Dr. Stark
moody and full of conversation. A kind of self-searching conversation, punctuated with queries for which the questioner also
furnishes the answers. Dr. Stark is worried and excited. Suddenly he has found his father-in-law a sinister person; one who

stirs him to depression.

"A man falls asleep in marriage," muses the Doctor. "And after a time he wants to keep on sleeping, undisturbed. "I'm surprised how little I've thought about it. Gee! What I don't know would fill a book."

"You look like helplessness personified."

"He tries to tell me I'm dissatisfied with my married life—"

"Maybe you are. . . ."

"He's very persuasive in some things, but I know he's incorrect. (*Suddenly grinning*.) Do I look like an unhappy man?"

"You'd know that better than me, Doc."

"Sonofagun! . . . Don't all married couples argue and disagree? Even the joke papers tell us that. A man would be a mad idealist to want a honeymoon all his life."

"No, he'd be a woman. A man can't be both lover and banker, enchanter and provider. But the girls want those combined talents. . . . The man who worries for the bucks is not the one to kiss his wife behind the ear."

The Doctor is puzzled. He can't understand how sometimes the most ordinary people suddenly become sinister.

Dr. Cooper is in, still discouraged, still looking for a telephone call. He doesn't know anything about women either. He's trying to make a living. Any man who has time to think about women in this generation is a loafer, according to Cooper. To Dr. Stark he reports his conversation with Mrs. Stark about the back rent. Dr. Stark is understanding. Belle had no right to talk to Dr. Cooper as she did. Stark will make his own decisions. Cooper at least had better stay until something happens. Perhaps if he could pay a little—Cooper will try—and is profuse in his gratitude. He is leaving hurriedly as Cleo comes through the door.

Dr. Stark would be firm with Cleo if he could, but a new attitude touched with humility disarms him. He apologizes to her instead for having shouted at her before. Cleo understands. The Doctor thinks, however, that she would be much more attractive if she did not use quite so much lipstick. It's because of the dark mirrors, Cleo explains.

"It's only my opinion, Cleo—"

"Do you realize that's the first time you've called me Cleo since I've been here?"

STARK (*taken aback*)—Is there any reason why I shouldn't?

CLEO—Oh, no! Certainly not!

STARK—How old are you, Cleo?

CLEO (*coquetting slightly*)—Don't you think that's a personal question?

STARK—I have no personal motives. . . .

CLEO (*smiling back*)—Mr. Prince asked me the same thing. He's a terrible flirt, isn't he?

STARK (*frowning*)—That's his way. He tries to be interesting—

CLEO—Lots of men are trying to be interesting.

STARK—Are they?

CLEO (*starting for office door but stopping short*)—Would you mind if I don't wear stockings in the office in the summer? Mr. Bernstein at Chelsea-Pontiac didn't mind.

STARK—Well . . .

CLEO (*hastily*)—If you say not to—

STARK—It's quite all right.

CLEO—Your wife might object.

STARK—Why should she?

CLEO—I may be wrong, but so many wives like to keep an eye on their husband's secretary.

STARK—Mrs. Stark runs my home. I run the office.

CLEO—After all, we must keep cool, mustn't we? May I say this?—I like you, Dr. Stark. Maybe that's too personal, but everything that's healthy is personal, don't you think?

STARK (*ponderously*)—Very possible. . . . (CLEO *stops at the side table on her way to the office again.*)

CLEO—Looking at this newspaper makes me think—the universe must be ruled by a committee; one man couldn't be so stupid.

STARK (*smiling*)—That's a very witty remark!

CLEO (*pleased*)—I'm glad you think so, Dr. Stark.

STARK (*looking at his watch*)—Mrs. Nelson will be here any minute. You'd better clean up the instruments, particularly the scalers.

CLEO—The scalers? . . . Which are those, Dr. Stark? I know, but I want to make sure.

STARK (*taking one from his top pocket*)—These.

CLEO—I'll cut some cotton rolls, too.

STARK—Always dry an instrument when you remove it from the sterilizer. It'll clean easier.

CLEO—That's a very good hint.

STARK—I wasn't hinting. Patients like clean instruments.

CLEO—Of course. (*Stopping at the operating room door.*) Your wife was very angry with me before.

STARK (*impatiently*)—Mrs. Stark is not the terrible person many people think she is!

CLEO (*dismayed*)—Oh, I didn't mean anything. . . .

STARK (*almost savagely*)—She's one of the most loyal, sincere and helpful persons I've ever met!

CLEO (*in a small voice*)—I'm sure she is, I'm sure of that. . . . (CLEO *disappears into the operating room. For a moment* STARK *stands there wagging his head. His eye falls on the dental magazine. He picks it up, looks at the ad and then throws the magazine across the room. As he begins to fill his pipe his glance turns to the window, right. He moves over to the window and looks out at the Hotel Algiers.* CLEO's *voice from the operating room threshold turns him around with a guilty start. In a small contrite voice.*) Pardon me . . . did I tell you before? Your wife expects you home at seven.

STARK (*annoyed*)—Yes, thanks—you told me—thanks!

CLEO (*meekly*)—You're welcome, Dr. Stark.

"Cleo disappears into the operating room again. Stark looks after her, annoyed. For a moment he stands reflectively. Finally he strikes a match and begins to light his pipe" as the curtain slowly falls.

## ACT II

It is July and still hot. Dr. Stark, Cleo and Frenchy are in the Doctor's office, finding such comfort as they can. Dr. Stark has been reading a favorite author—Shakespeare—and quoting from him occasionally. Frenchy, for some reason best known to himself, has been taking pot shots at Cleo. He has come to rue the day he picked her out of fifty-three applicants for the job she has, just to save the shy Dr. Stark from that task.

Cleo is at a loss to understand why Frenchy persists in picking on her; she's never done anything to him. She hasn't, admits Frenchy. And he doesn't propose that she shall do anything to any of his friends, either. . . .

Frenchy, with a parting shot at Cleo, has returned to his office. Dr. Stark again takes up his Shakespeare. As for Cleo, she can't read Shakespeare—the type's too small.

"Dr. Jensen don't seem to have any manners, does he?" Cleo is saying. "His personality is really nil, isn't it?"

"I wouldn't say that. . . ."

CLEO—An interesting personality must have a foundation of good character.

STARK—Who told you that?

CLEO—No one has to tell me such things. Dr. Jensen really offends. He does not know and obey the fundamental rules of etiquette.

STARK—He's a self-educated man—

CLEO—That don't cut no ice— So am I. My parents wanted to send me to a fashionable girls' college, but I went to secretarial school instead—just for the experience. Notwithstanding, I know the correct things to do and say. My husband, when I get married, will find me the perfect hostess.

STARK (*not knowing what to say*)—Do you intend to marry?

CLEO—I don't know—marriage is so sordid. I'd never marry for money. (*Abruptly.*) Do you love your wife?

STARK (*torn between her foolishness and attractiveness*)— Yes . . .

CLEO—That was a ridiculous thing to ask, wasn't it?

STARK—No.

CLEO—She must be an ideal wife.

STARK—You think so?

CLEO—I've often admired her for the way she manages and takes care of herself.

STARK—Do you like her?

CLEO—She has very good manners. God knows, there's not much courtesy left in the world! . . . May I be frank, Dr. Stark?

STARK—Yes.

CLEO—I've often resented the way she speaks to you.

STARK—How?

CLEO—Perhaps I better not mention it. . . .

STARK—You can. . . .

CLEO—Well, she seems angry with you, Dr. Stark.

STARK (*half smiling*)—Isn't that permissible?

CLEO—Permanently? I may be wrong. . . .

STARK—That's just your impression.

CLEO—It must be. . . . (*Seeing him smile.*) Everything amuses you, Dr. Stark.

STARK (*very close to her*)—Why?

CLEO—You're smiling.

STARK—It just seems that way. It's a habit. . . . When I can't meet a situation, I smile as if it amuses me. I don't mean to, but it comes out that way.

Cleo is afraid Dr. Stark is not a happy man—and she can't understand why. To her happiness is everything. What does

money matter if it doesn't bring happiness?  Take a Rockefeller
with a silver windpipe, for instance!  As for herself, Cleo is quite
happy.  She goes out a good deal.  Occasionally changing clothes
so often irks her.  But generally speaking she is happy.  Just
now most of her friends are away for the Summer, and the town's
dead.  That is why she didn't mind when Dr. Stark asked her to
work tonight.

Dr. Stark is interested, and amused, and finally a little suspicious that Cleo doesn't tell the whole truth when she is relating
her many social contacts and her adventures with pursuing males.
But he finds her curiously interesting.  If it is true, as she says
it is, that he has been staring at her for several weeks now—"as
if I belong in a museum"—perhaps it is admiration that prompts
his interest.

Cleo doesn't mind.  She knows Dr. Stark's interest doesn't
mean anything, and she has made up her mind that he needs her
there.  That's why she stays on.  She thinks, too, that Dr. Stark
likes her.  Does he?

The telephone is ringing. . . . It is Mrs. Stark. . . . She
wants to know the Doctor's plans. . . . Wants also to remind
him that Poppa has an appointment and that he should not forget to charge Poppa. . . .

"I never adjust my shoulder straps or girdle in public, as some
women do," announces Cleo, taking care of those items now.
"God knows it is so warm I'm practically naked underneath."

"You mustn't say things like that!" snaps Dr. Stark, with
surprising asperity.

"I'm sorry if I offended . . ."

"For your own good, Cleo, I mean.  Naïveness goes just so
far."

"I'm not naïve."

"May I tell you something?" asks Dr. Stark, after an uncomfortable pause.

"You have a right to tell me anything.  I work here; you
pay—"

"That would be terrible, if you really thought that—"

"Tell me whatever you want.  I don't care."

"Not if you feel—"

Again Mr. Prince has walked in upon them.  He is still restless in his mind.  He is piling up a fortune.  Why?  "To be
the richest man in the cemetery!"  He is late for his appointment.  What of it?  Another day will do.  And how is the Stark-
Singer affair getting on?  Will Cleo go with him to the stadium
concert to hear Jascha Heifetz?

Somewhat irritated by the trend of the conversation Dr. Stark leaves them, by which time Mr. Prince is ready to propose that Cleo should marry him. Perhaps she likes Dr. Stark—

"He's a very nice man," insists Cleo.

"But he lost his enterprise, years ago," Mr. Prince is quick to answer. "He's no more resourceful. I offered to put him in a swell office—he could become a big specialist—but he likes it here."

"Why?"

PRINCE—Afraid, no courage. My good daughter made him like that—afraid to take a chance. Keep what you got—"a half a loaf is better . . ." In life, my child, you must go forward. And if you don't go forward, where are you? Backward!

CLEO—You're trying to impress me. But I think you should help everybody you can. You don't have long to live—you're an old man.

PRINCE (*with a grand flourish*)—Miss Cleo, you're talking to a man with a body like silk. Every year he takes the waters at Saratoga. He possesses the original teeth, every one! (*As* CLEO *laughs.*) In all the multitudes of your acquaintanceship you won't find a man with younger ideas than your present speaker. How old are you, my child?

CLEO—How old do I look?

PRINCE (*ignoring her interpolation*)—I am speaking to you from wisdom, with a voice of velvet, as a past master of a Masonic Lodge: consort with an older man. In short, use your brains!

CLEO—It's lucky for me I don't take you serious. You're the biggest kidder on earth.

PRINCE (*smiling*)—Don't my young ideas reach out to your young ideas?

CLEO (*emphatically*)—I think you're flirting with me, that's all.

PRINCE (*winking*)—You see, you understand me to perfection! Tonight Heifetz is playing a piece by a famous author—

CLEO—I don't care for that.

PRINCE—Tomorrow night . . .

CLEO—Where?

PRINCE—You say where.

CLEO—Do you like me?

PRINCE—Truth is stranger than fiction: yes!

CLEO (*studying him*)—Where would you take me?

PRINCE—Anywhere. You're a girl like candy, a honey-dew

melon—a delicious girl. Yes, I like you. (*After a pause, the
veins suddenly standing out on his face.*) I'm serious . . . do
you understand that? I'm very serious, Miss Cleo. I'm talking
to you from the roots up!

CLEO (*hesitantly*)—I'd have to tell Dr. Stark.

PRINCE—What would I have against that? Yes, you give
me pleasure, Miss Cleo—just to talk.

CLEO—I'm glad you appreciate talk.

PRINCE—Why?

CLEO—Because you won't get more, Mr. Prince.

PRINCE—My child, it suits me to a T.

Prince has gone, calling gaily back at the door to remind Cleo
of their appointment. Dr. Stark is rather peeved when he hears
this, his effort to appear unconcerned intensifying his reaction.
Cleo can see through that. He has thoughts in his head and
then he blames her because he has them, she charges. He's
jealous—

Stark is stunned by the thought. And angry. Cleo is making
it very difficult for him to keep her on there, he says. She
really isn't the most efficient girl in the world— As for that,
Cleo is ready to leave any time. She doesn't have to work. Her
folks have money—

Cleo's romancing does not impress Stark, but when he would
re-establish their friendly relations she is stubborn. He has his
hands on her shoulders and is shaking her, and when he suddenly releases her at her command she stumbles and falls. For
a moment she lies on the floor crying.

Now Dr. Stark, melting completely, is all sympathy. She will
not let him help her up. When he stands by the door and she
gets to her feet slowly she repeats her intention of leaving as
soon as she can change her uniform—

"You know you need the job," Stark is saying.

"You never show anyone they're wrong by showing them
you're right. Don't you know that? Don't you? Does it make
you a great man to tell me I'm a liar? I know I'm a liar!"

"Cleo, I'm your friend . . . please believe me," insists the
Doctor earnestly, taking her hand, which she lets him hold.
"Everyone tells little fables, Cleo. Sometimes to themselves,
sometimes to others. Life is so full of brutal facts . . . we all
try to soften them by making believe."

CLEO (*tearfully*)—You're talking of somebody else.

STARK—We all like to have good opinions of ourselves. That's why we squirm around and tell stories and adjust ourselves. It's a way to go on living proudly—

CLEO—I don't care to talk about it!

STARK—Why, I lie, myself, a dozen times a day. You can tell me anything, Cleo. (*After a silent pause.*) Where do you come from?

CLEO (*defiantly*)—Madison Avenue! No more! I don't care to think. Sometimes I wish I didn't have a head. Last night I didn't have a wink of sleep. (*With sudden vehemence.*) Nobody loves me! Millions of people moving around the city and nobody cares if you live or die. Go up a high building and see them down below. Some day I'll fall down on them all!

STARK (*gently*)—Is that a right thing to say?

CLEO—My home life is fearful—eight in one apartment. My father had a very hard life; he ran the store. He, my father, he shrinked—shrank?—what is it?

STARK (*not sure*)—Shrunk or shrank.

CLEO—My father got littler and littler . . . and one morning he died right in bed while everyone was sleeping. Mom and Gert and two married sisters and their husbands and babies— eight in one apartment! I tell them I want to be a dancer— everybody laughs. I make believe they're not my sisters. They don't know anything—they're washed out, bleached . . . everybody forgets how to dream. . . .

STARK—I understand. . . .

CLEO—That's the biggest joke around the house: "Cleo, the dancer—the Queen of Sheba!" My sister Gert's a garment worker. We share one room. She's keeping company—she comes in late. I never sleep. I have all the inconveniences of love with none of the pleasure.

STARK—Yes. . . . You're tired. Go home. I won't need you tonight.

CLEO (*wanly*)—I never go home if there's another place— here, the office, I mean. Where can you go? Sit in the park till it's time to go to bed?

STARK—The park is nice, cool—

CLEO—Don't you know they molest you there? You're naïve. Even policemen.

Cleo likes Dr. Stark very much. He wouldn't laugh, she hopes, if she were to tell him that she wanted to be a dancer. Or a great actress. And he mustn't smile when she tells him things about himself. He isn't resourceful or enterprising, she thinks. He is too used to his life. He doesn't go out to things any

more. He is evasive and sideways. What has happened to his
courage?

"My mother's always trying to hold me back, not to have all
the experiences I can," reports Cleo, speaking rapidly and excitedly. "Those people think you can live on good advice.
Don't you think life is to live all you can and experience everything? Isn't that the only way you can develop to be a real
human being? Shouldn't a wife help a man do that? . . . They
won't hold me back. Their idea is to get married and have
babies right away. I want babies, three or four—!"

"Do you?"

"Sure. I'm healthy enough to have a dozen!"

"Are you?"

"Sure, but there's time for them. Must they come the first
year? Is that refined?"

It was Dr. Stark's wife that broke up his courage, Cleo has
decided, and she is not inclined to listen to his denials.

"You're hungry for expression, Cleo," says Stark. "That
makes you talk sometimes without thinking too much about
what you're saying. But don't ever hesitate to say what's on
your mind. . . . I like to hear it."

"Yes? . . . Well, I don't like your wife."

"Why?"

"I love you."

There is an embarrassed pause, broken by the Doctor's low-
voiced declaration that she is a fanciful girl. Then Cooper
barges in, unhappy with his own troubles, and the terrific heat.
The combination has made him a little wild. He has filled himself with ice water again and turned to them a little savagely—
"If only they invented hydrants in the street that give out milk
and honey! . . . we'd be happier people," he is saying. And
then with new belligerence he adds: "Don't I try? Can anyone
accuse me of indifference to my work? Why can't I make a
living? I'm falling apart by inches. (*Suddenly sobbing.*)
Where can I sail away? To where? I'm ashamed to live! An
ostrich can hide his head. Diphtheria gets more respect than
me! They coddle germs in laboratories—they feed the white
mice twice a day. . . . Why don't somebody coddle me? (*Controlling himself now.*) What did I do to my fellow man? Why
am I punished like this? (*Trembling again on the brink of sobs,
but holding them back.*) Where is the God they told me about?
Why should an innocent boy and an old lady suffer? I ask you
to tell me, what is the Congress doing? Where are they in the
hour of the needs of the people? (*Appealing to* STARK *person-*

*ally*.) Did you ever see such times? Where will it end if they can't use millions of Coopers? Why can't they fit me in, a man of my talents? The sick ones walk the streets, the doctors sit at home. Where, where is it? What is it? . . . what, what, what? . . . (COOPER *trickles off into silence.* CLEO *and* STARK *can be only helplessly silent in the face of this emotional speech. After* COOPER *blows his nose and wipes his eyes, a little ashamed of his feeling, he says with a faint bitter smile, mocking himself.*) Gaze on the Columbia University lunatic! The warrior of Ypres and Verdun! . . . (*He moves his trembling hand across his brow, at the same time taking a card from his pocket and handing it to* STARK.)"

The card is a record of Cooper's registration as a blood donor —type four. He is to get thirty dollars a pint for his contribution, and has visions of being out of debt in no time. He knows a boy who gave fifteen pints in one year. Suddenly Cooper has turned and snapped a protest at a remark of Cleo's, unleashing a wrath he has felt for weeks. And now he has walked up to her and is facing her furiously, and she pale and motionless. Stark would get between them, but suddenly the highly wrought Cooper drops his fist and throws his arms around Cleo, kisses her and runs from the office.

Cleo, overcome, sinks into a chair and is crying softly when Dr. Stark would comfort her, stroking her hair and telling her not to mind anything that Cooper has said. But Cleo is sorry for Dr. Cooper and fearful that he will do himself harm. There is little danger of that, Dr. Stark is convinced, considering Dr. Cooper's sense of responsibility to his family. He (Cooper) is a man of fine talent—a better talent than Dr. Stark's—though admittedly there are some who profess not to believe that. Mrs. Stark for one—

Cleo doesn't want to hear anything about Mrs. Stark, and he knows why. Nor will she forget what she has confessed, nor help him to forget it. He doesn't love his wife and she knows it—

"This is an office. I'm a married man. . . . You know I'm a married man, don't you?" Dr. Stark's tone is earnest but his voice is barely audible.

"Just because you're sad you can't make me sad," snaps Cleo, defiantly. "No one can. I have too much in me!"

"You're wonderful . . ."

CLEO (*almost dancing*)—Talent!—I'm talented. I don't know for what, but it makes me want to dance in my bones! Don't want to be lonely, never left alone! Why should I cry? I have a throat to sing with, a heart to love with! Why don't you love me, Dr. Stark? I was ten, then fifteen—I'm almost twenty now. Everything is in a hurry and you ought to love me.

STARK—Cleo, please . . .

CLEO—You're good, you're kind, you're like a father. Do you love your wife? I'm intuitive—I know you don't!

STARK (*making a last effort to stop her*)—Cleo!

CLEO—We're *both* alone, so alone. You might be like Cooper in a year or two. Maybe I lie. You know why. Because I'm alone—nobody loves me. But I won't have it that way. I'll change life.

STARK—You're wonderful. . .

CLEO—You don't deserve me. Not you or any other man I ever met.

STARK (*in an agony of indecision*)—Cleo, dear. . . .

CLEO (*shyly*)—I'll call you Benny in a minute! (*After a throb of hesitation.*) Ben! Benny! . . . (*They are standing off from each other, poised on needles.*) Don't be afraid. . . .

STARK— . . . No?

CLEO—Love me. . . . Love me, Ben.

STARK— . . . Can't do that. . . .

CLEO (*moving forward a step*)—Put your arms up and around me.

STARK—Cleo. . . .

"Now they move in on each other. Everything else gone, they are together in a full, fierce embrace, together in a swelter of heat, misunderstanding, loneliness and simple sex." The curtain falls.

By early August there had been some little relief from the heat, but not a great deal. It is late afternoon in Dr. Stark's office. There is a patient in the chair. When Cleo, who has been assisting Dr. Stark, comes into the outer office to answer the phone, the Doctor follows her a little excitedly. He is afraid it is his wife and he wants to answer. The day before, Cleo had told Mrs. Stark that the Doctor was busy and that was all he had heard from her that night.

This call, however, is from Mr. Prince and is for Cleo. It is another invitation for a concert date, but Cleo will not go. For one thing she does not like that kind of music. For another, she thinks once a week is enough to go out with an old man.

The patient in the chair, it transpires, is Willy Wax, the dance director, and Dr. Stark is hoping Cleo will refuse to go out with him, too. Cleo will make no promises.

Frenchy, who has followed a bit of this scene from the door-way, now interrupts it and Dr. Stark returns to his patient. Frenchy holds Cleo for a further drill in warning and good advice. He can see what is going on and he doesn't intend it shall go too far.

"Look, Cleo, for him there is sleep and day and work again," explains Frenchy. "He's not a happy man. He spends his days trying to exhaust himself so he can fall asleep quick. Not that he told me this. . . . I seen it with my two good eyes. Don't make trouble for him, Cleo. Don't take him over the coals. Unless you're serious, unless you love him . . ."

"And if I do?"

"Do you? See if you can understand this: through unhappy marriage he's lost power for accomplishment—he don't get much personal satisfaction out of his work; and the man who don't get that is a lost man. Lots of things he longs for he'll never take. And like millions of others he constantly feels worried, depressed and inadequate. But!—His unhappiness is a dangerous habit of which he is not fully aware—it may make him bust loose in some curious way . . . can you be it?"

"You must have read all that in a book."

"What goes on in the head of a moth?—Nothing! (*He reaches out and smacks an imaginary moth between his palms. Emphatically.*) That was you in effigy and promise!"

"Why don't you like me? Did I ever harm you or anyone else?"

"Cleo, I work like an antitoxin—before the complications come. And I know the difference between love and pound cake."

Mr. Willy Wax comes now from the operating room, affable, but somewhat irked because he cannot smoke. Now Frenchy has taken his place in Dr. Stark's chair and Cleo is showing Mr. Wax his X-ray plates, or offering to. Mr. Wax decides he will live without that touch.

Mr. Wax is confident that he has seen Cleo before, and perhaps he has. She was in the elevator when he entered one day last week. Anyway, Mr. Wax finds Cleo interesting, with a sort of "mazda glow" in her eyes. "There's a fever in you! You're talented! For what?" Mr. Wax would know.

"I don't want to spend the rest of my life in an office," Cleo admits.

Soon the acquaintance has expanded to the point where Mr.

Wax would have Cleo dine with him. Failing that, because of
Cleo's previous date, he would have her come to his office in
twenty minutes for luncheon of sandwiches and milk. Then
they will find out if Cleo has any real talent for dancing
routines—Frenchy is out of the chair and gone. Dr. Stark and Cleo
are alone. He has sat down beside her and kissed her shyly.
They try to make plans for the evening. There will be a lecture
first, and then perhaps the Planetarium. Cleo is getting a bit
fed up with the out-of-the-way places Dr. Stark chooses.

Mr. Prince takes her to interesting places, but Dr. Stark seems
a little ashamed of her. A little too cautious, thinks Cleo. But
that is the way it must be with the Doctor. He just can't do
everything he would like to do. Does he love her? She makes
him very, very happy. He would embrace her in demonstration,
but she eludes him. He is what she would call a regular old
kissing bug and she doesn't intend to let him creep up on her
like that. Stark is firm in his declaration of loyalty. Cleo is in
his thoughts all the time. But—yes—there is still Mrs.
Stark. . . .

Cleo recalls the engagement with Mr. Wax for luncheon in
his office. Is Dr. Stark jealous? He is—

"He's a very interesting man—I want to hear what he has to
say," says Cleo. "I can learn from him. He's interested in my
dancing."

"Wax makes propaganda for Willy Wax, dear. He's interested
in two things—himself and girls for himself. I know him—he's
been in this building for years."

"You act as if I was leaving. I'm not leaving you, Ben."

"Don't go down there," pleads Stark.

"Don't you know you're my best friend? My *only* friend?"
asks Cleo, earnestly.

"Being a friend is one thing. . . . (*Taking her hand.*) Cleo
. . . we don't belong to each other. . . . I mean I don't have
the right . . . this is like living in a subway and never getting
off the train. . . ."

"Is it fair for you to question my motives? Is it?"

"Cleo . . . (*Suddenly he kisses her hand.*)"

"That's right—kiss it. And kiss the fingers, every one. (*He
does so.*) And you do that of your own free will. (*With sudden
anxiety.*) Did I offend?"

"No, dear, no . . ."

"You have to always remember that you belong to me! Let

me pull your nose. (*She does.*) Your ears. (*She does.*) No, you can't kiss me. (*She eludes him.*) For another week, no kissing. . . . Now I have to go."

"Don't go. . . ."

"I have to, Ben. Don't worry. I'll be back soon." He has released her hand and started for the door. "Don't worry, Ben," she calls, turning, just as the door is opened by Mrs. Stark.

Mrs. Stark has come up from the beach because she is bored and lonely. She realizes that Ben has his clinic lecture and will be down Saturday—but with all the other husbands a week-end begins on Friday at the beach. Besides, Mrs. Stark is not altogether sure that she is not being a pest to Ben. If she is, let him tell her and she will go back to the beach and bury herself in the sand up to the chin, she cries, a little hysterically.

"Aren't you afraid I'll leave you, Ben?" Belle demands, suddenly growing a little awkwardly flirtatious. "Down there at the beach, alone? All day long? Suppose an interesting man came along? Don't you care?"

"You won't run away, dear. . . ." Ben is smiling a little uneasily.

"I might . . . or don't you think I'm attractive enough for a man—"

"You're as attractive as you ever were, Belle."

"Confess to your wife—aren't you ever afraid to leave her alone as much as you do?"

"Send me a wire before you elope."

"You'd *like* to get rid of me."

"Never, never!"

"Admit it—"

"Never, dear, not for a day. . . . And I don't want you to talk that way, even in a joke."

Belle Stark has a sudden idea: She will come into the office and take Cleo's place! In a week she will have the place on an efficient working basis. And she would work cheap. Ben is not enthused by the suggestion. After all, a man's office is his castle —and— Well, he has given in to her on most things, but about this he will be firm. He won't consider it.

Mrs. Stark changes the attack. Why does Cleo call him Ben? Let her be told to call him Dr. Stark, if that wouldn't be straining relations too much! Furthermore, Mrs. Stark has decided that she will go to the lecture. Will Cleo be there? Cleo takes notes, the Doctor explains—

"Will they be printed in a book, *Confessions of a Dentist?*"
Belle wants to know.

"Will you stop that stuff for a change?" demands Ben, blazing
out at her. "It's about time you began to realize there are two
ends to a rope. *I* have needs, too! This one-way street has to
end! I'm not going to stay under water like an iceberg the rest
of my life. You've got me licked—I must admit it. All right,
I'm sleeping, I don't love you enough. But what do *you* give?
What do you know about *my* needs?"

BELLE—Don't you dare speak that way to me!

STARK—You've been speaking like that for ten years!

BELLE—You won't throw me away for that dirty rag of a girl!

STARK—The hell with the girl! I'm talking of us. . . .

BELLE—I gave you too much of my life for that. You've used
me up. . . .

STARK—Belle, for Pete's sake . . . !

BELLE—And now you want to throw me off. But you're a
man, not an animal—you can't do that!

STARK—If you can't talk facts, keep quiet!

BELLE (*weeping*)—My mother sat crying by the window for
twenty years—

STARK—Every word is nonsense!

BELLE—But you can't do that to me. I wasn't born in Europe—I'm a modern woman—I don't weep, not me. . . . (*She
trails off into silence.* STARK *gruffly hands her a handkerchief,
which she uses.*)

STARK (*bitterly*)—Sonofagun. . . .

BELLE—Not weep, not weep. . . .

Mrs. Stark has bolted into the office and locked the door after
her. Nor will she unlock it when Ben calls to her. He is pleading with her when Dr. Cooper appears in a state of some excitement. He has come to bring his first blood donor check for
thirty dollars and to sign it over to the Starks. This, to Cooper,
represents history in the making and he calls to Mrs. Stark to
come out and observe the donation of "blood money."

Mrs. Stark is not interested. She comes from the room, but
only to continue on through the office on her way back to the
beach.

Cooper has gone back to his office happily. Dr. Stark stands
for a moment angrily thoughtful. He begins to pace the office.
At the window he looks out at the Hotel Algiers briefly. Now

Cleo returns, followed by Willy Wax. The dance director is mystified but gay. He could not hold Cleo in his office, he complains, she was so determined to get back to either the doctor or her work.

"Hinting—as if I belonged to him," protests Cleo.

"I beg your pardon, Cleo; that never crossed my mind," smiles Willy Wax. "Come to see me again—or I'll call you."

"Yes."

"Why are your brows bulging, Stark?" And with a wave and a pleasant "See you soon," Wax is gone.

"Close that door!" demands Stark, as a nervous and defiant Cleo protests that it is hot.

"I suppose you want me to melt into a little pool of water. Why're you looking at me like that?"

STARK—I don't want him calling you Cleo. Who is he?

CLEO (*sitting*)—Oh, you! . . .

STARK (*angrily*)—I didn't call you Cleo till I knew you for weeks. Why should he?

CLEO—What's the matter with you anyway?

STARK—Nothing, Cleo.

CLEO—This whole thing has to end!

STARK (*staring at her*)—Does it?

CLEO—It can't go on like this. I'll go out with other men.

STARK (*crossing to her*)—No, you won't.

CLEO—I was thinking about you and your wife in Mr. Wax's office—

STARK—After the lecture we're going to the Planetarium—

CLEO—What did she say?

STARK—I don't care what she said.

CLEO—But I do—

STARK—After we visit the Planetarium—

CLEO—You don't think of me, don't care for me. . . .

STARK—We're going to leave early and have a cool supper. . . .

CLEO—Have a party by yourself!—

STARK—Listen to me. . . .

CLEO—I used to think you cared for me. . . .

STARK—But I do, Cleo. . . .

CLEO—Since when?

STARK—Since now. Tu amo, Cleo. . . . That means "I love you." You're right, darling. The stars are useless. I'll take you to a different place tonight.

CLEO—Where?

STARK—They won't know us from Adam there.

CLEO—But you don't love me.

STARK—Only you.  Tonight we'll be together, Cleo. . . .
Alone, alone together. . . .

CLEO—I don't trust you.

STARK—You're more important to me than anything I know,
Cleo, dear. . . .

CLEO—What happened?

STARK—Nothing.  I only know I love you, Cleo.

CLEO (*after a pause, suddenly*)—Then hold me tight, Ben.
Kiss me, love me—kiss me till I can't be kissed no more.  Hold
me.  Don't let me be alone in the world, Ben. . . . Don't let
me be alone. . . .

"Stark moves to her and they embrace passionately" as the
curtain falls.

## ACT III

It is still hot at the end of August.  The Starks, Dr. Ben and
Belle, are having another of their frequent rows in the office.
It is time, complains Belle, for them to end the farce.  She is
not at all convinced that he has stayed at the office to seek out
an eighteen-dollar error in his vouchers.  Admittedly her mind
is still on Cleo, and she is suspicious.  Certainly he owes her
the common courtesy of telling the truth—

The phone rings, and they both jump for it.  Belle wins.  It
is not Cleo, however, but Belle's poppa who is calling.  He
wants to talk with Ben.  He should have been told that they
are going back to the beach, Belle thinks, but she knows Ben
doesn't want to go—

"No, Belle, I don't," admits Ben.  "That's a shack on the
beach, and this is a shack.  Don't be angry . . . it won't do
us no good to quarrel again.  I know you're my wife, but it's
like we're enemies.  We're like two exposed nerves!"

"It's my fault!"

STARK—Much more mine.  I don't know what happened.  I
thought about these things a lot these past few months.  You
expect many things from marriage, but I can't give them.  I
feel a moral obligation but I don't know what to do.  These
scenes go on.  We're always worried . . . we're two machines
counting up the petty cash.  Something about me cheats you—
I'm not the man to help you be the best woman it's in you to be.

So your attitude's justified.  I know I owe you a lot, Belle—
BELLE (*bitterly*)—Hallelujah!
STARK (*anger mounting despite himself*)—Now I realize I've
had a guilty feeling for years.  "Marriage is the only adventure
open to the coward," a certain man says.  He made a mistake;
you have to be a hero to face the pains and disappointments.
(*As she tries to speak.*)  No, let me finish.  Because now I'm
really guilty . . . I mean with this girl—
BELLE (*quickly*)—That's enough!
STARK—I can't lie any more—
BELLE—*That's enough!  Do you hear me?  Enough!*
STARK (*insistently*)—I have to tell you—
BELLE (*jumping up*)—But you don't love her!  You had an
affair, all right, but you don't *love* her!  (STARK *sits, head in
hands.*  BELLE *continues with fearful agitation.*)  The girl was
here all day.  You were close together and you fell into that
thing.  I can forget it, I can forget it, Ben.  I'm your wife.  It
doesn't involve our whole relationship.  We can have many
happy years together.  I'll do anything you want.  We're young
—we have our life together in common, our ten years.  We can
talk it out—we're civilized beings—I'll never mention it.  We'll
both forget it!  We need each other, Ben.  We . . .  (BELLE
*stands there, wavering, a spout of water.*  STARK *goes to her,
embracing her.  She is bloodless, stunned.*)
STARK—Belle, dear, dear, dear, dear. . . .
BELLE (*moving away and staring at him*)—It was only a thing
of the moment, wasn't it?  Wasn't it?  Do you hear me—
wasn't it?
STARK (*anything to blot out this pale ghost before him*)—
Yes, yes!  (*A pause, she wavers again, has to hold on to furni-
ture to steady herself.  Finally.*)
BELLE (*wildly*)—I'll wait for her.  When is she coming back?
STARK (*frightened*)—I'll take you home, Belle.  We'll go
home. . . .
BELLE—When is she coming back here?
STARK—I don't know.
BELLE (*wildly*)—You don't know?  Did you tell me you
don't know?  (*Sitting.*)  I'll sit and wait for her.
STARK (*after a pause*)—Belle, you can't do that. . . .  We'll
talk about it tomorrow—we'll be more sensible—
BELLE—Do you love her?
STARK (*twisting*)— . . . It can't be settled in a minute, Belle.
BELLE (*white to the lips*)—What can't be settled?

STARK—I don't know what . . . I have a responsibility. . . .

BELLE—Your first responsibility's to me! You hear that?

STARK—I have to know what to do, Belle, and . . .

BELLE—To do? . . . You don't know what to do? You're in doubts. You have the slightest doubt?

STARK (*writhingly*)—I don't know what . . .

BELLE (*instantly*)—Give me the key to the car!

STARK—I'll go down with you.

BELLE—Give me the key.

STARK (*giving her the key*)—It's across the street—I'll take you down. . . .

BELLE—Stay here.

STARK—Downstairs to the car. . . . (*She slaps him strongly across the face. He is silent.*)

BELLE—When you know what to do . . . I'll be at Milly Heitner's apartment.

Belle has gone now—"a blazing fury, but watery in the legs." For a moment Stark is stunned. He is literally shivering as he sinks into a chair. Now he has turned out a light and is sitting silently in the dark. He does not hear a knock at the door. Frenchy lets himself in. He would engage the Doctor in casual conversation, but the Doctor is not to be lured from his own pulsating thoughts. Where is Cleo? Cleo is out with Wax. Suddenly the Doctor is moved to confession. He is nearing 40, the Doctor is. Does Frenchy know that? Yet he feels like a boy. Does Frenchy ever think of having children? Frenchy doesn't. They break too easy. Doesn't Frenchy want to get married? When it's time, Frenchy agrees—

"When you fall in love, you mean?"

FRENCHY—Love? Depends on what you mean by love. Love, for most people, is a curious sensation below the equator. Love—as they call it—is easy—even the rabbits do it! The girl I want . . . she'd have to be made in heaven. That's why I wait—

STARK—You're that good, you think?

FRENCHY (*correcting him*)—That *bad,* Doc! *She'll* have to be the good one. This is why: Love is a beginning, a jumping-off place. It's like what heat is at the forge—makes the metal easy to handle and shape. *But love and the grace to use it!*— To develop, expand it, variate it!—Oh, dearie me, that's the problem, as the poet said!

STARK—Yes, I see your point. . . .

FRENCHY—Who can do that today? Who's got time and place for "love and the grace to use it"? Is it something apart, love? A good book you go to in a spare hour? An entertainment? Christ, no! It's a synthesis of good and bad, economics, work, play, all contacts . . . it's not a Sunday suit for special occasions. That's why Broadway songs are phoney, Doc! Love is no solution of life! Au contraire, as the Frenchman says— the opposite. You have to bring a whole balanced normal life to love if you want it to go!

STARK—Yes, I see your point.

FRENCHY—In this day of stresses I don't see much normal life, myself included. The woman's not a wife. She's the dependent of a salesman who can't make sales and is ashamed to tell her so, of a federal project worker . . . or a Cooper, a dentist . . . the free exercise of love, I figure, gets harder every day.

STARK—I see your point.

FRENCHY—We live in a nervous time. How can I marry? With what? . . . Unless the girl is with me, up to the minute on all these things. Otherwise they get a dirty deal, the girls.

Dr. Stark isn't listening—not very closely. Frenchy goes on. He has other observations to make, and now he plunges in. Does the Doctor know what he would ask himself?

"What can I do for the girl, for Cleo? What will she be in ten years with my help?" That's what Frenchy would ask.

"You talk as if a happy marriage isn't possible—"

"No, I don't. But they're rare, like the dodo bird, mostly extinct. You know it yourself, Doc."

"Frenchy, I love her, I love her! . . . I love that girl! I'm half out of my mind. I don't know what to do. (*Striding to the light switch.*) Look at me. My face is so twisted. It feels twisted—is it twisted? . . ."

With some effort Frenchy gets the now hysterical Stark into a chair. It is time for a practical discussion of problems, thinks Frenchy. "All my life I have been afraid to do something wrong," Stark is muttering; "and now I've done it!"

"Leaving Scriptures out. . . . Do you want the girl or your wife? That's problem No. 1."

"I don't know where I stand . . ." weakly answers Ben, mopping his brow.

Mr. Prince is at the door. He, too, has come to discuss problems. He has come to believe that it is unwise for men to live alone. He finds himself in love with Miss Cleo. He knows Dr. Ben is having an affair with her. Still he has selected Cleo as the one to renovate his life—

"You like to choke me?" Prince asks, blandly, as the two men face each other. "Do it . . . put your two hands on my old guzzle and squeeze! That's the only way you'll stop me!"

"No, you can't be sane!"

"Are you? What can you offer her? Did it ever enter your befuddled mind?"

"I won't discuss this! And leave the office!" The order is peremptory, but Mr. Prince does not heed it. "You dare to think you'll buy that girl," Stark continues, as a slow flush creeps over the face of Prince. "You're a damned smiling villain! Go home, get out!"

"Listen, a man in the fullness of his life speaks to you. I didn't come here to make you unhappy. I came here to make *myself happy!* You don't like it—I can understand that. Circumstances insulted me enough in my life. But *your* insults I don't need! And I don't apologize to no man because I try to take happiness by the throat! Remember, Dr. Benny, I want what I want! There are seven fundamental words in life, and one of these is love, and I didn't have it! And another one is love, and I don't have it! *And the third of these is love, and I shall have it!* (*Beating the furniture with his umbrella.*) De Corpso you think! I'm dead and buried you think! I'll sit in the long winter night with a shawl on my shoulders? Now you see my face, Dr. Benny. Now you know your father-in-law, that damned smiling villain! I'll fight you to the last ditch— you'll get mowed down like a train. I want that girl. I'll wait downstairs. When she returns I'll come right up, in five minutes. I'll test *your* sanity!—*You*, you Nobel prize winner!"

Mr. Prince, exhausted by the vigor of his effort, wipes his face with a large silk handkerchief and is gone. For a moment Stark walks nervously about the room, observing the rain through the window, mopping his fevered face with his handkerchief. At the rattle of the doorknob he rushes to open the door. It is Willy Wax.

The dance director is apparently making an effort to control an emotional over-intentness. He has come to report a recent encounter with Cleo, Stark-sky's "little neon light." That is where Mr. Wax got the scratches on his face. He had sent her home, but not before he had discovered that she was old-fashioned

and believed in love.  Yet he has no intention of keeping away
from Cleo, as Stark warns him to—

"Since when does a stinker dentist, a prime pinhead, have
the right to dictate the morals and manners of a Willy Wax?"
demands Willy with a sneer.

"You keep away from her!"

"You mind your goddam business!"

"Wax, for God's sake—!"

"Understand this for once and all; any white woman who
pleases me—"

Stark is at his throat.  Wax, frightened out of his wits, tries
to break the dentist's hold.  They are both breathing heavily.

Suddenly Stark has released him.  Wax recovers enough breath
to assume a bold air.  "That's how you act over a little pony
who can't stand on her own legs!" he is saying, trying to
straighten out his disordered clothes.  "You're walking around in
the shadow of the noose, Stark-sky.  Don't I know your type?—
A bourgeois balcony climber—married, prates of purity—gives
temperance lectures, but drinks and plays around—"

"Leave the office, please!"

Wax is taking his time when Cleo lets herself in.  The situation is plain to her.  Instantly she flashes out at Wax: "Mr.
Wax, we don't want you around this office.  You make love
very small and dirty.  I understand your type very well now.
No man can take a bite out of me, like an apple, and throw it
away.  Now go away, and we won't miss you."

"Yeah, I'm forming a Society for the Extermination of the
Superfluous.  You two are charter members." He slams the
door as he leaves.

Now Cleo and Stark try to work out an understanding.  Suddenly they find themselves in a close embrace, frightened of
what may portend.  Again Mr. Prince is at the door.  He, too,
has come for an understanding.  He finds Cleo annoyed and
puzzled, Stark sullen, nervous and angry.  He is himself determined and passionately desperate.  He has come to renew his
offer of marriage.  Nor will he be dissuaded by Cleo's warning or
Stark's bewildered defiance.

"Are you going to let him go on like that?" Cleo finally demands of the dentist.

"You are clay, Miss Cleo, on the way to great womanhood,"
Prince is saying.  "What can he offer you?  He loves you—his
memoirs are written on his face.  But I see a big chapter heading: 'No Divorce.'  Why not?  Ten years they're married.  She

runs his life like a credit manager. They lost a child together
. . . they're attached underground by a hundred different roots.
But if he left her—as he knows—could he leave his practice?
Never! Then *you'd* be a credit manager. . . . But why go on?
He won't leave her. That needs courage, strength, and he's not
strong."

CLEO (*to* STARK)—Why don't you answer him? (*There is a
momentary silence.* CLEO *is looking from one to the other, realizing that* STARK *has no case.*)

PRINCE (*finally*)—My girl, I studied you like a scientist. I
understand your needs.

CLEO (*not knowing what to do or say*)—What are they?

PRINCE—A man to help you learn and grow. A man of
maturity and experience in everything—love, what to eat, where,
what to wear and where to buy it—money to buy it—an eye
turned out to the world! You need a man who is proud to
serve you and has the means to do it. He knows how to speak
to the head waiter and the captain on the ship. He don't look
foolish before authority. He is a missionary in life with one
mission, to serve and love you.

STARK (*laughing desperately*)—How absolute the knave is!

PRINCE—Now let us come down to terra firma. You're a brilliant girl. . . . I'm old enough to be your father.

CLEO—Well?

PRINCE—But notice! Every president of this great country
is my age. Because this is the time he's at his best. . . . He
has learned how to serve. And there is a simple worldly con-
sideration—it has its importance. In twenty years you'll still
be young, a beautiful woman of the world. Cremate me, burn
me up and throw me away, and what have you got? A fortune!
And so you go, a great woman, scattering good as you go. . . .

CLEO (*after a pause*)—What do you say, Ben? (*After waiting.*) Don't stand there like a dead man. . . .

PRINCE—What can he say? He's as mixed up as the twentieth
century!

STARK (*turning wrathfully on* PRINCE)—You come here with
this lust!

CLEO (*shaking* STARK *by the arm*)—Don't fight with him.
Talk to *me*, Ben.

PRINCE—Time is of the essence.

CLEO (*almost crying*)—Don't discuss him, Ben. Tell me what
*our* plans are. What'll you do with me?

STARK—Cleo, I can't talk now. . . . This man standing here . . .

CLEO—No, you have to tell me now. Where do I stand? . . .

STARK—Stand? . . .

PRINCE (*harshly*)—In short, will you leave your wife? (STARK *is silent, unable to make an answer.* CLEO *looks at him appealingly.* PRINCE *stands in the background, unwilling to provoke* CLEO'S *wrath.*)

CLEO—What do you say, Ben . . . ?

STARK (*lost*)—Nothing. . . . I can't say . . . Nothing. . . .

CLEO—You'll let me go away? (*She gets no reply from him. Half stunned, she seats herself. Finally.*) I'd like to hold my breath and die.

PRINCE (*softly*)—He'd let you do that, too.

STARK (*to* PRINCE)—You're a dog, the lowest dog I ever met! (*To* CLEO.)  Do you know what this man is trying to do?

CLEO (*crushed*)—I don't care.

STARK (*gently*)—Listen, Cleo . . . think. What can I give you? All I can offer you is a second-hand life, dedicated to trifles and troubles . . . and they go on forever. This isn't self-justification . . . but facts are stubborn things, Cleo; I've wrestled with myself for weeks. This is how it must end. (*His voice trembling.*) Try to understand . . . I can't say more. . . . (*He turns away. There is a momentary silence, which is broken by* PRINCE.)

PRINCE (*approaching her*)—And I offer you a vitalizing relationship: a father, counselor, lover, a friend!

Cleo is wearied with the argument. She would have Prince stop. She would have him know that she doesn't love him. The statement does not deter him.

"Miss Cleo, believe me, life is lonely, life is empty," Prince is saying, a pleading note in his voice. "Love isn't everything. A dear true friend is more than love—the serge outlasts the silk. Give me a chance. I know your needs. I *love* your needs. . . . What do you have to lose?"

"Everything that's me," mutters Cleo.

Mr. Prince would continue his pleading and his argument, but Cleo is not convinced. She, too, has a problem to settle—

CLEO—I'm a girl, and I want to be a woman, and the man I love must help me be a woman! Ben isn't free. He's a citizen of another country. And you, Mr. Prince, don't let me hurt your feelings; you've lived your life. I think you're good, but you're too old for me. And Mr. Wax, his type loves himself. None of you can give me what I'm looking for: a whole full world, with all the trimmings! (*There is a silence.* PRINCE *sees he is licked. Finally he sighs and says softly.*)

PRINCE—Silence is better than rubies. . . .

CLEO—Experience gives more confidence, you know. I have more confidence than when I came here. Button my coat, Ben.

STARK (*coming right to her*)—Yes. . . . (*He quickly buttons the front of her coat with fumbling nervous hands. Then suddenly he embraces her strongly, tears in his eyes.*) How your heart beats, Cleo . . . how it beats. . . .

CLEO (*finally, as they separate*)—I understand you, Ben. . . . Good night. (STARK *is silent.* PRINCE *shakes his head.*)

PRINCE—I'll drive you home.

CLEO—No, I'll go alone. Don't follow me—stay here. Count a hundred till I'm gone. . . .

PRINCE—Good-by, Miss Cleo.

CLEO (*as they gravely shake hands*)—Good-by, Mr. Prince. If you close your eyes, you'd never know I'd been here. Count a hundred—

PRINCE (*closing his eyes*)—One, two, three . . . four, five . . . (CLEO *has left the room.* PRINCE *slowly opens his eyes.*) . . . fifteen, thirty-seven, eighty-nine . . . (*Then in a whisper.*) one hundred . . . Lebewohl! I'm a judge of human nature. She means it; why don't we walk with shut eyes around the world? . . . (*Looking at his watch.*) It's very late. . . .

STARK (*who has been listening intently*)—There! . . . The elevator took her down. . . .

PRINCE—Yes, you love her. But now, my iceberg boy, we both have disappeared.

STARK (*tremblingly*)—I don't believe that. This isn't disappearance, when you're living, feeling what you never felt before. . . .

PRINCE (*heavily*)—Yes. . . .

STARK (*eyes flooding with tears*)—I insist this is a beginning. Do you hear?—I insist.

PRINCE—I hear. . . . (*He slowly moves to the door.*) My mind is blank. Next week I'll buy myself a dog. . . .

STARK—You going home, Poppa?

PRINCE—It's Labor Day on Monday. In the morning I'm going to the mountains. I excuse you for the names you called me . . . as you excuse me.

STARK—Yes. . . .

PRINCE (*smiling faintly*)—You'll permit me to come around and disturb you, as usual. Good-by, Benny.

STARK—Good-by, Poppa. (*They smile at each other.* PRINCE *goes to the door.*)

PRINCE (*at the door*)—Go home, to my daughter. . . .

STARK (*slowly rises from his seat; calls* PRINCE *back*)— Poppa, wait a minute. . . . (*Gropingly.*) For years I sat here, taking things for granted, my wife, everything. Then for just an hour my life was in a spotlight. . . . I saw myself clearly, realized who and what I was. Isn't that a beginning? Isn't it? . . .

PRINCE—Yes. . . .

STARK—And this is strange! . . . For the first time in years I don't feel guilty. . . . But I'll never take things for granted again. You see? Do you see, Poppa?

PRINCE—Go home, Benny. . . . (*He turns out the lamp.*)

STARK (*turning out the other lamp*)—Yes, I, who sat here in this prison-office, closed off from the world . . . for the first time in years I looked out on the world and saw things as they really are. . . .

PRINCE (*wearily*)—It's getting late. . . .

STARK (*almost laughing*)—Sonofagun! . . . What I don't know would fill a book! (PRINCE *exits heavily.* STARK *turns out the last light, then exits, closing the door behind him.*)

"The room is dark, except for red neon lights of the Hotel Algiers and a spill of light from the hall."

### THE CURTAIN FALLS

# THE AMERICAN WAY
## A Drama in Two Acts

### By George S. Kaufman and Moss Hart

BROADWAY was abuzz with rumors concerning "The American Way" before that expansive drama of frankly patriotic propaganda was produced at the Center Theatre in January. The Rockefellers had ordered it written, some insisted, because they had to have something to fill the second largest theatre in New York, and also, because the family was convinced something should be staged in the American theatre that would serve to stimulate a saner patriotism and a healthier tolerance than the last few years have developed. For this purpose, rumor added, the Rockefellers had provided a fund of $250,000, and didn't care that whether the drama was financially successful or not.

As so often happens, there was little reason for and less truth in these rumors. "The American Way" was evolved in the usual manner to which play productions are subject. The play was written, the authors, George S. Kaufman and Moss Hart say, because Mrs. Kaufman was insistent that it should be written and pleaded with them until it was written. It stems from a play of similar form and content that Mr. Hart had fooled with and abandoned about the time Noel Coward's "Cavalcade" was produced in London. The Coward thought had not inspired Mr. Hart's experiment, but the production of "Cavalcade" served to discourage it.

The cost of the production did run close to the quarter million dollars mentioned, and this was subscribed by a half dozen optimistic showmen and perhaps a dozen friends and well wishers of the authors. Fortunately for all concerned, either sentimentally or financially, "The American Way" was a popular success from its first performance. Its first half takes rank as one of America's superior folk plays and its second half is a ruthlessly revealing arraignment of the American way of meeting or dodging, ignoring or grappling with current social, racial, economic and political problems.

In its reception the reviews of New York's professional play-goers may be described as being ecstatic, with reservations. Mr.

145

John Anderson, writing in the *Journal-American*, successfully summed up the case for a voting majority of his colleagues when he wrote: "No audience that I can remember in my time on the aisle has been so shaken with emotion as we all were at the Center Theatre Saturday night. . . . Here was no longer a theatre but a place of pilgrimage, no time to sit in judgment, but to stand at attention. Salute!" Later, when in conclave assembled for the selection of the best play of the season of American authorship, no one of the critics gave "The American Way" a nod. Which would seem to indicate that many of the drama's impressive virtues are imbedded in its staging and direction.

It is a misty morning in 1896 when the curtains are parted on "The American Way." The scene is Ellis Island and there is a crowd of people awaiting the arrival of an immigrant ship from overseas. Through the mist, appropriately, the Statue of Liberty can be seen and back of it the reflection of an early morning sun. The crowd, split into two groups by a gang-plank that will shortly be attached to the incoming ship, represents "a patient cross-section of American immigrant life: Italians, Portuguese, Russians, Lithuanians, Germans, Latvians, all kinds—men, women and children, all ages."

A half dozen immigration officials hold the crowd back, and a perfect babel of tongues grows more and more excited as the bellow of a fog-horn in the distance indicates the closer approach of the ship. One young German, a substantial type in his early 30's standing at the edge of the crowd, timidly importunes an officer for the latest news. He is near the front of the crowd, he explains, because he has been there all night. He is waiting for his wife and his babies—a little girl and a boy baby he has never seen.

Now the fog-horn is nearer, and now there is the muffled sound of the ship's band playing "My Country, 'Tis of Thee." Soon the black prow has come into view. A moment later the gang-plank has been run up to a great iron door "in the bowels of the ship."

"As the first immigrant sets foot on the gang-plank the waiting relatives can no longer be held in check. They rush forward, screaming the names of their loved ones. Laughter, tears, embraces, kisses. For a good interval the officials are helpless; the dock is a swirling mass of excited and joyous humanity. Then gradually the officials regain control."

"All right now! All right!" the officials are calling, as they

"THE AMERICAN WAY"

Martin: Liebchen! Liebchen! Are you all right?
Irma: Yah, yah! . . . Martin, who was elected President?
(*Frederic March, Florence Eldridge*)

try to herd the milling crowd toward the examination rooms. "Keep moving! Both sides! Both sides to the health officers! Examination of papers! Both sides to the health officers! Examination of papers!"

Presently we are conscious of the reappearance of the young German, his face beaming. He has found his family—"a wholesome-looking German girl in her late 20's, leading a little girl of three or four by the hand and carrying a baby in her arms."

They have come a little forward from the crowd and we hear a rush of excited German from both the wife, who is Irma, and from the little girl. The father, Martin, would stop the torrent of words. Anyway, he would have them speak English. Yes, they must try to remember always to speak English, now that they are going to be Americans. And Irma does try, haltingly, but with not too much success. Martin, in one year, has learned to speak pretty well and is very proud.

They are all so happy there must be another embrace all around, and the kindly official must have another look at the baby Karl. Karl is "Wunderbar." And Martin must reassure the protesting 3-year-old Lisa that she, too, is wonderful. They are on their way to Ohio, this family, Martin informs the official. Martin has already established a home there in Ohio.

"Well, when you get to be Governor of Ohio, don't forget who let you into this country," the official laughingly suggests. "Good luck, Fritzie!"

They have cleared the passageways now. The crowd has drifted away, in excited groups. Martin and Irma, Lisa and baby Karl are on their way to Ohio. The lights fade. The curtains close.

In a moment's darkness the scene is changed to the public square of Mapleton, Ohio. "The little park in the foreground can be found in a thousand American small towns—the Civil War cannon, the pile of cannon balls, the little monument, a few scattered benches, etc. Circling the square are the traditional landmarks of small-town life. There are the church, the bank, the post-office, the courthouse, the hotel."

There is also a familiar assortment of store signs, and above the stores the offices of Mapleton's professional men—lawyers, insurance agents, etc. At one end of the square a banner announces that that is Republican National Headquarters, and that the party's candidate for President is William McKinley. Down the street is Democratic National Headquarters, and here another banner as bravely proclaims the candidacy of William Jennings Bryan.

It is a mild October day. The sun has set and in the twilight a few lights have been turned on in the stores and offices. The citizen activity is normal and passive. A small boy emerges from the saloon with a can of beer and swings along toward home with it, picking up a chum on the way. Mrs. Kennedy and Mrs. White stop on the corner by the bank long enough to compare observations on the Indian Summer weather that has been prevalent. The Judge and the Doctor pause long enough to let us know that the Doctor has a feeling there is a lot of Bryan sentiment around. This is a distressing observation to the Judge, who certainly has no use for free silver and that radical sixteen-to-one platform Bryan stands on. After which the Judge buys himself a Lillian Russell cigar and goes on his way.

Two young blades who have just been finished off in a barber shop and are probably quite smelly, are ready for their evening dates. The popular song they are humming has a refrain that goes "I don't want to play in your yard, I don't like you any more—"

And now Martin and Irma Gunther, our German friends of the Ellis Island meeting, walk through the square. Martin is proudly showing Irma her new home town and explaining to her the new life he has taken up in this new country.

"See, Liebchen," Martin is saying, "there is the cannon of the Civil War, and the monument to the soldiers from this town. And there is the courthouse—see? That is where I went to get my first papers. Remember—I wrote you?"

"Yah, yah!"

"And in five years I go back, and then I am a citizen. You too, Irma. And there is the bank, Irma, where I have money. Almost two hundred dollars, even with what I sent you. In one, maybe two years, Irma, I have my own shop. Work for myself. I will not be just a cabinet maker, but—Martin Gunther, Cabinet Maker."

"Ein jahr! Das ist sehr schnell, Martin."

"No, no. In America it can happen. You will see . . ."

Otto and Clara Heinrich happen along. They are Martin's good friends, and they are very glad that Martin's wife has at last arrived. She will see that she will like America. Already in six years Otto has his own bakery. Otto thinks that the next day he and Clara will give a party for Irma. Otto will bake for her a great American dish—doughnuts . . .

From Republican Headquarters a man has appeared with a drum. That is a signal the parade is forming. Soon Irma will see that, too—

"In two weeks, Liebchen, comes an election for President of the whole country," Martin explains. "Think of it! Here in America the people say who shall be the man. There is no Kaiser, no King, no Czar. Everything is the people, Irma. And in five years, Irma, I vote too. Think of it!"

"Es ist wonderbar, Martin!"

"And our babies, Irma—Lisa and Karl—they grow up in a free country. They are Americans."

"It is good, Martin."

"Yah, Irma. It is good."

They meet Banker Brockton, who is keeping Martin's money —nearly two hundred dollars—in his bank. And now, in the distance, a band can be heard playing "There'll be a Hot Time in the Old Town Tonight." It is getting dark and the parade turns out to be a torch-light affair, boosting the candidacy of William McKinley, who, according to the transparencies, stands for a Full Dinner Pail and a Square Deal.

Once around the square and the marchers come to a halt. A speaker has jumped upon the base of the cannon and is prepared to assure the voters of the fair town of Mapleton that they will make no mistake when they vote for William McKinley, the working man's friend and a worker himself in the best interests of all the people.

A heckler appears. She is for "Votes for Women" and she would like to know how Mr. McKinley stands on that issue. The speaker would ignore her, but he cannot. There are cries and catcalls, and someone is chanting derisively, "I should worry, I should fret, I should marry a suffragette!" The heckler persists. She is, it develops, a Miss Baxter and she stands her ground. Finally at the speaker's suggestion, two constables are summoned to drag her away. She is still shouting "Votes for Women!" as she goes.

"Well, folks," the speaker continues, "after votes for women I suppose we ought to have votes for monkeys." There is a roar of laughter from the audience. "And now, gentlemen, to get back to serious matters. Don't forget, when you go to the polls on Tuesday, November third, that there is only one candidate who stands four-square and solidly—"

Around the corner of the square suddenly appears another procession headed by another and a louder brass band. This one is playing "John Brown's Body," and the crowd that follows is chanting advice to voters to vote for William Jennings Bryan.

In this parade the transparencies inform the people that Bryan and Sewall should be supported—"Don't be a Slave to Gold" reads one. "McKinley is the tool of Mark Hanna" declares another. "Bryan, the Man of the People" captions a flaring portrait of the people's candidate.

Now a Bryan speaker has reached the base of the soldiers' monument. "Gentlemen, my friend here has been telling you about William McKinley—" he begins.

"Just a minute, my friend!" shouts the McKinleyite. "I am addressing this meeting."

"So am I!! . . . Gentlemen, William Jennings Bryan has no Mark Hanna behind him. He has only the people behind him. And in front of him the Presidency of the United States."

"Well, here's something in front of you, Mister!" yells a man in the crowd. With that he aims a ripe tomato and hurls it directly into the speaker's face. In a second someone has thrown a rotten egg. In a minute the two factions have set upon each other and the square is in an uproar. The fight continues for several minutes, then the numerically stronger Republicans have chased the Bryan Democrats down the street.

At the edge of the crowd Martin has been able to hold Irma protectingly in his arms. "Liebchen! Liebchen! Are you all right?" he is asking, as the lights fade. "Yah, yah," answers Irma. "Martin, who was elected President?" The curtains have closed.

In the darkness a schoolbell is heard ringing. Soon out of the darkness a chorus of children's voices can be heard reciting an oath of allegiance in unison: "I pledge allegiance to my flag, and to the Republic for which it stands. One nation, indivisible, with liberty and justice for all."

The lights are up. The children are being formed into line. They are just finishing "My Country, 'Tis of Thee." The teacher addresses them. They are on their way to the station to greet Mark Twain, the great American writer. Just as last week they had greeted Admiral Dewey, the hero of Manila Bay. Little Irma Gunther, now six, is to present Mr. Twain with a bouquet. The children are singing "Oh, Mapleton, the gem of Ohio" as they march away. The lights fade.

Now the curtains have parted again. This is the workshop of Martin Gunther, cabinet maker. "It is a small, crowded room, in the rear of which, through a curtained archway, can be seen the Gunther living quarters."

The tinkle of a small bell over the door of the shop announces a customer. It turns out to be small Bobby who is seeking subscriptions to *St. Nicholas Magazine*. He hopes to win a magic lantern or perhaps an air rifle. Bobby gets a nickel and Mr. Gunther's best wishes for success.

Martin, at work at the bench, is pensive. He has eaten no dinner. He wants no supper. Irma is anxious. Martin, she knows, must be worried. And now it comes out. Mrs. Brockton has decided to buy her furniture in Chicago. Her order would have meant a Winter's work for Martin. But—Martin will find something. He may have to give up the shop for a little while—but he will find something. And he will not hear of their going back to Germany. No. No. "Whatever happens, we stay in America," he is telling Irma. "We do not want our Karl to be used just for an army, like me. Like my father. No, Irma, we do not give up. It is worth working for—these things—for our children and for us, both."

"You are right, Martin. Sometimes I forget. What difference does a little hardship make?" Irma has gone to put young Karl to bed. And, believe her, they would have had trouble with Karl in any army.

Another tinkle of the bell brings in Winifred Baxter, the women's rights heckler of the political meeting. She is wearing bloomers and evidently has left a bicycle outside.

"Good evening," calls Miss Baxter. And then, turning abruptly to Martin—"Mr. Gunther, if you don't mind my saying so, you're a fool."

"Perhaps you are right," agrees Martin, chuckling.

WINIFRED—I have just heard that Mrs. Samuel J. Brockton has canceled a large order because I am one of your customers. Is that right?

MARTIN—She did not exactly mention you by name, Miss Baxter.

WINIFRED—No, she probably said that insufferable suffragette. Well, why didn't you give up *my* business, which amounts to a good dollar and a quarter a year?

MARTIN—Maybe I believe in votes for women.

WINIFRED—No, I think I had it right the first time. You're a fool.

MARTIN—Maybe. But in a way I am like *you.* A little bit stubborn. I do not like even Mrs. Samuel Brockton to tell me who my customers should be.

Winifred—Well, that's fine if you can afford it, but remember I'm not exactly popular in this town. I'm considered not quite a lady. I'm what they call a radical, you know, and Mrs. Brockton and a number of other ladies don't approve of that. You're going to lose another customer every time I chain myself to a lamp-post, and you'll lose 'em by the dozen week after next, when I go on a hunger strike in Senator Fletcher's bedroom. Don't let that get around yet. . . . So you see, Mr. Gunther, I'm a pretty expensive customer. Think you can afford me?

Martin—Yes, you *are* a little expensive, Miss Baxter, but I cannot help it. This is a free country—no? You have the right to chain yourself to lamp-posts; I have the right to choose my customers. No?

Winifred—Oh, yes. Yes. But just this once, Mr. Gunther, suppose we cancel *my* order instead?

Martin—Miss Baxter, I took your order first. That is all I can say.

Winifred—I see. . . . Well, Mr. Gunther, you're not only a fool, but I'll go no further. You're the kind of a fool I like.

Martin (*the bell tinkles and* Samuel Brockton *enters*)— Good evening, Mr. Brockton.

Brockton—Good evening, Gunther. Mrs. Gunther. Good evening, Winifred.

Winifred (*pleasantly*)—Good evening, Samuel. . . . Good night, Mr. Gunther. Go right ahead with my order, even if you don't hear from me, because there's a good chance of my being in jail. In fact, I've already packed a bag and sent it over. (*And she goes.*)

Martin—It is nice to see you, Mr. Brockton. Can I do something for you?

Brockton—Well, I'd just like to talk to you for a few moments, if I'm not interrupting anything.

Irma—If you will excuse me, please . . . the children. (*She goes.*)

Martin (*after a pause;* Brockton *looking around, curiously*) —You have not seen my shop before, Mr. Brockton, have you?

Brockton—No, no. I haven't. It's very nice. . . . Tell me, Gunther, did you really throw my wife out of your shop this afternoon?

Martin (*astonished*)—Why, no, Mr. Brockton. Certainly not.

Brockton—You're sure?

Martin—Why, yes, Mr. Brockton. Of course I'm sure.

BROCKTON—Well, why *didn't* you?

MARTIN—I beg your pardon?

BROCKTON—That's what I would have done in your place.

MARTIN—Are you joking with me, Mr. Brockton?

BROCKTON—Not at all. The fact is, Gunther, you're entitled to a medal, but you'll have to be satisfied with just getting that furniture order back.

MARTIN—Mr. Brockton, you mean I have the order again?

BROCKTON—That's right.

MARTIN—Oh, Mr. Brockton—Mr. Brockton, that is wonderful. You do not know how much that means to me. It means everything. I can keep my shop. I can keep— Oh, Mr. Brockton, how can I thank you?

BROCKTON—You don't have to, Gunther. But tell me, did you really give up that order because of some silly obligation to Miss Baxter?

MARTIN—That does not matter now. Oh, Mr. Brockton, how can I thank you?

BROCKTON—You *did*, didn't you? You threw a thousand-dollar order away just because—(*He shakes his head, mystified.*) —why did you do it, anyhow?

MARTIN—I don't know, Mr. Brockton. I must do what I think is right. Do not misunderstand me—I did not like to throw away that order. But if you will forgive my saying so, Mrs. Brockton was not fair. Miss Baxter has a right to what she thinks, even if that is different from what Mrs. Brockton thinks. All my life, Mr. Brockton, my one idea was to come to America. Why? Because then no one can tell me what I must do, how I must think.

BROCKTON—I see. Well, it's brought a good many people to this country. My great-grandfather, among them. Only he died for just what you're talking about.

MARTIN—It is not a bad thing to die for, Mr. Brockton— freedom. You only understand what it means when you have not had it.

BROCKTON—Yes, I suppose so. Well, we've got a great country here. Young, and rich, growing all the time. No telling where it'll go.

MARTIN—I am proud to be even a little part of it, Mr. Brockton.

BROCKTON—Well, we need people like *you*, too, Gunther. . . . Tell me, have you ever thought of branching out a little?

MARTIN—Well, of course I like to dream. Some day a shop

twice as big.   Maybe a couple of helpers.

BROCKTON—No, no, I meant more than that.   Seems to me furniture is one of the everyday necessities.   Lots of little towns around here, all of them growing.   Everybody has to have furniture. . . . I meant a factory.   Ever think of that?

MARTIN—A factory, Mr. Brockton!   Do you know how much money that would take?

BROCKTON—Yes, I think I do.   But you see, Gunther, banks sometimes lend money on promising investments.   Seems to me you'd be a pretty good investment.   Anyway, it's something to talk about.   Drop into the bank some day—let's talk it over.

MARTIN (*considerably stunned*)—Yes.   Yes.   I will be—(*He has to swallow at this point.*)—I will be glad to.

BROCKTON—Good.   Come in right after the holidays.

MARTIN—Yes.   Yes.

BROCKTON—My, my!   Kind of wonderful to think we're starting a new century, isn't it?   Nineteen—hundred.   Certainly sounds strange, doesn't it?   Nineteen hundred.   Well, I guess by the time it's finished we'll be used to it. . . . Merry Christmas! (*And with a wave of his hand he is gone.*)

MARTIN (*quivering with excitement, can barely await the closing of the door.   He runs shouting into the room at the rear.*) —Irma!   Irma!   What do you think?   What do you think? (*The curtains close.*)

There is the sound of a factory whistle.   A group of workmen coming from the Gunther furniture factory sprawl on the steps to eat their noonday lunch.   For several minutes they pay pretty strict attention to their sandwiches and pie, their cake and fruit. A foreman appears from the factory and calls for attention.   He has an announcement to make.   The Cleveland order is behind. Mr. Gunther would like to have them work overtime until it is finished.   He expects to pay time and a half for everything over ten hours.   The men mumble a little, grumble a little and then agree.   After all, it's the first time that a time and a half offer has ever been made in that town.   That's probably because Gunther used to work at a bench himself.

The workmen finish lunch and turn to small talk.   One wants to put a little bet of five dollars on Jim Jeffries.   He gets no takers.   Another is excited because he has read in the paper that the Wright Brothers have actually stayed up in the air two minutes with their flying machine.   A third refuses to believe any such damfool thing.   Even if he saw a flying machine he wouldn't believe it. Automobiles? Yes. Electric light? Yes. You can believe them things. But flying machines? Nah! A fight threatens. So, the fellow who reads the papers is a liar! Perhaps he is! All right— Before they can get their coats off the foreman comes again from the factory. Because of the men's willingness to work overtime Mr. Gunther is setting up the beer. Wow!

It is the Fourth of July, 1908. Seemingly all of Mapleton is gathered in the picnic grove on the outskirts of the town. The Firemen's Band is playing in the bandstand, above which a huge banner bears the legend: "Mapleton Annual Outing, July 4, 1908." The crowd is milling about. At tables the more sedate citizens are gathered. The Martin Gunthers. The Samuel Brocktons. Judge Hewitt and Mrs. Hewitt. Dr. Squires and Mrs. Squires.

"The Martin Gunther we now see bears few of the marks of the young German immigrant. He is beginning to blossom into a successful American business man; his figure, of course, is a shade more substantial than in the early days, and there is about him that air of authority and assurance that comes with a little success. As for Irma, the eight or nine intervening years, plus a period of prosperity, have also done much to alter her appearance. Lisa and Karl, now fifteen and thirteen, are attractive youngsters very much in the American mold."

The band plays on. The children romp in and out. A leader of sorts is trying to induce the crowd to sing. Just over the hill there is a sound of exploding firecrackers. The songs range from "I'm Afraid to Go Home in the Dark" and "Because I'm Married Now" to "Down Where the Wurzburger Flows."

Now the crowd is yelling for "Jeff." When Jeff—"obviously the local Harry Lauder"—appears, the band swings into "I Picked a Lemon in the Garden of Love" and Jeff sings lustily. Two other town boys oblige with a little act. One is "Teddy" and the other is "Taft." The crowd adores them. The leader introduces the Mayor of Mapleton, Junius W. McEvoy, and J.W. makes a speech filled with fire and patriotism. Mapleton is the fastest little growing town west of the Mississippi. Mapleton is about to be paved for six blocks of its Main Street length with the same kind of asphalt that they use in New York. Mapleton is buying automobiles and having babies. Martin Gunther, their esteemed fellow citizen, is planning to build a new furniture factory. Let Cleveland watch out!

Dr. MacFarlane, Principal of the Mapleton school, awards the prizes for the term: To Alexander Hewitt, winner of the final-term debate, "Resolved, That the United States Should Finish the Panama Canal." To Betsy Davis, for elocution. To Miriam Squires for American History. To Karl Gunther for his English composition, "Could the San Francisco Earthquake Have Been Avoided?" After which intermission is called while the band eats. . . .

At the tables the talk is on family matters. Anna, the Gunther's hired girl, who has been so long with the Gunthers that she seems like one of the family, is leaving to marry a fireman. She had met him at a fire. It is going to be pretty hard to replace Anna, what with hired girls getting as high as two dollars a week and refusing to do the washing and ironing.

Winifred Baxter arrives. Winifred, the suffragette, has now gone mad about automobiles. A good deal of sputtering and exploding signifies the quality of her new Pope-Toledo which, with seven horse-power, can do thirty miles an hour as easy as anything. . . .

The leader of the day has announced the order of events for the afternoon. It starts off with a baseball game, includes races and pie-eating contests and is to end with a balloon ascension. And then in the evening there is to be the biggest fireworks display Mapleton has ever seen, featuring the Last Days of Pompeii and the Battle of Bunker Hill.

As the announcement is completed there are insistent calls for Martin Gunther and demands for a speech. Martin fumbles and blushes and admits that he can't make a speech, but he is glad to be there and awful glad George Washington and those others went across the Delaware. Martin would like to sing an old German song, "Ach du Lieber Augustine," if the crowd will help him out with the chorus. The crowd is doing its best when the sky begins to darken and the first faint roll of thunder is heard. In practically no time at all the inevitable Fourth of July thunder shower is there. Hats and pieces of newspaper blow through the air. Screeching, screaming, yelling and helter-skelter running set in gustily as the curtains close.

We are at the Mapleton Tennis Club in 1914. A pretty young girl of about twenty-one has come out on the porch in an effort to avoid a group of teasing companions. She is Lisa Gunther and the rumor has spread that she is engaged to Alex Hewitt. True? Of course it's true. Look at her face. And remember how Alex looked! Finally Lisa confesses, but it is to be a secret.

And it is a secret until a group of boys follow Alex to the porch humming the wedding march. Among the boys Lisa's brother Karl is the biggest tease of all—

"Mr. Hewitt, as your future brother-in-law, I feel it my duty to warn you that my sister talks in her sleep. In fact, that new wing we built on the house—"

"Karl Gunther, you shut up!"

"However, when you're walking the floor with that baby, you won't mind it. I trust you will name the first one Karl, the second one Karla, the third and fourth ones—"

"Karl Gunther, I'll—"

The engaged pair would rush Karl, and the others are piling after them as the lights fade.

It is a quiet Summer evening. On the piazza of the Martin Gunther home four people are rocking. They are Martin and Irma Gunther, Winifred Baxter and Banker Brockton. The men are smoking. The talk takes in a variety of subjects. Summer is going fast. In six weeks Lisa Gunther will be married. Think of that! Karl, too, has a girl, though Irma doesn't see how Karl can be thinking of such things when he is going to college and expects to be an architect.

Anna has brought a pitcher of iced tea. Anna has also heard the squeal of a small boy and recognized it as that of her son, Tommy. Tommy is all Anna got from the fireman she married. He had gone away with a band and had never come back. Winifred Baxter, it transpires, has also had a fling at marriage. Her Mr. Alexander had also left her, but without any Tommy. Mr. Alexander had gone away after six months, leaving Winifred with memories of an unhappy experience. Mr. Alexander, it seems, turned out to be a spiritualist and on the honeymoon every night at 10 o'clock he tried to get his mother back. . . .

Irma and Winifred have gone into the house to see Lisa's trousseau and give Winifred a chance to smoke. Irma wouldn't like to have her smoke on the porch. The children might come back from the movies—

Brockton is sentimentally reminiscent. He is a widower now, and in his loneliness he has become closely attached to the Gunther family. He is most grateful for Martin's and Irma's kindness, but Martin would make light of that—

"Samuel, everything that I have in the world I owe to you," Martin is saying.

"Nonsense, Martin."

"Yes, yes. That day you walked into the shop—when first

we talked together—that was the beginning of everything for me."

"Your idea of a factory was two helpers—remember, Martin?"

"If anyone had ever told me I would some day employ hundreds of men—it wasn't so long ago, either. Fourteen years. Remember—you said next week we start a new century, nineteen hundred. They have been a wonderful fourteen years for me . . . America. God has been good."

It is ten-thirty now. Martin and Brockton start their usual evening walk to the Square. The children coming from the movies take over the porch. They had seen Mary Miles Minter in a wonderful picture and Episode 13 of "The Clutching Hand." Very exciting.

One of the boys is strumming "You Made Me Love You" on a mandolin. And "Peg-o'-My-Heart." The young people hum the refrains. They have swung a little wildly into "When the Midnight Choo-choo Leaves for Alabam" when Martin Gunther suddenly returns. He has a newspaper in his hand. His face is grim—

"Children, children, stop a minute," he pleads.

"What's the matter, pop?" asks Karl.

"Something has happened! Something terrible!"

"What is it?"

"What's happened?"

"Austria-Hungary has declared war on Serbia."

"Oh, papa, how you scared me," says Lisa, greatly relieved. "I thought something really was the matter."

"Let me see," chips in Karl, reaching for the paper. He studies the headlines. "What's so terrible about that?"

"It's what it might lead to, Karl. It's what it might lead to," answers Martin, soberly. He has started up the steps. "I don't like it. I don't like it," Martin is muttering, as he goes into the house.

"Don't you worry about it, pop," Karl calls after his father, and adds, half to himself: "Gosh, I thought something had happened right here in Mapleton."

The mandolin player has got as far as "And then he'd row, row, row, way up the river . . ." as the lights fade and the curtains close.

And now all the feverish preparation for war and all the excitements of 1917 take possession of the scene. A band comes marching on playing "Tipperary." Behind it is a shouting, cheering, singing crowd bearing banners with well-remembered legends:

"Mapleton Will Do Her Bit," "Uncle Sam Wants You for the Army," "Mapleton's Victory Loan Goal: Two Million Dollars!" "Out to Lick the Kaiser," "Berlin or Bust," "Make the World Safe for Democracy," "I'm a Gold Star Mother," "Sugar Will Win the War," "Remember Meatless Monday." . . .

The music and the shouting are punctuated by the sudden appearance of Liberty Loan Speakers. "Sometimes it is a soldier who speaks; sometimes a Red Cross Nurse; sometimes a Gold Star mother; sometimes a Boy Scout; sometimes merely a civilian. The speeches, singing and cheering intermingle, never stopping. You hear a fragment of each speech: "The challenge is to all mankind. We are fighting for the rights and liberties of all small nations." . . . "Our beloved President has called this a war without hate. We are fighting to make this world safe for democracy." . . . "This is a war to end all wars, to end all tyranny." . . . "Every time you buy a Liberty Bond you are forging a link in the chain of freedom." . . . "My boy gave his life in France, and I am proud of it. I have two other sons fighting there now, and I only wish that I had more."

There are two bands now. They swing from one wartime song to another—"Keep Your Head Down, Fritzie Boy," "Over There," "Keep the Home Fires Burning," "Tipperary," "Long, Long Trail," "Pack Up Your Troubles." The end comes finally in one "great paroxysm of war hysteria." The bands are playing, the crowd is singing "Madelon" as the lights slowly fade and the curtains close.

A few weeks later we are again in the living room of the Gunther home. Martin and Irma are there, and Lisa, Alex, Karl and Helen. Helen is the girl from Chicago who is going to marry Karl. Alex wears a captain's uniform. Karl is pacing the floor. His father's eyes follow him intently. Irma is seated and is twisting and untwisting her handkerchief.

Suddenly Karl wheels on his mother. "Mama—mama, you have no right to do this to me," he cries. "I can't bear to see you suffer, but how do you think I feel when I walk down the street, and people yell 'Slacker!' after me? How do you think I feel?"

IRMA (*almost moaning it*)—I don't care, Karl. I don't care.

KARL—What can I say to them? That my mother doesn't *want* me to go? Other mothers have sons. We're no different from anybody else.

IRMA—Karl, Karl, I can't stand any more. I won't listen.

KARL—But, mama, can't you see—

MARTIN—Karl, wait! Wait a minute. You must try to understand how your mother feels.

KARL—I know, papa—I know. Why do you think I haven't just gone out and enlisted? Because I *do* understand. But I can't bear it any more—I can't. We're Germans, papa—Germans. Everybody knows it. What do you think they're saying?

LISA—Mama, he's right. People are saying terrible things.

ALEX—It's true, Mrs. Gunther.

IRMA—I don't care. I don't care.

HELEN—Mrs. Gunther, I love Karl too. We're going to be married. But I think he ought to go. I want him to go.

IRMA—I don't care. If Karl goes to this war he will be shooting at his own flesh and blood. My own brothers he may shoot down. My own brothers. I cannot stand it. Surely there must be some other way—that Karl should not have to go over there and kill his own people. (*In the distance the sound of a band is heard—"Pack Up Your Troubles."*) I won't do it. I will never say yes. My heart cries out against it. I grew up with those people. I love them. I have their letters—their pictures. How can I send my son over to shoot them?

LISA—But, mama, we're at war. That makes things different. You're wrong, mama. You're wrong.

IRMA—Wait until you have a son, Lisa. Wait until you and Alex have a son. . . . Wait until they ask you to send him out to shoot down his own people. Then you will know how I feel.

Outside a parade is approaching. There are occasional yells from excited people. "Hock the Kaiser! Hang him to a sour apple tree!" yells one. The Gunther doorbell has rung. Anna lets in Brockton and Winifred Baxter. Winifred is wearing the uniform of the overseas ambulance corps. Brockton is obviously proud of the picture she makes. Martin is admiring, too, but Irma cannot bring herself to look.

There is a crash. Someone has hurled a rock through the window. Outside there is jeering. "How do you like that, you dirty slacker?" yells a voice. "What's the matter? Are you afraid to enlist?" "We don't want any slackers in this town!" Karl, in white fury, starts for the door. Brockton and Alex hold him back.

Winifred breaks the silence that follows. She must leave to catch her train. But before she goes she wants Irma and Martin to know that she feels toward them just as she always has felt.

She kisses Irma and shakes Martin's hand. With a gay "Auf Wiedersehen!" she is gone, Brockton with her.

Now the Gunthers have returned to their problem. Martin has picked up the rock and put it on the table. Irma has been watching him. "I don't care! Let them throw rocks!" she bursts forth. "It is better than that Karl should kill our people!"

"They are not our people, Irma," declares Martin, turning finally to face her and the issue.

IRMA—Martin, what are you saying?

MARTIN—I have been silent long enough—because I knew how deeply you felt this. But they are not our people any more.

IRMA—No, no, Martin, I cannot tear these people out of my heart, just because now there is a war. I was born in Germany, Martin. I grew up there. So did you. I love this country— yes, but I love Germany too. I cannot help that. It is deep inside of me. My heart breaks enough when I think that these two countries I love must fight each other. But that Karl should go over there, a gun in his hand, and kill those people I grew up with—that I cannot stand.

MARTIN—Don't you think that I am tortured too, Irma? When I wake in the night and hear you crying beside me, don't you think my heart breaks? I love Germany too, Irma. Do you think I can forget the little town that we were born in? My mother and father, those boys and girls we went to school with— they must have sons now too, Irma, like our Karl. Do you think I *want* him to go over and kill those people?

IRMA—Then for God's sake, Martin, do not let Karl go! Do not let him go!

MARTIN—No, Irma—Karl *must* go. This country opened its arms to us, reared our children. Everything that we have and everything that we are, we owe to America. Lisa's baby is an American; the children that Karl will have will be Americans, and *I* am an American, Irma. And so are you!

IRMA (*brokenly*)—No, no! Don't let him go, Martin. Please! Please!

MARTIN—Irma Liebchen, he must go. This is our country, Irma, and I am proud that we *have* a son to go. We cannot divide our allegiance, Irma—we are either Germans or we are Americans, and I say we are Americans! . . . Karl! Karl!

Irma is sobbing convulsively as the lights dim and the curtains close. Then, out of the darkness, "immediately the ear is assailed by a cacophony of sound—factory whistles, automobile horns, sirens, bells. Every imaginable thing that can make a noise seems to be making it."

The noise has seemed to reach its peak and is slowly subsiding. Mapleton, being rudely awakened, is stirring itself. A man in nightshirt and bathrobe appears and calls excitedly back to his wife to join him. Across the street another pair appears, also in bathrobe and nightclothes. What is this racket? What can it be? It must be the armistice, ventures one! It *is*, they are agreed! It *is* the armistice! And back they dash to dress for it!

The celebration begins to take form. "Johnny, Ethel and Tom now appear. One of them is beating a frying pan with a big spoon; Ethel wears a lampshade over her head and has the bedclothes trailing behind her. They parade around singing 'We'll Hang the Kaiser to a Sour Apple Tree.' "

Over to the right Harry, Grandma and Amy have emerged. "One wears a saucepan on her head; Grandma is doing a jig. They start to sing 'Good Morning, Mr. Zip, Zip, Zip,' parading as they do so."

There is much shouting of joyous congratulations from one to another. Everything is wonderful! Now the boys will be coming home! Let's everybody go down to the Square! And off they go shouting, singing. The screech of factory whistles and sirens is deafening. The lights dim.

We are back in the Square. "Naturally the Square of 1918 is a far cry from the Square of 1896—chain stores have replaced both Mr. Mercer and the grocery store, a motion picture theatre now stands where Olsen and Olsen had sold harness and buggies, and an ice cream emporium now occupies the spot where Mr. Murphy's saloon had stood. Flags, bunting and banners gaily bedeck the buildings. WELCOME HOME, MAPLETON HEROES. . . . WE WELCOME OUR BOYS . . . MAPLETON HELPED WIN THE WAR . . . WAR HEROES, THE TOWN IS YOURS. . . . MAPLETON SURRENDERS TO THE A.E.F. . . . WELCOME, SOLDIER BOYS."

There are not many people in the Square at the moment. Practically everybody is down at the station waiting for the train that is bringing the boys back. Out of the church come Martin and Irma Gunther, Lisa, Alex and Helen. The women are in deep mourning and have been weeping. Irma is still in tears and Lisa would comfort her. Lisa thinks her mother should come to her house for a little. And Helen, too, has an idea. Let Irma come home with her. Together they will give Karl's baby his dinner.

Martin has stopped to survey the decorations of the Square. "Soldier heroes. . . . I hope it was not all a waste," he is saying. "I hope he did not die for nothing. . . . You are coming home with us, aren't you, Winifred? And you, Samuel? You can make Irma forget a little, maybe."

"Yes, Martin."

"Perhaps it is not all a loss, Martin," Irma finds voice to say, as she joins her husband. "Maybe the world learns a little bit from all this. Maybe when Karl's son is a man, he finds a better world than Karl knew."

"Karl's son. Karl will live for us again, Irma, in his son."

They have started on. Softly, from the distance, come the strains of a military band playing "Over There." There is a great cheering of the people.

"They are home, Martin," says Irma.

"Yes, Liebchen, they are home." He has put his arm around her. They are standing thus as the band and the crowd pour into the Square. In no time there is a great, seething, cheering mass. Every bit of standing room is occupied and most of the roofs. Excited faces appear at all the windows.

"Then come the soldier boys—band ahead of them, marching proudly and with smiles on their faces they swing into the Square. Flowers are tossed at their feet; kisses blown; children dodge excitedly in and out among the paraders; parents call out the names of their loved ones."

The company has come to a halt. The order is to break ranks. And now there is such a rushing of soldier boys into the arms of fathers, mothers and sweethearts as Mapleton had never seen before. Martin's arm is still around Irma as they stand and watch.

The curtain falls.

## ACT II

It is a Saturday night in 1927. At the Mapleton Country Club the regular Saturday night dance is being combined with a kind of watch party. A young man, having attempted to fly from New York to Paris, is somewhere out over the ocean and news from the radio announcers is eagerly awaited. The orchestra has just stopped playing "Ramona." The dancers, after half-hearted attempts at getting an encore, are drifting off the floor and through French windows to the porch of the club house. It is then that Station KDKA of Pittsburgh breaks in with an announcement. Everybody stops to listen—

"Here is the latest news on the sensational New York-to-Paris flight of Charles A. Lindbergh," confides a full, round voice. "This young American, who startled the world yesterday by taking off alone in his plane, The Spirit of St. Louis, has still not been sighted over Europe. An immense crowd is waiting at Le Bourget Field in Paris to give him the greatest welcome of all time, when and if he arrives, and all over America tonight his fellow countrymen are wishing Charles Lindbergh Godspeed and a happy landing. Station KDKA will keep you advised."

The announcement is followed by an excited chattering. "Boy, think of that! Flying over the Atlantic Ocean! All by himself!" . . . "Gee, I hope he makes it. Wouldn't it be terrible if he didn't make it?" . . . "Well, I've got a hunch he is going to make it!"

The dancers are beginning to drift back to the ballroom. Winifred Baxter is in with Judge Hewitt, but she doesn't have the Judge long. Mrs. Hewitt needs him for bridge. Anna, the Gunthers' girl is there, a little to Winifred's surprise, until she learns that Anna's boy, Tommy, is playing a horn in the band. Tommy's doing quite well as a musician. He gets that from his father and Anna is glad that that's all he gets.

Lisa appears from the clubhouse excitedly to report that her father and mother are actually dancing. Everybody should come and see. And everybody in sight does. "Well, it's the first time a schottische has ever been danced to 'Yes, Sir, She's My Baby,' " ventures Winifred.

The third generation has arrived. Lisa and Alex's two daughters are there with their governess to beg that they be allowed to stay up till Lindbergh gets to Paris, even if that takes all night. Soon they are joined by young Karl and his mother. Helen Gunther is now an attractive woman just turning thirty. Young Karl, aged nine, would stage a bit of rough-house fun with his grandfather if he were not suppressed.

"That little Karl. He is a devil," chuckles Martin, after the children have gone.

"Yes. It is like living over again, Martin, to have him with us," fondly admits Irma. "He talks just like our Karl used to. The same voice he has, Martin."

"Yes, sometimes I think I am back in the shop again. I have to pinch myself. You know what I did today, Irma? I went into the factory and made him a train. I can still make a pretty good train, Irma."

Irma kisses him gently. "Ah, Martin, God was kind to us. He took away our boy, but he gave us little Karl."

Winifred Baxter is back. She has been dancing with Brockton, but not too successfully. "No, Samuel, it has nothing to do with your dancing," Winifred is explaining. "It's just that I may want to walk again some day."

"Martin, I am afraid our dancing days are over. They don't play 'The Blue Danube' any more," sighs Brockton. "I am afraid the younger generation is always going to the dogs, Martin."

"Say, it wasn't so long ago that *I* was the younger generation," snaps Winifred. " 'Votes for Women'—remember? Shocked everybody. Well, that's all over now. The ladies have got their vote. And what was the first thing they did with it, after all my struggles? They elected Warren G. Harding President of the United States."

"Well, Winifred, you might have known something like that would happen."

"Yes, I suppose so. You know, the funny part of it is, except for a few fools like me, they didn't really *want* the vote. They don't care *now*. Just let 'em be feminine, and get their man— that's all they care about. Well, you can't say I haven't kept up with the times. Yes, sir, I opened up the first beauty shop in Mapleton."

"Yes, I thought you were crazy, Winifred," admits Irma. "That women should go to a store to get made beautiful, like you go to the grocer's for a pound of coffee—I thought you were crazy."

"Well, Irma, they do it. Facial, shampoo, henna rinse, mud pack, manicure, pedicure, neck massage—and they walk out looking just the same. Ah, me! Votes for women!"

Anna has come excitedly to tell them that Tommy is about to sing. Well, she admits, it isn't exactly singing—crooning they call it. The Gunthers go to hear. But Winifred and Brockton decide on a boat ride instead. It is a grand moonlight night for proposals of marriage and Samuel has an idea that Winifred may be in the mood.

Tommy's song is finished. Several young couples stroll in. They are hoping for news of Lindbergh. Martin and his three grandchildren come from the ballroom. They, too, are talking about flying. Grandpa is telling of the time no one would believe the Wright Brothers had stayed up two minutes.

"Was Lindy a boy just like me, Grandpa?" Karl would know.

"Yes, I imagine he was, Karl. He grew up in a small town,

went to school, played games—just like any little boy—and now he is going to be a great American."

"Maybe I can be a great American some day too, huh, Grandpa?"

"You couldn't fly an airplane. Aunt Helen wouldn't let you," warns Mary Hewitt.

"I could so."

"All right," quiets Grandpa. "Perhaps not airplanes, Karl, but maybe you can do something else. Just look at all the little boys who came from little towns and became great Americans. Benjamin Franklin, Thomas Edison, Lincoln—all the rest of them. Starting with nothing—not even as much as you have. But all of them had a spirit inside them that made them great Americans. That is the important thing. And now Lindbergh— flying all by himself over the ocean. Starting off in the dawn yesterday—just waving his hand good-by. And doing something no man has ever done before. Doesn't that make you feel proud, children? Isn't it a wonderful story? How a little boy, a boy just like millions of other Americans—"

There is a great cheering in the clubhouse. "He did it! He did it! Lindy did it!" The voices are booming. The dancers pour out onto the porch, cheering, dancing, embracing each other. Now everyone is dancing—including Martin and the children. The orchestra has begun to play "Yankee Doodle." Probably Tommy Nelson is singing it. The curtains close.

On a street corner in Mapleton a political speaker is haranguing a crowd of men and a few women. There are banners bearing huge pictures of Herbert Hoover. And other banners urging the crowd to vote the straight Republican ticket and for Herbert Hoover—

"Voters of Mapleton: On Tuesday of next week you will go to the polls to elect the next President of the United States." The speaker's voice is booming, his conviction insistent. "I have only this to say to you. If you want prosperity to continue, if you want good times such as you have never seen before, vote for Herbert Hoover. (*Cheers.*) Herbert Hoover is first and foremost a business man—the great executive. Let's put a business man in the White House, and in Herbert Hoover's own words there will be a chicken in every pot and a two-car garage for every American family."

The speaker urges the women especially to remember that Herbert Hoover considers them a great force in political life.

And he concludes with one grand last promise:

"Voters of Mapleton, one final word: If you think you have got prosperity *now*, elect Herbert Hoover President of the United States, and this country will never forget him. I thank you."

The crowd is dispersing, mumbling, shaking its head, busy with argument. The lights fade.

It is February, 1933. We are back in the Square at Mapleton. "It is a chill Winter's day, and the entire atmosphere is one of bleakness and despair." There are plenty of "For Rent" and "For Sale" signs and a banner strung between two buildings reads: "Give to the Community Chest. Remember the needy."

"The pedestrians that hurry by reflect the spirit of the times. Harried, forlorn, despair in their eyes. Here and there a few threadbare, shivering men are offering apples at five cents apiece."

One man has stopped another in the lee of Brockton's bank. He has been reading a paper. He has read that the First National in Mesalia had failed to open that morning. The Fidelity Trust in Alliance, too.

"Think Brockton's bank is all right?" the second man wants to know.

"I don't know. I guess so."

He hurries away. A woman stops him. What is that about the bank? He doesn't know. He hurries on. Another woman is coming into the Square. The first woman stops her.

"Myrtle! There's something wrong at the bank. Better take our money out."

"As they hurry toward the bank they stop to whisper to another woman. The rumor is under way. Like wildfire it spreads from one person to another. You see one dash for home to get a bank-book; another gathers a little knot of people around him, excitedly whispers the news. In no time at all a milling crowd has gathered in front of the bank. Grimly, a line forms, stretching out into the Square."

An employee of the bank rushes out. He calls a Boy Scout soliciting contributions for charity in the Square. It is Karl Gunther. "Go get your grandfather right away! Mr. Brockton wants to see him!" orders the clerk.

The line has broken. The mob would rush the doors of the bank. Samuel Brockton appears on the steps and raises a hand for silence: "There is absolutely no reason for this panic," he tells them. "I give you my word this bank is safe. You have known me for years; I know most of you. Please take my word.

This bank is absolutely solvent. Your money is safe."

"Well, if it's safe, give it to us. Give us our money!"
The crowd echoes these sentiments. "Please! Listen to me!"
Brockton continues. "No bank in the world can pay every de-
positor in cash. That is not the way a bank is run. But if you
will go to your homes—"

The crowd shouts him down. It is fast getting out of hand
when Martin Gunther appears, Karl running excitedly ahead of
him. Martin pushes his way to the steps and faces the crowd—
"People! People! Listen to me! Listen to me!" The crowd
is momentarily stilled. "You must believe Samuel Brockton
when he tells you this bank is safe. (*A voice from the crowd:
'We want our money!'*) You will get your money, but you
cannot have it all at once. (*'Give us our money.'*) Listen to
me! I have money in this bank, just like you. I am not drawing it out—not a penny of it. (*'We don't care! We want our
money!'*) Listen! Listen! You all know Samuel Brockton.
He is your friend as well as mine. I am going inside here now
and sign over to this bank everything that I have in the world.
My factory—everything! (*There is a scoffing roar from the
crowd.*) Please! Please! Stop this madness! Stop and think
this over! (*The crowd is almost silent, almost convinced.*) Do
you hear me! Do you understand what I am saying! I am
putting everything I have in the world in this bank."

The crowd seems impressed. Martin goes into the bank. "For
a moment the crowd is quiet—almost too quiet. With solemn
faces, men and women look at each other. Then, almost imper-
ceptibly, the line moves—each of them is a few precious inches
nearer to his goal. Quiet again—and then a hysterical woman
can stand it no longer. She breaks forth:"

THE WOMAN—I want my money! I'm a widow! It's all I've
got! What'll I do? What'll I do? It's all in that bank! I
want my money!

A MAN (*as the hysteria spreads*)—I've got a sick kid! I've
got to send him away or he won't live!

ANOTHER WOMAN (*weeping*)—My money! My money! Oh,
God! Oh, God!

THE MAN—What's the matter with this line? Why isn't it
moving? What are they keeping us out here for? I've got a
sick kid! I've got to have money or he'll die! I've got a sick
kid, I tell you!

THE FIRST WOMAN—What are you going to do? Why doesn't

somebody do something? My whole life—my whole life is in there—all my money! I want my money!

With a roar the crowd surges forward. There are more police, now, but they are powerless before the mob's onslaught. Clubs are wielded. There is shrieking and tearing of clothes. The riot is at its height as the curtains close.

Out of the darkness the voice of Franklin D. Roosevelt can be heard over the microphone:
"I am certain that my fellow Americans expect that on my induction into the Presidency I will address them with a candor and a decision which the present situation of our Nation impels," the President is saying. "This is pre-eminently the time to speak the truth, the whole truth, frankly and boldly. Nor need we shrink from honestly facing conditions in our country today. This great Nation will endure as it has endured, will revive and will prosper. . . . Our distress comes from no failure of substance. We are stricken by no plague of locusts. Compared with the perils which our forefathers conquered because they believed and were not afraid, we have still much to be thankful for. . . . The money changers have fled from their high seats in the temple of our civilization. We may now restore that temple to the ancient truths. . . . We face the arduous days that lie ahead of us in the warm courage of national unity. . . . In this dedication of a Nation we humbly ask the blessing of God. May he guide me in the days to come."
The lights gradually reappear. A crowd of WPA workers marches in. The men are on their way to do a bit of road fixing over in Mesalia. They stop to rest.
"I'm certainly glad I went to college," says one, laying down his shovel.
"Well, buddy, take a look at me. I'm what's left of the most brilliant research chemist in his class."
"How about me?" chips in a third. "I was voted the man most likely to succeed."
"Well, fellows, we're eating, anyway, and that's something. We were starving before."
A foreman appears with pay checks. The men swarm after him. The lights fade.

Across the way an American boy and girl appear. They are dispirited, dejected. The girl's name is Ruth. The boy is Karl

Gunther. Karl is sullen, embittered. This, he sneers, is certainly a big night. He has a whole dollar to spend. Ruth is distressed. She would not have him so bitter. What good can come of bitterness—

"Listen, Ruth, what's the use of kidding ourselves?" demands Karl. "Here I am—twenty-one years old. I've never had a job in my life—never had a *job*. I've been trying for three years, but I can't get one."

"I know, Karl, but it doesn't help being so bitter."

"What am I supposed to do—laugh? All right, I've got a home. A place to go and sleep nights, and listen to my grandfather tell me what a wonderful country this is. Still a wonderful country. Took everything he had. His business—money. Lost it all in one day that time the bank went under. But it's still a wonderful country. What's so wonderful about it, I'd like to know?"

"But—it's our country, Karl. You wouldn't want to be anywhere else, would you?"

"I don't know. There must be some place where a fellow's got a chance, where the cards aren't stacked against you right from the beginning."

"Darling, don't let it spoil everything for us."

"Oh, sure not—it'll be fine. In a couple of years things will be even worse, so we can get married and go right on relief."

"Karl, Karl, what can I do with you?"

"I'm sorry, Ruth. I don't give you much fun, do I? Why don't you get some rich guy that can take care of you?"

A couple of young men have strolled in. Evidently they are familiar with this situation, or others like it. They greet both Karl and Ruth as old acquaintances. One of them takes a pamphlet from his pocket and passes it to Karl. "Look this over when you have a minute," he says. "It's sort of what I was telling you about the other day."

Ruth would take the pamphlet from Karl. She knows what it is. It's vicious stuff. "Do you want the same kind of thing here that they have in Germany?" demands Ruth.

"Well, what are we going to do?"

"Karl, we'll solve our problems in our own way. We don't need those ideas."

"I'm not so sure about that. I only know I'm sick of waiting around."

One or two of the WPA workers have wandered back, folding their checks and still kidding about their wealth.

"Well, I can always do that, anyway," sneers Karl, as they pass on. "How about it, Ruth? If I can get on the WPA, will you marry me?"

"*Yes!* Yes, Karl, I would. That's the way *I* feel about it!"

"Well, I don't!" Karl answers. Both tone and manner are violent. "Come on—I'll treat you to a Coca-Cola. We'll make a great big night of it." They go on their way.

This time the parting curtains reveal the Gunther living room decorated with many flowers. It is Martin and Irma's Golden Wedding anniversary and all their children and their grandchildren, and all their old friends have gathered to celebrate it. There is a huge bell of flowers suspended from the ceiling, and flowers in profusion are all about the room.

Under the bell a Minister is waiting. Presently Lisa, who is an anxious mistress of ceremonies, gives a signal. A pianist and violinist start the wedding march and from the dining room Martin and Irma walk in together, arm in arm. Irma is wearing the veil in which she was married and is smiling happily. Martin, stalwart and proud, walks smartly beside her.

"Martin and Irma Gunther, on this the fiftieth anniversary of your wedding day, I give you the blessing of God," the Minister is saying. "You have shared together both the joys and sorrows of the years, and because you have shared them together each joy has been a greater joy, each sorrow a lesser sorrow. Now, together, you stand before me truly as one, and may it please God to continue His blessings in the years to come. (*He opens the prayer book and reads aloud.*) 'Set me as a seal upon thine heart, as a seal upon thine arm; for love is strong as death. Many waters cannot quench love, neither can the floods drown it.' (*He closes the book.*) My blessing upon thee, Martin and Irma Gunther."

Martin has taken Irma in his arms and kissed her tenderly, as the friends and guests applaud. And now from the dining room two men appear bearing a large satin-lined case. In it is a handsome gold tray. As the men set it down Samuel Brockton steps forward and addresses the Gunthers.

"Martin—Irma—your friends have asked me to present to you this token of their affection," says Brockton. "On it you will find inscribed the names of all those who love you and hold you dear. But I want to do more than just present this gift. I would like to tell you, Martin, and you, Irma, how much you mean to your friends, how much you mean to *me*."

With fervid sincerity the speaker recalls the beginnings of Martin and Irma's residence in Mapleton; his meeting with Martin; Martin's beginnings in business; Martin's valiant effort to save the bank; his years of gain and his years of loss—

"You may again have factories, Martin," Brockton concludes. "But what you have tonight is a rare possession for any man. Irma beside you, Lisa, your grandchildren, your friends. Martin —Irma—I am proud to have known you."

And now congratulations and kisses come in a shower until Anna, in great excitement, calls the company's attention to the radio. She has a surprise for them. As she turns the dials an orchestra is just finishing a popular tune. It is the orchestra of Tommy Nelson and the program is coming direct from the Rainbow Room, Radio City, New York. A moment later Tommy Nelson himself is sending a special greeting to his two friends in his home town—to Mr. and Mrs. Martin Gunther! His greetings and his wish that he might be with them are followed by Tommy's singing a little song in honor of the occasion—"Put on your old gray bonnet with the blue ribbons on it—" As Tommy finishes ". . . Through the fields of clover we will drive to Dover, on our Golden Wedding Day," the congratulations and the kisses start all over again.

The guests file happily into the dining room. Only Martin and Irma and their grandchildren have stayed a little back of the others for their own family greetings. The children gone, Martin and Irma have a moment or two of sentimental recollections and a renewal of the love and faith that has sustained them these fifty years. And now they have all gone into the dining room. Again the strains of the wedding march, followed by a good deal of cheering and laughter, the clink of glasses and the indistinct words of a toast. . . .

There is a ring at the doorbell. A maid lets in Ed Lorenz, the young man who had handed Karl the pamphlet. Ed has come to remind Karl of an important meeting, with initiations. Kamerling, who has been in this country for three months, is going to speak. Karl better—

Brockton comes from the other room. He recognizes Karl's friend. When they are alone Brockton hopes that Karl is not thinking of going to the meeting Lorenz represents. Brockton knows all about that young man's activities. Karl is defiant. Brockton thinks he had better call Martin. Martin, too, is distressed to think Karl should have anything to do with such things. But Karl is still defiant—

KARL (*turning on him*)—You've no right to stop me. How do *you* know—how does *he* know—what it's like for me? For millions like me. You're living in the past—the world's moving. You don't know what's going on. We've got different problems now. And the same old system can't meet them any longer.

BROCKTON—You see what's happening, Martin. No place is safe from it, even America.

KARL—Go ahead—wave the flag. Let the bands play. But if you stop listening to "The Star-spangled Banner" for a minute, you can hear this whole rotten system crashing around your ears.

MARTIN—Karl, Karl, do you know what you're saying?

KARL—You bet I do! The land of the free! Sure! Free to waste your life away looking for a job! What's the use of freedom if it doesn't get you anywhere?

BROCKTON—Karl, stop it. You ought to be ashamed of yourself.

MARTIN—No, no, let him go on. I want to hear this.

KARL—What's so wonderful about the American way of doing things, compared with any other way? Look at *you!* What have *you* got after all these years? Nothing!

MARTIN—I will tell you what I have got, Karl. I have got everything that I wanted from America, and more. I came over here a poor boy, with nothing, and I got from America riches and years of happiness. All right, the riches have gone. That does not matter. But freedom there still is, and that is what *does* matter. I don't care how they are trying to change this country, or what name they call themselves. They are all the same—all these things—they are un-American. What really matters, Karl, is that you, and the young people like you, should take over this country, and keep it what it has always been.

KARL—Try that speech when you're looking for a job, Grandpa, and see where you get. You're sentimental about this country, but I'm not. I tell you this country is in a bad way—you ought to talk to *my* generation. Just listen to them for a while. You've had your life, and everything that went with it. But I haven't. I'm just starting, and I'm going to fight for my chance.

MARTIN—You will not get your chance that way, Karl.

KARL—Oh, I know all about that.

MARTIN—If you have your way—you and your friends—and they change this country the way they want it—it will not be what they tell you now, Karl.

KARL—I don't care what it is, I'll have a job, anyway.

MARTIN—You will have a job—yes—but you will live your life in a country that is one great prison.

KARL—I'll take that chance. It's my life.

MARTIN—There will be no friends even that you can trust, that you can talk to. Your own children will not belong to you. They will be told from the cradle what to believe; at five they will have guns put in their hands.

KARL—I don't care what they do—they get results, don't they? Look at 'em!

MARTIN—Yes, look at them! Look what they are doing over there today. They have gone back to the Dark Ages. Don't think that I have not thought about you, Karl—how hard it is for you. I have. But your chance lies with the America that we have.

KARL—I know. Freedom! Well, it isn't enough. You can't marry a girl on freedom! You can't eat it if you're hungry!

MARTIN—Freedom! Freedom is a curious thing, Karl—you do not get up every morning saying, "Ah! I am free!" You do not even think about it, perhaps, but it is part of a man, as much as living and breathing. It is the very spirit of a man. To live where there is freedom, Karl, that is the greatest thing in the world. Yes—yes, I *am* sentimental about this country. If America meant liberty before, think what it means now.

KARL—Well, that's the way *you* feel about it. I'm going to that meeting!

With a toss of the head Karl has left. The laughter of the anniversary guests swells. Irma appears in the door to call Martin. Everybody is insisting that they shall dance "The Blue Danube." Martin doesn't hear. Irma takes him by the arm as the crowd comes pouring back into the room. The music is playing. Mechanically Martin lets Irma carry him into the dance. There is great laughter as the dance whirls on. The lights fade.

Out of the shadows a man comes forward. He wears a uniform, brown shirt, military belt. He is followed by another and another. Now there is a company of them. They are joined by three young men in civilian dress. Karl Gunther is one of the three. They move forward and disappear.

The curtains are parted. We are back in the picnic grove. It is night. In the distance there is the flicker of torches. Presently a body of men marches in, their faces dimly lit. They gather around the band stand. A leader, surrounded by three guards, mounts the stand. In the voice of a fanatic he addresses the crowd—

"You all know our mission. We must fulfill our part. Then and then only can America fulfill *her* destiny. There are forces in this country who accuse us of being un-American; in reality we are in the truest sense of the word Americans, the real patriots of this country."

There is a cheer from the men. The leader continues. The spiritual regeneration of the youth of America, to be followed by reorganization for economic reinforcement and the political schooling of youth is the party's aim—

"Let us not swerve from our high purpose; we must remake this country for Americans and Americans only. Other countries have cleaned their houses; the time is coming when we must do the same. Tonight we meet to initiate three new members, to pledge them, as we have pledged ourselves. Henry Williams, John Courtenay, Karl Gunther—step forward. (*The three figures step forth into the light.*) When you take this solemn oath, you pledge with your life to work for our cause—to free this country from the bonds in which it is now held. You! (*He points to* KARL.) Repeat these words after me. I, Karl Gunther—"

" 'I, Karl Gunther—' "

"Pledge with my life—"

" 'Pledge with my life—' "

He gets no farther. Suddenly there is a shout of "No! No!" from the fringe of the crowd. Now Martin Gunther has brushed aside those who would stop him and stands with Karl. The crowd would stop him. Karl would have his grandfather let him alone. But Martin is not to be stopped. He knows these men. Knows what they would do. Dares them to let him speak. The crowd jeers, but the leader motions his permission.

Above the cries and taunts of the crowd the voice of Martin Gunther rings out: "Think! *Think* what you are doing!" he shouts. "There are not many countries left that are free! If this country goes down, what will men do? Where else can men go? Do not do this thing, I beg of you! Do not bring this madness over here! You will not starve in this country. There will be jobs again, just as there have been in the past. This is not our first crisis! Read! Read the history of America! Again and again we have fought our way through. And now, just because one man—*one man*—stands over in Europe and tells us that democracy is finished, that this country is no good, are you going to believe him? Because if that is what you believe, you have no right to call yourselves Americans! Democracy is *not* finished; it still exists in many countries of the world, and we are not going to let it die! We are going to keep up the fight until this evil force is wiped from the face of the earth!"

The leader has taken Martin by the shoulder and roughly turned him around. "You're a German, aren't you?" he demands. The crowd jeers derisively.

"I am a German—*yes!*" screams Martin. "But that does not matter. I could be Russian, Italian, anything—I am *American!* My own son—*his father*—died for this country, and I would rather see this boy dead than here tonight!"

There is another yell from the crowd. The men are savage now. Martin faces them defiantly—

"I am ashamed that that flag—that pirate flag—flies over Germany today. I am—"

With a savage roar the leader takes off his belt and strikes Martin with it. The others crowd in, raining blows on the old man's head. Martin sinks to the ground. Karl tries to go to him, but is thrown back into the crowd. Suddenly the leader himself, looking down on the prostrate figure, motions the mob back. Karl, released, kneels to take his grandfather's head in his arms. "Grandfather! Grandfather!" he calls. There is no answer. The lights fade.

Out of the darkness the tolling of a church bell is heard. Slowly a straggling procession of simple people forms and moves across the scene. Now the curtains have parted. Again we are in the Square of Mapleton. It is packed solidly with Martin Gunther's friends and fellow townsmen, come to pay him their last respects. From out the church a flag-draped coffin is borne. Followed by the Minister, Irma, Brockton, Karl and the others. Now the procession has halted. Samuel Brockton has stepped forward—

BROCKTON—To you, his fellow townspeople, who have come to say farewell to Martin Gunther, I would say that you may bid him farewell not only sorrowfully but also joyously. Martin Gunther lived with tolerance and in peace among his neighbors. He had a deep and simple faith in the goodness of his fellow men, and he died fighting for that which he felt gave meaning to life—for that which made it rich and beautiful—Freedom. He died for the thing he loved—his country.

KARL (*suddenly and hysterically*)—Grandpa! Grandpa! It

wasn't all for nothing! If you could only know that! If you could only know that! (IRMA *puts a comforting hand on his arm.*)

BROCKTON—To Martin Gunther we pay a just homage. For it may be truly said that he was an American. He lived as an American; he died as an American. I can think of no finer epitaph. I see in the life of Martin Gunther, and even in his death, high hope for America. It will go on, this country, so long as we keep alive the thing that Martin Gunther died for. Let us keep this land of ours, which we love so dearly, a land of hope and freedom.

"The funeral procession again starts on its way. As it does so, a single voice starts 'The Star-spangled Banner.' Another joins in, then more and more, until every voice in the Square is uplifted in the national anthem. Men, women, children—their voices mount to a fervid finish."

THE CURTAIN FALLS

# NO TIME FOR COMEDY
## A Comedy in Three Acts

### By S. N. Behrman

THE production of "No Time for Comedy," which occurred in mid-April, stirred considerable interest and for a variety of reasons. It was the fourth production of the Playwrights' Producing Company of which Mr. Behrman is one of five associates. It marked the end of a two-year exile from New York of Katharine Cornell. And it ended a long search for the proper comedienne to play its chief role by the acceptance of an emotional actress who had, during her consistently successful career, had practically no time for comedy herself. Miss Cornell not only assumed her first major comedy part in Mr. Behrman's play, but she also jointly shared honors with the Playwrights' Company in its production.

There was a feeling among the playwrights who were casting it, and I suspect with the dramatist who had written it, that the heroine of "No Time for Comedy" offered a perfect role for a Lynn Fontanne or an Ina Claire. Neither was available. When it happened that Miss Cornell, having read the play, wanted to do it, there were a series of conferences ending in mutual agreement. The actress' success proved a further tribute, not only to the universality of her art, but to the basic versatility of her talent as well.

"Although the grand themes are probably the ones that stimulate her imagination most," wrote Brooks Atkinson in the *Times,* "she does not impose on the worldly ones. She gives a winning performance that makes friends for her and the play."

"No Time for Comedy" was the third success out of its first four ventures scored by the Playwrights' Company—Robert Sherwood's "Abe Lincoln in Illinois," with Raymond Massey, being the first, and Maxwell Anderson's "Knickerbocker Holiday," with Walter Huston, the second. Elmer Rice's fine but unwieldly "American Landscape" was their only failure, and Sidney Howard the only member of the organized quintet who did not have a script ready.

The Esterbrook tower apartment is on the forty-second floor

"NO TIME FOR COMEDY"

ay: Please, dear, don't let's go into the fundamentals tonight.
inda: O.K. No fundamentals.
ay: Every marriage goes through the doldrums sooner or later. We're in for ours. You've got
it tight until we're through it.

(*Laurence Olivier, Katharine Cornell*)

of a smart New York hotel. It is attractively furnished and at the moment of the play's beginning has but a single occupant— Clementine, Linda Esterbrook's colored maid. Clementine, a person of ample proportions and abundant good nature, is at the telephone. She is dialing a number from a list which she has before her. Evidently she has been at this for some time.

The first contact that Clementine makes by phone is with Jack and Charlie's. Is Mr. Esterbrook there? . . . No, Mr. Esterbrook is not there. . . . Will they ask him to call his apartment the moment he comes in? It's important.

Clementine takes another number from the list. It is that of the Ritz-Carlton. Will they connect her with the bar? Is Mr. Esterbrook there? . . . He isn't? . . . Will they have him call his apartment if he should come in? Thanks.

Clementine has got as far as the St. Regis Hotel when Linda interrupts her. Linda is a handsome young woman probably in her early 30's. She is an actress known on the stage as Linda Paige. She is not greatly surprised to learn that Clementine has not had any luck with her calls. Linda thinks perhaps Clementine might try Mr. Esterbrook's studio again, even though he never answers that particular phone. But Clementine has already covered that location. The building superintendent told her Mr. Esterbrook had left about noon.

"You might try the Club," suggests Linda. "Sometimes he feels athletic, goes to the Club for a fast workout and gets stuck at the bar."

No luck at the Club, either. Linda feels that they might as well give up.

"He's a chore, dat man, and dat's a fact," sighs Clementine.

"You understate it," smiles Linda.

"But he's a nacherel honey. I gets hoppin' mad at him. Den when he shows up, I jest loves him."

"Somewhat duplicates my experience."

"Oh, you'se jest plumb crazy about him. Let me jest call Mac's . . ."

"No. The hell with him," decides Linda lightly.

"Dat's the way I feel about my Joe on Saturday nights—the hell with him."

"Nice to have it timed for you like that."

There is a caller. Mr. Philo Smith would like to see Mrs. Esterbrook. Linda lets him come up. Mr. Smith "is between 45 and 50, quiet, keen-faced, well-possessed; he has made his major decisions in life and no longer permits himself to be agitated much about anything."

Mr. Smith's call is a little surprising to Linda, but flattering as well. They had met at a dinner and Linda had felt that she had not made a particularly good impression. Mr. Smith is reassuring. He was, and is, interested. He had not seen Linda's last play, but he hopes to see the next. And when will that be? That, says Linda, depends upon her husband.

"Does he write all your plays?" Mr. Smith would know.

"He's written the last three. I became a star in his first one."

"What does an actress do between plays?"

"Worries about her next. Gets depressed. Thinks she's through. Looks in the mirror and thinks: Better get on with it—have a good time. Has a good time."

Linda envies Mr. Smith. In his work he does not have to wait on anyone. "I can't do anything until I am given something to do," says Linda. "I am a secondary agent; you are primary. I am always telling my husband how lucky he is— for the same reason. But he grouses. He has to wait too, he says—for an idea. When he's between ideas he's very difficult to live with. When he's in the grip of one he's impossible."

The talk drifts toward the intimate and is lightly confessional. "I am a business man," admits Philo. "The most despised variety, a banker. I am also—the final epithet—what they call bourgeois."

"You have great power. There is something glamorous in that—just in the fact of power."

"What looks like power from the outside may be only a complex of strains and stresses from the inside."

"I met your wife for just a second the other night. She is lovely."

"Do you imply she is one of the strains and stresses?"

"Not at all. I don't know in the least what made me speak of her just now."

"Your intuition."

Now it is Linda's turn. "I have an errant husband," says she. "He's between ideas. When he's between ideas he makes an alcoholic tour of the town. It makes him forget he's between ideas. This is a list of his haunts. It's rather a game to track him down."

"What's the next place on your list?"

LINDA—An institution called the Blue Grotto. I'd just, if you don't mind, like to call the Blue Grotto. I have an irre-

sistible conviction that he's there. If he's not at one bar, you
think: Well, I'll catch him at the next. It's like chemin de fer.

PHILO—I can save you the call. He's not at the Blue Grotto.

LINDA (*amazed at his quiet assurance*)—What makes you
say that?

PHILO—You might try—Regent 4-9777.

LINDA—What place is that?

PHILO—It's my house.

LINDA—Really!

PHILO—Yes.

LINDA—Really?

PHILO—Yes.

LINDA—But—I don't quite see how . . .

PHILO—I told you my visit was not impromptu. (*A moment's
pause. She studies him.*)

LINDA—I didn't know that Gay and your wife . . .

PHILO—I don't suggest that they are . . .

LINDA—Well, thank you very much. You relieve me greatly.
I'm delighted to know he isn't on a binge.

PHILO—You are very much in love with him?

LINDA—I am. How do you know?

PHILO—The other night at the Wylers' you let it drop.

LINDA—I talk too much.

PHILO—Not for me.

LINDA (*after a moment*)—But I didn't know that . . . Gay
never met your wife, did he, till that dinner party at the Wylers'?

PHILO—He's known her for several months.

LINDA—Really?

PHILO—Yes.

LINDA—Stupid of him not to tell me. Why ever didn't he tell
me? Your wife is very charming—I should have loved to . . .
She's very young, isn't she?

PHILO—Yes.

LINDA—Is she your only wife? I mean—she isn't the mother
of the boy at Harvard?

PHILO—No.

LINDA—How long have you been married?

PHILO—Five years.

LINDA—Are you very much in love?

PHILO—I shouldn't like to be divorced a second time. It gets
to be undignified.

LINDA—Aren't you an alarmist, Mr. Smith?

PHILO—Do I look like an alarmist?

LINDA—My dear Mr. Smith, I found your wife adorable to look at and very gracious. If my husband is with her now, having a pleasant time, I am delighted. I'd infinitely rather have him with her than lushing at Jack and Charlie's. I shouldn't dream of interrupting him.

PHILO—That's a speech. You don't mean it. I beg of you, Miss Paige, not to be gallant. I dislike gallantry.

Past another series of irrelevancies they return to the more serious matter that concerns them both. It suddenly occurs to Linda that it would have been more seemly if Mr. Smith had first spoken to his wife rather than to her, but Mr. Smith doesn't discuss things with his wife. They are beyond that stage.

"Have you come here to tell me that my husband and your wife are having an affair?" Linda demands, flatly.

"Not at all. In the first place, that is unimportant. In the second place—though perhaps my wife still does not suspect it and I am sure your husband doesn't—the situation is far more dangerous than that. Really I have come here, not to warn you, but through you your husband."

"Of what?"

"Of being discovered."

"I beg your pardon."

"Quite casually my wife made a single remark about your husband. Knowing her as I do, this remark revealed to me in all clarity the danger your husband is in. This remark impelled me to come here to warn you, to warn him. I am interested in only two things in life, Miss Paige—my work and my hobby— and I don't want them disrupted. I don't want the routine of my life disturbed. I don't want divorces or sensations or scandals. I don't want my two children to read about their stepmother in the tabloid papers. I want peace. . . ."

"What was the remark?"

"When she said of your husband that he had latent possibilities as yet unrealized I knew that his position was perilous. My wife has a passion for developing latent powers. When they are not there she invents them. Her first husband was a mediocre but amiable man whom she utterly ruined by persuading him he was first-rate."

"My husband is not mediocre, Mr. Smith. My husband is brilliant."

"Then she will persuade him that he is profound."

Still, Linda cannot take Mrs. Smith seriously as a rival. In fact Mrs. Smith impresses her as being rather fluffy.

"She is a Lorelei with an intellectual patter," insists Mr. Smith.

"Insidious . . ."

"For certain types—fatal."

Now Mr. Smith is going. He hopes Linda will soon be doing a new play that he may come and see. Linda hopes so, too. She even hopes Mr. Smith's wife will inspire her husband to write one.

"If my husband is still at your house when you get home, please don't give him my regards," says Linda. "I don't care to intrude on his personal life unless he chooses to share it with me voluntarily."

"I understand, of course," says Mr. Smith. "My sense of your danger increases by the moment."

Philo Smith has left Linda in something of a state of mind. "She knows that at this minute her husband's unrealized possibilities are being probed by the intellectual Lorelei. She laughs a bit and meditates—she is between laughter and jealousy." Now she has gone to the table with the telephone on it and confirmed the Smith number—Regent 4-9777. Laughingly she adds it to the list of her husband's other haunts. "She looks at her watch. She thinks a moment. She gets up. She is by this time definitely upset. She has to admit to herself that she is angry and jealous. In fact she is very angry and very jealous. She implores God to damn her husband anyway." And now she has dialed a number on the phone and is talking with a Mr. Makepeace Lovell—

"Hella, Pym . . . This is Linda. What are you doing for dinner? . . . Oh, too bad . . . I'm at loose ends . . . Oh, no, don't do that! . . . You mustn't do that . . . Where were you going? . . . Well, it's pretty late to cancel now, I should think. . . . It's half-past seven . . . Don't bother . . . Just called you on the chance . . . No, no, I wouldn't think of it. I'll just go to bed with a book . . . All right, if you feel like it . . . Do what you can . . . Call me back."

Clementine has come in. She is ready to try the few remaining places on the list if Linda wants her to, but Linda isn't interested. "I wonder where dat travelin' man can be," muses Clementine. "I been about tru de list. He must of found a new place."

"I believe he has!" admits Linda.

A moment later Pym Lovell has called. He is free for dinner

and will be by for Linda in twenty minutes. Clementine doesn't think much of Mr. Lovell. For one thing he has a funny name. And for another he talks funny. Nor is she satisfied with Linda's explanation that the funny talk is due to the Oxford influence.

Now there is the sound of a key in the door. It can't be the boss. He never can open the door by himself when he's— But it is. Gaylord Esterbrook himself and cold sober. An attractive, rather boyish young man is "Gay," looking a bit weary but entirely in command of himself.

A second later he has thrown himself full length upon the couch. Sniffing for evidence, Clementine is still bewildered, but Linda is resigned. They will just have to accept Mr. Esterbrook sober and make the best of it.

Gaylord is in a pessimistic mood—such a mood, Linda declares, as he does not usually achieve without having been drunk for three hours and exhilarated for one. He cannot see why she cannot find a play in the stacks of them that are submitted to her. She could, if she would, pick one blind and act in it. The critics would still call her brilliant. As for him, he's through—

"What the hell's the use of kidding myself—I've got nothing to say," moans Gay.

"But you say it charmingly," counters Linda.

GAY—The hell with that. I'm sick of that. It's no time for that.

LINDA—Never was such a time. The world's depressed. This is the moment to be gay, if possible.

GAY—That's like calling for a minuet in a plague town.

LINDA—Why not?

GAY—You live in an aura of exhibitionism or you couldn't ask me a thing like that. Look around you. Pick up a newspaper. Look at the world. And you expect me to go on babbling lightly in a never-never land.

LINDA—You underestimate yourself. Your plays are gay, they're gallant and witty. Occasionally they're touching. What more do you want? Do another—for God's sake—and for mine. I'm a brilliant actress and on account of your gloomy introspections about the state of the world I have to sit around here and twiddle my thumbs and do nothing. What is this mania for under-rating yourself that's caught you lately? Is it bait for contradiction? I find it tiresome. I wish you'd snap out of it!

GAY—I'm written out.

LINDA—Nonsense.

GAY—This vein of mine is an anachronism. It's an overdrawn bank account. It's finished.

LINDA—Every writer feels that once in a while.

GAY—Mixture of glitter and disillusion—post-war—definitely dated.

LINDA—There's no reason to abandon the disillusion; and as for the gaiety, it's more precious—what you can distill of it—than ever. Despair is a last resort—anybody can succumb to that. I read that behind the siege-lines in Madrid the natives laugh and go about their business and see shows and have as good a time as they can. Right under the bombings! What are you grousing about?

GAY—I'm grousing about my indolence in a world that demands action.

LINDA—The world's full of action—too much action.

GAY—If I had any guts I'd go to Spain and join the Loyalists.

LINDA—And be killed? What then? There are enough people dying. Living's the stunt.

GAY—This kind of living's an acquiescence in horror.

LINDA—Not at all. A defiance. You snap your fingers in its face.

GAY—You snap your fingers before the gangster's machine-gun. Very effective! All over the world people are being murdered and tortured and humiliated. Death is rained from the sky on whole populations. I read an article the other day by the British biologist Haldane. He quoted from a famous German scientific journal of biology—what was formerly a journal of biology—an article by a storm-troop captain outlining a technique for the bombing of cities. You bomb the poorer sections because the massing of population makes your hits more effective. The scientific note comes in this way: the wiping out of the large masses will make it easier to lift the biological level in the rest after the city is occupied. At lunch today I saw John Gauthier—just back from the Far East. He told me of the mass execution in Nanking; 40,000 Chinese raked down by machine-guns—not tied or anything—just walked along submissively in front of the fire—never occurred to any of 'em to run away. Look at the glamorous Roto sections in the Sunday papers; next to the Spring fashions you see streetfuls of children in gas-masks looking like monsters. What sort of world is this? *Danse macabre!* And you expect me to sit in my room contriving stage-situations for you to be witty in! Or I go to Holly-

wood and sit in endless conferences agonizing over novel methods
for boy to meet girl. I tell you it's all an irrelevance, an anachronism, a callous acquiescence—

LINDA—I gather the besieged Spaniards love the American
films. If they enjoy seeing our glamor boys pursue our glamor
girls before they're knocked to bits, why grudge them? Why
grudge them a little fun in their last moments? What would
you have them do? Sit in their shelters and contemplate the
eternities? The eternities are a bore. They're inhuman. You
can't take them in. We can only laugh at our plight. That's
what distinguishes us from the animals and from the savages
you're so excited about. They can't laugh.

GAY (*reflectively*)—It's all right to laugh under fire—that's
courage—but not sitting on the side-lines—that's callousness.

LINDA—Sometimes I think that we here laugh less than those
in Europe who are right under the shadow, those on the firing-
line. I was told a charming story the other day about Sigmund
Freud in Vienna. An old man, eighty-two and mortally ill.
One afternoon people walked into his little apartment and cleared
it out—money, gold and silver ornaments, passports, bank-books,
everything. When they left he turned to his family and said:
"Well, those fellows earned more in this one visit than I make
in a year in fees!"

GAY—What does that prove? It's gallant—it's moving—it's
heroic even—but what does it prove?

LINDA—Is all this so new? Twenty years ago there was a war.
Was that an idyll? I don't know much history but I imagine
somewhere in the world there's always been war. There are two
sorts of people, that's all—the brutes and the decent ones—there
have always been and as far as I can see there's no hope of exterminating the brutes.

GAY (*moodily*)—You can keep them from exterminating you.

LINDA—On the other hand, if they exterminate us, so much the
worse for them. They'll kill each other off or they'll bore each
other to death. We've got to have as good a time as we can, be
as gay as we can, as delighted as we can—right under their
horrid snouts.

Linda has mixed him a drink. They have decided to be "gay
and delightful" for the moment. She has come to sit with him
and is cradling his head in her lap. Their talk is light and affectionate. They have paid each other compliments and found happiness in kisses inspired of their affection. And now Gay has
gone blue again—

"God, dearest, I'm blue. I'm low. I'm sunk. I'm bored with myself," he protests.

"Maybe that just means you're bored with me," lightly suggests Linda.

GAY (*looking at her, his hands on her face*)—You, darling—you're beautiful—you're wonderful . . .

LINDA—Nevertheless . . .

GAY—How long have we been married?

LINDA—I'm always telling you to the day. For once, you guess.

GAY—I don't know. Forever . . .

LINDA (*mock wistfulness*)—So long?

GAY—I mean—I don't remember not being married to you. What did I do before?

LINDA—You were married.

GAY—That was just an adolescent miscalculation.

LINDA—Maybe this is a miscalculation of your maturity. . . .

GAY—I get lonely for you walking in the street.

LINDA—You get over it when you come home.

GAY—Let's go out for dinner.

LINDA—I've made a dinner date.

GAY—Oh, have you?

LINDA—I had no means of knowing whether you were coming home or not—I didn't feel like eating alone.

GAY—Who with?

LINDA—Pym Lovell.

GAY—My God!

LINDA—I like Pym. He's a nice boy.

GAY—When you first meet Pym Lovell you think what a precocious boy and when you meet his father you realize it's his father who's precocious. Why don't you dine with his father?

LINDA—Because his father's in London. Dine with us.

GAY—No, thanks. I'll stick around here. (*He gets up, walks away from her, sits on the sofa.*)

LINDA—I'd cancel it but he's given up a date for me.

GAY—I'll stay in and gather my thoughts—both of them.

LINDA—I'll be back early.

GAY—No reason for that. (*A silence.*)

LINDA—Are we washed up, darling?

GAY—What?

LINDA—Are we washed up?

GAY—Please, dear, don't let's go into the fundamentals tonight. I'm in no mood for it.

LINDA—O.K. No fundamentals.

Gay, "feeling that he is being arbitrary, and irritated that she should make him feel arbitrary," tries to explain that every marriage goes through the doldrums sooner or later. Linda will just have to sit by until they are through theirs. Linda is prepared to agree. They love each other. That is admitted. But Gay would be happier if Linda were a little less "all-seeing, a little less all-wise, a little less clairvoyant." And Linda would be less anxious if she knew just what outside interest had suddenly inspired Gay's "abrupt concern over cosmic misery."

Gay would resent the suggestion. His concern has not been abrupt at all, even though he has gone on providing her with "vehicles" in which she has ridden to success—

"If there is anything profoundly irritating, it's the assumption that every general indignation may be traced to a private grievance," protests Gay. "It must be true that women have no capacity to absorb the abstract."

"I can absorb the particular and I'd certainly like to know who she is, this Miss Cosmos. Or Mrs. Maybe Mrs. Cosmos?" answers Linda.

Young Lovell has called and is waiting. Linda prepares to keep her engagement. But she must get in one more word about the play that Gay should be writing. They are much happier when she is working. Let him consider that.

"I'm sorry you're out of sorts," she says. "I love you very much. I'll be back early if you feel like seeing me. Don't mope. Call up somebody and have some fun. You might read one or two of those plays—they'll cheer you up—show you how good you are."

Linda has gone. Gay has begun to pace the room. "He is furious with himself and with her for not having given him more cause to be furious." "Christ Jesus!" he mutters, as he walks. Now he has reached the table with the telephone on it—and the list that Clementine has been following. His surprised eye suddenly comes upon the new number—Regent 4-9777. Now he has rung for Clementine. She comes, all wondering innocence.

"You'd been trying to get me on the phone before I'd got home, hadn't you?" demands Gay.

"Bless yer, boss. Called you ever' place but de police station."

GAY (*picking up the list*)—What about this number?
CLEMENTINE—What number?

GAY—Regent 4-9777.  How did that get on here?

CLEMENTINE—Is dat Mac's?

GAY—It is not Mac's!  You know it's not Mac's!

CLEMENTINE (*looking at the number*)—Whut you so hot about?  Dat ain't my writin'.  Miss Lindy, she must of put dat dere.

GAY—All right.  That's all I wanted to know!

CLEMENTINE—Shall I order you a bite to eat?

GAY—No, thanks.  I'm out.

CLEMENTINE—When'll you be back?

GAY—None of your God-damned business.

CLEMENTINE (*guffawing*)—Lordy, boss, you shu's got lousy manners, but I loves you anyhow!

"She goes out.  Gay is in a cold fury.  He has been spied on, he has been pumped.  His hand reaches for the telephone.  Reading from the slip before him, he dials Regent 4-9777" as the curtain falls.

## ACT II

The upstairs living room in the home of Philo and Amanda Smith is luxuriously furnished.  At the moment Amanda Smith and Gaylord Esterbrook are being served coffee by Robert, "a tall, blond, impeccable butler."

"Amanda is wearing an exquisite house dress—she looks ravishing.  She is quiet, slim and dark; she has what is known as a classic profile, of which she is aware and which she displays unobtrusively, without ever a flourish.  Her voice is gentle, low, musical.  She seldom raises it.  It is a rich voice rather; it vibrates with understanding and intimation.  She lets it vibrate."

Amanda, who is intensely musical, thinks perhaps Gay would like to hear some music.  And he would.  The slow movement of something.  She presses a button and a concealed Capehart obliges with the Schubert Trio.  The effect of the music is to lead Gay into a mildly rhapsodic description of Amanda—

". . . Harmony—that's your strong point, isn't it?" he is saying.  "Harmonious . . . not a discordant note anywhere. . . . All you have to do is sit here, digesting a perfect dinner, absorbing beautiful music through your ears and the bouquet of old brandy through your nostrils and harmony through every pore.  In fact, it's a nice little ivory tower you've got here. . . ."

"I know what you think of me, a spoiled rich woman, a dilettante.  I know that really in your heart you despise me.  It's true

I've built an escape for myself here.  But I don't want you to
yield to it.  Your rebellion against it, your indignation against it
and against me are what, in an odd way, I want to foster.  The
curious thing is . . ."

"What?"

"This indignation, this bitterness are what I miss in your plays.
How is it they don't get into your plays?"

"I suppose the plays are my ivory tower, my escape."

"They shouldn't be.  Not in that sense.  They should express
your struggle—not your escape from the struggle."

"I can't take my struggles seriously.  They're puny."

"That's where you're wrong.  They're the essential thing about
you."

There is, thinks Amanda, a discrepancy between Gay and his
work, and therein lies his dishonesty and the cause of his misery.
Gay combats the thought with the conviction that, forced by his
unconscious, a man expresses himself completely in his work.
Somewhere Gay has read that when a yearner says that he has
wonderful ideas if he could only express them he's a liar, because
he has no ideas to express.

"Nothing in it," declares Amanda, with some finality.  "Expression should be not yourself but an extension of yourself.  Not
what you are but what you might be."

"Living above your means artistically—inflation in the aesthetic
realm—disastrous as it is in the economic—or so the all-wise
columnists tell me," sighs Gay.  And then adds, a little fiercely:
"God damn it, Mandy, how little one knows first-hand—how
much we have to take on faith from what other people tell us.
How little we get down to First Principles.  Wish I had a First
Principle.  Haven't got one—not one measly First Principle."

"The truth is—you coddle yourself," Amanda is saying a moment later.  "You're lazy.  You permit yourself to be diverted
by circumstances."

What circumstances, Gay demands, and after a bit of fencing,
Amanda bravely tells him: "Well, then, the circumstance that you
are married to a very brilliant and brittle actress of comedy and
that you have written your plays not to express yourself but to
express her.  This is the first time really that you have broken
away from that circumstance in your work.  Did you tell her,
by the way?"

No, Gay had not told Linda.  Hadn't the heart to.  Linda has
been waiting six months for him to write a play for her.  He
couldn't bear to tell her there is no part for her in the new one.

She's been reading scripts, too, but hasn't found anything. Gay feels curiously guilty—

"You didn't set out not to write a part for her," Amanda consoles him. "You set out to do a serious play. That there will be no part in it for her is sad. It is also significant."

Gay has finished the first act of the new play. Amanda thinks it superb. With Amanda's encouragement Gay could be frightfully enthused by that first act. But then he suffers most awful fits of depression. He is heartsick about the second act—

"I've got a horrible suspicion that all I've got here is a one-act idea—one of those God-damned trick things that's insoluble once you spring it," Gay says. "Barrie had an idea like that once— a dilemma that couldn't be resolved—"

Amanda thinks "Dilemma" might not be a bad title for the play, and Gay agrees. But where's the play?

"You mustn't let yourself get discouraged," insists Amanda. "I won't let you give this up. I know—I feel—that this departure will mark a turning-point for you—be significant for all your future work—beyond what you realize."

Gay is not to be cheered. His first act curtain is good. He feels that. But from there on the idea's lousy. Amanda refuses to give up. She has fixed him another whiskey and soda. And now she is recapitulating the story for him, thinking it may restore his perspective on the whole thing—

"A distinguished scientist, whose reputation is unimpeachable— Nobel prize winner in chemistry and all that—has an only son who goes off to fight for the Loyalists in the Spanish war," Amanda begins. "The boy is killed. He is blown to bits by a German bomb at Guernica. The father finds this fact unbearable. He cannot reconcile himself to it. He simply cannot endure the fact that his beautiful boy—a poet, generous, gifted and sensitive—should be shattered, unrecognizably mangled, in a Spanish suburb. . . ."

Gay is listening, moodily. . . . "He begins to feel some resolution impending. . . . She observes this; her beautiful voice goes on, hypnotically—"

"Well, he goes on with his work, clings to his work, spends days and nights in his laboratory. One night he falls asleep on his cot for an hour or two—and his son appears to him, his son speaks to him. He wakes up, thinking it a dream, but the communication continues. He begins to investigate psychic phenomena and he becomes convinced that communication with the dead is possible. He is convinced by the messages he gets from

his son.  He writes a book and publishes these communications.
So that this man, this renowned scientist, this arch-skeptic, this
dealer in tested phenomena who has hitherto regarded all such
goings-on as the refuge of the distraught, the stamping ground
for border-cases, marginal hysterics, becomes himself a convert to
mysticism, a Prince of the Occult.  Because of his scientific emi-
nence this conversion becomes an international sensation.  All
over the world, the bruised, the grief-stricken, the disinherited,
those who, finding life unbearable, idealize death, flock to him
for comfort—just as, in another time, these same people followed
Christ."

There is another pause.  Gay sits listening, brooding.  He
swallows another drink.  Amanda continues.  And now the story
takes another turn.  The father delves deeper and deeper into
psychic phenomena, and the more he delves the more convinced
does he become.  Soon people from all over the world seek him
out.  His correspondence is tremendous.  He addresses great
crowds of investigators and converts.

Into one of his meetings in Albert Hall in London a young
man wanders.  "He listens.  Suddenly an area clears in his befuddled brain.  He remembers.  The gray-bearded man on the
platform is his father!"

The young man goes into the street, still bewildered.  He seeks
out his father's home in St. John's wood, recognizes it and realizes that he is himself.  He was not killed in the air-raid.  There
had been an error in identification.  He goes into the house.  The
old family servant does not recognize him.  He is waiting to see
his father when suddenly a horrid misgiving strikes him—

"Words spoken by his father in the meeting come back to him.
It is borne in on him that his father has a new career, that he
is delivering a message to the world and that this message is
based on a single fact—his own death.  Will his father want to
see him?  Dare he be alive?  This resurrection from the grave—
what will it do but expose to the world another in the long list
of the false messiahs. . . . He looks out of the window and sees
the bent old man, his father, his face lined with grief and lit by
faith, being helped out of his car.  Shall he face him?  Shall he
go away?  He hesitates, his hand on the latch of the door—
Curtain!"

For a moment Gay sits absorbed and quiet, the highball glass in
his hand.  Then, in a strained, tense, unnatural voice he calls—
"Mandy . . ."
"Yes, Gay."

"Mandy, darling. . . ."

"Yes, dear."

"I've got it!"

"Gay!"

"I've got it!"

"Gay . . . Gay, darling!"

"I've got the second act, Mandy—you adorable, wonderful creature, I've got it. I just see it. While you were talking—I felt it coming—and I've got it—I see my way out—I've got it!"

"I knew you would."

"You've saved my life, Mandy!"

Gay has taken Amanda into his arms. She is insisting that she has done nothing, but he will not have it. For weeks he has been struggling for this idea, and she has given it to him. Now he will have another drink and go on. Amanda is quivering with curiosity. And Gay returns to the play—

The boy does not leave the house. He waits. He realizes now that the reason the servant has not recognized him is because of the change plastic surgery has wrought. His face is all patched up. The boy waits for his father. When the father comes the boy hands him a letter from his son. It is a poem the boy had written on Spain. The mother and sister are sent for. They are moved to tears as they read the poem.

Amanda, too, is moved to tears. Gay hurries on. The boy realizes "that if his father did recognize him it would be a major tragedy for the father—because his whole life is now centered on this new illusion he has created—this method of communication with the dead—this proof of immortality. . . ."

"They none of them know him!"

"They none of them know him. They none of them want to know him. Ghosts make uncomfortable house guests. He takes tea and talks to them about their darling—describes what he did and said and felt in his last days. With complete sincerity the father shows him messages he has received from the dead boy— messages which confirm the spoken testimony of this miraculous eye-witness—the kind of coincidence made possible by any sensitive and powerful imagination. . . ."

"It's wonderful—Gay, darling—it's wonderful. . . ."

Gay goes on feverishly with his story. The boy stays among his people, "a ghost secure in his nonentity," and then his girl, his sweetheart, penetrates the mystery. By some trick of phrase she recognizes him. And she's fallen in love with another man, whom she is going to marry. It is at that moment of recognition, "when she finds out and the audience knows she's found out—that's my curtain for the second act!" declares the playwright.

Gay is keen in his confidence that he has solved his problem. The second act is wonderful. Amanda is sure of that. The third act will come. Gay is sure of that, too.

"Oh, Mandy, I love you!" he cries, taking her in his arms. "I do love you. You're good for me. You're wonderful for me! I'd never have gotten this idea if not for you."

"Nonsense. Of course you would!"

"It's you started me on this. I'd never have tried it at all, if not for you."

"While you're high on it—why don't you put it down? Go into the library and put it down before you forget it."

"All right. Darling . . ."

And now another problem intrudes. The problem of Linda. Linda knows about them. Gay is sure of that because of the telephone number on her table pad. She probably thinks they are having an affair. As they are not, Amanda is sure Gay's conscience should be quite clear on that point.

"God, what a chore sex is!" wails Gay.

"Some people find it entertaining," Amanda suggests demurely.

"Its penalties are out of all proportion to its delights," insists Gay.

The telephone has rung. It is Pym Lovell. He is with Linda Esterbrook. They had some thought of coming over and Amanda is insistent that they should.

Gay, however, is far from pleased. He resents Linda's spying on him. Linda doesn't have to know where he is. She guesses. Living with her is like living with a medium. And if Linda chooses to spy on him why shouldn't they justify her suspicions?

"The thing about Linda I can stand least is the unconscious censorship she exercises over me!" fumes Gay.

"How?" Amanda would know.

"Something damnable in our relationship which makes it impossible for me to be unfaithful to her."

"You're in love with her."

"What does that mean?"

"You must be."

"It may be because in my first marriage—whatever you may say—how did you find it?"

"What?"

"I don't know whether you cheated.—I did. And it does—

whatever you may say—it does something to the fabric of a marriage, coarsens it, rots it. Does that sound Victorian? Why the hell shouldn't I sound Victorian if I want to?"

"You're in love with her. I've felt that—"

"It's got nothing to do with love. I resent Linda. I resent her lucidity, her clarity, the absence in her of . . . I find myself becoming involved with another woman—I feel myself settling into the worn grooves of seduction—and I never fail—even when she is not there . . . (*His rebellion mounts at the injustice of it.*) even when she doesn't know. I never fail to hear her silent laughter reducing my ardor to platitude."

Philo Smith has opened the door and hesitated about coming in. "He had been told Amanda was dining out. He acts like a stranger, as if the house didn't belong to him."

Philo knows Mr. Esterbrook. Amanda explains that she and Gay had given up the theatre at the last minute. Philo would go through to the library, if they don't mind. He is in need of a few reference books. Shyly he crosses the room and disappears.

"Rich men give themselves a sense of intellectual distinction by buying first editions and collecting pictures," Gay observes, a little cynically. "They feel in their hearts that merely by the act of purchase they've written the books and painted the pictures."

Philo isn't like that, Amanda insists. He really reads his books. A moment later Philo has reappeared with an armful of them. Are they from behind the grilles? Are they first editions?

"I can't understand this passion for first editions," says Gay. "I'd just as soon read a book in the Modern Library. When you have to lock a book behind a grille like a teller in a bank there seems something strained about it."

"Some are unique texts," explains Philo.

"Then they should be in a museum."

"They will be. They are only waiting, as is customary with the relatives of rich men, for me to die."

Amanda would stab her husband with a look, but Gay "feels suddenly a curdled respect for him, but increased antagonism."

"Mandy tells me you write."

"Not exactly. I compile."

"Research must be fascinating. You get a sense of creation without the agony."

"There is something in what you say," admits Philo. "I hope you are not one of those authors who get a sense of creation merely because they agonize. At any rate the library is at your service now for either process—I trust for both."

"Thank you very much. I've never worked in a vault before. I may be outside the grilles now, but one day I'll be behind them. God, I'm getting pompous."

Gay has dashed through the library door. Philo, too, is about to go. Nor can Amanda's announcement that Mrs. Esterbrook is coming detain him. He remembers Mrs. Esterbrook very pleasantly, but right now he is very tired and will go to bed.

Amanda has called Robert and given him instructions to see that Mr. Esterbrook, in the library, is to be provided with hot coffee, and a drink, if he wants it, and is not to be disturbed on any account. When Mrs. Esterbrook and Mr. Lovell arrive Amanda is to be notified. She will be in the library.

And now Linda and Pym have arrived. Pym "is an attractive, wryly humorous young Englishman. He has a distinguished ancestry, a small income and does odd journalism." Linda is in high spirits. She has been home and changed to a lovely evening frock.

Young Lovell has a decidedly strong suspicion that he is being maneuvered to Linda's uses. Linda would reassure him that she has brought him to Amanda's with the thought that she may be altering the course of his whole life. Mandy's the girl for Pym. Mandy would see his latent possibilities and make the most of them. Pym, however, is not in love with Mandy. And he is in love with Linda.

The butler has come to give them Mrs. Smith's message. Mr. Esterbrook is in the library, working, and not to be disturbed. He will tell Mrs. Smith they are there.

This is bad news for Linda. Worse than she thought. Pym must make an excuse to get away. Linda must be left alone with Amanda. . . .

Amanda has arrived, "full of warmth and welcome." It is nice of Linda to come. Amanda had often asked Gay to bring her, but, being a genius, he must have been neglectful.

"Gay and I were sitting here quietly after dinner over coffee and listening to Schubert when he suddenly got an idea. . . . And nothing will do but he must rush into the library and set it down at once," Amanda explains, sweetly.

Her husband had been there, too, but he is such a creature of routine that, although he knew Linda was coming, he just had to go to bed with a book. And now Pym has been struck with an idea, too, and must go somewhere private to put it down. He thinks perhaps he is a genius, too—

"Besides, I asked him not to stay," confesses Linda.

"I should give thirty guineas to overhear your conversation," admits Pym, after having solemnly kissed them both good-by. "I shall pray for you, Mandy, to be victorious."

"What is he chattering about?" demands Amanda.

"I haven't the faintest idea."

"In any event, I shall marry the survivor. If you both die in combat, I shall retire to a nunnery."

With Pym gone the talk turns briefly to him. Linda adores Pym because he is gay and amusing. Amanda likes him too, but feels that he is rather wasting himself. Linda does not feel that waste is necessarily prodigal—

"I'm afraid that must have sounded malicious," Linda explains as she notices Mandy's raised eyebrows; "but what I mean is that if people want to waste themselves, why shouldn't they?"

AMANDA—I'm afraid I don't agree. That goes against my profoundest convictions. . . .

LINDA—Does it?

AMANDA—Yes. I believe that people have an obligation—it sounds priggish to say it—a profound moral obligation to live up to the best in them—to realize themselves to the limit of their capacities.

LINDA—Well, don't you think they do?

AMANDA—Obviously they don't.

LINDA—How can one be sure? If Pym wants to fool around and be agreeable to ladies and write superficial pieces about America for an English tabloid, don't you think perhaps that that's all Pym is meant for?

AMANDA (*with her most ravishing smile*)—I'm afraid I don't.

LINDA—Why does he do it then?

AMANDA—Because he thinks it's smart—environment—early influence—all sorts of reasons. Pym definitely has a father complex!

LINDA—Has he?

AMANDA—Yes. As his father is a great man he has always been obsessed by the fear of never being able to surpass his father. When his father was Pym's age he was already marked for a great career. Failing that, Pym takes refuge in deprecating achievement altogether.

LINDA—Perhaps he deprecates it because he feels unable to

achieve it, father or no father, and perhaps his instinct is justified.
AMANDA (*smiling patiently*)—I'm afraid I don't agree.
LINDA—Can one add a cubit to one's stature? Personally, I
agree with the authority that says you can't.
AMANDA—Oh, but I disagree. I disagree profoundly. People
do it all the time. Great occasions make them, crises make
them, love makes them. One is constantly called upon to extend
oneself beyond one's capacities.
LINDA—Inflation. Is that good?
AMANDA—One must unearth one's latent powers—develop
them.
LINDA—How nice to believe in these psychic trapdoors! Snap
them open, and lo and behold—hidden treasure!
AMANDA—You put it very well.
LINDA—It's all so comforting!
AMANDA—History is full of people who have exceeded their
capacities.
LINDA—No, perhaps they have merely expressed them.
AMANDA—We disagree. We disagree fundamentally. Isn't that
delightful?
LINDA—Great fun!

If Gay is in the library working Linda is interested in knowing
what he is working on. Amanda is pleased to tell her that he
is working on a new play, and quite surprised that Linda did not
know about it. What is the play about? It is about immortality.
And what does Gay know about immortality? Linda would
know. What does anyone know about immortality, except by
intuition, counters Amanda. This play is altogether different
from Gay's other work—"profounder, richer, more provocative."
"Is it profound or is it merely—obscure?" asks Linda.
"Wait till you read it," enthuses Amanda. "He got his second-
act line—in this very room—not more than thirty minutes ago.
And just now—he sent for me in the library—to tell me he'd
got his idea for the third act. He sees it through now—to the
end."
Naturally Linda wonders why Gay has not told her about the
play. Because, Amanda steels herself to report, because there is
no part in it for Linda.
"But that's so silly," protests Linda, after a moment's pause.
"Naturally, I love to act in Gay's plays. I love to speak his
lines. But if he's written a play and it's good I'll be very happy.
I can get another play. I can do a revival. The important thing

for Gay is to keep working. Surely he knows that and that I
know it. Surely . . ."

AMANDA—Perhaps he thought . . .
LINDA—What?
AMANDA—That you wouldn't be sympathetic to *this* play?
LINDA—But why shouldn't I be? I am really hurt.
AMANDA—I'm sorry—I'm terribly sorry—I shouldn't have . . .
LINDA—But you aren't in the least sorry. You are very happy.
You have probably never in your life been so ecstatically happy
as you are at this moment.
AMANDA—But, Mrs. Esterbrook, really . . .
LINDA (*cheerfully*)—Call me Linda! Shall we be honest with
each other? It's enormously difficult, I know. But shall we try?
What harm can it do you possibly? You enjoy inspiring Gay.
That is to say you enjoy sleeping with him. I can understand
that perfectly.
AMANDA—It's not true. I mean we haven't . . . It's not true.
LINDA—If it's not true already then it's imminent. You'll inspire him into it. I hate it and I don't mind telling you I'm
intensely jealous. Sleep with him if you like, but for pity's sake
don't ruin his style. Immortality! What on earth's Gay doing
writing about immortality! Why, when he can write about life
and about love and can make people laugh in the theatre, do
you push him off the deep end to write about immortality which,
at best, is dubious and inhuman? Really, Mandy!
AMANDA (*the cello vibrates slowly and richly*)—We can't
really talk because we have nothing—absolutely nothing—in
common.
LINDA—What about Gay?
AMANDA—In my poor puny way I am only trying—at a time
when life is a *danse macabre* . . .
LINDA—So that's where he got that!
AMANDA (*goes on tranquilly*)—An inferno of hatreds and
perils to bring his work into some relation to the period in which
he is living. I want him to stop fiddling while Rome burns. I
am afraid you are selfish, Linda.
LINDA—Of course I am. What are you?
AMANDA—I feel that Gay might be great. . . .
LINDA—What's the matter with him now?
AMANDA—His work is brilliant but—I have told him so my-
self—trivial.
LINDA—Why? Because he writes comedy? I'd rather have

him write trivial comedy than shallow tragedy. The truth is, Mandy—let's face it—you see yourself as an Influence—with a capital I— What vanity!

AMANDA—I do. I am not ashamed of it. It is the best a woman can be. To inspire a brilliant man to become a great one—I confess it—yes—this would be happiness for me. History is full of women who . . .

LINDA—I doubt it. They may have stimulated men—to réclame, to publicity, to success, yes—but I don't believe in First Aids to greatness. That's something else again. I don't believe in this romantic myth that men need women to inspire them. Oftener I think they succeed in spite of women—just as poets make music of their frustrations. And the same goes for women. They succeed—when they do—without men or in spite of them. I know my own poor case—I lifted myself up by the bootstraps, out of nothing, not for any man, but just to survive, just by obeying some irresistible spring of vitality within myself that wouldn't let me be!

AMANDA—But did you never think—when you were planning some piece of work, some piece of acting—unconsciously perhaps —did you never think: *he* will like this, *he* will like that. . . .

LINDA—No, I didn't. Men were a by-product, part of the dividend of success.

AMANDA—Look at the Curies!

LINDA—Their passion for science made their work inevitable. It's wonderful they found each other for personal reasons. It was a heaven-sent collaboration, but I am very much afraid, Mandy dear, that yours with Gay has a different source.

Amanda is convinced that she and Linda are at different poles, but the discussion doesn't stop there. Linda would know why it is that Amanda doesn't try to inspire her husband. Amanda has tried and failed. Linda would like to know why Amanda always picks "arrivés." Why doesn't she stimulate to greatness someone who is obscure? Amanda feels that the artist who has arrived and who begins to doubt his talent presents the most poignant tragedy of all. Linda would have Amanda honest for once—

"Come on, Mandy, let your hair down," she challenges. "It won't hurt you with Gay. You don't really believe this act of yours, do you? You can't possibly. You've got Gay through this mystic spray you shed about—this rainbow belief in the profundity of his literary powers. . . ."

"How dare you! How dare you!" cries Amanda, near to tears.

"It's all in fun—come clean," Linda persists. "I wish you could teach me the technique, Mandy—all this pastel theorizing —a wonderful dim lighting for sex."

"I understand now—I understand everything now," cries Amanda, hurt to the quick and suddenly throwing all discretion to the winds.

"What do you understand?"

"He's always talking about your clairvoyance, your critical faculty of which he's afraid, your pitiless clarity. . . ."

"My God, Mandy, you make me sound like an X-ray."

"You are! You've shriveled him!"

"Is Gay shriveled? He looked awfully well this afternoon."

"You have—in his soul! You can't understand faith or hope— you can't understand anything but foolish, empty laughter. You're destructive. You're merciless. If I have furnished him with an oasis where he can escape to brood and dream, I'm happy—do you hear—proud and happy!"

Amanda's emotion has mounted. She is near to breaking now. Linda looks at her in frank astonishment—

"It is inconceivable to you that anyone can be sincere," Amanda goes on, excitedly. "You can't believe the truth. You attribute the most sordid motives to everything—"

Amanda is in tears. Linda looks at her "with detachment, with admiration and wonder—"

"And besides all that—you can cry," mutters Linda, half to herself. "I am certainly and completely sunk!"

"You're horrid—you're hateful and horrid—I—I—hate you!"

With this Amanda rushes out of the room into the library. Linda stands for a moment staring after her. "She is unhappy and jealous—but she decides to make the best of it. Standing there alone in Mandy's beautifully lit living room she blows a valedictory kiss toward the library." As Linda turns to leave the library door opens and Gay, dark with anger, comes in.

What has Linda done to Mandy? What has she said to her? Mandy is sobbing! Linda has been spying on Gay. This is the end. Gay can't stand Linda any longer. He has come to loathe her "beautiful superiority." He hates her detachment, her coolness, her destructive critical nature. He is going to marry Mandy.

Linda has met his outburst calmly, even lightly, until now. She is looking at him wonderingly as she says—

LINDA—It's happened then, has it? We're through.

GAY (*definitely*)—Yes.

LINDA—I can't believe it somehow. Why? Why? You're not in love with her. You can't be in love with her. I simply can't believe you're in love with her!

GAY (*the more bitter, as what* LINDA *is saying is true*)—Can't you? Nevertheless, I am—madly in love with her!

LINDA (*wistfully*)—Would you love me, Gay, if I praised you for attributes you haven't got? Would you love me if I could cry? I'll practice.

GAY—Always clear! Always articulate! Sahara-lighting!

LINDA—No vaguely lit oasis, like this that Mandy offers. What can I do? I'm helpless against her. And the worst of it is —she's sincere—as fanatics are sincere. What can I do?

GAY (*bent on hurting her, bent on destroying her*)—I'll tell you what you can do! You can preen yourself! You can revel in your own superiority! You can pity us for this childish emotion which has involved us. You don't need me. You don't need anybody. You're self-sufficient. You can return to the narcissism which satisfies you really, though you pretend it doesn't!

LINDA (*deeply wounded, frightened at his bitterness*)—Gay! Please don't say things like that to me.

GAY (*beyond appeal*)—You can return to gaze at yourself forever in a full-length mirror!

LINDA—Gay—what is it? What's come over you? Gay . . . (*He says nothing, stands there trembling with anger, looking at her with hate in his eyes. A painful and at the same time comforting truth forces itself in on her.*) Gay! You're miserable! You're unhappy! This isn't the ecstasy of new-found love. . . .

GAY (*almost shouting his denial*)—It is!

LINDA—Gay, what is it? Gay . . . (*She is close to him, her arms extended out to him, to embrace him, to shield him.*)

GAY (*in a fury at being discovered—away from her*)—Don't come near me! Leave me alone! Don't question me! I can't bear you, I tell you. Quit spying on me!

Gay has flung himself out through the library door. Again Linda finds herself alone. "An overpowering and thrilling realization comes over her first of all—that Gay is not really in love with Mandy—that he wants only for some obscure reason to hurt her and punish himself. She is filled suddenly with hope, with a kind of joy, with a determination to fight."

Philo Smith comes through the door. Linda is delighted to see him. Her impulsiveness apparently leaves him quite cold, but

she does not care. She rushes on with what she is eager he
should know— Gay and Mandy are engaged! Yet Gay does
not love Mandy! Gay is just trying to hurt her (Linda) and
punish himself—
"He can talk out his misery to her because she isn't his wife,"
Linda is saying. "He can't talk to me because I am. Why is
that, Philo? Why can't married people talk to each other?"

PHILO—Don't ask me metaphysical questions.

LINDA (*all her resources rising to the surface*)—I am going to
fight, Philo. I am going to make a fight. Will you help me?

PHILO—Up to a point.

LINDA—Are you sleepy?

PHILO—If I were I shouldn't have come down. . . .

LINDA—Do you play games?

PHILO—Chess.

LINDA—I should have thought so. . . . I don't unfortunately.
Any other game? There's a backgammon board. Do you play
backgammon?

PHILO—Yes.

LINDA—Will you play backgammon with me? (*With a twinkle
in her eye, gay again.*) You see, Philo, I can't really leave here
tonight without saying good night to my hostess. I'm too well
bred. And I can't possibly interrupt her just now. She and
Gay are collaborating so hard. I mustn't interrupt the creative
process. (*During this she is getting the backgammon board into
place and the chairs.*) At the same time—I don't mind telling
you, Philo—I want a good excuse to outstay her. (*By this time
they are sitting at the backgammon board and have started a
game.*)

PHILO—Very well.

LINDA—Philo, you're a darling.

PHILO—Don't be familiar!

LINDA—How you enjoy being crotchety! You don't fool me,
you know. You don't fool me a bit! (*He says nothing.*)
Mandy says you and I are alike. Two strong characters. I don't
feel my strength just now. My strength is in abeyance. I don't
mind telling you, Philo darling, that I'm just hanging on by the
skin of my teeth! (*He still says nothing. Suddenly she finds
him looking at her, staring at her.*) Am I keeping you up by any
chance?

PHILO (*snapping irritatedly at her*)—You already have. . . .

LINDA (*amazed*)—What?

PHILO (*same voice*)—It's way past my bedtime! Why do you suppose I came downstairs?

LINDA (*her amazement growing that he is aware of her at all and for even a moment as a human being*)—Philo!

PHILO (*severely*)—Your move, Miss Paige!

"She moves abruptly, with only a quick glance at the counters and her eyes returning instantly to his. By this time, though, his gaze is fixed hard on the board." The curtain falls.

## ACT III

It is early afternoon of the following day. In her living room Linda Esterbrook is deep in a huge armchair, and also deep in a manuscript which evidently she has been reading for some time. She is about through with it. This is "the first act and a quick outline of the second and third acts of Gay's play 'Dilemma.' "

As Linda lets the manuscript fall in her lap she is lost in profound thought, and for some moments afterward she is deeply stirred "by an emotion which is undiscoverable until she expresses it later to Gay himself."

Although Linda has told Clementine that she is not home to anyone, the maid must interrupt to announce that a Mrs. Smith is in the lobby below insisting that it is absolutely necessary that she should come up. Clementine would like to deny her; in fact, if this is the Mrs. Smith the boss is playin' around with Clementine would like to "mutilate" her, but Linda orders that Mrs. Smith be allowed to come up.

Gay, it transpires, has not been home all night, but Clementine feels reassured that he has not been with this Mrs. Smith. "She sounded awful blue, de Lord be praised," exults Clementine.

Amanda is a bit tense when she appears. She dislikes greatly to seem so persistent, but she feels that her errand is important. She has come to apologize for her part of the scene the night before, but Linda is sure that she was quite insufferable herself. Amanda has come also to tell Linda something that she finds extremely difficult to tell because of her very sincere affection for her—

"You will end, I am sure, by not letting your affection for me stand in your way," Linda assures her sweetly. "You have such character, Mandy."

"Please don't let's quarrel. I really couldn't bear it," protests Mandy.

"But I am quite sincere, believe me. As I say, I've been thinking and thinking. And you've opened up for me new vistas,
undermined, so to speak, all the major premises on which I've
based my life. Last night I sat in your living room. I was determined to fight you for Gay. And suddenly I began to doubt
myself. I began to see myself as odious, destructive, un-adven-
turous. . . ."

"Linda!"

"I remembered your phrase—the great occasions love makes.
Was I obstructing one of them? You, I thought, were more
audacious than I, more adventurous, more exploratory. Here
you were, willing recklessly to enlist the impossible, admitting no
limitations, like the successful wonder-workers achieving miracles
by ignoring facts. Supposing that in your library Gay was giving birth—with you as *accoucheuse*—to a masterpiece? This, I
thought, might be one of those very great occasions which love
makes, and here was I standing in the way of it. I wavered. I
retreated. I took myself away. . . ."

"I came back to apologize to you. You were gone."

"I came back here and called up Pym. He's a darling, really.
He sat up with me till nearly dawn, holding my hand. I made a
new resolution. . . ."

"Did you?"

"To turn over a new leaf. To praise indiscriminately, to appreciate and inspire and convert myself, if ever I get the chance
again—into a general builder-upper! You see what an influence
you are, Mandy—not only on Gay—on me!"

Linda has not begun to work upon her new plan because Gay
had not put in an appearance the night before. The news is most
disturbing to Mandy. Especially as she, too, has been unable to
get in touch with Gay. Linda, however, has had word from Gay
—he has sent her his play, "Dilemma." She has been reading
that. It is, of course, only one act, with the second and third
acts outlined, but Linda has found it interesting as well as a
little startling, seeing that it is quite out of Gay's normal vein.

Amanda is convinced that "Dilemma" is marvelous. For the
first time in her life she feels justified. She can understand why
Linda, having had no part in the play's inspiration, would not
be able to appreciate it. "What made him send it to you?" wails
Mandy. "He felt always you wouldn't be sympathetic to it."

"I was very much surprised to get it," Linda admits.

"Please don't discourage him."

"Haven't I told you, Mandy, that I am, thanks to you, a reformed character?"

"You'll tell him you like it, won't you, that you think it's wonderful?"

"I'll try."

And now Amanda has come to the real point of her visit. Difficult as it is for her to tell Linda, and especially since Linda has
been so nice about it, she must report that she and Gay are
engaged—

"Linda! I beg you to believe me," begs Amanda. "I struggled
against this! (LINDA *gives her a quick look*.) Only last night—
just before he left—I told him it would be better for us not to
see each other any more—I begged him to see that he was
putting me in a false position—his play was well on the way—
my usefulness over. I entreated him to return to you—and suddenly, out of a clear sky, he asked me to marry him."

Linda pronounces the technique infallible, and understands.
She understands, too, when Amanda returns to worrying about
the absent Gay—

"You must get used to these little disappearances," warns
Linda. "Especially as you're going to marry him. If you find
him elusive as a lover, as a husband, I assure you, he'll be practically non-existent."

Philo Smith is on the phone. That, too, is a surprise to
Amanda, though she was sure that Philo liked Linda. Come to
think of it, Amanda is convinced that Linda and Philo were
probably made for each other.

Again the phone. This time it is Pym Lovell. Linda, answering, is very sweet and apologetic to Pym for having kept him up
all night.

"You're enormously popular, aren't you?" ventures Amanda.

"You exaggerate."

"I envy you. What a radiant career! It must be wonderful
to be an accomplished actress. . . ."

"It has its limitations."

"To appear every night before a thousand people, looking your
best, lit and made up to the best advantage—exquisitely dressed.
What a thrilling profession! Mass-seduction nightly. . . ."

"I, on the other hand, envy your profession—where the seduction is individual," sweetly answers Linda.

"You don't like me, Linda. You don't really like me. I feel
very unhappy about it."

"Let's hope that Gay will compensate you for that!"

Amanda realizes that everything about the divorce is going

to be difficult—unless Linda will help. Linda might persuade Philo— But Linda isn't interested. In fact Linda has no intention of giving up Gay, even though Gay has committed himself—

"It's a commitment I do not recognize," announces Linda, quite firmly. "I mean to stick to Gay—as long as possible. I think I can survive you, Mandy. . . . I mean to try!"

There is the sound of a door slamming as Gay comes in. "He has been drinking but is not in the least drunk. . . . Since we last saw him, Gay has undergone a thousand changes of mood and plan—but one emotion has remained constant: despair in a conviction that has crystallized in him that his play is no good. He would rather die than admit it, but he is here because he can no longer endure the suspense of waiting for Linda's opinion."

The discovery of Amanda with Linda is not pleasing to Gay. Nor is he prepared to make excuses for his failure to get in touch with her. In fact Gay very much resents being "spied on" and says so. Which reduces the startled Amanda to tears, which adds to Gay's irritation.

A moment later Linda leaves them. Now, the cry over and good feeling restored, Gay is ready to announce his plans. Amanda is clinging to him as he tells her that they are going to Spain and that they're going right away. Rather startling news for Amanda. As for the play—it's no good; to hell with it. Nor can the surprised and depressed Amanda alter this conviction. He has come for his things. He will not be long. He will meet Amanda in the cocktail bar downstairs.

Before she goes Amanda must know whatever impelled Gay to send the play to Linda. The fact that Linda has told infuriates him—

"She's a . . ." explodes Gay, controlling himself with an effort. "What did she say about it?"

"Not her dish, she said."

"That's a compliment!"

"Of course it is. The play is wonderful!"

"What the hell do you know about it?" shouts Gay, and Amanda goes dumb with surprise and misery.

Again Gay is contrite and apologetic. He is a brute, but he doesn't mean to be. He is awfully sorry, but—

"There are moments between people when they shouldn't discuss anything, when they shouldn't talk, when to exchange any but the most casual remarks is to run a gauntlet—like yachting in a mined area in war time," he explains.

Let her be a darling and go on down to the cocktail bar and have a drink. Soon he'll join her and they will plan their trip to Spain.

Amanda has gone. Clementine brings drinks on a tray and that is one thing Gay wants. Clementine, a little more impertinent than usual in her criticism of the departed Mrs. Smith, finally so exasperates Gay that he fires her—fires her with force and for good. But Clementine is not moved—

"Lord, boss, the way Miss Lindy feels about you right now you's lucky ef you ain't fired yosef," announces Clementine. "I know Miss Lindy and I'm warnin' you, boss, her patience is jest about run out. . . . You's jes like my man exackly—full o' entertainment but just nacherly no good. I hate to see you go. I'll do what I can fer yer wid Miss Lindy."

Clementine shuffles out. Gay paces the room, drink in hand. "His temper is demoniac but turned in on himself—a mood of terrific self-torture. Everything appears to have dropped away from him—every inner conviction and every objective support. He is lost in chaos!" He picks up the script of the play, examines it for evidence that Linda has read it and puts it back. He is standing, "staring into a vacant future," when Linda comes in.

Linda's spirit is light, with a kind of forced lightness. She inquires for Mandy. She is a little surprised that he should select Spain for a honeymoon. After all the world is wide—

"It's not wide," Gay blurts out, passionately. "It's narrow. It's close. It's a closet. And I've got claustrophobia. I'm shut in it with you. I've got to get away from you. I've got to break your hold on me. God damn it, Linda, I've got to marry Mandy or somebody because it's the only way I can be unfaithful to you!"

"That's the sweetest thing you ever said to me. Thank you, dear!"

"You're being very funny, aren't you?"

"Not at all. I had no idea we were so close. I had no idea we were in a closet together. I really didn't. I thought you were unfaithful to me regularly and with ease. I'm delighted to discover you have to marry to achieve it. It seems drastic—a cumbersome method—but I must say I find it highly flattering. Thank you, darling!"

They have come to the play now and Gay must know what Linda thinks of it. He knows it is terrible, but he must hear it

from her. Linda does not think it terrible. In a way it's fascinating, and the first act is awfully well written. But—

LINDA—I don't quite see the reason for doing a play like this.
What does it accomplish? Whom does it demolish? It tells
bereaved people who cling to a hope in immortality, because without it they must give themselves up to despair, that their hope
is an illusion. Why? Why go out of the way to do it?

GAY—Because the whole notion of immortality is destructive.
A powerful and impotent concept which keeps people from facing
reality. Spiritual dope-taking. People must learn to face the
real world, then perhaps they'll improve it.

LINDA—Who are you to say it's an illusion? How do you
know?

GAY—I say it's healthier—and more practical—to assume that
this is all we have.

LINDA—I don't like your last act. Why does the boy have
to die?

GAY—To save his father's face.

LINDA—I hate ghosts on the stage. People aren't necessarily
interesting because they're dead. You write so delightfully and
charmingly for living people; why write lugubriously for corpses?
I hate ghosts on the stage. Even Hamlet's father. He's quite a
bore. And above all, Gay . . .

GAY (*masochistic*)—Let me hear it—tell me everything. . . .

LINDA—I feel a revulsion from your play altogether because
it is dominated by the idea of death. . . .

GAY—But we are living in an era of death. We are pervaded
by death. Death is our hero, our protagonist—war and death—
death and the fear of death. Death purrs over us, a giant
bombing-plane—its shadow over the green pastures, darkening
the still waters. That is why my play is dominated by it—because we are.

LINDA—What if we are? Why should your play be? One
should keep in one's own mind a little clearing in the jungle of
life. One must laugh.

GAY—It is easy for us here in America to laugh. We have
the illusion of safety.

LINDA—This putting of dead people in plays does them a dis-
service really, strips them of the dignity of their silence. Aesthetic
body-snatching! We know nothing of death and can know nothing. When we describe it even, we are describing life. . . . I beg
of you, Gay, don't throw away your charming gift, don't despise

it. . . . Is it more profound to write of death of which we know
nothing than of life of which we may learn something, which
we can illuminate, if only briefly, with gaiety, with understanding? Gay, I beg of you, don't turn your back on the gift you
have, the instinct you have, the power you have. . . .

Gay knows what is wrong. It isn't the idea of the play but
his failure to pull it off. He knows that his play is "inadequate to its idea." "I wasn't equipped to do it," he says; "indignation without form—passion without authority—I saw exactly
what it would be—not tragic, but thin, petulant."

"But even if it were everything you wanted it to be I still
shouldn't be impressed," says Linda. "I am not impressed by
the dead. Your hero says to the girl that in Spain he learned
how to die and now he will practice what he has learned. . . .
That does not impress me—that he knows how to die— Stoics
and fanatics—the insensitive and the robots. In any case it is
an art that sooner or later Nature imposes on all of us. No, the
difficult thing, the admirable thing is to live. That requires in-
genuity, that requires skill, that requires imagination—that is the
index of civilization—the ability to live, not the ability to die.
Don't spin for me fantasias of death. Imagine for me variations
of life. . . ."

"I shall go to Spain—where death is not a fantasy—but a
reality!"

"But why? Why add to the holocaust? Why?"

"Why? I'll tell you why. Because I'm sick of improvising
these variations on life, as you call them. I'm sick of it! It's a
charming phrase—the kind of phrase I've written so often for
you to say on the stage. What does it mean actually? Skim-
ming for the eternal themes—sex plus what passes for sophistica-
tion. If this thing (*He indicates the manuscript on the table.*)
is no good it's because I haven't actually been through it—I
haven't been through anything. While I'm improvising these
charming variations people are dying—the innocents are being
slaughtered. And in my personal life I improvise variations also
—Mandy! No, I'm sick of it, sick of my work, sick of myself.
I want something clear and outside myself to be enlisted for. I'm
sick of the triviality, sick of ringing changes on what I've already
written, sick of the futility. If necessary, I swear to God, I want
it shot out of myself."

Linda understands now. It is Mandy he is trying to get away
from. "To avoid marrying Mandy you're leaving almost the only

country left in the world where one may still live with some independence, with some decency—not paralyzed by fear. You should stay here, live here where and while it is still possible to live. The more inhuman the rest of the world the more human we. The grosser and more cruel the others the more scrupulous, the more fastidious, the more precisely just and delicate we."

"That reminds me somehow of the aristocrats in the Bastille bowing to each other on the way to the scaffold."

"They are pleasanter to remember than the knitting women."

Linda has a plan. She will get Gay out of his mess with Mandy if he will let her, and without interfering with their friendship. "I know what you are running away from," repeats Linda. "Not only Mandy—but yourself. You feel sterile at the moment and that you'll fill in the vacuum with experience. I know perfectly well that if you had an idea you were excited about, you wouldn't go. . . ."

"But I haven't an idea I'm excited about. I haven't even an idea."

"I have. . . . Why don't you write a play about Mandy and me? Two opposite types of women in the life of a man, an artist, a writer—the builder-upper and the breaker-downer—the critical faculty versus the clinging vine— What Every Woman Knows in reverse."

"I see you allocate to yourself the superior role!"

"Not at all. A lot to be said for Mandy. Great crises, she says, great occasions, great loves make people extend themselves —exceed their capacities—whereas the other woman—I—is skeptical, critical. Stay in your little street, I say, cultivate your garden—don't try to make a forest out of it—if you are a miniaturist remain content with that and don't attempt the Michael Angelo frescoes—a playwright like you for instance caught between the upper and nether millstones of these two points of view . . . Which wins out in the end? Whom does he stay with?"

Almost before he knows it Gay's interest is attacked, first as a technician, then in the building of the story itself. And its climax. Which of the two would win out? Mandy or Linda? The builder-upper or the breaker-downer? And what would be the dramatist's feelings? If the play were a success it would be a toss-up. But if it were a failure? Naturally he'd turn to the builder-upper because he never could forgive the wife for being right.

"Gay, darling. . . . That's charming. You could have a lot

of fun with it. Why don't you try it? Please try it!"

Gay is pondering the theme. "I hate you often because you know more than I do. Mandy massages my ego. It's very pleasant."

"There you are! It's right in your hands. Do it, Gay. Do it for me."

Gay is still doubtful. Who's interested in actresses, anyway? Or playwrights? That's old stuff. People are only interested in themselves.

Philo Smith is announced. Gay is surprised. Whatever can Linda see in that stuffed shirt? But, counters Linda, Philo is not what Gay thinks. Philo is not stuffed, just suppressed. Philo had proposed to Linda the night before, and quite handsomely.

"Well, why don't you marry him?" demands Gay sharply. "Great marriage. The two critical faculties—the two skeptics. You'll produce a lot of question marks!"

Gay has flounced out to do his packing. A moment later Amanda is on the telephone. She is getting a little anxious in the cocktail bar. . . .

Philo Smith is apprehensive. He admits it. He is back to clarify the somewhat fantastic happenings of the night before. But not to take anything back. He had gone to sleep thinking of Linda, and wakened with her still in his thoughts.

"I am glad I told you the truth," Philo is saying. "I came to see you yesterday—not because I wanted to tell you about your husband and Amanda—that meant less than nothing to me. I came because I wanted to see you—to talk to you. I came because, since I saw you at the Wylers', I could not forget you. I couldn't get you out of my mind. I thought: I'll go to see her— I'll talk to her and this will cure me. The effect was the opposite. (*He smiles at her.*) Is this the onslaught of age? Is this senility?"

"You can't expect me to think so," says Linda.

Gay comes dashing back. Being jealous of Philo, "he thinks to conceal this by ignoring him." Gay can't find his passport. Linda thinks if he will look in the little black box, where he throws so many things, he will find it. But before he returns to the search Gay would sound Philo out as to his interest in Spain. Philo is admittedly not greatly interested and Gay resents his unfeeling detachment.

"My dear Mr. Esterbrook," Philo explains, "I am afraid you see the world not as it is but as you would like it to be. The history of the human race is a disgraceful history. Civil war is no new thing in Spain. They fought the Carlist wars for forty years. They kill each other because they want to—that is their pastime. You are like the sentimentalists who divorce the totalitarian rulers from their peoples. No such divorce is possible. They have the governments they want, the governments they deserve. The average man is bloodthirsty and contemptible. The great satirists, Voltaire and Swift, knew that. Your indignation is sentimental and romantic. It is infantile."

Gay is trembling with anger as he turns to Linda. "You were saying exactly the same things in different words just a few minutes ago," he says, quietly. "I see you both cuddled together in a cocoon of detachment. So happy!"

"Gay—Gay, darling . . . please . . ."

But Gay has dashed back into his room. The incident has served to clear Linda's mind. Now she knows that there could not be anything between her and Philo. She will always be waiting for Gay to come back. She is not angry at what Philo had said. He may be as right as he is logical. Certainly she does not despise him, as he fears she does—

"It isn't that," says Linda. "It's that you are independent, you are secure, you are islanded in contempt. Gay, for all his absurd little faults—whatever he may be—Gay feels. He bleeds. You don't bleed, Philo. I must be there, when he wants me, to staunch his grief."

Philo has gone and Clementine has announced that Pym Lovell is on his way. Clementine incidentally would also clear up the mystery of Mr. Gay and his passport. "De boss is ravin' mad, Miss Lindy. An' guess why? 'Cause he kain't find his passport. An' guess why he kain't find his passport? 'Cause I stole it an' it's right here," explains Clementine, fishing the missing document from her ample bosom.

Clementine is very pleased, until Linda takes the passport from her. Then she is depressed. "Don't give it to 'im, Miss Lindy," she begs. "He'll go over there where dey's fightin' an' get hisself into a mess o' trouble." But Linda is firm. . . .

Now Gay has come plunging in again. He is relieved to find Philo gone, but far from pleased to find Pym Lovell replacing him. Gay has come suddenly upon a terrific idea and he is all eagerness to tell it to Linda. Pym is frightfully in the way, and very irritating with his gay patter—

"I beg of you, Pym, don't be light and witty," Gay cautions. "I've written lightweight boys like you so often that I can anticipate your every remark."

Again the telephone has rung, and that is almost too much. "What the hell kind of a house is this?" demands the exasperated Gay. "Linda, I've got to talk to you. It's important."

Linda answers the phone. The impatient Amanda is calling again to know when Gay is coming. Linda suggests that she will send Pym down to hold Amanda's hand while Gay is finishing his packing. Pym is not keen for the assignment, but Linda, with a kiss and a promise to have dinner with him, persuades him to accept it.

"One thing I am grateful to you for, Gay," says Pym as he goes. "It will be so easy to be your successor. I'll seem so charming. Anybody would!"

And now Gay has returned to his great idea for the play. The idea Linda had given him. The idea of the two women—Linda and Mandy—

"But I see beyond it—way beyond it," says Gay excitedly.

"Really? Really? Tell me!" Linda is both excited and very happy.

GAY—I see refracted through it the disturbances and the agony of the times. The whole thing formed in my mind—in there— just now—while I was looking for a shoe . . .

LINDA—I'm glad, dear. I'm awfully glad . . .

GAY—And I've got a hell of a title for it.

LINDA—What?

GAY—"No Time for Comedy!"

LINDA (*considers a moment*)—Not bad!

GAY—I have a feeling—I have a feeling, Linda—if only I can pull it off . . .

LINDA—You can. I am sure you can!

GAY—It'll have some weight, some contemporary value—and a wonderful part for you.

LINDA—Don't worry about that. I'm going to revive "The School for Scandal."

GAY (*angry*)—Who the hell wants to see "The School for Scandal"? What the hell's it got to do with us now?

LINDA—It's a classic. I've always wanted to do it!

GAY—It's an anachronism.

LINDA—This isn't the only moment—just because we're so unfortunate as to be living in it. There were other times—and we should remember them. Here's your passport. (*She hands him passport.*)

GAY—What are you trying to do—get rid of me?

LINDA (*lightly*)—Why not?   (*The telephone rings.* LINDA
*goes to answer it.*)

GAY—Because I love you.   (LINDA *stops on the way to the
telephone. She turns, looks at* GAY, *smiles. She is moved. She
does not want to reveal how deeply she is moved. The telephone rings again.*)

LINDA (*on the telephone*)—Hello . . . Yes . . . Yes . . .
Of course . . . I'll tell him.   (GAY *knows the worst. His body
stiffens with apprehension. He leaps to his feet from the couch.*)
It's Mandy—for you.

GAY (*speech fails him. He makes the inarticulate sounds of
a wounded animal.* LINDA *is inexorable. He starts for the phone,
cannot face it. He implores* LINDA, *he beseeches her, hoarsely.*)
—What? . . . What? . . .

LINDA—You ought to know.  You've got to write it.  It's the
curtain for your last act, isn't it?   (GAY *recognizes the wisdom
of this: that there is nothing to be done; that he must face it.
He goes to the phone. He picks up the receiver. He prepares
to speak. His face is twisted in agony.*)

"No words come from between his parched lips.  Linda sits
watching him, a knowing smile on her face.  In the eternity of
his inarticulateness,

**THE CURTAIN FALLS**

# THE PHILADELPHIA STORY
## A Comedy in Three Acts

### By Philip Barry

IT seemed as though Philip Barry had been away from the theatre for a long time. That was because his last definite success was scored in 1932 with "The Animal Kingdom." But there had been Barry bids for success in 1934, with "The Joyous Season," in 1935 with "Bright Star" and in 1936 with a college play adapted from the script of a pair of graduate co-eds, Eleanor Golden and Eloise Barrangon, called "Spring Dance."

He missed the next two seasons and then last season came forward with two plays, "Here Come the Clowns" and "The Philadelphia Story." The first, as more fully appears in later pages of this issue, also failed of popular success, but "The Philadelphia Story," with the unpredictable Katharine Hepburn as its star, can fairly be described as an old-time Barry hit.

"That there have always been two Philip Barrys writing for our stage has long since been well known to those who have followed Mr. Barry's double life as a dramatist," John Mason Brown wrote in the N. Y. *Evening Post*. "One of these has been the cosmic Mr. Barry who has fought an anguishing, often arresting, inner struggle as he has gone searching for his God in such scripts as 'John,' 'Hotel Universe,' 'The Joyous Season' and this Winter's 'Here Come the Clowns.' The other Mr. Barry, the first to be heard from and the one his largest public has always doted upon, is the dramatist who has shown an extraordinary flair for badinage and written such charming and perceptive tearful comedies as 'You and I,' 'White Wings,' 'Paris Bound,' 'In a Garden,' 'Tomorrow and Tomorrow' and 'The Animal Kingdom.' It is this second Mr. Barry, the smiling one with a lump in his throat, who has tossed off 'The Philadelphia Story.' "

Miss Hepburn's success as the heroine of Mr. Barry's new play was supremely gratifying to that actress' friends. She had had an unhappy experience when she first came back from Hollywood triumphs to star in a much weaker play and before she was quite ready for the test. This was Dorothy Massingham and Murray McDonald's "The Lake," a failure in 1933. She had thought to test her later talents last season with Helen Jerome's "Jane Eyre," but changed her mind following a successful road tour. Her un- qualified success in the Barry play would indicate that the deci- sion was a wise one.

The Seth Lord home is one of the more attractive suburban places near Philadelphia. The sitting room, into which we are ushered at curtain rise in "The Philadelphia Story," "is nicely furnished in grand Victorian style." At the moment Dinah Lord, fifteen and plumpish, "is stretched out on a sofa reading three proof sheets." Tracy Lord Dexter, her sister, twenty-four and attractive, is sitting in an armchair with a leather writing port- folio in her lap, writing "Thank you" notes. There is a litter of gift boxes, indicating an approaching wedding.

Margaret Lord, the girls' forty-seven-year-old mother, pleasant, matronly and formal in the Philadelphia tradition, brings in still more gift packages to be acknowledged by Tracy, whose job grows irksome. She is even having trouble spelling omelet. "O-m-m-e-l-e-t," prompts Margaret. "I thought there was an- other 'l,'" admits Tracy. And then, fortunately, she discovers that it isn't an omelet dish after all, but an old Dutch muffin ear.

Dinah is making herself a bit pestiferous. For one thing she decides that the proof sheets she has been reading, and which she found in her brother Sandy's rooms, "stink," a word that greatly offends her mother. And for another she suddenly reveals that her sister Tracy's first husband, Dexter Haven, is home from wherever he may have been. Dinah has seen his car standing in front of his house. This news is exciting to Mrs. Lord, but not to Tracy—

"I'm not worried, Mother," says Tracy. "The only trouble Mr. C. K. Dexter Haven ever gave me was when he married me. You might say the same for one Seth Lord. If you'd just face it squarely as I did—"

"That will do," protests Margaret. "I will allow none of you to criticize your father."

"What are we expected to do when he treats you—"

"Did you hear me, Tracy?"

"All right, I give up."

"—And in view of this second attempt of yours, it might pay you to remind yourself that neither of us has proved to be a very great success as a wife."

"We just picked the wrong first husbands, that's all."

Tracy is ready to forget both her father and her first husband. She is going to be happy now. George Kittredge, her husband-to-be, is an angel.  A handsome angel, too.  Tracy is convinced that she is a lucky girl.

"I like Dexter," announces Dinah.

"Really?  Why don't you ask him to lunch or something?" suggests Tracy, flirting out of the room.

"She's awfully mean about him, isn't she?" Dinah persists.

"He was rather mean to her," says her mother.

"Did he really sock her?"

"Don't say 'sock,' darling.  'Strike' is quite an ugly enough word."

"But did he really?"

"I'm afraid I don't know the details."

" 'Cruelty and drunkenness,' it said."

"Dinah!"

"It was right in the papers."

"You read too much.  You'll spoil your eyes."

Dinah has returned to her proof sheets and soon these have caused another minor upheaval.  The proofs, it appears, are of a story about Dinah's father that is to be printed in the magazine *Destiny*.  They have been sent to Sandy Lord for approval.

"It's partly about Father's backing three shows for that dancer —what's her name—Tina Mara," reports Dinah in reply to her mother's excited queries; "and his early history—and about the stables—and why he's living in New York instead of with us any more, and—"

"Great Heaven—what on earth can we do?"

"Couldn't Father sue them for liable?"

"But it's true—it's all—"

Realizing her mistake Margaret Lord tries to divert Dinah's thought, but meets with little success.  Dinah has a feeling that the story is simply full of "innundo," especially the part about Tina Mara.  Also she thinks Tracy is pretty mean not to invite her own father to her wedding.  Tracy's hard, that's what she is.

"Not hard," corrects her mother.  "None of my children is that, I hope.  Tracy sets exceptionally high standards for herself, that's all, and although she lives up to them, other people aren't always quite apt to.  If your Uncle Willie Tracy comes in, tell him to wait.  I want to see him."

With her mother gone Dinah has another idea.  In a flash she is at the phone and has called Dexter Haven.  In aother minute she has greeted Dexter with amusing affectation and invited him to come right over to lunch.  She is speaking, Dinah says, for her sister—but perhaps he had better not say anything—

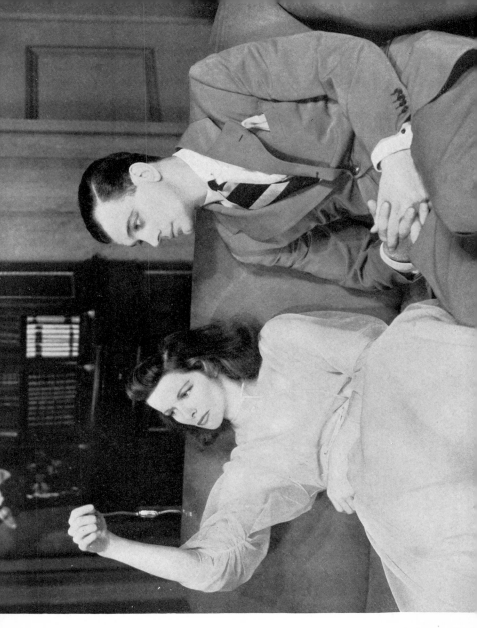

"THE PHILADELPHIA STORY"

Tracy is still puzzled. She can't understand why all the wedding plans are so far along. She doesn't even know whose wrist watch it is that she is wearing. She had found it in her room.

(Katharine Hepburn, Joseph Cotten)

Photo by Vandamm Studio, New York.

Tracy has come back. Dinah quickly hangs up and reports that the call was a wrong number. A moment later Sandy Lord, a pleasing young man of twenty-six, has arrived. He is a popular brother with these sisters, and reports his wife and baby fairly blooming with health in a hospital.

Sandy is also disturbed at the discovery that the family knows of the article about Mr. Lord which is to be printed in *Destiny*. Sidney Kidd is the publisher of *Destiny*, he reports, and he doubts if they could stop the story. But he has a compromise scheme. He has invited Macauley (Mike) Connor, author and special writer, and Elizabeth Imbrie, photographer, of *Destiny*, to stay with the Lords through Tracy's wedding. Connor and Miss Imbrie have been doing a series of stories for the magazine— "Industrial Philadelphia," "Historical Philadelphia" and one that they plan to call "Fashionable Philadelphia." Letting them on the inside for Tracy's wedding will mean a lot to them—

"A trade, eh?" snaps Tracy. "So we're to let them publish the inside story of my wedding in order to keep Father's wretched little affair quiet!"

"It's utterly and completely disgusting," thinks Margaret. And Tracy is frankly angry. "If they've got to have a story, I'll give them a story," she promises. "I'll give them one they can't get through the mails!" But neither her mother nor her brother is much worried by the threat. When it comes to the test Tracy will be acting her best.

"You don't know yet what being under the microscope does to people," warns Sandy. "I felt it a little coming out in the car. It's a funny feeling."

"It's odd how self-conscious we've all become over the worldly possessions that once made us so confident."

"I know; you catch yourself explaining away your dough, the way you would a black eye; you've just run into it in the dark or something."

The absence of Mr. Lord, Sandy admits, is likely to cause some questioning on the part of the reportorial visitors, but he has fixed that by leaving copy for a telegram that is to be sent by Susan Lord, Sandy's wife, just before dinner: "Confined to bed with a cold, unable to attend nuptials, oceans of love, Father."

"It'll come on the telephone and Thomas will take it and you won't have your glasses and he'll read it aloud to you," Sandy instructs his mother.

Uncle Willie Tracy is an early guest. Uncle Willie is 62 and still a little on the gay side. He is one for Sandy to consult about

the *Destiny* story and the possibility of collecting libel in case of
misstatement. Uncle Willie's advice is voluminous but not especially practical.

And now Mike Connor and Liz Imbrie are seen coming down
the hall and this serves to empty the sitting room quickly, save
for the presence of Sandy, left behind as a welcoming committee
of one. Connor is a handsome, well-set-up young man of 30,
Miss Imbrie an alert young redhead of 28, a bit on the ferret
order.

The attitude of the magazine representatives is plainly critical,
which inspires Sandy to suggest a sort of showdown—

"Your approach to your job seems definitely antagonistic,"
Sandy is saying. "I don't think it's fair. I think you ought to
give us a break."

MIKE—It's not a job I asked for.

SANDY—I know it's not. But in spite of it, and in spite of
certain of our regrettable inherited characteristics, we just might
be fairly decent. Why not wait and see?

MIKE—You have quite a style yourself. You're on the *Saturday Evening Post,* did you say?

SANDY—I work for it.

MIKE—Which end?

SANDY—Editorial.

MIKE—I have to tell you, in all honesty, that I'm opposed to
everything you represent.

SANDY—*Destiny* is hardly a radical sheet: What is it you're
doing—boring from within?

MIKE—And I'm not a communist, not by a long shot.

LIZ—Just a small pin-feather in the Left Wing. (MIKE *looks
at her.*) Sorry.

SANDY—Oh, I see; Jeffersonian Democrat?

MIKE—That's more like it.

SANDY—Have you ever seen his house at Monticello? *It's*
quite a place too.

LIZ—"Home Team One; Visitors Nothing"—Is this house very
old, Mr. Lord?

SANDY—No, there are a very few old ones on the Main Line—
The Gatehouse is, of course. Father's grandfather built that for
a summer place when they all lived on Rittenhouse Square.
Father and Mother did this about 1910—the Spring before my
brother Junius was born. He's the eldest. You won't meet him,
he's in the diplomatic service in London.

MIKE (*to* LIZ)—Wouldn't you know?

SANDY—I worked for Sidney Kidd once; what do you make of him?

MIKE (*after a short pause*)—A brilliant editor, and a very wonderful man.

LIZ—Also, our bread and butter.

SANDY—Sorry to have been rude.

MIKE—I suppose you're all opposed to the Administration?

SANDY—The present one? No—as a matter of fact we're Loyalists.

MIKE (*selecting a card from a sheaf taken from his pocket*)—Surprise, surprise. The Research Department didn't give us much data. Your sister's fiancé—George Kittredge—aged 32.—Since last year General Manager Quaker State Coal, in charge of operation.—Is that right?

SANDY—That's right.—And brilliant at it.

MIKE—So I've heard tell. I seem to have read about him first back in '35 or '36.—Up from the bottom, wasn't he?

SANDY—Just exactly—and of the mines.

MIKE—Reorganized the entire works?

SANDY—He did.

MIKE—National hero, new model; makes drooping family incomes to revive again. Anthracite, sweet anthracite.—How did your sister happen to meet him?

SANDY—She and I went up a month ago to look things over.

MIKE—I see. And was it instant?

SANDY—Immediate.

MIKE—Good for her. He must be quite a guy.—Which side of this er—fine aboriginal family does she resemble most, would you say?

SANDY (*rising*)—The histories of both are in the library; I'll get them out for you. I'll also see if I can round up some of the Living Members.

Sandy has gone to round up the family. Mike and Liz are left to their own devices. They are ready to begin a summing up of reactions and to proceed with the laying out of a plan of procedure. Neither is particularly enthusiastic. Mike had tried again to resign but without success. Liz takes the job as she finds it. Mike is still thumbing his research cards, and Liz begins investigating angle shots for pictures. Their comment is intimate and personal.

"C. K. Dexter Haven." Mike thinks a guy with a name like

that just must be different. ˏAnd the new fellow—Kittredge—
"man of the people"—

"From all reports quite a comer," comments Mike. "Political
timber. Poor fellow, I wonder how he fell for it."

"I imagine she's a young lady who knows what she wants when
she wants it."

"The young, rich, rapacious American female—there's no other
country where she exists."

"I'll admit the idea of *her* scares even me.—Would I change
places with her, for all her wealth and beauty? Boy! Just ask
me!"

"I know how I'm going to begin. (*He leans back on the sofa,
closes his eyes, and declaims.*) So much for Historical Philadelphia, so much for Industrial. Now, Gentle Reader, consider
an entire section of American Society which, closely following the
English tradition, lives on the land but in a new sense. It is not
the land that provides the living, it is—"

"You're ahead of yourself. Wait till you do your documenta-
tion."

Mike has thrown himself upon the sofa. He's tired. Let Liz
tell the four footmen to call him in time for lunch.

Dinah has appeared to entertain them. Dinah—real name
Diana, changed by her sister, she explains—would try out her
French and her society manners, but the guests are no more than
politely tolerant. . . .

Tracy Lord is "cool, collected and charming" when she greets
her new guests. She hopes they will stay for her wedding, and
they are sure they would love to.

"People have always been very nice about letting us live our
simple and uneventful little life here unmolested," Tracy is saying, smiling sweetly. "Of course, after my divorce last year—but
I expect that always happens, and is more or less deserved. Dear
Papa was quite angry, though, and swore he'd never let another
reporter inside the gate. He thought some of their methods were
a trifle underhanded. You're a writer, aren't you, Mr. Connor?"

"In a manner of speaking."

"Sandy told me. I've sent for your books. 'Macaulay Connor'— What's the 'Macaulay' for?"

"My father taught English history. I'm Mike to my friends."

"—Of whom you have many, I'm sure. English history has
always fascinated me. Cromwell—Bloody Mary, John the Bastard— Where did he teach? I mean your father—"

"In the High School in South Bend, Indiana."

" 'South Bend'!  It sounds like dancing, doesn't it?"

Tracy is sure Mike must have had a happy childhood in South Bend—even though Mike found it terrific.  And Liz— Is Liz married?  Liz isn't, exactly.  At least she hasn't been for years— not since she left Duluth.  That's news—even to Mike.

And are Liz and Mike living together now?  That's an odd question, bristles Liz.  But Tracy can see nothing odd about it—

"Miss Imbrie—don't you agree that all this marrying and giving in marriage is the damnedest gyp that's ever been put over on an unsuspecting public?"

"Can she be human?"  Mike makes bold to inquire of Liz.

"Please, Mr. Connor!—I asked Miss Imbrie a question."

"No.  The fact is, I don't."

"Good.  Nor do I.  That's why I'm putting my chin out for the second time tomorrow."

Presently George Kittredge arrives and is brought forward by a proud Tracy to meet the new guests.  George is big and blond, with a touch of the importance common to self-made men.  He modestly admits that he is the man who anticipated the workings of the Guffey Coal Act and was pretty generously written up some months back, and Tracy loses no chance to edge in additional endorsements of her true-love's prowess.

"I guess this must be love," Mike concludes.

"Your guess is correct, Mr. Connor," smilingly admits George.

"I'm just his faithful old dog Tray," adds Tracy.

"Give me your paw!" commands George.

"You've got it," laughs Tracy, as he takes her hand and kisses it.

Margaret Lord has arrived and bubbles with hospitality.  She is so glad to know them.  So glad to have them.  So sorry Mr. Lord isn't there.  But he had been detained in New York on business for the lovely Tina Mara.  He'll be down later.

"After lunch Sandy must show you some of the sights," suggests Margaret.  "The model dairy, and the stables, and the chicken farm—and perhaps there'll be time to run you out to some other places on the Main Line—Devins, St. David's,—Bryn Mawr, where my daughter Tracy went to college—"

" 'Til she got bounced out on her—"

"Dinah!"

And now Uncle Willie has reappeared, to be greeted effusively by Tracy as "Papa!  Dear Papa!"

"You angel—to drop everything and get here in time for lunch," enthuses Tracy, to Uncle Willie's complete amazement.

". . . These are our friends Mr. Connor and Miss Imbrie, Father —they're here for the wedding."

Tracy sends Uncle Willie out with her mother to get the latest changes in the wedding plans, and Willie is glad of the escape. And then Dinah's surprise is sprung. Dexter Haven arrives. He has come the short way, he explains, across the fields. And when both Margaret and Uncle Willie suggest that he go right back home he politely avoids the issue. He has been invited to lunch, and right nice it was of Tracy to include him—

"Of course I intended to come anyway," Dexter is saying, after Tracy has asked the butler to lay an extra place, "but it did make it pleasanter— Hello, Kittredge!"

"How are you, Haven?" responds the slightly depressed George.

DEXTER—What's the matter? You don't look as well as when I last saw you. (*He pats his arm sympathetically*.) Poor fellow—I know just how you feel. (*He turns to* TRACY, *gazes at her fondly*.) Redhead—isn't she in the pink, though!—*You* don't look old enough to marry anyone, even for the first time—you never did! She needs trouble to mature her, Kittredge. Give her lots of it.

GEORGE—I'm afraid she can't count on me for that.

DEXTER—No? Too bad— Sometimes, for your own sake, I think you should have stuck to me longer, Red.

TRACY—I thought it was for life, but the nice Judge gave me a full pardon.

DEXTER—That's the kind of talk I like to hear; no bitterness, no recrimination—just a good quick left to the jaw.

GEORGE—Very funny.

THOMAS (*in door*)—Luncheon is served, Madam.

MARGARET—Thank you, Thomas.

UNCLE WILLIE—I don't suppose a man ever had a better or finer family. (*Takes* MARGARET's *arm*.) I wake in the night and say to myself—Seth, you lucky dog. What have you done to deserve it?

MARGARET (*as they go*)—And what *have* you?

TRACY—Do you mind if I go in with Mr. Connor, Miss Imbrie?

LIZ—Why, not in the least.

SANDY (*taking* LIZ' *arm*)—Sandy's your boy.

TRACY—Because I think he's such an interesting man.

GEORGE—Come on, Dinah, I draw you, I guess.

DINAH (*taking* DEXTER's *arm also*)—Dexter—

DEXTER—Isn't snatching one of my girls enough, you cad?

GEORGE—You're a very bright fellow, Haven. I'll hire you.

TRACY (*to* MIKE)—That's very insulting—but consistently interesting. We must talk more. (*They are all up near door right when* SETH LORD *comes into the room.*)

SETH—I don't know how welcome I am, but after Sandy's note, I thought the least I could do was to—

TRACY—Uncle Willie! Please go on in to lunch, everyone. I want a word with Uncle Willie. (*They go on in—*DEXTER *turning back with a faint smile at* TRACY; *she crosses down left facing* SETH.)

SETH—Well, Daughter?

TRACY—Well?

SETH—Still Justice, with her shining sword—eh? Who's on the spot?

TRACY—We are; thanks to you—Uncle Willie.

The curtain falls.

## ACT II

The Lords' porch is more like a room than a porch. There are entrances from both the sitting room and the library. Now, in the early evening, with a clear sky, a bank of geraniums shielding one end of it and porch settees and chairs scattered about, the porch is particularly attractive.

Mike and Liz have found it and are taking advantage of the quiet and of the absent family. Mike is adding to his notes. Liz is reloading her camera. Occasionally they stop to compare notes. Mike has decided that Kittredge is quite a fellow. Liz isn't so sure. Mike can't understand why Tracy fell for Kittredge, and there are other things about Tracy that puzzle him a good deal. Mike's being puzzled, however, doesn't puzzle Liz. This new interest—

"Yeh? I get you, but you're wrong," insists Mike. "You couldn't be wronger. Women like that bore the pants off me—"

"For a writer you use your figures of speech most ineptly," says Liz.

Uncle Willie and Seth Lord have strolled in from the garden. Soon they are followed by Sandy with a warning that they had better be dressing for dinner. And now they are all gone except Mike, who is gathering up his research cards. He is about to follow the others when Tracy calls to him. She has come from the house with a book. It is one of the Connor books and her eyes are bright with the wonder she has found in it.

"I've been reading these stories. They're so damned beautiful!" says Tracy.

"You like? Thanks—"

"Why, Connor, they're almost poetry."

"Don't fool yourself—they *are!*"

"I can't make you out at all, now."

"Really? I thought I was easy."

"So did I, but you're not. You talk so big and tough—and then you write like this. Which is which?"

"I guess I'm both."

"No—I believe you put the toughness on to save your skin."

One story called "With the Rich and Mighty" is the one that Tracy likes best. Mike had that title from an old Spanish peasant's proverb: "With the Rich and Mighty Always a Little Patience." Why, when he can do things like that, does he do anything else, Tracy would like to know. Because, explains Mike, he has to earn a living. True, people buy books—but that one Tracy has been reading represented two solid years' work and netted Connor something less than six hundred dollars.

"Miss Imbrie is in somewhat the same fix," explains Mike. "She is a born painter, and might be an important one. But Miss Imbrie must eat. Also, she prefers a roof over her head to being constantly out in the rain and snow."

"Food and a roof—food and a roof—"

"Those charming essentials."

"Listen! I've got an idea!" Tracy is deeply in earnest as she faces Mike. "Listen! I've got the most marvelous little house in Unionville. It's up on a hill, with a view that would knock you silly. I'm never there except in the hunting season, and not much then, and I'd be so happy to know it was of some use to someone. There's a brook and a small lake, no size really, and a patch of woods, and in any kind of weather, it's the— And look at that sky now, will you! Suddenly it's clear as clear! It's going to be fine tomorrow! It's going to be fair! Good for you, God!"

There isn't time to consider Tracy's idea further. Dexter Haven is coming and she would prefer not to be left alone with him, if Mike doesn't mind standing by. She would like to add, however, that she'd never think of coming to the cottage except when she was especially sent for. Mike has time to protest, a little untactfully, that the idea of artists having a patron has more or less gone out—which plainly hurts Tracy—

Then Dexter is there with a small picture wrapped in tissue. He is in a gay, even a flippant mood, and Tracy is irritated by the intrusion. If he would like to do something for her he can get the hell out of there— But Dexter can't see that. He has a feeling that Tracy really needs him. At this personal turn Mike is again of a mind to move on, but again Tracy asks him to stay. "Do stay, Mr. Connor," Dexter adds. "As a writer this ought to be right up your street."

"Don't miss a word," warns Tracy.

DEXTER—Honestly, you never looked better in your life; you're getting a fine tawny look—

TRACY—Oh, we're going to talk about me, are we? Goody.

DEXTER—It's astonishing what money can do for people, don't you agree, Mr. Connor? Not too much, you know—just more than enough. Particularly for girls. Look at Tracy. There's never been a blow that hasn't been softened for her. There'll never be one that won't be softened— Why, it even changed her shape—she was a dumpy little thing originally.

TRACY—Only as it happens, I'm not interested in myself, for the moment. What interests me now, is what, if any, your real point is.

DEXTER—Not interested in yourself! My dear, you're fascinated! You're far and away your favorite person in the world.

TRACY—Dexter, in case you don't know it—I—

DEXTER—Shall I go on—?

TRACY—Oh, yes, please do, by all means—

DEXTER—Of course, she is kindness itself, Mr. Connor—

TRACY—Itself, Mr. Connor.

DEXTER—She is generous to a fault—that is, except to other people's faults. For instance, she never had the slightest sympathy toward nor understanding of what used to be known as my deep and gorgeous thirst.

TRACY—That was your problem.

DEXTER—It was the problem of a young man in exceptionally high spirits; who drank to slow down that damned engine he'd found nothing yet to do with— I refer to my mind. You took on that problem with me when you took me— You were no helpmate there, Tracy. You were a scold.

TRACY—It was disgusting. It made you so unattractive.

DEXTER—A weakness sure, and strength is her religion, Mr. Connor. She is a goddess, without patience for any kind of human imperfection. And when I gradually discovered that my relation to her was expected to be not that of a loving husband and a good companion, but— (*He turns away from her.*) Oh—

never mind—

TRACY—Say it!

DEXTER—But that of a kind of high priest to a virgin goddess, then my drinks grew more frequent and deeper in hue, that's all.

TRACY—I never considered you as that, nor myself!

DEXTER—You did without knowing it. And the night that *you* got drunk on champagne, and climbed out on the roof and stood there naked, with your arms out to the moon, wailing like a banshee— (MIKE *slides off the chaise and into the room left.*)

TRACY—I told you I never had the slightest recollection of doing any such thing!

DEXTER—I know; you drew a blank. You wanted to— Mr. Connor, what would you say in the case of— (*Turns and sees* CONNOR *gone.*)

TRACY—He's a reporter, incidentally. He's doing us for *Destiny*.

DEXTER—Sandy told me. A pity we can't supply photographs of you on the roof.

Tracy would dismiss all memory of the roof incident as trivial and childish. Dexter is convinced that it was important and revealing. Tracy would remind him that they were married for nearly a year. But marriage, Dexter insists, being an affair of the spirit and not of the flesh, doesn't change so true a case as Tracy represents.

Neither can Dexter understand what convinced Tracy that she should marry Kittredge. It can't be love, as Tracy insists. And it offends his vanity to think of anyone who was even remotely his wife marrying one so obviously beneath her in mind and imagination. Kittredge may be all that is claimed for him—but he's still not the man for Tracy. And let her realize that once she has taken him she will have to stick. "He'll give you no out as I did," Dexter warns.

"I won't require one," answers Tracy, with spirit.

DEXTER—I suppose you'd still be attractive to any man of spirit, though. There's something engaging about it, this virgin goddess business, something more challenging to the male than the more obvious charms.

TRACY—Really?

DEXTER—Oh, yes! We're very vain, you know— "This citadel can and shall be taken—and I'm just the boy to do it."

TRACY—You seem quite contemptuous of me all of a sudden.

DEXTER—Not of you, Red, never of you.  You could be the damndest finest woman on this earth.  If I'm contemptuous of anything, it's of something in you you either can't help, or make no attempt to; your so-called "strength"—your prejudice against weakness—your blank intolerance—

TRACY—Is that all?

DEXTER—That's the gist of it; because you'll never be a first-class woman or a first-class human being, till you have learned to have some small regard for human frailty.  It's a pity your own foot can't slip a little sometime—but no, your sense of inner divinity won't allow it.  The goddess must and shall remain intact.—You know, I think there are more of you around than people realize.  You're a special class of American Female now—the absolute tops, my dear.

TRACY—Damn your soul, Dext, if you say another—!

DEXTER—I'm through, Tracy—for the moment I've said my say.


George Kittredge has come from the living room.  He would, if he could, treat his discovery of this twosome lightly and with great good humor, but the going, for George, is a little heavy. Dexter, calling Tracy's attention to the little wedding present he has brought her as he passes the table, leaves them.

The present is a picture of the *True Love,* a boat which Dexter had designed and practically built, and which he and Tracy sailed up and down the coast of Maine the year they were married.  It was a lovely boat, and the memory it arouses is holding for an instant.  Then Tracy would put it out of sight and out of mind with a bitter "the hell with it."

And now it is George's turn to wonder whatever it was that could have induced Tracy to marry Dexter.  Tracy thinks it probably was a sort of hangover from their childhood, seeing that they grew up together.  George is going to change everything. He is going to build Tracy an ivory tower all her own.  Theirs is going to be a grand life together, with no wasting time on unimportant people.  Nor does the thought that Tracy had once belonged to Dexter bother George.  He doesn't choose to believe that Dexter ever possessed her—ever was her lord and master—

"I don't believe he ever was—not really.  I don't believe anyone ever was, or ever will be.  That's the wonderful thing about you, Tracy."

"What?  How?—"  She is looking at him, startled.

"You're like some marvelous, distant— Oh, queen, I guess.

You're so cool and fine and—and always so much your own.
That's the wonderful *you* in you—that no one can ever really
possess—that no one can touch, hardly. It's—it's a kind of beautiful purity, Tracy, that's the only word for it."

"George—" Tracy is really frightened now.

"Oh, it's grand, Tracy—it's just grand! Everyone feels it
about you. It's what I first worshiped you for, Tracy, from
afar."

"George, listen—"

"First, now, and always! (*He leans toward her.*) Only from
a little nearer, now—oh, darling!"

"I don't want to be worshiped! I want to be loved!"

"You're that, too. You're that all right."

"I mean really loved."

"But that goes without saying, Tracy."

"And now it's you—who doesn't see what *I* mean."

The butler has brought a tray of drinks, and Margaret has
come to warn them again that there is not much time if they are
to dress for the party. Tracy's father is with Margaret. He is
a little worried that Tracy is apparently taking things to heart
so. She will wear herself out. He is worried, too, about the
spectacle he thinks they are all making of themselves before the
young people who are representing *Destiny*.

At that suggestion Tracy's resentment flares again. Who is
responsible for the situation as it stands? She would like to know.
That, insists Mr. Lord, is beside the point. He is convinced the
least they can do is to inform Mr. Connor and Miss Imbrie that
the family is quite aware of their purpose in being there. Tracy
is prepared to tell them, but her father thinks it would be better
for the statement to come from the titular head of the family—

"Of course—inasmuch as you let us in for it in the first place,"
snaps Tracy.

"Do keep that note out of your voice, Tracy," begs Mr. Lord.
"It's most unattractive."

TRACY—Oh? How does Miss Mara talk? Or does she purr?

MARGARET—Tracy!

SETH—It's all right, Margaret.

TRACY—Sweet and low, I suppose. Dulcet. Very ladylike.—
You've got a fine right, you have—after the way you've treated
Mother—after the way you've treated us all—a magnificent right
you've got to come back here in your best county manner and
strike attitudes and make stands and criticize my fiancé and

give orders and mess things up generally just as if you'd done—
MARGARET—Stop it instantly, Tracy!
TRACY—I can't help it. It's sickening.—As if he'd done nothing at all!
MARGARET—It is no concern of yours. If it concerns anyone, it concerns—well, actually, I don't know whom it concerns except your father.
SETH—That's very wise of you, Margaret. What most wives won't seem to realize is that their husband's philandering—particularly the middle-aged kind—has nothing whatever to do with them.
TRACY—Oh? Then what has it to do with?
SETH—A reluctance to grow old, I think. I suppose the best mainstay a man can have as he gets along in years is a daughter—the right kind of daughter.
TRACY—That's interesting, to say the least.
SETH—One who loves him blindly—as no good wife ever should, of course. One for whom he can do no wrong—
TRACY—How sweet.
SETH—I'm talking seriously about something I've thought out thoroughly. I've had to. I think a devoted young daughter gives a man the illusion that youth is still his.
TRACY—Very important, I suppose.
SETH—Very—and without her, he's inclined to go in search of it again, because it's as precious to him as it is to any woman.—But with a girl of his own full of warmth for him, full of foolish, unquestioning, uncritical affection—
TRACY—None of which I've got—
SETH—None. You have a good mind, a pretty face and a disciplined body that does what you tell it. You have more wealth than any of us, thanks to one grandfather's name, and another's red hair, and a shameless play for both of them since about age three. In fact—
TRACY—I never! I loved them!
SETH—In fact, you have everything it takes to make a lovely woman except the one essential—an understanding heart. Without it, you might just as well be made of bronze.
TRACY—That's an awful thing to say to anyone.
SETH—Indeed it is.
TRACY—So I'm to blame for Tina Mara, am I?
SETH—If any blame attaches, to some extent I expect you are.
TRACY—You coward.
SETH—No.—But better to be one than a prig—and a perennial

spinster, however many marriages.

MARGARET—Seth! That's too much.

SETH—I'm afraid it's not enough.

TRACY (*staring at him*)—Wha-what did you say I was?

SETH—Do you want me to repeat it?

MARGARET—Seth—now I understand a great deal that I didn't.

SETH—It's all past now, Margaret. It has been for some time. Forgive me. You won't have to again. *I* understand a lot more than I did, as well.

TRACY—"A prig and a—" You mean—you mean you think I think I'm some kind of virgin goddess or something?

SETH—If your ego wishes to call it that, yes— Also, you've been talking like a jealous woman.

TRACY—A—? What's the matter with everyone all at once, anyhow?

They have gathered for the start to dinner. Seth Lord has tried to tell Mr. Connor and Miss Imbrie that their reason for being there is known to the family, and been met with a similar statement that was trembling as a confession on the tongues of the visitors. And then the butler arrives with a telegram. Sandy would stop it now, but Margaret has already asked Thomas to read it and he does—

" 'Most frightfully sorry will not be able to get down for the wedding as am confined to my bed with everything wrong. Baby better. It was only gas. Love, Father.' Is there any answer, Madam?"

"No, Thomas—none in this world," sighs Margaret.

"Now do you understand, Mr. Connor?" blandly questions Seth.

"I think we do."

"It's wonderful," insists Liz. "Lord only knows where we go from here."

SANDY (*excitedly*)—To Aunt Geneva's— Come on, everybody.

DINAH—My first party, and about time.

UNCLE WILLIE (*over* LIZ' *shoulder*)—Who'll come in my little car with me?

MARGARET (*cutting in*)—Seth and Dinah and I—Sandy, will you bring Miss Imbrie and Mr. Connor?

SANDY—Like a shot.

DINAH—The evening is pregnant with possibilities. (MAR-GARET *takes her gently by shoulders and ushers her out the door.* UNCLE WILLIE *starts out but hesitates long enough in passing to pinch* Liz' *behind, then goes out innocently.*)

Liz (*jumping forward*)—Ouch!

Seth (*to* Liz)—What was it?

Liz—N-Nothing. (*To* Sandy.) You know, I felt exactly as if I had been pinched.

Mike (*to* Tracy)—Aren't you coming?

Tracy—I'll follow along with George.

Mike—What's the matter with Tracy?

Tracy—You tell *me*, will you?

Mike (*looking at her intently*)—Damn if I know. I'd like to.

Tracy—Well, if you happen to find out—

Mike—I'll tell you. Sure.

Tracy—And remember, Mike—"With the Rich and Mighty"—

Mike—"Always a Little Patience"—Yes, I will.

Tracy—Do that. Please do.

"He goes out. She stands for a second then comes to table, pours a glass of champagne and drinks. Starts to pour a second as the curtain falls."

Several hours have intervened. Enough to cover a party at Aunt Geneva's. We are back on the porch at the Lords'. Sandy is just coming from the house with two bottles of champagne and a bottle of milk, with glasses to match. Tracy is waiting for him. Apparently these two have been hatching a conspiracy. Mike Connor, it appears, has been doing a good deal of raving, mostly about Mr. Sidney Kidd, the publisher, and Tracy has hit upon an idea that may cause Mr. Kidd to think differently about publishing the story of the Lords.

Sandy is to add what he knows about Kidd to what Connor has told them and write it for the *Post*. "Sidney Kidd—his habits—his habitat—and how to hunt him," is Tracy's idea. Sandy thinks he can do it in three thousand words if he can keep awake. And then he will offer to swap his story on Kidd for Connor's piece on the Lords. But Mike and Liz mustn't suspect.

For the present it is Sandy's idea that Tracy has had enough champagne. She mustn't boast that wine never affects her, just because she never takes it. It's unlucky to boast.

"George will spank!" warns brother.

"I could spank George for the way he behaved," answers Tracy.

"He had a right to be sore. You and Mike disappeared for two hours, at least."

"You were along."

"All the same, tongues were wagging like tails, George said—"

"George wanted to leave sharp at twelve—how could we?"

"They need a lot of sleep, those big fellows."

"They must.—Then at one, with Father and Mother and Dinah.—Then at two, then at three—every hour on the hour. We fought like wolves in the car coming home."

"I hope you explained."

"Certainly not. He should have known. He was extremely rude. You'd have thought I had been out with Dexter, or something.—(*A pause.*)—I wonder where Dext was? I half expected him to— I don't like the look behind Dexter's eyes, Sandy. It makes me sad."

"Don't be sad, Tracy."

"Oh, Sandy, if you knew how I envy you and Sue that darling fat creature you've just produced—"

"You'll probably have four or five of your own any day now."

"Six! Oh, I hope—I do hope—I hope I'm good for something besides knocking out golf balls and putting horses over fences."

Tracy is worried about George. Perhaps she *has* been mean to him. She admits she's in a mood. So many things she always thought were terribly important are—and the other way around. She probably had better be going to bed, but she doesn't want to. "I feel too delicious! Sandy, I feel just elegant," says Tracy.

Tracy has started into the house when she sees Mike coming. Mike is in fine fettle and lyrically explosive—

" 'No lightweight is balding, battlebrowed Sidney Kidd; no mean displacement, his: for windy bias, bicarbonate,' " recites Mike, drinking his wine and pausing to look quizzically at the glass. "This is funny stuff. I'm used to whisky. Whisky is a clap on the back. Champagne, entwining arms. . . ."

"I'll tell you what: let's all have a quick swim to brighten us up," Tracy is saying. "Go get Liz, Sandy." She has taken off her bracelet and two rings and laid them on the table.

"Not me; it's too cold this early," protests Sandy.

"It's the best hour of the day," insists Tracy. "Dexter and I always swam after parties."

"I haven't got any bathing suit," ventures Mike.

"But we won't need any. It's just ourselves," persists Tracy.

Mike thinks perhaps they had better continue to dip into the champagne instead. Sandy goes to get Liz, anyway. Mike and Tracy face each other. They find each other interesting, and looking fine. It was a grand party. "The prettiest sight in this fine, pretty world is the Privileged Class enjoying its privileges," admits Mike. ". . . Consider, Gentle Reader, they toil not, neither do they spin."

"Oh, yes, they do! They spin in circles!" corrects Tracy, illustrating with a spin that seats her finally down on the floor, where Mike joins her. Suddenly Mike is quite serious—

"Tracy, you can't marry that guy."

"George?—I'm going to. Why not?"

"I don't know; I'd have thought I'd be for it, but somehow you just don't seem to match up."

"Then the fault's with me."

"Maybe so; all the same you can't do it."

"No? Come around about noon tomorrow—I mean today."

They are pretty critical of each other now. Mike, says Tracy, is the worst kind of a snob—an intellectual snob. Tracy, insists Mike, is quite a girl. Tracy is sure Mike would find quite a number like her if he were to get around more. Mike hasn't the least interest in investigating Tracy's "Upper Clahss."

"You're just a mass of prejudices, aren't you? You've so much thought and so little feeling, Professor." There is the suggestion of a sneer.

"Oh, I am, am I?"

"Yes, you are, are you!" She stops and turns on him. "Your damned intolerance infuriates me. I should think, of all people, a writer would need tolerance. The fact is, you'll never—you can't be a first-rate writer or a first-rate human being until you learn to have some small regard for— (*Suddenly she stops. Her eyes widen, remembering. She turns from him.*) Aren't the geraniums pretty, Professor? Is it not a handsome day that begins?"

Mike doesn't like being called "professor," but Tracy gives little heed to his objection. What do classes matter, she would know, except for the people in them? George comes from the lower classes, Dexter from the upper—and there's a great deal to be said for Dexter, too.

"There aren't any rules about human beings, that's all," declares Tracy, pouring herself another glass of champagne. "You're teaching me things, Professor. This is new to me; thanks, I am beholden to you."

"There's magnificence in you, Tracy. I'm telling you," Mike is saying, a moment later.

"I'm—! Now I'm getting self-conscious again," admits Tracy. "I—it's funny—Mike, let's—"

"What?"

TRACY—I don't know—go up, I guess. It's late.

MIKE—A magnificence that comes out of your eyes, that's in

your voice, in the way you stand there, in the way you walk. You're lit from within, bright, bright, bright.  There are fires banked down in you, hearth-fires and holocausts—

TRACY (*turning to him*)—You—I don't seem to you—made of bronze, then—

MIKE—You're made of flesh and blood—that's the blank, unholy surprise of it.  You're the golden girl.  Tracy, full of love and warmth and delight—  What the hell's this?  You've got tears in your eyes.

TRACY—Shut up, shut up!—Oh, Mike—keep talking—keep talking!  *Talk,* will you?

MIKE—I've stopped.

TRACY (*deliberately, harshly; after a long moment looking at each other*)—Why?  Has your mind taken hold again, dear Professor?

MIKE—You think so?

TRACY—Yes, Professor.

MIKE—A good thing, don't you agree?

TRACY—No, Professor.

MIKE—Drop that Professor—you hear me?

TRACY—Yes, Professor.

MIKE—That's really all I am to you, is it?

TRACY—Of course, Professor.

MIKE—Are you sure?

TRACY (*looking up at him*)—Why, why, yes—yes, of course, Profes—  (*His kiss stops the word.  The kiss is taken and returned.  After it she exclaims softly.*)  Golly!  (*She gazes at him wonderingly, then raises her face to receive another.  Then she stands in his arms, her cheek against his breast, amazement in her eyes.*)  Golly Moses!

MIKE—Tracy, dear—

TRACY—Mr. Connor—Mr. Connor—

MIKE—Let me tell you something—

TRACY—No, don't—  All of a sudden I've got the shakes.

MIKE—I have, too.

TRACY—What *is* it?

MIKE—It must be something like love.

TRACY—No, no!  It mustn't be.  It can't—

MIKE—Why?  Would it be inconvenient?

TRACY—Terribly.  Anyway, it isn't.  I know it's not.  Oh, Mike, I'm a bad girl—

MIKE—Not you.

TRACY—We're out of our minds.

MIKE—Right into our hearts.

TRACY—That ought to have music.

MIKE—It has, hasn't it?—Tracy, you lovely—

Mike would kiss her again, but she breaks the embrace. There is the sound of someone coming. Tracy looks quickly toward the door and then back to Mike. "It's—it's not far to the pool," she whispers. "It's only over the lawn, in the birch-grove— it'll be lovely now."

"Come on—" He is holding out his hand.

"Oh, it's as—it's as if my insteps—were melting away— What is it? Have I—have I got feet of clay, or something?"

"—Quick—here they are!" He has taken her hand and hurried her down the steps and into the garden.

Sandy and Liz have come from the house. Sandy has acquired a collection of snapshots from Liz—all of Sidney Kidd. Some the publisher knew were being taken and some he didn't. She will let Sandy have three of them if he promises not to reproduce them without permission.

With a little more pleading Sandy is also in possession of Mr. Kidd's "sacred private number"—"the one by the bed and the bathtub"—and a moment later he is at the phone—

"Hello? . . . Mr. Kidd? This is Alexander Lord. . . . No. I'm in Philadelphia. . . . Yes, I know it is. . . . It's early here, too. Look, Mr. Kidd, I think you'd better get over here as fast as you can. What? I'm sorry to have to tell you, Sir, but Connor has had an accident—yes, pretty bad—he had a pretty bad fall—a pretty bad fall.—No, it's his heart we're worried about now.—Yes, I'm afraid so; he keeps talking about you, calling you names—I mean calling your name. How's that?—No, the eleven o'clock's time enough. We don't expect him to regain consciousness much before then."

With a promise to meet Mr. Kidd at North Philadelphia, Sandy's telephoning is completed. "Kidd doesn't want any publicity," he reports. Liz isn't worried. Mike's only hope was to get fired, anyway. Is Liz in love with Mike? Sandy would know. Liz is evasive on the subject. She wouldn't want to get in Mike's way, but if another girl should come along—

"Oh, I'd just scratch her eyes out, I guess—that is, unless she was going to marry someone else the next day."

Dexter Haven has joined them, but soon Liz has gone to bed and Sandy has excused himself on the plea that he has a little job of blackmailing to look after. Now George Kittredge strolls in.  He is looking for Tracy.  She didn't answer her phone.  He would like to know why Dexter is there, but he gets little satisfaction from the query.

Now Dexter has found Tracy's rings and bracelet on the table. With a quick glance in the direction of the swimming pool he turns to advise George to go to bed.  George, however, is staying right there.

A moment later Mike appears from the garden.  He is carrying Tracy in his arms.  They are both wearing bathrobes and slippers, and "there is a jumble of clothes, his and hers, slung over Mike's shoulder."  As Mike stops, Tracy stirs sleepily in his arms and mumbles in a low voice—

"Take me upstairs, Mike—"

"Yes, dear.  Here we go."

With an amazed "What the—" George starts for Mike.  Dexter steps quickly between them—

"Now easy.  Easy, old man!  (*To* MIKE.)  She's not hurt?"

MIKE—No.  She's just—

TRACY (*murmuring dreamily*)—Not wounded, Sire—but dead.

GEORGE—She—she hasn't any clothes on!

TRACY (*into* MIKE'S *shoulder*)—Not a stitch—it's delicious.

MIKE—It seems the minute she hit the water, the wine—

DEXTER (*glancing at* GEORGE)—A likely story, Connor.

MIKE—What did you say?

DEXTER—I said, a likely story!

MIKE—Listen: if—!

DEXTER—You'll come down again directly?

MIKE—Yes, if you want.

DEXTER—I want.

TRACY (*lifting her head limply*)—Hello, Dexter.  Hello, George.  (*She crooks her head around and looks vaguely up at* MIKE.)  Hello, Mike.

DEXTER (*opening the door drapery*)—The second door on the right at the top of the stairs.  Mind you don't wake Dinah.

TRACY—My feet are of clay—made of clay—did you know it? (*She drops her head again and tightens her arms around* MIKE'S *neck.*)  Goo'nigh'—sleep well, little man.

DEXTER (*calling off*)—Look out for Dinah.  How are the mighty fallen!—But if I know Tracy—and I know her very well —she'll remember very little of this.  For the second time in her life, she may draw quite a tidy blank.—Of course she may worry, though—

GEORGE—Good God!

DEXTER (*turning on him swiftly*)—You believe it, then?

GEORGE—Believe what?

DEXTER—The—er—the implications, of what you've seen, let's say.

GEORGE—What else is there to believe?

DEXTER—Why, I suppose that's entirely up to you.

GEORGE—I've got eyes, and I've got imagination, haven't I?

DEXTER—I don't know. Have you?

GEORGE—So you pretend not to believe it—

DEXTER—Yes, I pretend not to.

GEORGE—Then you don't know women.

DEXTER—Possibly not.

GEORGE—You're a blind fool!

DEXTER—Oh, quite possibly!

GEORGE—God!

DEXTER (*studying him*)—You won't be too hard on her, will you?

GEORGE—I'll make up my own mind what I'll be!

DEXTER—But we're all only human, you know.

GEORGE—You—all of you—with your damned sophisticated ideas!

DEXTER—Isn't it hell?

MIKE (*coming swiftly through the door*)—Well?

GEORGE (*advancing on him*)—Why, you lowdown—!

DEXTER (*quickly*)—The lady is my wife, Mr. Connor. (*His uppercut to* MIKE'S *jaw sends him across the porch and to the floor.*)

GEORGE—You!—What right have—

DEXTER—A husband's, till tomorrow, Kittredge.

GEORGE—I'll make up my mind, all right!

DEXTER (*after* GEORGE *is gone*)—Are you okay, old man?

MIKE (*nursing his chin*)—Listen: if you think—!

DEXTER—I know—I'm sorry. But I thought I'd better hit you before he did. (MAC, *the night watchman, comes along.*) Hello, Mac. How are you?

MAC—Hello, Dexter! Anything wrong?

DEXTER—Not a thing, Mac.—Just as quiet as a church.

MAC—Who is it? (*He looks at* MIKE.) Hell! I thought it might be Kittredge.

DEXTER—We can't have everything, Mac.

The curtain falls.

## ACT III

The Lords' sitting room is full of bright sunshine late next morning. There are also flowers everywhere. And Uncle Willie, in morning coat, fancy waistcoat and Ascot, is having a time interrogating Thomas the butler, in an effort to straighten out a situation that bothers him.

It is about Dinah. Dinah, it appears, had telephoned Uncle Willie at an absurdly early hour to rush over immediately, ahead of Aunt Geneva, because of something that had occurred. Uncle Willie would like to know what has happened.

Thomas doesn't know, but Dinah, who soon appears, knows and as soon as Thomas has gone takes Uncle Willie into a corner to tell him. It is about Tracy. Something has to be done and Dinah has no one but Uncle Willie to turn to. Uncle Willie, she feels, would be just as well pleased if Tracy did not marry George. So would Dinah. And she thinks she knows a way to stop it.

"Suppose she all of a sudden developed an illikit passion for someone?" suggests Dinah.

"Can you arrange it?"

"It doesn't need to be. It is already."

"Ah? Since when?"

"Last night—and well into the morning."

"You surprise me, Dinah."

"Imagine what *I* was—and just imagine what *George* would be."

"And—er—the object of this—er—illikit passion—"

"Let him be nameless." Uncle Willie is exasperated at this turn. "Only tell me, should I tell George—it's getting late."

Dexter Haven has come into the room from the porch and is standing by the piano.

"Maybe he'll want to marry her anyway," suggests Uncle Willie.

"But she can't! If she marries anyone, it's got to be Mr. Connor!"

"Connor? Why Connor?"

"She's just got to, that's all."

Dexter has stepped forward. This, he thinks, is a pretty big order to swing at this late date. And it is just possible that Dinah has only dreamed what she believes she has seen and heard.

When Tracy comes from the house she is wearing the dress she expects to be married in. She is a little puzzled. She thinks she must have had a touch of the sun the day before. It is so hard for her to get her eyes open. She wishes Dexter would go home, but Dexter is intent on staying—at least until Tracy's eyes are open.

Tracy is still puzzled. She can't understand why all the wedding plans are so far along. She doesn't even know whose wrist watch it is that she is wearing. She had found it in her room. Besides she had been robbed. The rings and bracelet she had worn to Aunt Geneva's party have been stolen. When Dexter produces the jewelry she is more puzzled than ever. Dexter wasn't at the party. At least she didn't think he was. Still, there were a lot of people—

"You should have taken a quick swim to shake them off," suggests Dexter. "There's nothing like a swim after a late night."

"A swim!" repeats Tracy. And now her eyes are open wide.

At Dexter's suggestion he and Uncle Willie have gone to investigate eye-openers in the pantry. And, suggests Dexter, as he is leaving, it might be a good idea if Dinah were to tell Tracy her dream, in case conversation lags.

Dinah is a little worried by the suggestion. Worried, too, by the thought of Tracy's marrying and going as far away as Wilkes-Barre to live. And finally she gets around to the dream—

"I thought I got up and went over to the window and looked out across the lawn," reports Dinah, with some suggestion of suppressed excitement. "And guess what I thought I saw coming over out of the woods?"

TRACY—I haven't the faintest idea. A skunk?

DINAH—Well, sort of— It was Mr. Connor.

TRACY—Mr. Connor?

DINAH—Yes—with both arms full of something. And guess what it turned out to be?

TRACY—What?

DINAH—You, and some clothes. Wasn't it funny? It was sort of like as if you were coming from the pool—

TRACY—The pool!—I'm going crazy. I'm standing here solidly on my own two hands going crazy. And then what?

DINAH—Then I thought I heard something outside in the hall, and I went and opened my door a crack and there he was, still coming along with you, puffing like a steam engine. His wind can't be very good.

TRACY—And then what—

DINAH—And you were sort of crooning—

TRACY—I never crooned in my life!

DINAH—I guess it just sort of sounded like you were.  Then he—guess what?

TRACY—I couldn't possibly.

DINAH—Then he just sailed right into your room with you and —and that scared me so, that I just flew back to bed—or thought I did—and pulled the covers up over my head and laid there shaking and thinking: If that's the way it is, why doesn't she marry him instead of old George?  And then I must have fallen even faster asleep, because the next thing I knew it was eight o'clock, and the typewriter still going.

TRACY—Sandy—typewriter—

DINAH—So in a minute I got up and went to your door and peeked in, to make sure you were all right and—guess what?

TRACY—What?

DINAH—You were.  He was gone by then.

TRACY—Gone?  Of course he was gone—he was never there!

DINAH—I know, Tracy.

TRACY—Well!  I should hope you did!

DINAH—I'm certainly glad I do, because if I didn't and if in a little while I heard Dr. Parsons saying, "If anyone knows any just cause or reason why these two should not be united in holy matrimony"—I just wouldn't know what to do.  And it was all only a dream.

TRACY—Naturally!

DINAH—I know.  Dexter said so, straight off.

TRACY—Dexter!

DINAH—Yes.—He said—

TRACY—You told Dexter all that?

DINAH—Not a word.  Not one single word.  But you know how quick he is.

TRACY—Dinah Lord—you little fiend; how can you—?

Seth Lord is there, worried because Dinah isn't dressed; eager to assure Tracy that everything is fine, or should be, between them.  And Mike has come to add his good morning and, after the others have gone, to try to straighten certain things out in his mind so far as Tracy is concerned.  It isn't the story he is writing that he wants to talk about.  He doubts if that will ever be finished, now that he has found himself getting so damned tolerant he has lost his angle.  The mark on his chin?  Oh, he thinks he must have got that when he stuck his chin out too far.

Mostly he would like to know if Tracy is all right.  After all it was a flock of wine that they had put away, and he is greatly relieved to hear that she is feeling fine—

"I—I guess we're lucky both to have such good heads," suggests Tracy.

"Yes, I guess."

TRACY—It must be awful for people who—you know—get up and make speeches or—or try to start a fight—or, you know—misbehave in general.

MIKE—It certainly must.

TRACY—It must be—some sort of hidden weakness coming out.

MIKE—Weakness?  I'm not so sure of that.

TRACY—Anyhow, I had a simply wonderful evening.  I hope you enjoyed it too.

MIKE—I enjoyed the last part of it.

TRACY—Really?  Why—why especially the last?

MIKE—Are you asking me, Tracy?

TRACY—Oh, you mean the swim!  We did swim, and so forth, didn't we?

MIKE—We swam, and so forth.

TRACY (*turning to him suddenly*)—Mike—

MIKE—You darling, darling girl—

TRACY—Mike!

MIKE—What can I say to you?  Tell me, darling—

TRACY—Not anything—don't say anything.  And especially not "Darling."

MIKE—Never in this world will I ever forget you.

TRACY—Not anything, I said.

MIKE—You're going to go through with it, then—

TRACY—Through with what?

MIKE—The wedding.

TRACY—Why—why shouldn't I?

MIKE—Well, you see, I've made a funny discovery: that in spite of the fact that someone's up from the bottom, he may be quite a heel.  And that even though someone else's born to the purple, he still may be quite a guy.  Hell—I'm only saying what you said last night!

TRACY—I said a lot of things last night, it seems.

MIKE—All right, no dice.  But understand: also no regrets about last night.

TRACY—Why should I have?

MIKE—That's it!  That's the stuff; you're wonderful.  You're aces, Tracy.

TRACY—You don't know what I mean!  I'm asking you—tell me straight out—tell me the reason why I should have!  (*But she cannot finish.  Her head drops.*)  No—don't—  Just tell me—what time is it?

MIKE (*glancing at his wrist*)—What's happened to my wrist watch?

TRACY (*without turning*)—Why?  Is it broken?

MIKE—It's gone.  I've lost it somewhere.

TRACY (*after a moment*)—I can't tell you how extremely sorry I am to hear that.

MIKE—Oh, well.  I'd always just as soon not know the time.

TRACY (*her back to him*)—There on the table—

MIKE—What is?  (*Finds his watch.*)  Well, for the love of—! Who found it?  I'll give a reward, or something.

TRACY—I don't think any reward will be expected.

Dexter has come to bring Tracy a little medicine that Uncle Willie had concocted in the pantry.  A stinger—guaranteed to remove the sting.  And that reminds Tracy—it is an awful thing she has done to Dexter.  Dexter thinks she must be thinking of George.  That reminds Tracy of something else.  She must talk with George before the wedding—bad luck or not.  She calls George on the phone, and discovers that he has already sent her a note.  So George had known about everything, too!

"I'm such an unholy mess of a girl," Tracy is saying.  And a second later she adds, "But never in all my life—not if I live to be one hundred—will I ever forget the way you tried to—to stand me on my feet again this morning."

"You—you're in grand shape," protests Dexter.

And what about his wedding present?  Did Tracy like that? Tracy did.  She was a good boat, the *True Love*.  And is. Tracy is quite distressed at the thought of Dexter's selling her. Or of building himself a *True Love II*.  If he should ever call another boat that she would blow both him and the boat right out of the water—

"*I'll* tell you what you can call it, if you like—" suggests Tracy, a little bitterly.  "In fond remembrance of me."

"What?"

"The *Easy Virtue*."

"Tray, I'll be damned if I'll have you thinking such things of yourself," protests Dexter, going to her.

"What would you like me to think?"

"I don't know.  But I do know that virtue, so-called, is no matter of a single misstep or two."

"You don't think so?"

"I know so.  It's something inherent, it's something regardless of anything."

"Like hell it is."

"You're wrong.  The occasional misdeeds are often as good for a person as—as the more persistent virtues.—That is, if the person is there.  Maybe you haven't committed enough, Tray. Maybe this is your coming of age."

"I don't know.—Oh, I don't know anything any more."

"That sounds very hopeful.  That's just fine, Tray."

The butler has brought in the note Tracy had sent for.  He would like to report, also, that the guests are practically all in the house, some of them standing, and that the help sends Miss Tracy its best wishes.  Then Sandy rushes in, considerably excited.  He has just had a talk with Sidney Kidd, the publisher, and shown him the profile he has sat up all night to write.

Things are getting near the deadline, but Tracy is more excited by George's note.  The others have gone and she is reading it to Dexter—

" 'My dear Tracy: Your conduct last night was so shocking to my ideals of womanhood, that my attitude toward you and the prospects of a happy and useful life together, has changed materially.  Your, to me, totally unexpected breach of common decency, not to mention the moral aspect—' "

George Kittredge comes in from the porch, but Tracy goes on reading.  "It's only a letter from a friend," she explains.  " '—not to mention the moral aspect, certainly entitled me to a full explanation, before going through with our proposed marriage.  In the light of day, I am sure that you will agree with me.  Otherwise, with profound regrets and all best wishes, yours very sincerely—'

"Yes, George, I quite agree with you—in the light of day or the dark of night, for richer, for poorer, for better, for worse, in sickness and in health—and thank you so very much for your good wishes at this time."

"That's all you've got to say?"

"What else?  I wish for your sake, as well as mine, I had an explanation.  But unfortunately I've none.  You'd better just say 'Good riddance,' George."

"It isn't easy, you know."

"I don't see why."

George feels that he had a right to be angry, and Tracy agrees that he had. She wishes she could explain to him that, despite everything that happened, she feels more of a person, but George admits it would be a little difficult. Finally Mike, who has been standing by with Liz, offers his bit—

"Kittredge, it just might interest you to know that the so-called 'affair' consisted of exactly two kisses and one rather late swim. . . . All of which I thoroughly enjoyed, and the memory of which I wouldn't part with for anything. . . . After which I accompanied her to her room, deposited her on her bed, and promptly returned to you two on the porch—as you will doubtless remember."

"Doubtless without a doubt," puts in Dexter.

"You mean to say that was all there was to it?"

"I do."

Tracy, who has been looking at Mike in astonishment, suddenly turns on him and demands: "Why? Was I so damned unattractive—so distant, so forbidding, or something, that—?"

"This is fine talk, too," protests George.

"I'm asking a question!" repeats Tracy.

"You were extremely attractive," admits Mike, softly; "and as for distant and forbidding, on the contrary. But you were also somewhat the worse—or the better—for wine, and there are rules about that, damn it."

"Thank you, Mike. I think men are wonderful," says Tracy.

George is greatly relieved, too. But that does not thrill Tracy in the least. If her "wonderful, marvelous, beautiful virtue" is still intact, it is no thanks to her, she assures him. "It's purely by courtesy of the gentleman from South Bend."

Of course, if Tracy admits that she may have had a little too much champagne, and is willing to promise that she will never touch the stuff again, George is ready to forgive and forget. But not Tracy. She admits that she does not think any too well of herself, but she had hoped that George at least would think the best of her.

"You're too good for me, George," admits Tracy. "You're a hundred times too good. And I'd make you most unhappy, most— That is, I'd do my best to."

With which admission George storms out. He is disgusted with Tracy and Dexter and their "whole rotten class."

And now what to do? There's the crowd waiting. There's the license. There are even two licenses, seeing Dexter had never destroyed the one he got the time he and Tracy eloped to Maryland, because it was quicker.

There is also Mike, who is ready, even eager, to marry Tracy, if she'll have him. Tracy doesn't think Liz would like that, but she is "most beholden" to Mike.

Tracy's father and mother also come to her support. They have met George in the hall and know what has happened. Mr. Lord is prepared to make any announcement Tracy would approve. Tracy, however, decides to make her own announcement. She is through with being helped out of scrapes. She throws the doors into the living room open, and faces her guests—

"I'm—I'm—hello! Good morning—I'm—that is to say—I'm terribly sorry to have kept you waiting, but—but there's been a little hitch in the proceedings. I've made a terrible fool of myself—which isn't unusual—and my fiancé—my fiancé—my fiancé, that was, that is—he thinks we'd better call it a day—and I quite agree with him."

There is a pause. Tracy, growing a little flustered, appeals suddenly to Dexter for help. A second later she is repeating lines that Dexter gives to her—

" 'Two years ago you were invited to a wedding in this house and I did you out of it by eloping to Maryland.' "

Again she turns to Dexter, but Dexter is busy borrowing a wedding ring from Margaret, and slipping it to Mike. Now he goes again to Tracy's aid—

" 'Which was very bad manners. But I hope to make it up to you by going beautifully through with it now—as originally—and most beautifully planned.' Because there's something awfully nice about a wedding, I don't know—they're gay, and attractive, and I've always wanted one—"

Dexter has gone back to Mike. "I'd like you to be my best man, if you will," he says, "because I think you're one hell of a guy." He goes back to Tracy and her speech—

"—And so if you'll just keep your seats a minute—That's all." She has closed the doors and turned to Dexter. The others have gone out.

"Dexter—are you sure?" Tracy is saying.

"Not in the least; but I'll risk it—will you?"

TRACY—You bet! and you didn't do it just to soften the blow?
DEXTER—No, Tray.
TRACY—Nor to save my face?
DEXTER—It's a nice little face.
TRACY—Oh—I'll be yare now—I'll promise to be yare!

DEXTER—Be whatever you like, you're my Redhead.—All set?

TRACY—All set! Oh, how did this ever happen? (*Gets hat from chair, looking in mirror, puts on hat.*)

SETH—Don't enquire.—Go on, Dinah, tell Mr. Dutton to start the music.

DINAH—I did it—I did it all. (*Exits.*)

SETH—Daughter—

TRACY (*over to* SETH)—I love you, Father.

SETH—And I love you, Daughter.

TRACY—Never in my life have I been so full of love before. (*The wedding march starts.*)

DEXTER—See you soon, Red—

TRACY—See you soon, Dext— (DEXTER *and* MIKE *exit.*) How do I look?

SETH—Like a queen—like a goddess.

TRACY—Do you know how I feel?

SETH—How?

TRACY—Like a human—like a human being.

SETH— —and is that all right?

TRACY (*taking his arm and slowly starting down toward door*) —All right? Oh, Father, it's Heaven!

THE CURTAIN FALLS

# THE WHITE STEED

## A Comedy in Three Acts

### By Paul Vincent Carroll

NOT often does a playwright blessed with a popular hit on the occasion of his emergence from obscurity score a second success his next time out. This happened to Paul Vincent Carroll, currently the outstanding dramatist of the Irish race. Last year he gave us "Shadow and Substance," which, with Sir Cedric Hardwicke, ran through the better part of the season. This season he came with "The White Steed" which approached though it did not duplicate that record.

There was divergence of opinion when it came to a question of comparing the plays, which is always a little foolish and quite unfair in establishing critical evaluations. Every play is written to stand or fall by its own faults and virtues. Those who thought "Shadow and Substance" the more sensitively spiritual and the more broadly appealing of the two were entirely justified in that conclusion. And those who contend that "The White Steed" has more body and is the more effective drama in a strictly theatre sense are also generously supplied with convincing evidence.

"The White Steed" is based on one of the folk legends of Ireland. This would be the story of Niam, the goddess who, meeting Ossian, the son of Finn, lifted him to a place beside her on her white steed and carried him away to the Land of Eternal Youth, where for three hundred years they lived an idyllic love life. Then Ossian became restless and Niam sent him back to the land for which he hungered, warning him not to dismount or touch the earth. But Ossian, disgusted with the efforts of the little black men whom he found infesting the land of his birth, sought to impress them with his strength, fell from the white steed and, on touching the earth, withered away with his accumulated years.

"When I try to make a play that will not have merely substance but beauty also," Mr. Carroll has written, "I go back invariably into the folk tales, into the wisdom of the old days, and having relearned something of simplicity I return to survey with much greater detachment the present maelstrom of egotism, perse-

249

cution and cruelty."

And so we have the story of a modern Niam who would lift up a vacillating Ossian of this day and make a man of him. The reception of "The White Steed" was generously favorable and with the popular Irish comedian, Barry Fitzgerald, playing the lead, the play ran through the better part of the season.

The sitting room of Canon Matt Lavelle's Parochial House in the seaside village of Lorcan, County Louth, Ireland, is a comfortable room, though the furniture and fittings are commonplace and typical. "A sideboard, a bookcase, a few heavy tables, a miniature altar of the Blessed Virgin, with a light." This is how Author Carroll sees it. "On the walls a collection of those sanguinary holy picture oleographs that make the atmosphere of the average Catholic house so oppressive."

On this afternoon of an autumn day Canon Matt himself, a small man, "frail and worn except in the eyes, which gleam with feeling and occasionally with humor," is sitting in a large armchair drawn up before the fireplace. "He has had a shock which has paralyzed his legs which rest on a cushioned footrest near the chair."

Canon Matt, who has been sleeping, awakes with a start and calls, in a bit of a panic, for his housekeeper, Rosieanne. It would be like her to let him doze off that way. And like her to be spending a great deal of time "blatherin' " with tradesmen at the door.

Rosieanne is quite equal to giving the Canon his replies in kind. She can't be all the time running in and out for him, and besides she'll be leaving him in a week. Not because, as the Canon suspects, she has any idea of marrying, but because she has come to believe no one but a saint could stand the new Father Shaughnessy who has been sent to take the Canon's place while he is incapacitated.

Canon Matt is sure he can adjust that matter. He is still the Canon, for all he's crippled, and he'll be speakin' to Father Shaughnessy. "Listen to me, Rosieanne: Where is he now?" the Canon would know.

"He's down in the church hall havin' a meetin'. Sure he's always havin' meetin's inside and outside and everywhere."

"The divil if such a man for meetin's I ever met."

"If you had to hear him last night below at the pier, standin' on the promenade wall. Down with the drink, down with the dancin', down with lovemakin', a solid Catholic nation for a holy

"THE WHITE STEED"

Canon: Now you're being silly and stupid, Nora. You're not going back to England, I hope.
Nora: No, I'll never leave Ireland again. There's something here that's nowhere else. It's away
ck far and away deep down.

*(Barry Fitzgerald, Jessica Tandy)*

Catholic people, and a dig at the wee handful of Protestants in every line."

There is a knock at the door. This may be Father Shaughnessy but if it is this is no time for Canon Matt to be speaking to him. "He'll only start on me with these new schemes of his and aggravate me," protests the Canon. Let Rosieanne wheel him to his bedroom that he may be out of the way.

It isn't Father Shaughnessy who is knocking. It is Phelim Fintry, the vegetable man. And Phelim has brought a bill—a bill for vegetables running back to 1925 and amounting to the grand total now of £17.4.6d! That's a poser—

"Did he not tell me fifty times that I'd get me vegetables free till the two of us were under the clay?" protests Canon Matt, with some excitement, as he checks the bill. "He's lost the grace of God, that's what it is." He turns to Rosieanne for an explanation. "What do you know about this?"

"Well, I didn't want to annoy you, Canon, but it's about Phelim's daughter, Nora, that's in the lendin' library," Rosieanne explains hesitantly. "The girl that was away in England. Father Shaughnessy put her out of the hockey team yesterday."

CANON—And what's he got agin *her?* Sure, Nora's a fine little bit of a girl.

ROSIEANNE—It was for going with—with a boy.

CANON (*impatiently*)—A boy! And what the hell does he want her to go with, an elephant?

ROSIEANNE—He has the girls in the team pledged agin boys an' courtin' an' kissin'.

CANON—And the marriage rate the lowest in Europe. And he had to pick on Phelim's daughter. There's me leeks and scullions and carrots and a grand wallop of cauliflower every week, all gone in the one sweep.

ROSIEANNE—That's little of it. Wait till this new Vigilance Committee of his gets to work.

CANON—What *is* this affair that I hear all the blatherin' about?

ROSIEANNE—It's men and women he is havin' roamin' about the place seein' there is no kissin' on the roads, or bad dancin' or mixin' with Protestants and that District Justice with the new Irish name—he used to be Danny Fitzpatrick—promises that all people brought before him by the Vigilance Committee will be severely dealt with.

CANON—Och, that oul' Bury-me-Grannie was in the Junior

School in Maynooth when I was ordained.  I think they put him out because he wouldn't wash his ears.

Now Father Shaughnessy has arrived.  He enters the living room briskly, carrying an armful of papers and books which he places on the table irascibly.  "He is a tall, thin figure, with dark features, circumspect and mathematically-minded.  There is under his equanimity the hint of cruelty.  He is in the early 30's."

The Father is in anything but a pleasant mood.  The books and papers he has brought he has confiscated from the free lending library, and he is primed for a serious talk with the Canon.

The Canon, however, is not feeling well and is in no mood for "discussin' and talkin'," as Rosieanne tries to explain.  When Father Shaughnessy would send her to the kitchen, she promptly gives in her month's notice.  Canon Matt couldn't think of trying to get on without Rosieanne, but Father Shaughnessy is quick to accept the notice.  He has been wanting to bring on his own servant from Derry City anyway.  And now Father Shaughnessy would return to the subject of his campaign.  First there is the question of the incredible laxity he has discovered at the library.

"Dean Swift's filth, Bernard Shaw's blasphemous humor, AE's pantheistic cant, and the ravings of a humbug called Henrik Ibsen, and a score of others here all either blasphemous or anti-Catholic, or both.  I may say that I received nothing but unwarranted liberties and impertinence from that girl assistant whose appointment *you* sanctioned in the library, so with the help of Mr. McGiolla Phadraig, the District Justice, I had her summarily censured and suspended."

CANON—In the name of God, do you mean the girl Nora Fintry?

FATHER SHAUGHNESSY—I believe that is her name.

CANON—But you put her out of the hockey team, too.

FATHER SHAUGHNESSY—Well, rules must be kept and spiritual laws respected.  (*Pause.*)  Do you realize, Canon, just how bad a way this parish is in?

CANON (*lamely*)—Well, the people's poor and we can't take blood out of a stone.

FATHER SHAUGHNESSY—I mean neither blood nor stones.  I mean moral laxity, spiritual carelessness and a general hardening of moral feelings.  (*He taps the table with his pencil.*)  I don't like it, Canon, and there's no use in mincing words.

CANON—There may be a little waywardness here and there, but bless me soul, the people's all right deep down.

FATHER SHAUGHNESSY—Not a bit. That old pretension won't do any longer. We have new enemies now to contend with like Communism, open godlessness and militant Atheism. And that's not mentioning four forced marriages here since I came two months ago.

CANON—There has always been a percentage of human weakness in every community since David dragged Bethsabee out of her bath.

FATHER SHAUGHNESSY—That is not an apologia I can accept. I mean to work in close conjunction with the Civil Law and I intend to make full use of the new law in the Constitution against public impropriety. I have already publicly announced that I will not, under any circumstances, baptize any illegitimate child or any child of a mixed marriage.

CANON—That's just being high-handed. You can't make Catholicism a mere code of morals wrapped up in the fear of God.

FATHER SHAUGHNESSY—Even if it were only a code of morals, that would be preferable to a sentimental puddle. I tell you, Canon, I have been all over England and I know what I'm talking about. There we have emotionalism in its worst forms, ruling head, heart and soul. No one there now thinks except in terms of how they feel at the moment, and they don't avoid evil because they love or fear God—they avoid it for ethical reasons. That is the reason why England has a percentage of goodness left, why her conduct is at times more reasonable than our own, but these methods are not good enough for us.

CANON (*mystified*)—It all seems very mystifying to me— maybe there's somethin' wrong with me and I still believe in poor human nature and the oul' grace of God.

FATHER SHAUGHNESSY—I'm afraid, Canon, there is a good slice of the clerical ostrich in you.

CANON (*a little heated*)—I am no ostrich, nor a ferret either, but I *am* an oul' Irish sheepdog. I may be blind in one eye and my fur is a bit tore with the furze and whins, but I know the dark well enough to round up me sheep and take them home.

Father Shaughnessy thinks perhaps the Canon is not well. He would suggest a glass of hot milk. But the Canon has suddenly discovered that he is in "good fightin' fettle the night," and is prepared to go on. He puts much of his faith in "time and the risin' grace of God to fix things back the way they were without our blunderin' fingers."

"That's just theological procrastination," insists Father Shaughnessy.

"Ach, you're afflicted with a mathematical mind. You did teach mathematics in some college in England, didn't you, or was it in Derry?"

"You say that to me because I feel conscientiously there are many abuses in this parish that should be stamped out."

"I say it to you because you are looking for mathematical exactitudes in the spiritual and you'll not get them here so long as the Irish mind re-echoes back to the oak tree and the wishing well. In this country of ours, with all respect to your psychology and ethics, in spite of Governments and laws, the people here are fundamentally free. What you want is to replace their old wayward love of God that is splattered with mud and blood and crudities, with a shrinking fear of God that'll knock all the life out of them. If you want that sort of thing, go and live in Scotland, where the people have measured every word in the Bible with a screw gauge and knocked every ounce of beauty out of their national life, and what have they achieved? Merely a reputation for the Bible amongst intelligent people as the most volatile and dangerous book ever written."

Father Shaughnessy is not to be diverted from his campaign. He is taking up the cases of the offenders in order, and he has called a meeting of his Vigilance Committee for this afternoon. He would suggest that perhaps Canon Matt would prefer to be wheeled into his bedroom. And if he is too unhappy in this house, perhaps he would consider the Bishop's offer of refuge and quiet in the Aged Priests' Home outside of Dublin—

"I shall accept no such offer and I am no aged priest," snaps Canon Matt. "I am only sixty-seven and I am fit as a fiddle if I could only walk. . . ."

Phelim Fintry has called to see the Canon and meets Father Shaughnessy as well. Not with any great enthusiasm, however. Phelim would know why his daughter Nora has been put out of the hockey team and out of the library as well. It is Father Shaughnessy who answers him—

"Nora was suspended for impertinence unbecoming to an Irish girl, and she was put out of the team by me, Phelim, for breaking one of the rules of membership."

What rule? Phelim would know. The rule that forbids a

member of the hockey team keeping company with a man, the Father explains. It would be no crime for a growing woman like Nora to want to keep company, but the lanes and byroads and dark places along the coast are not the proper places for furthering a Catholic courtship, says Father Shaughnessy. That should be conducted in the home. But, protests Phelim, the Father doesn't know the Fintry home—

"It's a white-washed hovel with two rooms in it," says Phelim, "built in 1829 with stone floors that killed me wife and the childer that were to be yet born to us. *I* sleep in the kitchen in a box bed and Nora sleeps in the wee room. It has a wooden bed and the bed-covers are not too new and the wee bits of furniture are wizened with the weather and there's a wee bit of curtain that Nora hangs her few Sunday belongings behind—a blue costume, a few pair of stockings, and a cheap little dance frock. She might show you all these, Father, because as a minister of God you might understand, but as a woman do you think she would like young fellows like Corr to see them?"

Father Shaughnessy has no time for these matters of minor importance. He would know whether Phelim is with him or against him and Phelim declares himself to be on the side of his own blood. He had come for his daughter's good name, and seeing he cannot get that, he will take the amount of his vegetable account. That will help make Nora's room more suitable for her friends.

There is a sharp knock at the door and in bursts Nora Fintry herself. "She is a finely made girl in the 20's, quiet and pensive, but quick in spirit and temper. She regards them all frankly and without self-consciousness."

NORA (*rather sharply*)—Father, what are you doing here?

PHELIM—I was talkin' to the Canon, sure.

NORA—Did you come here to beg for *me?*

PHELIM—I did not. You're puttin' a lie on me now.

NORA—I don't believe you. There's a bit of the oul' curryin' willie-wagtail about you, but I will beg from no man and I will have no man beg *for* me either. Come along home out of this.

PHELIM—Sure, if you let me draw me breath—

CANON—You are in the divil's own temper, Nora, and you never even asked me how I was.

NORA (*not unkindly*)—You know I wish you well, Canon.

FATHER SHAUGHNESSY (*crossing to her*)—Nora Fintry, I am disappointed. I was expecting a more satisfactory visit from you.

NORA—You mean, Father Shaughnessy, you expected me to crawl to the porch of your parochial door and beg my job in the library back?

FATHER SHAUGHNESSY (*with pain*)—I expected you to come here and correct your impertinent attitude to me, like any modest Irish maiden.

NORA—But I am not modest and some of your mob say I am not even a maiden, so I must live up to your opinion of me.

PHELIM (*interposing*)—Now there's no luck, Nora, in that sort of talk to the priest. Maybe I was a bit hasty meself with me tongue. If I was . . .

NORA—Aw, stop spilling your Irish dribbles, Father, and come home. (*She grasps him firmly by the arm and leads him out. FATHER SHAUGHNESSY stares fixedly after them.*)

CANON (*breaking out*)—Nora, I—I—I'm ashamed of you.

NORA (*as she goes*)—Oh, no, you're not, Canon. Am I ashamed of *you* because you stumped when they wanted to send you to a home for clerical grannies?

CANON (*as door closes*)—I—I—I, well, I— (*He subsides.*) M—m, she's a corker, right enough!

FATHER SHAUGHNESSY—That girl has been ruined by what Britain very shrewdly calls broadmindedness.

CANON—Och, is it fair always to be throwing the British stone at her? These people will do anything for you if you rub them the right way.

FATHER SHAUGHNESSY—Catholicism is not a matter of rubbing people any way. I wish, Canon, you would accept the Bishop's offer and cease confusing me here.

CANON (*vehemently*)—Didn't I say my say about that? You may get rid of certain evils in this parish, Father Shaughnessy, but *I* won't be one of them.

Donnachaidh McGiolla Phadraig, who before he took to the Gaelic was Dan Fitzpatrick, the District Justice of Lorcan, is an interested caller. He comes, prepared and preferring to talk Gaelic, only to find that the Canon will stick to English. He finds, too, that the Canon has no intention of entering any discussion of the sinners of the parish—

"What is the use?" demands the fiery little Canon. "I won't agree with anything you say. I don't agree with this new tide of ideas. I am human enough to want, like all ordinary people, a little sugar in my tea, a little soda in my whiskey, a wee bit

of coaxing in my dogma and a hot bottle in my bed on a frosty
night. I hate anything in the raw from raw poteen to raw men
like Calvin, whom I'd have strangled out of a sense of decency
to the humanity Christ died for. If our Lord had never been
human, had never drunk wine, had never allowed a woman's
hair to clean his feet, had never pitied a miserable little bitch
selling herself in a narrow street, half the people who now believe in Him would have sput on Him long ago. No, I am not
with you, I am agin you. You can laugh at me when I call my
servant Rosieanne, instead of Rose, when I go mad for fresh
vegetables and mashed potatoes, or when I read the *Independent;*
but I believe, when I go down on my knees on the stone floor of
that old church out there, and ask God in my own way to forgive the human weaknesses of these poor slaves of ours, that I am
doing more good than all the Calvinistic seekin'-out and spyin'
and Vigilance Committees you propose. There now, I have said
my say and in me heart I'm agin you."

Father Shaughnessy and the District Judge, who are strong
for making civil and ecclesiastical laws the same, soon find they
cannot change the ideas of Canon Matt Lavelle.

And now the Vigilance Committee has arrived. Sarah Hearty,
Brigid Brodigan and Patrick Hearty. Sure, the Canon knows
them all, and knows more about them than Father Shaughnessy
ever will. But he will not interfere with their meeting. Let
Rosieanne turn his chair around so his back will be to them and
he maybe will sleep a bit. . . .

Father Shaughnessy's talk to the assembled committee stresses
the point that while, in cleaning up the evils that surround them,
they must, each of them, have in him the simple love of God and
all his creatures, at the same time they must not confuse kindness with weakness. "We must fearlessly unfurl the banner of
the cross, ladies and gentlemen . . ." concludes Father Shaughnessy. He would have gone on, but just at that point Canon
Matt snored rather loudly and the next moment Rosieanne was
in to announce the arrival of Denis Dillon, the schoolmaster.

Mr. Dillon is "a young man in the 20's—ill at ease, awk-
ward and a little breathless." Nor does the attitude of Father
Shaughnessy serve to put him at ease. The Father had sent for
Mr. Dillon thinking perhaps he would be one to serve the
Vigilance Committee as secretary.

But it now appears that not only is Mr. Dillon ineligible as
Committee secretary but that in addition he is "very much at
variance with its aims and objects in your private life."

Mr. Dillon thinks perhaps it might be the drink, but Father Shaughnessy had had no report on that. No, it seems that Mr. Dillon had been keeping company with a girl of alien faith, a non-Catholic. Is that true? It is true, Mr. Dillon admits, but Dorothy Craig is a good girl. And so are plenty of Catholic girls, Brigid Brodigan is quick to protest.

"I would remind everyone here that we are doing the work of God," declares Father Shaughnessy. "Spite, envy and injurious words are not part of it."

Miss Brodigan is quieted, and Father Shaughnessy goes on with Mr. Dillon's examination. The admission the young man has made is regrettable. As a faithful servant of the Holy Church his duty is clear. "Come, Mr. Dillon, I am sure you have your answer ready for us!"

Mr. Dillon would take time. It is possible that Miss Craig might turn Catholic for him, a suggestion the women of the Committee are inclined to flout. Still, it must be considered and Father Shaughnessy is prepared to give Mr. Dillon time to make up his mind. If he should find himself "too weak-willed to pass the test of spiritual and moral sobriety" of course he can hand in his resignation from the school. This thought is fairly terrifying to Mr. Dillon and he retires to a corner to think it over.

The Committee goes on with its work. There is a complaint from the people who own the four waterfront hotels that Mr. McGiolla Phadraig refuses to issue them licenses unless their programs are exclusively Irish. On this complaint the Committee will take no action. Hadn't all four of the girls who had been forced into marriage the previous month been often seen in these places?

A letter from Dermot Corr, who had caused the trouble with Nora Fintry on the hockey team, explains that there was nothin' between him and Nora, and that if she was agin the priest he wanted to have nothin' to do with her. Father Shaughnessy is instructed to send Dermot Corr a pardon.

There is still the matter of Nora Fintry herself, but Father Shaughnessy will take that up with Nora—

FATHER SHAUGHNESSY—I will see the girl myself at her house. (*He rises and all rise after him.*) That, I think, will be all for the moment. Go out now, to your ordinary work in your ordinary way, but keep your eyes open and your ears, but at the same time, your hearts. (*He hands them all cards.*)

These cards, bearing my signature, and that of Mr. McGiolla
Phadraig will admit you to the dance halls and to the public
houses and invest you with special powers, as my moral policemen. You will each make a detailed report at our next meeting. (*Pause.*) And now, Mr. Dillon! (*All turn and look at*
DILLON. *He raises his head slowly. He rises weakly from the
chair and comes forward, a meek man. A long pause.*)

DILLON—I—I will do what you want. I will not see Dorothy
Craig again.

FATHER SHAUGHNESSY—Excellent. Your victory is an example to the rest. Give me your hand, Mr. Dillon. (DILLON
*gives his hand weakly.* FATHER SHAUGHNESSY *shakes it.*) I
congratulate you and, as a reward for your courage, I appoint
you secretary of this Vigilance Committee. (DILLON *nods ab-
jectly.*)

DILLON—I will do what I am capable of doing. Thank you.
I don't feel well. I'll go now if I may. (*He turns and goes
quietly. The rest follow him out except* FATHER SHAUGHNESSY
*and* MR. McGIOLLA PHADRAIG.)

PHADRAIG—Well, Father Shaughnessy, I think we have reason
to congratulate ourselves. The work is begun and we are on
the way to a purely Catholic State.

FATHER SHAUGHNESSY—True, but the battle that is to re-
echo outside this parish has yet to be fought. (*They go out
quietly together. The minutes pass.*)

CANON (*starting and muttering in his sleep, then sitting up,
rubbing his head and looking sleepily at the empty chairs.
Sniffing and calling fussily*)—Rosieanne, Rosieanne!

ROSIEANNE (*entering*)—Oh, you're wakened again, Canon,
are you? Do you want me?

CANON (*sleepily pointing to the window*)—Oscal an—an—an
fhuinneog.

The curtain falls.

## ACT II

The living room in Phelim Fintry's cottage is a shabby room,
"with wizened odds and ends of furniture; some chairs around
an open grate with hobs." Phelim is sitting on a low stool before the fire. Nora is making griddle cakes at the stove.

Their talk of the moment is of Dermot Corr and his appearance before the Vigilance Committee. Nora is not worried by
that, nor by the probability of her own summons either. She is
planning to go to work for Michael Shivers in the Stella Maris

hotel in the capacity of hostess. The thought frightens her
father. Look what has happened to Denis Dillon!

"Poor devil," sighs Nora. "Brave only when he gets the drink
he sneaks out of the Stella Maris, and he gets the shakers when
he sees a Roman collar in a shop window."

There is a knock at the door. It is Dillon himself, "maudlin
with drink" and defiant. "Can I come in for a minute?" he
asks from the door.

NORA (*belligerently*)—You may, if you bow three times to
the cat and beg the dog's pardon.

PHELIM—Come on in, Denis, an' don't mind her.

DILLON (*coming forward*)—The worst of it is, I can't answer
her. Nora, as a good Christian, I admire you and hate the sight
of you, because you are not afraid of your masters. There now,
in vino veritas.

PHELIM—You have been havin' a half one, Denis. Sit down
and rest yourself.

DILLON (*sitting*)—Yes, Phelim, I have been having a half
one. I have been having ten half ones. Half ones make me
brave. Half ones change me from a man who loves law and
hates life to a man who loves life and to blazes with law. Half
ones take away my fear of my holy masters, my fear of my
job and the road. That's it, the road. To you, Nora, the road
is a place winding out and upwards to the stars; to me it is a
lane down to an old pond where men drown themselves because
they have nothing to eat.

PHELIM—Get him a drop of tea, Nora, for to clear his head.

NORA (*looking at him*)—I suppose as a woman I should be
sorry for you, but I'm not. I despise you.

PHELIM—Can't you leave him alone!

DILLON—No, let her go on. I know she hates me. Hate and
love and fear, the real trinity under the statues and the prayers
and the hymns. I'm sayin' it. I'm tellin' you, mind, and I
wouldn't say it only for the whiskey in me makin' me brave.

NORA—It's a poor kind of bravery that whiskey gives. Have
you nothing better than that to bring out the good in you?

PHELIM—Nice good it's bringing out in him . . . blasphemy
an' blatherin'.

NORA (*giving him a cup of tea*)—Here, drink this. For two
pins I'd throw the damned thing about you.

PHELIM—Nora!

DILLON—Do! I implore you, do. Throw it about me. I

crave you to throw it about me.

NORA—That's right.   Self-abasement and belly-crawling.

DILLON—I know.  That and worse . . . the badge of all our tribe.  Spit on me, throw mud on me, so that one day I may maybe find the extreme and by the living Christ I can turn and wreck red ruin, that's it!   That's what's in me and I'd never have known it only the whiskey told me.

PHELIM (to NORA)—That's enough.  You'll only aggravate him and the drop in him.  (He claps DILLON on the back.)  No one will give you your breakfast for that kind of high talk, Denis.  You be a good sensible lad and mind your school.

DILLON (coming out of reverie)—School! (Melancholy.) "The very name is like a bell to toll me back . . ."  Och, I'm a fool, a poor idiot, a little black man.  The whiskey's dyin' in me.

NORA (humoring him)—I didn't know you were a poet?

PHELIM—There you are, startin' him again.

DILLON (morbidly)—Nevertheless, Nora, I am a poet.  I am a poet of unwritten poems, a wielder of sheathed swords, a lover of my dead mother born again as a young understanding maid and the father by her of men without fear, but when I finish this cup of Irish tea, this cup of stern disillusionment, I shall be merely Denis Dillon, the village schoolmaster, the clerical bell-boy who banks the parochial ha'pence.

Dillon still has a few things to say before he will let Phelim Fintry induce him to leave.  He would know, if he could, how much Nora really hates him.  And how much she would hate him if she knew that for giving up Dorothy Craig he had been made secretary of the Vigilance Committee.  Nora is unmoved. She can hate only what is important enough to be hated.

And now Denis recalls what it was that brought him to the Fintry cottage.  It was to report that he had seen Nora that day in a married man's car—the car of Michael Shivers it was— "the avowed enemy of the new clerical fascism" and she knows what that would mean if it were reported.

"You will say nothing of this, I want you to promise me that," pleads the distressed Phelim.

"I will promise you, Phelim, but in the morning when I stand naked . . . when the whiskey is dead and the sword of Don Quixote gone back to its castle in Spain, what then?  I will be Denis Dillon, tell-tale, maker of obeisances and currier of favors. If I could only show you my inside when I am sober!  Show you the meanness and the cowardice and the spite.  Lord, what an unholy picture I am. Even the cat dislikes me . . ."

"Take him away, Father; he makes me want to kick him," sneers Nora.

Phelim is about to lead young Dillon away when he notices a bunch of papers sticking out of his pocket—papers with weird drawings of skulls and crossbones on them, and "The Man Without Fear" printed under them. Immediately Denis is in a state of nerves, ready to deny that he knows anything about them; pleading with Nora to hasten to Shivers' snug and find out if he had given Shivers a letter to slip under a door.

"Some of these days he will get so brave that he will say boo to Paddy Slaven's goose," says Nora, starting for the door. "I'm telling Shivers I'm starting work with him in the morning, Father."

Dillon's panic is still active, and now he is filled with self-pity as well. But it is little sympathy he has from Phelim Fintry. Now there is another knock at the door. This time it is the new priest, as Phelim can see by a peek out the window. The news is bad for Dillon, who is all shivers and fear again and would be hidden.

It is better to face the situation, insists Phelim, and Dillon agrees. "The drink's dead in me, anyway," he says. "I'm Denis Dillon now . . . sober and despicable, the clerical message-boy."

Father Shaughnessy is thoughtfully, even suspiciously, inquiring, and a little disturbed to learn that Nora has gone alone to Michael Shivers' on an errand. It's a dark night and he could wish that she had been accompanied, whether she wanted to be accompanied or not.

"Faith, there's not much use in blamin' the schoolmaster," observes Phelim. "Nora is none too easy to handle at times."

"That explanation, Phelim, does not erase from the Fourth Commandment the words 'instruct and correct.' I will have a talk with her myself. I am convinced that apart from a little windy froth she has swallowed in England, she's a good girl."

"Froth or no froth, Father, Nora's a good girl," protests Phelim with some spirit.

"That's what I said, Phelim," answers the priest slowly and calmly. . . .

Again there is a knock at the door. It can't be Nora, reasons Phelim. Nora "knocks slow, as if she felt the hurt that she mightn't be wanted." And as he starts for the door he adds: "That's the knock of a woman who bates her husband."

It is Sarah Hearty who enters. She is carrying a letter and

is in a state of excitement. She would have Father Shaughnessy read the letter, but the Father turns it over to Dillon and Dillon, shivering now with fear, also begs off because of the bad eyes he's just had examined.

"I will read it, Father," calls the excited Sarah, holding the letter to the light. " 'To Mrs. Sarah Hearty. You fermenting big sack of moral barley, ignored by the birds of the air and rejected by Guinness's brewery, keep your wasp's nose to yourself at night or you will get a bullet in the part of you that comes after the rest of you. Signed: The Man Without Fear.' "

They are all standing as if turned to stone: Dillon a study of fear; Sarah a picture of wronged womanhood; Father Shaughnessy looking out into space, grimly. The door opens and Nora enters. For a moment she is nonplused. Sarah Hearty hands her the letter. Nora reads it slowly, wonderingly. "She looks from one to the other and then at Dillon, and finally breaks into uncontrollable giggles."

They stare at her, horrified. Suddenly Sarah Hearty would leap forward and strike Nora, but Phelim steps between them—

"My dear people," the Priest is saying, "this scurrilous outpouring of a mind abandoned to evil is intended to discourage and affright us on our march onwards to the achievement of a new state of things in our little village. All of us except one have been shocked by its indecency. That one has been abroad in a pagan country. We must be painstaking and forbearing until she has learned to re-adjust herself to the Christian State."

"The Christian State!" answers Nora, staring at him unflinchingly. "A schoolmaster that scrapes and bows, a father that is afraid of old shadows, a mean stupid old woman and a priest as cold as the mountain stones."

Consternation has seized the group. Phelim has grabbed his daughter's arm in protest. Sarah Hearty is accusing Nora of defying the Priest. Father Shaughnessy is visibly upset. Denis Dillon stands as one transfixed.

It is to Denis that Father Shaughnessy turns quietly. The wicked note, he says, will be entrusted to Denis. Has he ever seen it before? He has not, Denis is quick to answer. And he'll do his best to find the author of it.

"The man . . . or the woman who wrote it is a menace to our very souls," announces Father Shaughnessy. "He or she must go!"

As for Nora, it is Father Shaughnessy's hope that she will apologize for her unchristian attitude toward the note, and the hope of Phelim and Denis as well. But Nora will apologize only on one condition—

"We shall go together to the Canon and give him this note to read. If, in spite of his pain, he doesn't laugh at it, I will apologize."

Again there is great indignation and out of it comes Sarah Hearty's charge that Nora, the brazen hussy, has been seen many times in the Shivers car. And Denis Dillon's reluctant confirmation of the charge when Father Shaughnessy presses him for it. Nor is Nora one to deny the charge, much to the distress of her father—

"It's true, all true!" she suddenly breaks out. "I may have been born in the bed of a bondsman, but that doesn't make me a thing that creeps. Tomorrow morning I go to work with Michael Shivers."

Nor will Nora give heed to the advice of any of them, especially that of Denis Dillon. Once she had called Denis a worm, but now she wants to apologize to the worm and substitute a louse. Nor will she come to any meeting of the Committee prepared to humble herself and promise that she will never see the Shivers person again.

"The evil you assimilated in a pagan land is deep in you, woman," declares Father Shaughnessy.

"What I have in me that won't let me stoop I didn't get in England, for England hasn't got it to give," answers Nora. "I got it here. It was in Aideen when she rode by Oscar's side at the Battle of Garva. It was in Cu Chulainn when he tied himself to a pillar before he'd stoop to death, it was in Ossian when he rode back on Niam's white horse and found the land full of priests like you and little men like that poor schoolmaster there, and it's in me now, making me refuse to come to your council table and swallow the ancient draught of humility."

Again Sarah Hearty has rushed forward with intent to do physical violence to the "brazen bitch," but is checked with some force by Father Shaughnessy, who dismisses her forthwith from the committee and the room. And now he turns again to Nora with a last offer—

"I am leaving you the key of the eternal door, Nora Fintry," he says. "The centuries may have rusted your own."

Without a word or a look Nora goes into her bedroom. Phelim Fintry follows after. Father Shaughnessy is about to go when Inspector Toomey appears at the door, cap in hand.

Inspector Toomey has come to report a case of assault at

the Stella Maris hotel. One Patrick Hearty had, on the authority of a card given him as a member of the Vigilance Committee, tried to force his way into the Stella Maris after closing hours. He had been stopped and forcibly ejected by Michael Shivers and had just been taken with a broken jaw to a Dundooley doctor.

It is Father Shaughnessy's opinion that Patrick Hearty was well within his rights as an investigator for the committee and he will stand behind him if charges are preferred.

Inspector Toomey would remind Father Shaughnessy that the only ones with right to entry after hours are the police, and Father Shaughnessy would like to know how much the police are paid not to enter. Inspector Toomey resents the implication and Father Shaughnessy is stirred by what he terms the Inspector's impertinence. Mr. Hearty is threatening to bring charges of assault, dutifully reports the Inspector, and if he does Father Shaughnessy will be called as a witness. That will please Father Shaughnessy, and he hopes for great results, remembering the friendly McGiolla Phadraig.

When Inspector Toomey, very mad, and Father Shaughnessy, well pleased, have left the Fintrys', Denis Dillon sinks heavily into a seat before the fire. Soon Nora and Phelim come back into the room. Phelim is still actively protesting the foolishness of arguing against the Priest.

"The policeman we can always shoot down," Phelim is saying, "but the priest we must always leave to God and God is always too slow for the old venom that is in us."

It is Phelim's idea that Nora will be going back to England now, but it is Nora's intention to stay where she belongs. If her father is worrying about her staying at home, and being against the Priest, as she is, she would remind him that she will be sleeping in at Shivers' Hotel, and that should make it easy for him to disown her.

"Enemies . . . making enemies all the time," Phelim is muttering. "Now even your own father is an enemy." And then he adds in his worry: "I will dodge up and see the old Canon. Maybe he'll give me a grip again of the old things I knew. (*Pause.*) Will I tell him you were asking for him?"

"Do!"

PHELIM—You remember how he used to call you Noreen. He used to say, "You are too serious, Noreen. Let you leap over your own shadow and you'll hear fairy music," but you'd rather sit on the window sill longin' to be Niam on her white steed.

NORA—Yes! My white steed. (*She looks out in front of her, hidden emotion filling her eyes and face.*) How I would watch for it coming down from the fairy path and over the stream in Paddy Slaven's field. . . . Then one day the old packman that used to come on Fridays told me he saw it being sold by a little black man at the fair of Mullacrew. . . . And after that I . . . I felt the hate in me of all things black and little . . . (*Her voice breaks. There is a long pause.*) Don't charge the Canon that account for the vegetables, Father. There's no use in hurting an old man.

PHELIM—Sure, it was just a puff of the bad temper in me. I'll let it be. (*As he goes.*) God help me, and I with a daughter that's like a strange woman to me. (*He goes off. NORA looks out in front as if in a dream.*)

NORA—Niam and her white steed . . . "And when she looked on Ossian and saw how wise and tender he was and how beautiful and strong, she felt herself filled with a great love for him and longingly and with quiet hands, she drew the folds of her robe of gold more closely to her and made room for him behind her on the back of the white steed." (*NORA looks down at the miserable form of DILLON, his head still morosely in his hands.*) Well, "Man Without Fear," are you going home tonight?

DILLON—Why do you call me that?

NORA—Isn't that what you call yourself?

DILLON—Only when I'm drunk.

NORA—You poor devil.

DILLON (*lifting his head slowly*)—Look at me, Nora. Amn't I a miserable, despicable creature? If you could see the inside of me.

NORA—What do you want me to do, pity you?

DILLON (*almost sobbing*)—Give me one little word of sympathy, I need it.

NORA (*looking at him*)—God forgive me. My only impulse is to kick you. (*Sudden passion seizes her.*) Get up and get out of here before I murder you. Go on, get out! Get out! Get out!

DILLON (*rising and cowering away from her*)—Yes, I will . . . I will go. Just give me a minute to . . . to collect myself. God, the eyes you have! Pitiless, ruthless. You could strip me and flog me, couldn't you?

NORA (*between her teeth*)—Yes! Yes! Lay weals on you!

DILLON—Only a disappointed virgin could be like you, vicious

and merciless. If you were a woman, you would have taken
my head and given me a little word.

NORA—You little devil! You are shrewd, for all your coward-
liness.

DILLON—All cowards are shrewd. If only I was drunk I
could tell you more. I could tell you much more. It's not for
nothing I lie over the gutterin' candle at night and drink and
read when my holy master is in bed in the Chapel House. Little
does he know that I can rock his rafters with Rabelais and break
whiskey glasses with Boccaccio. And you lying in bed riding
over the billows on your white steed away from King and Pope
and the little men and their priests. Are we not a little like
each other, after all? When I am drunk with whiskey and you
are drunk with dreams, are we not the hidden Ireland the poets
in Dublin never write about; the wandering ghosts of what was
there when the priests and the little men came in from the seas?
(*Pause. They look at each other.*)

NORA (*softly*)—Maybe you're right, Denis. Maybe we *are* a
little like each other.

DILLON (*pathetically grasping her two hands*)—Nora, thank
you! Thank you for sayin' that. Oh, how much, how very
much that means to me. (NORA *brings her hand slowly to his
head and touches his hair.*)

NORA—There! Was that what you wanted?

DILLON—Yes, it lifts me up, like a drink, out of the grave.
It is all strange and terrible. When you spat on the floor tonight when I betrayed you, I knew in a flash that I would love
you to the end of everything. (*Sobbing.*) Don't send me away
out where I will be a little black man again, weeding the clerical
garden. Lift me on your white steed, Nora.

NORA—Every man, Denis, must lift himself on the white steed.

DILLON—That's what I fear and dread. That's why I will
never escape, never! I have come out of the Firbolgs . . .
I have come out of the little men that Ossian found in the place
of Finn. Help me, Nora!

NORA—What do you want me to do, Denis?

DILLON—I want to have courage. I want to break down this
fear that is in me. To be able to look at men, even at my masters
and not shiver with the cold.

NORA—But in the morning, it will be different. When they
say "come" to you, you will come, and when they say "go" to
you, you will go.

DILLON—It's true. From the moment I rise, I go in fear.

When I look up at the dark saints over my bed, when I look out of the window and see the priest's house and when I turn my key in the school door. And all my leisure is spent in dreamin' of things burnin', of things fallin', of things I see myself smashin'. And look at me, look well at me!

NORA—I have always loved the smashing of things too, since I was a little girl. Look, Denis, like you with your saints, I have suffered these cups for months past; they're coarse and thick and stupid and callous, and I hate the sight of them because they hurt me. Let's smash them into smithereens. (*They look at each other.*)

DILLON—You're crazy! Phelim would be ragin' mad!

NORA—I knew you'd say just that. (*She hurls a cup against the wall and smashes it.*) There! (*She smashes another one.*) And there! (*He looks at her fascinated, rushes across, seizes a cup and throws it.*)

DILLON—And there!

NORA (*smashing*)—And there!

DILLON (*smashing*)—And there!

NORA (*smashing*)—And there!

DILLON (*smashing*)—And there! It's wonderful. I feel as if there was the taste of blood in my mouth, the taste of the blood of my enemies, the taste of the blood of scoundrels who have taught me to love their laws and hate life. I, that have warm blood and the laugh of a giant.

"He laughs in abandonment, then suddenly he pauses and is quiet. He and Nora stare at each other bright-eyed and flushed, then with a cry they come to each other wordlessly. They are clasped in each other's arms passionately as the curtain falls."

## ACT III

Canon Lavelle is asleep in his living room chair while Rosieanne and Meg, "a comparatively young red-headed tartish servant" whom Father Shaughnessy has brought in, are trying to dust. They are antagonistic, these two, and spoiling for a fight. As both insist on dusting the same chair they fall to hair-pulling and the Canon wakens with a start.

The girls draw apart and straighten themselves up secretively. Rosieanne is all solicitude for the Canon's comfort. She would fetch him his tea if there were any milk in the house, but the Widow Whelan has quit sending both milk and butter since

Father Shaughnessy had refused to baptize her daughter's child because the daughter had married a Protestant. That's sad news for the Canon.

Father Shaughnessy is back, "flushed and triumphant." In the court at Dundooley, it appears, the forces of law and order have struck a great blow for Ireland. Still the Canon is not impressed.

"Och, great blows have been gettin' struck for Ireland since I was the size of a drumstick an' we're still livin' on spuds and buttermilk."

"These were the blows of politicians, men of froth and egotism. This is new and different. We have won our case, Canon, and this man Shivers was fined five guineas or thirty days. Do you know what that means?"

"It means a fine big hole in all our future quarterly collections."

"It means the State recognition of our Parochial Vigilance Committees—a new army of policemen who will steer this nation back to its Catholic heritage. Tomorrow, moral committees like ours will be functioning in every parish. That, Canon, is our solution of all the problems of youth in Ireland."

"Och, you're imagin' things. You should have been a Presbyterian clergyman born in Scotland and brought up on oat-cakes and Calvinism. When I was a young whipper before I got the call to the Church, I kissed me girl at the cross-roads, aye, and walloped Jeremiah Duggan on the public road for tryin' to do the same. That same girl since gave a son to the Easter rising, and a daughter to the Carmelites. It's not bad for what you'd call a brazen woman."

"Canon, these disclosures of yours are not—theologically dignified."

"Well, here's hopin' God's no theologian or we'll all get our backsides scorched. I'd rather a pennyworth of old Mary Cassidy's faith."

Michael Shivers has called to see Father Shaughnessy. He comes, not to make terms, but to remind the Father that the decision just handed down by McGiolla Phadraig decreeing that Patrick Hearty had the right to enter the Stella Maris hotel after hours, "is the ruling of a jackass." In view of which conviction Mr. Shivers feels that the only course open to him is to defend his premises with all the means at his disposal.

"There have been men in every country who have always resisted the pioneers. History shows us that such men have always been blasted out of the way. I will say no more than that."

"You have said enough," agrees Mr. Shivers.

Inspector Toomey is the next to arrive. He also would talk with Father Shaughnessy. "You are acquainted with the girl, Nora Fintry?" inquires the inspector.

"I am. She is one of my parishioners," answers the Priest sharply.

Toomey—Before being one of your parishioners, she is a citizen of this State with full citizen papers, and she has appealed to me for protection against your Vigilance Committee.

Father Shaughnessy—The sequence is not important.

Toomey—To me the sequence is very important. It determines whether she has or has not the right to secular independence.

Shivers—There's the damn thing I've been tryin' to say, and I hadn't the schoolin' to put it in words. I demand your protection, too. (*A pause.* Toomey *regards* Father Shaughnessy.) Well? How long more are you going to stand there silent before the priest?

Toomey—As long as I feel I can get a peaceful decision. As a man that's been through raids and ambushes with the flying squads in the revolution racket, I know what hate and venom are. I know what it feels like to want to tear the guts out of an enemy. I know what it is to shoot down men at point-blank range out of a sense of duty. That sense of duty is my ruling passion. Do you know now why I'm standing here without a word?

Father Shaughnessy—Do I understand that you are threatening *me*, Inspector Toomey?

Toomey (*grimly*)—I've never threatened a man in my life. Threats are an evasion of duty, and I never evade my duty.

Father Shaughnessy—Do you recognize that I too have a strong sense of duty?

Toomey—Of course I do, Father Shaughnessy.

Father Shaughnessy—Then need we be opposed?

Toomey—That is for you to say. I don't want to quarrel with you if I can help it. We both have dirty work to do, and nobody ever thanks us for it. Everyone has a bad word for both of us in the end. Why should we quarrel? You stick to your pulpit, and I'll stick to my barracks. What are they, after all, but the two strait-jackets of human nature!

Father Shaughnessy—You forget one important thing in

giving me advice, Inspector Toomey.

TOOMEY—And that?

FATHER SHAUGHNESSY—I never asked for it. I have work to do here and I will do it. Tomorrow the rest of Ireland will be doing exactly what I am doing. I am convinced of that.

TOOMEY—Take it or leave it. Come along, Shivers. You and Nora Fintry have certain secular rights under the common law, and it's my job here to see they're protected.

Father Shaughnessy is moved to action. He will write a letter to the Ministry of Justice revealing the impertinences of its agent. He is busy at that task when Nora Fintry comes with a basket of fresh vegetables for the Canon. She would stay and "blather" with her friend, as he suggests, but the sight of Father Shaughnessy discourages her. She is about to hasten along when Father Shaughnessy stops her. If she will not come to him he will go to her. He has decided, for one thing, to see that she is reinstated in her position in the library on two conditions. Before he can name them, however, Nora has announced firmly that there will be no conditions.

"You prefer defiance?" demands Father Shaughnessy.

"What *is* defiance?" softly inquires Nora. "If it is the struggle of a spirit to escape standardization and to preserve its integrity and humanity, then I *am* defiant. But I am not alone. The broken heart of humanity is defiant too, today. (*Breaking suddenly into tears*.) Oh, God, can't you see? Can't you see?"

"I can see nothing but a proud and intractable woman whom I will not tolerate as a living scandal in our midst."

They are facing each other defiantly when Denis Dillon knocks at the door. He has come to report to Father Shaughnessy, but at the Canon's suggestion he thinks he will be taking Nora Fintry home first. There is, as frequently happens, rebellion in Denis' soul, but he is still too weak to acknowledge it. Nora has noticed—

"Never mind, Denis," says she forbearingly, as they are leaving. "Some day the dark saints will fall—all over the world."

Patrick Hearty has come, also for orders, and it is to him that Father Shaughnessy reveals a new plan respecting Nora Fintry.

"Mr. Hearty," he is saying, gravely, "you know of the defiant and outrageous attitude of this girl Nora Fintry. We are now in the grave position that we have no alternative but direct action. That girl must be broken. (*Passionately*.) We must make an example of her, an example that will be the acid test of our determination, an example that by God's grace will be speedily followed all over Ireland. (*Turning.*) Our moral law is the only legitimate law in this land or in any land. Go out, on my authority, get Dillon and my men together and when you find this girl publicly associating with this married man Shivers, bring her here before me."

"By—by what means, Father?"

"By the only means that is left to us," replies the Priest, tensely, his fist clenched, his face grim.

CANON (*from his chair*)—That's the maddest order that was ever given, since the charge of the Light Brigade. You had a right to consult the Bishop first.

FATHER SHAUGHNESSY (*angrily*)—The Bishop is an old man, as you are an old man. The moral law of this country must be exalted by someone with sufficient moral courage, otherwise what is the use in our having a new Christian constitution?

CANON—The only thing you will exalt is the question whether the priest is or is not above the civil law. A nice how-do-you-do there will be then. And every shrewd churchman from Donegal to Dingle will call you a blunderin' ass.

FATHER SHAUGHNESSY—Tch! I am tired of your inanities. I am going to put down my foot in *your* case also and insist on your going to a home for old men. (*He goes out with an impatient wave.*)

CANON (*jumping about in the chair explosively*)—A—a—a home for old men! The cheek of him! The—the damned cheek of him!

The curtain falls.

Later that evening we are again in the living room. "The Canon is shuffling about irascibly in the invalid's chair. Rosieanne is sitting by him knitting."

Suddenly the Canon lifts his head decisively. He can stand, he says, and he will stand. Nor can any protest from the frightened Rosieanne stop him.

"I can, I know I can!" he is saying. "The Mother of God will let me walk. When I was dozing today I gave her a right straight talkin' to."

The next moment he has started to rise, and before Rosieanne can catch him he has lurched forward and collapsed in a heap on the floor. There he lies for a moment and then Rosieanne, with great straining and puffing, gets him back into the chair again.

He would have some tea and toast now, and with some real butter. Let Rosieanne try coaxin' some butter from the Widow Whelan. Let her tell the widow if she will bring her daughter's unbaptized baby to the house, and if Rosieanne will get a bit of holy water from the font and bring it to him in the bathroom, the Canon will see to the baby's baptizing himself. What does it matter if Father Shaughnessy should report him to the Bishop? What does it matter who's blamed or reported in the end?

Michael Shivers has called for a word with the Canon, and the word would naturally be concerned with his opposition to the autocratic rulings of Father Shaughnessy.

"How can you go easy with this sort of thing?" Michael demands. "It is a downright liberty, and his bullyin' and dragoonin' and refusin' to baptize the mixed marriage children are liberties, too. We are not being kicked down the lanes of the eighteenth and nineteenth centuries now, Canon."

"Sure, I'm always tellin' him. It's all routine now, and no faith. As if it was anything but faith that dragged us all out of the pit."

"Well, I'm tellin' you straight, Canon—that's why I'm here. I'm takin' my stand on my rights as a citizen and the majority of the people down there are quietly doing the same. Do you know what I mean, Canon?"

"I know it's never the right of anyone to do the wrong thing. You should keep away from Nora Fintry, Michael; she's not for *you*."

"Did I ever say she was? I don't care two straws for the girshe. I just get seen with her to uphold a principle; call it spite if you like."

"That's a terrible admission to make."

"That's human nature, and right well you know it, Canon."

Now Rosieanne is back. The unbaptized baby and its mother are waiting for the baptizing. It is satisfying to Michael Shivers to catch the Canon carrying on a bit of sedition on his own account, but before the baptism can be accomplished Father Shaughnessy breaks in upon the scene and is properly excited. He not only forbids Canon Matt to go through with the baptism, but has made arrangements with the Bishop to have him called for and taken to a quiet home in Dalkey this very day.

"You'll need at least another dozen along with yourself to shift *me* out of here," defiantly mutters the Canon. "I'm in with the bricks and I'm stayin' until they fall down."

But he is not so brave after Father Shaughnessy has stamped out of the room to send Widow Whelan's daughter and her child away.

"We're beat, Rosieanne," confesses the Canon, weakly. "If only the Blessed Mother would let me walk. . . . Wheel me in, Rosieanne, to the little altar, till I tell her the wretch and the villain that I am."

A moment later, when Father Shaughnessy returns with the news that the Bishop's car is waiting and that the Canon should be wrapped up and prepared for the journey, Rosieanne tells him that the Canon will not budge. He has locked himself in the Oratory, chair and all, and won't come out.

"This is ludicrous," storms Father Shaughnessy. "He must come out. I insist on his coming out. Go, give the Bishop's man some tea in the kitchen, and I'll have things arranged by that."

And now Denis Dillon arrives, albeit a little unsteadily. Denis, it appears, has been spending the Father's coppers for drink and with the drink his courage has returned.

"You have been drinking," suggests Father Shaughnessy with some effort at restraint.

"I have. I and Judas Iscariot drowned our remorse together," answers Denis.

FATHER SHAUGHNESSY—In the strict interests of morality, I summarily suspend you meantime from the school.

DILLON (*maudlinly*)—It is not new to me to be suspended, Father Shaughnessy. All my life I have been suspended by a piece of whip-gut over the edge of a precipice and all about me dark saints frown and jabber in my ears and away below me little black priests read their breviaries and see in me the justice of God.

FATHER SHAUGHNESSY—This is disgusting before me. (*Imperatively.*) Sober yourself, fellow, in my presence.

DILLON—To be sober is to be afraid again—afraid of your black cloth and your eyes and your collar.

FATHER SHAUGHNESSY (*suddenly striking him with the back of his hand across the face*)—Will that sober you?

DILLON (*wincing and stung. After a pause*)—A little, perhaps. Sufficient for me to recognize another Irish clerical privilege.

FATHER SHAUGHNESSY—You are insolent, incredibly insolent. Get out of here and report to me when you are sober. Then I will deal with you.

DILLON (*turning slowly*)—When I'm sober . . . when the mountains fall upon me. (*Sudden noise of cheering and shouting without.*)

ROSIEANNE (*entering excitedly*)—Father, Patrick Hearty is dragging the girl Nora Fintry up the street. They're coming in here.

FATHER SHAUGHNESSY (*calmly*)—Then admit them instantly and without concern.

ROSIEANNE—But there's a whole crowd of people followin' them, cheerin' and shoutin' at them.

FATHER SHAUGHNESSY—Take no notice of them. Admit only my officer and his prisoner. (*She nods and goes.*)

DILLON (*turning a little drunkenly and staring at the priest*)— Prisoner! A strange word that! Nora will never be anyone's prisoner.

FATHER SHAUGHNESSY—I will deal with this insolence at another time, Dillon.

The door has been flung open. Patrick Hearty drags in Nora Fintry and throws her forward. "He looks exhausted and is panting. Nora is disheveled, her clothes are torn and her hair tossed about her face."

Mr. Hearty is prepared to report that he has followed Father Shaughnessy's instructions and to charge that Denis Dillon had deliberately refused to help him. He had found Nora in the company of the man Shivers in a motor car. He had looked for Secretary Dillon to help him and found Denis drinking at Shivers' bar and singing a disgraceful ballad. Denis not only refused to co-operate with Mr. Hearty but he had called him a Firbolg. A Firbolg, he explains, would be "one of them little black men that you see in Joyce's History, Part I."

Mr. Hearty had thereupon thrown Mr. Dillon against the bar and called Officer Brigid Brodigan to help him bring Nora to the Priest. He had then ordered four of his fellow officers to arrest Michael Shivers. Michael and the officers were still battlin' below on the bridge. Hearty would have called on the people to assist him, but the people around Shivers' place were agin him. As for the Civil Police, the Inspector and his men just stood lookin' on. And so did Denis Dillon. Nora Fintry'll not be standing looking on, once she gets away from there, she assures them.

"A deplorable attitude, child," protests Father Shaughnessy.

"Will you please be silent and allow me to deal as gently as possible with you."

"Lift the crumb from the table of your master, Nora," advises Denis.

"No man is my master," answers Nora, with some violence. "No damned generation of clerics will hunt *me* down. I am a daughter of what was here before you all and a mother of what will be here after you are all gone."

Father Shaughnessy thinks perhaps Nora is tiring and suggests that she sit down, but when they bring her a chair she throws it violently from her. . . .

Now Rosieanne has come to report that the Bishop's man is growing restless and the Canon is still locked in the Oratory. Also that there is a crowd gathering outside wanting in, and that Nora's father "is standing crying at the door."

"Standin' cryin' at the priest's door. There's somethin' that echoes far back in that," says Denis Dillon.

"For that malicious remark, Denis Dillon, you are placed under arrest as an enemy of the Vigilance Committee," declares Father Shaughnessy, and Patrick Hearty moves toward Denis to carry out the arrest.

DILLON—What does it matter? I have been under arrest since I was born. I have been inside the netting wire that runs round the clerical gardens.

HEARTY—Enough of that cheek or I'll quieten you.

NORA—Keep your heart up, Denis. They can take our bread and butter, but they can't take what we had before they came to the land at all. (PHELIM FINTRY *enters, distressed.*)

PHELIM (*looking about him worried and downcast. Pathetically to* NORA)—There! What did I tell you! I could see this before me like a dog on the road. Enemies—always makin' enemies, didn't I say?

NORA—Stop whining, father, and take me home out of this place.

PHELIM—How can I take you home, and all hands here agin you?

DILLON—*I* will take you home, Nora.

HEARTY (*grimly*)—Aye, schoolmaster, when the priest says it.

DILLON—If only I was able, Nora.

NORA—You are able in the heart, Denis, never mind. (DILLON *hangs his head.*)

FATHER SHAUGHNESSY—Each of you must first openly express

sorrow before me for having publicly outraged the moral law, and for the grave scandal you have given, and you must both give an assurance to live a fit and proper life in the future and to co-operate in the spirit and in the letter with my Vigilance Committee.

NORA (*flashing out*)—I was not born to give you, or any of you, assurances.

DILLON—And that answer will do for me, too. (*Pause.*)

FATHER SHAUGHNESSY (*grimly*)—Nora Fintry, are you going to exhaust my patience with you?

NORA—What's your patience to me, Father Shaughnessy? You're just to me a man I rub shoulders with in a dark street, and forget.

PHELIM—For God's sake, Nora, don't anger the priest. You'll not be the better of it the morrow or the day after. Can't you say the word that he wants you to say? What's there in a word?

NORA—There's always been one in Ireland who thought the whole of life was in a word. I was born of such a one.

PHELIM—You were born of *me*, Nora, an' I didn't learn you that.

NORA—It's your old double bed you're thinking of, father. Only for that you'd swear you never saw me before.

DILLON—That's it. The double beds and the clerical gardens —the twin jailors that deny us life.

HEARTY—How far are we to put with this, Father?

FATHER SHAUGHNESSY—Do you two want to provoke me to the use of sterner measures? You are both a menace in my parish. You will either repent of your misdeeds and give suitable assurances or leave my parish.

NORA—I will give you nothing, and I will remain in my own home, where I belong.

DILLON—An' I will dig myself in beside you, Nora.

And now Phelim Fintry is ordered by Father Shaughnessy to refuse his house to his rebellious daughter until she consents to the promises Father Shaughnessy demands of her. And Phelim, though sore distressed, agrees. . . .

Inspector Toomey is knocking a little violently at the door. Cries are heard outside. The Inspector would report the arrest of four of Father Shaughnessy's peace officers and he has come to add Patrick Hearty to the quartet, charging him with "assault and battery and doing grievous harm to Nora Fintry and Michael Shivers."

"This is an outrage," protests Father Shaughnessy. "These moral officers acted expressly on my orders."

"Am I to take it then, Father Shaughnessy, that you aided and abetted these people in a breach of the civil law?"

"I want none of your police jargon. Put it that way if you like."

"Your admission leaves me with no alternative," angrily insists Inspector Toomey. "I warned you before I never count the cost of doing my duty clean or dirty. I'll probably pay for this but I'm doing it all the same. (*Pause.*) As an officer of the law, I arrest you, Father Shaughnessy, and charge you with being a menace to the public peace and with inciting people to acts of criminal violence in defiance of the civil law."

Patrick Hearty is greatly excited. The idea that a representative of the civil law should dare lay a hand on a priest of the Church is beyond his understanding. He stands ready to brain any man who attempts it. Inspector Toomey, however, stands firm. Even after Hearty has called to the crowd for support, and been assured by an angry answer that they stand ready to invade the place and take the "bloody bobby" into their own hands for punishment, he stands firm. Toomey, if necessary, will shoot his way through any attempt on the part of the crowd to interfere with him, and he so warns them.

For answer there is a shattering shower of stones against the windows. Father Shaughnessy steps to the window and, with hand upraised, addresses the crowd—

"My people, I want you to face this crisis calmly and with Christian dignity. You are now, as always, the custodians of the moral name and fame of our country, treasures which we store eternally in our souls. Don't be distressed, it is not the first time that one of your priests has gone to a prison cell . . ."

"The new Marc Antony!" shouts Denis Dillon. "You damn fool, Toomey. Have you no brains!"

"I will not allow this incitement," shouts the priest. "Stand back!"

The excitement spreads, both inside and outside the house. Toomey, continuing to stand his ground, is prepared to handcuff his prisoners together and face the crowd. But as they start for the door, Rosieanne, waving her hands hysterically, flings open the door leading to the Oratory and stands before them, shouting—

"The Canon! Father, the Canon!"

A second later Canon Lavelle appears in the doorway. He is

walking, a little unsteadily, with the aid of a stick. He is greeted with a shower of ejaculations.

"This—is incredible," weakly protests Father Shaughnessy, staring at him.

CANON (*crossing to* FATHER SHAUGHNESSY)—Faith is always incredible, Father Shaughnessy, to the mathematician. (*Cries of shouting and cursing without.*) What is still more incredible is that your blundering has made raving wolves out of my harmless sheep. Listen to that!

FATHER SHAUGHNESSY (*stopping the* CANON *as he moves towards the window*)—You can't interfere in this. I forbid it. You must await the Bishop's ruling.

CANON—I will do as I think fit. There are lives at stake. (*A tense pause as they regard each other.*)

FATHER SHAUGHNESSY (*in a temper*)—Very well, I have warned you. I withdraw as a protest. (*He slams the table angrily and sits down.*)

VOICES—The Canon! The Canon! Hurrah for the Canon!

CANON (*at the window, hammering with his stick sharply*)— I'll hurrah yous if I come out, the—the damned cheek of you all. Is that you I see there, Christy Lamb, and the poor cows below waitin' to be milked? And you, Sarah Pender, who's mindin' your children and you there like a brazen faggot? An' Peadar Coyne. I'll go down, Peadar, and raise you on me toe with a kick, so I will. An' you, Nancy Ryan, I never saw you with a clean house in my life and there you are, an' you, Phil Brady, that put the heel on my boot that came off in a week. A grand cobbler you are, standin' there, ravin' and shoutin', an' of course we wouldn't be right without you, Barney Comiskey. How did you manage to drag your elbow off the counter to come up and see me? An' you, you lazy imp, Aggie Slaven, an' the ashes meetin' me at the door whenever I go to your house. A fine set yous all are, makin' a public show an' laugh of my parish, an' the man from the *Independent* sittin' there on the wall writin' it all down and burstin' with the laughin'. Get home out of that this minute, to your work an' your children an' when I say Mass the morrow I will not have me tongue in me cheek when I'm talkin' to you. (*Noise of people moving away and then silence. The* CANON *slams the window tight, then crosses and confronts the others. Tapping with his stick.*) Patrick Hearty, when I was strong on me props, did I or did I not lead you home often of a night, when you had more drink in you than would stupefy a donkey?

HEARTY—You maybe did, Canon.

CANON—There's no maybe about it at all.

HEARTY—That's all over now, Canon.

CANON—I see. You're a drunkard no longer. You have changed all that to be a common hooligan, defyin' the law and assaultin' your neighbors.

HEARTY—I done it on the priest's orders.

CANON—You did it for your own glorification. Knocking the daylights out of your neighbors for the greater honor and glory of God is a worse disease than leprosy. Go home to your big ass of a wife an' I'll see if I can coax the Inspector here not to land you below in the jail.

HEARTY—All right, Canon, if you want me to go, I'll go. There's a devil the size of an elephant in that fellow Toomey, and I want nothin' to do with him.

TOOMEY—You're right, Hearty. I'd think as much of braining you as I would of strangling a weasel.

The Canon has suggested that Denis Dillon take the weakened Nora into the house for a cup of Rosieanne's tea. Now he has turned to Inspector Toomey and congratulated him extravagantly as "the grandest and the greatest idiot in all Ireland," for having actually arrested a priest for breaking the law—

"Honest men, Toomey, can sometimes be damned nuisances," answers the Canon when Toomey insists that he is an honest man. "That's why the Greeks killed Socrates, and quite right too. Did you ever hear of the law of come and go, of the law of Nelson and his blind eye? When the English, who have the wisdom of all mediocre people, are menaced by Communism, they don't shoot them down, do they? They picture them in the comic papers with beards and bombs and laugh them out of existence. We, who are more learned but less wise, should do likewise with our Holy Willies on the one hand like Hearty and his Vigilance men, and our pagans on the other hand like Dillon and our little firebrand Nora."

Toomey has gone, buoyed by the promise that the trouble is over. Father Shaughnessy, however, is still there and still angered. His blustering has no effect upon Canon Lavelle, however.

"Your blundering and old-fashioned heroics have ruined everything I have achieved," charges Father Shaughnessy.

"What have you achieved?" counters the Canon. "You have only succeeded in stupidly dragging into the light the things we old codgers grow in the dark in Ireland."

"I will allow nothing to grow in the dark in the new Ireland we are building."

"Of course you won't, because you're a hot-headed pioneer full of spiritual snobbery. Ten thousand sages of the Church have refused to write certain laws on paper, but you rushing in with a Gaelic tag in your mouth, scrawl them across a page with a schoolboy's pen. Let me tell you this, that we rule this nation with laws that no one writes but that everyone instinctively accepts. You can cross out a law that's on paper, but you can't cross out a law that has never been written. The day you put these laws on paper in this country, you and I and all we stand for will have to take the field and fight to the death for our continuance. You think I'm an oul' fool, because I speak to my people in their own language, but instead I am what Christ cautioned us to be, as simple as a dove, but as wise as a serpent."

And there it ends, with the Canon announcing that he has written the Bishop and Father Shaughnessy meeting this challenge by announcing that he will seek the Bishop for a personal conference.

"Go ahead," advises the Canon, "an' if his Right Reverence is half as shrewd as I think he is, he'll send you to Glasgow where Communists are two a penny and Holy Willies are nineteen to the dozen."

Father Shaughnessy has stamped his way out of the room. Rosieanne has come to urge the Canon to rest, that he may not overdo the triumph the Mother of God herself has vouchsafed him. And now Denis and Nora are in and the Canon has suggested that Denis make a point of sending a message to the Widow Whelan and the others that have unbaptized children to bring all the babies up to him to be baptized.

As for Denis' job as schoolmaster, that will be all right, too— but the Canon likes his teachers married. It settles them. Which gives Denis an idea—

"Nora, do you think if I went back to the school . . ." he begins. But Nora is not receptive—

"So, you want to go on being a message boy and the Canon's parish clerk," she queries vehemently. "Is that what it all comes to?"

CANON—Now, what kind of talk is that, Nora?

NORA—He must choose. This is one of the things must be said, Canon. You want him to run your messages and be your parish clerk, I want him to go out and meet life and not hide from it, to cease being a servant, and to begin being the giant that every man should build up within himself, yes, to charge windmills, if need be, to believe with me that no law is stronger than life. For these I want him, Canon, and I won't share.

DILLON—Then, neither will I share, Nora. (*Pause.*) Canon, I refuse your offer of the school.

CANON (*going to* DILLON)—It's easy, Dillon, to be heroic when the blood runs hot. But how hot is the blood when your wife is hungry and with child and the fire won't light because there's no coal.

DILLON (*aghast*)—God, don't say that to me, Canon.

CANON—Aye, I'll say it to you. It's another of the things must be said.

DILLON—I . . . I . . . I couldn't bear that. . . . It's all so uncertain. If I went back to the school for security, would you not try and see a little of the way with me?

NORA (*slowly*)—You asked me, Denis, to lift you up and set you free. I've tried and failed. Good-by, Canon. I'm going away.

CANON—Now you're being silly and stupid, Nora. You're not going back to England, I hope.

NORA—No, I will never leave Ireland again. There's something here that is nowhere else. It's away back far and away deep down. A man going down a moonlit road from a fair may know it, or a child reading on a broken window sill of Niam or Aideen or Maeve, but they will tell you no name for it. They will look away from you and the tears will come with a sudden wild rush, but the cry is within them forever, and neither money nor mating will make them happy. (*Pause.*) I am like that, Canon. It's my only sin, and this is my only true confession. Do you know now, why I could not say the wretched word for poor Father Shaughnessy . . . or why I can't be the wife of your parish clerk? (*Pause. She looks at the* CANON *with suffering eyes and goes to the door.*)

DILLON—Have pity on me, Nora.

NORA—I have no pity, Denis, for a man who wants to live on in servitude. I have been born out of warriors, poets, saints and heroes; and am I to bear children to a servant?

DILLON—But there's no way, Nora. Can't ye see there's no way?

NORA—When there's no way, what do all great people and nations do? They blaze a way. But cowards sit in the mud and

complain against God. There's my father's land that needs working and the field at the back needs draining and tilled. There's
the growing of things in the earth—the joy of seeing them flower,
and there's *me*. I will have a free man or no man. (*She pushes
him away*.) Out of my way, Denis, a shrewd old man sets a
penny mousetrap for you and you blunder into it. I will find
what I am seeking without you. (*She goes off with pride and
hauteur*. DILLON *turns from the door to the* CANON. *They look
at each other*.)

DILLON (*brokenly*)—I . . . I will go now, Canon. . . . I will
report for duty on Monday morning.

CANON (*as in a dream*)—So you will . . . and be sure not to
be late, for there's piles of parish work for you that's been
neglected.

DILLON—Very well, Canon, good night.

CANON (*slowly*)—Good night.

DILLON (*turning at the door with sudden spirit*)—Canon, if—
if you were me, what would *you* do?

CANON (*acidly*)—Go home, Dillon. I'm not you.

DILLON (*flashing in*)—You'd throw the school to hell, and go
out after her. You'd drain Phelim's fields for her and dig in
them till your back would break and you'd laugh through it all,
wouldn't you? Go on, Canon, tell me! Tell me the truth!

CANON—I'll tell you nothing.

DILLON—You're afraid—afraid I'll find out the truth of it all.

CANON—Damnation to your cheek, Dillon.

DILLON—And damnation to your slavery. To hell with your
school. I'm going out to find Nora and I'll drain and dig and
plant for her till my body aches. And Nora and I will fight you
to the last.

CANON (*looking at him, after a long pause*)—Now, you're a
man, Dillon, and there won't be any fighting to be done. I am
afraid neither of Nora nor of her children-to-be. And a wiser and
finer Ireland needn't be afraid of them either. I am toppling to
the grave, but that is my faith. I may be wrong but I don't
think somehow that I am. Now go, Denis, and even if she wants
you up on a pagan steed, get right beside her. It will not take
you astray—her white steed has not come down the centuries for
nothing.

DILLON—I will, Canon. And forgive me for bursting out
against you.

CANON—Och, your grannie. Stop asking people to forgive you
and begin telling them to go to blazes. (DILLON *goes off in*

*bright spirits. The* CANON *turns weakly, staggers a little and blunders to a chair, into which he settles himself pensively. He lifts his eyes slowly to the picture of the Blessed Virgin. To the picture, with conversational intimacy.*)    Well, Holy Mother, we're used to these little mountain storms, but sure, the mountains remain.    So we needn't be afraid, need we now?

**THE CURTAIN FALLS**

# HERE COME THE CLOWNS
## A Drama in Three Acts

### BY PHILIP BARRY

AMONG its other distinctions, Philip Barry's "Here Come the Clowns" is the only drama of the season of which this volume is a record that so interested the professional play reviewers that many of them paid it a second visit and reviewed it a second time. This interest was largely evoked because of the play's unusual theme—which is that of man's search for spiritual truth and enlightenment in a sadly muddled world.

Following the first performance in early December a majority of the critics confessed themselves moved by the beauty of many of Mr. Barry's scenes as well as his natural flights of eloquence, and vastly interested in the play and its author's approach to spiritual problems. But—just what did this or that mean?

The following Saturday Mr. Barry, having been stirred to a defense of his play by the reviewers' befuddlement, wrote his own review of "Here Come the Clowns," which he hoped would clear the critical minds. In this review, printed in the New York *World-Telegram,* the author began by saying: "It seems to me that 'Here Come the Clowns' is an extremely simple play, as easy to understand and as clear in its meaning as any fable might be. The entire action takes place at James Concannon's Globe Theatre and in the backroom of a speakeasy attached to it. If the word 'Globe' means the world, I am afraid that is just what I mean. If the backroom of Ma Speedy's Café des Artistes is a small cross-section of the world, populated by some of its apparently less important citizens, that, too, is what I mean. They are not unimportant to me. . . .

"I feel that Clancy is but one man ready and willing to go down in the battle with evil, which continues to be fought throughout the world; that all men should live and die fighting it. That it is infinitely better to die in this struggle than it is to live in fear or in the questionable security which follows any compromise with all these things in government and human society that we know in our hearts to be wrong. This at least was Clancy's answer. . . . Clancy at last finds God in the will of man."

With this statement of faith and understanding those who come upon "Here Come the Clowns" first in this volume are considerably better fortified for both the enjoyment and digestion of Mr. Barry's play than were those first audiences in New York. So let us proceed at once to the opening—

The back room of Ma Speedy's Café des Artistes, Mr. Barry would have you know, is Ma's special and secret pride. There is a miniature stage set in the back wall. Small booths on either side may be used either for the entertainment of the customers or, on occasion, as dressing rooms. "The artists are given to trying out new acts here in the presence of their critical fellows, and sometimes, when the spirit moves, spontaneous entertainments take place."

There is a narrow balcony that stretches the length of the room. It is reached by a steep staircase and leads to a dance-hall which occupies the upstairs front of the building. On the lower floor there are doors leading to the dining room and kitchen, and in the opposite corner a private entrance from the alley that connects the café with James Concannon's Globe Theatre.

The back room is rather dimly lighted at the moment. It is late Saturday night, after the show at the Globe. In one of the booths flanking the stage Major Armstrong, a vaudevillian, has a copy of *Billboard* propped up before him. In the opposite booth John Dickinson, a press agent, is resting his head on his folded arms, neglecting for the moment the bottle and siphon on the table before him.

At the alley door Walter, the waiter, is trying firmly to convince a persistent young woman that she cannot enter by that door, nor bring in her friend, however desperately in need of a stimulant the friend may be. That's the rule. This room is reserved strictly for artists from the Globe. "No one can come in without their private key or else accompanied," Walter explains.

"Listen! Tell Ma Speedy for me that Connie Ryan, head usher at the Globe, is here with her sister, who's had a shock," the young woman is protesting in a voice that is husky, but pleasing.

"I'm sorry, ladies," Walter answers, as firmly as before. "The proprietor is in the front. You'll have to ask there. And *strictly* within the law." With which final word he closes the door and moves back into the room, prepared to continue serving his guests. The Major will have a bottle of ale. Mr. Dickinson another double rye, and no advice from Walter.

For a moment the Major and Dickinson sit staring out into

the room. The Major is the first to speak. It must have been
Clancy's wife at the alley door, he ventures. Which would indicate that she had been in the theatre when Clancy had appeared
boldly on the stage and practically broken up the act of Cooper
and Farrell at the close of the show.

It is Dickinson's opinion that Clancy is crazy—"that crazy
stagehand," he calls him—but Cooper and Farrell were a pair of
flat-footed hoofers, so what if their act was stopped? A swell job
thinks Dickinson. But the nerve of Clancy! "Coming right on
stage in the middle of a turn and asking for someone! Who, for
God's sake?"

Clancy may be looking for his wife, suggests the Major. "All
those misfortunes, one after the other! I guess things got to happening just too fast for him."

"He was a good mascot for the Globe, but he was a bum one
for himself, all right," ventures Dickinson.

"He was always very religious. I hope it helps him."

"The poor dope—the poor, bewildered dope! I was there back-
stage a year ago when the baby-spot came loose and caught him
in the eye. It wasn't a week since his kid died."

"I'll never forget his white face tonight—staring out over those
footlights—"

"What I'll never forget is what that whoozis—that swine of an
illusionist—what he did afterwards," says Dickinson.

Max Pabst is the illusionist, but before we learn what it was he
did the door from the restaurant opens and a short, stout, pink-
and-white man comes in. "He wears a double-breasted dinner-
coat, which drapes gracefully over his curves. He has very small
feet and rotates upon them a trifle when he walks. . . . This is
Ma Speedy, and he is in an expansive mood."

Speedy is likewise a little excited over the Clancy episode.
Can't imagine who it is Clancy is looking for. Hopes he won't
come wandering in there. Anyway, his wife and her sister are
out front. He wonders if anyone would mind if he let them come
in to get some refreshment for Mrs. Clancy? Not Dickinson or
the Major.

Dickinson moves over to the Major's booth. They get a crib-
bage set from Walter and draw the curtains of the booth for
privacy.

And now Connie Ryan and Nora Clancy come in from the restaurant. "Nora is slight and frail, somewhere in her middle
twenties. Connie is two years older, without Nora's cheap refine-
ment of feature, but curiously vital and attractive. Her half-open

coat reveals the blue uniform of a Globe usher."

Ma Speedy is sweetly effusive in his greetings. Let them make themselves comfortable, and let them not mind if anyone should speak to them. They are all just one big family at Ma's little club—"artistes for artistes, you know," he tells them. So Connie orders a beer for herself and a double brandy for Nora, and Speedy goes back into the restaurant whistling happily.

Connie would reason with Nora. Clancy could never have seen her way up there in the balcony. It isn't for fear he saw her that Nora is worried. It was his voice and the crazy way he acted. And the fear she has that Clancy may be hunting Val Gurney. But, argues Connie, why should he go after Val? He doesn't even know it was Val for whom Nora had walked out on him.

"Someone might of wised him up—some busy-body," suggests Nora.

"Go on—it's nothing but your own guilty conscience," chides Connie.

NORA—It was only while I was with him I had a guilty conscience.

CONNIE—Half the time I don't get you at all.

NORA—We're different, that's all. We always have been.

CONNIE—I'll say we have. But don't kid yourself that if Clancy's gone off his nut it wasn't you who did it, because it was.

NORA—It was not! It was not!

CONNIE—All right, all right—calm yourself! Anyway, I don't believe for a minute that he has.

NORA—He was always half nuts—half the time he didn't make sense at all.

CONNIE—You mean the kind of sense *you* could understand. You never had his imagination.

NORA—Oh, my God—"imagination"—

CONNIE—You heard me.

NORA—I know I did. And I know how you've always stuck up for him, regardless.

CONNIE—Why shouldn't I have?—If ever a guy got a dirty deal from life *and* his wife—

NORA—Why? Lots of people have accidents and lose their jobs and have a kid die on them and—

CONNIE—*And* his wife, I said.

NORA—Maybe you should have married him instead.

CONNIE—Wha-at? (*She laughs shortly.*) Me marry Clancy? That's a good one. I should've sailed right up to him, I suppose. I should've said, "Mr. Clancy, I know you've got an eye for a pretty face, but I'm the girl for you, Mr. Clancy. Connie Ryan, good and dependable." Yes: I wouldn't've married him if he'd offered himself on a silver platter. Not if he'd come to me on his knees, I wouldn't've. Me married to Clancy! That really *is* to laugh.

NORA—Maybe yes, maybe no. At least you could of plowed through all those foolish books with him and talked big talk till two in the morning on one glass of beer about God knows what. And of course *you'd* never of wanted to go to dances and things.

CONNIE—Listen: I like dances just as much as you do! Clancy likes them too—if he goes with someone who sticks to him and doesn't roll her eyes around like a couple of hoops.

NORA—Oh, pooh! Tell me one thing: How'd you like to be married to someone who made you feel mean all the time?

CONNIE—Nobody could me.

NORA—When all you wanted was a little fun every other year or so.

CONNIE—Show me somebody funnier than Dan Clancy when he wanted to be.

NORA—I guess he just didn't want to be, with me: I guess that was it.

CONNIE—*I* never had to wait around for the laughs with him.

NORA—It's just what I'm telling you: you're the one who should of—

CONNIE—Here's your drink.

An alley door key is turned and Val Gurney lets himself in. "He is a sharp-featured little man in his middle thirties. He sails his natty hat onto a hook on the wall, adjusts his cuffs and makes directly for the table where Connie and Nora sit."

Gurney is jocular and confident. He is glad to see that his "baby" is taking her tonic and a little impatient with her that she should worry about Clancy. Nothing's going to happen. There's no way Clancy could know that they had been friends. "Friends!" echoes Connie, with the trace of a sneer. "If you don't like it you know what you can do," snaps Nora. And Connie does just that. Takes her things and starts to leave. But at the alley door she listens for a minute and then turns back quickly to the table.

"Get out! Get in there, quick! Get into the front!" she almost shouts. They are slow to move. Connie keeps after them until they are through the door. Then she sits down again and waits. Now another key has turned in the lock of the alley door and three people enter. They are Gert Marble, "a boyish, discontented young woman"; Jim Marble, "a lanky individual of about forty," and Dan Clancy. "Clancy is probably somewhere in his middle thirties, but with such lines of fatigue in his face, such anxiety in his fearsome eyes as to make any conjecture as to his actual age irrelevant and beside the point."

Marble's arm is about Clancy's shoulder and he is nearing the end of a long story to which Clancy evidently has been paying little attention. Finishing the story Marble unties the string of a small duffle-like bag he has been carrying under his arm and takes out a ventriloquist's dummy. This he sets up on a chair with a gay, friendly, professional air—

"There you are, Frank, my friend," he says to the dummy. "Now, mind you behave yourself."

The dummy's mouth flaps open and shut. "God, how you love to hear yourself talk," it says. Marble gives it a push in the face and "Frank" collapses on the chair.

Suddenly Clancy is conscious of the back of Connie's head. He calls her name and she answers without turning around. And then she turns and faces him. She's glad to see Clancy, and he to see her, though they're not over enthusiastic in the showing of it. He would know about Nora, and Connie tells him Nora is all right and working again.

"She's flighty, you know. Nora's flighty," says Clancy.

"You're telling me—who brought her up from a baby? Tell me—how's it been going with yourself?" inquires Connie, as Clancy sits down beside her. "I got to wondering about you once or twice, when I had a spare minute or two."

"I've been all over the place," reports Clancy.

"So I heard tell—from the stage of the Globe tonight."

"That's a bad thing I did," admits Clancy, guiltily.

"Only for Cooper and Farrell."

"All the same, it was bad and ill-mannered, interrupting the show that way. But I was almost out of my senses, Connie."

"And where are you now, would you say?"

"The sight of you brings me back into 'em. You're the real foul-weather friend, Connie."

"You'll turn my head with your compliments."

"I'm a queer duck, and there's no denying it."

"Who is it you're after, Dan? Who've you been looking for?" As Clancy looks away she adds: "I only thought I might, maybe,

## "HERE COME THE CLOWNS"

Clancy: Who is it? Tell me who it is! Because I'll render him null and void, so I will!
Nora: Don't be a fool! No one's anything to me but myself, and never has been.
Connie: That's nice of you. It's right sweet of you to leave him something.

*(Madge Evans, Dora Dudley, Eddie Dowling)*

give you a steer."

"No, there's no one can do that."

"You certainly got all the bum breaks there were."

"You have to take what comes."

"What they call 'resignation'?"

"They do, and they call it well."

"If I were you, I'd get good and sore, believe me I would," says Connie, with spirit.

"Why should I? God-damn it, it's the will of God!" answers Clancy, sharply, as he turns to welcome Walter, come to take their orders for drinks.

Now the others have discovered Clancy. Dickinson and the Major come from the booth to greet him and be introduced to Connie. Marble is adding a bit of clowning with Frank Frenzy, the dummy. The Major, no more than hip-high to any of them when he lets himself down from the cushion he was sitting on, is not disturbed by the surprise of those who do not know him as a midget. He has his satisfactions, too. "Do you know, they had General Tom Thumb in wax in Mme. Tussaud's museum in London for many years," he reminds them, when Marble introduces him jokingly as Tom Thumb the Second. "He stood there among other world notables, such as Napoleon and Nelson, and was the object of much interested comment." Dickinson has recovered the Major's cushion. "Let's all sit," he suggests, as he lifts the Major to his place. "For God's sake let us sit upon our bums and tell sad stories of the death of kings."

It is a philosophical conversation they fall into, and a little sad. Dickinson, deeper in liquor, is supremely pessimistic. Marble is inclined to believe that the world is full of unhappy humans. Clancy is heavy with resignation. The mood is too depressing for Connie—

"This is a real gay party," she says, sarcastically. "This is certainly an evening out! When do the Swiss Bell Ringers come on?"

" 'O, dry those tears, O calm those fears. Life was not made for sorrow,' " spouts Frank, the dummy.

"It's wonderful the way you do that, Mr. Marble," praises Connie. Marble is putting Frank back in his place.

"I'm a very wonderful feller," agrees Marble.

Clancy has heard the music in the dance hall upstairs and Connie has a strong urge for dancing. Let Clancy dance once with her, like in the old days. Clancy is reluctant to try. He's forgotten all he ever knew. But Connie is insistent. She finds a

carnation for his buttonhole and sees him again as gay and jaunty
as he used to be. Finally, though for a moment reminiscence has
clouded his mind with a memory of the carnations and lemon
trees that flourished back in the Glengariff days of his father—
"the flower of God" was what his mother called carnations—and
there was another who wore them always—he is finally persuaded
to try the dance with Connie.

They have just gone off the balcony into the dance hall when,
unnoticed by those on the floor, an unusual figure appears there.
"A stoutish man of uncertain age, wearing a dark suit of foreign
cut. His face is bland, and, in repose, curiously benevolent.
What hair he has is cropped short. He comes to the balcony
railing and stands there, looking out thoughtfully."

It has suddenly occurred to the Major that it was James Concannon, the old gentleman himself, that Clancy is looking for.
Old John always wore a carnation. And there was never a man
for whom Clancy had a greater reverence.

And what has become of Concannon? He's been a corporation
for a long time now, since others run the business, and no one
ever sees him. Even the private staircase that he used to use
back of the stage is dust-covered and long unused, and the door
is locked. Still, the Major is strongly suspicious it is Concannon
for whom Clancy is looking.

"Or I wonder—I wonder could it be me, simple Max Pabst, for
whom that poor, unfortunate fellow has been looking?" The
figure on the balcony is leaning forward, addressing them "in a
low, precise voice with a middle European accent."

Having delivered himself of his introductory query, Professor
Max Pabst walks calmly along the balcony and down the stairs.
Dickinson is disturbed, the Major startled.

"What's he doing here tonight, anyway?" Dickinson is demanding. "What's the point of arriving in town two days ahead of
time? He doesn't go on until Monday, does he? Whoever heard
of an act blowing in on a Saturday? Anyhow, I swear to God
I've seen him some place."

From the restaurant Ma Speedy appears, followed by Freddie
Ballantine, "a dapper little middle-aged man in a dinner coat,"
manager of the Globe. Speedy has mislaid the Professor, and is
a little startled now to discover him coming down the balcony
stairs. "Gracious! You're just everywhere at once, you are!"
protests Speedy.

"A little tour: I like to see things for myself," answers the
Professor, mysteriously, as he looks approvingly about the room.

Pleasant—how pleasant—a charming setting.  Anything could happen here—no?"

Ma Speedy is pleased that the Professor should like his pet Café des Artistes and when Pabst adds that it is full of "Gemüt-lichkeit" Ma is so completely overjoyed that he orders Walter to bring in the Scotch—and Perfection at that.  He also grows reminiscent, regaling them with the story of the days when for three years running he was held over for a second week at the Palace; when he had a special curtain and drop and Harry Collins made his gowns.  But—the war changed the audience's attitude toward Ma's kind of art.  He saw the writing on the wall, retired from show business and bought this little nest.

Gert Marble is back and with an experience to relate.  A young girl from whom she had had a fan letter the day before is in the restaurant.  She will be with them in Syracuse the next week, too—visiting friends.  The news is far from pleasing to Marble.  Throws him into a sort of rage of protest.  But Gert is unim-pressed.  "Try not to be more of a fool than God made you," she advises her husband, and sits down to join him and the Major dealing cold deck poker hands.

At the other table Ballantine has drawn Professor Pabst and the slightly alcoholic and indignant Dickinson into a conference on next week's press announcement.  The Professor has been brought on on short notice to take the place of The Thinking Horse.  He was glad to offer himself as a substitute—besides it happens that he owns a share or two of Globe stock, which is cer-tainly a surprise to them all, especially Ma Speedy.

Pabst, Dickinson now decides, may be the new Concannon for whom Clancy is looking.  That at least is an interesting idea, even to Pabst.  He had never met Concannon but once or twice.  "He was most impressive," admits the Professor.  "He seemed to me a very lonely man—but then who, of any importance, is not?"

At the other table the Marbles have resumed their quarrel.  Marble is insisting that Gert shall head her new admirer off.  "It's bad enough having to play a split-week in Syracuse without any of that going on!" he sneers.  "If you can't take it, you know what to do," answers Gert.

Dickinson has been looking over Prof. Pabst's press stuff and thinks it probably will be all right.  It is "just the usual crap."

PABST—You seem a trifle—shall we say, unfriendly?

DICKINSON—I guess the fact is I've never cared much for magicians.

PABST—But I am not a magician.

DICKINSON—Then what are you?

PABST—An illusionist.

DICKINSON—What's the difference?

PABST—There is a great one. Magicians are interested primarily in deception. I am interested only in truth. But truth is so often an illusion I must, you see, in truth call myself an illusionist.

DICKINSON—A new slant on the same old tricks; crap and double crap.

PABST—Not "tricks," I beg of you. I am not interested in tricks. I have a modest gift for eliciting the truth, that is all— For instance, you carry a gun. Is that not the truth?

DICKINSON—Yes. Very clever. How did you know?

PABST—That is not interestin'. What is interestin' is the purpose for which you carry it.

DICKINSON—And what might that be?

PABST—Yourself. (DICKINSON *stares at him.*)—But I wouldn't, if I were you. It would help nothing.

DICKINSON—Thanks for the advice.

PABST—Merely the truth. Amusing to audiences because one sees and hears so little of it—particularly about oneself, you know. (*Turns to* BALLANTINE.) Tell me more of your man Clancy. I find him most interestin' also. I should like to see more of him.

DICKINSON—You won't have to wait long: he's upstairs now.

SPEEDY—Here? You don't mean it!

DICKINSON—Upstairs, I said. Dancing.

PABST—So? I must have missed him.

BALLANTINE—Dancing! Absolutely!

DICKINSON—You know how they do—on volcanoes?

SPEEDY—Oh, dear—I don't like this at all!

PABST—He is a natural comic. I hope I may be able to do something for him—something, perhaps, to help him forget his troubles.

DICKINSON—I'm sure he'd appreciate that no end.

PABST—We shall see—we shall certainly see what we can do for that unfortunate clown. Such a curious search of his—for whom—for what?

DICKINSON—You tell us, Professor.

PABST (*a moment. Then he speaks in a brisk, matter-of-fact voice to* SPEEDY)—I hope my bag of effects will be safe in the coat-room?

SPEEDY—Don't you worry. No one's ever lost even a hat at Ma Speedy's.

PABST—And that was his wife in the Front, with her lover?

SPEEDY—Well, they do say she and Gurney are—of course *he* doesn't *dream*—

PABST—Shh! Jetz kommt er. Er ist punkt.

There is a burst of dance music from the balcony as Connie and Clancy, followed by a youthful and engaging pair of dancers, Lew Cooper and Fay Farrell, come in from the dance hall. They evidently have been having a grand time and are gay in their reactions. They had been together once before, three years ago Decoration day, at the Beach. They had entered a marathon then, and Connie and Clancy had won a doll. . . .

All is not harmony with the Cooper and Farrell duo. They are talking of given names when Lew Cooper reveals that he was named by "the top dame of an orphan asylum," and resents it bitterly. Fay doesn't care.

"You'd more or less like to know who you are though, wouldn't you?" demands Cooper.

"I wouldn't care! Really, I wouldn't!" insists Fay. "Are names the reason you won't marry me?"

"They might be—and that ugly mug of yours, of course."

"This guy has been crazy for me for five years, nearly," says Fay, turning to the others. "Ever since we teamed up and developed our act, he has. And still he won't marry me. He won't even sleep with me."

Connie has returned to her memories of the doll she won with Clancy. "Night and day he stands up there on my dresser like this," she says, shaping her napkin into a cone and standing it before her. " 'Dan Clancy,' I say to him, 'you keep out of trouble. You're always getting into trouble.' "

CLANCY—I must have been named after Daniel in the Lion's den.

CONNIE—"If you were troubled with lions," said the King, "you must have brought them yourself."

CLANCY—If my little Angela had been a boy, I was going to name *her* after Michael, the Archangel.

FAY—Who? What circuit does he play?

CONNIE—Listen to her!

CLANCY—The Universal! Up the heavens and down again.

He's Captain of the selfsame troops that defended the throne of God against the assault and battery of the Old Nick, that time there was the trouble.

DICKINSON—"And there was War in Heaven!"

CLANCY—There was that all right—and what a war! My mother told me all about it, over and over. Three hundred years it went on—of course, their time is not like ours.

CONNIE—Three days, most likely—or else three minutes.

DICKINSON—Michael and his angel fought against the dragon. And the great dragon was cast into the Earth. I thought you looked familiar, Professor.

PABST—You are so amusing.

CLANCY—Michael's the fine old bird, and without him God knows where we'd be now.

DICKINSON—And where are we?

CONNIE—And don't be so irreverent, calling him an "old bird."

CLANCY—I'm not. I know the Captain well. Once in the army—the time I got conked—I thought I saw him. (*He salutes.*) —Maybe I did.

FAY—I'll tell you what, Clancy: if Lew ever marries me and we have any kids, I'll name the first Michael Daniel, after you both.

CLANCY—You can leave out the "Daniel"—or call the next one it.

LEW—Oh, lay off this marrying-and-kids stuff! It's enough to drive a guy crazy!

FAY—Why, Lew—

LEW—Just lay off it! Talk sense.

FAY—He's been this way all week—some chip on his shoulder for everything and nothing.

LEW—Well, it's been one hell of a week—playing to empty houses—and on the same bill with a flock of midgets. Midgets—God!

CONNIE (*glancing in the direction of* THE MAJOR)—Hush, Lew—

LEW—I don't care. I hate 'em. I hate the sight of 'em. Hey, come on. Come on with those drinks, will you? I want a drink!

Lew has jumped up and helped himself to a drink from the tray that Walter is bringing in. Professor Pabst is immensely pleased with all these touches of human comedy that he is seeing. A moment later the Marbles have resumed their quarrel, intensified now when Walter brings in a note to Gert from the young woman in the restaurant. Marble grabs the note, reads it, pronounces it sickening and throws it to the floor. "What am I to do with you?" he cries to Gert. "How can I keep you off it, you filthy, underhanded little—"

Ma Speedy has again taken a hand, stopping Marble in his attack, for the sake of the rest of them. Gert boldly recovers the note and puts it in her bosom.

"As fine a collection of wretched, unhappy human beings as ever it has been my privilege to behold," observes Professor Pabst, and adds: "I am learning much." Ballantine would take him away but the Professor wants to stay and meet Clancy, who appeals to him strongly.

Ballantine negotiates this introduction later and also takes advantage of the opportunity it affords to lecture Clancy again about his having broken up the show. Again Clancy is apologetic. He regrets what he did, largely on Mr. Concannon's account. True, Mr. Concannon is no longer there. And it is not for Mr. Concannon that Clancy is searching—though to be sure he might take that form as well as any other— Suddenly Professor Pabst leans toward Clancy and says, very softly—

"Mr. Clancy— Unhappy and luckless Mr. Clancy—is it possible, by some curious chance, that he for whom you have been searching is no less a personage than—than God Himself?"

CLANCY (*after a moment's silence*)—It is!—And what's there curious about it?

CONNIE—Dan! What are you talking about?

SPEEDY—Good gracious!

DICKINSON—A still hunt for the Almighty! It's marvelous. Clancy, you certainly fly high.

CLANCY (*wheeling on him and demanding*)—And why not? Isn't He everywhere? Is there a nook or a corner where He's not? What's there so strange in going out to find Him? Others have done it, and others will again! (*Once more his head sinks and his wild eyes stare blankly at the floor. He goes on, half to himself:*) I have to find Him! 'Tis a necessary thing to me. I know it is His will that things happen as they do, but I've come to a place where I have to know the reason for certain of them. And know I will!

PABST—Of course, of course—

MARBLE—It's the damndest thing—

THE MAJOR—Why, Jim?

BALLANTINE—But in a vaudeville House—on a Saturday night!

Absolutely!

SPEEDY—Yes—that takes the cake, it certainly takes the—cake!

MARBLE (*to* CLANCY)—Why, of all places, did you think He'd pick the Globe for a personal appearance?

CLANCY—I don't know.—I was in Cleveland. I'd been many other places among the poor and lowly, where they say it's easiest to—where they say He spends much of His time—but nor hide nor hair of Him. I was out walkin' by myself when all of a crack it came over me, like a cat jumped down on me back from a wall: "Tomorrow night at James Concannon's Globe—Holy Saturday night—hurry, me boy, hurry!"—So I came as quick as I could. I don't know how I got here. I don't even remember the—the train, it must have been. It wasn't till near curtain-time did I arrive. The sweat was pouring from me, for fear of missing Him— (*His voice rises.*) But I can't have! I can't! I know in me bones He was there!

CONNIE (*swiftly moving to his side*)—Come along now, Dan. Come along with Connie.

CLANCY—Don't treat me as if I was bereft of me senses! I'm not! I'm sane as the next one, maybe more so. I could be a bit off on me reckoning, of course. Maybe it was tomorrow night—no, tomorrow's Sunday and the House will be locked fast, and dark.—Or maybe it was somewhere not precisely in the Globe, but roundabouts. Maybe it was even—even— (*He glances about him.*) —No, Connie—the night's not over yet.

CONNIE—Will you please to come along, please?

CLANCY—And maybe miss Him entirely?—After all this time render me search null and void?

PABST (*rising and touching his elbow, gently steers him into a chair at the table, then turns and calmly surveys the incredulous faces about him*)—This seems not at all as strange to me as it appears to seem to you. A man searches for the Truth and calls it "God"— Why not? It has many names, and as many faces.

CLANCY—It has one: and that's the name and the face of God!

DICKINSON (*to* PABST)—Maybe you can scare Him up for the poor guy, Professor. Maybe *you* can evoke Him.

PABST—The Truth, I can evoke.

DICKINSON—Who says?

PABST—You do not believe me.

DICKINSON—No.

PABST—You would like a demonstration, perhaps?

DICKINSON (*after a silence*)—Yes. Strut your stuff.

MARBLE—And be *sure you make it good.*

PABST—Very well.—But you must promise not to interfere.—Agreed?

The request is directed toward Dickinson, who replies with a gesture of consent. Professor Pabst has moved swiftly to the little stage and thrown back its curtains. What Ma Speedy would term a "small but tasty" interior is revealed. A rather elaborate and quite nondescript setting it is—a huge Italian chair, a Chinese table—"the loot of many years, and utterly unreal."

Ma Speedy is wriggling gleefully in his chair. They are going to have an entertainment and that is what he loves. Ballantine, on the other hand, has had enough for one week. He grabs his hat and out the alley door he goes.

On the stage a pair of portières at back have been parted, revealing the door marked "Private." Pabst tries it and it is locked. He carefully draws the portières closed again.

"And surely if He should choose to reveal Himself, Truth would prepare the way for Him, would it not? Shall we begin?" he says

"Look—he's going to do his act—" whispers Fay.

"Act? I have no act. It is you who have the acts." Pabst has come down the steps and turned to Marble. "Mr. Marble—please—"

"But—but aren't *you* going to do something?" asks Ma Speedy, disappointment in his tone.

"I? Oh, no—I shall merely be master of ceremonies." Pabst is smiling again at Marble as the curtain falls.

## ACT II

The scene is not changed. The action is continuous. At the front of the stage Professor Pabst turns his attention first to Mr. Marble, the ventriloquist. Marble would add a laugh or two by having Frank Frenzy, the dummy, answer for him, and often from the bag. Yes, he is married. Yes, this is his wife. Yes, she assists him in his act. She wears black tights and is said to have a very fine figure. "Don't fail to tell us everything," suggests Gert.

But when it comes to going up on the stage with the dummy, Marble rebels. He has already done twelve shows this week, and he is throat-sore and weary. Pabst, however, is insistent—friendly but insistent. This particular act will refresh both

Marble and Frank, the professor promises.

"Marble's too good for Number One on any bill," interposes Dickinson. "I'll do the opener. It's a recitation, very short and to the point. Listen, Clancy: This is for you—"

Marble is arranging his props on the stage as Dickinson proceeds, talking directly to Clancy—

"Once there was a little man in County Kerry—like you—and he led a little life—and one day he began to pack a little bag. And *They* said, 'Where are you off to? Where are you going?' And *he* said, 'I'm packing my bag and I'm going to Connemara.' And *They* said, 'You mean, you're going to Connemara, God Willing.' And he said, 'I mean I'm going to Connemara.' So God changed him into a frog and put him in a frog-pond and kept him there for seven years—" Connie laughs and asks what kind of a God would do that to a little man. Dickinson continues: "Oh—Clancy's—and other people's generally. And then God changed him back again—and what did the little man do? He began at once to pack his little bag. And *They* said, 'Where are you off to? Where are you going?' And he said, 'I'm going to Connemara.' And *They* said, 'You mean, you're going to Connemara, God Willing.' And he said, 'I mean I'm going to Connemara, or back to the frog-pond!'"

"I see what you mean," says Clancy.

"When you arrive there send me a postcard—with the answer," begs Dickinson.

"Apt—but we must have no more interruptions," cautions Pabst. He turns to Marble. "Shall we begin?"

Marble goes into his ventriloquial act with Frank, kidding the Professor, kidding Frank, kidding himself. "You seem depressed, Jim. What's the matter?" the dummy inquires. "Has the little witch been acting up again?" "The little—?—I don't know who you mean, Frank." "W-i-t-c-h—'w' as in 'butter.' She certainly runs you ragged. I don't see how you stand it—" "I don't care to discuss my domestic affairs." "You're going to, whether you care to or not," says Frank.

"Oh, lay off—" Gert is disgusted and a little mad.

But the dummy is not to be stopped. With each interrogation Frank becomes more and more revealing concerning this "chippie off the old block—Tenth avenue, between Fourteenth and—" Marble would appear to be defending Gert: "She is the soul of loyalty, kind, generous, sweet-tempered, loving and economical— in fact, the perfect help-meet," says he. "'Hell-cat?' did you say?" parries Frank. "'Help-meet!' Help-meet—hooey! Applesauce!"

The give and take grows more and more bitter. It is no time
for secrecy, insists Frank. There has been too much of that.
And why doesn't Jim quit Gert, knowing all he knows? "Why, I
guess I just don't want to," weakly insists Marble. "More
hooey," answers Frank. "You mean you're too soft-hearted to.
You know if you don't watch her like a hawk she'll go straight
to hell in a hack—well, why not let her?" "She was a sweet kid,
once." "You mean before the girls came around." "The what?"
"You heard me—the girls! The little ones—the soft ones—the
frilly ones—the girly-girls—"

Gert has jumped from her seat and is advancing threateningly.
"I'll kill you, you damned little—" she is shouting raucously.
"And what do you call yourself?" taunts the dummy. "What
could sink a man lower than to have to live with a woman who—"
Gert is standing over the pair of them now. "I won't stand it!
I don't have to listen to such talk! I—I'll—" She seizes the
dummy and shakes it violently—"You—you foul little, lying
little—" She flings the dummy to the floor, grabs her hat and
makes for the alley door—"You'll never see me again," she shouts.
"Never in this world—you hear me!" She is through the door
and gone, banging the door behind her.

Slowly Marble picks up the sprawling dummy, puts it back in
the black bag, hunches it under the crook of his arm and would
follow after. "Where are you going?" asks the Professor. "After
her. She'll just sit in there till I come," resignedly answers
Marble.

PABST—I would not, if I were you.

MARBLE—Why not?

PABST—Is that not just what she wants? Is that not just what
you have always done?

CONNIE—But the poor, misguided creature—who else is she to
turn to?

SPEEDY—She's got a right to her own life!

DICKINSON—Who says?

CLANCY (as MARBLE stares at PABST, hesitating)—Go on, Jim.
Go on, man!

MARBLE (gazing at CLANCY)—No. (He sinks into her chair
at the table, the black bag dropping at his feet.)

CLANCY—But she's your own wife! And she might do some
harm to herself.

MARBLE—Let her! Who gives a damn?

CLANCY—That's no thing to say!

PABST—Wise—at last he grows wise.

CLANCY—Wise, me foot! Who's to help her but him?

PABST—Never mind her. The Truth has set *him* free!

DICKINSON—The hell it has. It's only moved him into another kind of prison.

MARBLE—Shut up, the lot of you!

THE MAJOR—You shouldn't have done it, Jim.

PABST (*turning blandly to* THE MAJOR)—You, also did not care for the performance?

THE MAJOR—No, I did not.

PABST—Perhaps you and I might give a better one—you think?

THE MAJOR (*staring at him*)—How do you mean?

PABST—You could be *my* little man—no?

THE MAJOR—I don't understand you.

PABST—Would you be so kind as to come on stage with me, please?

THE MAJOR—No. No, thank you.

PABST (*moving closer to him, stands over him*)—But I must insist! It is very important to a friend of yours— (*Glances at* CLANCY.)

SPEEDY—Oh, go on, Major—it's all in fun.

MAJOR—But I don't see how—

PABST (*holding out a hand to him*)—Come—you will soon find out how. It is really as simple as what-you-say—a-b-c.

On the stage the Professor picks the Major up, swings him around and sets him down on his knee. "Now then! Attention, please—everyone attention! Good evening, Major."

"Well, what is it you want to know from me?"

"Just a few little things. Like our friend Clancy, there are small things that puzzle me—"

And the Professor has begun a new search for the truth. Once, when Clancy objects to a pointed reference to himself, he is bidden to come closer to the stage—and the truth that is to be revealed.

"Tell me about this Clancy," the Professor is saying to the Major, as Clancy seats himself on the second step of the stage-steps. "Acquaint me briefly with the facts of his decline and his fall."

THE MAJOR—From the beginning, his life has been a hard one. As a boy he knew cold and hunger, and he has known them since.

He never asked for much, and much was never given him.

CLANCY—Don't make me out sorry for meself now—for I'm not!

THE MAJOR—In fact, the little that he had, at last was taken from him. He lost his little home and he lost his little savings. He lost the sight of one eye.

CLANCY—Well, I never did any crying over meself with either of them. It's not such things alone—

THE MAJOR—He lost his job. His young brother and his little daughter. That was the worst. He was left with only his beloved wife to help him mourn all these things that had been so dear to him. Then he woke one fine morning and found that she was gone, too.

PABST—His wife? Where to? With whom—a lover?

CLANCY (*springing up*)—Put up your dukes! You get a poke in the nose for that!

PABST (*holding out his hands to* CLANCY)—Forgive me—

CLANCY—Then why did you say such a thing?

PABST—I was in error: forgive me.

CLANCY—The poor child left me because she thought she was bad luck for me. She said it to me once: "I bring you bad luck, Dan," she said.

PABST—Of course—of course—

CLANCY—"Of course" no such thing! She only thought it!

PABST—I understand.

CLANCY—See that you do! And in the future, mind your tongue!

PABST (*bowing his head, turns again to* THE MAJOR)—And his little girl—how old was she?

THE MAJOR—I don't know precisely—two—three—

CLANCY—Three years, four months, two days.

PABST—They are sweet at that age.

CLANCY—*She* was!—And she was good, too, and pretty as a picture and full of jokes and laughing. Never a tear out of her, except now and then when her little insides hurt her, with the wind or the like—or when she grew aware of the vast world about her and felt too small in it and needed comforting.

PABST—A bitter blow to lose her.

CLANCY—It was, that. How it happened, I don't know—or why it ever did. She was always well and strong, for all that she was a seven months' baby. It started with no more than a little cold—the same as any child might have in changing weather.

But it grew and grew until it was all the way through her and then the doctor could only shake his head and sit and watch her, fighting for breath, beating her little fists in the air.

PABST—What could be sadder?

CLANCY—There's little that could be—I don't know of anything could, now I think of it.—Angela was all that was ever all my own. My job could be taken any time—the eye is a delicate organ, subject to accidents—me house was never fully paid for— young Timmy, my brother, drank—and my Nora was me wife only so long as she was willing to put up with me. But Angela was all my own.

PABST—Still, all such deprivations mean something—don't you agree, Major? They all have some purpose in the scheme of life.

DICKINSON—Oh, sure, sure—they add zest.

CLANCY—But mean what? That's what I want to know! The purpose of 'em!—And I want to know other things!

There is no time for those other things at the moment. At the Professor's prompting the Major has begun the story of his own life. He, too, had had a child. A son. Born a good many years ago. Anna, his wife, had been a midget, too. Smaller, even, than he. Perfectly formed, perfectly proportioned, and with the bluest blue eyes! "The Vest-Pocket Venus" the newspapers called her, and they had adopted the title for their act, "Major Armstrong and His Vest-Pocket Venus."

"We—we thought that having a child would be like shouting from the housetops: 'Look! See how these small people have loved! Love is not denied the small in stature if their souls, if their spirits be—'" The Major pauses, and then, regaining control, goes on—"He was born as Caesar was, and the medical men in attendance were very interested and very pleased with themselves. He was normal in every way—like Anna's grandmother— like my father—"

The Major and Anna were very happy with their first-born but when, at four, he was nearly as tall as they, they began to worry and fear and plan. When the boy was five they "were like three children together" and when he was seven they decided to send him away—for his own good. But Anna could not endure a world without her child. "Month by month she dwindled away to nothing and one night she just turned on her pillow and died." The Major's voice has sunk to little more than a hoarse whisper. "It was here in the Sims' Hotel. I would have followed her but

Mr. Concannon gave me the courage to wait."

"And what became of the boy?" the Professor would know.

"The people he was with were not good people—they couldn't have been, because he ran away from them. I've never been able to find out where—or anything about him—though I've tried very hard to. He'd be a grown man now. I—I daresay he'd make a dozen of me." The Major is looking at the Professor. "And now may I get down, please?"

PABST—One moment. (*He turns to* CLANCY.) Well, Mr. Clancy—?

CLANCY (*looking up, his eyes dazed*)—Who—? Where? What did you say?

PABST (*turning to the others*)—It appears that our saddened friend does not yet realize that others among us also have our burdens to bear.

CLANCY—Ah, that I do! I do indeed! But what help is that to anyone? (*He turns to* THE MAJOR.) My heart is knotted up into a fist for you, Major.

THE MAJOR—Thank you, Clancy.

PABST (*frowning down on* CLANCY)—Which is the worse—to have the Almighty take a child, or to have to give it away to strangers? To have it safe in heaven—or to have it roam the world, nameless and alone.

CLANCY—The cases are not the same—nor the circumstances! But both are bad, both!

PABST—Which is better—to have one's wife die, wracked to the bone with grief—or to have her leave one, and live on?

CLANCY—It's not the same—there's no similarity!

And now it is Cooper and Farrell's turn. The Professor has asked them to step forward, which they reluctantly and hesitantly do. From Fay the Professor would know what has been her reaction to what she has heard. Would she still want to marry? And have children? Fay would. And why, then, pretty as she is, hasn't she taken Lew by the hand and led him to the altar? She can't because Lew won't have it so. In which case, the Professor agrees, Lew must have his reasons.

"Oh, can it!" shouts Lew. "What right have you got to mix in, anyway?"

"But this is impolite of you," protests Pabst. "It is not in the interests of a varied entertainment. Come, young man—come,

come—come—" The Professor is smiling and coaxing.
"That'll be all right," announces Lew, with finality.

PABST—He is stubborn, Little Major. It appears *we* must go
to *him*. (*With* THE MAJOR *he proceeds down the stage steps,
advances to* LEW *and stands directly facing him.*) Look at him,
Little Major. Gaze upon this strange contradiction: a young man
in love who will not marry. Talented, well-off, sound in limb and
in sinew, and still he will not marry.

LEW—That's my business, isn't it?

PABST—Ah, yes—deeply so. Look at him, Major—you are a
wise little man—perhaps you can account for this perverse attitude. All that we know of him is that he is a foundling, that he
is in love and that he will not marry.—Ah, yes! And one thing
more—

LEW—Shut up. Shut up, you!

PABST—Just one—a certain unaccountable distaste for very
small people, like yourself. Look at him closer—consider the
brow, the elevated cheek-bones. And the eyes—did you ever see
eyes so blue in a man's head? Where have you ever seen their
like before? (LEW *begins to tremble. His hands close and un-
close spasmodically.*) He seems to grow nervous—I wonder why?
Of what can he be afraid? (*His voice lowers.*) Little Major—
does it not grow more apparent why he will not marry? (*A sudden cry is wrung from* THE MAJOR *and he turns his gaze sharply
from the Dancer's face. But* PABST *goes on:*) Is it not now
somewhat more evident who he is?

LEW—You—you fishy, fat-headed slob, you—what the hell do
you think you're trying to pull off?

THE MAJOR—Let me go! Let me go!

PABST—But certainly. (THE MAJOR *totters toward the stage,
sinks down upon the lowest step and sits there, his head in his
hands, his narrow shoulders shaking.* FAY *looks wonderingly
from him to* LEW, *then back again.*)

FAY—Oh, Lew— Let me tell him!

LEW (*suddenly shouting*)—He lies! He's not!

PABST (*mildly*)—Who is not what? Have I said anything?

LEW—Plenty! But it's not true that I'm his—he's my—! And
you know damn well it's not!

PABST—Of course, of course—

LEW—Then why do you make it seem that it is? You, with
your oily roundabout way of—your cheap, ten-twenty-thirty trick
of piling it up, and then making it sound like it was the McCoy—!

(*He flounders and stops.*)

FAY—Lew—listen, Lew—

LEW—I tell you it's just his rotten idea of being funny! It's a stinking lie, the whole thing, cooked-up out of nothing! I'll be damned if I'll hang around and take any more of it! To hell with the lot of you— (*He storms out into the alley.* CLANCY *drops down upon the step and throws one arm protectingly about* THE MAJOR. FAY *moves to the alley door.*)

FAY—Lew! (*Turning, she faces* PABST.) I think—I think you're a living horror. God damn you to hell. (*She goes out.*)

PABST (*sighs, lowers his head and clasps his hands across his front.*) Dear, dear. It seems that even the semblance of truth is not popular.

There is a suggestion of rebellion in the audience. If it is only the "semblance" of truth that the Professor is producing, suggests Clancy, then he must be admitting himself that it is not true. And why, Dickinson would know, should he be taking all this from Pabst. Any small time ham could put on as good an act. Besides it happens that he (Dickinson) knows who Lew's father is and where he is. No, he won't tell.

"All I know is that if ever I did find him, it might—it might be like that," plaintively admits the Major.

"You tricky old wretch, you—Lew and Fay were better off as they were—and so was the Major," says Clancy, turning on Pabst.

"But, advise me seriously, Mr. Clancy—would you not rather your daughter were dead than that she had ever grown up to deny you?"

"She never would have! . . . And I say again, you shouldn't have done this to the Major. You've not done him good, you've done him ill."

"A matter of opinion," insists Pabst. And would Clancy rather it had happened to him? There's nothing more that could be done to him that hasn't been done, insists Clancy. And he has his consolations. He had had a wife who loved him, and maybe still does. He had his health and his small house with a garden round it and a little girl who was all his own. They're fine memories, these. And he is content.

"Connemara—to Connemara!" interjects Dickinson, rising a little uncertainly.

Connie would take Clancy away now, and Clancy is of a mind to follow her, until the insistent Professor challenges his willingness to give up his great search so easily. "The Irish are a soft race, really," says Pabst, a trace of contempt in his voice. "The bravery is all in front?"

"Who says it is?" demands Clancy. "Who says they are?"

"An Irishman without a cause—is there a sadder sight in the world?" prods the Professor.

"If me cause is a lost one, it's none the less me own, you old crook," shouts Clancy, and would turn again to follow Connie. Again the Professor stops him. Evidently some new plan is taking form in his mind. He has taken two chairs and placed them opposite each other. Then he calls Speedy and whispers a message to him. Speedy, puzzled but obedient, goes into the restaurant. The Clancy curiosity is excited. He decides to stay for a minute. He would have Connie stay, too, but Connie has no intention of letting Pabst worm any alleged truths out of her. She has nothing to tell—nothing—

"No?—Not one little word to the one man in the whole world—" The Pabst voice is suave and insinuating.

"That isn't so!" shouts Connie. "I don't! I don't at all!"

"Don't what? What have I said?"

"Never mind! Come on, Dan. I don't like it here. I—"

Clancy is staring at Connie as though he might be seeing her for the first time. There is something strange about her face. What is it? Why isn't she wearing her earrings? Surely she remembers the earrings her grandmother had given her—

"You're thinking of Nora," says Connie. As for Connie, she wouldn't wear earrings on a bet. Not if she had to—

The door to the restaurant has opened and Nora is standing there. Ma Speedy is bringing her in. Clancy's back is turned. Nora is protesting that she doesn't want to come. "Why should I be the stooge for a trick-man, for God's sake?" demands Nora. And now she sees Clancy. Speedy had told her that Clancy had left. At the sound of her voice Clancy turns and would embrace her joyously. Nora holds him off. Let him keep his distance. Clancy is startled but obedient. He goes back to his chair. Nora turns on Connie. "I suppose it's you I've got to thank for this," she says, resentfully. "I'd nothing to do with it," answers Connie. "I'd of done wonders to keep it off."

Nora has sat down defiantly in the chair opposite Clancy. There is a challenge in her voice as she demands to know what he wants. The others—Dickinson, Marble, the Major and Speedy—decide it were better for them to get out, but Nora had as soon they stayed. This is a free-for-all and she'd like to get it over with. Clancy can't understand. She's changed some-way. She's got hard. She has always been hard, says Nora. She was born hard—hard as nails. Naturally she took pains that he didn't learn that. He had a sweet little picture of her in his mind and she tried to live up to that. Nothing that he believed of her was true. He may as well know that once and for all.

"You're a blight on me, Dan Clancy, and you always have been," says Nora, and laughs at a memory of his trusting belief in her. "Something's just suddenly come over you," suggests Clancy. "Oh, tie it outside! You're a worse fool than I thought you!" snaps Nora.

"Why did you run away from me with never a word?" demands Clancy. "Was it because of all the misfortune that had suddenly come upon us, and you thinking you'd brought it?"

"That's what you told yourself, is it?" marvels Nora.

CLANCY—I'm asking you, Nora—and what's more, you're to tell me.

NORA—That was part of it, yes.

CLANCY—What else?

NORA—Because I couldn't stand you!

CLANCY (*looking at her aghast*)—You don't mean that all at once there was no more love in your heart for me—

NORA—I mean there never was any!

CLANCY (*frowning, unable to comprehend, turns to* CONNIE)—She's joking.—You hear her, Connie: she's trying to make some kind of a joke.

NORA—Joke, my eye! I'm saying what I mean now, for once—and I mean just that—never ever—never a scrap of love!

CLANCY (*looking at her from under his brows*)—For nearly four years we were man and wife—

NORA—You don't need to tell *me* that!

CLANCY—You can't fool me, Nora. I have too good a memory.

NORA (*seeing what he means and laughing shortly*)—Oh, I liked *that* part of it all right. I got round heels, you know.

CLANCY (*set face and angered eyes traveling her from head to foot and back again; finally very softly*)—From a dear and a loving and warm-hearted girl, full of grace and delight, something or someone has turned you in no time at all into a cheap, dirty-mouthed little piece. Someone has put a spell on you—who is it?

NORA—So there has to be someone *else*, does there? Listen, you—

CLANCY—Who is it? Tell me who it is. Because I'll render him null and void, so I will!

NORA—Don't be a fool. No one's anything to me but myself, and never has been.

CONNIE—That's nice of you. It's right sweet of you to leave him something.

CLANCY (*searching* NORA'S *impudent pretty face for something he wants desperately to find there*)—It's not that I don't love and cherish you as I always have— But you anger me. Your un-womanly talk and your vast impertinencies and the silly, hollowed-out sound of a laugh that used to be sweet like a string-orchestra—it makes me angry.

NORA—So what?

CLANCY—I don't know yet, but you must be made to unlearn your new tricks.

NORA—Oh? By who?

CLANCY—By me!—you fresh, brassy little jape, sitting there on your hard seat with that new chippie look in your shoe-button eyes and that two-for-a-dollar smile round your mouth, you were once my wife, you still are. And I'll have no wife of mine abroad on such behavior, and you can make book on it!

NORA—So what do you plan to do?

CLANCY—You know what I'd like to do this minute?—I'd like to give you one with the flat of me hand that'd send you spinning down the Ages.

NORA—Only you won't.

CLANCY—Don't be so sure, Miss.

NORA—You haven't it in you to. You're the original Mister Soft-heart, and your hands were made for love-pats. (*She rises.*) Well—save 'em for someone else. I'm not taking any. (*She drops back a step or two, opens her bag, peers into a mirror, powders her nose and addresses him with a fine air of finality.*) Anything more?—If not, I'll be getting along now.

But Clancy has stepped before her and ordered her to stay where she is. When Nora would appeal to Speedy he also avoids the issue. Speedy never comes between husband and wife. And then the door from the restaurant is opened and Val Gurney comes swaggering in. He's glad to see Clancy back, is Gurney. Glad to see him looking so well. A fellow'd hardly know there was anything the matter with his eye. But Clancy will have done of Gurney or his patter—

"I don't like you, Val Gurney, and I never did. All that I ever owed you was that it was through you that I first met up with Nora. But since she's left me I owe you no more."

"Why, Clancy, you surprise me. I thought we were old friends. What's the trouble between you and the Missus?"

"It turns out it was a stray cat I brought home," says Clancy, looking at Nora. "I buttered her paws and she stayed only to lick them off, and then strayed again."

"You don't say—and I thought you'd be the perfect match."

"I remember you said so." Clancy turns suddenly upon Nora and seizes her by the wrist. "Only, where did you stray to?" he demands. Professor Pabst and Ma Speedy decide this is a good time to depart. The others would urge Clancy to go easy. But Clancy is not to be stopped. He wants the name of the man and will have it—

"Val! Val!" cries Nora, when Clancy has forced her to her knees. And now Clancy knows. Nervously Gurney has put out his cigarette. Clancy is staring incredulously at him. Dickinson and Marble are closing in. Gurney is excitedly suggesting that there should be no rough stuff. Everything can be settled peacefully. What would a man want with a woman he couldn't hold, anyway?

Clancy is not to be stopped. He has moved in now, swiftly, ruthlessly. He has Gurney by the neck and is beginning to shake him slowly, like a sack. Nora is yelling her protest, but nobody is paying any attention. "He had it coming!" Connie is shouting. "You both of you had!"

With a twist of his arm Clancy has sent Gurney crashing against the alley door. He lies there for a minute, gets to his feet, brushes himself off and fumbles for the doorknob. Half through the door he turns and spits out his words at Clancy—

"You scum! You half-witted moron! Come around and ask me some more questions sometime. Ask me about your kid, for instance." Clancy has turned and started for Gurney again. "She came pretty quick, didn't she? Seven months, my foot— six was nearer it! Why else do you think she married you, you poor, dumb—"

Before Clancy can reach him Gurney has slammed the door. Again Clancy is facing Nora.

"It was him introduced us, him that brought us together. And from the first sight of you you knew it was all up with me. And you took me straight off—"

"He made me! He kept after me till I—"

"You put your head on my shoulder and said, 'Let's not wait, Dan. Let's not wait a week even.' Do you remember you did?"

"You don't know—"

"That was in April—and less than seven months after—on the second day of November—though we'd not looked for it till the first of the year, if that soon—and the doctor said often at seven months if the mother was not as strong as she might be—" His voice catches and he stops. His body is swaying, he is murmuring to himself—"And I told meself there was no more ill could happen to me!" He has turned slowly to Nora now, and touched her gently upon the shoulder—"You can go along now, Nora." He has laid her coat over her shoulder—"There now—there we are—" They are at the door—"Good-by, now. When I think of the frets and the worries you've had me heart aches for you, you bad girl, you— Good-by, now. Good-by, Nora—" She has gone through the door, pathetically crushed. Clancy comes heavily back to the table—"I think I'll have a small drink, now, if that's agreeable," he says, and Dickinson fixes one which he drains at a gulp. "That's what I needed," he says, drawing the back of his hand across his mouth. " 'There comes a time,' as they say—"

"Oh, yes—it's a small world. God's in his Heaven, all right, and he's going to stay there." Dickinson is bitter.

Clancy has slumped down into a chair and is gazing blankly at the table. Connie slips into the chair beside him and takes his hand in both of hers. "She was yours, little Angela was," comforts Connie. "She was all your own. Never have I known a baby to go so for any man. You were the one bright star in her little life. She was just a little fool for you, Dan—no one else ever counted with her."

He has swung around. His eyes are bright with tears, now, and he is half laughing. "D'you remember—? How she—? How she used to—? The way she would—? When I'd come in before supper and she heard me tread on the stairs, how she'd—?" He cannot finish. Connie's arm goes around his shoulder—"She was all yours," she is saying; "she was all your own—"

Clancy shakes his head. His mood has changed. "She was not," he says, positively. "And Nora never was, neither. And all me fine consolations are no more than a heap of angel-droppings, as me young brother Tim used to say."

"Hush, Dan—"

"I'll not! There's too much hushing done! We hush when

we should be—! (*He throws back his head and shouts:*) —You up there, why do you send such blank confusion upon the world? What's the earthly good of half the things that happen? Things that on the face of them are blundering injustices with no sense nor purpose—what's the reason for them? (*He drags himself to his feet and half-circles the room.*) Have You not said You'd come when we called You? Then where are You keeping Yourself?—What have You to lose by passing a moment or two with a man of Your own making in such unholy need of You? (*His arm lashes through the air in a peremptory gesture and his voice thunders the command:*) Can You not hear me? Then come to me! Come!"

There is sympathy for him, but little support among the group in the room—Dickinson, Marble and the Major. They would reason him out of his faith and his convictions. "Knock, and it shall be locked in your face," sneers Dickinson. "Seek, and you'll go on seeking." But Clancy will have none of their doubts. He still doesn't know where He keeps Himself, but—

It's sleep Clancy needs. Connie knows that. She is taking him now toward the door when "the portières at the back of the stage are opened a little and out upon it there emerges the figure of a man in a gray suit. He wears a soft white shirt with a flowing black tie. He has a gray mustache and a small, trim beard and his head is crowned with a great shock of white hair. His face is kindly, even benevolent. There is a white carnation in his buttonhole."

"Dan Clancy— Don't be in such a hurry, Clancy," the Figure calls.

Clancy has stopped and turned. He is startled by what he sees. "Mr. Concannon!" he calls, jubilantly. "Look, Connie—it's Mr. Concannon!"

"I—I see it is," says Connie.

Now Mr. Concannon has come down a little farther on the stage and greeted them amiably—the Major and Clancy. Clancy sits on the stage steps at Mr. Concannon's feet. Ma Speedy has come from the restaurant, a cunning look on his face.

It is a friendly talk that Mr. Concannon and Clancy are having. Things haven't been going too well with Clancy. Mr. Concannon is sorry to hear that, but he'll not believe Clancy's troubles have him down. He'll not believe that—

"And when did you get back?" Clancy is asking. "This very night! And didn't I do the same? Was there—? Did some-

body—don't take me amiss, sir— But was there something special that brought you? Just precisely on this very night, you
know—"

"It's hard to explain," admits Mr. Concannon, after a pause.
"Somehow, I felt impelled to come."

That pleases Clancy. It is easy for him to believe now that
Mr. Concannon has been sent to answer his questions for him.
Mr. Concannon is puzzled, but eager to please.

"Maybe *you* can tell me, sir—maybe you can tell me why, for
all its pretty scenery, the whole earth is full of human misery,
of death and tyranny and torture?"

Mr. Concannon—You are afraid of death?

Clancy—I don't savor the thought of it. Not while I've yet
to find the meaning of life.

Mr. Concannon—What else have you to ask?

Clancy (*after a pause*)—Well, sir, to come straight out with
it, if it's Good that rules over us, why is it Evil that always seems
to have the upper hand?

Mr. Concannon—There must be the occasions for sin, must
there not—that Virtue may hold her lovely head aloft? There
must be persecution, must there not—to fortify man's faith in
heaven? There must be slavery, must there not—that he may
know the priceless boon of freedom?

Clancy—Maybe there must be, but why must we *stand* 'em?
Why can't we fight 'em off the face of the earth?

Mr. Concannon—Submission: it is the Will of God. All must
be left to the Almighty Will.

Clancy—The same old—

The Major—Tell me if you will, sir—tell me His reason for—
for creating things like—tell me—why are—why are freaks?

Mr. Concannon—Would you deny Him a sense of humor?

The Major (*starting back as if struck*)—Oh, don't—please
don't—

Clancy (*springing up angrily*)—That's no thing to say! What
kind of a thing is that to be saying?—You're not the James Concannon *I* know! Who are you, you old devil? (*Suddenly advances up the steps and upon the stage.*) Maybe the old war in
Heaven came out the other way—maybe Michael the Archangel
lost the fight after all—and to a crafty old rat too smart to let
on that he'd won.—So we'd take his will as the will of God, eh?
(*He plucks the carnation from* Mr. Concannon's *buttonhole and*

*flings it away.*)    That would explain a lot of things, eh?    Holy
God, what wouldn't it?

As Clancy steps again toward Mr. Concannon the figure calmly
pulls off his wig and mustache and glasses.    Prof. Pabst stands
revealed before him.    He is leering at Clancy.

"Isn't he marvelous?"    Speedy is demanding, in great excitement, "he had his little kit in the coatroom and did the whole
change in less than——"

"Me lifelong I've thought it was Good ruled the world, but
from the way you've ruled us here this night——" begins Clancy.

Dickinson has drawn his revolver and is advancing threateningly upon the Professor.    ". . . All right, Professor—relax,
your act's over.    It stank, Professor!"

Speedy has tried to stop Dickinson without success.    Pabst, his
eyes glassy with the thrill of danger, is beckoning Dickinson to
come closer.    Once he stops to invite his attacker to come to the
theatre on Monday.    But Dickinson is not to be diverted——

"You don't open on Monday!    You're canceled—booked
out——" Dickinson is still advancing with the pistol before him.
Now Connie would stop him, but he pays her little attention.
Suddenly Pabst calls out——

"Help me, Clancy!"

Before Connie can stop him Clancy has leaped down from the
stage toward Dickinson.    He is a second late.    There is the
double discharge of the revolver.    Clancy buckles over, then
straightens again.    For a second he stands there, "his eyes round
with astonishment——"

"It was another trick," ventures Connie, hopefully.    "Dan—
are you all right?"

"For a second I felt as if something hit me, but I feel nothing
now," answers Clancy, again bearing down on Dickinson and
knocking the gun out of his hand.    Then he turns suddenly on
Pabst: "And you!    I see now it's no will of God things are as
they are—no, nor Devil's will neither!    It's the will of all them
like yourself, the world over—men bad by their *own choice*—and
the woods full of 'em!"    He has moved toward the table and
sunk into a chair.    Connie hurries to him.

"Dan!    What is it?"

"Answer?    The proud will of man is me answer!    The free will
of man turned the wrong way.    Free to make his own world was
he?    The fine job he's made of it!"

"Dan, what's the matter with you?"

"—Turning lies into truth and truth into lies till nobody clearly knows the one from the other. But know we will, know we *will*—for it's a fine instrument—the free will of man is, and can as easily be turned to Good as to Bad. Ah, it's the grand thing, is man's will! Whatever it's sunk to, it can rise again. It can rise over anything, anything!"

"Except one: Death, my poor clown!" corrects Prof. Pabst.

"Even that!" answers Clancy, exultantly. "Be the stars it can live and die and resurrect itself!"

The mention of Death has frightened them. They have gathered closer, now—Connie, Dickinson, and Marble. Ma Speedy has gone in search of help. Clancy would have them leave him alone. This is his own affair.

Professor Pabst, looking on, with some amazement, suddenly starts to leave. "He is fantastic! He is incredible!" he is muttering. Marble would stop him, but Clancy calls Jim back. "Let him go," he says, "there are bigger birds than him." "I'll be at the Globe on Monday," Pabst calls back.

Dan's head has fallen. He raises it with some effort and calls to Connie. She sinks into a chair beside him.

CONNIE—But *are* you hurt? Tell me!

CLANCY—Just give me a look at you.

CONNIE—But tell me!

CLANCY—Do you know something?

CONNIE—What?

CLANCY—I like it better without.

CONNIE—It?

CLANCY—Your face?

CONNIE—Without what?

CLANCY—The little gold earrings.

CONNIE—But what's that got to do with—? (*Then in spite of herself, she cries out happily.*) Oh, do you, Dan?

CLANCY (*nodding gravely*)—I do—and that's the truth—and me last word on the subject. (*For a moment they gaze at each other, saying nothing. Then his eyes half close and he draws a deep and satisfied breath.*)

DICKINSON (*bracing himself with both hands upon the table before him*)—Once there was a little man in County Kerry and he began to pack his little bag—

CLANCY (*turning slowly, a broad smile upon his face, his eyes merry*)—I'll send you the post card. (*He makes a half gesture toward* CONNIE, *then slumps forward upon the table.*)

CONNIE—Dan!  (*He does not reply.*)

THE MAJOR—The things that happen. Is—is he going to die?

CLANCY (*raising his head once more*)—Who is not going to?

DICKINSON—Those who live and die like you, Dan Clancy.

CLANCY—Thank you, John. (*His head sinks slowly and he is still.*)  I smell the lemon tree, the air is full of it!

THE CURTAIN FALLS

# FAMILY PORTRAIT

## A Drama in Three Acts

By Lenore Coffee and William Joyce Cowen

IT is the provocative dramas that most frequently give life and color to a dramatic season. In New York last winter there was more serious discussion among play reviewers and the steadier supporters of the theatre over the Coffee-Cowen Biblical play, "Family Portrait," and Philip Barry's "Here Come the Clowns" than any other two dramas the season produced. "Family Portrait" was also virtually the only dramatic novelty of the year.

When William Joyce Cowen was working with Cecil De Mille on that expansive Biblical canvas called "The King of Kings" many years ago, the urge was strong upon him to write a play that should tell the story of Jesus Christ as the Savior may have been seen through the eyes of his essentially commonplace family. The idea afterward took firm possession of Mrs. Cowen, who, as Lenore Coffee, long had been a writer for the screen. Together the Cowens evolved the simple story that is "Family Portrait," taking their inspiration and their argument from those verses in the Gospel According to St. Mark which begin: "And he went from thence, and came into his own country, and his disciples follow him. And when the Sabbath day was come he began to teach in the synagogue, and many hearing him were astonished, saying: 'From whence hath this man these things? . . . Is not this the carpenter, the son of Mary, the brother of James and Joses, and of Juda, and of Simon? and are not his sisters here with us?' And they were offended at him. But Jesus said unto them, 'A prophet is not without honor but in his own country, and among his own kin, and in his own house.' "

The authors determined to keep their dialogue as colloquial as possible and their argument as close to modern social trends as they could consistently, thus giving their play the spirit of timeliness and bringing it into convincing focus as a family portrait. They have been both praised and blamed for the results obtained.

There were no divided opinions, however, regarding the appealing performance of Judith Anderson in the role of Mary, mother of Jesus. Her triumph was complete and as the run of the play

318

continued well into the Spring the wonder grew that an actress whose chief successes had been won with roles of totally dissimilar character could so skillfully and beautifully embody the spiritual virtues of this beloved mother.

It is early morning in the village of Nazareth, in Judea. We stand in the courtyard of the house in which Jesus, Mary, his mother, and his brothers, James, Joseph, Simon and Judah, live. Joseph and Simon are married and their wives, Naomi and Reba, live here too. It is "a low plaster house with a wooden door in the center" and an outside stairway leading to the roof. In the yard there is a fig tree in full leaf, and around its base a circular seat has been built by this family of carpenters. At one end of the house a wooden shed is used as a shop, a sign over it proclaiming this fact professionally. A table and stools stand under the tree. There is a plaster wall around the place, through which a heavy wooden gate lets into the yard. Looking over the wall and beyond the house soft rolling hills may be seen. Just now a cock has crowed to herald a dull, gray day, and there is the sound of other animals stirring in adjoining sheds.

Mary, "a slight woman of about forty-five," has come from the house with a tablecloth over her arm and a tray of dishes in her hands. "There are understanding and humor in her face, as well as sweetness and great character." She proceeds methodically and carefully to lay the table for breakfast. It is not long before her family is stirring. Young Daniel, Simon's and Naomi's six-year-old, having been sent to bring in the goat, must stop to have his grandmother supply a pin for a missing button on his pants. Joseph, whose voice is not too pleasant, would remind his mother from indoors that breakfast should be hurried if they are to get to work on a particular job.

Now Naomi has come to help Mary. It is Naomi's suggestion that they give the boys an egg for breakfast, seeing that they will have quite a walk to their work.

Then Judah, who is seventeen and the youngest of the brothers, appears in fine spirits and with interesting news to report. Judah had been calling on Miriam, daughter of Aaron, the night before and Aaron had left them alone for practically five whole minutes. That, Judah is convinced, is a most favorable sign. He must get himself a good job now and begin to think seriously of marriage. . . .

It is Mary's sister-in-law, Mary Cleophas, "a rather large woman, shrewd of eye, aggressive in manner," who first discovers a suggestion of family disharmony in her sister-in-law's home. Mary Cleophas has come to borrow a bowl of barley, and she can see that her friend and neighbor is worried. It is, admits Mary, because Jesus has gone away again. His brothers are furious, but they could do nothing about it. Jesus just said he was going and went. The brothers have blamed Mary for encouraging Jesus. She would like to have Mary Cleophas stay for breakfast. That might help to keep Jesus' family pleasant.

"I never knew anyone to stop being unpleasant on my account," insists Mary Cleophas, pleasantly, "but I'll be glad to stay." She puts down her bowl. "So he left! How long will he be gone?"

"I—I don't know—exactly—"

"You mean he didn't say?"

"I don't suppose he *knew*. He'll stay until he's done what he set out to do. (*Then, with a little rising panic in her voice at Mary Cleophas' dubious expression.*) He's always come back before! That time he went away with John—he came back, didn't he? And the forty days he spent in the desert—he came back. He's *always* come back—"

"Of course. I was just wondering. (*Pause.*) I hope you did right letting him go."

"If you could have seen his face! I never saw anyone look so happy. As if he was *ready* for something."

Reba, wife of Joseph, "a little older than Naomi, handsome in a dark way," reports a bad night. Her child cried with the earache and Joseph tossed and worried. No one realizes how high-strung Joseph is or they would not upset him.

They have all come to breakfast now, and found their places at table. Joseph is a little irritable, but otherwise there is no suggestion of unpleasantness. The brothers greet their Aunt Mary amiably and listen as their mother tells a little jubilantly of Judah's prospects with Miriam. Judah is embarrassed and his brothers are inclined to tease him, though free to admit that the thought of Miriam's dowry is not without its satisfactions.

Mary, forgetting, had set a place for Jesus, and now Judah would know where his brother is. He had hoped to tell him first about Miriam.

"It seems, my dear Judah, that your favorite brother has decided that he has other work to do—work much more important than the mending of roofs and the building of barns—so he's left us with the Mordecai job on our hands without so much as a 'by your leave'!" complains Joseph.

Mary, who has been pouring a cup of milk for Daniel, turns quickly to answer him. "That's not fair!" she says with some spirit. "You know he's been going to do this other work. You've always known—but you've kept him here time after time when he wanted to go. And as far as this Mordecai job is concerned, you know perfectly well that Jesus told you right from the beginning that he wouldn't be here to do it. You're all my sons, but it's time you learned to stand on your own feet and not rely on him for everything. (*She pauses, a little breathless.*) Goodness knows he's the kind that'll carry as big a load as anyone'll give him!"

JUDAH—You don't mean he's gone for good!

MARY—No, dear—of course not—

JUDAH—When's he coming back?

MARY—Well, that's hard to say, dear—

JOSEPH—He hasn't taken *us* into his confidence. We don't count. We're just his family!

DANIEL—What has Uncle Jesus done, Mamma?

NAOMI—Nothing, dear.

DANIEL—Then *why* is everyone cross with him?

SIMON—Drink your milk—and don't ask questions. (*To* NAOMI.) I wish someone would teach the boy manners. Personally, I've nothing against his preaching—but I don't see why he can't do it on Sundays—or when work is slack.

JAMES—If he wants to preach, why isn't he a rabbi?

MARY—He doesn't agree with all their ideas.

JOSEPH—Oh, he's going to startle the world with something new, I suppose! (*Adds sourly.*) He's the best carpenter in the family. We won't get half the good jobs without him.

SIMON—And he knew how to get along with people. They liked to do business with him.

JAMES—Surely you must all see how unpleasant this is for *me*. After all, I stand for something in the community—

JUDAH—I'll miss him so! I'll be lost without him!

MARY—So will I!

JAMES (*disregarding this*)—His views and behavior are *so* irregular. It's embarrassing for *me*. After all, my friends are some of the most important men in town. As for these new ideas of his—we believe in the law, *according* to the law—and no deviation.

MARY—Then how's the world ever going to progress?

JAMES—It's better off without progress if you have to break

the law to do it.

NAOMI—Come along, Daniel, you'll be late for school. (*He kisses* MARY; *exits with* NAOMI.)

JUDAH—I don't see why he hasn't got a right to his own life! He's thirty years old. And he's got a lot of good ideas, too! If people would live the way he wants them to the world would be a fine place! Room for everyone. And he's practical. Believes in paying people decent wages. Says a man is worth his hire. But not to worry about being rich. That there's other kinds of *riches* besides money!

The brothers are not impressed. Joseph, in fact, is quite sarcastic. But Mary returns to Jesus' defense. Jesus has always had these ideas, even when he was a little boy. Doesn't Joseph remember what happened when his brother was twelve and they left him in the Temple?

"Suppose he has gone out to spread his kind of thinking?" says Mary. "After all, what is it? To be kind—to be fair—to love your enemies and do good to those that hate you. What *harm* can come of that?"

"Not to *him*, perhaps—but what about us?" demands Joseph.

"Yes—we've built up a good business here—" adds Simon.

"With his help," Mary reminds them. And then, Mary Cleophas adds: "Well, they say you never know a family till you've had breakfast with them. (*With decision.*) You're making too much of the whole thing. He's gone away before—and he'll go away again."

Jesus will never get anywhere preaching kindness. Joseph is convinced of that. "You've got to startle people if you want to get anywhere—and who's going to be startled by kindness!"

Breakfast is over and the women have started to clear the table when Mordecai arrives. Mordecai is "an excited, elderly man," who has given the brothers a contract to fix the roof of his barn. And why aren't they about it? And where is Jesus? It was largely on Jesus' account that he had given them the contract, Mordecai admits. Jesus is the best carpenter in all Judea. Without him Mordecai is ready to call the contract off. Then Mary Cleophas reminds him of the wording of his agreement—"that the work should be done by four sons of the House of Joseph—"

"Now, Mordecai," says Mary Cleophas, "if a man goes to a dealer and orders four donkeys and doesn't specify four white ones—and three brown and one gray donkey are delivered, the

"FAMILY PORTRAIT"

They have all come to breakfast now and found their places at table. The brothers greet their Aunt Mary Cleophas amiably, and listen as their mother tells a little jubilantly of Judah's prospects with Miriam.

(*Evelyn Vardon, James Harker, Judith Anderson, Philip Coolidge, Tom Ewell, Lois Austin, Norman Stuart, Ronald Reiss, Virginia Campbell*)

law will hold him to the agreement."

"I don't call that a very happy comparison," suggests James, stuffily.

It has started to rain. The brothers have rushed to get their tools and coats and have hurried away with Mordecai to roof the barn before the grain is spoiled. James, the oldest brother, "tall, austere and bigoted," has agreed to take Jesus' place, but only with the understanding that if Jesus doesn't give up his notion and come back to his job something shall be done to bring him back. Mary agrees.

"Did you mean that about bringing Jesus back," Mary Cleophas asks, when James has gone.

"Maybe they'll forget about it," Mary answers, hopefully. "Maybe it will all just—blow over." And then, as she glances anxiously at the sky she adds: "It's a cold rain. I begged Jesus to take his warm cloak. He'll be wet through."

Naomi has come to report that baby Esther is sleeping and to recall that Daniel's teacher has said he is doing ever so well in school. Because of the rain, Mary and Naomi have gone into the house to devote the day to putting up fruit as the curtain falls.

The scene has changed to a wineshop in Capernaum, built on a pier at the end of the Sea of Galilee. There is a bar with tables and stools in the wineroom proper and a kind of private room with table and stools at one end. There are bottles and jugs on the shelves back of the bar. At the moment the tables are full. Eben, a peddler, is displaying his wares to the curious and the interested. A hungry-looking waiter moves among the customers and Selima, the proprietress, is busy at the bar.

The fishing boats are not in yet, Eben reports, and there is no sign of them through the mist. Selima grows impatient. Business has been heavy and all her men folk are out in the boats. She will have to have more help if the rush keeps up. But suppose some other town—Choraizon or Bethsaida, for instance—should make Jesus a good offer? What would happen then? He is the biggest attraction Capernaum has ever had.

"Does he show any signs of moving on?" Eben would know.

"No, but you never can tell. When he gets talking or walking you can't say when or where he'll stop. Take this morning. The boys should have been back from their fishing hours ago—but Jesus decided to go with them, and if he gets to making lessons out of things they'll forget all about coming home. He may wind up on the other side of the lake and stay there! That's why I keep saying—'Sell now.' ''

"Well—I don't know. Since things are going so well I'd stick to it and take a chance."

"Take a chance! That's a regular man's argument. Why take chances? I said that to my brother when he talked about making our house larger. 'Why go to all the extra expense?' I said. 'Jesus doesn't mind where he sleeps.' (*She changes to a confidential tone.*) I *must* say we never had anyone who was less trouble. Why, we once had John the Baptist and his followers at our house and they nearly drove us crazy!"

Selima has gone to the kitchen to see that her help is not filling the wine cups too full when Mary, James, Joseph and Simon enter the shop. They evidently have come a great distance. Mary, accepting the strange scene a little timidly, decides to stay in the shop for the present. Let her sons continue their search if they will. She has no thought of embarrassing Jesus before a crowd of strangers. In spite of the stories they have heard, Mary does not believe that Jesus is out of his mind. She wants to see him alone. She will stay where she is. Let them go on. She is quite sure she will be all right.

The brothers have gone. Mary, looking through the crowded room for a place to sit down, can find none and is standing a little back by the wall when Selima returns from the kitchen to greet with commercial effusiveness the rich merchant, Mathias of Sidon, who has just come in. Selima finds a seat for Mathias by the simple process of ousting a young man she sees has about finished his meal. Mary, too, finds a seat at an adjoining table and is quietly listening as Selima describes to Mathias the change that has come over the town since Jesus has been there. It is in the hope that he can get some of the new business that Mathias has come.

"The old prophets used to pray and hope for God to do the rest," Selima is saying. "But do you know what this man does? He goes out and takes a hand at the nets. Like this morning. Whenever *he* pulls, the nets are always full. We only hope the price of fish keeps up."

A man has called from the door that the boats are in and there is considerable commotion. A fisherman is there to report that the boys have had a fine catch, with fish enough in their nets to feed hundreds of people.

Mathias is interested. He would like to meet Jesus. Where can he find him?

"He'll be preaching—but you'd better get there early if you

want to hear anything," Selima advises. "Otherwise you'll get caught in a tangle of beds and stretchers—"

"Beds and stretchers?"

"Cripples and invalids—they all go to him."

"And he cures them?"

"Certainly! And he's going to teach my boys how to do it, too. Then send them out by themselves. I don't see why they shouldn't be able to—once they've been shown how."

This gives Mathias an idea. He is more anxious than before to meet Jesus. But Selima, too, has grown cagy and will tell him no more.

On her way back to the kitchen Selima notices Mary. She stops to inquire how the soup is. Mary thinks it may be a little thin. That, allows Selima, indicates Mary's country taste.

"I suppose you've come here to see our Jesus?" queries Selima.

"Yes—I have—"

"Well, you've come to the right person if you want to get in touch with him. I can arrange it."

"You *can?*" Mary is quite impressed.

"You see—my two sons are with Jesus, and we think the world of him and he thinks the world of us," Selima explains. "I suppose you have some sons? (MARY *nods and starts to speak; SELIMA rattles on.*) Then I'm sure you will agree with me it's very important for a man's future to have people like him. The *right* people. Look at my father-in-law. When the Romans started the new aqueduct at Sidon, he knew a man whose daughter was the mistress of one of the officials—so he got a contract for stone that made him a fortune!"

Selima has gone back to the kitchen and Mary has turned to the interesting young man who has been busily writing at the next table.

"Does she really know so much about him?" she asks.

"Well, naturally, her sons being with him, she knows a little more than most people—but not as much as she pretends."

MARY—It's been wonderful to sit here and listen to all these things about him.

YOUNG MAN—If you're so interested, why don't you join the crowd and listen to *him?*

MARY (*confused*)—I'm waiting for someone. Besides, crowds frighten me a little—

YOUNG MAN—It's always like this. You'll never get a chance to see him alone.

MARY (*drawing him out*)—And they all believe in him.  They all think he's wonderful?

YOUNG MAN (*with glowing faith*)—For *me*—he's the beginning and the end.

MARY—Oh, I didn't mean *I* had any doubts about his being wonderful.  I only meant—did the *people* think so—

YOUNG MAN—I can only speak for myself.  I would *die* for him.

MARY—What does he *do*—that makes everyone follow him?

YOUNG MAN—Oh, nothing that I can explain. (*Searches for words.*)  He just sits out on a hillside—or in a field—and talks to people.  And when they go away—they feel better.

MATHIAS (*who has been listening intently between gulps of soup, gets up and comes to the table*)—Excuse me—but I couldn't help hearing what you were saying.  Perhaps you can give me some information I want.

YOUNG MAN—Well—I don't know—

MATHIAS—Do you know anyone who has real influence with this man Jesus?  One of the disciples?

YOUNG MAN (*simply*)—I'm one of the disciples. (MARY *looks at him with added interest.*)

MATHIAS (*eagerly*)—Well, I've got a proposition I want to make to you. (*He looks toward the kitchen and then hurries on.*) If you can get Jesus to leave this town and come to Sidon, I'll guarantee him all reasonable expenses—a salary for six months —and a nice bonus besides!

YOUNG MAN (*indignantly*)—No one would dare go to him with a proposition like that. (SELIMA *enters from the kitchen with* MATHIAS' *fish and stands listening.*)

MATHIAS—Why not?  It's perfectly sound.  I'm a respectable business man—my word's as good as my bond.

YOUNG MAN—He wouldn't be interested.

MATHIAS—Nonsense.  Everyone's interested in a good business deal. (*Lowering his voice.*)  If *you* could help me, I'd make it worth your while.  How much?  Come now—every man has his price— (*Suddenly becoming conscious that* SELIMA *is behind him,* MATHIAS *straightens up, greatly confused, and fumbles for a pepper grinder, then returns to his table.*)  Just borrowing the pepper—

SELIMA—How do you know it's going to need pepper when you haven't tasted it yet?  No, Mathias—I was standing right behind you—I heard every word you said. (*Banging fish down on table.*) And I know what you're up to! You've got your eye on Jesus and the business he brings. Well, let me tell you one thing—neither you nor anyone else is going to get that business away from here until we're good and ready to let it go!

MATHIAS—It seems to me you're taking a lot on yourself—

SELIMA—Not any more than's been given me. You seem to forget that my sons—

MATHIAS—Please, Selima—don't tell us about your sons again! And as to business—Jesus isn't going to spend the rest of his life here, is he? And when he does move on, he can move in *my* direction, can't he? (*He adds slyly.*) I might need a smart woman to run the place—someone who knows how to handle the crowds. (*He looks at the fish.*) And feed them right. (*There is a long pause—*MATHIAS *resumes pleasantly.*) How about my eating that fish while it's nice and hot? (*Sits down.*) There's no one can do a fish as well as you can, Selima. (SELIMA *stands watching him.*) Your brother's a lucky man. I hope he gives you a good cut out of the profits.

SELIMA (*complainingly*)—Not what he ought to—

MATHIAS (*mildly*)—You don't say? Well, that's what comes of doing business with relatives. (*Takes a mouthful of fish.*) My—my—what a fish! And what a sauce!

SELIMA (*solicitously*)—I thought maybe it might need just a scrap more lemon—

MATHIAS (*his mouth full*)—Not a thing—perfect!

YOUNG MAN (*seeing* MARY's *look of distress*)—Don't look so upset. These things happen all the time.

MARY—But what does Jesus think of it? Doesn't it make him angry?

YOUNG MAN—He knows how people are. How they have to struggle to make a living. He doesn't expect to change human nature overnight. Mind you—if anyone came to him *direct* with a proposition like that—(*He laughs.*)—well, they wouldn't forget it in a hurry! But, even while he was angry, he'd understand—and make excuses for them.

MARY (*smiling*)—Yes—that sounds like him. Just like him. I remember once when one of his brothers tried to drive a sharp bargain—

YOUNG MAN—His brothers? Then you know the family—you must come from Nazareth. Do you know Jesus, too?

MARY—I know him very well. You see—he's my son.

YOUNG MAN—Your son! (*Looks at her intently.*) Why,

you know—there *is* a resemblance. (MARY *smiles*.) And when
you smile—it's quite like him!

SELIMA (*turning as she hears this and crossing over*)—Quite
like who?

YOUNG MAN (*with innocent malice*)—Like our Jesus. There's
such a resemblance between them—

SELIMA—*I* don't see it! And certainly no one knows him any
better than I do—

YOUNG MAN—This lady is his mother.

Selima, considerably flustered by this revelation, would cover
her confusion by telling of what a time she has protecting Jesus
from all sorts of people. Soon she has escaped again to the
kitchen and is busy with the trade.

Mary is pleased with what she has heard. She is ever so glad
that she has come. Now she will be able to tell her sons some
things that will surprise them.

The Young Man is greatly interested. It is difficult for him to
believe that anyone, even Jesus' brothers, should ever think of
expecting Jesus to give up his work. Of course Mary never
approved of such a course.

Now the brothers have returned. They look disgruntled, especially James, and Mary's enthusiastic report that she has something to tell them is countered by their report that they have a
good deal to tell her, too.

They had tried to see Jesus, but could not get close to him
because of the crowd. And when they had sent him word that
his mother and brothers were there and wanted to see him he
had sent back word, by one of the common fishermen, too, asking: "Who *is* my mother—and who are my brothers?"

For a moment Mary is incredulous. Surely there must be
some explanation. She has James repeat this strange message,
and describe in detail the circumstances under which the message was delivered—

"There were people on all sides of him," reports James. "You
couldn't move edgeways—and what do you think he said, Mother?
After he got our message he looked around at all of them and
said, '*You* are my mother and *you* are my brothers!' To *them*,
mind you! To that ignorant crowd!"

"But that changes everything!" cries Mary, her mood changing completely. "Why didn't you tell me that in the first place?
Frightening me like this and making me think he didn't want to

see me! With all those people listening he used our message to make a lesson of! That's the way he teaches. Don't you see?"

JAMES—No, I don't see!

MARY (*her voice rising*)—But, James! That message wasn't for us—it was for the people who were listening. He was trying to tell them that because they followed him and his teachings *they* were his brothers and sisters—his mother, too!

SIMON—But, Mother—you don't understand—

MARY (*with increasing conviction*)—This thing about all men being brothers—why, he's said it to me hundreds of times! That's one of the things he believes in most! You'll see, when he's through talking to the crowd, he'll come here looking for us. And you ought to be glad you didn't get to him. What would you have said in front of all those people? "We want you to come home? We want you to come back and help us mend roofs and barns? We think you're out of your mind?"

SIMON (*timidly*)—I must say he seems to be doing well.

MARY—Doing well? Look at the crowds—that ought to tell you something!

JOSEPH—I'd like a chance to air my views and have a crowd follow me!

MARY—Why, an important man from Sidon was trying to get Jesus to come to his town—but the people here won't let him go. (*Her eye falls on the* YOUNG MAN *as she speaks.*) And you should have heard what that young man over there thinks of him! He thinks the sun rises and sets in him. He said he'd *die* for him! (*The* YOUNG MAN, *hearing himself referred to, turns and starts to rise.*) I'd like you to meet my sons— (*She pauses, then realizes she can't make the introduction and adds:*) Oh, I'm sorry—I'm afraid I don't know your name—

YOUNG MAN—Judas. Judas Iscariot.

Mary, her hand confidingly on Judas' arm, is saying, "This is James—and Simon—and Joseph—" as the curtain slowly descends.

## ACT II

There is great excitement in the house in Nazareth. The yard is bright with sunlight. Reba is collecting the freshly laundered sheets that have been drying on the back wall. Naomi is sitting under the fig tree shelling peas. From inside the house Mary's voice, a little tremulous, calls to them at intervals to hasten their

work that everything may be in readiness for the great event
that is pending.

Now Mary Cleophas has arrived to add her bit of flurry. In
her hand she carries four killed and plucked chickens. With
these she gestures freely as she reports that in the market place
literally everybody is talking and making such a fuss over the
return of a native as never has been made in Nazareth before.
People who had ignored Mary Cleophas for years had spoken
to her most amiably this morning, including a few whom she took
great delight in snubbing.

Now Mary, still a little fluttery, has come from her lamb roast-
ing to greet Mary Cleophas and to sort of check up the day—
"I know I've forgotten something," she is saying, half to herself.
"Clean linen, water for the bedrooms, new wicks for the lamps—
and I've my bread still to bake. Oh, yes—Reba, get out my best
hand towels—with the blue embroidery—and put them in his
room. And let me see—what else? Oh, dear—I must think!"

"She has been going on like this for hours," Naomi tells Mary
Cleophas. Then, turning to Mary, she advises—"Now, don't
worry, Mother. Everything's going to be lovely. And, Auntie—
you stay here and keep her from getting too excited."

Naomi has gone. Mary Cleophas is maneuvering Mary toward a stool. *"Coming home!* I just can't believe it! Coming
home!" Mary is exclaiming.

"If you don't sit down and rest a minute you won't be fit to
see him when he gets here."

MARY (*sitting*)—I was never so happy in all my life! When
I think how I worried about him. The nights I've lain awake
wondering if he was cold or hungry or—or *safe,* even. And now
he's coming home! And not just coming, either, but *invited!*
(*Pause.*) Has—has anyone said anything about it in town?

MARY CLEOPHAS—Anyone? You're joking, Mary! Why, no
one talks of anything else.

MARY—But we only knew it this morning—

MARY CLEOPHAS—They're certainly rushing to get ready for
him! You should see the streets and the food shops! And the
strangers that are here in town already! There won't be an
empty bed in any of the inns by nightfall. People are coming
in from the sea-coast, too.

MARY (*happily*)—And all to see my son! I've been wishing
all day I could be in two places at once. Home here fixing things
for him—and out in the street hearing what people are saying

about him. What *are* they saying?

MARY CLEOPHAS—I couldn't even begin to tell you! I don't suppose there's a mother in Nazareth that doesn't envy you, Mary.

MARY (*sighing—too happy to speak*)—If only Judah were home—how he'd love to see his brother! Still, if things go here anything like they did at Capernaum, they'll never let him get away! (*Sighs again with sheer happiness.*) You know, I'm trying so hard to be calm—to *look* calm, anyway—and then I suddenly remember the way he smiles and the way he speaks—and realize that I'll be actually seeing him—with my own eyes—*today!* And my heart just turns over! (*A little gasp.*)

MARY CLEOPHAS (*kindly*)—It's—it's been pretty hard for you, hasn't it?

MARY—Oh, I don't mean to complain. Other people need him. And, after all, I had thirty years. (*Pause.*) I hope there won't be too many people around *all* the time. I'd—I'd like to have him to myself for a while. At first, anyway.

MARY CLEOPHAS—You haven't a chance. The house will be full of people who never knew we existed before!

Mary Cleophas is right. The first neighbor, Hepzibah, "a large, voluble, middle-aged woman of dubious sincerity," has arrived with an armful of plates. With so famous a son coming home Mary is quite sure to be needing extra plates and table-cloths. And does Mary think, after a while, when he is settled, she could drop in for a minute?

James has appeared. He has been meditating and is visibly annoyed to come in from his meditations to find everybody running about in a state of the most unusual excitement. Why?

"Jesus is coming back—by special invitation—to preach in the synagogue," his mother informs him, with great dignity.

The idea is a little preposterous to James. He doesn't intend being taken in. Someone has been filling his mother's head with ideas. James is on his way to the gate to find out for himself when Mary faces him. "I might have known that something like this would happen to spoil things," she says, with spirit. "And I'm not going to have it. This is his first visit home. He's been invited back here as an honored guest—and if the town can treat him that way, I think his own brother might do as much! (MARY *continues to* SIMON *and* JOSEPH.) Come here, Simon! And you too, Joseph! You heard what I said just now to James? I mean that for you, as well! I want peace and quiet in this house while Jesus is here—and I mean to have it! (JAMES *stalks off, exiting through gate.*)

Simon and Joseph have come in while she was speaking and are quick to assure her of their sympathy and understanding. They, at least, are very proud of their brother. They are even considering what they should say if, during the reception, they should be called upon for a few words. Joseph would like to say something appropriate and still lead up gracefully to a mention of the business. In fact Joseph is very much concerned about the business just now. He has lined up a big job with the Romans, but he realizes that he is certain to face heavy family opposition. James, in particular, is not likely to be nice about it. And this is the day Joseph has appointed for a meeting with the Roman prospect, one Appius Hadrian.

A moment later a knock at the gate heralds the arrival of the Roman. He is rather a resplendent individual as, coming through the gate, he raises his right hand in the old Roman salute. "Hail Caesar!" hails Appius. "Hail, Roman!" hails Joseph. At which moment Mary Cleophas blows her nose "with a trumpet-like sound" that gives them both a start.

Appius Hadrian quickly makes himself at home. With a suggestion of a strut he walks over and picks a fig from the tree, eating it with such satisfaction that when Joseph offers him a basket of them he orders it sent to his house. As Reba starts up an outside stairway with a basket of linen the Roman stops eating figs long enough to notice that she has very good legs— like all hill country women.

But soon they are talking business. Appius Hadrian would like Joseph to figure on building three crosses a week for fifty weeks as a first order. "But understand—sound timber, and according to specifications," he warns. "We had trouble with one contractor last year. A number of his crosses broke in the joins and spoiled the show."

"You won't find that trouble with us. My father was an expert on joins. He always said, 'If the join is good, the job is good.'"

Appius is busy figuring in the fees and taxes with the price when the family opposition develops. James comes quietly through the gate just as Joseph is assuring Simon that he intends going through with the contract whatever James may say about it. But James is not so easily put aside. He strides directly to Appius Hadrian and firmly announces: "We don't do business with foreigners!"

"This is a *Roman* province," replies Appius, quite undisturbed.

"And wherever the *Romans* are the other people are the foreigners."

"In my elder brother's absence I am the head of the house and I forbid any dealings with the Romans."

"Now, look here, James! I'm not going to have you interfering!" Joseph protests. "It's none of your business how we run the shop!"

"You *are* being unreasonable, James—"

"I will not have this place contaminated!" firmly announces James.

Appius Hadrian thereupon takes himself off, suggesting that when they finish their wrangling they can communicate with him. "If Romans did menial work, such as carpentry, we wouldn't have come to you," is his parting shot.

Joseph turns angrily upon James, while Simon runs excitedly to call their mother. Mary is busy with her bread, her hands in the dough, but she comes finally and continues kneading the bread as she hears the dispute. Joseph explains at length and with spirit how, after great personal effort, he finally had the contract for a hundred and fifty crosses as good as in his hand, only to lose it when that "strait-laced old fogey" James, proceeded to insult Appius Hadrian.

Mary is inclined to accept the whole matter as trivial until she learns that the contract was for crosses that the Romans use in their executions. "They hang criminals on them—and nail their hands and feet," explains Simon, extending his arms in illustration. "Like this!"

"Don't, Simon!"

"Besides—that isn't what James objects to—it isn't the crosses —it's the Romans!"

"But I can't understand why the making of a few crosses is such a big contract—"

"A few? You don't call a hundred and fifty a year a few!"

"So *many!*"

"They ship them all over the country. And they don't use the same ones over again. They leave them standing until—"

"*Simon! Please!*"

"There wouldn't be any profit in it if the crosses were used more than once. (*Eagerly.*) So you see what a good thing it is!"

"No, I don't! I'm surprised at you, Joseph, wanting anything to do with it. (*He starts to speak but she halts him with a gesture.*) I'm not blaming you for trying to get ahead—it's your nature to be like that. But I don't believe in killing people—no matter what they've done."

"Only the lowest sort of criminals—"

"Even so. What have we to do with a business like that? And today—of all days! Jesus coming home—the whole town making ready to welcome him—and you sit here talking about Roman crosses! (JOSEPH *tries to speak but she cuts him short.*) Now, I'm not going to discuss it any further. I've got too much to do!"

Joseph and Simon find such solace as they can in the thought that they may not need the cross contract if Jesus should draw the expected crowds to Nazareth.

Little Daniel comes romping in to report with great pride the changed attitude of his playmates toward a fellow whose Uncle Jesus is going to preach in the synagogue. And another neighbor, Anna, has flung open the gate and brought Eben, the peddler, into the yard. It is Anna's conviction that the family of so famous a son will be eager to set itself out in the finest raiment to celebrate the home-coming.

Mary is reluctant to stop her work to look at Eben's goods, and convinced that she cannot afford any of them, however pretty and fashionable they may be. But she is tempted by a blue shawl. Blue is Jesus' favorite color! It would be lovely to have that to wear—but—ten pieces of silver—"It's lovely, but I can't afford it!" sighs Mary.

"If I was the mother of your son there's nothing I couldn't afford," tempts Eben.

"You know my son?" brightens Mary.

"Know him? I'd be starving to death if it wasn't for him."

"He helped you? Tell me about him."

"When I say he helped me—I mean—well, wherever he goes there's crowds—and where there's crowds there's money. Sometimes I get so interested in what he says I almost forget to sell my goods! He certainly knows how to hold people—right in the palm of his hand. (*Adds sheepishly:*) You know, I listen to him and I think to myself—I won't drive such a sharp bargain next time—think of the other fellow, like he says. Then I get away and get mixed up in a business deal—and, well, I guess I forget all about it. You know how it is. (*Then, with a burst of generosity.*) Look, since you're his mother—I'll make you special prices. The blue scarf—nine pieces of silver. Sunset—seven pieces—"

"I'll take it. The blue one. (*To* MARY CLEOPHAS.) Oh, dear—maybe I shouldn't! But I *do* want to look my best. (*She reaches in pocket of her dress and counts out the money; then picks up the shawl and throws it around her shoulders.*) Do you think he'll like it?" (*She turns around for* MARY CLEOPHAS *to get its full effect, her back to the gate.*)

And now Daniel has come shouting into the yard. "He's here! He's here!"

"Where? Where is he?" demands Mary, going eagerly toward the gate.

"Coming up the road! He's here! Mother! Father! Uncle Joseph! He's here!"

Mary has gone to the open gate. She stands there for a moment, peering down the road. "Then her arms fly out as she almost runs out into the road. The curtain starts down. The peddler kneels, doing up his pack, and Mary Cleophas picks up the forgotten shawl and starts out after her." The curtain falls.

A week later the yard at the house in Nazareth is deserted. It is early morning. There is a knocking at the gate. The knocking brings no one from the house, but shortly is followed by the appearance of the neighbors—Hepzibah and Anna. They are curious. What is happening with the family since the failure in the synagogue? No one comes to see them any more. As for Hepzibah, she is just as well pleased that the family was put in its place. They had all put on airs when they heard Jesus was coming. All except James. And now, look! A shop full of lumber and nothing to do with it—

"Anyone seen Mary since Sunday?" Hepzibah would like to know.

"I think she took it pretty hard," answers Anna, shaking her head. "She bought a new shawl. I talked to her the day he was coming home—and my, was she excited!"

Mary comes from the house. "She is pale and making an effort to be composed, and braces herself for the taunts she knows are coming." She has brought Hepzibah's dishes. She had meant to return them before, Mary explains. But there had been much to do, the girls were away and Judah had just come home. Judah would probably be marrying Miriam soon now—

"Oh, well—with a good match like that, people are bound to look up to you again," Anna begins, and then breaks off, embarrassed. "I'm sorry, Mary. I didn't mean to say that. (*Adds clumsily:*) Jesus might do better another time. We all have our off days. Ezra, the singer, tells me that sometimes he can't get a full note. He—"

"But he doesn't blame it on other people's lack of hearing!" interrupts Hepzibah. "I don't like to hurt your feelings, Mary— but I'm not one to hold back anything. And I must say you always spoiled him. Made him think he was something special—"

"It's not easy to bring up a lot of boys without a man in the family," says Anna, turning to Hepzibah. "You know, Mary, Jesus really ought to have known better than to come back here where everyone knows him. When a man's hammered on your cupboard doors and mended your roofs, you're not going to believe he's turned into a prophet overnight."

Daniel has been climbing up on the wall at the back of the yard. Suddenly he stops and demands: "Are the police really after my Uncle Jesus?"

"Why, Daniel!" Mary ejaculates in shocked tones.

"That's what they said in school. Why is everyone angry at him? He whittled me a swell boat while he was here."

"I don't know, Daniel. Your uncle does what he thinks is right," says Mary. Daniel has gone back to climbing the wall. He is teetering along its edge in imitation of a tight rope walker.

"Well, Daniel—trying to do tricks like your Uncle Jesus?" calls Hepzibah, as Daniel sways uncertainly.

A gasp of protest from Mary does not stop her.

"If you like magic, there's a wonderful fakir in town this morning—an Egyptian. You ought to see *him!* Makes flowers grow in a barren pot—tears a scarf in two and makes it all one piece again—"

Joseph has come from the house. In a moment he has ordered Daniel from the fence and made a great show of getting to work. There is so much to do these days there is no time in which to do it all, he explains. They had worked until midnight the night before getting a rush order through.

There has been no rush order. There has been no work. Mary knows this, but she tries to play up to Joseph. She thinks perhaps she had better call Simon to help with the work. Hepzibah and Anna may not have been completely convinced, but they decide they may be a little in the way and depart.

And now Joseph and Simon forsake all pretense and turn to blaming their present state of idleness on the failure of their brother Jesus. Mary will not listen. They were eager enough to have Jesus come, she reminds them, which Joseph admits. He had expected Jesus to "go over" in Nazareth as he had in other places. And if he had—

"Well, I guess it's easy to fool strangers," he sighs. And adds:

"I'll never forget the way they rose up against him in the synagogue and drove him out to the edge of that cliff! They'd have pushed him over, too, if—he hadn't got away."

"Joseph, how do you suppose he did it?" asks Simon, in a lowered voice. "There was a lot of talk about his—well—just vanishing—"

"His disciples slipped him away," confidently explains Joseph. Which reminds him: "And there's another thing! That crowd he got together for disciples. He couldn't pick people that might do him some good! A lot of ignorant fishermen! He'll never get anywhere with *them!*"

Joseph and Simon have gone. Mary has not been able to make much of an impression in her effort to cheer them.

"I sometimes wonder how Jesus would feel if, all the time he is preaching about peace and brotherly love, he knew the wrangling that's gone on in this house ever since he left," ventures Mary Cleophas.

MARY (*agitated*)—Oh, Mary Cleophas, I don't know—it's so difficult! (*Pause.*) I've always encouraged Jesus and stood up for him but lately I've wondered if I was doing right—if I was doing my duty to my other children. After all, they've got *their* lives to live— They're entitled to their share of happiness. Goodness knows what they ask is harmless enough! Just work to support their families.

MARY CLEOPHAS—Yes—the way things are—I suppose you can't blame them for taking it pretty hard.

MARY (*reluctantly*)—People weren't in the right frame of mind for him to come back just now. No one here had any real faith in him. But their local pride was stirred up. Then when he came—and you know how simple he is—and he went around without making himself important—just living here as he always did—well, they just couldn't accept him—that's all.

MARY CLEOPHAS—I suppose they expected to have him wearing a gold crown.

MARY (*absently*)—Something like that.

MARY CLEOPHAS—Still, you've always treated him as though he were different from the others.

MARY—He *is* different. Even before he was born I knew he was different. I— (*She breaks off—rises and walks away, lost in a memory too deep to put into words. When she speaks it is about something else.*) You know, I'm glad Judah didn't get home in time, after all. He loves his brother so—it would have hurt him to see how he was treated here. (*Pause.*) Well, *his* life is going to be happy—Miriam is a lovely girl—

Daniel runs in to report that the Rabbi and Mendel are coming up the road. And Judah not up yet! Mary is distressed. But Rabbi Samuel doesn't want to see Judah. He wants to talk with Mary alone first. The message he brings is not very pleasant, he tells her, when they are alone. Aaron, father of Miriam, has called off the wedding. But, why? Because, Mendel chips in, because Mary's family is getting a bad reputation. But why should Judah suffer for his brother? Mary demands. That's what they asked Aaron—but he just closed his shop and took the family away.

"Didn't even give us a chance to defend ourselves!" protests Mary. There is an exchange of looks between Mendel and Rabbi Samuel. Yes, Aaron did make one condition, albeit grudgingly. If Mary were to agree never to receive Jesus in her house again —disown him, cast him off—forget that he ever existed—

"It's a hard choice, Mary," the Rabbi admits. "But it's your responsibility. You're the one who must decide."

"So far as I'm concerned the whole transaction is a total loss," adds Mendel. "My commission gone—my time wasted—to say nothing of the money I spent arguing terms. No place but in the wine-shop would Aaron discuss it! You know, this business of Jesus upset Aaron from the very beginning. He always said— 'If he's a miracle worker—*I'm* a Roman Emperor!' I tried to tell him—Judah's a fine young man. Nothing like his brother. A little hot-tempered, perhaps, like all Nazarenes—but marriage will settle him down. I got him partly satisfied—then Jesus came back here with all that to-do about him and was a failure. That just finished Aaron!"

"Well, Mary?" The Rabbi is waiting.

"My house will be open to Jesus as long as I live," Mary answers, firmly.

RABBI—It seems pretty hard for Judah to pay for his brother's mistakes. You said so yourself, Mary—

MARY—I can't understand it! Why did they all turn against him? What is he teaching that could possibly do anybody any harm?

RABBI—He excites the people. Puts a lot of new ideas in their heads. Starts them thinking. You see, Mary—it's so easy to get off on the wrong foot. Mind you, *I've* no objection to his teaching even though he isn't a rabbi. I don't even mind his allowing people to *call* him Rabbi. After all, it only means "teacher." I think he's honest and sincere. But very *indiscreet*. And when people criticize him, see what he says—"Don't judge people if you don't want to be judged yourself—"

MENDEL—But then he goes on to make it worse with a deliberate dig at the Pharisees—and you know how touchy they are—calling them names—insulting them! Tells them they're full of hypocrisy and corruption!

RABBI—Word about him has got to Jerusalem and right now, when things are so unsettled, it's a bad time to talk about the equality of man and the oppression of the poor. But that's the history of all reformers. They go too far. I don't want to worry you, Mary, but you mustn't close your eyes and your ears to the danger he's in.

MARY (*flaring up as she rises and walks across the stage*)—That's all I've heard since the day he left home to preach! Everyone predicting he'd come to a bad end. And every day more and more people believe in him! Oh, what I've learned about human nature from this town! All my old friends and neighbors hardly able to wait until they get inside the gate to tell me some scandalous story about him! No wonder he was a failure here—surrounded by envy and hypocrisy and unbelief! And you—who invited him here— (*She breaks off, then returns and faces the* RABBI.) You were always a fair man, Samuel—but now you've put yourself on the side of the Pharisees who hate Jesus because they see their power and their influence slipping away from them—because word of him and his work is spreading all over the country! That it's even reached Jerusalem! And it'll go on! People like *you* can't stop him! No one can stop him!

RABBI (*furious*)—I came here as a friend—trying to spare your feelings—I didn't come here to be insulted! (*Springs up and crosses to* MARY.) Now, I'll tell you something! If someone doesn't get hold of that son of yours and stop him—he'll end up like his cousin John with his head on a harlot's platter. He's got the Temple and the Government so stirred up against him—why, I wouldn't give you that—(*snaps his fingers*)—for his safety! Not that! (*Snaps his fingers again. There is a dead silence as the* RABBI *breaks off, breathless.* MARY *walks over to the gate and opens it and stands there.*)

MARY (*almost in a whisper*)—I don't like to ask a rabbi to leave my house—but I can't have you talking like that about my son. The streets are free—you can say what you like in them.

But this is his home. (*Her voice breaks a little.* MENDEL *and the* RABBI *walk silently past her toward the gate.* MENDEL *exits but the* RABBI *pauses. He is profoundly moved and we must feel that he realizes her outburst was maternal, and not directed at him personally.*)

RABBI—I'm sorry, Mary. I lost my temper. (*Pause.*) All I know is—if he were my son—I'd be worried.

Mary, shaken by the Rabbi's last words, is pacing the yard, her hands clasped, as Judah comes clattering down the stairs from the roof. He is distressed at having slept so late. Half the day is gone and he has not seen Miriam. He would bound away, but Mary restrains him. And listens unhappily to his repeated tale of love for Miriam. Then gently, as tactfully as she can, Mary tells Judah of Aaron's decision. Reminds him that he is young. That there are lots of other girls; that Aaron has always been a difficult man, and very influential—

"But what have I done!" persists the unhappy Judah.

MARY—You haven't done *anything!* (*Searching desperately for reasons.*) It's just that—Aaron's ambitious and—and we aren't exactly what you would call a prominent family— (*She breaks off.*) There's nothing we can do, Judah. He's taken Miriam away.

JUDAH—But there must be a *reason,* Mother—what is it? He must have said something. Mendel and the Rabbi wouldn't come here on just nothing! They wouldn't dare!

MARY (*realizing that she can't evade the truth any longer, faces* JUDAH *with as much courage as she can muster*)—I don't know how to tell you! (*Puts her hand on his arm.*) The only one of my children who never gave me a moment's worry! (*Pause.*) Judah—he won't let you marry her—because of your brother—

JUDAH—My *brother?*

MARY—Because of Jesus. (*There is a silence while* JUDAH *stares at her.*)

JUDAH—You mean they've called off my *wedding* because of Jesus?

MARY—Yes. (*She puts her arms around him.*) Oh, Judah—I don't know what to say to you—I know how hard this is on you! It's hard on *me,* too— (JUDAH *shakes her off, half mad with grief and resentment. He is young enough to be nearly in tears.*)

JUDAH—It's easy to talk! But I'm young! And my life's going to be ruined just because I've got a brother with crazy ideas!

MARY—Judah! Oh, I know how hurt and upset you are, dear —but try to remember how fond you were of each other! Why, Jesus was your favorite brother! He used to carry you around—

JUDAH—I don't care what he was! He's ruined my life! (*Pause.*) Wasn't there *anything* you could do—

MARY—Aaron did make one condition—

JUDAH—Why didn't you tell me? What was it?

MARY—It was something impossible—

JUDAH—What *was* it?

MARY—He wanted us to disown Jesus—forbid him the house—

JUDAH—Well, why didn't you do it!

MARY—Judah!

JUDAH—What does he care about us? He goes his own sweet way—running around the country doing as he pleases! Why should we worry about him?

MARY—Judah—*don't!*

JUDAH—I hate him! I *hate* him! I wish he were dead!

"He brushes past Mary, flings open the gate and goes out into the road. The gate closes sharply behind him. Mary stands alone on the stage; then with a gesture of complete and utter defeat, she crosses with leaden feet to the table, sinks down on the bench and lays her head on her arms and weeps brokenly" as the curtain falls.

## ACT III

We have come to Jerusalem with Mary and Mary Cleophas. It is night. In the moonlight a narrow square in a poor district of the city is revealed. There are the fronts of houses in the background. Arches lead from the square to other narrow streets. In the center of the square is a small pump. Here two towns-women are filling pitchers.

Mary Cleophas is sitting on the edge of the sidewalk. She has taken off her shoes and is rubbing her tired feet. She and her sister, Mary Cleophas confides to one of the women, are in search of her nephew. He is having supper somewhere around there. They have been looking for the place.

"I don't suppose you know my nephew, do you?" hazards Mary Cleophas. "This is a big place—but he's quite a figure—

from what they tell me—"

"What's his name?"

"Jesus. Jesus of Nazareth."

The woman has set her pitcher down with a clatter. Her whole attitude has changed. *"That man!"* she exclaims.

MARY CLEOPHAS—Then you do know him?

WOMAN—Don't insult me! I wouldn't have anything to do with him!

MARY CLEOPHAS—But I thought he created such a stir here last week—rode through the city—

WOMAN—Broke the Sabbath to do it!

MARY CLEOPHAS—But the people waved palms and cheered. I heard they made a real demonstration.

WOMAN—A lot of idlers and roustabouts! I haven't any use for him! Stirring people up—turning families against each other! Telling them what to do and what to say! Who does he think he is?

MARY CLEOPHAS—Did you ever see him?

WOMAN—I don't have to! I've heard enough about him.

MARY CLEOPHAS—I've known him since he was a little boy. I don't agree with everything he says. But he's a good and honest man. (*The Roman soldiers' trumpet is heard offstage.*)

WOMAN—You wouldn't say that if you knew what he did here last week! Drove the money-changers out of the Temple with a whip! Where they've been since anyone can remember! That was a fine thing to do with old Annas getting a percentage on all the money that changes hands! And if that wasn't enough—he told them they could tear down the Temple—*tear it down, mind you*—and he'd rebuild it in three days!

MARY CLEOPHAS (*startled*)—He didn't say that?

WOMAN (*with satisfaction*)—That and worse! He called himself the Son of God! A blasphemer. I maybe shouldn't have said so much—with you his relative—

MARY CLEOPHAS—Speech is free. I'm not one to stop anyone from speaking their minds. But I'm glad his mother didn't hear you. He's the apple of her eye. Besides, I've heard these things before and nothing ever came of it. (*The Roman soldiers' trumpet is repeated offstage.*)

WOMAN (*roused again*)—He's going too far now! Even though they're used to fanatics here.

MARY CLEOPHAS—Fanatic—so that's what they call him!

WOMAN—And the class of people he has for followers! That

red-headed dancer from Magdala—at least, that was *one* of her professions—

MARY CLEOPHAS—I've heard of *her*.

WOMAN (*acidly*)—She makes a show of herself! Breaking alabaster jars of perfume over his feet and bathing them with it and wiping them off with her hair!

MARY CLEOPHAS (*reluctantly*)—It does sound kind of pagan.

WOMAN—They tell me that back in Magdala she had more servants than she could count. Gold plates to eat off—and silk sheets to sleep under—

MARY CLEOPHAS—You don't say! (*Breaks off as she sees* MARY *approaching.*) Here's my sister now— (*She rises.*) —Well—it's—it's been nice—having this little talk—good night.

WOMAN (*picking up pitcher*)—Good night. (*She eyes* MARY *curiously as she exits.*)

Mary is weary. She has walked far and looked at all the two-storied houses. Selima had said they would be having supper in an upper room. Everywhere Mary had met soldiers. They have made her very uneasy, but Mary Cleophas tries to be reassuring. There is always something going on in Jerusalem. "Mary, I know how important Jesus is to you," says Mary Cleophas, "but they're scarcely calling out the Roman Army for him!"

Mary Cleophas doesn't think much of Selima's directions, even if her sons did make the dinner arrangements.

"The way she trails them around the country! Her James and her John!" Mary Cleophas' tone is a bit contemptuous. "I should think it would drive them crazy. And what was that business about who'd sit where?"

MARY—I didn't quite understand. Something about wanting to know when Jesus became king—if he'd promise seats on each side of the throne to her sons. (*Suddenly serious.*) All this talk of thrones and kingdoms—he never cared for things like that— (*Breaks off.*) I can't get those soldiers out of my mind!

MARY CLEOPHAS—If there was anything really wrong— wouldn't the girls have told us at Bethany? Surely, they'd be the ones to know—with him sleeping there every night!

MARY—Nice girls, weren't they? And they all seem so fond of Jesus. I'm glad he gets to a quiet place at night—and it's just walking distance from Jerusalem.

MARY CLEOPHAS—That Martha's a fine housekeeper. The other one moons around. Martha was telling me that it nearly

drives her crazy. Meals to get for all those men—but do you
think her sister helps? No—she just sits and admires Jesus and
never lifts a finger. Martha even went so far as to complain to
him about it—and what do you think he said? That Martha
worried about the house too much—that her sister had her mind
on better things! That's a fine way to talk about a lazy girl with
her head in the clouds!

MARY (*not listening*)—You know, it's been years since I was
in Jerusalem. But I don't remember it's ever being so—so unfriendly.

MARY CLEOPHAS—That's because you're tired.

MARY (*slowly*)—No. It's something else. Everything is so
still—and yet it isn't peaceful. As if something were waiting.
The way it is before a thunder storm. (*Adds impulsively:*) You
know, I thought once I got to Jerusalem I'd feel better, knowing
he was so close. But I don't. I shouldn't even say this, but for
the first time in my life—I'm *frightened*.

Someone can be heard approaching. A second later a young
man wrapped in a dark cloak hurries into the square and would
pass quickly through if Mary had not recognized him. It's Judas
Iscariot! The young man she had met in Capernaum. Surely
Judas will know where Jesus and the others are having supper!

Judas is a little confused. It is very late— Yes, Jesus is all
right. Everything has been going about as usual—

"But they say he is upsetting law and order in Jerusalem,"
Mary says.

"People use words lightly," answers Judas, evasively.

MARY—And that he breaks the Sabbath!

JUDAS—He doesn't know the meaning of time.

MARY—You're hiding something from me! What is it?

MARY CLEOPHAS (*chidingly*)—Mary! After all, his safety
must mean as much to Judas as it does to you— (*To* JUDAS.)
She's been so worried.

MARY (*barely hearing* MARY CLEOPHAS)—He isn't in trouble—
with important people, that is—who might do him some harm?

JUDAS (*haltingly*)—It's—it's hard to say—such a mixed crowd
here in Jerusalem. You're bound to offend someone—sooner or
later. Of course, he knows he runs that risk—but he won't listen
to anyone— (*His voice trails off.*)

MARY—When did you see him last? Did you have supper with
him and the others?

JUDAS—I left early.

MARY—Oh, then they're still there! (*To* MARY CLEOPHAS.) We'll get to him after all!

MARY CLEOPHAS—Is it very far?

JUDAS—About fifteen minutes' walk.

MARY CLEOPHAS—*Fifteen minutes!* (*To* JUDAS.) All right, lead the way.

JUDAS—I can't. I'm—I'm—in a hurry. I have an errand— (*His voice trails off.*)

MARY—If you'll just tell us how to get there—

JUDAS (*quickly and nervously*)—You go down that way— (*points across stage*)—until you come to a wide cross-street—and there's a fountain in the middle—a square one. You turn left there and go straight along until you reach the street of the water-sellers—

MARY CLEOPHAS—How'll we know it?

JUDAS—There're always donkeys tied to the racks.

MARY CLEOPHAS—Not at *this* time of night!

JUDAS (*desperately*)—There'll be a lot of water jars standing about. You can't miss it!

MARY CLEOPHAS—Now let's get this straight. I've had all the wrong directions I want in one evening. (*She repeats directions slowly, to his intense nervousness.*) We go down that way— (*points*)—until we get to a wide street. (*She stops.*) I didn't know there *were* any wide streets in Jerusalem.

JUDAS—I mean—wider than this.

MARY CLEOPHAS— —and there's a fountain—

JUDAS (*with increasing emotion*)—Then you turn left—

MARY CLEOPHAS— —and find the street of the water-sellers. And the house is there. Which house is it?

JUDAS—The third house—it has a balcony. (*He turns to go.*)

MARY CLEOPHAS—What's the man's name?

JUDAS—*Nathan!*

MARY (*to* MARY CLEOPHAS)—Can't you see he's in a hurry? (*To* JUDAS.) Don't worry about us. We'll find it quite easily now. (*Pause.*) I hope we haven't made you late.

JUDAS (*in a strangled voice*)—No. There is still time.

MARY CLEOPHAS—Good night.

MARY—Good night. And thank you. (*Takes his arm.*) And you're sure no harm can come to him?

JUDAS—He says no one can destroy him.

MARY CLEOPHAS—What does he mean by that?

JUDAS (*with growing panic*)—I don't know! *I don't know!*

(*He rushes from the scene.*)

MARY CLEOPHAS—Another fifteen minutes!

MARY—Oh, it doesn't matter—now that we know where we're going. (*They start to cross stage.*) I'm so glad that Judas left early!

"As they exit, the soldiers' trumpet sounds offstage and is answered from a distance." The curtain falls.

Mary and Mary Cleophas have found the house of Nathan in Jerusalem. But they have arrived too late. In a room on the upper floor a table, set for thirteen, with the candles still burning, has been recently deserted. A large silver goblet and a flagon of wine are prominent. It is a pleasant room, a replica of da Vinci's painting, "The Last Supper." There are windows at the back through which the roof of the house across the street may be seen.

Mary is bitterly disappointed, and would go on, if they can learn where Jesus and his friends have gone. Mary Cleophas rebels. Not a step farther will she go on those cobblestones until she knows where she is going and *why*.

Someone is coming up the stairs. "The door opens and Mary Magdalen enters, pausing in surprise and alarm. She is plainly dressed, but carries her clothes with a certain air. She has beautiful red hair."

"We're looking for Jesus of Nazareth," Mary explains, simply, in answer to the Magdalen's obviously suspicious inquiries.

"Who told you he'd be here?" demands the Magdalen.

"Judas. He showed us the way—"

"Judas! I thought he'd gone with the others—"

"We met him in the street alone."

"Where was he going?"

"He didn't say. He seemed in a great hurry. He just told us how to get here— Surely this is the place. (*Pause.*) Hasn't Jesus been here?"

"They've all gone!" That should end the conversation so far as the Magdalen is concerned.

"Why, I know who you are! You're from Magdala, aren't you?" persists Mary Cleophas.

"I *was* from Magdala."

"Selima told me about you."

"Selima talks too much. Who are you?"

"This is the mother of Jesus," Mary Cleophas explains, gesturing in Mary's direction.

For a moment the two face each other, the one smiling and gentle, the other dismayed and a little awed. "Oh—I'm—I'm so sorry—I had no idea—" the Magdalen is muttering.

"I'm glad to know you," says Mary, extending her hand. "I've heard about you— You're a friend of my son—"

The Magdalen has bowed her head, genuinely touched. And before she can reply Nathan has come rushing up the stairs in a state of excitement. "Magdalen! Magdalen!" he calls. "They bought swords tonight! Jesus told them to even sell their clothes if they had to—but to get swords!"

And then he sees Mary and Mary Cleophas and is mystified. With a warning look the Magdalen explains who the strangers are. When Mary would have more of his news, would know if it concerns her son, Magdalen is quick to change the subject.

Mary had heard the soldiers in the street getting orders to go some place. They wanted to see someone named Pilate. It was his house they were going to.

"Probably to quiet some disturbance," ventures Magdalen. "There's always something happening in Jerusalem—"

Nathan would hurry them on. But where? "They've just gone for a walk. In the hills, I guess," says Nathan. "They often go up Gethsemane way," adds Magdalen. "There's some gardens there."

Mary would go in search of them, and Nathan would have her go, but Magdalen advises sharply against it. Let Mary send Nathan's boy to tell Jesus that she is there. That would be best. And let Mary give the boy the message herself—

"You must get her out of Jerusalem!" the Magdalen tells Mary Cleophas, as soon as Mary has gone with Nathan. "Get her away from here! Take her home!"

"You mean—there's going to be trouble?"

"Yes."

"What kind of trouble?"

"None of us knows! That is, none of us—except—"

"Except who?"

"I think Jesus knows. He tried to tell the disciples tonight. To prepare them. (*Pause.*) He was like a man going on a far journey."

Mary has come back now, and is much relieved because she has sent the message. She has found a stool in front of the table and would have the Magdalen tell her of her son. They hear such mixed-up stories in Nazareth.

"I've always tried to think of my other children," Mary is saying. "To see their side of it. Suddenly I couldn't any longer. It was as if they all just—melted away. I didn't have any other children. Only this one—and he was in trouble."

On a hassock by the table Magdalen has found Jesus' cloak, and is worried. "Isn't that just like him?" says Mary, reaching eagerly for the cloak. "Never thinks of himself. But I don't see why all those disciples can't think of him once in a while."

Mary has discovered a tear in the cloak and would mend it. Thread is found and as Mary sews a light of tender reminiscence fills her eyes—

"How this takes me back!" she muses. "When he was a little boy his knees went through everything! He played so hard. And when he grew up and went into the carpenter shop he worked the same way. Never knew when it was time to stop."

MAGDALEN (*sitting down near* MARY)—He's the same now. Works until he drops. He has so much he wants to say—he seems almost afraid he won't have time to say it. (*She quickly covers this ominous note by adding:*) The other day it grew dark without his even knowing—and the people stayed on and listened —way into the night.

MARY CLEOPHAS (*yawning*)—He always was a good talker. It's a real gift.

MARY—What did he talk about that time? (MARY CLEOPHAS *nods.*)

MAGDALEN—About a shepherd who lost one sheep. And how he left the whole flock and searched and searched the night through until he found it. And how happy he was and what it meant to him to bring one—to bring one lost sheep back into the fold. I love that story. (MARY CLEOPHAS *falls asleep.*)

MARY—How I wish I could have been here and heard these things! But I feel easier in my mind about him—talking to you. Please tell me more. Do great crowds gather when he preaches?

MAGDALEN—I should think so! You know how fond he is of children? Well—the other day when he was preaching, a lot of them gathered around and someone complained. But Jesus said if having the children running about shouting and laughing while he preached annoyed the older people—then *they* could leave. That Heaven itself was made up of the innocent and the simple-hearted.

MARY (*hesitantly, looking around at her sleeping sister-in-law*) —There's something I want to ask you—while my sister's asleep. I want to ask you—about the miracles.

MAGDALEN—I—I can't say much about the miracles. They just *were*. (*Pause.*) Of course, he performed a great many more in the beginning when he first started out on his work. But lately he's turned more and more to teaching. Telling people the way to live. And a great deal about understanding and forgiveness. And the beauty of human life. I don't believe he thinks miracles are very important. He always says a man isn't really any better after seeing something spectacular than he was before. He'd much rather talk about loving them that hate you than raise the dead. After all—he's not concerned with the death of the body. But the disciples—they'd like more miracles. Excitement—and the crowds. But he does less all the time. There is one thing he wants them to believe above everything. It underlies every word he says—it is the very foundation on which his whole teaching is built.

MARY—And what is that?

MAGDALEN—The dignity—and the greatness of man. People criticize him for calling himself the Son of God. They forget how much more often he calls himself the Son of Man. Because Man is God—and God is Man. (*The Roman trumpet is heard outside.* MAGDALEN *rises in instinctive alarm.* MARY *sees this and puts her sewing down.*)

MARY—You feel you owe a great deal to my son, don't you?

MAGDALEN—Without him I am nothing.

MARY—Then you must tell me the truth about him. Is he in danger?

MAGDALEN (*searching for an evasion*)—There is no greatness without danger.

MARY—But why? But why? What does he *say* or *do* or *teach* that anyone could possibly find fault with?

MAGDALEN (*she sits—then speaks almost bitterly*)—He blesses the poor and the meek. And the hungry. And those who weep. And he tells them all the same thing—rich and poor alike. "If you love me—take up your cross and follow me."

MARY (*apprehensively*)—Cross?

MAGDALEN—That's a figure of speech he uses. He means— self-denial. (*Pause.*) And then—he blesses those who have sinned. I—I don't want to—to embarrass you—or bore you by telling you about myself. You probably know already—

MARY—Only what I've heard—and you can't judge people by that.

MAGDALEN—You looked just like him as you said that. But, you see, it's his acceptance of people like me that they condemn!

This whole idea of repentance and forgiveness. No one ever taught it before. Being *born* again! Think what that means!

MARY—I can *see* what it means.

MAGDALEN—He raised me from the dead. I was blind—and now I see. I was deaf—and now I hear. The world will never be the same because he has lived! (MAGDALEN, *overcome with emotion, sinks down, her head in her hands. MARY, seeing her shivering, puts the cloak of Jesus around her shoulders, then takes the silver chalice from the table and offers it to MAGDALEN.*)

MARY—Drink a little of this wine. It will warm you. (MARY *holds the chalice to MAGDALEN's lips. In the silence that follows we hear the Roman soldiers' trumpet repeated—then suddenly the growing murmur of a crowd. MARY and MAGDALEN look at each other. Neither speaks. Now there is shouting and an angry rise to the voices outside. Both women are rigid with fear. MARY puts the chalice down on the table with a trembling hand.*)

MARY CLEOPHAS (*awaking*)—What's that? Someone call me? (*Neither MARY nor MAGDALEN answers.*) They're certainly worked up over something— (*The noise grows in volume and nearness. Suddenly the name "Jesus of Nazareth" is clearly heard shouted derisively. MARY springs to her feet and rushes to the window. At the same moment, NATHAN bursts into the room. MAGDALEN rises, the cloak of Jesus falling to the stool. MARY is at the window when NATHAN seizes her and thrusts her away.*)

NATHAN—Get away from that window! They've arrested him! I don't want my house mixed up in this!

MARY—Arrested!

NATHAN—They're taking him to Pilate.

MAGDALEN (*to NATHAN*)—How did they know where he was? Who told them?

NATHAN—Judas Iscariot.

MAGDALEN—Judas! But the other disciples—what were they doing?

NATHAN—Running for safety!

MARY CLEOPHAS—Deserted him—

MARY (*stunned*)—*Arrested!* I must go to him!

MARY CLEOPHAS (*trying to make her voice gentle*)—No, no! They've only trumped up some charges against him— (NATHAN *exits as MAGDALEN, MARY and MARY CLEOPHAS cross to the door. MARY makes no answer to her sister. At the doorway she stops, turns and goes across the room to the hassock, and picks up his cloak.*)

MARY—He'll need this. They may keep him all night.

"As she starts again for the door the shouts in the street reach a crescendo and Mary stands, Jesus' cloak clasped in her arms as she hears the words—'Crucify him! Crucify him!' " The curtain falls.

It is several years later. A bright sunlight floods the dooryard of the house in Nazareth. The fig tree is in full bloom, "heavy in green leaves and purple fruit." There is someone at work in the carpenter shop. Naomi is finishing setting the table under the fig tree, spread now with a fine cloth and the best plates and bowls as for a celebration. There is happiness again in the house in Nazareth.

Daniel, a full sixteen years now, vaults the wall he used to have difficulty climbing. He has seen his Uncle Judah hurrying down the street. He may be looking for old Beulah—seeing that his wife, Deborah, is about to have a baby.

And now it appears that the celebration is to be a betrothal party for Esther, the daughter of Joseph and Reba. The prospective bridegroom and his father are coming all the way from Damascus by camel. No wonder there is excitement in Nazareth!

Mary has come down the stairs. A softer gentleness has settled upon her with her years, but she is still one with her family and interested in all their activities.

"I can't get used to it," she smiles, when they tell her of Judah's going for Beulah. *"My* baby rushing after a midwife for *his* baby! (Pauses.)* It's nice, though. I never get over being grateful that Judah found a good wife after all. *(Another pause.)* Nearly time for the guests, isn't it? *(With a smile for ESTHER.)* Someone's getting impatient."

Esther blushes prettily under the chiding of her grandmother and is happy. A little sad, though, when she thinks of living so far away.

"Damascus *is* a good ways off," admits Mary. "But, just think! You'll be the head of your own house—no old mother-in-law to make life miserable, the way I do around here. *(She smiles at ESTHER who smiles back a bit shakily.)* And then, before you know it, your babies will be coming along. Wait till you have your first one! Nothing makes you feel so important as your first baby. I'll never forget mine. . . . *(She breaks off—a shadow crossing her face.)* Look—there's the first star! Like the one at Bethlehem. *(Pause. Throws off mood with effort.)*

There now, don't let me start talking about—about when I was young—or the company won't get any supper!"

And now there is a loud knocking at the gate, and a great scurrying of preparation in the yard. But it turns out to be only Judah and Beulah. "Be sure to make it a boy," Judah calls happily after the midwife as she mounts the stairs. "I'll do my best—but you should have thought of that sooner," laughs Beulah.

Mary Cleophas has come through the gate with a jug of wine, and a moment later Mendel, the marriage broker, who has run himself out of breath, appears. Mendel has come ahead to see that all is in readiness. He has left Leban, the merchant, and Joshua, his son, at the inn in charge of an assistant. Apparently there is one thing about which he is anxious. He has a whispered conversation with Joseph and is obviously relieved at Joseph's answer. But Mary has noted this. She calls to Mendel, who turns a surprised look upon her.

"Mary!" he exclaims, heartily. "Oh, I'm sorry—I didn't see you in all the rush. My, but you're looking well—and on a busy day like this! Your hands full with the engagement supper—and if I remember your housekeeping rightly, it'll be something to make our visitors open their eyes. (*Rattles on nervously.*) I'll never forget—"

"Never mind about the supper, Mendel. (*A hush falls on the group.*) When you first met Leban and his son in Damascus last year—did you tell them all about our family?"

"I should say I did! What a wonderful woman you are—what a fine man their father was, God rest him! (*Switches subject cannily.*) I was thinking this morning—if he could only have lived to see this day! Esther was just a baby when he died, wasn't she?"

"She wasn't born."

"Oh, I thought she was."

"You're sure you told them about everyone?"

"I was at my best! You should have heard me! I went back five generations. I got them so tangled up in the family tree—"

"You left no one out?"

"They're here!"

"You haven't answered me, Mendel."

"Why stir that up again, Mary? You're a respectable family. You've lived it down."

Joseph has opened the gate and the guests are entering. Mary Cleophas has edged her way over to Mary's side. "I'd be awfully sure I was right before I said anything, Mary," suggests Mary Cleophas, with an affectionate pat of Mary's arm.

And now, with a great show of hospitality and neighborly friendliness the guests are introduced. Leban is a bearded merchant of middle years. Joshua, his son, tall and handsome, is shyly stealing glances at the blushing Esther. Soon Joseph has concluded the introductions and suggested that they all go into the house and have a glass of wine, which seems a happy thought. Joseph has waved the party on when Mary stops him. They all turn back as she speaks—

MARY—Just a moment, Joseph. (*To* LEBAN.) I'm sorry to interfere at the last minute like this—but since no one else will speak, I'm afraid I'll have to. I can't let this go on without saying something.

MENDEL—Please, Mary—don't be unreasonable!

MARY CLEOPHAS—Be quiet, Mendel. (JOSEPH *looks at his wife and makes a helpless gesture.*)

LEBAN (*puzzled*)—I don't understand. (*There is a buzz of whispering among the family.* MARY *silences it with a little gesture. A dead silence follows.*)

MARY—What I have to say isn't easy. You see—(*There is a painful pause.*)—we had a little trouble in our family— (*She falters.*)

LEBAN—Yes?

MARY (*summoning her courage and forcing herself to a complete statement in one sentence. As she speaks the light begins to slowly soften*)—My oldest son—he got into some difficulty with the authorities.

LEBAN (*hesitantly, to* MENDEL)—Is that James—the one who's away?

MARY—No, not James. The one I mean is dead. (*Pause.*) He was killed.

LEBAN—Oh, I'm sorry. An accident?

MARY—They thought he was trying to stir up trouble and they —they crucified him.

LEBAN—*Crucified* him!

MARY (*with sudden desperation*)—Don't you understand? Don't you see what I'm trying to tell you? My son was Jesus of Nazareth! (*Her voice breaks and she makes a gesture of helplessness and turns away.*) Now you know! (*There is a long pause.* LEBAN *looks questioningly from one face to another but the family avoid his gaze, not knowing that he is trying to conceal the fact that the name means nothing to him. Suddenly* JOSEPH *breaks into the silence, anxiously.*)

JOSEPH (*eagerly*)—You're not going to let this come between the young people, are you? After all, it's a long time ago, and outside of that, no one can say a word against us. Everything we told you about our family is true.

MENDEL—Absolutely true!

JOSEPH (*continuing*)—I admit we did leave that out—about my brother. Maybe we shouldn't have—but my daughter's happiness means a lot to me. (*His voice breaks a little.*) I didn't want to spoil her chances.

MARY CLEOPHAS (*watching* LEBAN)—Save your breath! The man's never heard of him! (*The others stare at* LEBAN *with incredulity.*)

LEBAN (*mumbling in his embarrassment*)—Well—you see—I'm afraid—I—I—I live so far away—

MARY—He was quite well known.

The family is plainly upset, and perhaps a little indignant, at such ignorance. They would have Leban know that their brother was the talk of the country at one time, and had many offers from neighboring places. No, he was not a rabbi—at least not a regular rabbi. He preached, and had disciples who hung on his every word, and scurried away like rabbits when he got into trouble—

"I hear that some of them are keeping on with the work," says Mary. "I *hope* it's true. It'd be a shame to have it all lost. He worked so hard—never took any care of himself. You know—looking back—I've often thought he knew he wasn't going to live long."

"There was some talk of people seeing him again—*after*—" Simon adds.

"I used to wait for him," says Mary. "I thought surely if he came anywhere it would be here, to his home. But he never came."

"What did he teach?" Leban's tone is kindly as he notes Mary's emotion.

"Why—to—love your enemies—never to judge or condemn anyone—to be *forgiving*. And to make life as easy as you could for other people. (*Pauses, groping for the most important things.*) To live for a purpose in which you believe and never let anyone

keep you from your belief—not even your own family. You must
be willing to die for it. And not to be afraid of people who—
who kill the body. Because, after that, there is nothing more
they can do. And to be kind to little children—he loved little
children. (*A pause in which she feels she must make this last
point dreadfully clear—and searches for the right words.*) And
to remember always that human life is beautiful—and noble—because it houses God. (*She is aware of the little startled look on*
Leban's *face—and hastens to extend the idea.*) I mean—when—
when you degrade or dishonor human life—you degrade and dishonor God. (*There is a moment of dead silence.*) That was all
he taught."

"Has anyone ever tried it—to live the way he taught?"

"I don't think so."

"Might be interesting to see what would happen if they did,"
ventures Leban.

"It's too simple," thinks Mary Cleophas.

"You know, I think that's what caused all the trouble," Mary
says. "They couldn't understand that it was all just as simple
as that. That there wasn't something behind it. So they accused
him of trying to attack the government."

"Then it was a political offense?" says Leban, plainly relieved.

"I guess you'd call it that," Mary admits, embarrassedly. "I—
I never really quite understood. (*Pause.*) They hurried me out
of the city. I think he told them to. I never saw him again."

But now the Rabbi has arrived and the business of the betrothal
is resumed. Joseph has again taken charge and at last gets them
all started for the house, leaving only Mary and Judah alone.

"If the baby's a boy—what are you going to name him?" asks
Mary, with careful casualness.

"We haven't decided."

"I wish—"

"What, Mother?"

"Will you do something for me, Judah?"

"Of course I will! What is it?"

"Judah!" It is Beulah's voice calling from upstairs.

"Coming!" He has started for the stairs. For a step or two
Mary walks with him. At the foot of the stairs she stops him—

"If it's a boy, will you name him after your brother— After
Jesus, I mean?"

"Why—why, yes, Mother. I'll talk to Deborah about it—"
He has leaned over the staircase and kissed her.

"It's a nice name," says Mary, as Judah starts running up the stairs. "I'd like him not to be forgotten."

"Mary is alone. The light has faded and it is nearly dusk. She turns and goes toward the table, picks up the taper and starts to light one of the seven-branched candlesticks."

**THE CURTAIN FALLS**

# KISS THE BOYS GOOD-BYE

## A Comedy in Three Acts

### By Clare Boothe

THERE had been a good deal of talk about the coming of "Kiss the Boys Good-bye" early in the season. It was Clare Boothe's first comedy following her success with "The Women," for one thing, and for another it was, by report, a pointed satire on the Hollywood ballyhoo concerned with the search for an actress to play Scarlett O'Hara in the screen production of Margaret Mitchell's *Gone with the Wind*.

The stage was set for either a quick failure or a sensational success. Happily "Kiss the Boys Good-bye," produced in late September, was a little on the sensational side. Its reviewers were not raving in their praise, but they were frankly enthusiastic and the buying public that followed was even more enthusiastic than the reviewers.

"Kiss the Boys Good-bye" ran through the holidays to a consistently crowded theatre. A second company was organized for Chicago, and scored a success in the West. Everything, as might be said, was rosy. In the midst of which ideal state Miss Boothe wrote a preface for the printed version of the play published by Random House.

In the preface she completely astounded the play's critics and admirers alike by declaring that her play was, in reality, a most important social document, "a political allegory about Fascism in America," no less.

"We are not, perhaps, sufficiently aware that 'Southernism' is a particular and highly matured form of Fascism with which America has lived more or less peacefully for seventy-five years," reads the Boothe foreword. "Indeed 'Southernism' may possibly have been the inspiration or forerunner of Fascism. At any rate those who like to draw political analogies, which means all those of us whose intellectual ability to cope with historical processes consists in reciting innumerable rather too pat analogies between 'Then and Now,' 'Over Here and Over There,' may surely with profit trace the Black or Brown Shirt idea to the White Shirts of the Ku Klux Klan. And although 'industrial capitalism' had relatively little to do with their problem, the White Shirts, like the Brown and Black Shirts, also brought order out of a post-war era of chaos. The Southern chaos of 1865 being worse than the German chaos of 1932, it is notable that the order was even more quickly and brutally brought. The carpet-bagger-inspired Communism of the Negro was ruthlessly and passionately stamped out as the 'Jew-Inspired' Communism of the laborer in Germany has been. Indeed the swastika never burns more brightly or savagely in the Schwarzwald than the Fiery Cross of the Klan once burned in the bayous and the cypress swamps of Dixie."

Miss Boothe's slightly belated revealing of her more serious purpose in writing "Kiss the Boys Good-bye" as an exposé and a warning caused a day's excited talk and provided a party argument for weeks. But her comedy ran on and made friends as a good evening's entertainment. No one in her audiences cared more than a light hoot as to whether it was seriously intended or not. Now, with the text available, every reader is privileged to read his own opinions into the script.

As "Kiss the Boys Good-bye" comes into view we are shown into the drawing room of a Dixie Flyer, northbound. The table has been set up between the berths. On one side, a Pullman Conductor is checking a sheaf of telegrams handed him by Lloyd Lloyd, "a sadly soured youngish man," seated across the table. The floor is littered with a mess of previously discarded efforts.

The Conductor, an amiable and observing human, is greatly interested in Mr. Lloyd's efforts as well as his creations. The telegrams are long and as sparkling as Lloyd can make them. Most of them are addressed to motion picture executives in Hollywood. They, Lloyd explains, like long wordy telegrams. "Gives them a chance to practice reading," he explains.

" 'Herbert Z. Harner, President of Harner Pictures, care Newark Airport—and the Mercy of God,' " reads the Conductor from one wire.

"You gotta gag 'em up, or the word gets 'round on the coast— you're slipping," again explains Lloyd, burping dolefully as a relief from a chronic stomach disturbance.

There are other wires, one for Horace Rand, in Westport, Conn. One for Myra Stanhope, the picture star, at the Waldorf-Astoria. The Conductor is practically atwitter with curiosity. Can it be possible that Myra Stanhope is going to play the part of Velvet O'Toole?

The Conductor wouldn't care for that choice. "I got a preconceived notion," he admits. "Something half Hepburn, half Bette

Davis, half Myrna Loy—"

"Stir, and add a dash of bitters—" finishes Lloyd.

There is, it appears, a young woman traveling with Mr. Lloyd and the Conductor has deduced from the Lloyd telegrams that she also is a candidate for the part of Velvet O'Toole. From what he has seen of the young woman he doesn't think she would do. Lloyd is inclined to agree with him. He has, he intimates, been searching for a favorite daughter of the South for the role, and he is bringing this one North for a sort of preliminary preview. If she lasts out the week-end he has planned, this Georgia find may be the girl they're looking for. Otherwise Myra Stanhope should be swell in the part.

Now the Conductor has gone with the telegrams and Cindy Lou Bethany, the "Georgia find," has come to talk with Mr. Lloyd. Cindy Lou "is a pretty girl, about eighteen or twenty years old, and Southern, very Southern. She is wearing a thin chiffon frock, with quantities of pink ruching at the throat and arm. Cool and colorful, this costume is nevertheless incorrect even in midsummer for train travel. She is carrying a thick book. If we could read the starred-and-barred, red, white and blue jacket, we would see that it is titled 'Kiss the Boys Good-bye.' "

Several things are worrying Cindy Lou. For one, she and her Aunt Lily Lou, who is traveling with her, would like a glimpse of Philadelphia. She can't understand why it is so important that they should be kept hidden in their compartment for fear the reporters might sneak up on them. For another thing, Cindy Lou is beginning to worry about spending a week-end in Connecticut and leaving Aunt Lily Lou alone in New York. Being a regular chatter-box, Aunt Lily Lou is bound to be mighty lonesome—

"Stop worrying about Auntie," protests the irritated Lloyd. "I've got her a swell suite at the Plaza. She can yammer to the bellboys 'til she's blue. Say, she can go have it out with General Sherman's statue in the park."

"Is there a statue of General Sherman?"

"Right outside her window."

"Mercy guide me! Aunt Lily Lou won't sleep a wink!"

Cindy Lou would like to take her aunt with her to the Rands', but that can't be done for several reasons, though one is enough: She hasn't been asked.

Again Mr. Lloyd tries to explain: Cindy Lou is getting a break. Herbert Z. Harner (quite privately referred to as God Almighty) is giving her the once-over at a quiet little house party where she will be among friends. If Herbert Z. likes her, fine. If he doesn't that settles it.

"But you said I was the only girl in the whole South—" protests Cindy Lou.

"Cotton-Blossom, you suit me fine. But Harner's the producer."

"You mean he's a . . . a typical motion picture man?"

"He's got a Z in his name," Lloyd calmly assures her.

And yet Cindy Lou just can't help worrying. Who are the Rands? Are they nice people? "There must be nice people up North," she muses. "I'm not nearly as intolerant as Aunt Lily Lou. She says whenever a lil Yankee baby's baptized, the clergyman removes its horns and tail in the vestry."

Cindy Lou does not consider the news that Horace Rand is the editor of the mgaazine, *Manhattan Man,* reassuring. Aunt Lily Lou insists *Manhattan Man* is lewd. "Lewder and funnier," gags Lloyd, gently urging her toward the door. And then he gives her some little hope by mentioning the fact that Mrs. Rand is really what is known as a lady. A Rumson, in fact, and "veddy, veddy longguyland."

"Any kin to the Atlanta Rumsons?" Cindy Lou would know.

"I'm not Cholly Knickerbocker, Toots, but Top Rumson, the ten-goal polo player is her cousin."

"Top Rumson?"

"Yeah."

"Oh, everybody home knows about him. His horse won the Kentucky Derby!"

"Yeah, the boy was born with a silver bit in his teeth."

Cindy Lou is quite excited about the Top Rumson news, but also a little worried. She has seen pictures of Top in a rotogravure section sitting in a night club with Myra Stanhope. Myra, she feels positive, would not be Top's type at all.

Cindy Lou is also a little worried about Mr. Lloyd. He must be terribly in love or something. All the other men she's ever met who were heart whole and fancy free have paid court to her—

"Oh, I don't mean it immodestly," she hastens to explain. "It's not 'cause I have any unusual charm, for a Southerner. I guess it's just 'cause I'm kin to practically everybody in Georgia."

"Maybe you're kin to the Amoebas, the way you subdivide."

"Honey, are you loved for yourself alone?"

"Am I— When a man's nuts about a bi— about a charming woman, he don't ask himself embarrassing questions."

"Oh, I apologize, if I've caused you to embarrass yourself. But do you feel Duty should always triumph over Love?"

"Haven't checked with the Hays office for two months, Toots. Go ask Auntie."

"Oh, she says Duty is the cornerstone of our Southern aristocracy. Else she'd never allow me to set foot in a sink-hole . . ."

"In what?"

"Hollywood."

It is a telegram of consolation that Lloyd is sending Myra Stanhope. For five years she has been Producer Harner's favorite star and she feels as though she was getting a pretty raw deal in the Velvet O'Toole matter. Cindy Lou is terribly, terribly sorry.

"You're getting a chance to be what every girl wants—movie star," Lloyd assures her.

"Oh, I don't want to be a movie star," protests Cindy Lou, "but Aunt Lily Lou says I must remember: I'm a true Daughter of the Confederacy."

LLOYD—Did you say you don't want to be a movie star?

CINDY LOU—Hon, whatever made you think I did?

LLOYD—Creepers. I didn't have to coax you to sneak out of Athens, Georgia.

CINDY LOU—I felt it was my duty.

LLOYD—Your what?

CINDY LOU (*clutching her book passionately*)—Mr. Lloyd, *Kiss the Boys Good-bye* is the finest book America has ever produced. The Georgia Star Monthly Book Reviewer, Miss Ida Mae Stonewall Jackson, says it's the only unbiased account of the Confederate War ever written. I owe it to the Albemarles and the Covingtons and the Culpeppers and the Bethanys, my kin—

LLOYD—You don't want to be a movie star?

CINDY LOU (*in almost a whisper*)—My. Lloyd, sir, my daddy says Hollywood is the Abattoir of Decency and the Outhouse of Civilization.

LLOYD—Daddy sounds like a re-write man!

CINDY LOU—My daddy says—

LLOYD—You mean—you won't be disappointed if you don't get the job?

CINDY LOU—"Job," Mr. Lloyd? I consider it the command of Destiny!

LLOYD—That's a damn fine speech. You make it to Herbert Z.

CINDY LOU—That's no speech; that's a sacred confession you dragged out of me.

LLOYD—Skip the trailer. What in hell *do* you want to be?

CINDY LOU—What every true Southern girl aspires to—and if I may say it—what every Bethany woman has always been: a loving wife and the mother of famous sons.

LLOYD—Jesu! May I never have another option renewed! Lloyd Lloyd, the greatest Director in the Outhouse—forgive my immodesty, Sugar—spends months combing the South for a new personality to play the greatest role that ever led to stardom, and he uncorks an incubator. Don't kid me.

CINDY LOU—Bethanys don't lie.

LLOYD—No-o-o-o!

CINDY LOU—Sometimes I have the distinct feeling you'd rather somebody else played the part.

LLOYD—Cindy Lou, I think it's a hell of a risky business to put an unknown inexperienced girl into a picture like this, with two million bucks at stake. But Herbert Z. is for it. So I excavate you. Now, if you make the grade with him, it's jake with me. It's got to be. But if you don't, I'm for somebody like Hopkins or Hepburn. I'll even vote for Stanhope, see? So it's all up to you, Toots, if the South gets in on the vindication of Dixie.

CINDY LOU (*coldly*)—Vindication? The South needs no vindication, I thank you. Why, everybody knows we could have won that war if you Yankees hadn't cheated.

LLOYD—Cheated? For God's sake, how?

CINDY LOU—Oh, Honey—! *I* don't know how you all cheated —but *you all* must know how you all cheated.

The train whistles as the curtain falls.

The Rands' living room in Westport is large, irregular and pine-paneled. "It is possibly a converted barn, but the conversion is of an expensive order." There is a book-lined alcove and a fireplace; a bar, a game closet filled with implements of sport and a table arranged for backgammon. "The furniture is a gay, easy combination of costly 'old New England junk' and well-upholstered modern 'overstuffed.' . . . On the walls a Van Gogh print or two verify the hint given by the bar, that we are in the country retreat of urban sophisticates."

George, a Negro butler, is behind the bar wiping glasses and reciting Shakespeare. Maimie, his wife, an anti-Shakespearian

*Photo by Lucas & Pritchard Studio, New York.*

"KISS THE BOYS GOOD-BYE"

Cindy Lou: . . . But what I can say about him—and all the rest of you poor white trash is aplenty. . . . Oh, you don't know my daddy.
Breed: Would Daddy hold Herbie for rape or high treason?
Cindy Lou: A Bethany, sir, wouldn't quibble about such technicalities!

*(Helen Claire, Hugh Marlowe, Carmel White, John Alexander)*

from instinct, protestingly answers the doorbell. The first callers
are Breed, a person of considerable corpulence and a manner that
is positive without being assertive, and Wickfield, a smaller, more
aggressive type, who is assertive without being positive. Their
relations would appear to be those of employee and employer, but
of uncertain authority in each case. Breed is declaring his intention of writing what he damn pleases in his column and Wickfield is protesting that, despite a long-term contract, what is
written for his publication shall not reflect upon his (Wickfield's)
personal integrity.

George and Maimie are interested, but not equally. George is
eager to accept Mr. Breed's invitation to call him "Comrade" but
Maimie is strongly in opposition. The previous Sunday, Mr.
Breed, it appears, had sneaked into Maimie's kitchen and "comyu-
mized" her Sunday supper ham.

"So, you admit you're a Communist?" snaps Wickfield.

"No, I'm a liberal. In other words, an average and an honest
man," answers Breed, appropriating a bowl of potato chips from
the bar and settling down with a drink.

The debate is for the moment interrupted by the appearance of
the hostess, Leslie Rand, "an attractive woman in her early
thirties." "She is one of those unfortunate admirers of the Bright
Boys and Girls who tries so hard to be wittier than her essentially simple nature allows."

Wickfield continues protestingly that he is there to thrash out
certain fundamental questions quietly, and he doesn't propose to
be fenagled into a carnival mood. He is, in fact, fed up. And if
Horace (that would be Horace Rand, the host) thinks he can
laugh off a showdown indefinitely he's a fool.

"I pay Rand $30,000 a year and a juicy block of stock for
editing jokes—jokes that give me a pain in the neck," protests
Wickfield, picking up a copy of *Manhattan Man* from the table.
"Ten years ago I bought this magazine—by mistake. Then jokes
were jokes. Now every wise-crack's analyzed for social satire."

"You don't honestly believe that *Manhattan Man* is a Revolutionary force?" queries Breed.

"Give me a single issue of this in which every man in a top
hat isn't shown as a moron, and every woman in an ermine coat
as a slut!"

"Give me an issue in which the upper classes are shown in anything but B.V.D.'s and brassières."

"And what effect has that on the *masses?*"

"Makes 'em strive like hell to succeed."

"Ridiculous!"

This time it is Horace Rand who interrupts. He is "a lean saturnine, attractive man of about thirty-four or -five, with a half-grin, a brusque manner and a maddeningly soft voice."

Rand is no more successful than was his wife in stopping the discussion, but the character of it is slightly changed by Leslie's intimation that there is to be a surprise guest or two. Including, perhaps, "the greatest unknown quantity in American life today." Not, however, as Breed suggests, "the 1940 Republican candidate."

"Read those headlines," commands Rand, producing a paper. And Wickfield reads: " 'Roosevelt tells business to co-operate. Market falls!' "

"So will the *Blade's* circulation if that's your idea of news," snaps Rand. "Read a good paper—*The Daily News*."

" 'Mystery Girl chosen to play Velvet O'Toole—'  The devil—"

" 'An unknown girl from the deep South has been definitely chosen for the screen heroine of "Kiss the Boys Good-bye," ' admits Herbert Z. Harner on arrival today at Newark Airport—' "

And now the truth is out: Herbert Z. Harner is going to preview his Southern find at the Rands' over the week-end!

Wickfield will be out, too. Let them order his car! He is not going to be trapped again. Last week it was the Women's Clubs. This week it is the movies. Let them make moving picture history if they want to. He, Wickfield, does not propose to be drawn into argument with any Hollywood pants presser. Order his car!

"Aw, Chief, I'm a loyal guy," pleads Rand. "Could I let an old '21' pal like Harner down who asked sanctuary from the press?"

"The press? What am I?"

"Pompous bastard, isn't he?" suggests Rand, with a smile for the crowd. "Say, this will be a swell exclusive story for the *Blade*." Playfully he hands Wickfield a cocktail. " 'Oo is my poor ickle boss, what's dot no nose for news."

"Well—" Wickfield has taken the glass and turned, defiantly. "Well 'oo get that marked copy of *Manhattan Man* I brought. I'll give 'oo ten minutes to make me guffaw. But if I frow up—which I probably shall—'oo's fru, doddam 'oo."

With which final fling Wickfield seeks the seclusion of the terrace, leaving Rand pretty mad, and Leslie, his wife, eager to console him. Leslie, in any showdown, will be found on her husband's side, but she, too, doubts whether inviting the Hollywood folks was so clever an idea.

"I don't like Herbert, either, darling," she confesses. "He's all right for an evening in '21' but need we inject him into the home?"

There is some little adjustment of the Rands' attitude toward each other, and a sort of armed truce established between Breed, the columnist, and Rand, the editor, both of them looking to the advancement of their own interests at the expense of Wickfield, their boss, if necessary. And then the expected guests arrive.

These include Top Rumson, with "a big blonde at the wheel," she turning out to be Myra Stanhope the picture star. Also Herbert Z. Harner himself—a very angry Herbert Z. because he feels right now that he has been framed. Why is Myra Stanhope always trailing him? And why can't he get a little rest from the press when he wants rest?

Also there has been a collision. Myra has driven her car into the rear of Harner's car, bumped her head and fainted. Top carries Myra into the room and puts her upon the sofa. They had, he explains, bumped heads and a bump like that can cause concussion.

There is much excitement over Myra's accident. The whole thing, to Harner, is a frame-up and he doesn't propose to be a victim.

"Where am I?" Myra asks, faintly, opening her eyes.

"About two hours from Brooklyn, where you came from," answers Harner, savagely.

"Miss Stanhope knew nothing about your being here," protests Top. "When she feels better, we'll leave at once."

"If she don't, I will," announces Harner.

"This is my house," declares Leslie Rand, with some spirit. "And Top is my cousin. His friends are welcome—"

"O.K., Leslie, let her stay for the whole damn week-end," snarls Harner.

"Harner, you're making a mistake not to give Myra that role," protests Top. "She's a great actress."

"And you're a great polo player," agrees Harner, elaborately shaking hands with each of them in turn; "and Rand's a great editor. And Breed's a great writer. And Wickfield's a great publisher. And I'm a great producer. And I've got a hunch Lloyd's found me a great Velvet." He shakes hands hopefully with himself at that thought.

"And I'd like my car *before* it becomes colossal," interjects Wickfield.

Harner would hate to see Wickfield go. It is only when he comes East that he has a chance to converse with intellectual equals. Being a Vanderbilt University man has its drawbacks.

"Now take this epic I've got in the works now, 'Kiss the Boys.' It's going to mean to the South what 'Uncle Tom's Cabin' meant to the North. . . . Stow the razz by presenting the South for the first time in a charitable historical perspective—"

"They got licked and couldn't take it," blurts out Top.

"Nuts, the South won that war," insists Breed.

"Sure," agrees Rand. "Lee just lost his sword to Grant in a strip poker game."

Now the insulting becomes particularly lively. Breed would insult the world. Harner would insult the press and Wickfield in particular. Myra would insult Harner if she could, and Rand has a try at anything and anybody to which he can attach a gag.

"Delighted you invited yourself," Rand says to Myra, when the pace slackens. "You'll find us just one big, unhappy family. We'll do our best to make you uncomfortable."

Leslie has figured out the room plan. Harner and Lloyd will be in the Yellow Room. The little Southern Flower down the hall. No connecting doors. Myra will have the room first assigned Breed and Wickfield. They will have to go into the bathhouse, where the laryngitis comes from.

The guests are pretty well scattered now. Myra has gone to get into a bit of scenery suited to the pool and her personality. Top and Leslie are left alone to exchange a moment's confidences. Leslie is worried about Top. Surely he isn't in love with Myra! Top isn't sure. But what if he is? He's been out of college three years and he hasn't found a job. He's too dumb, he suspects, to get a job. He thinks perhaps he should go out to Hollywood—

"Myra says Hollywood's the one place where they don't hold a wealth background against you," says Top. "She'll help me start a producing company of my own."

"Yes? Well, young man, you and Myra are staying right here. I'm joining the anti-Southern movement."

"Why?"

"I want Myra to have that part."

"You do?"

"I most certainly don't want Myra to have *you*. She's—she's— Oh, Top— (*Shaking him by the shoulders.*) Don't be an ass; you know she's not the sort of a girl you were raised to marry."

"Well, the sort of girl I was raised to marry, *ain't* the sort of girl I was raised to marry any more."

The company is dressing for a dip in the pool when Lloyd and Cindy Lou arrive. This rather spoils Cindy Lou's prepared entrance. She was all set for a "I declare I'm mighty glad—" before she realizes there's no one except Maimie and George to declare it to. But, decides Lloyd, the situation gives them a real break. Cindy Lou will have time to get into the outfit she brought for the occasion.

"Honey, do you really think I ought?" she demands, hesitantly.

"Do I know producers?" counters Lloyd excitedly. "You got to shoot 'em the climax first or they don't stay for the overture."

Maimie, ready to take Cindy Lou to her room, is proud to discover an old Bethany family tie. Maimie's grandpappy was a Bethany—a Bethany of Magnolia Hall—and buttled in the Big House. "An' when de wo' was ober, he got his freedom, so he was out of work for a long time," adds Maimie.

Maimie is glad to take care of Cindy Lou; glad to tell her about these No'therners, who ain't 'xactly No'therners. "George say dey's de powerfullest people in dis world," explains Maimie. "He says dey jes' clap deir hands an' say 'do dis,' 'do dat'—and de cameras click and de presses roll—" But Cindy Lou isn't going to like them—Maimie is sure of that. They may be what George calls 'em—"de intelligantchy"—but— "We calls it po' buckra where I come from," says Maimie. . . .

With some little suppressed excitement Myra Stanhope and Lloyd Lloyd manage a confidential moment. Myra is eager to have the blueprints. What has Lloyd done? How far has he gone?

Lloyd tries first to embrace her and then to satisfy Myra's curiosity. His little Southern find is there, getting into a number designed to knock Herbert Z. for a gool. Is she pretty? She is. Otherwise Harner would never fall for her. Will she scream? She'll never get a test.

Myra is partly convinced, but not entirely. She must take Lloyd's word for the way the conspiracy is working to her advantage, and she is ready to keep her part of the compact—when she gets the part. Meantime she has had to be pretty nice to Top Rumson to get him to bring her to the party. Lloyd will have to understand that.

Lloyd does and he doesn't. For a moment he is inclined to doubt Myra. He's probably a fool to expect her to be on the level. She is pretty sure to ditch him in the end. "You're not worth the glue that keeps your eyelashes on," he storms, pushing her away from him as Breed and Wickfield come down the stairs. The publisher and the columnist are still loud in argument. They pick themselves a brace of croquet mallets and start for the terrace. Breed gets through the door, but Myra calls Wickfield back.

Myra is worried about what is happening. Wickfield is sympathetic. Myra would like to feel sure that if it should happen that Harner is impressed with this Southern girl she could still depend on Wickfield. Harner still might be swayed by a publisher as powerful as Mr. Wickfield.

Mr. Wickfield thinks they could at least talk things over. Of course he is a married man—but they might take a little walk before dinner. At seven, say? At seven Myra will be waiting. And then Harner appears and Wickfield disappears.

"Woman at work!" sneers Harner.

"Oh, Herbert, let bygones be over," pleads Myra, when they are alone.

"So far as I'm concerned, the past is buried—along with your contract when it expires."

Nor can Harner be won over. Myra turns on the lure, offers her mouth for his salute and makes herself as completely possessible as possible. Still she is spurned.

"If Lloyd weren't the best director on the coast—I'd have given that schnitzel the gate long ago," growls Harner.

"I told him you wouldn't like it, but he said he couldn't put himself into it if we had to work on a Platonical vein," Myra explains. "You know you grossed a million in 'Snow Bound Souls.'"

"I would have grossed two if I'd starred that blizzard—You're P.B.O."

"What?"

"Poison at the box-office, dear."

"Damn you, Herbert. I was your first star. I made your studio."

"Yeah, and my whole studio's made you."

With which remark Harner disappears through the terrace door. He may or may not have heard himself referred to as a "college gorilla." Rand, coming in for a mallet, hears it and is amused. Also sympathetic. It is exaggerations like that, Myra insists, that wound a girl's sensibilities. Rand can understand. Rand can understand practically everything. He, too, has fallen for Myra and is hopeful of her favor, being frank and bold in his

approach. Myra's mouth is also for Rand, but the salute is interrupted. Top Rumson is looking for his friend.

Myra's mood has changed. She has found it difficult, she explains to Top, to swallow her personal revulsions to Harner, even
though she may owe it to the screen. Perhaps she doesn't care
so much about playing Velvet after all—

"The public's got such an idolized idea of this part, maybe no
star can make the grade," suggests Myra. "Listen, I played
Camille—and the hours I spent rehearsing that damn cough!"

"Gee, Myra, you're certainly easy to take! You know, you're
the only absolutely honest gal I know."

"Poor Top!" sighs Myra, stroking Top's hair. "Has all his
scheming itsy-bitchy debutantes got him down? Of course, I've
nobody's interest at heart but yours, Top. If this deal falls
through—say, let's get married Monday!"

"Maybe we ought to get out to Hollywood first."

"Oh, I don't give a damn about marriage myself—it's just—
I can do so much more for you if we're—"

"I don't want you all on the giving end of this."

"But if we don't get married quick, it might hurt your prestige."

"My prestige?"

"Well, my God, if I don't get Velvet I'm finished. (*Recover-
ing*.) I mean—I—if we eloped, the paper would say I'd chucked
it to marry you."

"Oh, well—"

"But all right, play-boy, I guess you weren't serious about
wanting to work in Hollywood."

"Why, of course I was serious!"

"You're cute. Take my mouth. It is yours—"

And then, just as Myra enfolds Top in a crushing embrace,
Cindy Lou appears at the stair landing all rigged out in hoop-
skirt and frills and carrying a tiny lace parasol.

Cindy Lou is quite apologetic. She had no intention of intrud-
ing. And of course she knows them, even before they introduce
themselves. She has always wanted to know Top—because, she
hastens to assure Myra, of his interest in horses. Myra Stanhope, too— Yes, Cindy Lou can see that Myra does resemble
her pictures dimly. And she would like to offer her congratulations— For what?

"I reckon I know when a couple is engaged," says Cindy Lou,
with a knowing smile.

"Guess that does it, Myra," admits Top, a little resignedly.

"No! I mean, listen, you!" interjects Myra, quickly. "This is a big secret. Nobody here knows about it, and for particular reasons of our own, we don't want them to."

"Cos I promise. I feel awfully important sharing a romantic secret with you international celebrities. I wouldn't embarrass you for the world."

Now Leslie has appeared on the stairs, caught sight of Cindy Lou and hastened to make her welcome. Cindy Lou is certainly grateful for Mrs. Rand's wonderful hospitality. "Meeting Mr. Harner in a bare hotel room—would positively have scared the pin feathers off of me. I'm so shy and unobtrusive."

And now Horace Rand has come from the yard, and, taking in the situation at less than a glance, has turned back to shout—

"Look away! Look away! Dixie's landed!"

"My husband—" Leslie is saying, by way of introduction, when Harner comes impressively through the door. "Mr. Herbert Z. Harner—Miss Cindy Lou Bethany, to you," she adds. Cindy Lou curtseys deeply. "At your service, sir—"

HARNER—I am—er—delighted—

CINDY LOU (*rising*)—And I am proud— Proud of the opportunity you have given me to play Velvet.

RAND (*at the bar*)—Lights, camera. Quiet, please. Carry on.

CINDY LOU—In the person of Velvet, it will be my rare privilege to portray at last all the miserable sufferings of the South at the unjust hands of the North. Cos, I mean the historical North.

HARNER—Is this—er—your native costume?

CINDY LOU—Oh, I knew you would want to see me first as I will appear on the screen. This is the very dress my great-grandmother Albemarle wore at the inauguration of Jefferson Davis in Montgomery, Alabama, on February 18, 1861.

HARNER—What time of day?

CINDY LOU—From two-thirty to three, sir, on a very fine afternoon. (*As* RAND *puts the parasol over his head.*) Uh-uh, that's unlucky, sir! (*Then circling and turning she goes to divan, billowing her skirts and sitting.*) And now, with your kind permission, I will play you a song which is a great favorite down home, by Miss Lili Strickland, the composer of "My Loverman Is a Fisherman," and many others. It's entitled by a strange coincidence, "Mah Lindy Lou," though my name is *Cindy* Lou. (*Playing the guitar as she sings.*)

"Honey, did you hear dat mocking bird sing last night?
Oh, Lawd, he wuz singing so sweet in de moonlight,
In de old magnolia tree,
Bustin' his heart wid melody . . ."

"Harner, naturally feeling trapped by this uncommand performance, looks wildly around, catches Lloyd's eye. . . . Lloyd smiles,
dead pan. The others, overcome by the sudden tragic premoni-
tion of exquisite boredom, sink, flabbergasted before Cindy Lou's
saccharine effrontery, in chairs . . . All but Myra, who softly begins to hum 'Flat Foot Floogie.' "

MYRA (*singing low and hot through* CINDY LOU'S *cool tempo*)
—"Good evening, friends. . . ."
CINDY LOU (*oblivious*)—

"I know he was singin' of you,
Mah Lindy Lou! Lindy Lou!
Oh, Lawd, I'd lay right down and die—!"

MYRA (*loud, killer-diller, as she breaks into a wild shag*)—
"Shoot the liquor to me, John Boy!"
Lloyd begins to sneak two steps at a time upstairs as the cur-
tain falls.

## ACT II

Later that afternoon, just before dinner, the Rand guests are
gathering in the living room for cocktails. Lloyd and Top are
playing backgammon. Leslie is passing pretzels and her husband
is starting his evening drinking.

The talk is concerned for the most part with the hilarious introduction of Cindy Lou and the riding they have all been giving
Herbert Harner because of his inability to take it. Harner has
fled to his room and asked George to bring his cocktail to him
there.

Cindy Lou, it appears, had no more than got well started with
her guitar when the whole room emptied and her audience made
a dash for the pool. "I asked her to hop out of that dirndl and
join us," protests Leslie, justifying herself as hostess.

" 'Befo' the sun goes down,' " chants Rand, in imitation of
Cindy Lou. " 'Yawl know how we-all are about our-all's camellia-
like complexions! Mah complexion wuz the first thing Mistah
Lloyd commented on when he interviewed me. Didn't yawl,

honey-sugar-foot-suh-Mistah Lloyd?' "

"Yeah. (*Bitterly.*) How'd you like to be clouted in the teeth for six weeks with that candied sauerkraut!"

Harner has come down stairs to suggest that, if dinner's on, they can all clear out and give him a chance to talk with Cindy. Again the riding begins. They are all, as Lloyd says, a-quiver to know what Harner thinks of her.

Evidently Harner doesn't think much, and he has made up his mind. He admits Cindy's pretty and probably would screen. So much could be said for thousands. She has a voice and she fairly "oozes purity," according to Rand—

" 'Ah-all's never been more than three acres from Magnolia Hall in mah-all's life—' "

"The girl's a washout, see?" That is the Harner decision. "She couldn't act in a hundred years."

"Gives her a pretty good head start on the Hollywood field," suggests Rand.

And now Cindy, who has insisted on staying in her room all afternoon, appears and is brightly greeted. She had not been lonesome in her room. She had been watching them all from her window. She is a little afraid she sang too long—but hadn't Mr. Lloyd told her to "go right into it"? No, she doesn't want a cocktail. She doesn't drink. Though, at the moment, she is so low she might try a small glass of "tea punch" or "scupper-nong wine." The Rands being out of those brands, Cindy thinks she might try a little sherry. Or port. No wine, either? Then she will have a "slight go."

"That's what my Daddy calls a little straight corn," explains Cindy.

Columnist Breed has appeared. He is not at all surprised to discover that Cindy is the daughter of Congressman Albemarle Bethany—once referred to in a certain column as "a bosom-beating, hypocritical, hill-billy, bladder-mouth, rink-stink, wind-bag—" Cindy Lou had cried herself into a "snit" when she read that.

"A snit?" queries Leslie.

"I do deplore it," explains Cindy, "but when I'm in a snit I'm prone to butt the object of my wrath plumb in the tummy."

"What a quaint trick!"

"My ole mammy, Dazzlene—she learned it from a she-goat and she passed it on to me."

"Oh, I see. By word of mouth, I trust."

Publisher Wickfield is the next to meet the Southern Flower.

Owning a small place of about 8,000 acres on the Peedee practically makes Wickfield a fellow Southerner, so far as Cindy is concerned. She knows the Peedee—

"My great-uncle Covington's plantation was on the Peedee. It's owned now by some big, rich, tax-evading Yankee, just for the ducks!"

"How barbaric!" says Leslie.

"It *is* barbaric to care less for the history of one's country than for shooting ducks. . . . (*Brightly.*) Though everybody in my family was born with a gun in his hand."

"Not to say a rope," suggests Breed.

"I do hope some day, someone who really appreciates *Covington Hall* will get it!"

"I hope so," agrees Wickfield, with a twisted sort of grin. "I intend selling Covington Hall—as soon as I've *shot* it out!"

"Oh, hush my mouth!" Cindy is covered with confusion. Her hand is across her mouth and she is backing away rapidly. "I wouldn't have hurt your feelings— My Daddy brought me up never to hurt the feelings of a *flea.*"

And now Breed remembers that old "Boom-Boom Bethany," the congressman, is the author of an amendment proposing a censorship for motion pictures, which is rather startling news to Harner.

Her Daddy doesn't know that Cindy is where she is or planning what she is planning. "But Mr. Lloyd says when Daddy hears I've been chosen to play Velvet he's going to feel quite differently about your industry," ventures Cindy, confidently. "Cos, there's several episodes in the book Daddy wants changed."

"Oh, does he?"

CINDY LOU—That part where Velvet goes in the dead of night to visit the Northern general?

HARNER—Considers that immoral, eh?

CINDY LOU—Immoral, no—just insulting to the South. Daddy says the Northern general's got to pay the visit on her.

MYRA (*coming from the terrace*)—Well, you're going great, honey chile.—How do you like her, Herbert?

LLOYD—Now, Myra, it's a little soon to say.

CINDY LOU—No, it isn't. Mr. Harner, I do realize I don't *look* terribly like Velvet, who's described as being so beautiful and all—much more like Miss Stanhope.

HARNER—Oh, I wouldn't say *that*—

CINDY LOU—What else could I say, with her standing right

here?  But I *do* know I qualify in every other way.

HARNER—Indeed.

LLOYD—State your qualifications, Toots!

CINDY LOU—Huh?

LLOYD—Shoot him the family tree.

CINDY LOU—Oh— Well . . . Like Velvet, I come of a very old Southern family.  My great-great-grandfather was an Albemarle.  My great-great-grandmother was a Covington.

WICKFIELD (*rousing from a nap*)—Uh—Covington!

CINDY LOU—My great-grandfather was a Culpepper, my great-grandmother was a County Clare O'Grady.  Both my grandparents were—

RAND—You're fine for breeding purposes.  But how are you as an actress, Miss Bethany?

CINDY LOU—Oh, I can't act for a hill of sour beans.  But Mr. Lloyd said you don't have to act to be a movie star.  He said if that was necessary, nobody in Hollywood could cast a picture.

HARNER—Quite an interesting point of view, for a director.

RAND—And shared by a great many of those who are not.

BREED—Lloyd, I hear taps in the distance.

HARNER (*turning to* CINDY LOU)—Well, why are you so damn sure you're like Velvet?

CINDY LOU—Mercy guide me, boastfulness comes mighty hard to me—

LESLIE—Oh, Herbert, you can see she's modest.

CINDY LOU (*gratefully*)—Yes, I'm a Bethany . . . Well, like Velvet, I'm young and patriotic—and like Velvet— (*She looks from one hostile, smiling, cynical face to another. A thin note of anger creeps into her voice.*) I have the quality of righteous indignation—when aroused. (*Apologetic.*) Though generally people do just call it the Culpepper temper.

MYRA—Ooh!  Herbie, the little lady's got temperament, too.

CINDY LOU (*the note of anger unmistakable now*)—Oh, my Daddy says, "Cindy Lou, you *look* mighty soft, but there's more of the Culpepper in you than meets the eye."  Though how I'd work myself into a snit with nothing to work myself into a snit about—

HARNER (*glaring at* LLOYD)—That's what great directors are for.  To develop *snit*—

Cindy Lou is a little discouraged.  She just knows that Mr. Harner doesn't think she's a "wow."  And she knows he isn't going to give her the part.

"I'll tell you right off," agrees Cindy Lou, with spirit, "I'll willingly step aside for any *other* Southern girl whose ancestors owned more slaves and plantations and all, and whose men made the supreme sacrifice at Antietam, too!"

But she is also convinced that if he should give Velvet to any of those ordinary Hollywood actresses—not meaning Myra Stanhope of course—or any of those actresses with affairs and a foreign accent—

"Well, I'm presuming to warn you, sir! If you give it to such a woman, why, *the South will positively secede!*"

Harner is impressed. When Cindy Lou decides to leave as soon as Maimie can pack for her he adds a light protest to those of the others. His attitude may be explained, he thinks, by the fact that Cindy Lou had proved what might be called a distinct surprise to him.

"Honey, you're a surprise to me, too," sympathizes Cindy Lou. "Mr. Lloyd gave me quite the *wrong* impression of you. (*Hastily.*) Though I know, unintentionally."

"Oh, he did!"

"So, I expected you'd be—well, loud and fat—"

"Like those bad boys Daddy wants to eradicate," suggests Breed.

"Yes. But you're right young and good-looking. And you've got a *wonderful* figure. . . . And practically no accent at all—that is, not much more than all Northerners."

Harner is quick to report that he is a college man—"a wolf with a sheepskin," confirms Rand—and an alumnus of Vanderbilt College. Which to Cindy Lou accounts for a lot of things, she having been engaged to scads of Vanderbilt men.

"Honey, I am consoled. Now I know 'Kiss the Boys Goodbye'—why, it's the South's Bible, without being irreverent—is perfectly safe with a Vanderbilt man. I *knew* the minute I looked at your fine *sensitive* face—"

Harner, under this barrage of flattery, moves uneasily toward the bar. A moment later George announces dinner, but first Cindy Lou must take a telephone call from her Aunt Lily Lou in New York.

"Hello, honey," Cindy Lou is saying at the phone. "No, you're all wrong about Northerners. The Rands are lovely . . . There's a little man here—vaguely connected with the news . . . who owns Uncle Covington's place on the Peedee . . . cos I'll make him tear down the power plant and restore the camellia gardens."

The guests are gathering for dinner. Top, Lloyd and Myra come in from the terrace and pause on their way to the dining room.

". . . And Mr. Rumson, that famous young polo player," Cindy Lou is reporting to Aunt Lily Lou. ". . . No, he's not flirting with *me* the teeniest bit. . . . Honey, that Myra Stanhope's here. Oh, honey, I'm looking at her *now*. She *can't* be that *old!* . . . Mr. Harner? Oh, he's wonderful. I have nothing to fear from him. He's wonderful. He's a *Vanderbilt* man. . . . No, nothing's decided yet—"

HARNER—You can tell her I say you'll screen.

CINDY LOU (*on the telephone again*)—Cos they all like me, precious—

HARNER—My dear, they *obviously* adore you.

CINDY LOU—Cos I'll do my duty. I'll phone you 'fore I go to bed. . . . What, Aunt Lily Lou? (*Giggles.*) 'Bye-i-e-ee . . . (*She hangs up and steps down.*) Now wasn't that sweet of them all to leave so we could talk confidentially.

HARNER—They're sweet people.

CINDY LOU—I said they were. (*Giggling again.*) I've just *got* to tell you what Aunt Lily Lou said 'cause you're practically a Southerner. . . . Her window faces the Plaza, where there's a gold statue of a general on a horse—

HARNER—General Sherman.

CINDY LOU—But—a lady is *leading* the horse.

HARNER—Victory, dear.

CINDY LOU—Maybe so! But Aunt Lily Lou says it's just like a damn Yankee to let the lady *walk*.

HARNER—Well, we damn Yankees always give a lady her choice, dear.

They exit arm in arm to the hall as the curtain falls.

After dinner that evening the Rands' house guests are variously disposed. In the living room Breed is occupying most of the sofa. Lloyd and Rand are playing backgammon, and through the door letting onto the terrace Cindy Lou can be seen with her guitar. She is singing softly to Harner, who sits on the wall beside her. Occasionally Rand breaks into the wafted melodies— "Carry me back to Ole Virginny, that's where the cotton and the sweet potatoes grow—" Now he is imitating what evidently

was Cindy Lou's conversation at table.  It is an amusing imitation, but Breed objects—

"You're a fine bunch of squeamers," he sneers.  "You want to
carve out this girl's gizzard, but not one of you wants to be
caught with the knife in your hand.  Kerensky was made out of
stuff like you."

Myra agrees with that, but the others are not interested.
Myra can see Harner playing right into Cindy Lou's hand, and
she is worried.  Breed is worried, too.  He is afraid Myra is forgetting whose houseparty she is on—and their hostess is a lovely
person!

Myra is in no mood to discuss her own campaigns.  She is
for squelching Cindy Lou before Harner is able to accomplish
what evidently to Myra is a fell purpose.  She is pretty sore at
everybody who won't help her.  Especially Lloyd.

"I get Velvet before I leave this house, or you and I are
finished," says she.  "Rumson wants to make an independent
picture with me."

It is an ultimatum so far as Myra is concerned.  And she wants
nothing to do with Rand's suggestion that she meet him down
where the rhododendrons grow an hour after everyone else has
turned in.  She is intent upon but one thing: how can she stop
Cindy Lou?

Now she finds that even Top Rumson is beginning to weaken
in his loyalty to her and to feel a little sorry for the way they
all have been treating Cindy Lou.  Someone, he thinks, should
warn the kid—

Cindy Lou seems to be doing all right.  She comes in from the
terrace with Harner now.  He is carrying her guitar and he has
decided that he will have some songs worked into the script of
"Kiss the Boys Good-bye."  And now she has sent Harner for
her wrap, which, because she had insisted on trading rooms with
Mr. Wickfield, is in the bath-house.  Cindy Lou has promised
to walk in the "copper moonlight" with Mr. Harner.  Seeing
Top she thinks it would be fine if he would go along, too.  Top
is pleased, but no one else thinks much of the idea.

As for sleeping in the bath-house, Cindy Lou is not at all
timid.  "Aunt Lily Lou says, in the North there's nothing in the
shape of a man to fear," she quotes.

"And I'm the only man in the house that hasn't got designs
on you," mutters Breed.

Cindy is worried about Breed.  Probably his old dyspepsia
has got him low again.  Breed is also a little fussed about Cindy

Lou and the Bethany influence in the South. Isn't it true that her Daddy has one of those nightgowns of the Klan in his attic. If he has, explains Cindy Lou, it must be that old one that belonged to her Grand-daddy 75 years ago. Cindy Lou doesn't know about such things—

"But my Daddy says he won't argue the rights or wrongs of it, but that the class he was born to is the class he wants to survive."

"Your father is a realist," suggests Wickfield.

"You call it realism here. You call it Fascism over there," growls Breed. ". . . Heil the 1938 Dictatorship out of the Ku Klux Klan by the spook of Robert E. Lee!"

These Northerners are funny to Cindy Lou. Just a little while ago she had heard Breed carrying on thataway with Mr. Rand about liquidating Mr. Wickfield, too. But of cos he didn't mean it. Mr. Wickfield is not so sure.

"You're not so dumb as you seem," allows Myra Stanhope when the men have gone to the terrace to talk this revelation out.

"Oh, I'm pretty dumb, Miss Stanhope," sighs Cindy Lou. "I just don't know how to make acceptable conversation with you-all. Everybody in this house says the most dreadful things to and about each other. And I repeat just one thing: I seem to have done wrong."

This is Myra's chance to tell Cindy Lou a few things that should be good for her. For one thing Harner is just playing, says Myra; he knows she (Cindy Lou) can't act, and would he be likely to risk two million dollars on her? Harner is just making a play for Cindy Lou to get even with Myra and Lloyd, as Myra sees it. Of course Lloyd brought Cindy Lou to meet Harner because he knew she would be a bust. And then Myra would get the part. "Who wouldn't want me after a dose of Dixie like you?" queries Myra.

"I realize everybody here is for you," admits Cindy Lou meekly. "But Mr. Harner *is* for me."

"You make me sick," sneers Myra. "Screen material! Wait till he gets you alone in a hotel bedroom."

"I know why you're telling all this."

"Hmm? I'd like to see you get home with your pride and reputation intact."

"You're not interested in my pride and reputation—"

"I want to be Velvet, eh?"

"Any woman in the world would nearly die for the great privilege of being Velvet. Velvet is a real lady—which is something

I'm finding it very difficult just now to be."

Myra sniffs. She isn't interested in Cindy Lou's acting. Of course she wants to play Velvet—but she's got more than one string to her bow. She's got Rumson, too—

"Listen! You haven't got a chance—not with him—not with Lloyd—and God knows not with Herbert Z.! Go on home. Or work yourself into a—snit. You'll see how serious Herbert is about you."

Cindy Lou is very unhappy and crying a little when Top Rumson comes back with her wrap. He is all sympathy, but there isn't anything he can say except "You've got to be a sport."

CINDY LOU—Yes, but I don't want to *face* anything for a minute. (*Turns to him eagerly*.) What I want to get in is— I can see that *you* aren't at all like them. They're all so rude and mean—

TOP (*surprised*)—You know it? Then *why* do you take it?

CINDY LOU—Oh, I've discounted it— They're so rude and mean to each other too. Why, I don't see how a wonderful young man like you, who's interested in constructive things—

TOP—Now wait: These people are intellectual tops just the same.

CINDY LOU—Being rude isn't clever. It's the easiest thing in the world. I know, 'cause I'm using all my Covington control on my Culpepper temper!

TOP—Why don't you go *home?* (*A pause.*)

CINDY LOU—Honey, are you very *much* in love with—*her?*

TOP—Hm? Oh. Well, you've got to forgive Myra. She's in a spot, too.

CINDY LOU—She's awful clever. (*Smiling.*) She guessed how much I like you.

TOP—Me?

CINDY LOU—You're the handsomest young man I ever saw!

TOP—Nobody's ever admired me for my brains.

CINDY LOU (*indignantly*)—You have lots of brains!

TOP—What for?

CINDY LOU (*earnestly*)—You know more about horse-breeding than any young man in the world.

TOP—Oh, *that.*

CINDY LOU—That's frightfully important. Breeding's what makes great horse races, and my Daddy says, great civilizations, too. Mr. Wickfield says you make a lot of money out of your stable—

Top (*wonderingly*)—I do at that.

Cindy Lou—Well! It takes just as much brains to make money out of raising horses as out of raising cotton, or—making movies, or—writing lewd jokes—

Top—I'm not interested in money—

Cindy Lou (*apologetically*)—Oh, I wouldn't have mentioned the money part, except you Northerners attach so much importance to it. Though my Daddy says that's one of the things the President is doing for you all up here: teaching you the futility of money-grubbing.

Top—Look, I inherited my stables. Running them well comes as natural to me as—as—

Cindy Lou (*helpfully*)—Being a gentleman?

Top—"Gentleman!" That word has such a phony sound.

Cindy Lou—You're not *ashamed* of being a gentleman?

Top (*smiling*)—I'm ashamed of most of the people I know who say they are.

Cindy Lou—We're not ashamed of our gentlemen back home.

Top—Maybe you raise a different kind.

Cindy Lou—My Granddaddy used to say, if you can shoot like a South Carolinian, ride like a Virginian, drink like a Kentuckian, make love like a Georgian, and be proud of it as an Episcopalian, you're a Southern gentleman, my boy!

Top admits to being an Episcopalian, but that doesn't completely satisfy him. He doesn't think he would have much chance in politics, being a Republican. So he thinks he will follow Myra's advice and have a try at the Hollywood game. Is he in love with Myra? Well, at least she's the most honest person he knows. Already she has told him everything about herself. And she was the only one with the courage to tell Cindy Lou that Harner was stringing her.

"Harner's a sadist," declares Top. "Making Myra suffer because she wouldn't—er—marry him. Naturally he thinks she's crazy for the part. She's not really. Why, just today, she was willing to chuck it, and marry *me*. But she *is* a great actress— that's why Lloyd pulled his dirty trick on you. That's the *only* reason why we helped him. We *had* to convince Harner by showing him the contrast— (*Now Cindy Lou's sobs are almost audible.*) Aw, I'm a flat-foot— Aw, don't cry!"

Now Cindy Lou seems to be crying again, but she isn't really. She is only laughing because what Top has brought for a wrap

is really her little old Juliet costume. She had worn it when
she acted in Athens, and she really can act "better'n any girl
in the Athens Junior League!" Just saying so gives her the
urge to act for Mr. Harner, who has come to take her for the
promised walk.

Before they really know what's happening Cindy Lou has
darted upstairs to change to her Juliet costume. Then there is
great discussion as to whether or not the house party should let
her go on. Harner is frank to say that he has no intention of
risking money on Cindy Lou. But if he sends her home how
will he entertain himself till Monday? Anyway, he didn't let
the kid in for what's happening. They are the ones who had
ganged up on her.

Top is pretty mad. He would like to sock Harner. But he
thinks the least they can do is to give Cindy Lou a chance to
show what she can do. Leslie Rand is of much the same mind.

"I won't stomp on the child when I know she's down," says
Leslie.

"Not down, Leslie, until Myra knocks her out," prompts
Harner.

And then Cindy Lou appears at the turn of the stairs dressed
as Juliet. She realizes now, she says, that Mr. Lloyd had not
been sincere with either her or Mr. Harner, and—

"Let's let the whole thing be decided by your acting, babe,"
suggests Myra, sweetly.

"We Bethanys always play fair," explains Cindy Lou. "And
that's what I'm asking you all to do. I don't *want* to be Velvet
if I'm going to do injustice to her. That would be a betrayal
of the South— So all you got to say is yes or no."

"The girl's a sport," announces Wickfield.

Now Cindy Lou has turned to the bar. That, she thinks, will
make a lovely balcony, if Mr. Harner will lift her onto it. Which
he does—

"I declare you're strong," purrs Cindy Lou, assuming a pose.
"Well, you know where I'm leaning on the balcony, on my
gloved hand? It begins where I say, 'Ah, me, . . . Ah, me.'
After that Romeo says something, I don't remember what. . . ."

"'Shall ah hear more or shall ah speak at this?'" prompts
George, the colored boy, who loves his Shakespeare.

"Why, *yes*, George, that's it. Do you reckon Maimie would
mind your being Romeo?"

"Not if *you* says so, Miss," smiles George, radiantly.

With which encouragement Cindy Lou goes on—

" 'Tis but thy name is my enemy:
Thou are thyself, though not a Montague.
What's a Montague? It's not hand,
Nor foot, nor arm, nor face—"

"Nor eyes, ears, nose nor throat," interjects Rand.

"Cos it's silly," agrees Cindy Lou. "Montague is just a name.
Well, then— 'Be some other name. What's in a name?' It's
plain Juliet isn't a Southerner. Family names are very important back home. So, anyway—'What's in a name?' "

"You asked that. We'll bite." This from Harner.

"She does say it twice."

"I pay for my sins as I go."

". . . 'what's in a name? That which we call a rose by any
other name would smell as sweet!' Cos it wouldn't! 'And doff
thy name and for thy name, which is no part of thee, take *all*
my self!' "

Myra has practically fallen off her chair with suppressed joy.
Cindy Lou pays no attention. On she goes with her lines, calling to George for cues, refusing to be put off by the funny side
remarks of her critics. She is getting along wonderfully until
Maimie barges in from the kitchen in hot pursuit of Breed, who
has lifted a leg of lamb—

"Maimie, don't blame him if he prefers cold mutton to Southern ham," cracks the irrepressible Rand.

And still Cindy Lou and George go on with their scene. Now
George would scale the bar to reach the balcony if Cindy Lou
did not push him back. " 'And whut love kin do, dat dares love
a-temp'. Therefore they kinsmen are *no* let to me!' " announces
George, and there is great applause.

"Ah's called de Harlem Guilgood," modestly explains George.

"You'se a Harlem no-good, that's whut you is," announces
Maimie, and reaches for him. "Niggah, you cum heah!"

"I declare—you all are the meanest I've ever seen!" snaps
Cindy Lou, her Culpepper temper rising. "But it's downright
skunky, just to hurt me, to make fun of a poor colored man that
way. You all know he can't act any better than I can."

"Dat's de truf," echoes Maimie. "You is a passel of smart-
Aleks! Mizz Rand, ah done reach fo' mah hat, and ah's gone
frum hyar!"

"But, Maimie, not tonight. There's no train!"

"Den . . . Ah'll take de counsel ob Mr. Breed. Ah'm having
a sit-down strike in mah kitchen!"

The excitement is general, with everyone trying to say something either smart or constructive. Cindy Lou's temper grows from what it feeds on. She has finally leveled her attack at Breed, whose Communist ideas have broken down Mrs. Rand's household.

"Haven't any of you the guts to tell this kid to shut her trap?" yells Breed. And when they put the job up to him he takes it—

"Little Miss B.—You're through—finished—out for the count. Now, hop down and go home."

CINDY LOU—Oh, I'm going. I've had enough of your Northern hospitality.

BREED—Well, as one who's busted many a molar on a beaten biscuit, it hasn't much over Southern hospitality.

LESLIE—Please! We're all going sour on this.

CINDY LOU—Oh, *what* have you all got against me personally?

RAND—Personally, darling, nobody's got anything against you, darling, except you're a god-awful bore.

TOP—That's damned unnecessary.

MYRA—Can that Galahad talk.

CINDY LOU—You have no cause to talk to me this way—

BREED—You're spoiling for it, child.

CINDY LOU—A Bethany welcomes criticism, but they don't take insults, sir!

BREED—Be just a gal with nice legs and good eyes. You'd get by. But for the love of Lee, can the aristocratic bromides—

CINDY LOU—You own a place on the Peedee, Mr. Wickfield. Are you standing there and hearing this?

WICKFIELD—Oh, leave the girl alone.

BREED—I'm trying to put her wise to herself. So she'll stand a chance against you tricky gang of sniggering nose-thumbers.

CINDY LOU (*angrily*)—You're as helpful as General *Sherman*—

BREED—Ouch! The Legend!

CINDY LOU—. . . who destroyed the South to bring us to our senses.

BREED—The Ogre of Dixie! 'Orrible William Sherman! The only Civil War soldier who acted like a soldier, and not a sponge-cake imitation of a gentleman!

LESLIE—That's enough!

BREED—Southern aristocrats! The Bayou Bourbons, the Coca-Cola Cunnels! The sub-thyroid progeny of three generations of rum-swilling, slave-driving cotton racketeers!

CINDY LOU (*with cold fury*)—Sir! Am I given to understand you are not attacking *me*, but my native South?

BREED (*smiling*)—Boys, she's got it.

CINDY LOU—May the good Lord smite you if I don't first!

BREED—The Old South, the last illusion of the New North—

CINDY LOU—Lift me down. (TOP *lifts her down*.)

BREED—. . . destroy *that*—and comes the Revolution!

CINDY LOU—I declare you're strong. . . .

BREED—Personally, I think she's cute as a button—

CINDY LOU—Why, you damn Yankee pole-cat! Here I come! (*She lowers her head and charges the length of the room, as* BREED *turns . . . and gets a well-aimed butt from a small blonde head smack in the abdomen. He lies gasping, his wind knocked neatly out*.) You're a mighty vulgar, two-faced man! You accept these people's hospitality and then turn their own servants against them! You take Mr. Wickfield's money here, and aim to call a sit-down strike on his *very own paper!*

WICKFIELD—Is that true?

CINDY LOU—Cos it's true! Why, he's not even a damn Yankee. He's what my Daddy calls the . . . *alien element!*

WICKFIELD—You alien element! You're fired! You can't pull a sit-down strike on me. Get up!

CINDY LOU—He can't. Oh, I haven't got the brains for argument, but I don't need them as long as my head is harder than his viscera!

Breed is pulling himself slowly to his feet. The others are still a little dazed, and Cindy Lou continues her onslaught, insisting frankly that she has never known a more snide, cheap, ungracious lot than they are. "Just high-sounding words and fast living," that's all they represent. Aside from any question of morals these Yankees just aren't smart. They will never catch up with the South, "cos you've got absolutely no sense of hospitality." Now she has burst into tears and Top has impulsively taken her in his arms. . . .

Cindy Lou is sorry she had to butt a guest in Mrs. Rand's home, and now she is ready to say good-by. She turns shamefacedly to Harner, who is beaming with a suppressed fever of excitement—

HARNER (*eagerly*)—Cindy Lou—

CINDY LOU—Sir, don't say it. I know I'm a flopperoo.

HARNER—Cindy Lou— (*He goes to her, takes her hands in*

*his, very warmly.*)  You've got it!

CINDY LOU—What?

HARNER—Youth, beauty, fire, temperament!  That damn-Yankee pole-cat touch!  (*To* LLOYD *and* MYRA.)  My God, isn't she tremendous!

LLOYD (*grudgingly*)—She gets her ideas across.

HARNER—Girl, we're going to New York tomorrow.  We'll take the afternoon plane for the Coast—

CINDY LOU (*incredulously*)—I'm—going to be Velvet?

HARNER—You *bet* you are!

CINDY LOU (*to* TOP)—He's not stringing me now?

TOP (*taking her hand*)—No, you've topped everybody.  You've got the job.

CINDY LOU (*overjoyed*)—Well, Mr. Harner, then I say, I thank you!  Good night, Mr. Rumson.  Oh, if I never see you again—I've got something to remember you by—both my little ole arms are black and blue.  (*Exits hastily to terrace.*)

HARNER (*to* LLOYD)—She's the find of the century!  For a while there, I had my doubts.  (*Thumping him heartily on the back.*)  But you struck fire out of her.  Boy, am I in your debt!

LLOYD (*weary and sour*)—Ah declare, Mistah Harner, you say the *loveliest* things—

The curtain falls.


## ACT III

The bath-house is small and rectangular, with white-washed wooden walls.  There are two small, high windows at back, one on either side of a door leading to a shower.  A man's bathrobe is hanging in the shower.  The rubbing table in the center of the room has been made up into a bed.

Cindy Lou, wearing a pair of girlish sleeping pajamas, is brushing her hair, counting the strokes between dabs at her eyes and convulsive little intakes of breath indicating that she has been crying.

She has finished her hundred strokes, wound her clock, daubed on the cold cream, turned out the light and is pulling down the shades when out of one window she sees something in the rhododendron bushes that gives her a start.  "For pity's sake," she gasps.  "No choice in a basket of rotten eggs—  Poor Mr. Rumson—"

She has just sat down on the bed and taken off her slippers

when there is a soft rap at the door. Wonderingly, and a little
frightened, she turns the light on again and moves toward the
door, demanding to know who's there. It is "just Herbert, dear,"
according to the muffled voice that replies, and he "just Herbert"
wants to come in.

"I must talk to you, child," he whispers hoarsely.

"I'm just 'fore going to bed."

"I know."

"So you can't come in."

"But, dear . . . I'm a *producer*."

Informality is an everyday affair in Hollywood, Herbert explains. Another moment he is in the room.

The Harner approach is a little mystifying to Cindy Lou, but
she is grateful for what he has done for her and will defend him
before the whole household. "I've had my eyes opened to what
disgusting lengths jealousy and envy will carry ill-bred people,
who shall be nameless, like Miss Stanhope and Mr. Lloyd," she
says.

"They were cruel. But listen! You copped off the prize plum
of years," Harner reminds her. "The biggest part in the biggest
picture— What you went through tonight is just one-two-three
with the run-around the boys and girls in *my* studio will try to
give you."

"But, sugarfoot, aren't *any* of your own people loyal to you?"

"Nobody's loyal to anybody in this game. The picture business knows only one god: the Box Office, see?"

That is why Mr. Harner would stress the fact that loyalty
must beget loyalty. "That's why I mean—if I'm for *you*, you've
got to be for *me*."

CINDY LOU—A Bethany disloyal could never be.

HARNER—I mean something besides loyalty. (*He presses her
hand between both of his.*)

CINDY LOU—I'll act to the best of my ability, be sure.

HARNER—Yes. (*He's got to try a new line.*) Look, poten-
tially you're a fine actress. You want to be a great actress, don't
you?

CINDY LOU—I want to do my *best* by Velvet.

HARNER—If you're going to give it what it *needs*, you've got
to learn to feel something besides— (*Irritated.*) righteous indignation!

CINDY LOU—I don't understand. . . .

HARNER (*putting his hand softly on her silk knee*)—The way

Velvet O'Toole feels for the Northern general, see?  Passion, desire, *esctasy*—

CINDY LOU—I must fall in love with the man who plays the part?  Oh, I can't—

HARNER—It doesn't make a bit of difference *who* you fall in love with.  But that camera's got to know you've felt—the hot and tender passion.

CINDY LOU—Mr. Harner—I mean, Herbert, honey, can I make a confession to you?

HARNER—Terrapin, of course you can.

CINDY LOU (*sitting beside him*)—I *am* in love! . . .

HARNER (*delighted*)—That's the girl.

CINDY LOU—Cos—I can't truthfully say I'm bursting into flames at the moment.  I only fell in love *tonight*—

HARNER (*hugging her a little*)—Baby, I know *just* when it happened—

CINDY LOU—But, honey, I'm terribly apprehensive—

HARNER—Baby . . .  It's the most *natural* thing in the world—

CINDY LOU (*embarrassed, she now begins to twiddle a ring on his free hand*)—Cos it's natural.  But it is kind of—inopportune.  I just instinctively know love *isn't* compatible with what I'm about to do.

HARNER (*patting her hand*)—Love and Hollywood—they go together like gin and ginger ale.

CINDY LOU—But I'd like to get *married,* honey.

HARNER (*dropping her hand*)—Yes.  Now, take it easy.  You don't want to get married until you've finished playing Velvet—

CINDY LOU—But what *am* I going to do about Myra Stanhope—

HARNER—Oh, forget that tramp—

CINDY LOU—But she's the real thing between us. . . .

HARNER—She has no mortgage on me just because we had an affair.

CINDY LOU—Mercy guide me, she's busier than a cat on a tin roof in a high wind!  Has she had an affair with *you* too?

HARNER—Say, that was so obvious it wasn't necessary for a gentleman to mention it.

Finally the truth is told—  It is Top Rumson with whom Cindy Lou is in love and she doesn't know how she can tell him she has seen Myra Stanhope in the rhododendrons with Horace Rand.  Rumson interest is a shock to Mr. Harner.  And dis-

gusting as well.  No little fool is going to play him for a sucker!
Cindy Lou had better forget Rumson pretty quick—

"Do you think I came down here to have you bawl all over
my shoulder about another guy?"

"Oh, honey, lots of men just do fall in love with me.  Daddy
says, wherever I am there'll be men, like flies around a jam
pot . . . I know I've gotten into the careless habit of just saying, 'Shoo.' "

"What about those three Vanderbilt men you were engaged
to at one time!"

"Oh, I confess to a weakness to being wooed.  But always
on a very high plane."

Again a light rap on the door.  This time it is Top.  He, too,
feels that he must talk with Cindy Lou.  There are nervous
signals with Harner, who has decided to retire to the shower
room from where he indicates that he wants Cindy Lou to let
Rumson in.  She does open the door a little way, but promptly
puts herself against it when Top would come all the way in.  She
is sure he can talk just as well from where he is.

Top has come because he was alarmed for her.  He was out
for a walk when he saw a man making his way toward the swimming pool.  He has an idea that he would like to sit around
and break the fellow's neck if necessary.

Cindy is properly excited by the suggestion.  She doesn't want
Top to wait.  She knows who it was that he saw—it was Mr.
Rand.  Rand had been around about ten minutes ago, and was
worried about her, too.  But he had gone for a walk afterward.
And now Top should go back to bed before Rand finds him there
and begins to wonder about that.

But Top has other ideas.  He grabs Cindy Lou's hand, the
one that is holding the door, and kisses it with fervor.  Then
he would explain about that.  And how he wanted to tell her
that he was related to the Atlanta Rumsons.

"Honey, I knew you must have inherited your seat from the
South—but I can't rave about it now," pleads Cindy Lou.  "This
has been a nerve-wracking day.  Please be sympathetic.  Good
night now."

"I was being—sympathetic.  Forget I ever came here, if that's
all it means."

"It means an awful lot."

"Does it?"

"*Don't,* honey!  Do I have to say it?  I'm one small garment
from being nude."

"Oh, gee, you're the nicest girl! . . . Well, say just one nice thing—"

"Well . . . 'Parting is such sweet sorrow. I could say good night until tomorrow.' But I can't tonight. Good night, now."

She has closed the door now and gone back to her dressing table, calling to Harner to come out and apologize. When Harner appears, a little sheepishly, he is wearing the bathrobe he found in the shower room. He has left his clothes hanging in its place.

Cindy Lou is pretty mad. Let him get that bathrobe off or she'll scream. No ole Hollywood carpet-bagger is going to compromise her. If her father were there he would horsewhip Harner. She is ready to scream, but doesn't. Anyway, screaming time's past, Harner assures her.

"Honey, let's back off and take a fresh start," suggests Cindy Lou, desperately. "This feeling about me may interfere with your judgment."

"Don't get me wrong. I'm no heel," the producer assures her. "This doesn't alter the fact you play Velvet. It will clinch it— maybe—" He has started around the bed after her.

"Now, I'm sorry to ask you; but I've just got to get my ducks in a row!" calls Cindy Lou. "Are you here to seize my virtue?"

"You make it sound so melodramatic."

"It may be just everyday Hollywood business to you, but so help me, it *is* melodramatic to me."

The chase around the bed has been resumed, Harner lumbering after the more agile Cindy Lou and missing her as she successfully keeps the bed between them. Finally he gives up and lies down. Cindy Lou has worked her way around to the dressing table and picked up her pearl-handled revolver. Now she has become suddenly calm and stands at the foot of the bed surveying him menacingly.

"Mr. Harner, sir, I'm *mighty* sorry I've got to do what I've got to do—"

"What have you got to do now?" he asks, preparing to protect his stomach with a pillow against another butting.

"Mercy guide me, I guess I've got to shoot you!"

Harner, slowly sitting up, yells to her to put the gun down, but Cindy has no such intention. Even as he offers to leave she continues to rationalize her act. It would look terrible if Mr. Rumson were to see him leaving. He wouldn't believe the truth! She'll just have to shoot—and she is a terrible shot, too! She will aim at a leg, but she hasn't any idea what she'll hit!

Harner springs toward her! There is a shot! Harner's legs

buckle under him and he goes down.  Cindy Lou has rushed
to the door and is shouting wildly—

"Help, murder, please!  Somebody!  Help!"

She has returned to Harner and bends over him.  In reply to
her solicitous inquiries she gets nothing but sepulchral groans—

"It'll be *worse* if you die . . ." she wails.  "That'd be terribly
embarrassing for me . . .  Please roll over, Sugar, and let me
see what I can do for you. . . ."

Now Top Rumson has rushed in, all excitement and worry
for Cindy Lou, who relievedly throws herself into his arms.

Top takes the gun from her and turns to Harner, still doubled
up on the bed, clutching his forearm.  Top urges him to a sitting
position to an accompaniment of further groans.  When Harner
sees the blood on his hand he collapses again.

"Lovely!  He can talk!" says Cindy Lou.

"It's just his arm—" Top explains reassuringly.

CINDY LOU—Well, I only aimed at his *leg* . . .  (*Gaily.*)
Mr. Harner, sir, wouldn't you be more comfortable if you lay
down on the bed—

TOP (*raising* HARNER *to his feet*)—You might have killed
him—

CINDY LOU (*going to get towel*)—That's what I *said*, honey,
but he *would* move.  (HARNER's *legs buckle under him.*)

TOP—Easy now—

CINDY LOU—Maybe he's just suffering from shell-shock—

TOP—Pull yourself together.  It's just a surface—  (*An expression of outrage comes over his face.  He points an accusing
finger at* CINDY LOU.)  Oh!  He—you—  (*He drops the limp*
HARNER *who falls half across the bed.*)

HARNER—Hey!  Ooooooh!  (*Doubles up on bed in pain.*)

TOP (*indignantly*)—He *was* the man I saw—

CINDY LOU (*soothingly*)—Cos he was.  (*To* HARNER, *folding
towel.*)  Let me bind it for you—my daddy says I have fairy
fingers—

HARNER (*coming to life*)—Keep that damned little screwball
away from me!

TOP—Then he *was* here—

CINDY LOU—Yes, Top, but—

TOP—He was here—when you were talking to me.  You lied
to me!

CINDY LOU—Yes, honey, but—

TOP—He was in here, *laughing* at me—!

HARNER (*mocking*)—"Parting is such sweet sorrow—"
CINDY LOU—No, Top—
TOP—. . . making love to you!
CINDY LOU—No! No! He—he was just explaining to me
how Velvet should act—
TOP—Naturally.
CINDY LOU—You don't understand—
TOP—Then *why* didn't you let me in—
CINDY LOU—Oh, thank heavens I didn't, honey—
TOP—What?
CINDY LOU—I mean, *that* was when he was in the shower
taking off his clothes—
TOP (*bitterly*)—I see.
CINDY LOU—No, you *don't*. I mean, *how* would it have
looked—
TOP—Just the way it looks now—!
CINDY LOU—Top, honey, you've got to listen—
TOP—. . . holding yourself *cheap*. For a movie part. God,
*Myra* wouldn't do that—
CINDY LOU—Top! You can't believe—
TOP—. . . but I suppose *that* comes under your duty to Dixie,
too!
HARNER—That's right. Worry about her duty to Dixie while I
bleed slowly to death—
CINDY LOU (*angrily*)—You *can't* say I hold myself cheap!
Why, you heard him, he's *bleeding* to death 'cause I didn't,
isn't he?
LESLIE (*in a dressing gown, running*)—Miss Bethany, I heard
a—scream . . . My God! Herbert—!
TOP (*noble but fierce*)—I shot him, Leslie—
HARNER—The hell he did—
LESLIE—But why—
TOP—He came down here—
LESLIE—But what for—
TOP (*savagely*)—A—slight go!

Top has put Harner's good arm around his shoulder and is
preparing to help the injured man back to the house. Leslie is
sure they should call a doctor to avoid complications. It would
help if she knew where she could find Horace.
"Ask that little false-face," screams Harner. "She'll tell you
where Horace is . . ."
Now there is more excitement; Harner repeating his charge

with interesting details; Cindy Lou shouting denials and Top putting in several confirmatory statements. Finally Cindy Lou is cornered. Yes, she admits, she did say she had seen Mr. Rand—but—

"Why did you tell such a malicious lie?" demands Top.

CINDY LOU—I—I thought Mr. Harner might leave—
TOP—All you had to do was call me—
HARNER—All she had to do was say "go"—
TOP—. . . making up a rotten story like that—
HARNER—Say, she made it up so I *would* tell you—and sour you on Myra, see?
LESLIE—You're an ambitious, dangerous, evil-tongued little girl!
CINDY LOU—I'm a lamb among the wolves!
LESLIE—Pack your bags—
CINDY LOU—A whirlwind couldn't get away from here so fast!
LESLIE—Did you say . . . rhododendrons? (*The echo of the word sounds in her mind. She makes a sudden move to the window where, during* TOP'S *speech, she pulls up the shade and stands with her back to them, tiptoe, rigid.*)
TOP—Well, a lot you care about this mess you're leaving— you certainly have soured me—on *you!* (*He exits so rapidly he almost knocks* HARNER *down.* LESLIE *turns from the window. She has been crying.*)
LESLIE (*urgently*)—Cindy Lou, forgive—
CINDY LOU (*fiercely*)—Get out of my boudoir, all of you! (*She takes* HARNER'S *clothes, flings them at* LESLIE *and* HARNER. LESLIE *runs out.*) Did *I* ask to come here? Did *I* seek the role of Velvet!
HARNER (*savagely*)—Baby, if you get it, the *North* will secede!
CINDY LOU—If I could count on that!

Harner leaves and Cindy Lou slams the door as the curtain falls.

A moment later, in the Rands' living room, Madison Breed is in the midst of a debate with Maimie, who is continuing her sit-down strike in the kitchen. Breed, disheveled and definitely drunk, has not been able to make any progress at all with Maimie. Disgusted, he recovers a half-filled bottle from the bar and throws himself heavily upon the couch.

Lloyd, who has heard the racket, has appeared on the stairs

in pajamas, as Top Rumson rushes up from the bath-house to report the shooting of Harner by Cindy Lou. Neither Lloyd nor Breed is particularly excited, even after the groaning Harner is helped in by Leslie Rand. They seem even a little pleased.

Nothing can move Maimie, who has shouted through the door that if they don't all go to bed she will turn off the lights. She has the telephone receiver off the hook in the pantry and they can't telephone for the doctor. To add to the excitement one Oscar, a trim and snappy reporter from the New York *Daily News,* carrying a loaded flashlight camera, has barged into the room. Oscar has come for a flash or two of the new Velvet O'Toole. It seems Aunt Lily Lou had telephoned the night editor of the *News* and told him everything—even about General Sherman's not letting her sleep. The *News* couldn't get the Rands on the phone, so Oscar had come running. Now he wants to know what's amiss. When he catches sight of the revolver on the table he is even more excited. And when there is a racket at the pool indicating another rumpus of some sort Oscar is for dashing down.

He is stopped by Top, who warns him to get out. Oscar won't get out until he gets the story. Now Maimie has put out the lights and Top and the reporter go into a clinch. Out of the clinch Top emerges victor and Oscar is out cold. They roll him in the closet with the croquet sets and shut the door.

"I don't give a damn about *myself,*" Top explains to Breed. "You know what the papers would do to *her.*"

"Might be interesting to see what she'd do to them," allows Breed.

The others are drifting in. It seems that the row at the pool had started when Lloyd had tried to toss Myra into the pool in revenge for her rhododendron flirtation with Rand. He had missed Myra but knocked Wickfield in instead. Which was fun for everybody except Wickfield.

Now Top must warn them of the reporter in the closet. What are they going to do about him? How much of the story is he going to hear, and how much of it will find its way into print?

"I'd like to see all you double-crossers smeared in every tabloid," snarls Harner; "but I've got my studio to consider. There's one thing that girl wants more than trouble—"

"Velvet!"

"I've got a little contract I'll sign here in three minutes—" and he has dashed upstairs to get it, followed by an excited Myra and Lloyd.

Breed has sunk a little deeper into his bottle and the daven-port. The Rands have talked out the revelations of the rhodo-dendron episode and agreed to call it a day so far as their mar-riage is concerned. And then Cindy Lou arrives, dressed as she was when she first came to Westport and carrying her book, her fitted bag, her hat and gloves. She is ready to go to jail, she announces, where she will be safe from the Yankee mob that is sure to gather to lynch her once they hear what she has done.

"But Herbert doesn't want this to get out—" Leslie is trying to explain.

"Oh, *doesn't* he!"

"You've got to listen—" pleads Top.

CINDY LOU—Sir, I don't care to hear anything you've got to say—

TOP—But I know what you said about Myra—

CINDY LOU—Sir, I wish you every happiness with the lady of your dubious choice and I bid you good-by *indefinitely*. Now, can George get my bags?

LESLIE—No. Because—

CINDY LOU (*moves to terrace, setting down bag*)—I'll get them myself—

LESLIE (*hurriedly*)—. . . Maimie is still—uppity.

CINDY LOU—Oh, she is! Well, I refuse to be trapped behind your lines any longer. (*Moves toward pantry.*)

LESLIE—But Mr. Harner wants to talk to you.

CINDY LOU—I have nothing to say to Mr. Harner. But what I can say about him—and all the rest of you poor white trash is aplenty.

TOP—Cindy Lou, you can't do that. You're the one who would suffer—

CINDY LOU—Oh, I know what I've got to do, sir. I don't *like* it but I've got to do it—

LESLIE (*frightened*)—What have you got to do?

CINDY LOU—Oh, you don't know my Daddy—

BREED—Would Daddy hold Herbie for rape or high treason?

CINDY LOU—A Bethany, sir, wouldn't quibble about such technicalities.

Cindy Lou has gone to the pantry to reason with Maimie. Top takes occasion to come to her defense. Is he in love with her? Who wouldn't be, with a girl like that? Well, Breed wouldn't be, for one.

"She hasn't done anything to you—to any of us!" declares Top, with fervor. "What's happened here—oh, it wasn't in her, it was in *us*. She just brought it to the surface."

Top has gone for his car and Leslie is for getting Cindy Lou started for town as soon as possible. Maimie has dutifully opened the door for Cindy Lou, and now she is explaining that while she is mighty homesick for Gawja, she just doesn't want to work there. Her feet won't stand it. George backs her up. They have examined themselves and decided that they will go back on relief.

"Yassum," explains George, "Mr. Breed he say dere gotta be a equal distribution ob ebbyt'ing— . . . An' relief is de onliest place where a po' colored man kin hab *his* share of dis hyar intellecshal integrity!"

Cindy Lou is forced to fend off a proposal of marriage from the prostrate but eager Breed. When they are about to open the closet and release the reporter, Harner comes charging down the stairs with a contract in his hand and a warning to Cindy Lou that she is not to make any statements.

He is prepared to sign a six-month contract with her at a thousand a week—with options. When she remains cold, he raises it to two thousand a week—with options—and the role of Velvet—if she doesn't tell the reporter why she shot Mr. Harner.

The presence of the reporter is news to Cindy Lou. The only reason she had demanded that the closet be opened is because she wanted to get her guitar—

"Great day in the morning! It never occurred to me, just cause I shot Mr. Harner . . . though Daddy does say the only way to treat a Yankee is wallop him so hard he apologizes to you— . . . Why, I was just 'fore going home and lying out of the whole thing to Daddy."

"What?"

"Why, he'd never forgive me when he heard you were still alive! (*Sighs.*) But, I declare, it's confusing. One minute I'm Velvet; the next I'm not. Well, now I am—"

Now Cindy Lou has the pen poised and is about to sign the contract when Lloyd, burning under Harner's declaration that he is fired, snatches the contract from her with the statement that it is an option-studded phoney, and submits another that is a straight seven-year O'Toole contract. But before she can sign that one Myra has burst into another bit of hysterics—

"No! No! All my life I've worked for a part like this. Why, in ten long years I haven't eaten a potato. And for what? A series of damned Gorgonzola sex-lure parts.  Sure I was born Hannah Green.  But I have ideals.  Which, if you'd had *my* early life—"

"But, Miss Stanhope, you and Mr. Rumson are going to form your own company," Cindy Lou reminds her, sweetly.

Top—No.  We're through—  (*He sinks on the divan, his face in his hands.*)  I'm just a sap.  So I'll just breed horses—pot ducks—get potted.  Who cares?

Cindy Lou (*going to him, urgently*)—Honey, tell me *quick*. Is something troubling you?

Top (*lifts his face*)—Cindy Lou.  If I—Oh, damn all these people—I'd be as proud as a pope to make love to you like a Georgian.

Cindy Lou (*eagerly*)—Honey, do I understand you are proposing to me?

Top—If I said, would you marry me now—  (*Turns away.*) Aw, you'd say *no*.

Cindy Lou (*emphatically*)—*No*, I wouldn't.

Top—Yes, you would.

Cindy Lou (*fiercely*)—No, I wouldn't!  (*He looks up surprised.*)  How *could* I, sugarfoot, when you're sweeping me off my feet now!

Top (*rising, eagerly*)—You mean—?

Cindy Lou—Maybe, Top, I'm letting down the South.  But I have my higher duty—

Lloyd—A loving wife and the mother of famous sons?

Cindy Lou—That's a solid principle for a lady to work on. But I can't postpone it seven years and do it justice—

Top—Cindy Lou!  (*They embrace.*)

Lloyd (*disgusted*)—Well, if that's not the cherry on the charlotte russe!

Rand (*goes to closet and opens it*)—Gentlemen, the press.

Oscar (*crawling out on his hands and knees*)—Oh, I'll fix you birds for this . . .

Harner (*rushing to him in a vain effort to separate him from his camera which* Breed *has handed him*)—Listen, I can explain anything . . .

Oscar—Statement, Miss Bethany?

Cindy Lou (*putting on her hat*)—No, sir.  Just say I'm too unobtrusive for Hollywood. . . .

Lloyd—Nuts, dear.  Hollywood's too unobtrusive for you. . . .

Cindy Lou (*hands contract to* Myra)—And the South does

deserve a great actress— (*Picks up fitted bag, hands it to* TOP.)

HARNER (*snatching the contract from* MYRA)—Over my dead body!

CINDY LOU—That reminds me. Couldn't *she* tell this reporter as much as I could?

MYRA (*triumphantly to* HARNER)—Honey, how's mah Southern accent?

OSCAR—As much as you could about *what*, Miss Bethany?

HARNER—Geez, Cindy Lou, on my honor as a producer . . . (*Agonized.*) Good-by, now!

ALL—Good-by, now!

CINDY LOU (*half hurt*)—Oh, you-all still don't trust me. (*To* HARNER.) Honey, I wasn't going to tell him I had to *shoot* my way through you to happiness!

"Top picks her up, bag and baggage, in his arms, and carries her waving happily over his shoulder to the terrace, as the reporter clicks his camera."

**THE CURTAIN FALLS**

# THE PLAYS AND THEIR AUTHORS

"Abe Lincoln in Illinois," a drama in twelve scenes by Robert E. Sherwood. Copyright, 1937, 1939, by the author. Copyright and published, 1939, by Charles Scribner's Sons, New York and London.

This happens to be the sixth appearance of Robert Emmet Sherwood as a best play author in this series of year books. He should, therefore, be pretty well known to the book's readers, and the facts of his life also. For latecomers, however, we may repeat that Mr. S. was born in New Rochelle, N. Y.; that he left his classes at Harvard to join the Black Watch in Canada for service in the Great War; that he was wounded and gassed and finally sent home. Thereafter he took to writing, serving *Vanity Fair*, *Life* and *Scribner's* as both contributor and editor. He gave up editing after he had won his first success as a playwright with "The Road to Rome" (1926-27). Last year he was elected president of the American National Theatre and Academy. He has also been president of the Dramatists' Guild and was a charter member and organizer of the Playwrights' Producing Company, which produced his "Abe Lincoln." Other Sherwood plays to be included in "The Best Plays" volumes were "Reunion in Vienna" (1931-32), "The Petrified Forest" (1934-35), "Idiot's Delight" (1935-36) and "Tovarich" (1936-37), which he adapted from the French of Jacques Deval. Mr. Sherwood is 44 years old, spends a good deal of his time in England and some part of it in Hollywood.

"The Little Foxes," a drama in three acts by Lillian Hellman. Copyright, 1939, by the author. Copyright and published, 1939, by Random House, Inc., New York.

Lillian Hellman headed the list of Best Play authors in 1934-35, when her first play, "The Children's Hour," was a sensation of the New York theatre season. Her second play to be produced was a study of family traditions and labor troubles in a New England town entitled "Days to Come" (1936-37). It failed and Miss Hellman went back to Hollywood chores for

another two years. When she emerged it was with the script of
"The Little Foxes," for which Dorothy Parker had suggested the
title. This play won a quick success in New York, with Tallulah
Bankhead playing its heroine. It afterward led the voting when
the New York Drama Critics' Circle failed to agree on a single
play that should be the choice of the circle as the best play of
the season written by an American author. Miss Hellman was
born in New Orleans, is in her early thirties, and came to playwriting through a varied experience as book reviewer, short-story
writer, play and scenario reader.

"Rocket to the Moon," a drama in three acts by Clifford Odets.
    Copyright, 1939, by the author. Copyright and published,
    1939, by Random House, Inc., New York.

Clifford Odets is also becoming a more or less regular contributor to these volumes. He earned inclusion in the issue of
1934-35 with his first full-length play, "Awake and Sing." He
was nominated for a second appearance in 1937-38 with "Golden
Boy." Mr. Odets is a Philadelphian by birth, but lived the better
part of his life in the Bronx, New York, from whence stem his
authoritative studies of Jewish family life. He was an actor with
the Theatre Guild companies for some years, and one of the or-
ganizers of the Group Theatre when that producing unit was first
evolved from Theatre Guild juniors. His first play to attract
attention was a one-act labor drama, "Waiting for Lefty." He
has done a good deal of work in Hollywood.

"The American Way," a drama in two acts by George S. Kauf-
    man and Moss Hart. Copyright, 1939, by the authors.
    Copyright and published, 1939, by Random House, Inc.,
    New York.

Here again we have two old contributors among the Best Play
authors. Mr. Kaufman began his contributions as far back as the
issue of 1921-22, which was the third volume of the year books
to be published. His first play, "Dulcy," written with Marc
Connelly, was then included. He has been represented in a majority of the issues that have followed. Mr. Hart came in as a
Kaufman collaborator in 1930-31 with "Once in a Lifetime," and
again in 1934-35 with "Merrily We Roll Along." They were

both represented the season of 1936-37 with "You Can't Take It with You." Mr. Kaufman is a Pennsylvanian, born in Pittsburgh, and Mr. Hart a New Yorker. Mr. Kaufman approached the theatre through a newspaper apprenticeship as dramatic editor of the New York *Times*. Mr. Hart started as a boy in the offices of a play producer. He wrote a play for his employer and submitted it anonymously. It was produced and ran for five weeks in Chicago. The Kaufman-Hart combination suffered its first failure last season with an elaborate dramatization of the last thirty years in American theatre history called "The Fabulous Invalid."

"No Time for Comedy," a comedy in three acts, by S. N. Behrman. Copyright, 1939, by the author. Copyright and published, 1939, by Random House, Inc., New York.

S. N. Behrman's last appearance in these volumes was as the adapter of "Amphitryon 38" (1937-38), from the French of Jean Giraudoux, and a Theatre Guild success of its season. Previous to that, however, Mr. Behrman had been a frequent Best Play contributor on his own. He started in 1931-32 with "Brief Moment," followed the next year with "Biography" and came back in 1935-36 with "End of Summer." Mr. Behrman is another of the five playwrights who this year formed the Playwrights' Producing Company—his associates being Robert Sherwood, Sidney Howard, Maxwell Anderson and Elmer Rice. He was born in Worcester, Mass., had a brief experience as an actor in a vaudeville sketch he wrote, was brought home by a distressed family and induced to finish his college course. He finally made good to the family's complete satisfaction by taking degrees at no less than three universities. He has had both happy and unhappy experiences as a scenario writer in Hollywood, but frankly prefers the living theatre. He wrote "No Time for Comedy" with Ina Claire in mind as the heroine, but previous commitments interfered with Miss Claire's acceptance of the role, and Katharine Cornell adopted it.

"The White Steed," a drama in three acts. Copyright, 1939, by the author. Copyright and published, 1939, by Random House, Inc., New York.

Paul Vincent Carroll this year, for the second time, won the New York Drama Critics' Circle citation as the author of the most distinguished play of foreign authorship to be produced during the season in New York. He won last year's award with his first full-length play to be produced in America, though he had been represented in the repertory of the Abbey Players of Dublin. Mr. Carroll is a schoolmaster in Glasgow, Scotland. He was born in Dundalk, County Louth, Ireland, in 1900. He was tutored by his father, also a schoolmaster, and trained as a teacher in Dublin. He did his first writing for the theatre for the Abbey Players in Dublin, his first play being a one-acter, "The Watched Pot." Following his American success with "Shadow and Substance," which at one time paid him $1,000 a week in royalties, he spent a month in New York and then returned to Glasgow and resumed his teaching job. He has since given up his school work and is devoting his time to playwriting.

"The Philadelphia Story," a comedy in three acts by Philip Barry. Copyright, 1939, by the author. Copyright and published, 1939, by Coward-McCann, Inc., New York.

"Here Come the Clowns," a drama in three acts by Philip Barry. Copyright, 1939, by the author. Copyright and published, 1939, by Coward-McCann, Inc., New York.

Philip Barry's first full-length play was one called "You and I." It won a Harvard prize, was successfully produced on Broadway, achieved a considerable run and was one of the ten best plays selected for the 1922-23 issue of "The Best Plays." Mr. Barry in the years following contributed five additional plays to these volumes, "The Youngest" (1922-23), "Paris Bound" (1927-28), "Holiday" (1928-29), "Tomorrow and Tomorrow" (1930-31) and "The Animal Kingdom" (1931-32). For the following six years, so far as this work is concerned, he embraced the silences. He makes up in part this year by having two plays included, thus equaling a record achieved but once before and then by Sidney Howard in the 1932-33 issue with "Alien Corn" and an adaptation from the French, "The Late Christopher Bean." Mr. Barry was born in Rochester, N. Y., forty-three years ago. He was a student at parochial schools before he went to Yale, where he was graduated in 1919. He studied drama with Prof. George

Pierce Baker at Harvard, has had experience writing advertising copy and in being an embassy attaché in London. He spends much of his time and does most of his writing in Cannes, France.

"Family Portrait," a drama in three acts by Lenore Coffee and
    William Joyce Cowen. Copyright, 1939, by the authors.
    Copyright and published, 1939, by Random House, Inc.,
    New York.

Lenore Coffee and William Joyce Cowen, as happens frequently with the more successful collaborators, are Mr. and Mrs. W. J. Cowen. They have been working together for fifteen years, most of the time of recent years in Hollywood, where Mrs. Cowen is one of the best-known and best-paid of scenario writers, and Mr. Cowen doubles scenario writing with novel writing, short story writing and picture direction. Miss Coffee is a native San Franciscan and, with pardonable pride, traces her family back to 1690, when the mission business was one of California's most active industries. Mr. Cowen hails from New York. Mrs. Cowen, having been educated at Dominican College, in San Raphael, thought some of becoming a lawyer, but tried writing advertising copy first and was practically lost to writing as a career when she submitted "The Better Wife" and Clara Kimball Young, star of the silent screen, accepted it as a starring vehicle. Mrs. Cowen has been on the picture pay rolls ever since. Mr. Cowen was in Santa Monica getting ready to sail for Manchuria when he met Miss Coffee. This gave him pause. In practically no time at all he had proposed marriage, been accepted, canceled his passage and settled down. Two of Mrs. Cowen's recent scripts were "Four Daughters" and "White Banners." She is at work on a sequel to the first to be called "Four Wives." Mr. Cowen has been busy with a couple of books, *They Gave Him a Gun* and *The Man with Four Lives*. It was Mr. Cowen who first had the idea for "Family Portrait." He got it while working with Cecil De Mille on the Biblical picture, "King of Kings." Hearing about it, Mrs. Cowen, something of a Bible student, became enthusiastic and they decided to do a play together with Mary, Mother of Jesus, as their subject. They gave seven months to research before they started writing. The Cowen home is in California, and when they are not writing, and often when they are, they find time to direct the activities of two growing children.

"Kiss the Boys Good-bye," a comedy in three acts by Clare Boothe. Copyright, 1939, by the author. Copyright and published, 1939, by Random House, Inc., New York.

Clare Boothe made her first "Best Play" appearance in the 1936-37 volume with "The Women," which lived up to expectations and became something of an international success. "The Women" was her second play to be produced, the first being a pretty serious drama entitled "Abide with Me" and concerned with the domestic activities of a deep-drinking husband. Fifteen years ago Miss Boothe was popular as a New York socialite. Being restless she took to writing, drifted into editing *Vanity Fair*, produced a novel called *Stuffed Shirts* and otherwise kept friends and kinfolk wondering as to what she might do next. With "Kiss the Boys Good-bye" she scored her second Broadway success.

# PLAYS PRODUCED IN NEW YORK

## June 18, 1938—June 18, 1939

### (Plays marked with asterisk were still playing June 18, 1939)

## COME ACROSS

### (13 performances)

A comedy drama in two acts by Guy Beauchamp and Michael Pertwee. Produced by George Bushar and John Tuerk in association with William A. Brady at the Playhouse, New York, September 14, 1938.

Cast of characters—

| | |
|---|---|
| Janet Kemp | Helen Trenholme |
| Probationer | Mary Heberden |
| Lacey | Cameron Hall |
| George | Byron Russell |
| Dr. Peter Willens | Richard Waring |
| Sir John Twining | Claude Horton |
| Mark Ryder | Arthur Vinton |
| Scratch | Richard Taber |
| Ratkin | Don Costello |
| Duggan | Charles Jordan |
| Lefty Grey | Owen Martin |
| Sister | May Marshall |
| Dr. Richards | David Orrick |
| Chief Inspector Wentworth | A. P. Kaye |
| Detective Sergeant Foray | Arling Alcine |
| Constable Mahon | Bernard Savage |
| Attendant | Harold Thomas |

Act I.—Scenes 1 and 3—Private Room in Wentley Hospital, London. 2—Clinical Laboratory. Act II.—The Operating Room.
Staged by Edward Clarke Lilley; settings by Watson Barratt.

Mark Ryder, Chicago gangster, is in London trying to escape the avengers of a rival mob who have put a slug in his chest. When Mark enters a nursing home, and forces the surgeon to operate by having his young son kidnaped and held as hostage, the avengers follow. Mark dies on the operating table, stabbed by a knife held with a rubber glove. The surgeon, the avengers and an involved nurse are all suspected, but it was really a jealous pal who did the job.

## LIGHTNIN'

### (54 performances)

A comedy in a prologue and three acts by Winchell Smith and Frank Bacon. Revived by John Golden at the Golden Theatre, New York, September 15, 1938.

Cast of characters—

| | |
|---|---|
| Lightnin' Bill Jones | Fred Stone |
| John Marvin | Henry Richards |
| Raymond Thomas | John Griggs |
| Lemuel Townsend | Walter Gilbert |
| Rodney Harper | Buford Armitage |
| Everett Hammond | Franklyn Fox |
| Sheriff | Orland James |
| Oscar Nelson | George Spelvin |
| Fred Peters | William Phillips |
| Walter Lennon | Roger Hundley |
| Zeb Crothers | Hugh Norton |
| Liveryman | Michael Markham |
| Reporter | Robert Lowes |
| Mildred Buckley | Helen Brooks |
| Mrs. Jones | Mrs. Priestly Morrison |
| Mrs. Margaret Davis | Muriel Hutchison |
| Mrs. Harper | Harriet E. MacGibbon |
| Freeda | Ann Hazzard |
| Emily Jarvis | Marjorie Garrett |
| Mrs. Moore | Virginia Copeland |
| Mrs. Jordan | Augusta Wallace |
| Mrs. Preston | Ruth Burton |

Prologue—John Marvin's Cabin in Nevada.  Acts I and III.—Office of the Calivada Hotel on the State Line Between Nevada and California.  Act II.—Superior Court at Reno.
Staged by John Golden; settings by Cirker and Robbins.

Mrs. Bill Jones is running a tourist hotel that straddles the California-Nevada line.  The hotel has become a divorcees' haven. Lightnin' Bill Jones, her husband, a hefty drinker, a good liar and a lovable ne'er-do-weel, helps with the house chores when able.  Certain real-estate sharpers seek to swindle Mrs. Jones out of her property and the power rights to a waterfall.  When Bill refuses to sign the deed and balks the sale Mrs. Jones determines to divorce him.  Bill, paying his attorney friend, young John Marvin, a surprise visit from the Soldiers' Home, learns of the suit and fights mother's claim for a divorce, effects a reconciliation, saves the hotel and the water power and promises to quit drinking.

## MISSOURI LEGEND

### (48 performances)

A comedy in three acts by E. B. Ginty.  Produced by Guthrie McClintic in association with Max Gordon at the Empire Theatre, New York, September 19, 1938.

Cast of characters—

| | |
|---|---|
| Aunt Belle | Clare Woodbury |
| Billy Gashade | Jose Ferrer |
| Frank Howard | Richard Bishop |
| Jim Cummins | Russell Collins |
| Charlie Johnson | Karl Malden |
| Bob Johnson | Dan Duryea |
| Mrs. Howard | Dorothy Gish |
| Thomas Howard | Dean Jagger |
| The Widow Weeks | Mildred Natwick |
| Hosea (Pop) Hickey | Joseph Sweeney |
| Sam | John Woodworth |
| George | Vincent Copeland |
| Asa | James Craig |
| Old Timer | John Philliber |
| Police Commissioner Gregg | Ben Roberts |
| The "Reverend" | Cliff Heckinger |

Acts I and III.—A Room in the Home of Thomas Howard in Missouri. Act II.—Scene 1—The Widow Weeks' Cabin in the Ozarks. 2—Office in a Small Bank.
Staged by Guthrie McClintic; settings by John Koenig.

Jesse James, outlaw, alias Thomas Howard, is living in a small town in Missouri with his wife, his brother Frank and such members of the James robber band as drop in from time to time. It is the last eight days that Mr. James ever lived anywhere. In this community he is accepted as a devout and loyal Baptist, and has come to believe that there is something to religion so long as God is understanding. He does his bank and train robbing on the side. Jesse stops on the way to one job to befriend the Widow Weeks. He pays off her mortgage and then takes the payment away from the collector. He robs a train, robs a bank, returns to his town house and is shot in the back by Bob Ford, alias Bob Johnson. Billy Gashade, loyal follower, sings, "The dirty little coward that shot Thomas Howard and laid poor Jesse in his grave" at the funeral services ending the play.

## YOU NEVER KNOW

### (78 performances)

A musical play in two acts by Cole Porter; adapted by Rowland Leigh from the original by Robert Katscher, Siegfried Geyer and Karl Farkas; orchestrations by Hans Spialek. Produced by Messrs. Shubert in association with John Shubert at the Winter Garden, New York, September 21, 1938.

Cast of characters—

| | |
|---|---|
| Gaston | Clifton Webb |
| Baron Ferdinand de Romer | Rex O'Malley |
| Chauffeur | Eddie Gale |
| Ida Courtney | Toby Wing |
| Maria | Lupe Velez |
| Henri Baltin | Charles Kemper |

Mme. Baltin (Jeanne Montaigne)...................Libby Holman
Headwaiter........................................Roger Stearns
Louis.............................................Wesley Bender
Geoffrey..........................................Dan Harden
General Carruthers................................Truman Gaige
Comptroleur.......................................Ray Dennis
The Debonairs: Edwin Gale, Buddy Hertelle, Harold Murray, Paul
    Pierce, Harold Voeth and Jack Voeth.
Showgirls: Cynthia Cavanaugh, Dorothy Compton, Jacqueline Dahlia,
    Virginia Daly, Natasha Dana, Barbara Elliott, Tilde Getze, Chris
    Gustafson, Billie Hill, Helen Hudson, Alice McWhorter, Mildred
    Riley, Lee Stephenson, Arlene Stone, Ellen Taylor.
Dancers: Joanna Allen, Helen Bennett, Marion Broske, Mary Ann
    Carr, Louise De Forrest, Enes Early, Helen Ecklund, Grace
    Gillern, Irene Kelly, Edith Lambot, Mary Ann O'Brien, Mildred
    Ramey.
Boys: Wesley Bender, Gus Schirmer, Jr., Ray Dennis, Robert Smith,
    Jack Richards.
    Act I.—Scenes 1, 5 and 7—Baron de Romer's Home, Paris.
2—Madame Baltin's Boudoir. 3 and 4—The Club Bali. 6—Outside
Madame Baltin's House. Act II.—Scene 1—Swimming Pool Adjoin-
ing Baron de Romer's. 2—Gare de Lyon. 3—Outside Madame
Baltin's Home. 4—Baron de Romer's Home.
    Staged by Rowland Leigh; dances by Robert Alton; settings by
Albert Johnson and Watson Barratt.

The Baron de Romer pretends to be Gaston, his man, the better
to carry on an assignation with Mme. Baltin, while Maria,
madame's maid, becomes involved with madame's husband. All
with singing and dancing.

## * HELLZAPOPPIN

### (336 performances)

A vaudeville revue in two acts assembled and produced by Ole
Olson and Chic Johnson at the 46th Street Theatre, New York,
September 22, 1938.

Principals engaged—

| | |
|---|---|
| Ole Olson | Chic Johnson |
| Dewey Barto | George Mann |
| Hal Sherman | Shirley Wayne |
| Bettymae Crane | Beverly Crane |
| Ray Kinney | Dorothy Thomas |
| Walter Nilsson | Bonnie Reed |
| Billy Adams | Mel Reed |
| Sidney Dean | Roberta and Ray |
| Radio Rogues | Aloha Maids |
| The Starlings | The Charioteers |
| Berg and Moore | Whitey's Steppers |

Staged by Edward Duryea Dowling; musical supervision by Harold
Stern, assisted by Edward A. Hunt. Music and lyrics contributed
by Sammy Fain and Charles Tobias.

## SING OUT THE NEWS

### (105 performances)

A revue in two acts by Harold Rome and Charles Friedman;
orchestrations by Hans Spialek; ballet music by Will Irwin. Pro-

duced by Max Gordon in association with George S. Kaufman and Moss Hart at the Music Box, New York, September 24, 1938.

Principals engaged—

| | |
|---|---|
| Philip Loeb | Mary Jane Walsh |
| Rex Ingram | Dorothy Fox |
| Hiram Sherman | Ginger Manners |
| Michael Loring | Daisy Bernier |
| Will Geer | Leslie Litomy |
| Burton Pierce | Jean Peters |
| Joey Faye | Christina Lind |
| Charles Lawrence | Kathryn Lazell |
| Jimmy Lydon | Eleanor Eberle |
| Jane Fraser | June Allyson |
| Thelma Lee | Madelyn White |
| The Virginians | Lewis and Van |

Staged by Charles Friedman; dances by Ned McGurn, Dave Gould and Charles Walters; settings by Jo Mielziner; costumes by John Hambleton.

## DAME NATURE

### (48 performances)

A comedy in three acts adapted by Patricia Collinge from a French play by Andre Birabeau. Produced by the Theatre Guild at the Booth Theatre, New York, September 26, 1938.

Cast of characters—

| | |
|---|---|
| Old Max | Thomas Coffin Cooke |
| Beer | Charles Bellin |
| 2nd Boy | Fredrick Bradlee |
| Very Small Boy | Peter Miner |
| Concierge | Hale Norcross |
| Doctor Faridet | Harry Irvine |
| Leonie Perrot | Lois Hall |
| Andre Brisac | Montgomery Clift |
| Batton | Morgan James |
| Nanine | Kathryn Grill |
| Madame Brisac | Jessie Royce Landis |
| Monsieur Brisac | Onslow Stevens |
| Uncle Lucien | Forrest Orr |
| Paul Marachal | Wilton Graff |

Acts I and III.—The Shop of Leonie Perrot, Paris. Act II.—The Library of the Brisac Home.

Staged by Worthington Miner; settings by Norris Houghton.

Andre Brisac and Leonie Perrot, she a country girl of 15 who has inherited a Paris stationery shop, he a schoolboy, also 15, who buys his supplies there, find themselves drawn together by a mutual loneliness. When it is discovered later that Leonie is to have a baby Andre is proud rather than frightened and Leonie maternally hopeful and happy. When Andre's silly quarreling parents discover what has been going on the shock serves to reveal the mistakes they have made in Andre's upbringing and to bring them close to a reconciliation.

## KISS THE BOYS GOOD-BYE

### (286 performances)

A comedy in three acts by Clare Boothe. Produced by Brock Pemberton at the Henry Miller Theatre, New York, September 28, 1938.

Cast of characters—

| | |
|---|---|
| Conductor | Wyman Holmes |
| Lloyd Lloyd | Millard Mitchell |
| Cindy Lou Bethany | Helen Claire |
| George | Frank Wilson |
| Maimie | Ollie Burgoyne |
| Madison Breed | John Alexander |
| B. J. Wickfield | Edwin Nicander |
| Leslie Rand | Carmel White |
| Horace Rand | Philip Ober |
| Herbert Z. Harner | Sheldon Leonard |
| "Top" Rumson | Hugh Marlowe |
| Myra Stanhope | Benay Venuta |
| Oscar | Lex Lindsay |

Act I.—Scene 1—Drawing Room on Dixie Flyer, Northbound. 2—The Rands' Living Room, Westport, Conn. Act II.—The Living Room. Act III.—Scene 1—The Bath House. 2—The Living Room. Staged by Antoinette Perry; settings by John Root.

See page 357.

## 30 DAYS HATH SEPTEMBER

### (16 performances)

A farcical comedy in three acts by Irving Gaumont and Jack Sobell. Produced by Kirby Grant, Inc., at the Hudson Theatre, New York, September 30, 1938.

Cast of characters—

| | |
|---|---|
| Grandma Henny | Alison Skipworth |
| Robert Barnes | Harry Antrim |
| Ella | Leyla Tyler |
| Edward | Gene Gericke |
| Mathilda | Julia Johnston |
| Mr. Seamon | Otis Sheridan |
| Vera | Elisabeth Wilde |
| Dr. Parson | William Crimans |
| Mrs. Johnstone | Alice Fleming |
| Mrs. Gleason | Rose Flynn |
| Mrs. Hartford | Florence Vroom |
| Jay Carter | Nat Burns |
| Chic Collins | Willis Claire |
| Punk | David Evans |
| Rork | Thomas Patrick Dillon |
| Kane | Douglas McMullen |
| Hospital Interne | Earl Brisgal |

Acts I, II and III.—Suburban Home of Robert Barnes. Staged by Bertram Harrison; settings by Jules Laurents Studios.

Grandma Henny, thinking to help a favorite grandson to marriage and a happy life by arranging a loan for him against an expected legacy tied up in his grandfather's will, finds herself in the grip of crooks. She is, however, smart enough to outwit them.

## VICTORIA REGINA

### (87 performances)

A play in three acts by Laurence Housman. Revived by Gilbert Miller at the Martin Beck Theatre, New York, October 3, 1938.

Cast of characters—

| | |
|---|---|
| A Footman | Raymond Johnson |
| Lord Conyngham | Wallace Widdecombe |
| Archbishop of Canterbury | Harry Plimmer |
| A Maidservant | Augusta Roeland |
| Duchess of Kent | Babette Feist |
| Victoria | Helen Hayes |
| Lord Melbourne | Charles Francis |
| Prince Albert | Werner Bateman |
| Prince Ernest | Alexander Clark |
| Mr. Richards | Albert Froom |
| Mr. Anson | Oswald Marshall |
| 1st Queen's Gentleman | Guy Moneypenny |
| Royal Footman | William Bishop |
| A Court Usher | Edward Martyn |
| Lady Muriel | Pamela Henry-May |
| Lady Grace | Izetta Jewel |
| Lady-in-Waiting | Beatrice Moreland |
| 2nd Queen's Gentleman | Fothringham Lysons |
| Mr. Oakley | James Bedford |
| Duchess of Sutherland | Eva Leonard-Boyne |
| Lady Jane | Kate Warriner |
| General Grey | Tom Woods |
| 3rd Queen's Gentleman | Edward Jones |
| John Brown | James Gibson |
| Benjamin Disraeli (Earl of Beaconsfield) | Abraham Sofaer |
| A Footman | Robert Von Rigel |
| Sir Arthur Bigge | Herschel Martin |
| An Imperial Highness | Felix Brown |
| His Royal Highness | Tom Woods |
| 1st Princess | Merryl Boyden |
| 2nd Princess | Edith Carew |
| 3rd Princess | Elsie Grant |
| 4th Princess | Frances Hunt |
| 2nd Foreign Prince | George Denham |
| 3rd Foreign Prince | Ian Maple |
| Queen's Granddaughter | Shirley Poirier |
| Queen's Grandson | Eugene Schiel |
| Queen's Attendant | Hitous Gray |

Act I.—Scene 1—Entrance Hall, Kensington Palace. 2 and 3—Sitting Room, Windsor Castle. 4—Prince Albert's Dressing Room, Windsor Castle. Act II.—Scenes 1 and 4—Prince Albert's Writing Room, Buckingham Palace. 2—Room Overlooking Park, Buckingham Palace. 3—Ante-Chamber, Windsor Castle. Act III.—Scene 1—Garden Tent, Balmoral Castle. 2—Buckingham Palace.
Staged by Gilbert Miller; settings by Rex Whistler.

After a run of 517 performances, following its first performance December 26, 1935, "Victoria Regina" was revived for a limited engagement with the above cast. It was planned to send the play on a brief tour later, but a renewed popularity kept it in New York past the holidays.

## THE GOOD

### (9 performances)

A play in three acts by Chester Erskin. Produced by Norman and Irvin Pincus at the Windsor Theatre, New York, October 5, 1938.

Cast of characters—

| | |
|---|---|
| Knucky (Archie) Payne | John Raby |
| Rose Dubrowski | Florence Sundstrom |
| Whitey | Warren Bryan |
| Harriet Eldred | Frances Starr |
| Alice Witte | Elwyn Harvey |
| Malcom Eldred | Robert Keith |
| Clarabelle Witte | Eleanor Pasner |
| Rev. J. Luther Wendell | Herbert Yost |
| Israel Baruch | Frederick Kaufman |
| Howard Eldred | Jarvis Rice |
| Francis Duncan | Eric Kalkhurst |
| Norma Babcock | Leona Powers |
| Dr. Vincent Ten Broek | Harry Bannister |
| Eli Baruch | Douglass Parkhirst |

Acts I and III.—Front Porch of the Eldreds' Home. Act II.—Living Room.

Staged by Chester Erskin; settings by Donald Oenslager.

Harriet Eldred, like her minister father before her, is a hard, unyielding and thoroughly "good" person who would hold all her neighbors to a strict accounting of the moral laws. Her coldness drives her sensitive son into an abnormal friendship with a choir master, and pushes her unloved husband into the arms of a house-maid. Because she refuses to deal sympathetically and under-standingly with a lad who has borrowed from the church funds the boy kills himself. The tragedy of her own unlovely life is complete.

## THE DEVIL TAKES A BRIDE

### (11 performances)

A play in three acts by Joe Bates Smith. Produced by Mont-gomery Ford at the Cort Theatre, New York, October 7, 1938.

Cast of characters—

| | |
|---|---|
| Meslie Bilby | Evelyn Byrd |
| Margaret Submit Quimby | Jeannette Chinley |
| Herbert Vanick Clauson | J. Arthur Young |
| Louisa Polly | Helen Shields |
| Gregory Jaried | Anthony Ross |
| Hermes Bilby | Philip Wood |
| George Rensley Quimby | Louis Hector |

Reporter................................................Robert Lindsey
Todd..................................................Frank Harvey
Hulbern...............................................Cledge Roberts
Acts I, II and III.—Parlor of George Rensley Quimby, Brooklyn.
Staged by John Hayden; settings by Lawrence L. Goldwasser.

Margaret Quimby, after thirty years of brutal treatment at the hands of her father, who blames her birth for her mother's invalidism, plots with her lover to cause the old man's death. A favorite uncle is caught and killed in the trap they prepare. Margaret, however, is able to convince the police that her father, whose past is filled with suspicious actions, is the guilty one and sees him sentenced to be hanged. Her lover deserts her, and she is left to loneliness and her conscience in the old Quimby mansion.

## THE FABULOUS INVALID

### (65 performances)

A play in two acts by Moss Hart and George S. Kaufman. Produced by Sam H. Harris at the Broadhurst Theatre, New York, October 8, 1938.

Cast of characters—

| | |
|---|---|
| John W. Carleton | Richard Gordon |
| Paula Kingsley | Doris Dalton |
| Laurence Brooks | Stephen Courtleigh |
| The Valet | Walter Beck |
| The Maid | Vera Fuller Mellish |
| The Character Man | William Dorbin |
| Ushers | { Edward Fisher / Donald Baker |
| George Haskell | William E. Blake |
| The Coroner | Sydney Grant |
| The Doorman | Jack Norworth |
| Bill | Ernest Lawford |
| Carleton's Secretary | Barna Ostertag |
| Bradley | Brant Gorman |
| An Office Boy | Edward Elliott |
| A Manager | John Moore |
| Another Manager | Richard Lloyd |
| A Motion Picture Man | David Leonard |
| An Author | George Lloyd |
| An Actress | Mona Moray |
| Saunders | Percy Helton |
| Sheridan | Charles King |
| Curtis | John Lorenz |
| An Announcer | Jay Velie |
| A Policeman | Ferdi Hoffman |
| Newsboys | { Alec Courtney / Jerome Thor |
| A Delivery Boy | Jack Arnold |
| Usherettes | { Amy Revere / Joy Hathaway / Virginia Burke |
| Prize Winners | { Bobbe Arnst / Ada Sinclair |
| A Boy | Philip Truex |
| A Girl | Marion Edwards |
| Goldie | Ruth Clayton |

```
Mr. Jamison...................................James MacDonald
The Auctioneer.......................................Solly Ward
His Assistant.......................................Al Amato
A Vendor......................................Robert Rhodes
A Photographer....................................Paul Payne
A Ticket Girl.......................................Elsa Ersi
Solinsky.........................................Curtis Karpe
The Stage Manager..............................Eddie Nelson
Daisy LaHiff.......................................Iris Adrian
A Comedian.....................................Clancy Cooper
A Plainclothes Man..............................Milano Tilden
A Salesman......................................Sid Stone
Jessie.......................................Jeanne Wardley
Annie..........................................Grace Valentine
A Director.........................................Louis Howard
```
In Various Other Roles, Equally Important to the Action, Will Be:
Beth Waller, Eileen Burns, Gladys Conrad, Dora Sayers, Ethel
Colby, Doris Jenkins, Sydna Scott, Ruth Strome, Meg Mundy,
Gerry Jones, Dorothy Waller, Katherine Duncan, Bonnie
Roberts, Louise Blackburn, Janice Joyce, Peggy Strickland,
Norman MacKay, Roy Johnson, Melvin Parks, Douglas Bedding-
field, Robert Regent, Alan Handley.
Acts I and II.—In and around the Alexandria Theatre, N. Y.
Staged by George S. Kaufman; settings by Donald Oenslager;
costumes by John Hambleton.

Paula Kingsley, a popular actress of the early nineties, appears successfully with her husband and leading man, Laurence Brooks, at the dedication of the Alexandria Theatre, New York. The night of the gala opening Paula dies of a heart attack. Brooks, immersed in grief, takes his own life. The ghosts of these two thereafter haunt the theatre, which is still the actors' heaven. They see the Alexandria pass through various experiences, sinking ever lower, until it becomes a cheap burlesque house and is raided by the police. At which point a brave band of new and youthful enthusiasts march in, take over the old house and start it again on the way to recovery.

## OSCAR WILDE

### (247 performances)

A play in three acts by Leslie and Sewell Stokes. Produced by Norman Marshall at the Fulton Theatre, New York, October 10, 1938.

Cast of characters—

```
Lord Alfred Douglas...........................John Buckmaster
Louis Dijon.......................................Edward Trevor
An Arab Boy..................................Richard Charlton
Oscar Wilde.....................................Robert Morley
An Hotel Waiter...............................Kenneth Treseder
Eustace.........................................Wyman Kane
A Waiter.......................................Reginald Malcolm
Frank Harris...................................Harold Young
Charlie Parker.....................................John Carol
A Butler.........................................Colin Hunter
Allen.......................................Arthur Gould-Porter
Sir Edward Clarke, Q.C..........................J. W. Austin
Mr. Justice Henn Collins......................Frederick Graham
```

```
Clerk of the Court.................................Lewis Dayton
Mr. E. H. Carson, Q.C.............................Mark Dignam
The Solicitor-General..........................Gordon Richards
Mr. Justice Wills................................Oswald Yorke
Jules.............................................Jean Del Val
```
    Act I.—Scene 1—Terrace of Hotel in Algiers.  2—Private Room in
London Restaurant.  3—Wilde's Study, Tite Street, Chelsea.  Act
II.—Scene 1—The Old Bailey During Trial of the Marquis of
Queensbury.  2—During Trial of Oscar Wilde.  Act III.—Scene 1—
Wilde's Study, Tite Street.  2—A Café in Paris.
    Staged by Norman Marshall; settings by Raymond Sovey.

Oscar Wilde is in Algiers with Lord Alfred Douglas as his traveling companion when he learns that the Marquis of Queensbury,
father of Lord Alfred, is threatening to make trouble if the friendship is continued.  Returned to London Wilde brings an action
for libel against Queensbury, which he loses.  He is in turn sued
by Queensbury and convicted of moral delinquencies that send
him to prison for two years.  Released, he lives and finally dies
miserably in Paris.

## HAMLET

### (96 performances)

A tragedy in three acts by William Shakespeare; incidental
music by Lehman Engel.  Revived by Maurice Evans in association with Joseph Verner Reed and Boris Said at the St. James
Theatre, New York, October 12, 1938.

Cast of characters—

```
Francisco..........................................Donald Arbury
Bernardo...........................................Wesley  Addy
Marcellus.........................................Donald Cameron
Horatio...........................................Donald Randolph
Claudius, King of Denmark.........................Henry Edwards
Gertrude, Queen of Denmark.......................Mady Christians
Hamlet.............................................Maurice Evans
Polonius...........................................George Graham
Laertes............................................Sydney  Smith
Voltimand.........................................Reynolds Evans
Cornelius..........................................Emmett Rogers
A Page.............................................William Prince
Ophelia...........................................Katherine Locke
Ghost of Hamlet's Father.........................Augustin Duncan
Reynaldo...........................................Henry  Jones
Rosencrantz......................................Alexander Scourby
Guildenstern......................................Everett Ripley
Player King.......................................Rhys  Williams
Player Queen........................................Paul Nevens
Third Player......................................Donald Arbury
Fourth Player......................................Emmett Rogers
A Lady in Waiting...................................Irene Tedrow
Fortinbras, Prince of Norway........................Wesley Addy
A Captain.........................................Alfred Paschall
A Gentleman........................................George Keane
Two Sailors.................................... { Richard Janaver
                                               { Emmett Rogers
A Gravedigger.....................................Whitford Kane
Second Gravedigger.................................Henry Jones
A Priest..........................................Reynolds Evans
```

Osric.........................................Maury Tuckerman
Ambassadors...................................
$\Big\{$ Rhys Williams
Paul Nevens

Lords, Ladies, Soldiers and Attendants: Irene Tedrow, Carmen
Mathews, Constance Friend, Ruth Wilk, Richard Janaver,
William Prince, Charles Bowden, Frederick Carney, Alfred
Paschall.
Act I.—Scenes 1 and 4—Platform Before the Castle at Elsinore.
2, 7 and 8—Rooms in the Castle. 3 and 6—Polonius' House. 5—
Another part of Platform. Act II.—Scene 1—Courtyard. 2—
King's Apartments. 3—Queen's Apartments. 4 and 5—Rooms in
Castle. 6—Frontiers of Denmark. Act III.—Scenes 1 and 5—
Room in Castle. 2—Corridor. 3—Polonius' House. 4—Churchyard.
6—Courtyard.
Staged by Margaret Webster; settings by David Ffolkes.

The first staging of the full-length text in New York. Ben
Greet had previously played the full play in the West. Mr.
Evans' revival took in at 6.45 and continued until 8.15. Following a half-hour's supper recess it was resumed at 8.45 and continued until 11.15. Later in the engagement the supper interlude
was increased to an hour. Three of Mr. Evans' 96 performances
of "Hamlet" were devoted to the shortened, or conventional, version of the tragedy.

## I HAVE BEEN HERE BEFORE

### (20 performances)

A drama in three acts by J. B. Priestley. Produced by Gilbert
Miller at the Guild Theatre, New York, October 13, 1938.

Cast of characters—
Sally Pratt..........................................Eileen Beldon
Sam Shipley.........................................Harry Rousby
Dr. Gortler.........................................Ernst Deutsch
Oliver Farrant......................................Eric Portman
Janet Ormund.......................................Lydia Sherwood
Walter Ormund......................................Wilfrid Lawson
Acts I, II and III.—Sitting Room of Black Bull Inn, Grindle
Moor, North Yorkshire, at Whitsuntide.
Staged by Lewis Allen; setting by Laurence Irving.

Walter Ormund and Janet, his wife, select an inn in North
Yorkshire for a Whitsuntide holiday. Ormund, a prominent industrialist, is nerve-shot and in need of a rest. At the inn the
Ormunds meet Oliver Farrant, a young schoolmaster, and Dr.
Gortler, a German scientist. Gortler has, in a vision, anticipated
this meeting. He knows that Mrs. Ormund and young Farrant
will be attracted to each other on meeting and that Ormund,
after certain experiences, will try to make way with himself. It
is the Gortler theory that all human beings live a succession of
lives through rebirth and achieve spiritual progress only as they

learn the lessons of each successive life and are able to project themselves spiritually to successively higher planes. All things happen as Gortler predicted. Ormund does try to kill himself, but through Gortler's elucidation of the time theory, is able to give up his wife to Farrant and prepare himself for further spiritual progress.

## DANCE NIGHT

### (3 performances)

A drama in two acts by Kenyon Nicholson. Produced by Robert Rockmore at the Belasco Theatre, New York, October 14, 1938.

Cast of characters—

| | |
|---|---|
| Ella Gantz | Maida Reade |
| Cliff Gantz | Edward Hodge |
| Buzz Johnson | Del Cleveland |
| Winfield Stout | Melbourne Ford |
| Homer Diltz | Anthony Dwyer |
| Arlene Hooper | Marian Leach |
| Wallace Tinsman | Edwin Mann |
| Grover Paxton | Charles Mendick |
| Rhoda Carver | Josephine McKim |
| Leonard Kerr | Frank Maxwell |
| Irma Lucas | Terry Fay |
| Frances Hight | Judy Parrish |
| Lloyd Pedrick | David Paul |
| Claude Swayze | Perry Bruskin |
| Harvey Bodine | David Wayne |
| Miss Spangelman | Mary Boylan |
| Blanche Hendricks | Mary Servoss |
| Jewel Hendricks | Mary Rolfe |
| Roy Titus | Lyle Bettger |
| Reba Clark | Lillian Green |
| Ruth Tabor | Darthy Hinckley |
| Earl Hendricks | Fred Herrick |
| Hobie Morgan | Bert Conway |
| Dora Roach | June Curtis |
| Marvin Kinney | Richard Clayton |
| Albie Kline | Robert Mayors |
| Midge Opdyke | Frances Carden |
| Leona Skillman | Gail de Hart |
| Otis Skillman | Gordon Peters |
| Art Manson | Harry M. Cooke |

Act I.—Scenes 1 and 3—The Veranda at Gantz's "Grove Dansant," Hunterdon County, New Jersey. 2—The Grove. Act II.— Scenes 1 and 3—The Grove. 2—The Veranda.

Staged by Lee Strasberg; settings by Raymond Sovey.

Hobie Morgan, quick-tempered, took a shot at Roy Titus in a quarrel. Hobie was sent to reform school, later paroled, and returned to the old town to find that Roy had also taken Jewel Hendricks, who had been Hobie's girl. The gang at the Grove Dansant, hearing that Hobie is back, spend the best part of one dance night trying to bring the enemies together in the hope that there will be a little bloodletting. Jewel does everything she can to keep the boys apart, even to giving herself to Hobie. This sacrifice changes everything. Hobie doesn't want to fight after that. He just wants to live for Jewel.

## * ABE LINCOLN IN ILLINOIS

### (287 performances)

A drama in three acts by Robert E. Sherwood. Produced by The Playwrights' Company (Maxwell Anderson, S. N. Behrman, Sidney Howard, Elmer Rice and Robert E. Sherwood) at the Plymouth Theatre, New York, October 15, 1938.

Cast of characters—

| | |
|---|---|
| Mentor Graham | Frank Andrews |
| Abe Lincoln | Raymond Massey |
| Ann Rutledge | Adele Longmire |
| Judith | Iris Whitney |
| Ben Mattling | George Christie |
| Judge Bowling Green | Arthur Griffin |
| Ninian Edwards | Lewis Martin |
| Joshua Speed | Calvin Thomas |
| Trum Cogdal | Harry Levian |
| Jack Armstrong | Howard daSilva |
| Bab | Everett Charlton |
| Feargus | David Clarke |
| Jasp | Kevin McCarthy |
| Seth Gale | Herbert Rudley |
| Nancy Green | Lillian Foster |
| William Herndon | Wendell K. Phillips |
| Elizabeth Edwards | May Collins |
| Mary Todd | Muriel Kirkland |
| The Edwards' Maid | Dorothy Allan |
| Jimmy Gale | Howard Sherman |
| Aggie Gale | Marion Rooney |
| Gobey | Hubert Brown |
| Stephen A. Douglas | Albert Phillips |
| Willie Lincoln | Lex Parrish |
| Tad Lincoln | Lloyd Barry |
| Robert Lincoln | John Payne |
| The Lincolns' Maid | Iris Whitney |
| Crimmin | Frank Tweddell |
| Barrick | John Gerard |
| Sturveson | Thomas F. Tracey |
| Jed | Harry Levian |
| Phil | Kevin McCarthy |
| Kavanagh | Glenn Coulter |
| Ogleby | John Triggs |
| Donner | David Clarke |
| Cavalry Captain | Everett Charlton |

Soldiers, Railroad Men, Townspeople: Stuart McClure, Allen Shaw, Phillip Caplan, David Hewes, Dearon Darnay, Harrison Woodhull, Robert Fitzsimmons, Joseph Wiseman, Walter Kapp, George Malcolm, Bert Schorr, Augusta Dabney, Bette Benfield, Ann Stevenson.

Act I.—Scene 1—Mentor Graham's Cabin near New Salem, Illinois. About 1830. 2—The Rutledge Tavern. 3—Bowling Green's House. Act II.—Scenes 1 and 3—Law Office of Stuart and Lincoln on Second Floor of Court House, Springfield. About 1840. 2 and 5—Parlor of the Edwards House. 4—On the Prairie about 1847. Act III.—Scene 1—A Speaker's Platform in an Illinois town. 1858. 2—Parlor of the Edwards Home, now used by the Lincolns. 3—Lincoln Campaign Headquarters, Illinois State House. November 6,

1860. 4—Yards of Railroad Station, Springfield, Feb. 11, 1861.
Staged by Elmer Rice; settings by Jo Mielziner.

See page 31.

## KNIGHTS OF SONG

### (16 performances)

A musical play in two acts by Glendon Allvine, based on a story by Glendon Allvine and Adele Gutman Nathan. Produced by Laurence Schwab at the 51st Street Theatre, New York, October 17, 1938.

Cast of characters—

| | |
|---|---|
| Harris | Victor Beecroft |
| William Schwenk Gilbert | Nigel Bruce |
| Arthur Seymour Sullivan | John Moore |
| Richard D'Oyly Carte | Reginald Bach |
| McManus | John Adair |
| Wardrobe Woman | Shirley Gale |
| Mrs. Gilbert | Rosalind Ivan |
| Maid | Carrie Glenn |
| Mrs. Cynthia Bradley | Natalie Hall |
| His Royal Highness, Albert Edward, Prince of Wales | Monty Woolley |
| Oscar Wilde | Robert Chisholm |
| George Bernard Shaw | Winston O'Keefe |
| Sarah Burnside | Martha Roberts |
| Vera Tracy | Shannon Dean |
| Mary Lou Simmons | Eva Paul |
| Butler | Robert Collins |
| Her Majesty, Queen Victoria | Molly Pearson |
| Flunkey | Leonard Rocky |
| His Grace, The Archbishop of Canterbury | Henry Mowbray |
| Ponsonby | Orlo Rexford |
| Lady-in-Waiting | Dorothy Johnson |
| Officer of the Deck | Karl Holly |
| His Imperial Highness, Crown Prince Wilhelm | Rex Williams |
| Times Reporter | Gladstone Waldrip |
| Herald Reporter | Norman Gray |
| Tribune Reporter | David Showalter |
| Organ Grinder | Burr Crandall |
| James Caldwell Bradley | Bruce Evans |
| Union Delegate | William Foran |
| Clara | Myrtis Jackson |
| Thomas | Everett West |
| Lord Ansel | David Showalter |
| James McNeill Whistler | Charles Atkin |
| Perkins | Bruce Evans |
| David, Grandson of Edward VII | Edward Ryan, Jr. |

Ensemble—Anthony Ferrara, Leonard Rockey, Edward Hayes, Paul Davin, Jay Amiss, Remington Olmstead, Jr., Freeman Bloodgood, Angus Cairns, Earl Ashcroft, Norman Crandall; Davie Gladstone, Virginia Cole, Sally Hadley, Beulah Blake, Sandra Nova, Lois Kirk, Ruth Wenton, Vera Dean, Betty Sparks, Emily Marsh, Ann Francis.

Singers—Ralph Bunker, Shirley Dale, Earl MacVeigh, Myrtis Jackson, Mary Dyer, Everett West, Orlo Rexford, George Vaughan, Laurence Siegel, Martha Burnett, Annamary Dickey, Mary Hoppel.

Act I.—Scene 1—Stage of Opera Comique, London, 1878. Dress Rehearsal of "Pinafore." 2—Upstairs Library of Gilbert's London Home. 3—Mrs. Bradley's Drawing Room. 4—Queen Victoria's Private Reception Room, Windsor Castle. 5—Deck of the Yacht *Hohenzollern.* 6—Stage of Fifth Ave. Theatre, New York. Dress Rehearsal of "The Pirates of Penzance." 1879. Act II.—Scene 1—Arthur Sullivan's Study. 1883. 2—Mrs. Bradley's Drawing Room. 1889. 3—D'Oyly Carte's Office in Savoy Theatre. 1900. 4—Stage of Savoy Theatre—"The Mikado" Revival. 5—King Edward's Private Reception Room, Windsor Castle. 1907. 6—Grand Ballroom, Windsor Castle.

Staged by Oscar Hammerstein; Gilbert and Sullivan musical excerpts staged by Avalon Collard; settings by Raymond Sovey; costumes by Kate Lawson.

Gilbert and Sullivan work together and quarrel through rehearsals of "The Mikado," "The Pirates of Penzance" and "Pinafore." A Mrs. Cynthia Bradley of Baltimore represents an Arthur Sullivan romance with a married American woman. It is she who does much to strengthen the composer's favor with Queen Victoria, and she also patches up many of the famous quarrels. Action begins with the staging of "Pinafore" and ends with the belated knighting of Gilbert after Sullivan's death.

## A WOMAN'S A FOOL—TO BE CLEVER

### (7 performances)

A comedy in three acts by Dorothy Bennett and Link Hannah. Produced by John J. Wildberg at the National Theatre, New York, October 18, 1938.

Cast of characters—

| | |
|---|---|
| Eddie Sommers | Edwin Phillips |
| Major | Eddie Green |
| Jeff Foster | Ian Keith |
| Christine Foster | Vera Allen |
| Minerva Himmelman | Sandra Stanton |
| Nina Suffieva | Haila Stoddard |
| Lew Lerner | Donald Foster |
| Josephine Lerner | Edith Meiser |
| Rosemary Littleproud | Margie Ann Kaufman |

Acts I, II and III.—Terrace of Bermuda Home of Christine and Jeff Foster.

Staged by Frank Merlin; settings by Donald Oenslager.

Jeff Foster, matinée idol, has quit the stage and gone to Bermuda with Christine, his wife, determined to devote his time to playwriting. Nina Suffieva, a Russian amateur with big ideas, follows the Fosters, determined to lure Jeff back to the stage if not to her apartment as her leading man. Christine meets Nina's challenge by being both firm and generous and wins in the end.

## KNICKERBOCKER HOLIDAY

### (168 performances)

A musical comedy in two acts by Maxwell Anderson; music by Kurt Weill. Produced by The Playwrights' Company at the Ethel Barrymore Theatre, New York, October 19, 1938.

Cast of characters—

Washington Irving...............................Ray Middleton
Anthony Corlear..................................Harry Meehan
Tienhoven.............................................Mark Smith
Vanderbilt.........................................George Watts
Roosevelt........................................Francis Pierlot
DePeyster..........................................Charles Arnt
DeVries...............................................John E. Young
Van Rensselaer..................................James Phillips
Van Cortlandt, Jr..............................Richard Cowdery
Tina Tienhoven..................................Jeanne Madden
Brom Broeck....................................Richard Kollmar
Tenpin........................................Clarence Nordstrom
Schermerhorn....................................Howard Freeman
Pieter Stuyvesant................................Walter Huston
General Poffenburgh............................Donald Black
Mistress Schermerhorn.............................Edith Angold
Citizens of New Amsterdam—Helen Carroll, Jane Brotherton, Carol
    Deis, Robert Arnold, Bruce Hamilton, Ruth Mamel, William
    Marel, Margaret MacLaren, Robert Rounseville, Rufus Smith,
    Margaret Stewart, Erika Zaranova, William Wahlert.
Soldiers—Albert Allen, Matthias Ammann, Dow Fonda, Warde
    Peters.
    Act I.—The Battery. 1647. Act II.—Scene 1—Interior of the
Jail.——The Battery. Prologue to Scene 2—Washington Irving's
Study. 1809.
    Staged by Joshua Logan; settings by Jo Mielziner; costumes by
Frank Bevan; dances by Carl Randall and Edwin Denby.

On the day of Peg-leg Peter Stuyvesant's arrival to take over
the governorship of New Amsterdam the corrupt and worried
Councilors look about for someone to hang to divert the new
governor's attention. They hit upon Brom Broeck who is a problem, both because he is determined to marry Tina Tienhoven,
Councilor Tienhoven's daughter, and because he is too independent to take orders from anybody. Brom is thus established
as the first American. Peg-leg Peter pardons Brom, but denies
his right to Tina. Peter plans to take Tina himself, but later re-
considers that decision. Peter is eager to stand well with pos-
terity.

## CASE HISTORY

### (11 performances)

A drama in three acts by Louis S. Bardoly. Produced by
James Troup at the Lyceum Theatre, New York, October 21,
1938.

Cast of characters—

Dr. Jim Baker.......................................Ned Wever
Emily Pardee........................................Ruth Abbott
Frank Pardee.......................................G. Pat Collins
Margaret Pardee......................................Ruth Lee
Barbara Pardee....................................Evelyn Mills
Dorothy Pardee....................................Babs Savage
Miss McKee............................................Grace Fox
Ann...................................................Muriel Starr
    Acts I, II and III.—Living Room of the Pardees' Suburban Home
in a Middle Western City.
    Staged by Adelyn Busnell; setting by James Morcom.

Emily Pardee's daughter, Dorothy, has been unable to walk for two years following an attack of infantile paralysis. In desperation Emily appeals to Miss McKee, a Christian Science practitioner. The next day Dorothy walks, which she could have done at any time she had been stimulated to the effort, according to Dr. Jim Baker, the Pardees' friend. Mrs. Pardee's stepdaughter, Barbara, is then seized with an attack of appendicitis and dies because Mrs. Pardee, depending again on Science, calls Dr. Baker too late. Mrs. Pardee thereupon goes into a decline mixed with liquor and melancholia. In the end Dr. Baker calls in the Science practitioner to restore Mrs. Pardee's faith. He can heal the body but not the soul. Science and medicine should work together, says he.

## MADAME CAPET

### (7 performances)

A drama in three acts, adapted by George Middleton from the French of Marcelle Maurette. Produced by Eddie Dowling at the Cort Theatre, New York, October 25, 1938.

Cast of characters—

| | |
|---|---|
| A Young Girl | Barbara C. Brown |
| Campan | Leslie King |
| Joseph II, Emperor of Austria | Frederic Tozere |
| Count De Mercy | Harold Gould |
| Marie Antoinette | Eva Le Gallienne |
| Madame de Misery | Alice John |
| Augeard | Nelson Welch |
| Rose Bertin | Blanche Ring |
| Sylvia | Phyllis Holden |
| Fanette | Carol Evans |
| Axel De Fersen | William Post, Jr. |
| Marie-Therese (aged ten) | Helen Renee |
| The Dauphin (Louis) | Diana Donnenwirth |
| Madame Brunier | Merle Maddern |
| Count De Vaudreuil | Staats Cotsworth |
| Baron De Besenval | George Baxter |
| The Duchess De Polignac | Mary Michael |
| First Lackey | Harvey Welch |
| Second Lackey | Fred Rendulic |
| First Guard | William W. Sanders |
| Second Guard | W. J. Hackett |
| A Market Woman | Suzanne Steell |
| Another Market Woman | Diane de Brett |
| A Court Lady | Elizabeth Dewing |
| Another Court Lady | Merle Maddern |
| A Third Court Lady | Phyllis Holden |
| Leonard | Le Roi Operti |
| Count De La Marck | Bram Nossen |
| Mirabeau | George Coulouris |
| Madame Elizabeth | Marian Evensen |
| Simon | Louis Veda Quince |
| Marie-Therese (aged fifteen) | Charita Bauer |
| The Dauphin (Charles) | Warren Mills |
| First Deputy | W. J. Hackett |

Second Deputy..................................Richard Bengali
Lamorliere.........................................Earle Mitchell
Rosalie..............................................Anne Baxter
Bault..............................................Craig Williams
Fouquier-Tinville..................................George Baxter
Herman, President of the Tribunal..................Harold Gould
Fabricius.........................................William Sanders
Chauveau-Lagarde..............................Staats Cotsworth
Reine Millot......................................Mary Michael
La Tour Du Pin..................................Frederic Tozere
Guard at the Tribunal.............................Nelson Welch
Another Guard...................................Harvey Welch
Sanson, the Executioner..........................William Sanders
A Priest..........................................Bram Nossen
A Bailiff............................................Fred Sears
Another Bailiff..................................Richard Bengali
Guard at the Conciergerie..........................Nelson Welch
Another Guard...................................W. J. Hackett
     Act I.—Scene 1—Queen's Private Apartments, Versailles. 1777.
2—A Corridor. 3—French Pavilion at the Trianon. 1787. Act
II.—Scene 1—The Tuileries, Paris. 1790. 2—Outside St. Cloud.
3—St. Cloud. Act III.—Scene 1—Tower of the Temple. 1793. 2—
Outside the Conciergerie. 3—The Revolutionary Tribunal. 4—
Queen's Cell at the Conciergerie.
     Staged by José Ruben; settings by Watson Barratt; costumes by
Helene Pons.

Marie Antoinette, following frivolous and extravagant days at
court, settles down to the enjoyment of her children and a hoped-
for correction of the life that has brought her unpopularity with
the French people. She is unable to stem the tide of revolution,
is tried, sentenced and sent to the guillotine.

## THE GIRL FROM WYOMING

### (86 performances)

A burlesque in three acts by J. Van Ostend Van Antwerp (John
Krimsky). Produced by John and Jerrold Krimsky at the American Music Hall, October 29, 1938.

Cast of characters—

Ben Longwood...................................Philip Huston
Mrs. Longwood..................................Nellie Thorne
Sheriff Peters...................................Billy M. Greene
Sleepy, a cowboy...................................Tony Kraber
Marcy Desmond..................................George Petrie
Alkali, a prospector...........................Donald Macdonald
The Girl from Wyoming...........................June Walker
Chiquori.........................................Anne Hunter
Pedro.............................................James Russo
Bartender.........................................Jack Goldie
Cow Belles.—Ruth Mann, Mary LaRoche, Jackie Susanne, Polly
     Smiley, Sherrand Pollard and Irene Mann.
Cow Hands.—Bruce Gordan, Walter Reed Smith, Alfred Brower,
     Norman Barcliff, Duncan Baldwin and Jack Riley.
     Act I.—Scene 1—Sitting Room in Boston's Back Bay. 2—A West-
ern Plain. 3—Main Street of El Reno, Nevada. 4—Desmond's
Elysian Fields. Act II.—Scenes 1 and 3—Western Plain. 2—
Prairie at Night. 4—Desmond's Elysian Fields Saloon. Act III.—
Scene 1—Main Street of El Reno. 2—Mountain Cabin. 3—Western
Plain. 4—Mountain Pass. 5—A Gulch.
     Staged by Robert Ross; settings by Eugene B. Dunkel.

Sex in the Purple Sage is the theme of this comedy. Ben Longwood of Harvard, following the Greeley advice to go West, finds himself surrounded by cowhands, harlots and a crowd of gambling toughies. Thanks to the interest his curly hair inspires in the Girl from Wyoming, Ben is saved in the nick of time several times.

"Naughty Naught," the Yale burlesque, was revived January 25, 1939, and alternated with "The Girl from Wyoming" for several weeks, ending after the forty-second performance.

## WALTZ IN GOOSE STEP

### (7 performances)

A drama in three acts by Oliver H. P. Garrett. Produced by Julien Chaqueneau at the Hudson Theatre, New York, November 1, 1938.

Cast of characters—

| | |
|---|---|
| August, The Leader | Leo Chalzel |
| Count Gottfried Von Laidi | Henry Oscar |
| Schmutzi | Harold Johnsrud |
| Josef Straub | John Boruff |
| Rudolf | Barrie Wanless |
| Colonel Heist | John Harwood |
| Tessie Konstantin | Mariana Fiory |
| General Von Straffen | Maurice Manson |
| Berthold Sprecher | Henry Sherwood |
| Dr. Sturm | Palmer Ward |
| Herr Schilling | France Bendtsen |
| Bruder | Charles Furcolowe |
| Heinrich | Howard Fischer |
| Mrs. Straub | Marjorie Dalton |
| Colonel Masch | Walter Davis |
| 1st Trooper | Turnley Walker |
| 2nd Trooper | John Rustad |

Act I.—Interior of Cabin Plane Used as The Leader's Flying Office. Acts II and III.—Apartment of Count Von Laidi in the City. Staged by Arthur Hopkins; settings by Norris Houghton.

August, the fuehrer, is flying home from a recent purge when he becomes actively conscious of opposition in his own staff. The pilot of the machine is contemplating a personal rebellion that will crash the plane and do away with August and Von Laidi, his Minister of Defense, once and for all. August and Von Laidi talk the pilot out of his intentions. Whereupon August's suspicions center on Von Laidi, an eloquent lieutenant of Machiavellian tendencies. Knowing that he is suspected, Von Laidi tries to start a counter revolution. He is stopped and handed a gun with which to make way with himself.

## DANTON'S DEATH

### (21 performances)

A drama in individual scenes vignetted by spotlight translated by Geoffrey Dunlop from the German of Georg Buchner; songs by Marc Blitzstein. Produced by Orson Welles and John Houseman at the Mercury Theatre, New York, November 2, 1938.

Cast of characters—

| | |
|---|---|
| Julie | Anna Stafford |
| Danton | Martin Gabel |
| Camille Desmoulins | Edgar Barrier |
| Lucile | Evelyn Wahl |
| Herault De Sechelles | Morgan Farley |
| Philippeau | Erskine Sanford |
| Lacroix | Guy Kingsley |
| Robespierre | Vladimir Sokoloff |
| 1st Old Man | George Duthie |
| 2nd Old Man | Erskine Sanford |
| Marion | Arlene Francis |
| Rosalie | Ruth Ford |
| Legendre | Richard Wilson |
| St. Just | Orson Welles |
| Christine | Mary Wickes |
| Fouquier | Eustace Wyatt |
| Barrere | Joseph Cotten |
| Gaoler | John Berry |
| President of the Convention | George Duthie |
| Servants to Danton | William Alland, Edgerton Paul, Stanley Poss |
| Convention Attendants | Richard Baer, Ross Elliott |

Members of the Convention—William Mowry, Sparke Hastings, Stephen Roberts

Voices in the Street—Arthur Hoffe, Sanford Siegel, Fred Thompson, Ellen Andrews, Fay Baker, Helen Coule.

Staged by Orson Welles; setting by Jan Tichacek.

Danton, following his earlier triumphs, continues to woo liberty of life and expression against the opposition of the fanatical puritan, Robespierre. The rising tide of Robespierre's popularity finally engulfs Danton, nor can his eloquence in defense save him from the guillotine.

## RUN SHEEP RUN

### (12 performances)

A comedy in three acts by Raymond Knight. Produced by Donald Blackwell and Raymond Curtis at the Windsor Theatre, New York, November 3, 1938.

Cast of characters—

| | |
|---|---|
| Wilkes Potter | Hugh O'Connell |
| George | Peter Goo Chong |
| Leila Stuart | Ruth Weston |
| Claude Pratt | Alan Bunce |

Mrs. Potter....................................Beatrice Herford
William Potter.......................................John Kirk
Nine..........................................Dickie Von Patten
Eighteen.......................................Alfred Alderdice
Phyllis Goodspeed.............................Virginia Campbell
Edith Pratt......................................Edith Gresham
Mrs. Kenneth Goodspeed.........................Regina Wallace
Steve Bellows......................................James Corner
Kenneth Goodspeed..............................Leo Kennedy
Mrs. Hopple...................................Zamah Cunningham
Mrs. Buker.........................................Hilda Bruce
Mrs. Frisbie....................................Peggy Coudray
Emily Terhune.....................................Enid Markey
Charlie Foster...................................John Maroney
Cochrane.........................................Paul Porter
Fred Buker....................................William Bendix
Hermy Rogers..................................George Ewing, Jr.
    Act I.—Scene 1—Living Room of Wilkes Potter's Penthouse, New
York City. 2—Bedroom in the Potter Home, Parksburg, Illinois.
Act II.—Scene 1—Front Porch of Potter Home. 2—Sunset Inn,
Outskirts of Parksburg. 3—Corridor off Main Lobby of Hotel
Parksburg. Act III.—Wilkes Potter's Penthouse.
    Staged by Donald Blackwell; settings by John Root.

Wilkes Potter is a small-town boy who goes to the big city,
becomes a famous columnist, but never loses (in print) his sentimental belief in and longing for the old home town. After
twenty-five years he goes back home. The people give him a
reception. His high school class holds a reunion. The old grads
get tight and start a fight. Potter is completely disillusioned and
hops quickly back to New York, only to be followed by the
daughter of the girl he once was engaged to. She is a young
sophisticate and would like to become his mistress, but can't. He
already has one.

## * LEAVE IT TO ME

### (259 performances)

A musical comedy in two acts by Bella and Samuel Spewack;
music and lyrics by Cole Porter. Produced by Vinton Freedley
at the Imperial Theatre, New York, November 9, 1938.

Cast of characters—

First Secretary.....................................Ruth Bond
Second Secretary.................................Beverly Hosier
Buckley Joyce Thomas............................William Gaxton
First Reporter.....................................William Lilling
Second Reporter.................................Walter Monroe
Dolly Winslow.....................................Mary Martin
J. H. Brody....................................Edward H. Robins
Mrs. Goodhue....................................Sophie Tucker
⎧ April
⎪ Mildred Chenaval
Mrs. Goodhue's Daughters.................⎨ Ruth Daye
⎪ Audrey Palmer
⎩ Kay Picture
Reporter...........................................Chet Bree
Photographer...................................George E. Mack
French Conductor...............................Walter Armin

```
Chauffeur............................................James W. Carr
Alonzo P. Goodhue..................................Victor Moore
                                                   ┌ Gene Kelly
                                                   │ Maurice Kelly
Secretaries to Mr. Goodhue................ ┤         Roy Ross
                                                   │ Jack Seymour
                                                   │ Jack Stanton
                                                   └ Walter B. Long, Jr.
Prince Alexander Tomofsky.........................George Tobias
Jerry Granger.....................................Dean Carlton
Colette ...............................................Tamara
Kostya............................................Joseph Kallini
Peasant...........................................Peter Lopouhin
Sozanoff..........................................Alexander Asro
Military Attache...................................John Eliot
Naval Attache.....................................John Panter
                                                   ┌ Roy Ross
Secretaries....................................... ┤ Jack Seymour
                                                   ┌ Michael Forbes
Decorators........................................ ┤ Thomas Jafollo
Waiter.............................................Don Cortez
German Ambassador................................Hans Hansen
French Ambassador................................Walter Armin
Latvian Minister..................................Peter Lopouhin
British Ambassador...............................J. Colville Dunn
Italian Ambassador...............................Thomas Jafollo
Japanese Ambassador.............................George E. Mack
Mackenzie.........................................Charles Campbell
Graustein.........................................Eugene Sigaloff
Folkin.............................................Ivan Izmailov
Secretary.........................................Stanton Bier
Foreign Minister..................................Alexis Bolan
Stalin.............................................Walter Armin
```

The Buccaneers—Don Cortez, John Eliot, Michael Forbes, Eddie Heisler, Tom Jafolla, William Lilling, Walter Monroe, John Panter.

Act I.—Scene 1—City Room of the Paris and Chicago *World-Tribune.* 2—Gare de l'Est, Paris. 3—A Park in Moscow. 4—Anteroom in the American Embassy, Moscow. 5—Goodhue's Bedroom in the Embassy. 6—Thomas' Hotel Suite in Moscow. 7—The Balcony. 8—Red Square. Act II.—Scene 1—Red Square. 2—A Droshka. 3 and 6—Thomas' Room. 4—A steppe. 5—Drawing Room in the Embassy. 7—Railroad Station, Moscow.

Staged by Samuel Spewack; dances by Robert Alton; settings by Albert Johnson; costumes by Raoul Pene Du Bois.

Alonzo P. Goodhue, socially and politically the best horseshoe pitcher of Topeka, Kansas, is made ambassador to the Soviet republic, largely through the maneuverings of his ambitious wife. Alonzo doesn't want to be an ambassador any place except in Topeka, and conspires with a bright newspaper correspondent, Buckley Joyce Thomas, to get himself discredited and recalled. He kicks the Japanese ambassador in the belly. Cordell Hull likes that. He shoots at a Russian diplomat and hits a Trotskyite. That makes him a hero. At last he tries idealism and one good deed a day. That puts him in bad with everybody and he is recalled.

## WHERE DO WE GO FROM HERE?

(15 performances)

A comedy in three acts by William Bowers. Produced by Oscar Hammerstein and Dwight Taylor at the Vanderbilt Theatre, New York, November 15, 1938.

Cast of characters—

| | |
|---|---|
| Frank | James Fuller |
| Blackie | John Laird |
| Nels | Ralph Holmes |
| Rennie | Don DeFore |
| Jack Hanley | Michael Owen |
| Tex | Stanley Becker |
| Perc | Edmund Glover |
| Ken | Gilbert Fates |
| Jones | John James |
| Einie | Will Dean |
| Phil | Hugh Martin |
| Bill | James Truex |
| Ted Miller | Charles Mendick |
| Doc Saunders | George Carleton |
| Harry Harris | Theodore Leavitt |
| Bailiff | Richard S. Bishop |
| Butch | Ed. Sabol |
| Joe King | Paul Hammond |
| Carole Lester | Cathie Bailey |

Acts I, II and III.—Living Room of Fraternity House, Small Mid-Western College.

Staged by Anatol Winogradoff; setting by Hugh Willoughby.

The boys of the Alpha Tau fraternity are in a spot. An old grad is about to foreclose a $10,000 mortgage on them. This will mean that they will have to get out of the venerable ruin that has been home to them for at least a couple of years. They attempt to raise the $10,000 by an appeal to the alumni and are laughed at, by wire, collect, for their pains. In the end a Jewish brother from another fraternity shows them how they can forestall foreclosure and loans them the $700 interest money. Which goes to prove that brothers are brothers under the skin.

## GOOD HUNTING

(2 performances)

A satire in three acts by Nathanael West and Joseph Schrank. Produced by Jerome Mayer and Leonard Field at the Hudson Theatre, New York, November 21, 1938.

Cast of characters—

| | |
|---|---|
| William Lewis | Guy Spaull |
| Corporal Thompson | Dennis Gurney |
| Hank Russo | George Tobias |
| Courier | James Larmore |
| Lt. Colonel Jarvis, D. S. O. | Nicholas Joy |

```
Corporal Bowker...................................J. P. Wilson
Major Fitzsimmons, M. C. ..........................Ben Smith
Lieutenant Frenique...............................Marcel Journet
Captain Stuart Stewart, the Laird of Kilbrecht......Edward Harvey
Captain Ram Singh, the Nizam of Ladore.........John Barrington
2d Lieut. Gerald Forsyte.........................Derek Williams
Brigadier General Hargreaves.....................Aubrey Mather
Marie.........................................Susi Lanner
Grace Hargreaves...............................Estelle Winwood
Monsieur Jervais.................................LeRoi Operti
Major General Sir Arthur Reynolds, D. S. O.......Horace Sinclair
Lieutenant Max von Auster......................Jess Thomassen
Colonel von Shimmelpfenig......................George Brandt
Captain Ras Mahamoud.........................Tracy D. Rutledge
General Liebfrau...............................Alfred Kappeler
     Acts I, II and III.—Church of the Twenty Virgins, Millefleurs,
France.
     Staged by Jerome Mayer; setting by Norris Houghton.
```

Brigadier General Hargreaves, in command of a British division at the front, has a terrible time sleeping late because of the noise made by the guns. He orders the gunners to be more considerate. Neither does the General permit his staff to talk shop before breakfast. It is a nice, picnicky sort of war, as the Hargreaves division conducts it along the lines the General was taught at war college; the same attack every morning at the same hour. One day the attack is accidentally made at another hour and the troops go right on into German trenches. They get a bit too far, however, and the Germans close in back of them.

## RINGSIDE SEAT

### (7 performances)

A melodrama in three acts by Leonard Ide. Produced by Rufus Phillips at the Guild Theatre, New York, November 22, 1938.

Cast of characters—

```
Laundryman.......................................Casper Kuhn
A Deputy..........................................Pass Le Noir
Another Deputy..................................William Balfour
Sam Hodge........................................Leo Herbert
Hingham...........................................John Adair
Jenny.............................................Marion Sittler
A Young Man......................................Richard Abert
Hattie.............................................Lorene Scott
Tuttle.............................................Harry Young
Phillipson.........................................Frederic Clark
Siever.............................................G. Pat Collins
Dodd...............................................Dave Mallen
Mrs. Burton.......................................Louise Larabee
Haskell............................................Frank Rothe
Fitzgerald..........................................Harry Antrim
Mrs. Sturgis.......................................Lucia Seger
Mary Sturgis.......................................Mary Rolfe
Orrin Sturgis......................................Grant Mitchell
Feeny.............................................Garnay Wilson
Harold.............................................Haldor de Becker
His Mother........................................Jean Croix
```

```
Berg..............................................Sanford  Bickart
Mother Jones......................................Jacquelyn  Green
George  Winston.....................................Roy  Roberts
Hazelton.........................................Russell  Morrison
A  Socialite.........................................Roc  Galvann
```
Jurors, Socialites, Hotel Guests, Nurse, Interne, etc.
    Acts I, II and III.—Lobby of the Commercial House, in a small
town in New York State.
    Staged by Rufus Phillips; setting by Lawrence L. Goldwasser.

Orrin Sturgis is a murder trial fan.  Loading his family into a
trailer he travels from one sensational trial to another.  In an up-
state town in New York he runs into the Burton trial and a New
York mob of gangsters trying to keep important evidence from
the court and also to maneuver the conviction of an innocent man.
After the exposure and his big moment Orrin starts for another
trial, but his daughter Mary remains behind to marry George
Winston, a reporter.

## THE BOYS FROM SYRACUSE

### (235 performances)

A musical comedy in two acts based on Shakespeare's "The
Comedy of Errors," by George Abbott; lyrics by Lorenz Hart;
music by Richard Rodgers.  Produced by George Abbott at the
Alvin Theatre, New York, November 23, 1938.

Cast of characters—

```
Singing Policeman..................................Bob  Lawrence
Another Policeman..............................James  Wilkinson
Antipholus of Ephesus............................Ronald  Graham
Dromio of Ephesus...................................Teddy  Hart
Dancing Policeman...............................George  Church
Tailor.........................................Clifford  Dunstan
Tailor's Apprentice...................................Burl  Ives
Antipholus of Syracuse............................Eddie  Albert
Dromio of Syracuse.................................Jimmy  Savo
Merchant of Syracuse..............................Byron  Shores
Duke of  Ephesus.................................Carroll  Ashburn
Aegeon........................................John  O'Shaughnessy
Luce...............................................Wynn  Murray
Adriana.........................................Muriel  Angelus
Luciana..........................................Marcy  Wescott
Sorcerer...........................................Owen  Martin
Courtezan...........................................Betty  Bruce
Secretary to Courtezan...........................Heidi  Vosseler
Assistant  Courtezan...........................Dolores  Anderson
Angelo..............................................John  Clarke
1st Maid.........................................Florine  Callahan
2nd Maid...........................................Claire  Wolf
3rd Maid.............................................Alice  Craig
Merchant of Ephesus............................Clifford  Dunstan
Seeress............................................Florence  Fair
```
Singers: Grace Albert, Laura Kellogg, Dolores Anderson, Armonce
    Wilkins, Marguerite Benton, Margaret Walsh, James Wilkinson,
    Joseph Scandor, Joe Granville, Herbert Wood.
Dancers: Libby, Bennett, Ruth Brady, Renee Cettel, Stella Clausen,
    Alice Craig, Bee Farnum, Ruth Gormly, Claire Harvey, Lita
    Lede, Connie Leslie, Vivien Moore, Florine Callahan, Mildred

Solly, Anna Mae Tesslo, Davenie Watson, Betty De Elmo, Claire
Wolf, Micky Alvarez, Sidney Gordon, Dan Karry, Tommy
Lynch, Jack Malis, Edwin Mills, Harry Peterson, Joe Harris,
Lee Tannen, Beau Tilden, Robert Howard.
Harry Levant, Conductor of Orchestra.
Act I.—Scene 1—Before the Temple of Justice, Ephesus.  2 and
4—Inside the House of Antipholus.  3—A Square.  5—Outside the
House of Antipholus.  Act II.—Scene 1—Outside House of Antipho-
lus.  2 and 4—A Square.  3—Inside House of Antipholus.
Staged by George Abbott; settings by Jo Mielziner; costumes by
Irene Sharaff; choreography by George Balanchine.

The racy story of how the Antipholus of Syracuse, and his
Dromio, without knowing that their twin brothers, the Antipholus
and Dromio of Ephesus, existed, were dragged into performing
the marital obligations of the Ephesus twins before the doubles
were discovered.   Larded with modern tunes and Broadway ver-
nacular.

## ROCKET TO THE MOON

### (131 performances)

A drama in three acts by Clifford Odets.   Produced by The
Group Theatre at the Belasco Theatre, New York, November 24,
1938.

Cast of characters—
Ben Stark, D.D.S. .................................. Morris Carnovsky
Belle Stark. .......................................... Ruth Nelson
Cleo Singer. ......................................... Eleanor Lynn
Phil Cooper, D.D.S. ................................... Art Smith
Mr. Prince. .......................................... Luther Adler
Frenchy. ............................................ Leif Erickson
Willy Wax. ......................................... Sanford Meisner
A Salesman. ........................................ William Challee
Acts I, II and III.—Dr. Stark's Waiting Room.
Staged by Harold Clurman; setting by Mordecai Gorelik.

See page 110.

## GLORIANA

### (5 performances)

A comedy in three acts by Ferdinand Bruckner; music by
Thomas Jefferson Scott.   Produced by Theatre House, Inc., at the
Little Theatre, New York, November 25, 1938.

Cast of characters—
Elizabeth of England. ............................. Blanche Yurka
Essex. ............................................. Boyd Crawford
Cecil. .............................................. Sayre Crawley
Bacon. ............................................. Tom Powers
Mountjoy. .......................................... Leslie Denison
Southampton. ................................. Anthony Kemble Cooper
Lady Ann. .......................................... Alice John
Lady Mary. ......................................... Celeste Holm

Northumberland..................................Robert  Breen
A Tavern Wench...............................Nancy Cushman
A Tavern Singer...............................Francis Swann
Barmaid..........................................Marjorie  Tas
Plantagenet...................................Philip Faversham
Philip of Spain...............................Harold Vermilyea
Tajo...........................................George  Cotton
Isabella.............................................Betty  Young
The Cardinal..................................Ainsworth Arnold
Idiaquez........................................John  McKee
Pater Mariana............................Benedict McQuarrie
The Archbishop..............................Edwin Cushman
Ladies in Waiting—Helen Edwards, Beatrice Graham.
English Soldiers—Stephen Deere, Hugh Franklin, Eric Franson,
    Philip Merrick, John Norton, Royal Rompel, Frederick Ross,
    Randolph Wade.
Spanish Grandees—Conrad Cantzen, Arthur Davison, Joseph R.
    Mann, P. J. Rollow.
Spanish Soldiers—Kenneth Ferrel, Edward Stanbury.
    Act I.—Scenes 1 and 3—Elizabeth's Room in Whitehall. 2—Room
in Essex's House. Act II.—Scene 1—The Mermaid Inn. 2—Gar-
den at Whitehall. 3—The Escorial: King Philip's Room. Act III.—
Scenes 1 and 3—Elizabeth's Room. 2—On the left, St. Paul's Cathedral, London; on the right, the Spanish Basilica.
    Staged by Tom Powers; production manager, Garret H. Leverton;
settings by Harry Horner.

Elizabeth of England at 60 is playfully and a little ponderously
flirting with the Earl of Essex, in his early twenties. When Essex
sees Elizabeth without her flaming red wig, and is completely disillusioned, he is quick to join Mountjoy in an abortive attempt to
abduct the Queen and start a revolution. Failing, Essex is sent to
the Tower and Elizabeth turns to the war with Philip of Spain.
Her navy is victorious in crushing the Spanish armada and Elizabeth resumes her restless and unsatisfied life.

## GLORIOUS MORNING

### (9 performances)

A drama in three acts by Norman Macowan. Produced by
Oscar Hammerstein in association with Michael Hillman at the
Mansfield Theatre, New York, November 26, 1938.

Cast of characters—

Ann...............................................Vera  Allen
Katrina Hoefler..............................Margaret Randall
Woden...........................................John  Balmer
Anton Veerkind.....................................Lee Baker
Leda...............................................Jeanne  Dante
Professor Hans Skaedia..........................Winston O'Keefe
General Gurgani................................Frederic Tozere
Hansen...........................................Bruce  Evans
Rutzstein.....................................St. Clair Bayfield
Buloff.............................................Len  Mence
Duren........................................Donald  Campbell
Nekell...........................................Harry Mestayer
Jacob Kellner...................................Maurice  Wells
Ruth Kellner...................................Frances Nabors
First Soldier....................................Herschel Cropper
Second Soldier..................................Eugene Francis

An Officer...........................................Arling Alcine
    Act I.—A Room in Anton Veerkind's House, Burglitz, the Capital
of Burglitzia, a province of Zagnira. Act II.—Scene 1—A Room in
the Town Hall. 2 and 3—Anton Veerkind's Room. Act III.—Scene
1—Room in the Town Hall. 2—A Corridor in the Prison.
Staged by Oscar Hammerstein; settings by John Koenig.

Leda Veerkind, a young girl, hears voices telling her that for
her people to deny God at the insistence of the dictator who runs
the mythical government of Zagnira is a sin. Returning from
school with her message she strengthens the people's faith. After
seven years under a dictator over a hundred citizens, being called
to account, refuse to recant their Christian religion. They, with
Leda and her grandfather, Anton, are taken to the public square
and shot down with machine guns.

## SOLILOQUY

### (2 performances)

A drama in two acts by Victor Victor; music by Adrian Mack.
Produced by Henry Weissman at the Empire Theatre, New York,
November 28, 1938.

Cast of characters—

Jimmy's Thoughts ⎫
Jimmy Mimms      ⎬ ...................................John Beal
                 ⎭
Ella Mimms.......................................Ellen E. Lowe
Mrs. McCorkle....................................Daisy Belmore
Ann Jenkins.........................................Helen Craig
Eddie Page.....................................Alexander Lockwood
Sidney Tarleton....................................Gwyllyn Ford
Mr. Danvers.....................................Clarence Derwent
Lieutenant Simmons.............................John Rutherford
Medical Examiner...................................Robert Dolan
Mr. Braithwaite................................Edward Broadley
Stenographer........................................Paul Marion
Girl at Summer Resort............................Ruth Meredith
Miss La Rue.........................................Joan Blair
"Honey" Blake..............................George L. Spaulding
Reporter Johnson...............................George Reynolds
Miss McGill.............................Grace Virginia Howard
First Chorus Girl...............................Katherine York
Second Chorus Girl............................Helen Le Berthon
Turnkey.............................................Paul Marion
Al Graumann..........................................Jack Duval
Mr. Sloman.......................................Elmer Jerome
Jury Foreman........................................Louis Labey
Subway Passengers, Office Workers, Neighbors, Chorus Girls, Jurors,
    Photographers, etc.
    Act I.—Scenes 1, 5 and 7—Jimmy's Apartment, Large American
City. 2—Subway. 3 and 6—Office. 4—Ferris Wheel. 8 and 16—
D.A. Headquarters. 9—Street Corner. 10—Bench at Summer Re-
sort. 11—Chinese Restaurant. 12—Jimmy's Roadster. 13—Club
Rivoli. 14—Roulette Table. 15—Nightstroll. Act II.—Scene 1—
Mrs. McCorkle's Rocking Chair. 2—Roulette Table. 3—Chorus
Dressing Room. 4—Detention Cell. 5—Before a Jury. 6 and 8—
Street Corner. 7—Soliloquy.
    Staged by Eugene Schulz-Breiden; settings by Norman Rock.

Jimmy Mimms, unhappy bookkeeper, grows increasingly discouraged when Ella, his slatternly wife, tells him they are to have a child.  At the office he bets $2 on a long shot, wins $100 and takes the new file clerk, Ann Jenkins, to Coney.  Love follows.  Next day Jimmy cuts Ella's throat with a bread knife.  Thereafter he suffers conscience pains.  The District Attorney pretends to believe Ella committed suicide.  Jimmy, acquiring a small inheritance from Ella's relatives, leads a gay life and finally gives himself away.  The police pick him up and a jury sends him to the chair.  (During the performance Jimmy's unspoken thoughts are relayed to the audience by sound track effects.)

## LORELEI

### (7 performances)

A drama in three acts by Jacques Deval.  Produced by Richard Aldrich and Dennis King in association with Sir Cedric Hardwicke and Richard Myers at the Longacre Theatre, New York, November 29, 1938.

Cast of characters—

```
Robert.............................................Jack Merivale
Louise.............................................Murial Williams
Eric Rumpau........................................Philip Merivale
Minna Rumpau.......................................Viola Roache
Antoine............................................Larry Bolton
Simone.............................................Cobina Wright, Jr.
Renie..............................................Joan Tetzel
Ruprecht Eisenkranz................................Dennis Hoey
Dora Bennett.......................................Edna Holland
Samuel Kronberg....................................Bernard Lenow
Julia..............................................Elizabeth Heckscher
Karen Von Singall..................................Doris Nolan
Gendarme...........................................Charles Atkins
Priest.............................................A. G. Andrews
Conrad Von Ritterbach..............................Arnold Korff
Elsa Von Ritterbach................................Esther Mitchell
Colonel Mitthaufer.................................Boyd Davis
```
Act I.—Hotel Terrace, Longemer, French Summer Resort in the Vosges Mountains. Act II.—A Schoolroom. Act III.—Scene 1—The Terrace. 2—A Road.
Staged by Jacques Deval; settings by Lee Simonson.

Eric Rumpau, dean of the University of Leipsic, winner of the Nobel prize for scientific research, universally acclaimed as a world scientist, goes into voluntary exile across the French border in the hope of doing something to save the old Germany from the new.  He is proclaimed a traitor by the Nazi government and faces death should he return.  Karen Von Singall, a favorite pupil in Leipsic, follows Rumpau to his exile, hoping to lure him home.  Instead she falls desperately in love with him, overstays her time and finally is called home to save the life of a young man who is standing hostage for her.   Rumpau, distressed by the turn of events, walks across the border and gives himself up to the Nazis.

## GREAT LADY

### (20 performances)

A biography with music in two acts by Earle Crooker and Lowell Brentano; music by Frederick Loewe; orchestrations by Hans Spialek.   Produced by Dwight Deere Wiman and J. H. Del Bondio by arrangement with Frank Crumit at the Majestic Theatre, New York, December 1, 1938.

Cast of characters—

| | |
|---|---|
| Office Boy | Anthony Albert |
| Stenographer | Hortense Kahrklin |
| Stenographer | Charlotte Sumner |
| Office Boy | Fernando Alonso |
| Stenographer | Muriel Gratton |
| Stenographer | Joan Mann |
| Managing Editor | Edward Kane |
| Office Boy | Basil Galahoff |
| Bill Adams | Wm. Chambers |
| Sub-Editor | Frederick Schweppe |
| Eliza Bowen (Later Elsa de la Croix) | Norma Terris |
| Jailer | William Mende |
| Pierre de Moreau | Shepperd Strudwick |
| Rene Lorraine | Jules Epailly |
| Captain Jacques | Joseph Macaulay |
| Freelove Clark | Helen Ford |
| Nicky Clark | Edward Craven |
| Waitress | June Forrest |
| Floorwalker | Andre Eglevsky |
| Waiter | John Young |
| Stephen Jumel | Tullio Carminati |
| Madame Colette | Irene Bordoni |
| Prologue | Joseph Macaulay |
| Organ Grinder | William Mende |
| Poor Girl | Leda Anchutina |
| Rich Boy | Annabelle Lyon |
| 1st Admirer | Basil Galahoff |
| 2nd Admirer | Anthony Albert |
| 3rd Admirer | Russel Protopoff |
| Jonathan | Robert Shanley |
| Elizabeth Clark | Jeanne Elkins |
| Maid | Katherine Mayfield |
| A Doctor | William Fariss |
| A Minister | Frederick Schweppe |
| A Caretaker | John Young |
| Butler | Walter Cassel |
| First Assistant Dressmaker | Katherine Mayfield |
| Second Assistant Dressmaker | Beverly Kirk |
| Decazes | Gage Clarke |
| Major Domo | Walter Cassel |
| Marquise | Grace Panvini |
| A Duchess | Isabel Girard |
| A Countess | Doris Moore |
| Louis XVIII | Robert Greig |
| Housekeeper | Christine Johnson |
| Maid | Dorothy Kirsten |
| Premier Danseur | Andre Eglevsky |
| Premier Danseuses | Leda Anchutina, Annabelle Lyon |

Act I.—Scene 1—Offices of *Live* Magazine, New York, 1939. 2—The Stocks, Providence, R. I.  1793.  3—Clark's Ordinary, Providence. 4—Pierre's Room in Bordeaux. 5—Madame Colette's Dressmaking Shop. 6—Jumel's Suite, Paris Hotel. 7—John Street Theatre, New York, 1804. 8—A Carriage Ride. 9—Elsa's Boudoir, New York. Act II.—Scenes 1 and 5—Drawing Room, Jumel Mansion, 1939, 1814 and 1852. 2—Madame Colette's Dressmaking Shop. 3—Cabin Aboard the *Elsa*. 4—Room in Jumel House, Paris.

Staged by Bretaigne Windust; settings by Albert R. Johnson; choreography by William Dollar; costumes by Lucinda Ballard and Scott Wilson.

Eliza Bowen, a loose lady of Providence, R. I., follows Pierre Moreau to France. After he has left her she meets numerous other light-hearted gallants, but finally marries Stephen Jumel, merchant prince, with whom she comes to America. The Jumels buy a mansion on the Heights in New York and entertain lavishly, for all society tries to snub Mme. Jumel. She was a patroness of the Bonapartes and when she was 56 she married the then 78-year-old Aaron Burr.

## AMERICAN LANDSCAPE

### (43 performances)

A drama in three acts by Elmer Rice. Produced by The Playwrights' Company at the Cort Theatre, New York, December 3, 1938.

Cast of characters—

| | |
|---|---|
| Captain Anthony Dale | George Macready |
| Betty Kutno | Patricia Palmer |
| Frances Dale Spinner | Rachel Hartzell |
| Gerald Spinner | Donald Cook |
| Carlotta Dale | Phoebe Foster |
| William Fiske | Howard Miller |
| Captain Frank Dale | Charles Waldron |
| Constance Dale | Sylvia Weld |
| Joe Kutno | Theodore Newton |
| Captain Samuel Dale | Charles Dingle |
| Klaus Stillgebauer | Alfred A. Hesse |
| Moll Flanders | Isobel Elsom |
| Captain Heinrich Kleinschmidt | Con MacSunday |
| Harriet Beecher Stowe | Lillian Foster |
| Paul Kutno | Jules Bennett |
| Abby Kutno | Ethel Intropidi |
| Nils Karenson | Aage Steenshorne |
| Henri Dupont | Pierre d'Ennery |
| Patrick O'Brien | J. Hammond Dailey |
| Reverend Jasper Washington | Emory Richardson |
| Abraham Cohen | Philip Singer |

Acts I, II and III.—Living Room of the Dale House, near Dalesford, Connecticut.

Staged by Elmer Rice; setting by Aline Bernstein.

Captain Frank Dale of the Dales of Dalesford, Conn., is torn with temptation to sell out the shoe factory that has been in the Dale family for generations. Being 75, Captain Frank wants to spend his remaining years in Florida and in retirement. His sale intentions also include the Dale estate, which is to go to the representative of a German-American bund who is suspected of wanting to use it as a Nazi camp. Distressed by the possibilities, all the Dale descendants reason strenuously with the Captain and the ghosts of other family representatives return to earth to add the weight of their arguments to those of the living. Before he arrives at a decision Captain Frank dies of a stroke and the remaining Dales decide to hold on.

## HERE COME THE CLOWNS

### (88 performances)

A drama in three acts by Philip Barry. Produced by Eddie Dowling at the Booth Theatre, New York, December 7, 1938.

Cast of characters—

| | |
|---|---|
| Walter | James Hagan |
| Major Armstrong | Jerry Austin |
| John Dickinson | Russell Collins |
| Ma Speedy | Ralph Bunker |
| Connie Ryan | Madge Evans |
| Nora Clancy | Doris Dudley |
| Val Gurney | Bertram Thorn |
| Dan Clancy | Eddie Dowling |
| Jim Marble | Frank Gaby |
| Gert Marble | Hortense Alden |
| Max Pabst | Leo Chalzel |
| Freddie Ballantine | A. H. Van Buren |
| Lew Cooper | Thomas Palmer |
| Fay Farrel | Eve March |

Acts I, II and III.—The Back Room of Ma Speedy's Café des Artistes in an American City.

Staged by Robert Milton; setting by John Koenig.

See page 285.

## SPRING MEETING

### (98 performances)

A comedy in three acts by M. J. Farrell and John Perry. Produced by Gladys and Philip Merivale in association with Lee Ephraim and George Jessel at the Morosco Theatre, New York, December 8, 1938.

Cast of characters—

| | |
|---|---|
| Joan Furze | Shelah Richards |
| Baby Furze | Aideen O'Connor |
| James | James Woodburn |
| Bijou Furze | Jean Cadell |
| Michael Byrne | Denis Carey |
| Sir Richard Furze | A. E. Matthews |
| Johnny Mahoney | Arthur Shields |
| Tiny Fox-Collier | Gladys Cooper |
| Tony Fox-Collier | Robert Flemyng |

Acts I, II and III.—The Hall and Dining Room of "Woodrooff," County Tipperary, Ireland.

Staged by John Gielgud (production under direction of Lee Ephraim); setting by Roger K. Furse.

Sir Richard Furze is a tight-fisted, hard-riding country gentleman of Tipperary, Ireland. He will spend anything for the maintenance of his hunting stable, but money to keep the house warm and stocked with food has to be pried out of him. His two daughters, Joan and Baby, are eager to marry and get away from home. Baby boldly sets her cap for Tony Fox-Collier and Joan, getting the upper hand of her father through an inheritance, defiantly marries Michael Byrne, a groom in the stables. Mrs. Tiny Fox-Collier takes Sir Richard unto herself and promises to reform him.

## *OUTWARD BOUND

### (215 performances)

A drama in three acts by Sutton Vane. Revived by The Playhouse Company at the Playhouse, New York, December 22, 1938.

Cast of characters—

| | |
|---|---|
| Scrubby | Morgan Farley |
| Ann | Helen Chandler |
| Henry | Alexander Kirkland |
| Mr. Prior | Bramwell Fletcher |
| Mrs. Clivedon-Banks | Florence Reed |
| Rev. William Duke | Vincent Price |
| Mrs. Midgit | Laurette Taylor |
| Mr. Lingley | Louis Hector |
| Rev. Frank Thomson | Thomas Chalmers |

Act I.—In the Harbor.  Acts II and III.—At Sea.
Staged by Otto Preminger; setting by Watson Barratt.

Sutton Vane's story of the steamer load of released souls that were started on a voyage toward Heaven and Hell was first produced in January, 1924, and achieved a run of 144 performances. It has been done as a picture by Warner's and there have been numerous stock company revivals. The original cast included Alfred Lunt, Leslie Howard, Dudley Digges, Beryl Mercer, Margalo Gillmore, J. M. Kerrigan and Charlotte Granville.

## WINDOW SHOPPING

### (11 performances)

A comedy in three acts by Louis E. Shecter and Norman Clark. Produced by Thomas Kilpatrick at the Longacre Theatre, New York, December 23, 1938.

Cast of characters—

| | |
|---|---|
| Jack Garfield | Philip Huston |
| Secretary | Patricia Rice |
| Janet Dixon | Ruth Lee |
| Ned Korn | Richard Taber |
| Mr. Talbot | George Spaulding |
| Miss Miller | Jean Mann |
| Mr. Frisby | Mortimer Weldon |
| Miss Doolittle | Alice Fleming |
| Mrs. Snodgrass | Ruth Conley |
| Mr. Simpson | Franklyn George |
| Trudy Huber | Gerta Rozan |
| Nurse | Marjorie Blair |
| Herman Garfield | George Sidney |
| Photographer | George Spelvin |
| Molly Moran | Ann Thomas |
| Penelope | Edith Leslie |
| Inspector Kennedy | W. J. Hackett |
| Matson | Solly Ward |
| Walsh | Philip Sheridan |
| McGinty | Tony Lord |
| Mrs. Stansbury | Ethel Strickland |
| Judge Polk | Donald MacKenzie |

Act I.—Scene 1—Office of Herman Garfield. 2—Hospital Room.
Act II.—Scenes 1 and 3—Store Window. 2—Garfield's Office.
Act III.—Scene 1—The Office. 2—The Window.
Staged by Arthur Sircom; settings by Tom Adrian Cracraft.

While Herman Garfield, proprietor of Garfield's Department Store, is in the hospital his progressive son adopts a lot of modern methods of attracting trade. One of them is to engage Trudy Huber, Viennese actress, to live in one of the store windows for two weeks, doing a strip-tease at night and a dress-tease in the morning to attract the crowds. Herman agrees to the stunt, though doubtfully, and a series of complications, involving union trouble, ensue. The stunt is finally abandoned and young Garfield marries Trudy to prevent the immigration authorities sending her back where she sailed for.

## BLOSSOM TIME

### (19 performances)

An operetta in three acts adapted from the original of A. M. Willner and H. Reichert by Dorothy Donnelly; music by Franz Schubert, adapted by Sigmund Romberg. Revived by the Messrs. Shubert at the 46th Street Theatre, New York, December 26, 1938.

Cast of characters—

| | |
|---|---|
| Kuppelweiser | Neville Landor |
| Vogel | Allen Raymond |
| Flower Girl | Betti Davis |
| Von Schwindt | Joseph Toner |
| Bellabruna | Charlotte Lansing |
| Count Sharntoff | Wheeler Dryden |
| Schubert | Everett Marshall |
| Mitzi | Mary McCoy |

```
Fritzi..............................................Marjorie Ford
Kitzi...............................................Gracie Worth
Erkman.........................................Ernest Goodhart
Binder...........................................Burt Raeburn
Domeyer...........................................John Wheeler
Kranz...........................................Douglas Leavitt
Schober.............................................Roy Cropper
Rosi..............................................Virginia Vonne
Mrs. Kranz.......................................Zella Russell
Emmy.............................................Alyce Chapelle
Novotney........................................Harry K. Morton
Mrs. Coburg.....................................Ruth Lockwood
Danseuse..........................................Alyce Chapelle
```
Act I.—Domeyer's Prater in Vienna. Twilight in May, 1826. Act II.—Drawing Room in the House of Kranz. Act III.—Franz Schubert's Lodgings.

Staged by Edward Scanlon; settings by Watson Barratt.

"Blossom Time" was first produced in New York at the Ambassador Theatre, September 29, 1921, with Howard Marsh, Olga Cook, William Danforth and Roy Cropper singing the leading roles. It was revived in 1924, 1926, and 1931.

## BRIGHT REBEL

### (7 performances)

A drama in three acts by Stanley Young. Produced by William Kilcullen at the Lyceum Theatre, New York, December 27, 1938.

Cast of characters—

```
Harrington.......................................Francis Swann
Peachey........................................Mary McCormack
Fletcher..........................................Robert Vivian
Mrs. Byron......................................Jeanne Caselle
Tom Moore.....................................James MacGuire
John Cam Hobhouse............................Maurice Manson
Scrope Davies....................................Michael Wills
Lord Byron.......................................John Cromwell
Annabelle Milbanke...........................Francesca Bruning
Lady Caroline Lamb............................Janice Hanford
Lord Melbourne.................................Lewis L. Russell
Lady Melbourne.................................Beatrice Terry
Lady Oxford......................................Helena Glenn
Lady Jersey.........................................Dana Dale
Jarvis..........................................Richard Aherne
Nicholas Kondylis................................Daniel Krewe
Augusta Leigh.......................................Ann Loring
Mrs. Minns....................................Marie de Becker
Dr. Lee Mann...................................Henry Vincent
Dr. Millengen....................................Francis Swann
Colonel Stanhope..............................Richard Aherne
```
Act I.—Scene 1—Newstead Abbey, 1809. 2—Melbourne House, London, 1812. 3—Byron's Rooms, London. Act II.—Scene 1—Melbourne House. 2—Byron's Rooms, 1816. Act III.—Scene 1—Byron's Rooms. 2—Byron's Military Headquarters, Missolonghi, Greece, 1824.

Staged by William Kilcullen; settings by Yellenti; costumes by Lucielle Samuels.

Lord Byron as a young man celebrates with his friends the publication of his first book of poems. He is rebellious and greatly disliked by his mother. He is sensitive and made miserable by the physical infirmity of his lameness. He gains the enmity of the women who pursue him and the politicians who accuse him of deserting his class when he turns to the defense of the weavers of Nottingham. He marries Annabelle Milbanke, whom he does not love, because Lady Melbourne, his friend, believes the experience will help in the development of his character. He is miserably unhappy as a result, the victim of malicious gossip because of his fondness for his half sister, Augusta Leigh. He flies to Greece in disgust and dies of a fever while fighting the Turks.

## MICHAEL DROPS IN

### (8 performances)

A comedy in three acts by William Du Bois. Produced by Marie Louise Elkins and Edward Massey at the Golden Theatre, New York, December 27, 1938.

Cast of characters—

| | |
|---|---|
| Irene Lawrence | Miriam Jordan |
| Michael Dwyer | Onslow Stevens |
| Timmie Lawrence | G. Albert Smith |
| Judy Morton | Arlene Francis |
| Frank McNeil | Edmund Dorsay |
| Hattie | Gee Gee James |
| Philip Adams | James Todd |
| Nan McNeil | Lee Patrick |

Acts I, II and III.—The Lawrences' Apartment, New York City. Staged by Edward Massey; setting by Eleanor Farrington.

Judy Morton of Idaho has written a book and spends all her money coming to New York in search of a publisher. She rents the furnished penthouse apartment of a friend. Michael Dwyer, publisher, lives in the apartment above and is in the habit of dropping down by rope ladder on the lady who rented Judy the apartment. Not knowing of the new tenant, he drops in on Judy. Judy is pretty scared, but becomes accustomed to the change. Before the evening is over both she and the publisher are honestly in love.

## DON'T THROW GLASS HOUSES

### (15 performances)

A comedy in three acts by Doris Frankel. Produced by Contemporary Stage at the Vanderbilt Theatre, New York, December 27, 1938.

Cast of characters—

```
Chet Smith..........................................John Raby
Nita Marx.......................................Margaret Randall
Burke Morgan.......................................Jack Yule
Meat Man..........................................Louis Latzer
Murray Tserk....................................Hayden Rorke
Jean Wilson....................................Joan MacCarthy
Mrs. Wilson Pratt Honifeather....................Rosalind Ivan
    Acts I, II and III.—Living Room of Farm House in Upper New
York.
    Staged by Leo Bulgakov; setting by Louis Kennel.
```

Chet Smith, Nita Marx and Burke Morgan are the editors of
a Communist magazine.  Mrs. Wilson Pratt Honifeather, Jean
Wilson and Murray Tserk represent the tiresome rich.  The rich
are deposited at the door of the Communists by a motor car
accident.  For three acts the two forces play upon each other,
the Communists trying to wangle supper money, the rich trying
to keep it.  Nothing much happens.

## THE MERCHANT OF YONKERS

### (39 performances)

A farce in three acts by Thornton Wilder, based on a comedy
by Johann Nestroy which was taken from an English original.
Produced by Herman Shumlin at the Guild Theatre, New York,
December 28, 1938.

Cast of characters—

```
Horace Vandergelder.............................Percy Waram
Ambrose Kemper..............................Bartlett Robinson
Joe Scanlon.....................................Philip Coolidge
Gertrude.........................................Carrie Weller
Cornelius Hackl...................................Tom Ewell
Ermengarde.....................................Frances Harison
Melchior Stack.................................Joseph Sweeney
Mrs. Levi...........................................Jane Cowl
Barnaby Tucker......................................John Call
Mrs. Molloy.......................................June Walker
Minnie Fay.....................................Nydia Westman
A Cabman..................................Edward F. Nannary
Rudolph...........................................Max Willenz
August............................................Peter Struwel
A Cook............................................Maida Reade
Miss Van Huysen.................................Minna Phillips
    Act I.—Vandergelder's House in Yonkers, N. Y.  Act II.—Mrs.
Molloy's Hat Store, New York.  Act III.—The Marmonia Gardens
Restaurant on the Battery.  Act IV.—Miss Van Huysen's House.
    Staged by Max Reinhardt; settings by Boris Aronson.
```

Mrs. Levi is a bright Irish widow who undertakes to arrange
the affairs of Horace Vandergelder, a merchant of Yonkers, who
is very close with his money, frankly vain and slightly lecherous
at 65.  Horace thinks he would like to marry Mrs. Molloy, a
New York milliner.  Mrs. Levi arranges a meeting.  Two of

the merchant's employers go to New York on a toot. All six meet by accident in the same gay restaurant. There are exposures and revealments. In the end Mrs. Levi gets the merchant herself.

## EVERYWHERE I ROAM

### (13 performances)

A play in three acts by Arnold Sundgaard and Marc Connelly. Produced by Marc Connelly and Bela Blau at the National Theatre, New York, December 29, 1938.

Cast of characters—

| | |
|---|---|
| Schoolmistress | Vera Deane |
| Jeremy | Royce Blackburn |
| Samuel | Ormond Lydon |
| Prudence | May Grimes |
| Pupils | Dorothy Littlejohn, Kathleen Slagle, Frank Westbrook |
| The Man | Dean Jagger |
| The Wife | Katherine Emery |
| Johnny Appleseed | Norman Lloyd |
| Clinton | Robert Collins |
| Barrel Rollers | Phil Brown, William Howell, William Matons, Frank Maxwell, Robert Breen |
| Jim | Paul Huber |
| Lady | Joan Wetmore |
| Gentleman | Erik Walz |
| Little Boy | Royce Blackburn |
| Buttermilk Man | Robert H. Harvey |
| Sandman | Charles S. Clarke |
| Jay | Arthur Barnett |
| Little Man | Frank Westbrook |
| Newsboys | James F. Burrell, Phil Brown, William Howell, William Matons, Frank Maxwell, Robert Breen |
| Direct Action Man | Frank Maxwell |
| Mayor | Earl Weatherford |
| Martyrs | Robert Breen, Frank Maxwell, Frank Westbrook, Phil Brown, William Howell, James Burrell, Peggy Anne Holmes |
| Cyrus McCormick | Robert Porterfield |
| Joseph | Robert H. Harvey |
| Pete | Tony Kraber |
| Jacob | Bill Benner |
| Map | Kathleen Slagle |
| Swedish Girl | Kalita Humphreys |
| Swedish Boy | Richard Bortin |
| Norwegian Girl | Hannah Lee Childs |
| Norwegian Boy | Judson Best Hall |
| Danish Girl | Camilla Hull |
| Danish Boy | John Dickens |
| Train Announcer | Meredith Johnston |
| Train Guards | Charles S. Clarke, Jon Urban, Robert Collins |
| Merchant | Earl Weatherford |
| First Celebrator | Robert Breen |
| Second Celebrator | James G. Burrell |
| Third Celebrator | Dorothy Johnson |
| Fourth Celebrator | Anne Francis |
| Jim Jr. | Fred Lawrence |
| Jay Jr. | Jay Owen, Jr. |
| Joe Jr. | John A. Kennedy |
| Travel Agent | Earl Weatherford |
| Accountant | Robert Collins |
| Gloria | Camilla Hull |
| Perry | Judson Best Hall |

```
Decorator.........................................William Howell
Lecturer...........................................Joan Wetmore
Nurse.............................................Annamary Dickey
Doctor............................................Earl Weatherford
Lawyers.........Laurence Siegle, Charles S. Clarke, John Dickens,
                                                  James G. Burrell
Senators..........................................⎰  Erik Walz
                                                  ⎱  Robert Breen
Process Server....................................Frank Maxwell
```

Act I.—Scene 1—Schoolroom, 1833. 2, 5 and 7—The Prairie. 3 and 4—Varick Street, New York, 1838. 6—Virginia. Act II.—Scenes 1 and 4—The Prairie. 2—Scandinavia. 3—Depot, St. Paul. 5—New York, Christmas, 1926. 6—At a Mailbox. 7—New York, New Year's Eve, 1927. Act III.—Scene 1—Travel Agency and Business Office. 2—The Farm. 3 and 7—The Wife's Room. 4 and 8—The Man's Room. 5—Lecture Hall. 6—The Club. 9—The Picnic. 10—The Storm. 11—In front of the Capitol, Washington. 12—Marching to New York. 13—A Graveyard. 14—Home of the Man and Wife. 15—The Prairie.

Staged by Marc Connelly; settings and costumes by Robert Edmond Jones; choral arrangements and direction by Lehman Engel; dances by Felicia Sorel.

The Man and the Wife, born to the soil, go West and make their home. Johnny Appleseed comes along to cheer them. The wheat grows and the apples grow. Comes the mechanical reaper and the Man and the Wife and all their neighbors rejoice. Now they have more time to play. Come the railroads, and the booms, and the Man and the Wife buy stocks and prosper. Come selfishness and greed and high living. Comes the crash, and the Man and the Wife go back to the land and plant more wheat and more apple trees.

## MAMBA'S DAUGHTERS

### (162 performances)

A drama in prologue and two acts by Dorothy and DuBose Heyward, dramatized from novel of same name by DuBose Heyward. Produced by Guthrie McClintic at the Empire Theatre, New York, January 3, 1939.

Cast of characters—

```
Mamba (Hagar's Mother).......................Georgette Harvey
Gardenia.........................................Anne Brown
Tony.............................................Jimmy Wright
Jane.............................................Maud Russell
Tessie...........................................Dorothy Paul
Slim..........................................Reginald Beane
Policeman........................................Bob Coogan
Another Policeman...............................John Rustad
Clerk of the Court..............................John Cornell
The Prosecuting Attorney.......................Oliver Barbour
St. Julien DeC. Wentworth (Saint)................Jose Ferrer
The Judge......................................Harry Mestayer
Hagar...........................................Ethel Waters
Davey............................................Al Stokes
Ned............................................Hayes Pryor
Mingo...........................................Louis Sharp
```

Drayton..................................................Canada Lee
Maum Vina (The Island Matriarch)................Ethel Purnello
Eva................................................Georgia Burke
Willie May.........................................Helen Dowdy
The Reverend Quintus Whaley...............J. Rosamond Johnson
Gilly Bluton.......................................Willie Bryant
Dolly.............................................Alberta Hunter
Lissa (as a Child).................................Joyce Miller
Martha........................................Rena Mitchell
Lissa.........................................Fredi Washington
Charleston Courtroom Visitors and Ediwander Island Field Hands,
    Church Members: Edna Beane, Altunar Branan, Inez Branan,
    Doris Champion, Rebecca Champion, Mary Holmes, Ella Mae
    Lashley, Assotta Marshall, Fredi Marshall, Henry May, Arthur
    McLean, Robert Raines, Edna Waters, Bradley Wilson.
    Prologue.—Mamba's Room in a Tenement on the Charleston, S. C.,
Waterfront.    Act I.—Scene 1—The Courtroom, Charleston. 2—The
Commissary of Brick House Plantation, Ediwander Island. 3—The
Church. 4—Mamba's Room, Charleston.   Act II.—Scenes 1, 3 and
5—The Commissary. 2 and 4—Gilly's Cabin, Ediwander Island.
    Staged by Guthrie McClintic; settings by Perry Watkins.   Song,
"Lonesome Walls," by Jerome Kern.

Hagar, a rangy colored woman down Charleston way, is haled
to court charged with attempted murder. She explains dumbly
that she had only tried to collect a $2 laundry bill from a cheater
who tried to sail away and leave her on a wharf. She had pulled
him ashore with her hands around his throat. Hagar's sentence
of five years in jail is suspended so long as she stays out of town.
She works dutifully for four years on a plantation, sending her
money to Mamba, her mother, for the support of an illegitimate
child. Then she does a good deed by taking a wounded gambler
to a hospital and is picked up by the police and jailed. Out of
jail she learns the gambler she befriended has attacked her
daughter. After Hagar attends to killing the gambler she shoots
herself.

## THE PRIMROSE PATH

### (166 performances)

A comedy in three acts by Robert Buckner and Walter Hart.
Produced by George Abbott at the Biltmore Theatre, New York,
January 4, 1939.

#### Cast of characters—

Eva Wallace....................................Marilyn Erskine
Grandma.......................................Helen Westley
Homer Wallace....................................Philip Wood
Davy Wallace....................................Leslie Barrett
Clare Wallace........................................Betty Field
Maggie Wallace.................................Florida Friebus
Emma Wallace....................................Betty Garde
Bayard Lawrence................................Russell Hardie
Augustus Cummings................................Clyde Fillmore
A Police Matron....................................Teresa Dale
    Act I.—Scenes 1 and 3—The Shanty in a Small Town Near
Buffalo. 2—A Boat House.  Act II.—Scenes 1 and 3—The Shanty.
2—Room in the Canandaigua Hotel in Buffalo.  Act III.—Scenes
1 and 3—The Shanty. 2—A Jail.

Staged by George Abbott; settings by Cirker and Robbins. Costumes by Helene Pons.

The Wallaces are a family living in Erie County, New York, hard by Buffalo. Grandma Wallace, the matriarch of the tribe, was a gay lady in her day and proud of it. Emma, her daughter, is continuing the family tradition, meeting her gentlemen friends in Buffalo and generously bringing home bacon and presents to her three daughters, a son and an incapacitated husband—a Harvard man who turned to Aristophanes and gin after leaving college. The second generation Wallace daughters, Clare and Maggie, become somewhat conventionalized. Clare accepts marriage with a noble smuggler and Maggie insists on a legal ceremony with another fellow. But Eva, 12, representing the fourth generation, is starting cheerfully toward the primrose path of dalliance at the play's end.

## THE GENTLE PEOPLE

### (141 performances)

A drama in three acts by Irwin Shaw. Produced by The Group Theatre at the Belasco Theatre, New York, January 5, 1939.

Cast of characters—

| | |
|---|---|
| Jonah Goodman | Sam Jaffe |
| Philip Anagnos | Roman Bohnen |
| Harold Goff | Franchot Tone |
| Magruder | Karl Malden |
| Stella Goodman | Sylvia Sidney |
| Eli Lieber | Elia Kazan |
| Florence Goodman | Lulla David |
| Angelina Esposito | Katherine Allen |
| Judge | Grover Burgess |
| Clerk | George Skelton |
| Lammanawitz | Lee J. Cobb |
| Polack | Martin Ritt |
| Flaherty | Harry Bratsburg |

Act I—Scenes 1 and 3—Steeplechase Pier, Coney Island. 2 and 4—Living Room of Goodman House. Act II.—Scenes 1 and 3—The Pier. 2—Night Court. 4—Steam Room of Russian Bath. Act III.—Scenes 1 and 3—The Pier. 2—Out in the Bay.

Staged by Harold Clurman; settings by Boris Aronson.

Jonah Goodman, Jewish, and Philip Anagnos, Greek, are two old pals who fish off Steeplechase pier in lower New York bay. Along comes Harold Goff, Brooklyn racketeer, and charges them $5 a week for protection. Goff also would seduce Stella, the daughter of Jonah, and when he learns that the old men have saved $190 toward a new boat he takes that, too. Jonah and Philip decide that they can have no peace until Goff is put away.

They take him out in the boat, knock him on the head and toss him over. When they recover his wallet they find their savings plus an additional $400.

## D'OYLY CARTE OPERA COMPANY

### (77 performances)

Presenting a repertory of Gilbert and Sullivan operettas at the Martin Beck Theatre, New York, beginning January 5, 1939. Musical Director, Isadore Godfrey.

## TRIAL BY JURY

Cast of characters—

| | |
|---|---|
| The Learned Judge | William Sumner |
| Counsel for the Plaintiff | Leslie Rands |
| The Defendant | Leonard Osborn |
| Foreman of the Jury | T. Penry Hughes |
| Usher | Richard Walker |
| Associate | C. William Morgan |
| The Plaintiff | Margery Abbott |
| First Bridesmaid | Maysie Dean |

Scene—A Court of Justice.

### FOLLOWED BY

## THE PIRATES OF PENZANCE

*or*, THE SLAVE OF DUTY

Cast of characters—

| | |
|---|---|
| Major-General Stanley | Martyn Green |
| The Pirate King | Darrell Fancourt |
| Samuel | Richard Walker |
| Frederic | John Dean |
| Sergeant of Police | Sydney Granville |
| Mabel | Helen Roberts |
| Edith | Marjorie Eyre |
| Kate | Ivy Sanders |
| Isabel | Maysie Dean |
| Ruth | Evelyn Gardiner |

Act I.—A Rocky Seashore on the Coast of Cornwall. Act II.—A Ruined Chapel, by Moonlight.

## THE MIKADO

Cast of characters—

| | |
|---|---|
| The Mikado of Japan | Darrell Fancourt |
| Nanki-Poo | John Dudley |
| Ko-Ko | Martyn Green |
| Pooh-Bah | Sydney Granville |
| Pish-Tush | Leslie Rands |
| Go-To | Radley Flynn |
| Yum-Yum | Viola Wilson |
| Pitti-Sing | Marjorie Eyre |
| Peep-Bo | Maysie Dean |

Katisha...............................................Evelyn Gardiner
    Act I.—Courtyard of Ko-Ko's Official Residence.   Act II.—Ko-Ko's Garden.

# IOLANTHE
## *or*, THE PEER AND THE PERI

Cast of characters—

The Lord Chancellor............................Martyn Green
Earl of Mountararat............................Darrell Fancourt
Earl Tolloller......................................John Dean
Private Willis.....................................Sydney Granville
Strephon.........................................Leslie Rands
Queen of the Fairies.............................Evelyn Gardiner
Iolanthe..........................................Marjorie Eyre
Celia.............................................Margery Abbott
Leila.............................................Ivy Sanders
Fleta.............................................Maysie Dean
Phyllis { ........................................Helen Roberts
         { ........................................Viola Wilson
    Act I.—An Arcadian Landscape.   Act II.—Palace Yard, Westminster.

# COX AND BOX

Cast of characters—

Cox.............................................William Sumner
Box.............................................John Dean
Bouncer.........................................Richard Walker
    Scene—A Room in Bouncer's House.

### FOLLOWED BY

# H.M.S. PINAFORE
## *or*, THE LASS THAT LOVED A SAILOR

Cast of characters—

The Rt. Hon. Sir Joseph Porter, K.C.B.............Martyn Green
Captain Corcoran.................................Leslie Rands
Ralph Rackstraw.................................John Dudley
Dick Deadeye....................................Darrell Fancourt
Bill Bobstay.....................................Richard Walker
Bob Becket......................................Radley Flynn
Josephine........................................Helen Roberts
Hebe............................................Marjorie Eyre
Little Buttercup..................................Evelyn Gardiner
    Acts I and II.—Quarter-Deck of *H.M.S. Pinafore* (off Portsmouth).

# THE GONDOLIERS
## *or*, THE KING OF BARATARIA

Cast of characters—

The Duke of Plaza-Toro..........................Martyn Green
Luiz.............................................Richard Dunn
Don Alhambra Del Bolero.........................Sydney Granville
Marco Palmieri...................................John Dudley

Giuseppe Palmieri...................................Leslie Rands
Antonio...........................................William Sumner
Francesco........................................Leonard Osborn
Giorgio...........................................Radley Flynn
Annibale.......................................T. Penry Hughes
The Duchess of Plaza-Toro.......................Evelyn Gardiner
Casilda...........................................Margery Abbott
Gianetta.......................................⎰ Helen Roberts
                                               ⎱ Viola Wilson
Tessa.............................................Marjorie Eyre
Fiametta.........................................Marjorie Flinn
Vittoria............................................Ivy Sanders
Giulia............................................Maysie Dean
Inez..............................................Ella Halman
Scene—Venice. Pavilion in the Palace of Barataria.

## THE YEOMAN OF THE GUARD

*or*, THE MERRYMAN AND HIS MAID

### Cast of characters—

Sir Richard Cholmondeley..........................Leslie Rands
Colonel Fairfax.......................................John Dean
Sergeant Meryll................................Darrell Fancourt
Leonard Meryll.....................................Tom Hancock
Jack Point.........................................Martyn Green
Wilfred Shadbolt...............................Sydney Granville
First Yeoman....................................Leonard Osborn
Second Yeoman......................................Mansel Dyer
First Citizen..............................C. William Morgan
Second Citizen...................................William Sumner
Elsie Maynard....................................Helen Roberts
Phoebe Meryll.....................................Marjorie Eyre
Dame Carruthers................................Evelyn Gardiner
Kate.............................................Margery Abbott
Acts I and II.—Tower Green.

## PATIENCE

*or*, BUNTHORNE'S BRIDE

### Cast of characters—

Colonel Calverley.............................Darrell Fancourt
Major Murgatroyd................................William Sumner
Lieut. the Duke of Dunstable........................John Dean
Reginald Bunthorne...............................Martyn Green
Archibald Grosvenor...............................Leslie Rands
Mr. Bunthorne's Solicitor...........................Wynn Dyson
The Lady Angela..................................Marjorie Eyre
The Lady Saphir.....................................Ivy Sanders
The Lady Ella...................................Margery Abbott
The Lady Jane..................................Evelyn Gardiner
Patience (a Dairy Maid)............................Viola Wilson
Act I.—Exterior of Bunthorne Castle. Act II.—A Glade.

## THE WHITE STEED

### (136 performances)

A drama in three acts by Paul Vincent Carroll. Produced by
Eddie Dowling at the Cort Theatre, New York, January 10, 1939.

Cast of characters—

| | |
|---|---|
| Canon Matt Lavelle | Barry Fitzgerald |
| Rosieanne | Leslie Bingham |
| Father Shaughnessy | George Coulouris |
| Phelim Fintry | Ralph Cullinan |
| Nora Fintry | Jessica Tandy |
| Donnacaidh McGoilla Phadraig | Roland Bottomley |
| Patrick Hearty | Farrell Pelly |
| Sarah Hearty | Grace Mills |
| Brigid Brodigan | Elizabeth Malone |
| Denis Dillon | Liam Redmond |
| Inspector Toomey | Thomas P. Dillon |
| Meg Magee | Florence Barrett |
| Michael Shivers | Tom Tully |

Acts I and III.—Canon Matt Lavelle's Parochial House in the Seaside Village of Lorcan, County Louth, Ireland. Act II.—Phelim Fintry's Cottage.

Staged by Hugh Hunt; settings by Watson Barratt.

See page 249.

## DEAR OCTOPUS

### (53 performances)

A comedy in three acts by Dodie Smith. Produced by John C. Wilson at the Broadhurst Theatre, New York, January 11, 1939.

Cast of characters—

| | |
|---|---|
| Charles Randolph | Reginald Mason |
| Dora Randolph | Lucile Watson |
| Hilda Randolph | Phyllis Joyce |
| Margery Harvey | Phyllis Povah |
| Cynthia Randolph | Rose Hobart |
| Nicholas Randolph | Jack Hawkins |
| Hugh Randolph | Peter Robinson |
| Gwen (Flouncey) Harvey | Shirley Poirier |
| William (Bill) Harvey | Warren Mills |
| Kathleen (Scrap) Kenton | Helen Renee |
| Edna Randolph | Ivy Troutman |
| Kenneth Harvey | Robert Craven |
| Laurel Randolph | Naomi Campbell |
| Belle Schlessinger | Margaret Dale |
| Grace Fenning (Fenny) | Lillian Gish |
| Nanny | Alice Belmore Cliffe |
| Gertrude | Georgia Harvey |

Act I.—The Hall, Randolph's Country House in North Essex, During Week-End in Late Autumn. Act II.—The Nursery. Act III.—The Dining Room.

Staged by Glen Byam Shaw; settings by G. E. Calthrop.

The Randolphs have gathered at the old homestead in North Essex to celebrate the parent Randolphs' golden wedding. During the celebration Nicholas, the unmarried son, discovers that he has loved Fenny, his mother's docile companion, for many years and didn't know it. Fenny is thrilled. Mother Randolph also discovers that Cynthia, who has not been home for seven years, has been living in sin in Paris with a married man whose wife would not divorce him. Now he has gone back to the wife and Cynthia agrees to stay home for awhile.

## THE IMPORTANCE OF BEING EARNEST

### (61 performances)

A comedy in three acts by Oscar Wilde. Revived by Richard Aldrich and Richard Myers at the Vanderbilt Theatre, New York, January 12, 1939.

Cast of characters—

Lane...............................................Guy Spaull
Algernon Moncrieff...............................Derek Williams
John Worthing, J. P...............................Clifton Webb
Lady Bracknell....................................Estelle Winwood
Hon. Gwendolyn Fairfax.........................Helen Trenholme
Miss Prism........................................Hope Williams
Cecily Cardew.....................................Florence McGee
Rev. Canon Chasuble, D.D......................Ainsworth Arnold
Merriman..........................................A. G. Andrews
　　Act I.—Algernon Moncrieff's Flat in Half Moon Street, London,
W. Act II.—The Garden at the Manor House, Woolton. Act III.—
Drawing-Room of the Manor House, Woolton.
　　Staged by Estelle Winwood; settings by Watson Barratt.

Played first in New York in 1895, "The Importance of Being Earnest," Wilde's story of the thoughtful young man who invented a sick friend on whom to blame his own peccadillos, was revived in 1910 with Hamilton Revelle, A. E. Matthews and Jane Oaker in the cast. It was done again in 1926 with Reginald Owen, Vernon Steele and Lucille Watson. A year later it was made into a musical comedy called "Oh, Ernest," Hal Ford and Dorothy Dilley being featured.

## WHERE THERE'S A WILL

### (7 performances)

A comedy in three acts adapted by Edward Stirling from a French play by Sacha Guitry. Produced by Edward Stirling at the Golden Theatre, New York, January 17, 1939.

Cast of characters—

Jean Marcelin....................................Edward Stirling
A Butler..........................................A. P. Kaye
Mademoiselle Morot...............................Anita Bolster
Lucie Marcelin....................................Jessie Royce Landis
Juliette Lecourtois...............................Frances Reid
Fernand Worms....................................Donald Baker
Marguerite Worms...............................Margaret Irving
Adrien Worms.....................................Clifford Brooke
　　Acts I, II and III.—The Study of Doctor Marcelin in Paris.
　　Staged by Edward Stirling; setting by Albert A. Ostrander.

Dr. Jean Marcelin, suspicious of his wife, draws up his last will and testament in which he reveals not only these suspicions but also his own past.  The will, left in a coat, is returned to the Marcelin home by a tailor.  Madame Marcelin reads the will, thinks her husband has killed himself and is preparing to take steps when M. Marcelin returns to confuse the situation.  The Marcelins now face each other knowing that the husband's former mistress is now his wife's best friend, and that the son of this mistress is now his wife's lover.  To give the situation a chance to clear Dr. Marcelin goes on a trip with his secretary, who turns out to be his own illegitimate daughter.

## SET TO MUSIC

### (129 performances)

A revue in two acts by Noel Coward.  Produced by John C. Wilson at the Music Box, New York, January 18, 1939.

Principals engaged—

| | |
|---|---|
| Beatrice Lillie | Richard Haydn |
| Eva Otega | Hugh French |
| Agnus Menzies | Anthony Pelissier |
| Moya Nugent | Kenneth Carten |
| Florence Britton | Ray Dennis |
| Tilda Getze | Anna Jackson |
| Penelope Dudley Ward | Gladys Henson |
| Sarah Burton | Anne Graham |
| Laura Duncan | Rosemary Lomax |
| Maidie Andrews | Laura Douglas |
| Ruby Green | Leonard Gibson |
| Bronson Dudley | Sanders Draper |
| Carol Louise Wanderman | Robert Shakelton |
| Victor Cutrar | John Mathews |
| Gilbert Wilson | Mary Ann Carr |

Staged by Noel Coward; settings and costumes by Gladys E. Calthrop.

## ONE-ACT REPERTORY COMPANY

### (3 performances)

A trio of one-act plays produced by the One-Act Repertory Company in association with Sam H. Grisman at the Hudson Theatre, New York, January 20, 1939.

## THE COGGERERS

Cast of characters—

Charles Stewart Parnell..............................Lionel Ince
Wolfe Tone.....................................Robert Wallsten
Lord Edward Fitzgerald.............................Roc Galvann
Robert Emmet....................................Horton Foote
John Mitchell....................................Ross Matthew

Eamonn O'Curry..............................Clement O'Loghlen
Mrs. Galgoogley....................................Irene Oshier
Oweneen....................................Evan Stephen Evans
    Scene—Entrance Hall of a Dublin Library.

## THE RED VELVET GOAT

Cast of characters—

Mariana........................................Barbara Robbins
Esteban.........................................Walter N. Greaza
Lorenzo............................................Horton Foote
Nimfo...........................................George Kossoff
Ester...........................................Frances Dworken
Lola.............................................Vera Visconti
Carmen.........................................Dorothy Maris
Ramon.............................................Roc Galvann
Don Pepe.......................................Ross Matthew
Dona Berta......................................Esther Mitchell
Ambrosio........................................Robert Payson
Saturnino..........................................Lionel Ince
    Scene—In Mexico.

## MR. BANKS OF BIRMINGHAM

Cast of characters—

King's Lieutenant...................................Lionel Ince
Quartermaster Solander........................Clement O'Loghlen
Valao...........................................George Kossoff
Mr. Banks.........................................J. P. Wilson
Matamua...........................................Roc Galvann
Chief Outourou...............................Walter N. Greaza
Amaroura........................................Dorothy Maris
Pomaretoota......................................Vera Visconti
Tahiriri.......................................Barbara Robbins
Mrs. Banks.......................................Esther Mitchell
Chief Outourou's Brother..........................Horton Foote
Chief Outourou's Uncle..........................Robert Payson
Vaiturou........................................Robert Wallsten
    Scene—In Tahiti.
    Staged by Emjo Basshe; settings by Manuel Essman.

In "The Coggerers" the statuary honoring old-time Irish heroes comes to life to welcome a recruit from the Easter uprising of 1916 named Oweneen Galgoogley. . . . In "Mr. Banks of Birmingham" a British conservative is sent to Tahiti in 1769 on a mission to civilize the natives. . . . In "The Red Velvet Goat" a simple Mexican peasant stages a show to raise money to buy a goat. The show is terrible. His wife takes the money and buys a red-velvet gown.

## THE AMERICAN WAY

### (164 performances)

A spectacle play in two acts by George S. Kaufman and Moss Hart; music by Oscar Levant. Produced by Sam H. Harris and Max Gordon at the Center Theatre, New York, January 21, 1939.

## Cast of characters—

| | |
|---|---|
| Martin Gunther | Fredric March |
| Immigration Official | James MacDonald |
| Irma Gunther | Florence Eldridge |
| Lisa Gunther as a child | { Lorna Lynn, Norma Clerc, Virginia Lodge } |
| A Boy | Bobby Barron |
| Another Boy | Bob White |
| Judge Hewitt | Bradford Hunt |
| Mrs. Kennedy | Jeanne Wardley |
| Mrs. White | Grace Valentine |
| Dr. Squires | Sydney Grant |
| Otto Heinrich | Maurice Wells |
| Clara Heinrich | Elsa Ersi |
| Samuel Brockton | McKay Morris |
| A Political Speaker | Robert Rhodes |
| Another Political Speaker | James Moore |
| Winifred Baxter | Ruth Weston |
| A School Teacher | Mary Murray |
| Antonio Coletti | John Long |
| Alex Hewitt as a child | { Buddy Buehler, Robert Cushman } |
| Karl Gunther as a child | { Teddy Casey, Buddy Irving } |
| Bobby | Tommy Lewis |
| Anna | Janet Fox |
| Factory Workers | Edward Fisher, Sidney Stone, Brant Gorman, James Russo |
| Mrs. Brockton | Eileen Burns |
| Mrs. Hewitt | Jean Shelby |
| The Chairman | John Lorenz |
| Mayor McEvoy | Hugh Cameron |
| Dr. MacFarlane | Le Roi Operti |
| Jeff | Allen Kearns |
| Mrs. Squires | Mary Brandon |
| Tennis Girls | Mona Moray, Ruth Strome, Gerry Carr, Katherine Duncan, Marion Edwards |
| Lisa Gunther | Adrienne Marden |
| Alex Hewitt | Alan Hewitt |
| Karl Gunther | David Wayne |
| Tommy | Walter Kelly |
| Mandolin Player | Stephen Sands |
| Helen | Dora Sayers |
| A Young Man | Alex Courtney |
| Another Young Man | Edward Elliott |
| Karl Gunther, Age 9 | Dickey Van Patten |
| Julia Hewitt, Age 11 | Elinor Pittis |
| Mary Hewitt, Age 10 | Claire Howard |
| A Political Speaker | Richard Lloyd |
| A Minister | Walter Beck |
| Julia, Age 21 | Barbara Woodall |
| Mary, Age 20 | Gretchen Davidson |
| Karl, Age 19 | Witner Bissell |
| Ed Lorenz | Jack Arnold |
| John Williams | George Herndon |
| Henry Courtney | Ward Tallmon |

Opening scene—Ellis Island, 1896. Other scenes—Small American Town.

Staged by George S. Kaufman; lighting and technical direction by Hassard Short; settings by Donald Oenslager; costumes by Irene Sharaff.

See page 145.

# HENRY IV

## (Part I)

### (74 performances )

A comedy in three acts by William Shakespeare; musical score by Rupert Graves. Revived by Maurice Evans at the St. James Theatre, New York, January 30, 1939.

Cast of characters—

King Henry the Fourth..........................Henry Edwards
Earl of Westmoreland...........................Alexander Scourby
John of Lancaster..............................William Prince
Sir Walter Blunt...............................Donald Cameron
Sir John Falstaff..............................Maurice Evans
Henry, Prince of Wales.........................Edmond O'Brien
Page...........................................George Keane
Poins..........................................Emmett Rogers
Earl of Northumberland.........................Charles Dalton
Earl of Worcester..............................Donald Randolph
Henry Percy, surnamed Hotspur..................Wesley Addy
First Carrier..................................Rhys Williams
Second Carrier.................................Alfred Paschall
Gadshill.......................................Donald Arbury
Peto...........................................Maury Tuckerman
Bardolph.......................................Reynolds Evans
Francis........................................Henry Jones
Mistress Quickly...............................Irene Tedrow
A Sheriff......................................George Graham
Lady Percy.....................................Mady Christians
Servant to Hotspur.............................Richard Janaver
Edmund Mortimer, Earl of March.................Everett Ripley
Owen Glendower.................................Rhys Williams
Lady Mortimer..................................Carmen Mathews
Justice Shallow................................George Graham
Justice Silence................................Henry Jones
Recruits:
   Mouldy......................................Maury Tuckerman
   Shadow......................................Charles Bowden
   Wart........................................Frederic Carney
   Feeble......................................Everett Ripley
   Bullcalf....................................Alfred Paschall
Earl of Douglas................................Sydney Smith
Sir Richard Vernon.............................John Kennedy
Lords, Officers, Soldiers, Travelers, etc.: Donald Arbury, Charles Bowden, Robert Brooks, Frederic Carney, Richard Janaver, George Keane, Alexander Nicol, Alfred Paschall, Everett Ripley, Maury Tuckerman.
   Prologue. Act I.—Scene 1—Westminster, the Palace. 2—An Apartment of the Prince's, London. 3—Windsor, the Palace. 4—Rochester, Outside an Inn. 5—The Highway. 6—The Boar's Head Tavern in Eastcheap. Act II.—Scene 1—Warkworth Castle. 2—Glendower's Castle, Wales. 3—London, the Palace. 4—The Boar's Head Tavern, Eastcheap. Act III.—Scene 1—Village in Gloucestershire. 2 and 4—The Rebel Camp Near Shrewsbury. 3—The King's Camp Near Shrewsbury. 5—Plain Between the Two Camps.
   Staged by Margaret Webster; settings by David Ffolkes.

As far back as 1761 David Douglass, who built the John Street Theatre in New York, was a popular Sir John Falstaff in Shakespeare's "Henry IV, Part I." In the fifties and sixties the part was played frequently and successfully by James H. Hackett, father of James K. Hackett. The only outstanding twentieth century revival was that of the Players' Club of New York in 1926, when Otis Skinner was the Falstaff, Philip Merivale the Hotspur, Basil Sydney the Prince of Wales and William Courtleigh the King Henry.

## JEREMIAH

### (35 performances)

A tragedy in three acts by Stefan Zweig, translated by Eden and Cedar Paul; acting version by John Gassner and Worthington Miner; music by Chemjo Vinaver. Produced by The Theatre Guild at the Guild Theatre, New York, February 3, 1939.

Cast of characters—

| | |
|---|---|
| Jeremiah | Kent Smith |
| Mother | Effie Shannon |
| Zebulon | Hannam Clark |
| Baruch | Alfred Ryder |
| Leah | Elizabeth Royce |
| Issacher | Ernest Rowan |
| Rebecca | Katherine Murphy |
| Laban | Robert Thomsen |
| Jochebed | Kathryn Grill |
| Her Husband | Robert Malcolm |
| Her Older Son | Paul Tripp |
| Her Younger Son | Vincent J. Donehue |
| Ruth | Joan Adrian |
| A Huckster | Henry Levin |
| Uriah | Mark Schweid |
| His Wife | Kay Wilt |
| Zephania | Charles Furcolowe |
| His Wife | Mary Fischer |
| Micha | John McKee |
| His Mother | Nell Harrison |
| A Merchant | David Rosen |
| His Wife | Virginia Gregori |
| His Nephew | Cameron Mitchell |
| Solom | Gordon Nelson |
| His Wife | Roberta Bellinger |
| His Daughter | Katharine Bard |
| His Son-in-Law | Theodore Paul |
| The Elder | John Hendrick |
| His Niece | Betty Young |
| Her Husband | George H. Lee |
| Gad | Charles Jordan |
| His Wife | Marian Rudley |
| Zilpah | Mary Perry |
| Hananiah | Harry Irvine |
| Pashur | Benedict McQuarrie |
| Abimelech | Robert Harrison |
| First Sentry | John O'Connor |
| Second Sentry | Byron McGrath |
| First Guard | Arthur Sachs |
| Second Guard | Harold Hoha |
| Third Guard | Alexis Tcherkassky |
| Zedekiah | Arthur Byron |
| Herald | Philip Lewis |
| Ahab | Byron Russell |
| His Father | Arthur Villars |
| Nahum | St. Clair Bayfield |

```
Imre.............................................Henry  Bennett
Joab.............................................Morgan  James
Nehemiah.........................................Cornell  Wilde
Aaron............................................Tom  Morrison
Shephan..........................................George  Petrie
Assyrian Captain.................................Mervin  Williams
Second Assyrian Officer..........................Byron  Russell
Third Assyrian Officer...........................David  Rosen
First Assyrian Soldier...........................Theodore  Paul
Second Assyrian Soldier......................Vincent  J.  Donehue
```
Act I.—Scene 1—"The Awakening," Roof of Jeremiah's Home.
2—"The Prophet's Ordeal," Bedroom of Jeremiah. 3—"Rumors,"
Bedroom. Act II.—Scene 1—"The Watch on the Ramparts."
2—"The Prophet's Ordeals," Bedroom of Jeremiah's Mother.
3—"Voices in the Night," Chamber of the King. Act III.—
Scene 1—"The Supreme Affliction," Market Square. 2—"The Mind
and the Spirit," A Crypt.
Staged by Worthington Miner; settings by Harry Horner; choreography by Felicia Sorel.

"Jeremiah" was written by Stefan Zweig in Austria during the
Great War. It was produced in Switzerland by German players,
but was later banned by Germany. It follows in story the Bible
tales of the prophet Jeremiah, whose lamentations were directed
largely against war and who, as a leading pacifist of his time, was
damned by the people, imprisoned by King Zedekiah and generally pushed around. Jeremiah curses God in his wrath but has
his faith restored in the end.

## ONE FOR THE MONEY

### (132 performances)

A revue in two acts by Nancy Hamilton; music by Morgan
Lewis. Produced by Gertrude Macy, Stanley Gilkey and Robert
F. Cutler at the Booth Theatre, New York, February 4, 1939.

Principals engaged—

| | |
|---|---|
| Nancy Hamilton | Philip Bourneuf |
| Nell O'Day | Alfred Drake |
| Ruth Matteson | Robert Smith |
| Maxine Barrat | Don Loper |
| Grace McDonald | Gene Kelly |
| Nadine Gae | George Lloyd |
| Brenda Forbes | Keenan Wynn |
| Frances Comstock | William Archibald |

Ray Kavanaugh and his Orchestra
Staged by John Murray Anderson; musical numbers by Robert
Alton; sketches by Edward Clarke Lilley; settings and costumes by
Raoul Pene Du Bois.

A collection of Nancy Hamilton skits having to do with life
among the upper classes and café society.

## * I MUST LOVE SOMEONE

### (151 performances)

A play in three acts by Jack Kirkland and Leyla Georgie. Produced by Jack Kirkland at the Longacre Theatre, New York, February 7, 1939.

Cast of characters—

| | |
|---|---|
| Marg Keston | Melba Deane |
| Ann Gibson | Dorothy Libaire |
| Maude Schultze | Jean Casto |
| Mrs. Long | Ethel Jackson |
| Ed Long | John Dilson |
| Bess McClintock | Claire Carleton |
| Joe Kelly | Jack Sheehan |
| Paul Strand | Charles Ansley |
| Jennie Sneed | Marion Pierce |
| Charles Sheldon | James Rennie |
| Sam Graves | Harry Bannister |
| Birdie Carr | Martha Sleeper |
| Bill Green | Theodore Corday |
| Bob Goesling | Scott Colton |
| Joshua Quackendall | Frank McCormack |
| Mark Blair | Robert Bernard |
| Moses | John T. Ricks |
| Ira Pond | Harry Koler |
| Mike Flaherty | Lew Eckels |

Six Clerks: Richard Burdette, Vane Carlin, Jack Douglas, Meredith Johnston, Jack Spinelly, Turnley Walker.

Act I.—Scenes 1 and 3—Chorus Dressing Room, Casino Theatre. 2—On Stage. Act II.—Scene 1—The Stage Door. 2—Carriages in the Night. 3—Private Room at Canfield's. Act III.—Birdie's Apartment.

Staged by Frank Merlin; settings by Karl O. Amend; costumes by Alfred Stern; dances by Ned McGurn; music arranged and directed by David Mordecai.

Birdie Carr, one of the prettiest of the Florodora sextette girls, decides to cut out the vulgarities and the loose living she and her chorus pals indulge, and go straight with Bob Goesling who, in the early days of the century, drives the first automobile from Detroit to New York. Before Birdie can negotiate this reformation her friend, Ann Gibson, kills her protector, a loathsome person, and the other girls and their men are kept busy trying to keep Ann out of jail. Then Birdie discovers that Bob is not as noble as he pretends to be. He was only trying to acquire a Florodora girl so he would have an amour to boast of back home.

## MRS. O'BRIEN ENTERTAINS

### (37 performances)

A comedy in three acts by Harry Madden. Produced by George Abbott at the Lyceum Theatre, New York, February 8, 1939.

Cast of characters—

Timothy Callahan.................................James Lane
Susan McGowan.........................Katherine Meskil
Michael O'Brien...............................Kirk Brown
Mary O'Brien.................................Margaret Mullen
Evangeline Van Iseldyke...........................Marie Brown
Terry Flanagan..................................John Carmody
Patrick O'Toole................................Harry Shannon
Marta O'Toole.............................Maureen McManus
Thomas Delaney...............................Walter Kinsella
Daniel O'Donnell................................Robert Conrey
Molly O'Day......................................Gene Tierney
Heinrich Wertheimer...........................Paul Ballantyne
Barney McFadden................................Richard Keene
Annie Dubrinsky..................................Aileen Ernst
Joseph Mulhern..................................Fred Sumner
Jerry Madigan.................................Robert Williams
Guiseppi.........................................Daniel Ocko
Papa Van Iseldyke..............................Asher Smith
Mama Van Iseldyke............................Emerin Campbell
Papa Wertheimer.............................Ralph Morehouse
Mama Wertheimer.............................Maidel Turner

    Acts I, II and III.—Parlor of the O'Brien House on Nassau Street, New York, 1848.
    Staged by George Abbott; settings and costumes by Jo Mielziner.

Mary O'Brien, sister of and housekeeper for Timothy Callahan, back in the New York of 1848, has little sympathy with the "foreigners" that are pushing their way past Ellis Island and into the new land of America which the Irish have taken over. She would sweep all the emigrants her brother Timothy invites to stay in his house, including Patrick O'Toole, politician, out the door, but Timothy is truly patriotic and has great plans for pairing off the newcomers. He introduces the marriageable Irish to the marriageable Swedes, Dutch and Italian neighbors. And Patrick becomes a leader of Tammany. Thus are the traditions of the melting pot sustained, and Timothy makes an eloquent speech about the new race that is to be born in the new land.

## STARS IN YOUR EYES

### (127 performances)

A musical comedy in two acts by J. P. McEvoy; lyrics by Dorothy Fields; music by Arthur Schwartz. Produced by Dwight Deere Wiman at the Majestic Theatre, New York, February 9, 1939.

Cast of characters—

Assistant Director.................................Ted Gary
Second Assistant Director.......................Davis Cunningham
Third Assistant Director.........................Edward Kane
Fourth Assistant Director.......................Robert Shanley
Fifth Assistant Director.........................Dan Dailey, Jr.
Sixth Assistant Director...........................Roger Stearns
First Girl..........................................Edith Grant
Second Girl........................................Thekla Horn

Third  Girl.........................................Nancy  Wiman
Wardrobe  Woman...............................Johanne  Hoven
Carpenter.........................................David  Morris
Fourth  Girl.....................................Frances  Rands
Electrician.......................................Anthony  Albert
Soundman.......................................Rennie  McEvoy
Babe.............................................Dawn  Roland
Wilder.........................................Clinton  Sundberg
Cameraman.......................................Walter  Wagner
Assistant  Soundman............................Ambrose  Costello
Fifth  Girl.........................................Phyllis  Roque
Sixth  Girl.......................................Natasha  Dana
Dancing  Girl.......................................Nora  Kaye
Leading  Man.....................................Walter  Cassel
Script  Girl.......................................Gloria  Clare
Bess.............................................Mildred  Natwick
Jeanette  Adair...................................Ethel  Merman
Voice  Coach.......................................Mary  Wickes
Maid.........................................Kathryn  Mayfield
Bill.............................................Jimmy  Durante
Jockey...........................................Basil  Galahoff
Darrow...........................................Robert  Ross
John  Blake....................................Richard  Carlson
Tata....................................Tamara  Toumanova
Dawson.......................................Richard  Barbee
Photographers.................Walter  Cassel,  Edward  Kane,  Davis
                        Cunningham,  Robert  Shanley
Russian  Consul................................Russel  Protopoff
French  Consul..................................Dwight  Godwin
Italian  Consul..................................Fernando  Alonso
English  Consul..................................David  Morris
German  Consul...............................Ambrose  Costello
            Al  Goodman  and  his  Orchestra
Ladies  of  the  Ballet:  Alecia  Alonso,  Peggy  Conrad,  Maria  De
   Galanta,  Jane  Everett,  Gail  Grant,  Marion  Haynes,  Thekla
   Horn,  Johanne  Hoven,  Marjorie  Johnstone,  Nora  Kaye,  Maria
   Karniloff,  Frances  Rands,  Audrey  Reynolds,  Olga  Suarez,
   Margaret  Vasilieff,  Mary  Jane  Williams.
Gentlemen  of  the  Ballet:  Anthony  Albert,  Fernando  Alonso,  Paul
   Alvin,  Savva  Andreieff,  Dwight  Godwin,  Basil  Galahoff,  George
   Kiddon,  Russel  Protopoff,  Richard  Reed,  Newcombe  Rice,
   Jerome  Robbins.
   Acts  I  and  II.—Sound  Stage  "7"  of  the  Monotone  Picture  Corp.,
Hollywood,  California.
   Staged  by  Joshua  Logan;  settings  by  Jo  Mielziner;  costumes  by
John  Hambleton;  choreography  by  Carl  Randall.

Ethel Merman is a Hollywood glamor star in pursuit of her
handsome and reasonably innocent leading man, Richard Carlson,
who decides to love Tamara Toumanova. Jimmy Durante is a
"wienie," or idea man for the studio. Miss Merman and Mr.
Durante concoct many schemes to achieve certain desired objec-
tives, but few of them work, which leads to interludes and music
cues.

## LEW LESLIE'S BLACKBIRDS OF 1939

### (9 performances)

A revue in two acts assembled by Lew Leslie; lyrics by Johnny
Mercer and others; music by Rube Bloom and others. Produced

by Lew Leslie at the Hudson Theatre, New York, February 11, 1939.

Principals engaged—

| | |
|---|---|
| Lena Horne | Bobby Evans |
| Beryl Clarke | Al Bledger |
| Joyce Beasley | Taps Miller |
| Kate Hall | Frank Riley |
| Lavinia Williams | Dewey Markham |
| Dorothy Sachs | Louis Haber |
| Vic Mizzy | Irving Taylor |
| Rosalie King | Tim Moore |
| Mitchell Parish | Sammy Fain |
| Atta Blake | Norman McConney |
| Laurene Hines | Jerry Laws |
| Mickey Jones | William Downes |
| Rosetta Crawford | Robert Clarke |
| Louisa Howard | Coleman Hill |
| Norma Miller | George Greenridge |
| Edith Ross | Ralph Brown |
| Lorenza Roberson | Hamtree Harrington |
| Charles Welch | Joe Byrd |
| Whitey's Lindy Hoppers | Van Grona's Swing Ballet |

J. Rosamond Johnson's Choir

Staged by Lew Leslie; settings by Mabel A. Buell; costumes by Frances Feist.

## * THE LITTLE FOXES

### (143 performances)

A drama in three acts by Lillian Hellman. Produced by Herman Shumlin at the National Theatre, New York, February 15, 1939.

Cast of characters—

| | |
|---|---|
| Addie | Abbie Mitchell |
| Cal | John Marriott |
| Birdie Hubbard | Patricia Collinge |
| Oscar Hubbard | Carl Benton Reid |
| Leo Hubbard | Dan Duryea |
| Regina Giddens | Tallulah Bankhead |
| William Marshall | Lee Baker |
| Benjamin Hubbard | Charles Dingle |
| Alexandra Giddens | Florence Williams |
| Horace Giddens | Frank Conroy |

Acts I, II and III.—Living Room of Giddens House, Small Town in South, 1900.

Staged by Herman Shumlin; settings by Howard Bay.

See page 75.

## MISS SWAN EXPECTS

### (8 performances)

A comedy in three acts by Bella and Samuel Spewack. Produced by William Harris, Jr., at the Cort Theatre, New York, February 20, 1939.

Cast of characters—

| | |
|---|---|
| Ethel | Joyce Arling |
| Harold | O. Z. Whitehead |
| Silvermine | William Bendix |
| Expressman | Wylie Adams |
| Josie Swan | Peggy Conklin |
| Miss Dawson | Esther Mitchell |
| Perry Weel | James MacColl |
| Sloane | Kurt Richards |
| Bretherton | Eduard Franz |
| Michael Borodin | Boris Belostozky |
| Judge Thomas | C. Norman Hammond |
| Bert Nansen | John Beal |
| Stenographer | Vera Matthews |
| Cashier | Sanford McCauley |
| Cunningham | John Williams |
| Elsie | Ann Andrews |
| Crampton | George Nash |
| Jason | William Hess |
| Doctor | William Bock |

Act I.—Reception Room of the House of Bretherton. Act II.—Scene 1—J. J. Crampton's Study. 2—House of Bretherton. Act III.—Scene 1—House of Bretherton. 2—Crampton's Study.
Staged by Samuel Spewack; settings by Raymond Sovey.

Miss Swan is a highly imaginative reader in a book publishing house. She also is an expectant mother. Because her young husband has been commissioned to write the biography of an eccentric New England industrialist Miss Swan goes fantastically into debt, buying a farm and furnishing it extravagantly on credit. When the industrialist decides not to publish his biography Miss Swan slips a fascinating adventuress into his home to persuade, if not to blackmail, him. She succeeds finally in re-establishing some little hope that her husband will get his advance and that her threatened publishing firm will be saved.

## OFF TO BUFFALO

### (7 performances)

A comedy in three acts by Max Liebman and Allen Boretz. Produced by Albert Lewis at the Ethel Barrymore Theatre, New York, February 21, 1939.

Cast of characters—

| | |
|---|---|
| Harry Quill | Hume Cronyn |
| Tuni | Luba Wesoly |
| Evelyn Quill | Elizabeth Love |
| "Pop" Clifford | Frank Camp |
| Barkas | Matt Briggs |
| Mannheim | Richard Taber |
| Sprung | Edmund Dorsay |
| McChesney | G. Albert Smith |
| Johnny Melba | Fred Lightner |
| Gus Delaney | Joe Cook |
| Gabby O'Keefe | Otto Hulett |
| Maxie Kromm | Nat Cantor |
| Fanny Franum | Fay Courtney |
| Gill | Henry Tobias |

```
Bloom..........................................Harold  Whalen
Blossom.....................................Peggy  Chamberlain
Lottie..............................................Joan  Engel
Pepe  Brothers................................Martell  Brothers
The  Flying  Martels..................William  and  George  Dewey
Phil  Gordon.......................................James  Kelso
Delivery  Boy.....................................Burton  Lewis
Johnson.......................................Dudley  Clements
Laundry  Man.......................................Albert  West
```
Act I.—Scene 1—Living Room of Harry Quill's Home in Flatbush.
2—Gus Delaney's Hotel Room in the West Forties.  Acts II and
III.—The Quill Living Room.
Staged by Melville Burke; settings by Donald Oenslager.

Harry Quill of Brooklyn has a budget of $600 with which to
stage a vaudeville show for his lodge.  He approaches Gus Delaney, a $3,000-a-week headliner in his day, and suggests that
Gus work as Master of Ceremonies.  Gus is delighted.  So delighted that he invites a half dozen fellow artists to move into
Harry Quill's startled home and there prepare for the big event
by eating all the food in sight and making free with the furnish-
ings that get in the way of rehearsals.  Then the lodge declares
the party off.

## CLOSE QUARTERS

### (8 performances)

A drama in three acts by Gilbert Lennox, adapted from the
play "Attentat" by W. O. Somin.  Produced by Ann Seranne and
Edmund L. Anderson at the Golden Theatre, New York, March
6, 1939.

Cast of characters—

```
Liesa  Bergman.................................Elena  Miramova
Gustav  Bergman....................................Leo  Chalzel
```
Act I.—Kitchen-Living Room of the Bergmans' flat in Working-
Class Tenement in a Continental Capital.  Acts II and III.—Parlor
of Bergmans' New Flat in Model Block of Workers' Dwellings.
Staged by Leo Bulgakov; settings by Watson Barratt.

Gustav Bergman, a radical engaged in political work in a continental capital, comes home to announce to a happy wife that the
committee is going to send him to London.  In the midst of their
joy news is broadcast over the radio that a political leader has
been murdered in the park.  He was one of Gustav's enemies.
Gustav has come home through the park about the time of the
murder.  The Bergmans are frightened.  They move, but their
fright follows them.  One incriminating bit of circumstantial evidence is piled upon another until the Bergmans decide upon suicide.  After they are dead the real murderer is discovered.

## AWAKE AND SING

### (45 performances)

A comedy in three acts by Clifford Odets. Revived by The Group Theatre at the Windsor Theatre, New York, March 7, 1939.

Cast of characters—

| | |
|---|---|
| Ralph Berger | Alfred Ryder |
| Myron Berger | Art Smith |
| Hennie Berger | Phoebe Brand |
| Jacob Berger | Morris Carnovsky |
| Bessie Berger | Julia Adler |
| Schlosser | William Challee |
| Moe Axelrod | Luther Adler |
| Uncle Morty | J. Edward Bromberg |
| Sam Feinschreiber | Sanford Meisner |

Acts I, II and III.—An Apartment in the Bronx.
Staged by Harold Clurman; setting by Boris Aronson.

"Awake and Sing" was first produced February 19, 1935, at the Belasco Theatre, New York. It achieved a run of 209 performances at that time. In the original production Jules Garfield (since become John Garfield in Hollywood) played Ralph Berger, Stella in place of Julia Adler was the Bessie and Roman Bohnen was the Schlosser in place of William Challee. Otherwise the cast was the same.

## FAMILY PORTRAIT

### (111 performances)

A drama in three acts by Lenore Coffee and William Joyce Cowen; incidental music by Lehman Engel. Produced by Cheryl Crawford in association with Day Tuttle and Richard Skinner at the Morosco Theatre, New York, March 8, 1939.

Cast of characters—

| | |
|---|---|
| Mary | Judith Anderson |
| Daniel | Ronald Reiss |
| Joseph | Norman Stuart |
| A Shepherd | Max Leavitt |
| Naomi | Virginia Campbell |
| Juda | James Harker |
| Mary Cleophas | Evelyn Varden |
| Reba | Lois Austin |
| Simon | Tom Ewell |
| James | Philip Coolidge |
| Mordecai | William Foran |
| Selima | Kathryn Grill |
| Eben | Philip Truex |
| Mathias | Hugh Rennie |
| A Disciple | Leonard Elliott |
| Hepziba | Eula Guy |

```
Appius Hadrian....................................Guy Spauli
Anna....................................Ruth Chorpenning
Rabbi Samuel........................................Bram Nossen
Mendel................................................Will Lee
A Woman of Jerusalem..........................Lois Jameson
Mary of Magdala............................Margaret Webster
Nathan........................................Ronald Hammond
Daniel, aged 16..................................Philip Truex
Esther.......................................Josephine McKim
Leban of Damascus.................................Guy Spaull
Joshua...............................................Neal Berry
```
Act I.—Scene 1—House in Nazareth. 2—Wineshop in Capernaum. Act II.—House in Nazareth. Act III.—Scene 1—Street in Jerusalem. 2—House in Jerusalem. 3—House in Nazareth.
Staged by Margaret Webster; settings and costumes by Harry Horner.

See page 318.

## FIRST AMERICAN DICTATOR

### (9 performances)

A play in three acts by Jor Marcy (Nathan Sherman) and Jacob A. Weiser. Produced by George Lewis at the Bayes Theatre, New York, March 14, 1939.

Cast of characters—
```
Representative Buckley..........................Humphrey Davis
Representative Saunders..........................Oscar Jacobson
Governor Huey P. Long..........................Conrad Noles
Gus.............................................Edmond LeComte
Oscar................................................Thomas Daly
Frank Darcy......................................Gilbert Green
Representative Madden..........................John Culbertson
Senator Wheatley..................................Lewis Fisher
```
Staged by Humphrey Davis.

Presumably the story of the late Huey P. Long's life, beginning with his fight against impeachment as Governor of Louisiana and ending with his 13-hour filibuster and harangue favoring a share-the-wealth program in Washington. He is assassinated by political enemies shortly after.

## TELL MY STORY

### (1 performance)

A drama in two acts and seven scenes by Richard Rohman. Produced by Freeman Theatre Group at the Mercury Theatre, New York, March 15, 1939.

Cast of characters—
```
Police Clerk....................................Frederic Giuliano
Domino...........................................Harry Bellaver
Thiero...............................................Lee Hillery
De Bello..........................................Richard Bengali
Mateo.............................................Gordon Nelson
```

```
Mendola.........................................David   Turk
Silvestra.................................William  H.  Chambers
Vulpi.....................................Sydney  Andrews
Violetta.................................George  Beban,  Jr.
Ricoremo....................................George   Moss
Malacro........................................Franklin  Klein
Filippo.......................................William  Toubin
Finzo...............................William  Webb  Sanders
Marino...........................................Arthur   Spencer
Rosso.............................................Edwin   Rand
The  Duke....................................Robert  H.  Harris
A  Boy........................................Richard  Benedict
A  Girl...........................................Beth  Cantreau
Clerk.............................................Joseph  Olney
    Staged  by  Marcel  Strauss.
```

Mateo (Giacomo Matteoti?) and the Duke (Benito Musso-lini?) are rivals in a contest for power in a European state. Mateo is a conservative who hopes to bring about reforms that will bring the people greater liberty by peaceful and well-ordered means. The Duke is a ruthless opportunist who is ready to use any and all means to further his ends. When the Duke fears that Mateo's suavity and wit are gaining an upper hand he en-gages an American gunman to take his enemy for a ride. There-after the Duke has everything his own way.

## PLEASE, MRS. GARIBALDI

### (4 performances)

A comedy in three acts by Mary McCarthy. Produced by Hall Shelton at the Belmont Theatre, New York, March 16, 1939.

Cast of characters—

```
Mrs.  Forbes.................................Minnie  Ashe  Hill
Endora.........................................Laura  Bowman
Ethel  Forbes.................................Christine  Arden
Rosa  Garibaldi..............................Dorothy  Emery
Gino  Garibaldi..............................Giuseppe  Sterni
Maria  Garibaldi...............................Ruth  Amos
Joe  Garibaldi...............................Barnard  Hughes
Paul  Manning...................................William  Rice
Bertha  Coe....................................Odette  Le  Roy
Mrs.  Ogden...................................Gwen  Emerson
    Staged  by  Hall  Shelton.
```

Rosa Garibaldi's first false step was discovered by her mother and her father. They were noble and forgave her. This gave Rosa the courage to refuse the boy who had seduced her when he offered marriage. That, thought Papa, was being a little too noble. Papa then swore that he would have the seducer's life and Rosa decided to marry the boy to save him.

## STOP PRESS

### (1 performance)

A drama in three acts by John Stradley. Produced by the Acting Company, Inc., at the Vanderbilt Theatre, New York, March 19, 1939.

Cast of characters—

| | |
|---|---|
| Jerry | Carl Johnson |
| Johnson | Charles Mendick |
| Webber | Clancy Cooper |
| The Gent | Lewis Gilbert |
| Mary Kendall | Edith Tachna |
| Mulrooney | Tony Kraber |
| Kitty Blake | Marguerite Walker |
| Matty | John Marlieb |
| John Snell | Ralph Bell |
| Alfred Snell | Houseley Stevens |
| Kendall | Al Jenkins |
| Deputy | Russ Conway |
| William Gore | Norman Porter |
| Larry | Archie King |
| Wilson | Gilbert Fates |
| White | Bernard Kaydison |
| Harkinski | Juan Root |
| A Man | Lou Turkil |
| Ann Thomas | Phillipa Bevans |
| Smyth | Frederick Olmstead |
| Hereford | Frank Maxwell |

Staged by Charles de Sheim.

Alfred Snell owns a newspaper in a small town in which a steel strike has been called, and sides with the steel mill owners in a campaign to drive certain dirty agitators and strike breakers out of town. John Snell, the newspaper owner's son, more on the liberal side, comes back from an exile to fight his father and induce the reporters on the Snell paper to write the true story back of the strike. There is considerable conflict. In the end the governor intervenes and the reporters decide to get out a paper of their own.

## THE HOT MIKADO

### (85 performances)

A swing version adapted from "The Mikado" of Gilbert and Sullivan; orchestral arrangements by Charles L. Cooke. Produced by Michael Todd at the Broadhurst Theatre, New York, March 23, 1939.

Cast of characters—

| | |
|---|---|
| Nanki-Poo | Bob Parrish |
| Pish-Tush | James A. Lillard |
| Ko-Ko | Eddie Green |
| Pooh-Bah | Maurice Ellis |

Yum-Yum......................................Gwendolyn Reyde
Pitti-Sing.........,..............................Frances Brock
Peep-Bo.........................................Roseeta LeNoire
Messenger Boy..................................Freddie Robinson
Katisha...........................................Rosa Brown
The Mikado.......................................Bill Robinson
Red Cap.........................................Vincent Shields
Singing Girls, Singing Boys, Dancing Girls, Jitterbug Girls, Jitter-
  bug Boys, "Tap-a-Teers," Guards, Quartette: Travers Crawford,
  Otho Gains, Harry Lewis, Elmaurice Miller.
  Acts I, II and III.—Somewhere in Japan.
  Staged by Hassard Short; choral direction by William Parson;
dances by Truly McGee; settings by Nat Karson.

The professional showman's answer to the swing adaptation of
"The Mikado," made originally by the Federal WPA Theatre in
Chicago. (See page 480.) This number is handsomely dressed
and expertly "swung."

## * THE PHILADELPHIA STORY

### (96 performances)

A comedy in three acts by Philip Barry. Produced by The
Theatre Guild, Inc., at the Shubert Theatre, New York, March
28, 1939.

Cast of characters—

Dinah Lord......................................Lenore Lonergan
Margaret Lord.......................................Vera Allen
Tracy Lord..................................Katharine Hepburn
Alexander Lord......................................Dan Tobin
Thomas.............................................Owen Coll
William Tracy......................................Forrest Orr
Elizabeth Imbrie..................................Shirley Booth
Macaulay Connor....................................Van Heflin
George Kittredge..................................Frank Fenton
C. K. Dexter Haven................................Joseph Cotten
          (Courtesy of the Mercury Theatre)
Edward...........................................Philip Foster
Seth Lord.......................................Nicholas Joy
May...........................................Myrtle Tannahill
Elsie...........................................Lorraine Bate
Mac..............................................Hayden Rorke
  Acts I and III.—The Sitting Room at Seth Lord's House in the
Country, near Philadelphia. Act II.—The Porch.
  Staged by Robert B. Sinclair; supervised by Theresa Helburn and
Lawrence Langner; settings and lighting by Robert Edmond Jones.

See page 216.

## THE FLASHING STREAM

### (8 performances)

A drama in three acts by Charles Morgan. Produced by Victor
Payne-Jennings at the Biltmore Theatre, New York, April 10,
1939.

Cast of characters—

```
Commander Henry Carr, R.N...........................Leo Genn
Corporal Denham, Royal Marines..................Roger Maxwell
Lieut.-Commander Peter Brissing, R.N.............Anthony Ireland
Commander Edward Ferrers, R.N.................Godfrey Tearle
Lieut.-Commander Richard Sandford, R.N..........Laurier Lister
Lady Helston.................................Patricia Godfrey
Rear Admiral Sir George Helston, Bart., C.B., R.N...Patric Curwen
The Rt. Hon. Walter Harrowby, P.C., M.P..........Felix Aylmer
Karen Selby...............................Margaret Rawlings
Capt. Winter, D.S.C., R.N.........................George Cross
    Acts I, II and III.—Old Spanish Fortress, Now Used as a Naval
Experimental Station in the British Atlantic Island of St. Hilary.
    Staged by Peter Cresswell; setting by the Harkers.
```

Commander Edward Ferrers, one of the British navy's ablest mathematicians, is stationed with a group of the Navy's scientists and mechanics on an island in the Atlantic working out a secret formula for the creation of aerial torpedoes. In a test that has failed, Ferrers' friend, Selby, has been killed. The Admiralty sends Selby's sister, Karen, herself a great mathematician, to take his place. The introduction of sex interest in the more or less monastic island causes an upheaval. Ferrers and Karen fall in love. Ferrers fights against a relinquishment of his vow of celibacy until his scientific experiments are completed. Again failure follows a test. The Admiralty would discontinue experiments, unless Ferrers will admit error in his calculations. Ferrers refuses. Karen Selby lies to save him. She has discovered an error. The Admiralty allows the experiments to go on. Karen and Ferrers determine not to wait.

## THE HAPPIEST DAYS

### (7 performances)

A drama in two acts by Charlotte Armstrong. Produced by Courtney Burr at the Vanderbilt Theatre, New York, April 11, 1939.

Cast of characters—

```
Norman.........................................Jimmy Lydon
Alfred Chapin..............................William Harrigan
Dorothy Chapin.............................Kathryn Givney
Jeff...............................................John Craven
Edith...............................................Uta Hagen
Ellen Donovan....................................Ethel Wilson
Brian Donovan..................................Russell Collins
Katty..........................................Dorothea Eller
    Act I.—Scene 1—The Chapin Living Room. 2—Jeff's Room.
3—The Donovans' Kitchen. 4—The Library Reference Room.
Act II.—Scenes 1, 3 and 4—The Living Room. 2—Jeff's Room.
    Staged by Marc Connelly; settings by P. Dodd Ackerman.
```

Jeff Chapin and Edith Donovan, 17, students in the same High School, fall deeply in love. Their trusting and somewhat blind parents have permitted them to do their home studying in Jeff's studio bedroom. When the situation becomes complicated by Edith's discovery that she is to have a baby the young lovers try to induce a Justice of the Peace to marry them. The justice laughs at them. When they try to tell their parents they are embarrassed and defeated. To them the world is cruel and its people ignorant and misunderstanding. In their dilemma they agree upon a suicide pact. Jeff is to shoot Edith and then himself. Before they can carry out their plan Edith decides that Jeff should live to inform the world of their discovery of the great happiness that nothing can change, not even death. Jeff kills Edith. He is arrested and, being tried for murder, acquitted by an understanding jury.

## MY HEART'S IN THE HIGHLANDS

### (44 performances)

A play in one act by William Saroyan; music by Paul Bowles. Produced by the Group Theatre at the Guild Theatre, April 13, 1939.

Cast of characters—

| | |
|---|---|
| The Boy | Jackie Ayers |
| Ben Alexander, the Poet | Philip Loeb |
| Johnny, his Son | Sidney Lumet |
| Jasper MacGregor, the Actor | Art Smith |
| Mr. Kosak, the Grocer | William Hansen |
| Johnny's Grandmother | Hester Sondergaard |
| Rufe Apley | James O'Rear |
| Philip Carmichael | Loren Gage |
| Henry | Phil Brown |
| Mr. Wiley | Harry Bratsburg |
| Real Estate Agent | Nicholas Conte |
| Husband | John O'Malley |
| Wife | Catheryn Laughlin |
| Esther Kosak | Mae Grimes |
| Two Guards | Peter Leeds, Charles de Sheim |

Good Friends and Neighbors: Eda Reis, Eileen Detchon, Undine Forrest, Charles Henderson, Mary Liles.

Scene—Fresno, California. In and Around Ben's House, 1914. Staged by Robert Lewis; settings and costumes by Herbert Andrews.

An allegory in which Ben Alexander, a struggling poet, refuses to give up his Muse and take a job. With his son and his Armenian mother-in-law he lives from hand to mouth until he is forced to rent his shack and take to the road. His spirits meantime are buoyed greatly by a slightly crazed old man, an actor from the poor farm, who plays comforting old tunes on a golden bugle.

## * NO TIME FOR COMEDY

(72 performances)

A comedy in three acts by S. N. Behrman. Produced by The Playwrights' Company at the Ethel Barrymore Theatre, New York, April 17, 1939.

Cast of characters—

Clementine........................................Gee Gee James
Linda Esterbrook................................Katharine Cornell
Philo Smith.......................................John Williams
Gaylord Esterbrook..............................Laurence Olivier
Amanda Smith.................................Margalo Gillmore
Robert............................................Peter Robinson
Makepeace Lovell................................Robert Flemyng
    Acts I and III.—Living Room of Linda's Tower-Apartment in a New York Hotel.  Act II.—Upstairs Living Room of the Smiths' New York House.
    Staged by Guthrie McClintic; settings by Jo Mielziner.

See page 178.

## * PINS AND NEEDLES 1939

(680 performances)

A revue in two acts by Harold Rome, Arthur Arent, Charles Friedman, David Gregory, John La Touche and Joseph Schrank; music and lyrics by Harold Rome. Presented by International Ladies' Garment Workers' Union at Labor Stage, New York, April 20, 1939.

Principals engaged—

| | |
|---|---|
| Al Eben | Millie Weitz |
| Harry Clark | Anne Brown |
| Paul Seymour | Nina Harary |
| Murray Modick | Ruth Rubinstein |
| Hy Gardner | Dorothy Tucker |
| Sam Dratch | Jean Nicita |

    Staged by Robert H. Gordon and Felicia Sorel; settings by Sointu Syrjala.

The original "Pins and Needles" was produced by Labor Stage, November 27, 1937, and has been running ever since. The revised version scheduled above included a number of new sketches and several new actors. The production was transferred in the Spring to the Windsor Theatre.

## MEXICANA

### (35 performances)

A musical extravaganza in two acts. Presented by the Republic of Mexico at the 46th Street Theatre, New York, April 21, 1939.

Principals engaged—

| | |
|---|---|
| Commentator | Graziella Parraga |
| Conductor | Paul Baron |
| Rosita Rios | Tito Coral |
| Carmen Molina | Enrique Pastor |
| Elisa | Jose Molina |
| Maria Luisa Lopez | Jose Luis Tapia |
| Estela | Rene |
| Eva Perez Caro | Rolando |
| Chucha Camacho | Amparo Arozamena |
| Lila Kiwa | Rafael Gutierrez |
| Marissa Flores | Jose Fernandez |
| Beatriz Ramos | Victor Novarro |
| Cuates Castilla | Consuelo Solorzano |
| The Trio Nacional | The Trio Lee |
| Vincente Gomez | Eduardo Hernandez Moncada |

Staged under General Supervision of Celestino Gorostiza, director of Department of Fine Arts of Mexico; music directed by Eduardo Hernandez Moncada and Mario Ruiz; dance by Gluck Sandor; settings by Julio Castellanos; costumes by Augustin Lazo.

## THE MOTHER

### (4 performances)

A drama in three acts by Karel Capek; English version by Paul Selver and Miles Malleson. Produced by Victor Payne-Jennings in association with Kathleen Robinson at the Lyceum Theatre, New York, April 25, 1939.

Cast of characters—

| | |
|---|---|
| The Mother | Nazimova |
| The Father | Reginald Bach |
| Andrew | Stephen Ker Appleby |
| George | Carl Norval |
| Christopher | Alan Brixey |
| Peter | Tom Palmer |
| Tony | Montgomery Clift |
| The Old Man | Edward Broadley |
| Man's Voice on Loudspeaker | Marvin Wells |
| Woman's Voice on Loudspeaker | Agnes Young |

Acts I, II and III.—Father's Room of the Mother's Home.
Staged by Miles Malleson; setting by Lester Polakov.

The Mother, having lost a husband and her first-born son in the wars, seeks to keep her four remaining boys from the battlefields. One by one she loses them all and their ghosts return to recite the virtues of war. In the end, seeing her country invaded,

she hands a rifle to her last and youngest boy and bids him go
do his part.

## WUTHERING HEIGHTS

### (12 performances)

A drama in three acts by Randolph Carter, based on Emily
Brontë's novel. Produced by Robert Henderson and Harry
Young at the Longacre Theatre, New York, April 27, 1939.

Cast of characters—

```
Ellen Dean.......................................Viola  Roache
Joseph..........................................Francis  Compton
Heathcliff...........................................Don   Terry
Hindley Ernshaw................................Robert  Bartron
Catherine  Ernshaw................................Edith  Barrett
Edgar Linton....................................Sherling  Oliver
Isabel Linton....................................Peggy  Converse
      Acts I and III.—Wuthering Heights.  Act II.—The Grange.
   Staged  by Stewart Chaney; settings by Mr. Chaney.
```

Picking up the romance of Heathcliff and Catherine Ernshaw
when the star-crossed lovers are well advanced toward maturity.
They stage several pitch battles, Heathcliff leaves, Catherine marries the stuffed and stilted Edgar Linton, and there is great misery
from then on to the tragic finale.

## THE SWING MIKADO

### (24 performances)

A 1939 version of the Gilbert & Sullivan operetta conceived by
Harry Minturn; swing orchestration and arrangements by Charles
Levy and Gentry Warden. Porduced by The Marolin Corpora-
tion at the 44th Street Theatre, New York, May 1, 1939.

Cast of characters—

```
Nanki-Poo.......................................Maurice   Cooper
Pish-Tush..........................................Lewis  White
Ko-Ko..........................................Herman  Greene
Pooh-Bah........................................William  Franklin
Yum-Yum.......................................Gladys  Boucree
Pitti-Sing.........................................Frankie  Fambro
Peep-Bo...........................................Mabel  Carter
Katisha...........................................Mabel  Walker
The  Mikado...................................Edward  Fraction
      Act I.—A  Coral Island  in  the  Pacific.  Act II.—The  Town
Meeting Place on the Island.
      Staged  by Harry Minturn;  dances  by Sammy  Dyer and  Hazel
Davis;  song  direction by Viola Hill; settings by Clive Rickabaugh;
lighting  by Oscar Ryan;  costumes  by John Pratt;  music  direction
by Edward Wurtzbach.
```

"The Swing Mikado," produced originally by the Chicago unit
of the WPA Federal Theatre, enjoyed successful runs in both Chi-

cago and New York before it was taken over by this commercial group. (See page 480.)

## DAY IN THE SUN

### (6 performances)

A comedy in three acts by Edward R. Sammis and Ernest V. Heyn. Produced by Forbes Dawson at the Biltmore Theatre, New York, May 16, 1939.

Cast of characters—

| | |
|---|---|
| Ed Hubbell | Matt Briggs |
| Postman | Royal Cutter |
| Gert Hubbell | Maida Reade |
| J. D. Crabshaw | Edward Butler |
| Ann Sumner | Elizabeth Reller |
| Brickie Hubbell | James Truex |
| Charlie Sumner | Taylor Holmes |
| Judge Livingstone | St. Clair Bayfield |
| Dick Blanchard | Ralph Holmes |
| Horace Grogan | Frank McCormack |
| Martin Mallon | Franklin Fox |
| Frank Burroughs | James Todd |
| Radio Commentator | Jack Hasler |
| Photographer | Sorele Sayer |
| Miss McLean | Jacqueline de Wit |

Acts I, II and III.—Living-Room of Summer Home in Small Town Near New York.
Staged by Arthur Sircom; setting by Louis Kennel.

Charlie Sumner is a fiend for slogans and advertising contests but not much of a provider. He lives hopefully on his relatives and happens to be able to furnish an alibi for a man accused of murder and about to be convicted on circumstantial evidence. Charlie had seen the man in the city library the day and hour of the crime.

## BROWN DANUBE

### (21 performances)

A melodrama in three acts by Burnet Hershey. Produced by Bonfils & Somnes, Inc., at the Lyceum Theatre, New York, May 17, 1939.

Cast of characters—

| | |
|---|---|
| Elsa | Gertrude Barton |
| Ludwig | Edward Fielding |
| Heinrich | Damian O'Flynn |
| Zita | Gladys Hanson |
| Erika | Jessie Royce Landis |
| Hedwig | Alice John |
| Anton | Albert Bergh |
| Stefan | George Macready |
| A Trooper | William Shea |
| Prince Otto von Tornheim | Ernest Lawford |

```
Franz....................................Robert  Vivian
Mr.  Mueller............................Edgar  Stehli
Lieut.  Schultz..........................Edward  Franz
Waldmann..............................Norman  Porter
Ernest  Hammaka.......................Dean  Jagger
Cardinal  von  Urbas....................John  McKee
Johann.................................Paul  Ballantyne
Lieut.  Grenzel........................Francis  Cleveland
Reineke................................Robert  Lindsey
Dahlmann..............................Frank  Richards
1st  Inspector..........................Albert  Ward
2nd  Inspector.........................William  Shea
Troopers:  Fred  Cotton,  F.  Byron  Gulden,  William  Hallowell,  Lisle
    Scott  and  Randolph  Wade.
```

Act I.—Scene 1—Interior of the Vienna-Paris Express. 2—Room at Tornheim Castle Near Vienna. Act II.—Erika's Apartment in Vienna. Act III.—Scene 1—Room at Tornheim. 2—Interior of the Express.

Staged by George Somnes; settings by John Root.

Prince Otto von Tornheim is taking the remnants of his family, including his daughter Erika, out of Vienna hoping to escape the Hitler invasion. Fifteen minutes from the Swiss border the Von Tornheims are stopped and sent back by Nazi order. In Vienna the Nazi in command, Ernest Hammaka, having once been an employee of the Von Tornheims, and always having a longing for Erika, agrees to save the life of Erika's brother if she will marry him. Erika agrees, but Prince von Tornheim knows that Hammaka's mother was of Jewish blood and that defeats Hammaka and brings about a happy ending for the Von Tornheims.

## THE AMERICAN LYRIC THEATRE

A repertory of music and dance drama. Produced by the American Lyric Theatre in association with The League of Composers at the Martin Beck Theatre, New York, May 18, 1939. Robert Edmond Jones, Managing Director.

## THE DEVIL AND DANIEL WEBSTER

### (6 performances)

A musical folk play by Stephen Vincent Benét and Douglas Moore.

Cast of characters—

```
Jabez  Stone...........................John  Gurney
Mary  Stone............................Nancy  McCord
Daniel  Webster........................Lansing  Hatfield
Mr.  Scratch...........................George  Rasely
Old  Man..............................Lee  Couch
Old  Woman...........................Alice  Tobin
School  Teacher........................Telete  Lester
A  Fiddler.............................Fred  Stewart
Justice  Hathorne......................Clair  Kramer
```

```
Simon Girty.....................................Ernice Lawrence
King Philip.......................................Philip Whitfield
Teach...........................................Lawrence Siegle
Walter Butler.......................................Don Lee
Men and Women of Cross Corners, New Hampshire.
    Scene—Cross Corners, New Hampshire.
```

Staged by John Houseman; music directed by Fritz Reiner and Lee Pattison; chorus under direction of May Valentine; settings and lighting by Robert Edmond Jones; choreography by Eugene Loring; associate producer, Richard Aldrich.

"The Devil and Daniel Webster" is an adaptation of the Faust legend taken from Stephen Vincent Benét's short story of the same title. Jabez Stone, having sold his soul to the Devil, is called upon for payment on his wedding night. Daniel Webster, being a neighbor and guest, agrees to defend Jabez before any jury the Devil can summon. Even a jury out of hell cannot withstand Daniel's eloquence.

PRECEDED BY

## FILLING STATION

A ballet-document in one act by Virgil Thomson.

Cast of characters—

```
Mac: Filling Station Attendant...................Lew Christensen
Roy: Truck Driver..............................Erick Hawkins
Ray: Truck Driver..............................Eugene Loring
State Trooper....................................Ray Weamer
Motorist.....................................Harold Christensen
His Wife........................................Anne Campbell
His Child........................................Ruby Asquith
The Rich Boy....................................Fred Danieli
The Rich Girl.............................Gisella Caccialanza
The Gangster....................................Michael Kidd
    Staged by Lincoln Kirstein; music directed by Fritz Litzinger;
costumes by Paul Cadmus; choreography by Lew Christensen.
```

## SUSANNA, DON'T YOU CRY

### (May 22, 1939)

### (4 performances)

A musical romance in two acts by Sarah Newmeyer and Clarence Loomis, based on melodies of Stephen Foster; special music by Hans Spialek.

Cast of characters—

```
Brian Tolliver...................................Lansing Hatfield
Susan Eliot.........................................Bettina Hall
Carter Reynolds................................Michael Bartlett
Eulalie Bland.....................................Hope Manning
Judge Bland......................................George Lessey
Mrs. Bland......................................Merle Maddern
Grandfather.........................................John Kirk
```

Cato..............................................J. Louis Johnson
Lem..............................................Robert Clarke
Grandmother (Ghost)............................Helen Mestelle
First Houseman.................................Jonathan Brice
Second Houseman...............................James Armstrong
Angie............................................Avis Andrews
A Young Composer...............................Richard Clark
Stage Doorman..................................Peter Chambers
Jeb Martin.....................................Lawrence Bolton
Jonathan Lamphrey.............................Robert Chisholm
Jeannie June (Age 4)..........................Diana Donnenwirth
Bradley........................................Frank Chamberlin
Jeannie June (Age 8)..............................Helen Renee
Mrs. Stoddard.....................................Mary Perry
Mary Lou.........................................Helen Mestelle
Randy...............................................Paul Roberts

Act I.—Scenes 1 and 4—Judge Bland's Plantation Home Near Covington, Kentucky, Christmas Eve, 1851. 2—Eulalie and Susan's Bedroom. 3—The Stage of the Melodeon Theatre, Cincinnati. 5—The Levee. Act II.—Scene 1—Ballroom of the Eliot Hotel, San Francisco, April, 1861. 2—Mrs. Stoddard's Boarding House, New York City, May, 1865. 3—Before the Bland Plantation.

Staged by Jose Ruben; music directed by Lee Pattison and Andre Polah; settings by Robert Edmond Jones.

"Susanna, Don't You Cry" is a romance evolved from Stephen Foster songs and relates the adventure of Susanna, who ran away hoping to join the actor Tolliver in Cincinnati. She is followed by Carter Reynolds, who accidentally kills Tolliver. Susanna and Carter are married and go to California to start a hotel and escape the police.

## THE BALLET CARAVAN

### (May 24, 1939)

### (2 performances)

Three ballets directed by Lincoln Kirstein; music conducted by Fritz Kitzinger.

### AIR AND VARIATIONS

A classic ballet in one act with choreographic arrangement by William Dollar of fifteen of Bach's Goldberg Variations; orchestrated by Nicolas Nabokoff.

Principals engaged—

Ruby Asquith                        Lew Christensen
Marie-Jeanne                        Todd Bolender
Lorna London                        Erick Hawkins
Misses Campbell, Heater, Tompkins and Vallon.

### POCAHONTAS

A ballet-legend in one act by Lew Christensen; music by Elliott Carter, Jr.

Cast of characters—

| | |
|---|---|
| Princess Pocahontas | Leda Anchutina |
| The Emperor Powhatan | Erik Hawkins |
| Pipisco | Eugene Loring |
| Captain John Smith | Harold Christensen |
| John Rolfe | Fred Danieli |

Indian Girls: Misses Asquith, Campbell, Colbath, DeKova, Friedlich, Heater, London, Quarequio, Shea, Tompkins, Tucker, Vallon.
Indian Men: Messrs. Bolender, Godwin, Kidd, Lahee, Weamer.
Costumes by Karl Free.

## BILLY THE KID

A character-ballet in one act by Eugene Loring; music by Aaron Copland.

Principals engaged—

Eugene Loring                    Marie-Jeanne
Todd Bolender                    Lew Christensen
Misses Campbell, Heater, London, Asquith, Colbath, Quarequio, Tompkins, DeKova, Friedlich, Shea, Tucker, Vallon and Wagner.
Messrs. Godwin, Hawkins, Kidd, Lahee and Weamer.
Costumes by Jared French.

## CLEAN BEDS

### (4 performances)

A drama in three acts by George S. George. Produced by Cled, Inc., at the Golden Theatre, New York, May 25, 1939.

Cast of characters—

| | |
|---|---|
| Murrey | Nat Burns |
| Lodger | Edwin James |
| Worth | Joseph Holland |
| Goldie | Sheila Trent |
| Kelcy | William Balfour |
| Mrs. Murrey | Fifi Louise Hall |
| Jack Letton | Pat Gleason |
| Donald Tabor | Alfred Alderdie |
| Charlie | James Welch |
| Officer Ryan | Tom Gorman |
| Ira Skyse | William Phinney |
| Joe | Raymond Maxwell |
| Blowsy Mag | Emma Hunting |
| Petroni | Anthony Raimond |
| Barbara | Helen Beverly |
| Daisy | Mara Brooke |
| Callahan | William Hunter |
| Mrs. Perkins | Leila Romer |
| Mary | Geraldine Cooke |

Acts I, II and III.—Bill Murrey's Rooming House for Transients in a Large American City.
Staged by Vadim Uraneff; setting by Watson Barratt.

Murrey is the proprietor of a flop house in a large Eastern American city. Mrs. Murrey runs a bawdy house on the side. Donald Tabor, a nice young man who has quarreled with Barbara, his wife, comes to the flop house to rent a bed. Murrey and a couple of other crooks plan to drug Donald, entrap Barbara and sell her into shame at Mrs. Murrey's. It works that way until late evening, when Donald conquers the drug and sends for the police.

## PRODUCTIONS BY WPA FEDERAL THEATRE PROJECT

### THE BIG BLOW

#### (157 performances)

A drama in six scenes by Theodore Pratt; music by Hans Bruno Meyer. Produced by the WPA Federal Theatre at Maxine Elliott's Theatre, New York, October 1, 1938.

Cast of characters—

| | |
|---|---|
| Wade Barnett | Kendall Clark |
| Aunt Jane Barnett | Elizabeth Malone |
| First Cracker | Leslie Hunt |
| Deefy | George Mathews |
| Orey | Thurman Jackson |
| Sarah Barnett | Dorothy Raymond |
| Celie Partin | Amelia Romano |
| Ony Mell | Burton Mallory |
| Clay | Doe Doe Green |
| Carney Jelks | Edwin Cooper |
| Holy Roller Preacher | Gregory Robbins |
| Preacher's Daughter | Frances Ware |
| First Woman | Melba Palmer |
| Her Husband | Jack Smith |
| Second Cracker | William Gallagher |
| Third Cracker | George Probert |
| Second Woman | Elizabeth Hawkins |
| Woman with Baby | Kate Cloud |
| Rusty the Kitten | Herself |

Additional Crackers: Fred J. Burke, Pell Dentler, Josephine Smith, Maurice Fallet, George Fay, Edward J. Fleischer, Julian Garfield, Agnes Gildea, Alec Guin, Fay Keen, Ruth Hoffman, Sam Lewis, Albert McWilliams, Myron Paulson, Wilda Pratt, Aage Steenshorne, Julian Taliaferro, Eugenia Woods, John McCormack, John Morrisey, Lise Rembova and Edward Wright.

Scene 1—Yard of a South Florida Farm. 2—Celie Partin's Cabin. 3, 4 and 6—The Barnett Log House. 5—A Holy Roller's Tent. Staged by Anton Bundsmann; settings by Samuel Leve; costumes by Mary Merrill; lighting by Feder. Production under the direction of Morris Ankrum, in association with George Brewer.

Wade Barnett has traded his Nebraska farm and brought his mother and his aunt to Florida for his mother's health. Arrived in Florida Wade discovers that he has been cheated in the deal, but is determined to go through with the adventure. He builds himself a stout log cabin and goes in successfully for scientific farming. His industry arouses the ire of the lazy Florida crackers. When he befriends a Negro named Clay they turn on him. Along comes a hurricane and Wade's log house is the only one that stands. The stability of the house and that of Wade's character turn the crackers in his favor.  His chief enemy is killed and he marries an interesting native girl.

## ANDROCLES AND THE LION

### (104 performances)

A play in a prologue and two acts by George Bernard Shaw. Revived by the WPA Federal Theatre at the Lafayette Theatre, New York, December 16, 1938.

Cast of characters—

| | |
|---|---|
| The Lion | Add Bates |
| Androcles | Arthur Wilson |
| Megaera | Hilda Offley |
| Lavinia | Edna Thomas |
| Centurion | Thomas Mosely |
| The Captain | P. Jay Sidney |
| Ferrovius | Daniel Leo Haynes |
| Spintho | Wardell Saunders |
| Lentulus | Percy Verwayne |
| Metellus | Al Moore |
| Ox Driver | Julian Costello |
| The Editor | J. Louis Johnson |
| The Call Boy | John Milton Lacey |
| Retiarius | Joseph Pope Jones |
| Secutor | Paul Johnson |
| Menagerie Keeper | Alonzo Bosan |
| Caesar | Maurice Ellis |
| Beggar | Charles Johnson |

Prologue—A Jungle Path.  Act I.—A Square at the Gates of Rome.  Act II.—Behind the Emperor's Box at the Coliseum.

Staged by Samuel Rosen; music by George Couvreur; settings by Manuel Essman; lighting by Feder; costumes by Perry Watkins, produced for the WPA by Philip Barber.

"Androcles and the Lion" was first produced in New York by Granville Barker at Wallack's Theatre, January 27, 1915, with O. P. Heggie as Androcles and Phil Dwyer as The Lion.

## * PINOCCHIO

### (149 performances)

An extravaganza with music in three acts adapted for the stage by Yasha Frank from the Italian of C. Collodi.  Revived by the WPA Federal Theatre at the Ritz Theatre, New York, December 23, 1939.

Cast of characters—

| | |
|---|---|
| Gepetto | Allan Frank |
| His Cat | Ettore Maggioni |
| Town Crier | Emil Hirsch |
| Mice | Jean Harper, Gretchen Karnot |
| Young Father | Vito Scotti |
| Pinocchio | Edwin Michaels |
| Juggler | Archie Onri |

```
Tumbler...........................................Anthony J. Salo
Grandpa ................................................Bill Swan
Puppeteers........................Ernest Moore, Elizabeth Roberts
Marionette....................................Gabrielle  Duval
Warrior Puppet....................................George Cohan
Rag Doll.......................................Helen Galuback
Hansel and Gretel...................Anne Wheeler, Mary Shannon
Beggar Women....................Anya Kubert, Francena Scott
Blue Haired Fairy Queen........................Georgiana Brand
The Cat.............................................Sam Lewis
The Fox..........................................Edward Lalor
Jolly Coachman.............................Robert Williamson
Ringmaster.......................................David Manning
The General......................................Hans Schweng
Pinocchio, the Mule.............................Mickey Kane
The Maestro........................................Sam Lewis
The Fireman...................................Sherman Dirkson
Mlle. Fifi..........................................Kohana
Capt. Fried Meatty...............................Harry Duncan
Lion ..............................................Phil Dwyer
Ship Figurehead.......................................Christiani
Male Goldfish........................................Kohana
Female Goldfish.............................Elizabeth Reydova
Blind Woman..................................Sonia Raskov
```

Act I.—Scene 1—Gepetto's Workshop, Italy. 2—Street. 3—A
Marionette Stage. Act II.—Scene 1—Fork in the Road. 2—Land
of the Boobies. 3—Under the Big Top. 4—Bottom of Sea.
5—Within the Whale. Act III.—Gepetto's Cottage.

Staged by Yasha Frank; music by Eddison von Ottenfeld and
Armando Loredo; choreography by Alexander Mamlet; settings by
Perry Watkins, lighting by Moe Hack; costumes by James Cochran;
special effects by Stephen Jan Tichacek.

## THE SWING MIKADO

### (62 performances)

The Chicago Federal Theatre version of the Gilbert and Sullivan operetta in two acts, conceived by Harry Minturn; swing
orchestration by Charles Levy; swing arrangements by Gentry
Warden. Produced by WPA Federal Theatre at the New Yorker
Theatre, New York, March 1, 1939.

Principals engaged—

```
Nanki-Poo.......................................Maurice  Cooper
Pish-Tush...........................................Lewis White
Ko-Ko...........................................Herman Greene
Pooh-Bah.......................................William Franklin
Yum-Yum.........................................Gladys Boucree
Pitti-Sing.........................................Frankie Fambro
Peep-Bo .............................................Mabel Carter
Katisha........................................Mabel Walker
The Mikado.....................................Edward Fraction
```

Acts I and II.—A Coral Island in the Pacific.

Staged by Harry Minturn; dances by Sammy Dyer and Hazel
Davis; vocal direction by Viola Hill; music directed by Edward
Wurtzebach; settings by Clive Rickabaugh; costumes by John Pratt;
lighting by Oscar Ryan; general supervision by George Jackson,
Emil Neiglick and Margaret Rand.

The idea of "jazzing" Gilbert and Sullivan originated in Chicago in the Fall of 1938. "The Swing Mikado" was produced
there in September and ran for the better part of the season. It

was transferred to New York March 1, 1939, and was later acquired by commercial interests.

## * SING FOR YOUR SUPPER

### (44 performances)

A musical revue compiled by Harold Hecht; lyrics by Robert Sour; sketches by Dave Lesan, Turner Bullock, Charlotte Kent and John Latouche; music by Lee Wainer and Ned Lehac. Produced by the WPA Federal Theatre at the Adelphi Theatre, New York, April 24, 1939.

Principals engaged—

| | |
|---|---|
| Gordon Clarke | Paul Jacchia |
| Virginia Bolen | Edward Fuller |
| Peggy Coudray | Carl Chapin |
| Bidda Blakeley | Edward Hemmer |
| Paula Laurence | Edwin Whittner |
| Coby Ruskin | Hansford Wilson |
| Rose Poindexter | Harry Hart |
| Roslyn Harvey | Bowen Tufts |
| Carol Coult | Walter LeRoy |
| Genora English | John Campbell |
| Allan Tinney | William Tinney |
| Muni Diamond | Frank Newton |
| Richard Finlayson | Rufus Finlayson |
| Lily Verne | Edwin Cooper |
| Edith Groome | Theresa Alvarez |
| Violet Smith | Costello Woolridge |
| Augusta Joseph | Arthur Donaldson |
| Trudy Goodrich | Israel Lansky |
| Louise Kelly | Edward LeDuc |
| William Britten | James Mordecai |
| Walter Franklyn | Ernest Pavano |
| Theodora Peck | William Myron |
| James Eakins | George Whittington |
| Edward Gutter | Maurice Siegel |

Staged by H. Gordon Graham and Harold Hecht; sketches staged by Robert H. Gordon; dances by Ned McGurn; choreography and ensembles by Anna Sokolow; settings by Herbert Andrews; costumes by Mary Merrill; lighting by Feder.

## * LIFE AND DEATH OF AN AMERICAN

### (29 performances)

A dramatic biography in two parts by George Sklar. Produced by the WPA Federal Theatre at the Maxine Elliott Theatre, New York, May 19, 1939.

Cast of characters—

| | |
|---|---|
| Michael Dorgan | John Pote |
| Kathleen Dorgan | Helene C. Ambrose |
| Slim (As a Boy) | Everett Spencer |
| Jerry Dorgan (As a Boy) | Danny Greene |
| Mrs. Ives | Josephine Morse |
| Spike | Nat Loesberg |
| Jerry Dorgan (As a Man) | J. Arthur Kennedy |

```
Mary Buckley.....................................Mary Rolfe
Waitress.......................................Dorothy Dunsby
Peasoup.......................................Eleanor Scherr
Slim (As a Man)................................Kendall Clark
Blues Singer..................................Blanche Collins
Doctor........................................Judson Langill
Lieut. Forbes....................................Robert Lowe
Danny Dorgan..................................Donald Cafarella
```
    Parts I and II.—Small Eastern City and Chicago, Ill.
    Staged by Charles K. Freeman; music by Alex North and Earl
Robinson; choreography by Lily Mehlmann; settings by Howard Bay;
costumes by Alexander Jones; lighting by Moe Hack; technical director, George Crowley.

Jerry Dorgan was born twelve seconds after the new century
had been ushered in. His parents were of the poor but honest
type. His life was conventional and commonplace. He was an
average student in grammar school, an athletic hero in high school,
an inquisitive but healthy adolescent. His bent was scientific and
he was making progress when his father died. He went to work
in an automobile factory. He was getting along promisingly
among the younger executives when the crash came and he had
to go back to work in the factory. At the second pay cut he
joined with the workmen who were protesting, became involved
in strike troubles and was killed in a brush with the police.

## OTHER FEDERAL THEATRE ACTIVITIES

At the close of the 1937-38 season four Federal Theatre plays
were still running in New York: ". . . one-third of a nation . . ."
which closed October 22, 1938, with 237 performances to its
credit; "Haiti," by William Du Bois, which took a couple of
short vacations in the Summer and closed September 24, 1938,
with 168 performances, which were very nearly continuous; "Prologue to Glory" by E. P. Conkle, which closed at the Maxine
Elliott Theatre August 13, 1938, and reopened at Daly's September 19 with Erford Gage in Stephen Courtleigh's role of Abraham Lincoln. The play had been presented 169 times before it
finally closed November 5, 1938; Shaw's "On the Rocks" which
was revived for fifteen performances between June 15 and July 1,
reopening October 7 to increase the number of performances to
sixty-six.

At Daly's Theatre December 22, 1938, a Yiddish adaptation
by Chaver Paver of the Clifford Odets "Awake and Sing" was
produced by Lem Ward for the Federal Theatre and continued
until April 9, 1939, chalking up ninety-five performances. It was
staged by Jacob Mestel, the settings were designed by Wood Mc-
Lane, lighting by Moe Hack and the cast included Isadore Ver-

nick, Emilie Adler, Gustave Schacht, Lyda Slava, Louis Brandt, Louis Coppersmith, Morris Dorf, Harold Schutzman and Jack Tammy.

During the Christmas holidays, in addition to the major presentation of "The Story of Ferdinand" and "Spring Fever," the WPA Marionettes gave twenty performances and the vaudeville players gave several shows. Two companies, Negro and white, sang the story of the birth of Christ in an adaptation by Hedley Gordon Graham on street corners during the holidays, starting December 19, 1938, in front of the Federal Theatre Workshop. Other performances, the last of which was on December 23, were on the steps of the Public Library, in front of the New York *Daily News* and at other points in Harlem and Manhattan.

Beginning January 30, 1939, at the Nora Bayes Theatre a Doris Humphrey-Charles Weidman dance program was given six performances, including "To the Dance," "With Red Fires," with music by Wallingford Riegger, and "The Race of Life," a dance based on the Thurman drawings with music by Vivian Fine. The dancers included: Doris Humphrey, Charles Weidman, Katherine Litz, Lily Mann, Eva Desca, Mildred Tanzer, Saida Gerrard, Kathleen O'Brien, Nadia Chilkovsky, Sophie Mintz, Hilda Sheldon, Lee Sherman, Marvin Marzoff, José Limon.

This was followed April 4, 1939, by another dance program on a Spanish theme called "Adelante" at Daly's Theatre where sixteen performances were presented. This included poems from the Spanish translated by Eli Siegel and Rolfe Humphries with additional verse by Bob Whittington and music by Genevieve Pitot. Narration was directed by Brett Warren; settings and costumes by Alexander Jones and lighting by Harry Peters. Charles K. Freeman staged the production which was under the technical supervision of George Crowley. The cast included: Bill Matons, Helen Tamaris, Alfredo Allegro, Paula Bass, Pauline Bubrick, Florence Cheasnov, Mura Dehn, Fanya Geltman, Ailes Gilmour, Ida Little, Lulu Morris, Klarna Pinska, Vivian Manet, Selma Rubin, Hilda Sheldon, Janet Schaff, Selma Schneider, Alex Tairoff, Mildred Tanzer, Roger Dodge, Donald Knapp, Rajah O'Hardino, Richard McMurray, Marvin Marzoff, Al Rosenblum.

# OFF BROADWAY

The Fifth Avenue Repertory Company started the season June 21, 1938, with "She Went to Town," written by George D. Batson and staged by Richard McCracken at the Fifth Avenue Theatre. Dorothy South, Dale Jordan, Robert Morrow, June Dae, Charles Paul, Bonnie Donohue and others made up the cast. On the same date The Washington Heights Actors Guild produced "American Caravan," a comedy by Frank Hilliard and Violet Rodda, and in late August this group produced "Love Is a Simple Thing" by Paul Showers. A third offering, "Slumbering Gods," by Louise Vaupel, ran for a week at Colonial Manor Theatre. All three plays were staged by Frank Hilliard. On June 23, 1938, a group calling themselves Six and Company produced "Death of Spring" by Alfred D. Geto at the Nora Bayes Theatre. J. J. Robbins directed and in the cast were Betty Comden and E. Monro Brown.

The Irish Repertory Players at the Heckscher Theatre, with Augustin Duncan directing and also playing in John M. Synge's "The Well of the Saints," continued from the former season into 1938-39 and was followed by "The White-Headed Boy" by Lennox Robinson, staged by J. Augustus Keogh, November 6, 1938, and in February of 1939 they gave one performance of George Bernard Shaw's "Widowers' Houses" which, by the way, was last seen in New York at the Herald Square Theatre March 8, 1907.

The International Ladies' Garment Workers' Union achieved such noted success with "Pins and Needles" that other labor groups went into the business of producing plays. The Furrier Workers' Union gave a performance of Clifford Odets' "Waiting for Lefty" at the Hotel Center Theatre July 19, 1938, with Milton Luban directing, and June 9, 1939, the Retail Drug Store Employees Union produced "Professional Men," by Charles Shillet and I. J. Alexander, at the Heckscher Theatre with a cast of thirty-five players. Howard da Sylva directed and Henry Andrews designed the settings.

At the New School for Social Research "The Cradle Will Rock" was given one performance by the Flatbush Players early in the season with Lou Cooper in the Marc Blitzstein role. January 15, 1939, it was again produced on this stage together with Albert Maltz's "Rehearsal," this time by the New Theatre League who followed it in February and March with an anti-Fascist satirical operetta called "Maid in Japan," written by Maurice Stoller with music by Elie Siegmeister. It was staged by Kumar Goshal. Also in the repertory of the Social Research School were "A Life in the Day of a Secretary," a one-act musical by Alfred Hayes and Jay Williams with the score by George Kleinsinger and staged by Peter Frye; "Press Time," by Stedman Coles and Jerome Brookman, staged by Joseph C. Pevny, February 26 and March 11, 1939; "America Sings," a revue produced by Theatre Arts Committee, March 18, 1939; "I've Got the Tune," a one-act music play by Marc Blitzstein; "Plant in the Sun," by Ben Bengal, and "Rehearsal," by Albert Maltz, in April and May, 1939, by members of the Flatbush Arts Theatre.

Edward Stanton, Ruth Simon and Edward Fitzgerald, known as the New Actors Group, produced "Desire to Live" at the Nora Bayes Theatre, August 4, 1938. The play was written by Jessie Lou Marvin, staged by George Lyons and included in the cast were Valesca Momerty, Alan Jason, Gloria Brown, Katherine Quinn, Lucille Banner, etc. The New Actors Group also produced "People Like Us" by George Salvatore and Joseph La Gattuta, at the Nora Bayes Theatre, September 16, 1938. John J. Robbins was the director.

The East Side Dramatic Group, which was playing Arthur Smith's "End of a Cycle" at the end of 1937-38, carried it into the new season and followed it at the Grand Street Playhouse with "Nether-World," by the same author, a living newspaper analysis of slum forces and crime among youth.

The Stage Crafters produced "One Woman's Way," by Tracy Kingman at the Nora Bayes Theatre August 29, 1938, staged by James R. Garey. We the Players gave one performance of "Recount," a political satire by Louis Wilderman and Arthur Block, at the Nora Bayes Theatre September 20, 1938. The Village Drama Group produced "They Fought for What" by Julius Muscari in September and in the same month Jay Strong produced "Thanks for Tomorrow" by Le Roy Bailey at the Nora Bayes Theatre, Walter Brooks directing and Louis Kennel designing the settings. The veteran May Vokes was in the cast which also included Francis de Sales, Eleanor Wells and Ralph Holmes.

In early October Butler Davenport revived his own play, "Difference in Gods," and played in it at the Davenport Theatre. Leighton Rollins, who had presented his dramatic experiment staging eighty-five tragic Goya etchings at the Laboratory Theatre, East Hampton, was encouraged to make a New York production and November 14, 1938, produced the poetic phantasy called "Disasters of War," with tableaux presented by the Studio Players, at the Finch Theatre.

December 20, 1938, the Metropolitan Players presented "Jail for Sale," a comedy by Samuel J. Park, which had been tested at the Barter Theatre, Abingdon, Va., and at the Bandbox Theatre in Suffield, Conn. The author staged the play and Lucille La Verne was in the cast. "Policy Kings" by Michael Ashwood opened at the Nora Bayes Theatre December 29, 1938. Music was written by Sam Manning; songs by James P. Johnson; staged by Winston Douglass, and the author was also the producer.

The Little Theatre Players produced "Afternoon of a Faun" by David Wiltshire and "Beyond Help" by Andrew Russell at the Lenox Hill Auditorium January 28, 1939.

The Playgoers Theatre presented several plays at the Barbizon Playhouse. Among these: "The Spring Returneth," a play with music by Alfred Allegro staged by William Vaughan, February 9, 10 and 11, 1939, "The Goslings" by Henry K. Moritz, staged by Ann Lobowe March 31, and "Bound to Happen" by Elswyth Thane, staged by Sola Staw May, 1939. In late March and early April the Balfour Players produced Martin Rost's "Soil," staged by Benno Franck. Another March production was "Stop Press" at the Vanderbilt Theatre, produced by The Acting Company, Inc., an organization composed of professional actors many of whom are in Broadway productions.

At the Barbizon-Plaza Theatre the Keynote Theatre sponsored a revue called "Sunday Night Varieties," opening April 9, 1939. It continued once a week through April at the Keystone Theatre. The sketches were by Berenice Kazunoff and Sylvia Fine, the lyrics by John La Touche and David Greggory and the production was conceived and directed by Nat Lichtman.

The Snarks gave their thirteenth annual performance at the Heckscher Theatre March 29, 1939. The play, which was "The Aunt from England" by Cosmo Hamilton and Anthony Gibbs, was directed by Arthur Sircom. The Gateway Players presented Laurel Rex's "American Cartoon" and Theatregate, a company of professional players, produced "Duet in a Dark Forest," by Mears Pitcher in the early Spring. The New York Players directed by Anne Gerlette produced four one-act plays in April at the Master Theatre: "The Informer" and "Justice" by Bertholdt Brecht, "Rehearsal" by Albert Maltz and "Happy Journey" by

Thornton Wilder. Three groups of the Harry Meloff Theatre Festival gave a series of Sunday night showings at the Nora Bayes Theatre in the Spring of 1939 under the auspices of the International Workers Order. The one-act plays included Ben Bengal's "Plant in the Sun," "Rehearsal" by Albert Maltz and a cut version of Maxim Gorky's "Lower Depths."

"The Ascent of F 6," a poetic drama by W. H. Auden and Christopher Isherwood, once held by the Theatre Guild, was produced for the first time in America by the Drove Players at their studio home April 23, 1939, for one performance. The Cooperative Players produced "Hell's Half Acre" by Abram Hill, staged by Joseph Orbato at the Transport Playhouse in late April. In early June this group produced "The Black Messiah" by Dennis Donoghue and James H. Dunmore. This comedy which was once called "The Demi-God" concerns the life of Father Divine. At the Henry Street Settlement in late April and early May "Medicine Show," a living newspaper written by the members of the Settlement House, was staged by Chouteau Dyer and Betty Lord.

The Group Theatre tried out two experimental plays on Broadway: William Saroyan's "My Heart's in the Highlands," later produced at the Guild Theatre and taken over as a Theatre Guild subscription offering, and "Quiet City" by Irwin Shaw which had two Sunday evening previews April 16 and 23, 1939, at the Belasco Theatre. It was then withdrawn for revision.

The Vagabond Players produced "The Great Magician" by Lawrence Carra with music by Wenner Laise. It was staged by Edward Padula at the Cherry Lane Theatre in late April and early May of 1939. This was a modern conception in play form of the Commedia dell'Arte routine. They also revived Benn Levy's "The Devil Passes" earlier in the season and later R. C. Sherriff's "Journey's End" which was directed by William Marwood. In the cast were William Hawley, Frank Thune, Daniel Cedrone, Robert Farquhar and John Morgan. "A Right Angle Triangle" by Ferdinand Voteur, a play about Negro Metropolitan life, was put on at the Workshop Theatre in late May by the Rose McClendon Players. The Workshop Theatre earlier in the season had presented three one-act plays under the collective title of "Curtain Time" at the Nora Bayes Theatre with Cyril Easton, Ty Cheney, Sheila Hunt and David Human in the cast.

The Modern Repertory Company with a non-Equity cast produced "War Scare," a drama by Joseph Moore, at the Rand School of the Theatre late in May, 1939. Another non-Equity cast played at the Cherry Lane Theatre in a play called "Reserve Two for Murder" by John Randall. This play was produced by two playwrights, James Reach and Tom Taggart, who formed a company called Manning Productions, leased the Cherry Lane Theatre in Greenwich Village and May 22, 1939, started a program of pre-Broadway tryouts with non-Equity casts.

The Lighthouse Players of the New York Association for the Blind, which has presented plays successively for the past 13 years, offered during the 1938-39 season at the Lighthouse Little Theatre, Marjorie Benton Cooke's "A Court Comedy," Mae Howley Barry's "The Bond Between" and Babette Hughes's "If the Shoe Pinches." Six blind young actresses formed the cast. Twenty members of the Guild Center Players, another company of blind players, presented Helen Pitts Parker's "The Raveled Sleeve," "A Good Girl in the Kitchen" by F. G. Johnson and A. L. Kaser, "The Great Suggestion" by Bertram Marburgh and Bennett Musson and "The Marriage Proposal" by Anton Chekhov at the Theresa L. Kaufmann Auditorium May 18, 1939. Alice Henry's "Fugitives" was given one performance at the Greenwich House by the Contemporary Theatre Group in early June, and about the same time The Actors Repertory Company gave Dan Garrison's Oklahoma oil field drama called "Boom" at the A C A Galleries.

Antoinette Perry gave a public audition at the Henry Miller Theatre for the Apprentice Theatre of the American Theatre Council June 1, 1939, after intensive work through the season which began in January. Fifty-six young actors and actresses remained after the eliminations from 2,000 applicants, tried out during the five months. The final performance consisted of fourteen short sketches directed by Theron Bamberger, Paul A. Foley, Frances Fuller, Harry Wagstaff Gribble, Auriole Lee, Arminta Marshall, Jean Munsell, Lea Penman, Philip Ober, Arthur Sircom, Blanche Yurka and Anton Hardt.

## MONODRAMA

Cecilia Loftus, under the management of Martin Jones, Judson O'Donnel and Clay Shaw, gave a series of impressions and impersonations at the Vanderbilt Theatre, starting October 30, 1938, and continuing until after the holidays.

Ruth Draper, after an absence from New York of two years, returned during the holidays and gave 26 performances of character sketches and monologues at the Little Theatre, beginning

December 26, 1938.

Elsie Janis started a series of Sunday evening programs at the Music Box January 1, 1939, under the management of Bernard Hart, Bill Doll and Joseph Hyman. Miss Janis, who had been absent from the New York stage for ten years, imitated many stage celebrities  There were four performances.

Miss Dorothy Crawford, who has made several tours in America and England, made her New York debut as a character monologist March 12, 1939, at the Guild Theatre, giving a program of six sketches of her own authorship.

## PUPPETS

The Wallace Puppeteers presented a series of marionette shows at their theatre in East 58th Street, New York, from October 15, 1938, to March 3, 1939. Original scripts for these plays were written by Harold Preston and the music was by Morris Singer.

The eleventh season of the Yale Puppeteers started with a performance of a topical musical revue, "It's a Small World," presented by Bernard Hart and Bill Doll at the Lyceum Theatre, November 6, 1939. The revue, which was in nineteen scenes, was written by Forman Brown and directed by Harry Burnet and Richard Brandon. Minnie Prescott Smith assisted with the costumes.

The Federal Theatre presented "Spring Fever" and a reproduction of "Florodora Sextette" at the Heckscher Theatre August 10, 1938, and "The Story of Ferdinand" in November and December at the Federal Music Theatre.

The Sue Hastings Marionettes were shown during the Christmas and Easter holidays at the McMillin Theatre of Columbia University. Beginning November 12 and ending December 31, 1938, "Winnie-the-Pooh," "Jack and the Beanstalk," "Alice in Wonderland" and "The Prince and the Hobgoblins" were shown. From March 25 to April 8, 1939, "Cinderella," "Robin Hood" and "Peter Rabbit" were the plays exhibited.

The Marionette Guild, which produced "The Emperor Jones," tried another Eugene O'Neill play, "Marco Millions." It was staged by Jerome Magon at the Carnegie Chamber Music Hall November 23 and 24, 1938. On December 18, 1938, it was repeated at the Barbizon-Plaza Theatre where Theodore Tiller's Marionettes made their New York debut February 23, 1939.

Tony Sarg's Marionettes, with Gilbert Josephson directing,

presented "Treasure Island," "Alice in Wonderland," "The
Mikado" and "Caspar's Circus" at the MacDowell Club December 29, 30 and 31, 1938.

### CHILDREN

Broadway paid its usual annual respects to the children of
New York during the Christmas holidays. The Federal Theatre
staged "Pinocchio," adapted and directed by Yasha Frank, at
the Ritz Theatre just before Christmas. The day after Christmas at the Mercury Theatre, under the management of Joseph
Lawren and Samuel N. Benjamin, a Children's Christmas Festival
started with George Blumenthal's production of the Winthrop
Ames version of "Snow White and the Seven Dwarfs," under the
stage direction of Eva Leoni. This was followed by the Children's Repertory Ballet's production of "Cinderella," a four-act
dance pantomime directed by Annette Van Dyke. December 29,
1938, "Little Women," dramatized by Marian de Forest from
the Louisa M. Alcott novel, was played by the Juvenile Actors'
Repertory Company and staged by Ester Dordoni.

The Clare Tree Major Children's Theatre did "Nobody's
Boy," a dramatization of "Sans Famille" by Hector Malot, at
the Waldorf-Astoria December 27, 1938, and in January repeated
the performance at the Heckscher Theatre, beginning its fifteenth
anniversary subscription series. "The Little Princess," an adaptation of the Frances Hodgson Burnett story, was the second attraction and "The King of the Golden River," a dramatization
of John Ruskin's fairy tale, was the last of the series.

At the Radio Music Hall the Christmas presentation included
"The Twelve Dancing Princesses," a pantomime based on the
Grimm fairy tale by Florence Rogge and Leon Leonidoff's
pageant of "The Nativity." Marco Montedoro designed the
settings and Willa Van the costumes for the pantomime for which
Maurice Baron wrote an original score. Eleanor Tennis was
the prima ballerina. Also at Radio Music Hall the Vienna Boys'
Choir made its New York debut in the Leonidoff Christmas
pageant. This chorus came from the Cathedral of St. Stephen
in Vienna.

The Children's Art Theatre gave a program of one-act plays
at the Nora Bayes Theatre consisting of "Fortunatus," "Mother
Holla" and "Little Red Riding Hood" early in December. Near
the end of the month the New York Hippodrome Opera Company
gave a series of matinees for children beginning December 27,

1938, with "Hansel and Gretel."

The King-Coit Children's Theatre presented "The Golden Cage," arranged by Catharine Cook Smith from the poems of William Blake, with music by Arthur Whiting, during February and March, 1939.

## COLLEGE PLAYS IN NEW YORK

The Hasty Pudding Club of Harvard University presented "Fair Enough" at the Waldorf-Astoria, New York, April 8, 1939, as its ninety-third annual theatrical production. The book was written by David Lannon, Alan J. Lerner and Morgan O. Preston; music by Elliott Forbes, Francis C. Lawrence, Alan J. Lerner and Sherwood Rollins; lyrics by Vinton Freedley, Jr., and David Lannon. The settings were designed by Calvin H. Eliot, George Smith and Howard Turner; music directed by Richard Lewine; dances arranged and directed by William Holbrook. Edward Clarke Lilley staged the revue.

The Princeton Triangle Club celebrated its fiftieth anniversary with a revue called "Once Over Lightly" at the 51st Street Theatre, New York, December 16, 1938. The book was written by Alexander Hays Lehmann, Richard Uhl and Robert Marshall McClung; music by Henry H. Hughes, Jr., Richard H. Gordon, Jr., Mark Lawrence and Tallman Bissell; songs by Sanders Maxwell; dance fantasies and musical settings by Carl E. Davis, Jr.

The Yale Dramatic Society presented a satirical revue "1066— And All That," at the Windsor Theatre, New York, December 19, 1938. This burlesque of English history by Reginald Arkell was based on a book by W. C. Sellar and R. J. Yeatman. The score was by Alfred Reynolds. The revue had been produced in London in 1935, and was given its American premiere by the Yale Dramatic Association at the Yale Theatre in March of 1938. The New York production was designed by Halsted Welles and the costumes by Koral Vaughn.

The University of Pennsylvania's Mask and Wig Club gave "All Around the Town," a musical show in two acts and twenty-one scenes at the Center Theatre, New York, November 19, 1938. The dialogue was mostly by George Elliott Hess and the songs by Clay A. Boland and S. Bickley Reichner. Robert F. Brown staged the revue, Walter F. Keenan, Jr., the dances and Clay Boland directed the choir.

The National Catholic Theatre Conference gave two cycles of Catholic plays at the Barbizon-Plaza Theatre, New York, called the New York Catholic Drama Festival, under the management of Rev. John W. Mahoney. "Cradle Song" was presented by the College of New Rochelle, May 6, 1939; "Murder in the Cathedral" by St. John's University and College of New Rochelle, May 7; "Mary Adelaide" by Our Lady of Good Counsel College, "Monsignor's Hour" by Manhattan College and College of Mt. St. Vincent and "Slayer of Dreams" by Fordham University, May 8; "The Far-Off Hills" by the College of St. Elizabeth and St. Peter's College, May 9.

The Fordham Mimes and Mummers staged Ben Jonson's "The Silent Woman" February 2 and 3, 1939. "Fair Enough," the annual Columbia varsity show, was staged at the Hotel Astor March 29 and 30, 1939. "The Beaux Stratagem" was presented by the Dramatic Society of the New York University Washington Square College at the Washington Square Playhouse, December 14, 17 and 20, 1938. Hunter College Make-Up Box presented "They Refuse to be Resurrected" and a puppet show called "One Summer's Day" in March. The Hunter College Italian Club presented a dramatization by Katherine Kunz-Schmidt of "I Promessi Sposi," the novel by Alessandro Manzori, at the Casa Italiana of Columbia University March 26, 1939; Barnard College Juniors presented "Forty Winks," a musical comedy in three acts by the Class of 1940, at Brinckerhoff Theatre March 10, 1939. Jane Mantell directed the performances.

### FOREIGN LANGUAGE PLAYS

The Theatre des Quatre Saisons opened its fourth New York season November 28, 1938, at the Barbizon-Plaza Theatre with Jean Anouilh's comedy "Le Bal des Voleurs." Other plays presented were "Le Precieuses Ridicule" and "Les Fourberies de Scapin" by Molière, "Le Faiseur," a comedy by Honoré de Balzac, adapted by Simone Jolliver; "L'Occasion," a tragedy in one act by Prosper Merimee, followed by Charles Vildrac's "Paquebot Tenacity."

The French Strollers, a repertory company of professional French actors including Suzanne Caubaye, Marcel Journet, Auguste Aramini, Michelette Burani, Antoinette Giroux, Mounette Roussel, Aljan de Loville and Germaine Giroux, under the management of Michael Barroy, made their first New York appearance April 29, 1939, at Washington Square Theatre of the New York University. The group, formed to present contemporary plays in cultural centers, produced "Tovarich," by Jacques

Deval, directed by Aljan de Loville, and repeated the performance May 5, 1939, at the McMillan Theatre, Columbia University.

At the New Chinese Theatre the Sin Sow Nin Opera Company of Canton presented "The Parting of the Angel's Child" as the first production of a three months' run starting in January of 1939.

The Chinese Cultural Theatre Group, under the direction of Mrs. Ernest S. H. Tong, presented five performances of "An Evening in Cathay" at the Mercury Theatre, New York, in early February, 1939. The program consisted of classical music, dances and drama of ancient China. The costumes were designed by Mei Lan-Fang and the performers were all Chinese.

The Yiddish Art Theatre (now in its twentieth year), under the direction of Maurice Schwartz, produced "Three Cities" by Sholem Asch with music by Sholem Secunda, October 10, 1938. The settings were designed by Samuel Leve and in the cast were M. Schwartz, Jacob Ben-Ami, Bertha Gersten and Michael Goldstein. In December "Who is Who," by H. Leivick, began alternating with "Three Cities" playing at the old Jolson Theatre. Miriam Riselle, Jacob Ben-Ami, Genia Schlitt, Zvee Scooler and Samuel Goldenberg supported Mr. Schwartz in "Who is Who."

In February "The Yiddish Bande" made its New York debut in a musical revue called "The World Trembles" under the management of Ignati Son and M. Schwartz. After playing until April at the Yiddish Art Theatre the Warsaw-Jewish group opened at the Belmont Theatre.

At the National Theatre a musical melodrama called "Scwartse Mamme" by Louis Freeman with music by Ilia Trilling was presented and staged by Julius Nathanson, January 14, 1939. The lyrics were written by Chaim Tauber and the principal players were Gertrude Stein and Leo Fuchs.

"Mazel Tov, Rabbi!," an operetta by Anschel Schorr and Joseph Rumshinsky, was presented in November at the Public Theatre by a company of players headed by Menashe Skulnik and Menachim Rubin. "A Wise Fool" and "Three Men and a Girl" by Isidore Lash were also presented at the Public Theatre during the season.

At the Second Avenue Theatre "My Baby's Wedding," an operetta by William Siegel with music by Alexander Olshanetsky and lyrics by Jacob Jacobs, was presented by Itzik Feld in October, 1938. Rose Gordon directed the dances and Michael

Saltzman was responsible for the scenery. Itzik Feld, Miriam Kressyn, Muni Serebrov, Vickie Marcus and Gloria Gold were members of the cast. In late December Mr. Feld presented "Long Live America," a musical in two acts by Abraham Blum, music by Alexander Olshanetsky, lyrics by Jacob Jacobs. The production was staged by Abe Gross and the dances directed by Marty Baratz. Dinah Halpern and Itzik Feld played the leading parts. "The Polish Rabbi," also by Siegel and Olshanetsky, was produced in March, 1939.

At the Irving Place Theatre, New York, the Yiddish Dramatic Players opened their season with "Round the Family Table" by Nathan Stutchkoff, staged by Lieb Kadison, October 9, 1938. Harry Lubin directed the music and Louis Bromberg designed the settings. Judah Bleich, Celie Adler, Mischa Stutchkoff, Sol Eisikoff and Muriel Gruber were in the cast. "One Sabbath Afternoon," adapted by Jacob Fishberg from James Hagan's English original, was produced and staged January 29, 1939, by Joseph Buloff. The settings were by Harry Saltzman. Buloff, Kurt Katch, and Fanny Lubritsky were featured. February 12, 1939, Chono Gottesfeld's "Topsy-Turvy" was presented at the Irving Theatre. Leib Kadison directed a cast which included Joseph Shoengold, Sylvia Fishman, Mae Schoenfeld, Isaac Hoff and Irving Jacobson. Later in the month this same company revived Gottesfeld's "Parnusseh."

## STATISTICAL SUMMARY

(LAST SEASON PLAYS WHICH ENDED RUNS AFTER JUNE 18, 1938)

| Plays | Number Performances | Plays | Number Performances |
|---|---|---|---|
| Bachelor Born | 400 | Room Service | 500 |
| I'd Rather Be Right | 290 | Shadow and Substance | 274 |
| I Married an Angel | 338 | The Two Bouquets | 55 |
| On Borrowed Time | 321 | The Women | 657 |
| Our Town | 336 | Whiteoaks | 112 |
| You Can't Take It with You | 837 | | |

# LONG RUNS ON BROADWAY

## To June 18, 1939

(Plays marked with asterisk were still playing June 18, 1939)

| Plays | Number Performances | Plays | Number Performances |
|---|---|---|---|
| Abie's Irish Rose | 2,532 | Adonis | 603 |
| *Tobacco Road | 2,357 | Street Scene | 601 |
| Lightnin' | 1,291 | Kiki | 600 |
| The Bat | 867 | Blossom Time | 592 |
| You Can't Take It with You | 837 | Brother Rat | 577 |
| Three Men on a Horse | 835 | Show Boat | 572 |
| The Ladder | 789 | The Show-Off | 571 |
| The First Year | 760 | Sally | 570 |
| Seventh Heaven | 704 | Strictly Dishonorable | 557 |
| Peg o' My Heart | 692 | Good News | 551 |
| The Children's Hour | 691 | The Music Master | 540 |
| Dead End | 687 | The Boomerang | 522 |
| *Pins and Needles | 680 | Blackbirds | 518 |
| East Is West | 680 | Sunny | 517 |
| Irene | 670 | Victoria Regina | 517 |
| Boy Meets Girl | 669 | *What a Life | 514 |
| The Women | 657 | The Vagabond King | 511 |
| A Trip to Chinatown | 657 | The New Moon | 509 |
| Rain | 648 | Shuffle Along | 504 |
| The Green Pastures | 640 | Personal Appearance | 501 |
| Is Zat So | 618 | Bird in Hand | 500 |
| Student Prince | 608 | Sailor, Beware! | 500 |
| Broadway | 603 | Room Service | 500 |

# DRAMA CRITICS' CIRCLE AWARD

Organized in 1935 with the avowed purpose of selecting each year the best play of the season written by an American author, the New York Drama Critics' Circle stipulated that any play chosen to represent the circle as a whole must receive a three-fourths vote of the active membership. For three years a choice was comparatively simple. At the April meeting in 1939, however, the Circle membership found itself in disagreement. Ten ballots were taken without a choice, and four plays were mentioned for the honor. Robert Sherwood's "Abe Lincoln in Illinois" and Lillian Hellman's "The Little Foxes" led the voting on all ballots. On the final ballot "The Little Foxes" received six votes, "Abe Lincoln" five votes, Clifford Odets' "Rocket to the Moon" two votes and William Saroyan's "My Heart's in the Highlands" two votes.

Paul Vincent Carroll's "The White Steed" received the unanimous endorsement of the Circle as the most distinguished play of foreign authorship to be produced during the season. Mr. Carroll's "Shadow and Substance" was similarly approved last season.

Previous awards of the Circle have been as follows:
1935-36—Winterset, by Maxwell Anderson
1936-37—High Tor, by Maxwell Anderson
1937-38—Of Mice and Men, by John Steinbeck

# PULITZER PRIZE WINNERS

"For the original American play performed in New York which shall best represent the educational value and power of the stage in raising the standard of good morals, good taste and good manners."—The Will of Joseph Pulitzer, dated April 16, 1904.

In 1929 the advisory board, which, according to the terms of the will, "shall have the power in its discretion to suspend or to change any subject or subjects . . . if in the judgment of the board such suspension, changes or substitutions shall be conducive to the public good," decided to eliminate from the above paragraph relating to the prize-winning play the words "in raising the standard of good morals, good taste and good manners."

The committee awards to date have been:

1917-18—Why Marry? by Jesse Lynch Williams
1918-19—None
1919-20—Beyond the Horizon, by Eugene O'Neill
1920-21—Miss Lulu Bett, by Zona Gale
1921-22—Anna Christie, by Eugene O'Neill
1922-23—Icebound, by Owen Davis
1923-24—Hell-bent fer Heaven, by Hatcher Hughes
1924-25—They Knew What They Wanted, by Sidney Howard
1925-26—Craig's Wife, by George Kelly
1926-27—In Abraham's Bosom, by Paul Green
1927-28—Strange Interlude, by Eugene O'Neill
1928-29—Street Scene, by Elmer Rice
1929-30—The Green Pastures, by Marc Connelly
1930-31—Alison's House, by Susan Glaspell
1931-32—Of Thee I Sing, by George S. Kaufman, Morrie Ryskind, Ira and George Gershwin
1932-33—Both Your Houses, by Maxwell Anderson
1933-34—Men in White, by Sidney Kingsley
1934-35—The Old Maid, by Zoe Akins
1935-36—Idiot's Delight, by Robert E. Sherwood
1936-37—You Can't Take It with You, by Moss Hart and George S. Kaufman
1937-38—Our Town, by Thornton Wilder
1938-39—Abe Lincoln in Illinois, by Robert E. Sherwood

# PREVIOUS VOLUMES OF BEST PLAYS

Plays chosen to represent the theatre seasons from 1909 to 1938 are as follows:

## 1909-1919

"The Easiest Way," by Eugene Walter. Published by G. W. Dillingham, New York; Houghton Mifflin Co., Boston.

"Mrs. Bumpstead-Leigh," by Harry James Smith. Published by Samuel French, New York.

"Disraeli," by Louis N. Parker. Published by Dodd, Mead and Co., New York.

"Romance," by Edward Sheldon. Published by the Macmillan Co., New York.

"Seven Keys to Baldpate," by George M. Cohan. Published by Bobbs-Merrill Co., Indianapolis, as a novel by Earl Derr Biggers; as a play by Samuel French, New York.

"On Trial," by Elmer Reizenstein. Published by Samuel French, New York.

"The Unchastened Woman," by Louis Kaufman Anspacher. Published by Harcourt, Brace and Howe, Inc., New York.

"Good Gracious Annabelle," by Clare Kummer. Published by Samuel French, New York.

"Why Marry?" by Jesse Lynch Williams. Published by Charles Scribner's Sons, New York.

"John Ferguson," by St. John Ervine. Published by the Macmillan Co., New York.

## 1919-1920

"Abraham Lincoln," by John Drinkwater. Published by Houghton Mifflin Co., Boston.

"Clarence," by Booth Tarkington. Published by Samuel French, New York.

"Beyond the Horizon," by Eugene G. O'Neill. Published by Boni & Liveright, Inc., New York.

"Déclassée," by Zoe Akins. Published by Liveright, Inc., New York.

"The Famous Mrs. Fair," by James Forbes. Published by Samuel French, New York.

"The Jest," by Sem Benelli. (American adaptation by Edward Sheldon.)

"Jane Clegg," by St. John Ervine. Published by Henry Holt & Co., New York.

"Mamma's Affair," by Rachel Barton Butler. Published by Samuel French, New York.

"Wedding Bells," by Salisbury Field. Published by Samuel French, New York.

"Adam and Eva," by George Middleton and Guy Bolton. Published by Samuel French, New York.

### 1920-1921

"Deburau," adapted from the French of Sacha Guitry by H. Granville Barker. Published by G. P. Putnam's Sons, New York.

"The First Year," by Frank Craven. Published by Samuel French, New York.

"Enter Madame," by Gilda Varesi and Dolly Byrne. Published by G. P. Putnam's Sons, New York.

"The Green Goddess," by William Archer. Published by Alfred A. Knopf, New York.

"Liliom," by Ferenc Molnar. Published by Boni & Liveright, New York.

"Mary Rose," by James M. Barrie. Published by Charles Scribner's Sons, New York.

"Nice People," by Rachel Crothers. Published by Charles Scribner's Sons, New York.

"The Bad Man," by Porter Emerson Browne. Published by G. P. Putnam's Sons, New York.

"The Emperor Jones," by Eugene G. O'Neill. Published by Boni & Liveright, New York.

"The Skin Game," by John Galsworthy. Published by Charles Scribner's Sons, New York.

### 1921-1922

"Anna Christie," by Eugene G. O'Neill. Published by Boni & Liveright, New York.

"A Bill of Divorcement," by Clemence Dane. Published by the Macmillan Company, New York.

"Dulcy," by George S. Kaufman and Marc Connelly. Published by G. P. Putnam's Sons, New York.

"He Who Gets Slapped," adapted from the Russian of Leonid Andreyev by Gregory Zilboorg. Published by Brentano's, New York.

"Six Cylinder Love," by William Anthony McGuire.

"The Hero," by Gilbert Emery.

"The Dover Road," by Alan Alexander Milne. Published by Samuel French, New York.

"Ambush," by Arthur Richman.

"The Circle," by William Somerset Maugham.

"The Nest," by Paul Geraldy and Grace George.

### 1922-1923

"Rain," by John Colton and Clemence Randolph. Published by Liveright, Inc., New York.

"Loyalties," by John Galsworthy. Published by Charles Scribner's Sons, New York.

"Icebound," by Owen Davis. Published by Little, Brown & Company, Boston.

"You and I," by Philip Barry. Published by Brentano's, New York.

"The Fool," by Channing Pollock. Published by Brentano's, New York.

"Merton of the Movies," by George Kaufman and Marc Connelly, based on the novel of the same name by Harry Leon Wilson.

"Why Not?" by Jesse Lynch Williams. Published by Walter H. Baker Co., Boston.

"The Old Soak," by Don Marquis. Published by Doubleday, Page & Company, New York.

"R.U.R.," by Karel Capek. Translated by Paul Selver. Published by Doubleday, Page & Company.

"Mary the 3d," by Rachel Crothers. Published by Brentano's, New York.

### 1923-1924

"The Swan," translated from the Hungarian of Ferenc Molnar by Melville Baker. Published by Boni & Liveright, New York.

"Outward Bound," by Sutton Vane. Published by Boni & Liveright, New York.

"The Show-off," by George Kelly. Published by Little, Brown & Company, Boston.

"The Changelings," by Lee Wilson Dodd. Published by E. P. Dutton & Company, New York.

"Chicken Feed," by Guy Bolton. Published by Samuel French,

New York and London.

"Sun-Up," by Lula Vollmer. Published by Brentano's, New York.

"Beggar on Horseback," by George Kaufman and Marc Connelly. Published by Boni & Liveright, New York.

"Tarnish," by Gilbert Emery. Published by Brentano's, New York.

"The Goose Hangs High," by Lewis Beach. Published by Little, Brown & Company, Boston.

"Hell-bent fer Heaven," by Hatcher Hughes. Published by Harper Bros., New York.

### 1924-1925

"What Price Glory?" by Laurence Stallings and Maxwell Anderson. Published by Harcourt, Brace & Co., New York.

"They Knew What They Wanted," by Sidney Howard. Published by Doubleday, Page & Company, New York.

"Desire Under the Elms," by Eugene G. O'Neill. Published by Boni & Liveright, New York.

"The Firebrand," by Edwin Justus Mayer. Published by Boni & Liveright, New York.

"Dancing Mothers," by Edgar Selwyn and Edmund Goulding.

"Mrs. Partridge Presents," by Mary Kennedy and Ruth Warren. Published by Samuel French, New York.

"The Fall Guy," by James Gleason and George Abbott. Published by Samuel French, New York.

"The Youngest," by Philip Barry. Published by Samuel French, New York.

"Minick," by Edna Ferber and George S. Kaufman. Published by Doubleday, Page & Company, New York.

"Wild Birds," by Dan Totheroh. Published by Doubleday, Page & Company, New York.

### 1925-1926

"Craig's Wife," by George Kelly. Published by Little, Brown & Company, Boston.

"The Great God Brown," by Eugene G. O'Neill. Published by Boni & Liveright, New York.

"The Green Hat," by Michael Arlen.

"The Dybbuk," by S. Ansky, Henry G. Alsberg-Winifred Katzin translation. Published by Boni & Liveright, New York.

"The Enemy," by Channing Pollock. Published by Brentano's,

New York.

"The Last of Mrs. Cheyney," by Frederick Lonsdale. Published by Samuel French, New York.

"Bride of the Lamb," by William Hurlbut. Published by Boni & Liveright, New York.

"The Wisdom Tooth," by Marc Connelly. Published by George H. Doran & Company, New York.

"The Butter and Egg Man," by George Kaufman. Published by Boni & Liveright, New York.

"Young Woodley," by John Van Druten. Published by Simon and Schuster, New York.

### 1926-1927

"Broadway," by Philip Dunning and George Abbott. Published by George H. Doran Company, New York.

"Saturday's Children," by Maxwell Anderson. Published by Longmans, Green & Company, New York.

"Chicago," by Maurine Watkins. Published by Alfred A. Knopf, Inc., New York.

"The Constant Wife," by William Somerset Maugham. Published by George H. Doran Company, New York.

"The Play's the Thing," by Ferenc Molnar and P. G. Wodehouse. Published by Brentano's, New York.

"The Road to Rome," by Robert Emmet Sherwood. Published by Charles Scribner's Sons, New York.

"The Silver Cord," by Sidney Howard. Published by Charles Scribner's Sons, New York.

"The Cradle Song," translated from the Spanish of G. Martinez Sierra by John Garrett Underhill. Published by E. P. Dutton & Company, New York.

"Daisy Mayme," by George Kelly. Published by Little, Brown & Company, Boston.

"In Abraham's Bosom," by Paul Green. Published by Robert M. McBride & Company, New York.

### 1927-1928

"Strange Interlude," by Eugene G. O'Neill. Published by Boni & Liveright, New York.

"The Royal Family," by Edna Ferber and George Kaufman. Published by Doubleday, Doran & Company, New York.

"Burlesque," by George Manker Watters. Published by Doubleday, Doran & Company, New York.

"Coquette," by George Abbott and Ann Bridgers. Published by Longmans, Green & Company, New York, London, Toronto.
"Behold the Bridegroom," by George Kelly. Published by Little, Brown & Company, Boston.
"Porgy," by DuBose Heyward. Published by Doubleday, Doran & Company, New York.
"Paris Bound," by Philip Barry. Published by Samuel French, New York.
"Escape," by John Galsworthy. Published by Charles Scribner's Sons, New York.
"The Racket," by Bartlett Cormack. Published by Samuel French, New York.
"The Plough and the Stars," by Sean O'Casey. Published by the Macmillan Company, New York.

### 1928-1929

"Street Scene," by Elmer Rice. Published by Samuel French, New York.
"Journey's End," by R. C. Sherriff. Published by Brentano's, New York.
"Wings Over Europe," by Robert Nichols and Maurice Browne. Published by Covici-Friede, New York.
"Holiday," by Philip Barry. Published by Samuel French, New York.
"The Front Page," by Ben Hecht and Charles MacArthur. Published by Covici-Friede, New York.
"Let Us Be Gay," by Rachel Crothers. Published by Samuel French, New York.
"Machinal," by Sophie Treadwell.
"Little Accident," by Floyd Dell and Thomas Mitchell.
"Gypsy," by Maxwell Anderson.
"The Kingdom of God," by G. Martinez Sierra; English version by Helen and Harley Granville-Barker. Published by E. P. Dutton & Company, New York.

### 1929-1930

"The Green Pastures," by Marc Connelly (adapted from "Ol' Man Adam and His Chillun," by Roark Bradford). Published by Farrar & Rinehart, Inc., New York.
"The Criminal Code," by Martin Flavin. Published by Horace Liveright, New York.
"Berkeley Square," by John Balderston. Published by the Macmillan Company, New York.

"Strictly Dishonorable," by Preston Sturges. Published by Horace Liveright, New York.

"The First Mrs. Fraser," by St. John Ervine. Published by the Macmillan Company, New York.

"The Last Mile," by John Wexley. Published by Samuel French, New York.

"June Moon," by Ring W. Lardner and George S. Kaufman. Published by Charles Scribner's Sons, New York.

"Michael and Mary," by A. A. Milne. Published by Chatto & Windus, London.

"Death Takes a Holiday," by Walter Ferris (adapted from the Italian of Alberto Casella). Published by Samuel French, New York.

"Rebound," by Donald Ogden Stewart. Published by Samuel French, New York.

### 1930-1931

"Elizabeth the Queen," by Maxwell Anderson. Published by Longmans, Green & Co., New York.

"Tomorrow and Tomorrow," by Philip Barry. Published by Samuel French, New York.

"Once in a Lifetime," by George S. Kaufman and Moss Hart. Published by Farrar and Rinehart, New York.

"Green Grow the Lilacs," by Lynn Riggs. Published by Samuel French, New York and London.

"As Husbands Go," by Rachel Crothers. Published by Samuel French, New York.

"Alison's House," by Susan Glasgow. Published by Samuel French, New York.

"Five-Star Final," by Louis Weitzenkorn. Published by Samuel French, New York.

"Overture," by William Bolitho. Published by Simon & Schuster, New York.

"The Barretts of Wimpole Street," by Rudolf Besier. Published by Little, Brown & Company, Boston.

"Grand Hotel," adapted from the German of Vicki Baum by W. A. Drake.

### 1931-1932

"Of Thee I Sing," by George S. Kaufman and Morrie Ryskind; music and lyrics by George and Ira Gershwin. Published by Alfred Knopf, New York.

"Mourning Becomes Electra," by Eugene G. O'Neill. Published by Horace Liveright, Inc., New York.

"Reunion in Vienna," by Robert Emmet Sherwood. Published

by Charles Scribner's Sons, New York.

"The House of Connelly," by Paul Green. Published by Samuel French, New York.

"The Animal Kingdom," by Philip Barry. Published by Samuel French, New York.

"The Left Bank," by Elmer Rice. Published by Samuel French, New York.

"Another Language," by Rose Franken. Published by Samuel French, New York.

"Brief Moment," by S. N. Behrman. Published by Farrar & Rinehart, New York.

"The Devil Passes," by Benn W. Levy. Published by Martin Secker, London.

"Cynara," by H. M. Harwood and R. F. Gore-Browne. Published by Samuel French, New York.

### 1932-1933

"Both Your Houses," by Maxwell Anderson. Published by Samuel French, New York.

"Dinner at Eight," by George S. Kaufman and Edna Ferber. Published by Doubleday, Doran & Co., Inc., Garden City, New York.

"When Ladies Meet," by Rachel Crothers. Published by Samuel French, New York.

"Design for Living," by Noel Coward. Published by Doubleday, Doran & Co., Inc., Garden City, New York.

"Biography," by S. N. Behrman. Published by Farrar & Rinehart, Inc., New York.

"Alien Corn," by Sidney Howard. Published by Charles Scribner's Sons, New York.

"The Late Christopher Bean," adapted from the French of René Fauchois by Sidney Howard. Published by Samuel French, New York.

"We, the People," by Elmer Rice. Published by Coward-McCann, Inc., New York.

"Pigeons and People," by George M. Cohan.

"One Sunday Afternoon," by James Hagan. Published by Samuel French, New York.

### 1933-1934

"Mary of Scotland," by Maxwell Anderson. Published by Doubleday, Doran & Co., Inc., Garden City, N. Y.

"Men in White," by Sidney Kingsley. Published by Covici, Friede, Inc., New York.

"Dodsworth," by Sinclair Lewis and Sidney Howard. Published by Harcourt, Brace & Co., New York.

"Ah, Wilderness," by Eugene O'Neill. Published by Random House, New York.

"They Shall Not Die," by John Wexley. Published by Alfred A. Knopf, New York.

"Her Master's Voice," by Clare Kummer. Published by Samuel French, New York.

"No More Ladies," by A. E. Thomas.

"Wednesday's Child," by Leopold Atlas. Published by Samuel French, New York.

"The Shining Hour," by Keith Winter. Published by Doubleday, Doran & Co., Inc., Garden City, New York.

"The Green Bay Tree," by Mordaunt Shairp. Published by Baker International Play Bureau, Boston, Mass.

### 1934-1935

"The Children's Hour," by Lillian Hellman. Published by Alfred Knopf, New York.

"Valley Forge," by Maxwell Anderson. Published by Anderson House, Washington, D. C. Distributed by Dodd, Mead & Co., New York.

"The Petrified Forest," by Robert Sherwood. Published by Charles Scribner's Sons, New York.

"The Old Maid," by Zoe Akins. Published by D. Appleton-Century Co., New York.

"Accent on Youth," by Samson Raphaelson. Published by Samuel French, New York.

"Merrily We Roll Along," by George S. Kaufman and Moss Hart. Published by Random House, New York.

"Awake and Sing," by Clifford Odets. Published by Random House, New York.

"The Farmer Takes a Wife," by Frank B. Elser and Marc Connelly.

"Lost Horizons," by John Hayden.

"The Distaff Side," by John Van Druten. Published by Alfred Knopf, New York.

### 1935-1936

"Winterset," by Maxwell Anderson. Published by Anderson House, Washington, D. C.

"Idiot's Delight," by Robert Emmet Sherwood. Published by Charles Scribner's Sons, New York.

"End of Summer," by S. N. Behrman. Published by Random House, New York.

"First Lady," by Katharine Dayton and George S. Kaufman. Published by Random House, New York.

"Victoria Regina," by Laurence Housman. Published by Samuel French, Inc., New York and London.

"Boy Meets Girl," by Bella and Samuel Spewack. Published by Random House, New York.

"Dead End," by Sidney Kingsley. Published by Random House, New York.

"Call It a Day," by Dodie Smith. Published by Samuel French, Inc., New York and London.

"Ethan Frome," by Owen Davis and Donald Davis. Published by Charles Scribner's Sons, New York.

"Pride and Prejudice," by Helen Jerome. Published by Doubleday, Doran & Co., Garden City, New York.

## 1936-1937

"High Tor," by Maxwell Anderson. Published by Anderson House, Washington, D. C.

"You Can't Take It with You," by Moss Hart and George S. Kaufman. Published by Farrar & Rinehart, Inc., New York.

"Johnny Johnson," by Paul Green. Published by Samuel French, Inc., New York.

"Daughters of Atreus," by Robert Turney. Published by Alfred A. Knopf, New York.

"Stage Door," by Edna Ferber and George S. Kaufman. Published by Doubleday, Doran & Co., Garden City, New York.

"The Women," by Clare Boothe. Published by Random House, Inc., New York.

"St. Helena," by R. C. Sherriff and Jeanne de Casalis. Published by Samuel French, Inc., New York and London.

"Yes, My Darling Daughter," by Mark Reed. Published by Samuel French, Inc., New York.

"Excursion," by Victor Wolfson. Published by Random House, New York.

"Tovarich," by Jacques Deval and Robert E. Sherwood. Published by Random House, New York.

## *1937-1938*

"Of Mice and Men," by John Steinbeck. Published by Covici-Friede, New York.

"Our Town," by Thornton Wilder. Published by Coward-McCann, Inc., New York.

"Shadow and Substance," by Paul Vincent Carroll. Published by Random House, Inc., New York.

"On Borrowed Time," by Paul Osborn. Published by Alfred A. Knopf, New York.

"The Star-Wagon," by Maxwell Anderson. Published by Anderson House, Washington, D. C. Distributed by Dodd, Mead & Co., New York.

"Susan and God," by Rachel Crothers. Published by Random House, Inc., New York.

"Prologue to Glory," by E. P. Conkle. Published by Random House, Inc., New York.

"Amphitryon 38," by S. N. Behrman. Published by Random House, Inc., New York.

"Golden Boy," by Clifford Odets. Published by Random House, Inc., New York.

"What a Life," by Clifford Goldsmith. Published by Dramatists Play Service, Inc., New York.

# WHERE AND WHEN THEY WERE BORN

(Compiled from the most authentic records available.)

Abba, Marta ............... Milan, Italy ............ 1907
Abbott, George ............. Hamburg, N. Y. ........ 1895
Abel, Walter ................ St. Paul, Minn. .......... 1898
Adams, Maude ............. Salt Lake City, Utah ..... 1872
Adler, Luther .............. New York City .......... 1903
Adler, Stella .............. New York City .......... 1904
Aherne, Brian ............. King's Norton, England ... 1902
Akins, Zoe ................ Humansville, Mo. ........ 1886
Alexander, Katherine ........ Arkansas .............. 1901
Alexander, Ross ............ Brooklyn, N. Y. ......... 1904
Allenby, Peggy ............ New York .............. 1905
Allen, Adrianne ............ Manchester, England ..... 1907
Allgood, Sara ............. Dublin, Ireland .......... 1883
Anders, Glenn ............. Los Angeles, Cal. ........ 1890
Anderson, Judith ........... Australia .............. 1898
Anderson, Maxwell .......... Atlantic City, Pa. ........ 1888
Andrews, A. G. ............ Buffalo, N. Y. ........... 1861
Andrews, Ann .............. Los Angeles, Cal. ........ 1895
Anglin, Margaret ........... Ottawa, Canada ........ 1876
Anson, A. E. .............. London, England ........ 1879
Arling, Joyce .............. Memphis, Tenn. ........ 1911
Arliss, George ............. London, England ........ 1868
Ashcroft, Peggy ............ Croydon, England ...... 1907
Astaire, Fred .............. Omaha, Neb. ........... 1899
Atwell, Roy ................ Syracuse, N. Y. .......... 1880
Atwill, Lionel .............. London, England ........ 1885

Bainter, Fay .............. Los Angeles, Cal. ........ 1892
Baker, Lee ................ Michigan .............. 1880
Bankhead, Tallulah ......... Huntsville, Ala. ......... 1902
Banks, Leslie J. ........... West Derby, England .... 1890
Barbee, Richard ............ Lafayette, Ind. .......... 1887
Barrett, Edith ............. Roxbury, Mass. ......... 1904
Barry, Philip .............. Rochester, N. Y. ........ 1896
Barrymore, Ethel ........... Philadelphia, Pa. ........ 1879
Barrymore, John ............ Philadelphia, Pa. ........ 1882
Barrymore, Lionel .......... London, England ....... 1878

Barton, James .............. Gloucester, N. J. ........ 1890
Baxter, Lora ................ New York ............. 1907
Beatty, Roberta ............ Rochester, N. Y. ......... 1900
Beecher, Janet ............. Chicago, Ill. ............ 1884
Behrman, S. N. ............. Worcester, Mass. ........ 1893
Bell, James ................ Suffolk, Va. ............ 1891
Ben-Ami, Jacob ............ Minsk, Russia ........... 1890
Bennett, Richard ........... Cass County, Ind. ........ 1873
Bergner, Elisabeth .......... Vienna ................ 1901
Berlin, Irving .............. Russia ................ 1888
Best, Edna ................. Sussex, England ........ 1900
Binney, Constance .......... Philadelphia, Pa. ........ 1900
Blackmer, Sidney ........... Salisbury, N. C. ........ 1896
Boland, Mary .............. Detroit, Mich. .......... 1880
Bolger, Ray ................ Dorchester, Mass. ........ 1906
Bondi, Beulah .............. Chicago, Ill. ............ 1892
Bordoni, Irene .............. Paris, France ........... 1895
Bowman, Patricia ........... Washington, D. C. ...... 1912
Brady, Alice ............... New York ............. 1892
Brady, William A. .......... San Francisco, Cal. ....... 1863
Braham, Horace ............ London, England ........ 1896
Brent, Romney ............. Saltillo, Mex. ........... 1902
Brian, Donald .............. St. Johns, N. F. ......... 1877
Brice, Fannie .............. Brooklyn, N. Y. ......... 1891
Broderick, Helen ........... New York ............. 1891
Bromberg, J. Edward ........ Hungary ............... 1903
Bruce, Nigel ............... San Diego, Cal. ......... 1895
Bryant, Charles ............ England .............. 1879
Buchanan, Jack ............ England .............. 1892
Buckler, Hugh ............. Southampton, England ...1886
Burke, Billie .............. Washington, D. C. ....... 1885
Burton, Frederick .......... Indiana ............... 1871
Byington, Spring ........... Colorado Springs, Colo. ...1898
Byron, Arthur ............. Brooklyn, N. Y. ........ 1872

Cabot, Eliot ............... Boston, Mass. .......... 1899
Cagney, James ............. New York ............. 1904
Cahill, Lily ............... Texas ................ 1891
Calhern, Louis ............. New York ............. 1895
Cantor, Eddie .............. New York ............. 1894
Campbell, Mrs. Patrick ...... England .............. 1865
Carlisle, Alexandra .......... Yorkshire, England ...... 1886
Carlisle, Kitty ............. New Orleans, La. ........ 1912

Selwyn, Edgar .............. Cincinnati, Ohio ........ 1875
Shannon, Effie .............. Cambridge, Mass. ........ 1867
Shean, Al .................. Dornum, Germany ...... 1868
Shepley, Ruth .............. New York .............. 1889
Sherman, Lowell ............ San Francisco, Cal. ....... 1885
Sherwood, Robert Emmet ..... New Rochelle, N. Y. ..... 1896
Sidney, George .............. New York .............. 1876
Sidney, Sylvia .............. New York .............. 1910
Sinclair, Arthur ............ Dublin, Ireland ......... 1883
Sitgreaves, Beverly ......... Charleston, S. C. ......... 1867
Skinner, Cornelia Otis ....... Chicago ............... 1902
Skinner, Otis ............... Cambridgeport, Mass. ... 1857
Smith, Ben ................. Waxahachie, Texas ...... 1905
Smith, Kent ............... Smithfield, Me. .......... 1910
Smith, Queenie ............. New York .............. 1898
Sondergaard, Gale .......... Minnesota ............. 1899
Sothern, Edward H. .......... New Orleans, La. ........ 1859
Spong, Hilda ............... Australia .............. 1875
Stahl, Rose ................ Montreal, Canada ....... 1872
Standing, Sir Guy ........... London ............... 1873
Starr, Frances ............. Oneonta, N. Y. .......... 1886
Stickney, Dorothy ........... Dickinson, N. D. ........ 1903
Stone, Fred ................ Denver, Colo. .......... 1873
Stone, Dorothy ............. New York .............. 1905
Strudwick, Sheppard ......... North Carolina ......... 1905
Sullavan, Margaret .......... Norfolk, Va. ........... 1910
Sunderland, Nan ............ Fresno, Cal. ............ 1898
Sydney, Basil .............. London ............... 1894

Taliaferro, Edith ........... New York .............. 1892
Taliaferro, Mabel .......... New York .............. 1887
Taylor, Laurette ........... New York .............. 1884
Tearle, Conway ............ New York .............. 1878
Tearle, Godfrey............ New York .............. 1884
Tell, Alma ................ New York .............. 1892
Tell, Olive ................ New York .............. 1894
Terris, Norma ............. Columbus, Kansas ...... 1904
Thomas, Frankie ........... New York .............. 1922
Thomas, John Charles ....... Baltimore, Md. ......... 1887
Thorndike, Dame Sybil ...... Gainsborough, England ... 1882
Tobin, Genevieve .......... New York .............. 1901
Tobin, Vivian ............. New York .............. 1903
Toler, Sidney ............. Warrensburg, Mo. ....... 1874

# NECROLOGY

## June 18, 1938—June 18, 1939

Aug, Edna, comedienne, 60. Character actress and vaudeville comedienne; first appearance in New York in "Dangerous Maid"; retired fifteen years ago. Born Cincinnati, Ohio; died Willow, New York, November 30, 1938.

Backus, George, actor and playwright, 81. Member of original cast of "Way Down East"; started forty-year career on stage in "The Celebrated Case" with James O'Neill; with Kate Claxton in "The Two Orphans"; supported William Gillette, William Crane and others. Born Columbus, Ohio; died Merrick, N. Y., May 21, 1939.

Bergere, Valerie, actress, 71. Played in musical comedy, vaudeville, screen and stage forty-three years; first English speaking part, 1892, San Francisco stock; last stage appearance "Moon over Mulberry Street," 1935. Born Metz, Alsace-Lorraine; died Hollywood, Calif., September 16, 1938.

Boag, William, actor-manager, 72. Twenty-five years with David Warfield and thirty years with David Belasco as stage manager. Born Charleston, S. C.; died Dongan Hills, Staten Island, N. Y., June 1, 1939.

Capek, Karel, dramatist and producer, 48. First play "The Robber" written in 1911; plays produced in New York, "R U R," "The World We Live In," "The Macropoulous Affair," "The Creators," "The Mother"; art director and producer at National and Municipal Theatre and his own theatre in Prague. Born Malé, Svatonovice, Bohemia; died Prague, Czechoslovakia, December 25, 1938.

Cliffe, H. Cooper, actor, 76. Widely known Shakespearian actor; London debut with D'Oyly Carte Company 1879; toured United States 1894; supported Henry Irving, Mrs. Fiske, Laurette Taylor; last stage appearance "Aged 26," 1936; recently in radio and pictures. Born Oxford, England; died New York City, May 1, 1939.

Cooke, Thomas Coffin, actor, 65. Veteran Shakespearian; started forty-four-year theatrical career with touring company of Wagenhals and Kemper; played with Mme. Modjeska, Kathryn Kidder, Annie Russell, Louis James, Laurette Taylor. Born Montgomery, Ala.; died Bayside, N. Y., June 10, 1939.

Dempsey, Clifford, actor, 73. On stage and screen more than fifty years; first appearance (1882) with Olga Nethersole; was rehearsing for "Abe Lincoln in Illinois" when he died. Born Winsted, Conn.; died Atlantic Highlands, N. J., September 4, 1938.

Fawcett, George D., actor, 77. Fifty years on stage and screen; Broadway debut in "The Maid and the Moonshiner" at Standard Theatre, 1886; star, feature and character roles until 1915; played with Tomasso Salvini, Alexander Salvini, Nat Goodwin and Maude Adams; with Percy Haswell founded stock company in Baltimore. Born Fairfax County, Va.; died Nantucket, Mass., June 6, 1939.

Frederick, Pauline, actress, 53. Stage and screen actress thirty-five years; debut as chorus girl, 1902, in "Rogers Brothers in Harvard"; last appearance in "Masque of Kings" in 1937; prominently cast in "When Knights Were Bold," "Samson," "The Fourth Estate," "Joseph and His Brethren," "Mrs. Dane's Defense" and "Madame X." Born Boston, Mass.; died Beverly Hills, Calif., September 19, 1938.

Gale, Zona, playwright and author, 64. Won Pulitzer Prize (1921) with "Miss Lulu Bett"; other plays "Mister Pitt," "The Neighbors," "Uncle Jimmy," "Evening Clothes" and "The Clouds." Born Portage, Wisc.; died Chicago, Ill., December 27, 1938.

Garvie, Edward, character actor and comedian, 73. Started stage career in 1885 in "In Old Kentucky." Appeared as black-face comedian in varieties and minstrels; starred in "Forbidden Land"; last appearance with Walter Hampden in "Achilles Had a Heel" in 1935. Born Meriden, Conn.; died New York City, February 17, 1939.

Gluck, Alma (Reba Fiersohn), opera singer and concert artist, 54. Studied with Arturo Buzzi-Peccia; Toscanini recommended her to the Metropolitan; debut in 1909 as Gilda in "Rigoletto," Philadelphia; with Metropolitan Opera Company until 1913; married Efrem Zimbalist, violonist. Born Bucharest, Roumania; died New York City, October 27, 1938.

Hale, Dorothy, actress, 33. Debut in "Lady Be Good"; subsequently in "Russet Mantle" and "Red Harvest"; in pictures "Cynara" and "Catherine the Great." Born Pittsburgh, Pa.; died New York City, October 21, 1938.

Hatch, Frank, actor, author and director, 74. Stage debut, California in the eighties; first New York appearance, 1890, in "The Bells of Hazelmere"; organized western stock companies; directed plays for William A. Brady; co-author of "Putting It Over" and "The Blue Envelope." Born Marysville, Calif.; died Richmond Hill, N. Y., October 25, 1938.

Heath, Thomas K., comedian and minstrel, 85. For more than fifty years in team of blackface comedians of McIntyre and Heath playing "Ham Tree," "The Georgia Minstrels," "Chickens" and "The Man from Montana." Born Philadelphia, Pa.; died Setauket, N. Y., August 18, 1938.

Irwin, May, actress, 76. Famous American comedienne; debut with sister Flo Irwin in vaudeville, 1875, Buffalo; long engagement with Tony Pastor; starred in Augustin Daly and Charles Frohman companies; introduced many popular songs: "The Bully," "After the Ball," "Hear Dem Bells," etc. Born Whitby, Ontario; died New York City, October 22, 1938.

Juch, Emma, singer, 78. Grand Opera and concert soprano in America and England in the eighties and nineties; debut London and New York in "Mignon," 1881; final appearance in New York Saengerfest, 1894. Born Vienna, Austria; died New York City, March 6, 1939.

Kalich, Bertha, actress, 64. Noted tragedienne; debut 1890 in Galicia; well-remembered roles in "Marta of the Lowlands," "Monna Vanna," "Magda" and "The Kreutzer Sonata." Born Lemberg, Poland; died New York City, April 18, 1939.

Kelly, Walter C., actor, 65. Famous as "The Virginia Judge," first presented in Marie Dressler's vaudeville act and continued for thirty-five years in America and Great Britain; played in "Huckleberry Finn," "Both Your Houses," and "The Passing Show." Born Mineville, New York; died Philadelphia, Pa., January 6, 1939.

Lederer, George W., producer, 76. Started as actor in "The Naiad Queen" in 1873; wrote vaudeville skits; was drama editor for the *New York Journal;* originated revue style of entertainment with "The Passing Show of 1894," "The Merry Whirl," "In Gay New York" and "The Rounders"; widely known productions "Florodora," "The Belle of New York," "The Lady Slavey" and "The Wild Rose," last production "The Pyjama Lady," 1930. Born Wilkes-Barre, Pa.; died Jackson Heights, N. Y., October 8, 1938.

May, Olive, actress, 65. Appeared in support of Maude Adams; remembered as ingénue in "Arizona." Died Beverly Hills, Calif., July 26, 1938.

Mitchell, Dodson Lomax, actor, playwright, 71. Fifty-three years on stage; first appearance in New York in "Fanchon the Cricket" in 1885 with his famous aunt, Maggie Mitchell; thirteen seasons with Julia Marlowe's company; four years with Arnold Daly; supported John Drew, Nazimova, George Cohan and others. Born Memphis, Tenn.; died New York City, June 2, 1939.

Moore, Owen, actor and producer, 52. Stock player until 1910; leading man with Mary Pickford in silent film, "The First Misunderstanding"; with Blanche Sweet in "The Escape"; with Greta Garbo in "As You Desire Me"; with Gloria Swanson in "What a Widow"; headed Owen Moore Film Corporation; last appearance in "A Star Is Born." Born Ireland; died Beverly Hills, Calif., June 9, 1939.

Moulan, Frank, singer, 63. Choir boy in Trinity Chapel, N. Y.; first stage appearance with Calhoun Opera Company; subsequently Castle Square Opera Company, Boston; scored success in "The Sultan of Sulu" in 1902; well known for Gilbert and Sullivan repertory. Born New York City; died New York City, May 13, 1939.

Oland, Warner, actor, 57. Fourteen years touring America and Europe; specialized in Ibsen and Shakespeare; started screen career with Theda Bara in "Jewels of the Madonna"; played with Pearl White in "Perils of Pauline"; best remembered as Charlie Chan. Born Umea, Vesterbotten, Sweden; died Stockholm, Sweden, August 6, 1938.

Osterman, Jack (Rosenthal), comedian, 37. Stage, screen and night club entertainer; in vaudeville and revues; appeared on Broadway in "Oh, Boy," "Parlor, Bedroom and Bath," and "A Night in Paris." Born Toledo, Ohio; died Atlantic City, N. J., June 8, 1939.

Rose, Edward E., playwright, 77. Dramatized romantic novels including "Janice Meredith," "Richard Carvel," "Alice of Old Vincennes," "A Gentleman from Indiana" and "David Harum." Born Stanstead, Quebec; died Fremont, Wisc., April 2, 1939.

Sargent, Epes Winthrop (Chic), drama critic, 66. Was on original staff and served *Variety* for many years; wrote for *Musical Courier, Dramatic News* and *Morning Telegraph*. Born Nassau, Bahamas; died Brooklyn, N. Y., December 6, 1938.

Stanislavsky, Constantin, actor, producer and director, 75. Co-founder Moscow Art Theatre with Nemirovitch-Dantchenko; called father of modern Russian theatre; with Moscow Art in New York, 1923-24. Born Moscow, Russia; died Moscow, August 7, 1938.

Tearle, Conway, actor, 60. Stage and screen star; son of the late Osmond Tearle, English tragedian; first appearance, England, 1901; played in support of Ellen Terry, Grace George, Billie Burke and Ethel Barrymore; recently in "Dinner at Eight" and with Tallulah Bankhead in "Antony and Cleopatra." Born New York City; died Hollywood, Calif., October 1, 1938.

Thornton, James, actor, song writer, 76. Debut as singer, Boston, 1881; in vaudeville team of Lawlor and Thornton; won *New York World* song-writing contest in 1894; songs included "My Sweetheart's the Man in the Moon," "When You Were Sweet Sixteen," "It Don't Seem Like the Same Old Smile" and "She Never Saw the Streets of Cairo"; last professional appearance in "Sweet Adeline" in 1929. Born Liverpool, England; died Astoria, N. Y., July 27, 1938.

Toller, Ernst, poet and dramatist, 45. Plays produced in America include "Man and the Masses," and "No More Peace"; books include "Learn from My Youth," "Look Through the Bars," and "I Was a German." Born Samotschin, Prussia; died New York City, May 22, 1939.

Tree, Viola, actress, author and singer, 54. Eldest daughter of Sir Herbert Beerbohm Tree; first appearance in father's production of "Twelfth Night" in Edinburgh, 1904; debut New York (1930) in "The Truth Game"; co-author with Gerald du Maurier of "The Dancers." Born London, England; died London, November 15, 1938.

Ware, Helen, actress, 61. Debut in 1899 with Maude Adams in "The Little Minister"; had been instructor of swimming and teacher in vacation schools of New York; played with Blanche Bates, Rose Stahl, Robert Edeson and Blanche Walsh; leading lady for Arnold Daly; starred in "The Third Degree." Born San Francisco, Calif.; died Carmel, Calif., January 25, 1939.

Wathall, Alfred G., composer, 58. Wrote "Sinbad the Sailor" and scores for many musical comedies including "Sultan of Sulu"; taught at Northwestern University School of Music. Born England; died Chicago, Ill., November 14, 1938.

Weadon, Percy (Frank Preston), producer and press agent, 79. Associated in late eighties with J. A. McCaull, Bartley Campbell and Steele MacKaye; co-producer with Fred Whitney of "The Chocolate Soldier"; general manager for Henry W. Savage, David Belasco, Klaw and Erlanger and the Shuberts. Born Greensburg, Ind.; died Long Island, N. Y., May 29, 1939.

Woolsey, Robert, comedian, 49. Once well-known professional jockey; started stage career at Alcazar Theatre, San Francisco; played leading roles in Gilbert and Sullivan operettas; New York debut in "Nothing but Love," 1919; teamed by Ziegfeld with Bert Wheeler in "Rio Rita"; became internationally known in vaudeville and pictures. Born Oakland, Calif.; died Malibu Beach, Calif., October 31, 1938.

Yeats, William B., poet, playwright, 73. Winner of Nobel prize for literature, 1923; first poetic play "The Countess Cathleen," 1892; prose plays "Kathleen ni Houlihan," "The Pot of Broth," "The Hour Glass" and "The Words on the Window Pane"; organizer and director of Abbey Theatre in Dublin. Born Sandymount, Ireland; died Roquebrune, France, January 28, 1939.

Yohe, May, actress, 77. Started as chorus girl in Philadelphia; appeared in "The Crystal Prince," Chicago Opera House, 1887; became vaudeville favorite in London, Paris and New York; married Lord Francis Hope; was famous as owner of Hope diamond; married Captain Putnam Bradley Strong and Captain John A. Smuts. Born Bethlehem, Pa.; died Boston, Mass., August 28, 1938.

# THE DECADES' TOLL

(Persons of Outstanding Prominence in the Theatre
Who Have Died in Recent Years)

|  | *Born* | *Died* |
|---|---|---|
| Aborn, Milton | 1864 | 1933 |
| Ames, Winthrop | 1871 | 1937 |
| Bacon, Frank | 1864 | 1922 |
| Baker, George Pierce | 1866 | 1935 |
| Belasco, David | 1856 | 1931 |
| Bernhardt, Sarah | 1845 | 1923 |
| Coghlan, Rose | 1851 | 1932 |
| Crabtree, Charlotte (Lotta) | 1847 | 1924 |
| Crane, William H. | 1845 | 1928 |
| De Koven, Reginald | 1861 | 1920 |
| De Reszke, Jean | 1850 | 1925 |
| Dillingham, Charles Bancroft | 1868 | 1934 |
| Ditrichstein, Leo | 1865 | 1928 |
| Dressler, Marie | 1869 | 1934 |
| Drew, John | 1853 | 1927 |
| Drinkwater, John | 1883 | 1937 |
| Du Maurier, Sir Gerald | 1873 | 1934 |
| Duse, Eleanora | 1859 | 1924 |
| Fiske, Minnie Maddern | 1865 | 1932 |
| Galsworthy, John | 1867 | 1933 |
| Gershwin, George | 1898 | 1937 |
| Goodwin, Nathaniel | 1857 | 1920 |
| Gorky, Maxim | 1868 | 1936 |
| Greet, Sir Philip (Ben) | 1858 | 1936 |
| Hawtrey, Sir Charles | 1858 | 1923 |
| Herbert, Victor | 1859 | 1924 |
| Hopper, De Wolf | 1858 | 1935 |
| Irwin, May | 1862 | 1938 |
| Lackaye, Wilton | 1862 | 1932 |
| Mantell, Robert Bruce | 1854 | 1928 |
| Miller, Henry | 1858 | 1926 |
| Morris, Clara | 1848 | 1925 |
| O'Neill, James | 1850 | 1920 |
| Patti, Adelina | 1843 | 1919 |

|                                   | *Born* | *Died* |
|-----------------------------------|--------|--------|
| Pinero, Sir Arthur Wing           | 1855   | 1934   |
| Pirandello, Luigi                 | 1867   | 1936   |
| Rejane, Gabrielle                 | 1857   | 1920   |
| Rogers, Will                      | 1879   | 1935   |
| Russell, Annie                    | 1864   | 1936   |
| Russell, Lillian                  | 1861   | 1922   |
| Schumann-Heink, Ernestine         | 1861   | 1936   |
| Sembrich, Marcella                | 1859   | 1935   |
| Shaw, Mary                        | 1860   | 1929   |
| Smith, Winchell                   | 1862   | 1933   |
| Sothern, Edwin Hugh               | 1859   | 1933   |
| Terry, Ellen                      | 1848   | 1928   |
| Thomas, Augustus                  | 1857   | 1934   |
| Warde, Frederick                  | 1851   | 1935   |
| Whiffen, Mrs. Thomas              | 1845   | 1936   |
| Wilson, Francis                   | 1854   | 1935   |
| Yeats, William Butler             | 1865   | 1939   |
| Ziegfeld, Florenz                 | 1869   | 1932   |

# INDEX OF AUTHORS

531

# INDEX OF PLAYS AND CASTS

536

# INDEX OF PRODUCERS, DIRECTORS AND DESIGNERS

542

## DATE DUE

| | | | |
|---|---|---|---|
| | | | |
| | | | |
| | | | |
| | | | |
| | | | |
| | | | |
| | | | |
| | | | |
| | | | |
| | | | |
| | | | |
| | | | |
| | | | |
| | | | |
| | | | |
| | | | |
| | | | |
| GAYLORD | | | PRINTED IN U.S.A. |